Center for Hellenic Studies Colloquia 2

Democracy, Empire, and the Arts in Fifth-Century Athens

Democracy, Empire, and the Arts in Fifth-Century Athens

EDITED BY

Deborah Boedeker
&
Kurt A. Raaflaub

HARVARD UNIVERSITY PRESS
Cambridge, Massachusetts • London, England

Printed in the United States of America

Photo Credits: Cover, Attic red-figure cup, Onesimos, 500–480, Deeds of Theseus. Amphitrite. Paris, Louvre G 104; Beazley 1963.318.1. After Furtwängler & Reichhold 1904–1932, vol. 3, pl. 141; vol. 1, pl. 5.

Library of Congress Cataloging-in-Publication Data

Democracy, empire, and the arts in fifth-century Athens / Deborah Boedeker & Kurt Raaflaub, eds.
p. cm. — (Center for Hellenic Studies)
Includes bibliographical references and index.
ISBN 0–674–01258–5 (pbk.)
1. Athens (Greece)—Civilization. 2. Greece—History—Athenian supremacy, 479-431 B.C. 3. Democracy—Greece—Athens. 4. Arts. Greek—Greece—Athens—Political aspects. I. Boedeker, Deborah. II. Raaflaub, Kurt A.

DF135.A53 2001
305.8'009495—dc21

2001028410

CONTENTS

PREFACE . . . . *vii*

CHAPTER ONE
Introduction *Deborah Boedeker and Kurt A. Raaflaub* 1

CHAPTER TWO
The Transformation of Athens
in the Fifth Century *Kurt A. Raaflaub* 15

CHAPTER THREE
Accounting for Culture
in Fifth-Century Athens *Lisa Kallet* 43

CHAPTER FOUR
Beyond Democracy and Empire:
Athenian Art in Context *Ian Morris* 59

CHAPTER FIVE
Democracy, Empire, and Art: Toward a Politics
of Time and Narrative *Eric Csapo and Margaret Miller* 87

CHAPTER SIX
Autochthony and the Visual Arts
in Fifth-Century Athens *H. Alan Shapiro* 127

CHAPTER SEVEN
Images and Political Identity:
The Case of Athens *Tonio Hölscher* 153

CHAPTER EIGHT
Presenting the Past in Fifth-Century Athens *Deborah Boedeker* 185

CHAPTER NINE
The Sophists in Athens *Robert W. Wallace* 203

CHAPTER TEN
The Constraints of Democracy and the Rise of the Art of Rhetoric *Harvey Yunis*. 223

CHAPTER ELEVEN
Democracy and Sokratic-Platonic Philosophy *Christopher Rowe* 241

CHAPTER TWELVE
Attic Old Comedy, Frank Speech, and Democracy *Jeffrey Henderson* 255

CHAPTER THIRTEEN
Tragedy and Politics *Suzanne Saïd* 275

CHAPTER FOURTEEN
The Panathenaic Procession: Athens' Participatory Democracy on Display? *Lisa Maurizio* 297

CHAPTER FIFTEEN
Reflections and Conclusions: Democracy, Empire, and the Arts in Fifth-Century Athens *Deborah Boedeker and Kurt A. Raaflaub* . . 319

ENDNOTES 345

BIBLIOGRAPHY 427

THE CONTRIBUTORS 493

INDEX. 497

PREFACE

Center for Hellenic Studies Colloquia

The Center for Hellenic Studies (CHS), located on a wooded campus in Washington, D.C., is a privately endowed residential research institute affiliated with Harvard University. At its core is a specialized library devoted to ancient Greek literature, history, philosophy, and related fields. Each academic year the Center offers fellowships to an international group of Hellenists in the earlier stages of their careers, and sponsors a summer session for scholars who need ready access to a strong research library. In addition, the Center has recently begun an annual colloquium series.

The CHS colloquia are devoted to examining significant topics that will profit from extended interaction of experts in various fields within and outside of Ancient Greek studies. These projects have a distinctly collaborative character. The organizers first formulate their proposed topic in consultation with the Center's Directors and its academic advisory board of Senior Fellows. They then invite participants to prepare original papers that will address designated aspects of the topic. In addition to those who are writing papers, several experts are invited to contribute to the process as discussants. At the colloquium itself, in the relaxed and intimate atmosphere of the Center, participants present and discuss the papers over the course of five or six days. Each chapter is then rewritten in light of the discussion, again in collaboration with the organizers. The goal is to achieve, at the end of this long process, an integrated volume that will be of interest to specialists and nonspecialists alike.

This volume contains the revised papers of the second CHS colloquium, which we organized ourselves in August 1995. We thank all who have contributed to the process: the Center's Senior Fellows for their support and constructive advice, all participants for their cooperative spirit and intellectual energy, Harvard University Press (in particular Margaretta Fulton) for its enthusiastic acceptance of the new series, and not least the entire CHS staff (including Brown University graduate students Carolin Hahnemann, Matthew Munich, and Suzanne Abrams, who served as our research assistants, and Dr. Hartmut Melchert), whose support and commitment made the colloquium a practical reality, and who assisted in many ways in the production of this volume. We hope that this book will convey to its readers some of the sense of excitement and mutual illumination that was experienced by all who participated in our meeting of 1995.

The first volume in the series, *Written Voices, Spoken Signs: Tradition, Performance, and the Epic Text,* edited by former CHS fellows Egbert Bakker and Ahuvia Kahane, was published in 1997.

Deborah Boedeker and Kurt Raaflaub
Directors, Center for Hellenic Studies

CHAPTER ONE

Introduction

DEBORAH BOEDEKER AND KURT A. RAAFLAUB

In planning this project, we started from two observations.[1] First, fifth-century Athens witnessed three unprecedented and truly remarkable phenomena: the first fully developed democracy in world history, the first empire created and ruled by a Greek polis, and an enormous upswing and flourishing of the arts; moreover, these three phenomena seem to have evolved roughly parallel to one another. Second, scholars frequently assume, often without substantiating it, that these developments were not only parallel but also interconnected, especially that the rapid and impressive cultural upswing that has given the fifth century the glory of the "golden" and "classical" age of Greek civilization was a function of democracy. The task we set ourselves and presented to the contributors when we initiated this project was to investigate whether and to what extent there really was a connection between the Athenian democracy and empire on one hand and, on the other, the development of the arts in the fifth century and, if so, how such a connection should be conceptualized and explained.

All components of this volume's title need explanation. We do not hesitate to use "democracy" for the political system (*dēmokratia*) prevailing in fifth-century Athens, at least from the late 460s, despite the obvious and often-criticized participatory limitations that only recent history has been privileged to overcome.[2] "Empire" and "imperialism," though laden with modern connotations, are used commonly for Athens' rule (*archē*) over its former allies and the concomitant attitudes; we use the terms here in this loose and nontechnical sense.[3] We understand "arts" comprehensively in the sense of all types of deliberate figural, performative, and literary expressions, although in the present context public forms of expression will receive more attention than more private ones. Finally, our decision to limit ourselves to the fifth century was guided by the observation that it was only in this period that a fully organized Athenian empire existed long enough to have a substantial and perceptible impact on the arts. To be sure, it is accidental that the Peloponnesian War ended in 404, and good arguments have been presented for the unity especially of Athenian democracy across the "artificial" threshold of the end of the century. But defeat, loss of empire, the bloody "tyranny" of the Thirty, and the violent restoration of democracy, with their traumatic repercussions visible not least in the trial of Sokrates, mark the end of an epoch, and those who emphasize the different character of fourth-century Athens have good reasons to do so. These differences need not be judged negatively, and the long-standing prejudice against the fourth century as a period of mere decline and crisis is definitely outdated. Still, overall, a conscious focus on the fifth century seems to us well justified for the purposes of our present inquiry.[4]

The questions this volume addresses are essentially modern questions, seldom raised in the period under study. Although from the fourth century the cultural rather than the political sphere increasingly served as a focus in praising democracy, the contemporaries of the fifth-century developments discussed here paid little attention to the questions and had a rather simple perception of the connections we are investigating. They were aware of a connection between democracy and empire, at least on a factual level.[5] And some of them thought that the size and splendor of buildings and monuments could serve as indicators of power.

Herodotus, the crown witness for this opinion, uses *erga* (works) for both human deeds, achievements, or actions and concrete artifacts and monuments. In the latter sense, *erga* prove greatness.[6] For example, Egypt is worth an exceptionally long description "because of the number of remarkable things which the country contains, and because of the fact that more monuments which beggar description are to be found there than anywhere else in the world" (2.35.1, tr. de Sélincourt & Marincola). Similarly, the historian justifies "a rather full account of the history" of Samos with the fact that the Samians "are responsible for three of the greatest building and engineering feats in the Greek world": the Eupalinos tunnel, the artificial harbor, and the Heraion, "the biggest of all Greek temples known" (3.60). Monuments represent power and thus importance in history; the conquest of states that are thus marked as important and powerful enhances the power of the conqueror. Hence the attention Herodotus pays to monuments serves two purposes: to preserve the memory of memorable achievements and to describe and explain the growth and power of the Persian empire.[7]

Thucydides is well aware of such historical interpretations of monuments and rejects them. He warns against taking present-day appearances as evidence for past greatness or unimportance, using the ruins of Mycenae as an example (1.10.1), and continues: "Suppose . . . that the city of Sparta were to become deserted and that only the temples and foundations of buildings remained, I think the future generations would, as time passed, find it very difficult to believe that the place had really been as powerful as it was represented to be . . . Since . . . the city is not regularly planned and contains no temples or monuments of great magnificence . . . , its appearance would not come up to expectation. If, on the other hand, the same thing were to happen to Athens, one would conjecture from what met the eye that the city had been twice as powerful as in fact it is" (1.10.2, tr. Rex Warner).

As Simon Hornblower observes, this passage "is virtually unique in Thucydides . . . for its mention of the great buildings which we regard as one of Athens' most memorable achievements . . . This whole passage is in fact polemic against Herodotus' conception of *ergon*, 'work': don't worry about *opseis*, the visual evidence, look at *dynameis*, power."[8]

Not surprisingly, then, praise of the arts receives minimal attention even in the Funeral Oration Thucydides attributes to Perikles. Although Perikles chooses not to recount in detail the great military deeds of the ancestors and the present heroes but rather to describe "the way of life (*epitēdeusis*) . . . , the form of government (*politeia*) and the habits (*tropoi*) which made our great achievements possible" (2.36.4, tr. Rhodes 1988), he does not explicitly mention the city's culture as part of these achievements. Any effort to discover even implicit allusions seems hazardous. For example, Thucydides lets Perikles say that the great number of occasions providing relaxations for the spirit (*anapaulas tēi gnōmēi*)—including public competitions (*agōnes*) and sacrifices throughout the year—cause daily pleasure (*terpsis*) and help overcome sadness (*to lypēron*, 38.1). Competitions and sacrifices mean festivals, and commentators are quick to point out that Athens had more festival days than any other Greek city—a fact confirmed by contemporary sources[9]—but what seems to matter more here is the *function* assigned to all such forms of relaxation: to create pleasure and joy and so to balance the sad and troublesome aspects of life in a city that was at war more often than not and in which political conflicts were frequent and intense. *Terpsis* is one of the purposes of poetry (*cf.* 41.4), and poetry was performed at festivals as part of the *agōnes*. Comedy, of course, was especially suited to serve this function.[10] This would have been a superb opportunity for the historian to extol the excellence of Athens' poets and theatrical performances, famous throughout the Hellenic world, but he does not take advantage of it.

In another passage, Perikles says, *philokaloumen* with moderation in expense (*euteleia*) and we are lovers of wisdom (*philosophoumen*) without becoming soft (40.1). The second point is clear enough: philosophers and other intellectuals were often criticized for being soft, and sophists were banned from Sparta;[11] the Athenian, by contrast, is interested in learning and welcomes those who offer it, but does not therefore neglect his *aretē*. But *philokaloumen* has caused much debate: we love what is beautiful—with *euteleia*. One naturally thinks of works of art, especially the Parthenon, completed by 431 (the date of the Funeral Oration), with its impressive sculptural programs, and of other decorated buildings that beautified the city. But these were certainly not inexpensive, and the term used here (*euteleia*) "in fact seems to be just the wrong word": *eutelēs* "means either 'cheap because economical, inexpensive' . . . or 'cheap, because of poor quality'."[12] Recent commentators thus assume that Perikles is not alluding to public buildings at all and that *philokaloumen* means "not 'we love beauty' . . . but 'we love what is noble' . . . a virtual synonym of *philosophoumen*."[13] Moreover, the word *philosophein*, though potentially very broad in its application, was recent at the time and referred to learning, intellectual curiosity, a desire to know and understand, or simply cleverness. That the Athenians were proud of their *sophia* soon became a commonplace; to read broader cultural significance into this claim seems unwarranted.[14]

Finally, "We do not need the praise of a Homer, or of any one, whose poetry gives immediate pleasure but whose impression of the facts is undermined by the truth. We have compelled the whole of sea and land to make itself accessible to our daring, and have joined in setting up everywhere undying memorials both of our failures and of our successes" (41.4, tr. Rhodes). "Memorials" (*mnēmeia*) can be understood both in the sense of the memory of events[15] and, concretely, of memorials erected, especially of course in the case of victories. Such *mnēmeia* might include monuments and temples in the city, and memorials of successes *and* failures were lined up in a long row in the public cemetery (*dēmosion sēma*), for all of Perikles' listeners to see—but this is not, or not primarily, what Thucydides seems to have in mind when he talks about memorials set up *everywhere*. Rather, "the whole earth is the tomb of famous men, and it is not only inscriptions on slabs in their own country which tell of them: even in countries not their own there dwells in every man an unwritten memory, a thing of the mind and not of a monument (*ergon*)" (43.3). Here *ergon* means "monument," but otherwise, throughout the oration, the word designates the achievements and deeds of men, especially those to be buried.[16]

True, in an oration at a "national" memorial service we should perhaps not expect to hear too much about arts and culture, and among the *epitēdeusis* and *tropoi* that make great accomplishments in war possible we might not assign high prominence to the arts either. Yet it is still noteworthy that even in Perikles' speech, which contains the most comprehensive praise of Athens' achievement surviving from the fifth century and is given by Thucydides to the leader whom we identify with Athens' "Golden Age," this aspect of Athenian life does not receive more explicit and comprehensive attention. But then, like much else we consider historically important, culture and the arts fell outside the limits of the task Thucydides had set for himself.[17] What seemed to him to matter most is expressed in another of Perikles' speeches, delivered to discouraged and weary citizens who had seen the Attic countryside ravaged by Peloponnesian invaders and suffered through the first onslaught of the plague: "You must remember that you are citizens of a great city and that you were brought up in a way of life suited to her greatness . . . Remember too, that the reason why Athens has the greatest name in all the world is because she . . . has spent more life and labour in warfare than any other state, thus winning the greatest power that has ever existed in history, such a power that will be remembered for ever by posterity" (2.61.4, tr. Warner).

To our knowledge, no other general statement survives from the fifth century on the issues under consideration in this volume. Several fourth-century speeches, however, address them in more detail. An interesting passage in Isokrates' *Panegyric* from ca. 380, which in many ways echoes a Funeral Oration, emphasizes among the benefits bestowed by the Athenians upon the other Hellenes the skills or know-how (*technai*) they either invented or approved of, "both those which are useful in producing the necessities of life and those which have been devised to give us pleasure" (*hēdonē*, 4.40).[18] Isokrates then speaks of the festivals with their sacrifices and competitions. Athens excels in these as well: its spectacles (*theamata*) surpass those of others in number and quality, cost and artistic worth (*technē*, 45), and competitions are held not only in athletics but also in eloquence (*logoi*), wisdom (*gnōmē*), and all the other arts (*erga*, 46). These claims represent a combination of Thucydides' reference to perennial sacrifices and competitions (2.38.1, discussed above) and elements typical of addresses to a panhellenic festival assembly (*panēgyris*).[19] Similarly, Isokrates' use of Athens' claim to be "an example to Hellas" goes beyond Thucydides' similar statement (2.41.1: *tēs Hellados paideusis*). In Thucydides it is a purely political claim; in Isokrates it is based on the city's gift of philosophy and rhetoric—in short: of culture (*paideusis*)—to the world (47–50).[20] On the whole, Isokrates clearly pays more attention to Athens' cultural achievement than Thucydides does, but his reasons lie in his interest in education and the role played in it by philosophy and rhetoric, and in his effort to prove Athens' festival culture superior to those of other panhellenic festivals, especially those of Olympia and Delphi. In fact, as far as we know, it was in those festivals that competitions in *logoi* and *gnōmē* (concert orations in prose) had their place, and not in Athens—despite what Isokrates asserts. For the rest, Isokrates remains vague: spectacles (*theamata*) distinguished by costliness and skill (*technē*) in all kinds of disciplines (*erga*), but no word of tragedy or public buildings as a cause of Athens' pride and reputation.

Later speeches, dating to the 350s, correct this picture. One credits Perikles, "because he was both a good leader and superb politician," the other the democracy in general with so adorning "the city with temples and public buildings that even today visitors from other lands consider that she is worthy to rule not only over Hellas but over all the world; while the Thirty neglected the public buildings, plundered the temples, and sold for destruction for the sum of three talents the dockyards upon which the city had spent not less than a thousand talents."[21] Conversely, in his first forensic speech on a public issue, delivered in 355, Demosthenes describes the great public monuments as products of the Athenian demos' moral qualities: their modesty in personal affairs and their striving for communal glory and honor. "Once they possessed greater wealth than any other Hellenic people, but they spent it all for love of honor (*philotimia*); they contributed from their own fortunes, and recoiled from no peril for the sake of glory (*doxa*). Hence the people continue to inherit possessions that will never die; on the one hand the memory of their achievements (*erga*), on the other the beauty of the memorials (*anathēmata*) set up in their honor—the Propylaia there, the Parthenon, the porticoes, the shipsheds" (22 [*Against Androtion*] 76, tr. J. H. Vince, modified). Monuments, then, stand as reminders of undying glory (*athanaton kleos*, ibid. 77).

In such statements, Herodotus' argument, linking splendid monuments and greatness or power, is resumed and developed further. This is the view, too, that, despite Thucydides' polemic, prevailed in posterity, as witnessed, among others, by Plutarch's statement in the *Life of Perikles:* "There was one measure above all which at once gave the greatest pleasure to the Athenians, adorned their city and created amazement among the rest of mankind, and which is today the sole testimony that the tales of the ancient power and glory of Greece are no mere fables. By this I mean his construction of public monuments (*anathēmata*); and yet it was this, more than any other action of his, which his enemies slandered and misrepresented" (12.1, tr. Ian Scott-Kilvert, modified). The best-documented political debate about domestic policy in the fifth century concerns precisely the building program on the Akropolis.[22] Remarkable as this is, the debate was more about imperial policy and relations with the allies than about the arts as such, and the report is preserved, with some anachronistic distortion, in Plutarch—by whose time Athens' unique cultural accomplishment had long been generally acknowledged.[23]

Thucydides' thinking about these questions, then, clearly is not typical of his time. Had Herodotus chosen to write about the post–Persian Wars period, our impression of contemporary perceptions of the issues we are concerned with might be slightly different. Even so, when Herodotus and Isokrates emphasize the connection between monuments and power, they merely link two facts, explaining one through the other, just as the "Old Oligarch" links empire and democracy: democracy corresponds to and is justified by the contribution of the lower-class citizens to Athens' naval power;[24] great monuments attest to great power and historical importance; that is, great powers set up great monuments. Such factual links imply causal connections but the latter are not pursued, differentiated, or conceptualized, even when, in Isokrates' case, Perikles or the democrats in general are identified as responsible for the glorious monuments of Athens. Why a democracy would be interested in doing the same as tyrants (such as Polykrates of Samos) or monarchs (such as the Egyptian pharaohs) did remains unexplored. Thucydides merely mentions fifth-century Athenian monuments to reject misleading appearances, and Isokrates' purpose is not to investigate why democrats might have been particularly interested in adorning the city with such monuments; it is only to contrast, schematically, the positive image of the democrats with the negative one of the oligarchs: the former built temples, monuments, and dockyards, and the latter neglected and destroyed them, just as the former created the empire and defended liberty and justice, while the oligarchs sacrificed the empire, violated justice, and enslaved the city.

Now monuments and public buildings with sculptural or painted decorations represent only one segment in a wide range of artistic achievements. What about the others? Are there any contemporary or near-contemporary statements that establish specific links, directly or indirectly, between democracy and/or the empire and other artistic genres or cultural phenomena that were conspicuously successful in fifth-century Athens? We think not, although opportunities were not missing. For example, the Old Oligarch comments on the multitude of festivals in Athens (above n.9) and on how the demos participates in them and profits from them (Pseudo-Xenophon, *Constit. of the Athenians* 2.9), but the connection of these phenomena with democracy remains unspecific and superficial: since the author argues that democracy is nothing but self-interested rule by the masses (1.2–9, 2.20), he considers it typical that they take advantage of the city's many festivals but he does not use democracy to explain the large number of festivals. In the *Frogs* of 405, Aristophanes virtually identifies the death of Euripides with the death of tragedy. Dionysos descends to Hades to bring back a real poet (66ff.) but ends up returning with one who, he hopes, can save the city (1417ff.). In this play the comic poet pleads most emphatically for the tragedian's role as a teacher of the city[25]—and assumes that role himself in a highly political address of the chorus to the audience (in the parabasis, 686ff.). But neither here nor anywhere else—although problems of both democracy and the empire are discussed intensely in many comic and tragic plays[26]—do we find in fifth-century Athens a specific expression of the idea that the glorious achievements of the Athenian dramatic theater had anything to do with the fact that Athens was a democratic or imperial polis.

As far as we can tell, there is only one exception, rhetoric. Certainly, excellence in speaking and counsel was part of elite education already in Homer's epics. In the fifth century, teachers of rhetoric were active in many parts of Hellas and the art of speaking well in public must have been practiced and appreciated throughout the Greek world. Moreover, Gorgias seems to have claimed that this skill gave its practitioner power over others in just about every situation of life, not only in politics.[27] Yet Athenian authors, foremost among them Thucydides, Euripides, and Plato, were keenly aware of an especially close connection between democracy as it evolved in Athens and the rising importance and rapid development of rhetorical skills, to the point where rhetoric became an all-powerful tool to impose one's will on the people, crush one's opponents in politics and law courts, and reach the pinnacle of power and influence in the city. This connection is made explicit, for example, in the "constitutional debate" in Euripides' *Suppliants,* when the opponent of democracy points to demagoguery as one of its fatal flaws: in a monarchy, he says, nobody has the power

> by loud-mouthed talk to twist the city this way and that
> for private profit—today popular, loved by all,
> tomorrow, blaming the innocent for the harm he's done,
> getting away with every crime, till finally
> the law-courts let him off scot-free! (412–16, tr. Philip Vellacott)

Thoughtful and polemical comments on the powerful role of speaking in democracy abound in the literature of the late fifth century[28]—with far-reaching consequences.

Overall, on the extant evidence, it seems that throughout the fifth century and beyond the Athenians' pride in their accomplishments rested more on military victories and imperial power than on culture and the arts. Confirmation comes from two documents. One, well known, is Aeschylus' funeral epigram, supposedly composed by the poet himself: "It is Aeschylus, son of Euphorion, an Athenian dead, that this monument in wheatbearing Gela hides. Of his noble courage the sacred field of Marathon could tell, and the longhaired Mede, who had good cause to know" (Anon. *Life of Aeschylus* 11, tr. John Herington, modified). Already Pausanias (1.14.5) noted the remarkable fact that Aeschylus, the most famous poet of his time, did not mention his poetry at all, only his participation in the glorious victory of Marathon. The other document, less familiar, is a comic fragment:

> Mistress of the world, august city of Athens,
> how perfectly beautiful (*pankalon*) appears your arsenal (*neōrion*),
> how beautiful (*kalos*) the Parthenon, and how beautiful (*kalos*) the Piraeus!
> What other city ever had such parks?
> It stands, as they say, in the beauty of heaven. (Adesp. fr. 340 Kock)

As Walter Miller observes, "The Parthenon was 'beautiful' in the eyes of this unknown comic poet; but the ship-yards and docks and slips of the harbors about Munychia receive a more enthusiastic epithet!"[29]

These statements correspond to a widespread attitude. Again, Plutarch offers an example. In his essay "The Glory of the Athenians" (*Moralia* 345c–351b), he observes, "If you take away the men of action, you will have no men of letters" (345c). Without heroes, there is no history, no heroicizing paintings or poetry. More importantly, great as such artistic achievements might be, no one would ever think of rating them higher than the actual deeds. Even tragedy, the crown jewel among Athens' cultural achievements—what profit did it bring the city "to compare with the shrewdness of Themistocles which provided the city with a wall, with the diligence of Pericles which adorned the Acropolis, with the liberty which Miltiades bestowed, with the supremacy to which Cimon advanced her? If in this manner the wisdom of Euripides, the eloquence of Sophocles, and the poetic magnificence of Aeschylus rid the city of any of its difficulties or gained for her any brilliant success, it is but right to compare their tragedies with trophies of victory, to let the theatre rival the War Office, and to compare the records of dramatic performances with the memorials of valour" (348c–d, tr. F. C. Babbitt).

On the Roman side, Sallust and Cicero attest to the same experience: try as they might, there simply was no way to deny that the prestige and glory accruing to military achievement prevailed over that resulting from rhetorical, juridical, or literary excellence.[30]

Given all this, it is understandable that we scrutinize the ancient sources in vain for more than most general and superficial connections between democracy, empire, and the arts. Such connections, however, have been proclaimed and taken for granted in modern times both by scholars and the public. To document the latter, it suffices to refer to the exhibition on *The Greek Miracle: Classical Sculpture from the Dawn of Democracy*, on display in 1992 in Washington and New York. In its catalogue, both in the title and in statements by politicians and contributors, the achievement of classical sculpture is directly and causally linked to democracy.[31]

Scholars have expressed similar views both for individual disciplines and the arts in general. For example, the rise of rhetoric, political theory, or historiography and, more broadly, the "sophistic movement" have all been explained by a direct and necessary connection with democracy.[32] T. B. L. Webster's well-informed and stimulating 1973 study of the relation between society and culture in classical Athens—a study that proceeds from questions similar to those posed in this volume—claims such connections more generally. Webster reaches the conclusion, among others, that the needs of the rich who from the time of Kimon were involved in political and legal struggles "called the sophists and the rhetoricians into existence and produced political theory as a kind of background. The patronage of the rich Kallias and his like gave Protagoras, Hippias, and their like a means of existence. But what is admirable and goes far beyond the immediate needs of the patron, is the width of knowledge shown by the sophists. This kind of patronage was not only interested in immediate results."[33] Yet in the patronage of art and literature politics was variously involved as well. "The Stoa Poikile and the Theseion were propaganda for the kind of democracy and the kind of policy in which Kimon believed, and the Parthenon was propaganda for the kind of democracy in which Pericles believed. But little compulsion was exercised on the artist," and in the case of Perikles, in contrast to Kimon's earlier projects, the citizens in the assembly had to approve the plans and the expenditures involved. In sum, a "small city with many meeting places, an open society, a viable social structure, intelligent patronage, educated audiences, the spirit of competition, these are things that classical Athens offered to artists, poets, and thinkers, and they are partly responsible for the flowering of culture."[34] Hence, although Webster focuses more on aristocratic than democratic patronage, in his view the unique "flowering of culture" in classical Athens was directly related to the unique conditions existing in democratic Athens.

Other studies of Athenian culture put the balance between art and politics rather differently, arguing that fifth-century art was largely driven by quite specific historical circumstances and ideological concerns.[35] To cite J. J. Pollitt, "Not all Classical art is Athenian nor are all the characteristics of Classical Athens attributable to Pericles, but without Athens Greek art would not have become what it did and without Pericles Athens would not have been what it was." Pollitt explains the classical style in Greek art as giving artistic form to Athenian democratic idealism and the enlightened humanism represented by poets and thinkers in fifth-century Athens. This style spread far beyond Athens, of course: "It was really Pheidias who, by forging a style which gave external symbolic form to the Periclean vision and by carrying it abroad to the panhellenic sanctuaries, particularly through the Olympian Zeus, made it possible for the rest of the Greeks to appreciate and to an extent participate in the Athenian experience." Even Polykleitos, the Argive sculptor second in fame only to Pheidias, although independent and more of a traditionalist, was increasingly influenced by Pheidias' style. Overall, then, despite his disclaimer cited above, Pollitt comes close to equating Greek classical art with Athenian classical art and classical art with democratic art. Such strong "Athenocentrism" is rare nowadays; it is contested by many in this volume, especially by Tonio Hölscher, Eric Csapo and Margaret Miller, and, in general terms, Ian Morris.[36]

We fully sympathize with ongoing efforts to overcome narrow Athenocentrism. Such efforts include intensified study of long-neglected parts of Hellas: poleis in what might be called "the Third Greece" beyond Athens and Sparta, and other forms of state such as especially the "tribal states" (*ethnē*).[37] From another perspective, attempts have been made to reconsider how uniquely Athenian were certain features that have long been considered such and thus interpreted as a direct consequence or reflection of democracy. Prime examples of such reevaluation concern democracy itself and one of the pillars of its ideology, the concept of equality, which had a much longer history and was much more common especially in the late sixth and fifth centuries than is usually assumed.[38] In one spectacular case, a recent attempt to tie to democracy the appearance of town planning with row houses on equal plots in many cities of the fifth and fourth centuries faltered after thorough scrutiny: whatever the reason for the widespread popularity of such "housing projects," it was not, or not only, democracy.[39] Nevertheless, as far as our present project is concerned, the extant evidence enables us (though often with difficulty) to discern interactions among democracy, empire, and the arts in Athens, the only polis with both a democracy and an empire over a sufficiently long time to have affected the development of the arts. Hence our focus on this city is inevitable—though, we are confident, it is not a narrow one.

In November of 1992, an international colloquium took place in Athens, organized by the Athenian Academy in cooperation with UNESCO, within the framework of the latter's "Décennie mondiale du développement culturel" and suggested by the "Forum of Prague" devoted to the theme of "culture et démocratie."[40] As Michel Sakellariou, the colloquium's organizer, emphasizes, democracy was to be taken seriously as a "sociocultural creation" that incorporates and reflects values and ideals of the surrounding culture and constantly interacts with this culture.[41] The volume with the proceedings of this colloquium was published too late to be integrated into the individual chapters of the present volume but in time to be referred to here.[42] It offers a broad panorama of discussions on many aspects of Athenian culture. Several authors reach conclusions that are comparable to Webster's. In several cases, however, the connection between democracy and culture is postulated rather than demonstrated; it certainly deserves more thorough examination.

This volume sets a different agenda from the Athens volume in three ways. First, our colleagues at the conference in Athens, very broadly concerned with culture, included in their discussions aspects such as religion, festivals, citizenship, the role of coined money, and public meals and banquets. This volume, by contrast, confines itself to the arts in the sense mentioned above (primarily public visual, performative, and intellectual expressions of ideas). Second, the Athens volume only rarely considers the empire. In our view, the empire is a crucial component in the complex set of interactions and developments in Athens, and this in every respect: politically, financially, socially, and ideologically; without giving this factor due consideration, we can understand neither democracy nor the role of the arts in the democratic city. And third, this in turn explains our concentration on the fifth century, while the Athens volume covers the entire "classical" period.[43]

To conclude, then, it is the goal of this volume to explore in detail to what extent and how the fifth-century "cultural revolution" depended on and interacted with Athenian democracy, and to what extent and how it was influenced by the fact that Athens was an imperial city. In pursuing this goal, we hope to disentangle, to the extent possible, the complex web of cause and effect involving empire, economic upswing, democracy, related social and religious changes, and developments in the arts.

Four chapters provide analysis of background and wider context. In chapter 2, Kurt Raaflaub sketches social, political, economic, and religious aspects of the transformation of Athens in the fifth century and thus establishes the social climate in which artistic developments took place. In chapter 3, Lisa Kallet presents the financial conditions on which at least the public cultural activities depended: state income and expenditures, and the various methods by which culture was financed. In chapter 4, Ian Morris looks beyond Athenian democracy and empire, emphasizing the need to include in such analyses not only "high" forms of culture and to take into consideration similar developments, especially increasing egalitarianism, occurring widely across the Hellenic world and even beyond.

Eric Csapo and Margaret Miller argue in chapter 5 that fundamental changes in art result from this new political and social milieu and its new ideology: democratic art, interested in possibilities inherent in the present moment and the future it will shape, comes to coexist and compete with aristocratic art with its focus on a paradigmatic past.

The authors of subsequent chapters discuss individual art forms or disciplines, focussing on specific aspects but keeping the common questions in mind: Alan Shapiro (chapter 6), using the example of autochthony, pursues the development of public ideology as it is reflected in vase painting. In chapter 7, Tonio Hölscher examines the changes of political identity as they are visible in public monuments and buildings as well as the political uses the Athenians made of such monuments. Deborah Boedeker (chapter 8) opposes a timeless, analogic, and essentially encomiastic view of history prevailing in Athenian public art and oratory to the initially non-Athenian, multifocal, potentially critical genre of narrative historiography. In chapter 9, Robert Wallace challenges traditional views of the sophists as being an essentially Athenian and homogeneous cultural phenomenon, thus again drawing our attention to cultural developments outside of Athens. Harvey Yunis (chapter 10), distinguishing sharply between practical oratory and the development of rhetorical theory, explains the latter, emerging at the very end of the fifth and in the fourth centuries, as a reaction to the deficiencies of democratic political oratory. Christopher Rowe traces in chapter 11 the beginnings of political philosophy, also at the very end of the period covered in this volume, relating it to strong reactions to democratic practices and the intellectual discourse fostered by these. In chapter 12, Jeffrey Henderson analyzes relations between Old Comedy and democracy, especially with respect to freedom of speech. After reviewing how scholars have tried to conceptualize and explain the political content of fifth-century tragedy, Suzanne Saïd (chapter 13) examines conflicts between concerns of the family or household (*oikos*) and those of the city, as they change from Aeschylus to Euripides. In focusing on the Panathenaic procession and its representation on the Parthenon frieze, Lisa Maurizio (chapter 14) presents an example of how religion and ritual can both integrate the citizen community and offer to noncitizen groups opportunities to participate in communal competition for honor and prestige.

In the final chapter, the editors review the conclusions of the individual chapters, consider how some of these ideas might be integrated into a coherent argument, and offer preliminary answers to the questions posed by this volume, showing as well areas on which future discussions might focus and directions in which more complete answers might be found.

CHAPTER TWO

The Transformation of Athens in the Fifth Century

KURT A. RAAFLAUB

In order to understand the nature and causes of the cultural upswing that took place in Athens in the fifth century we need to think not only about the various "arts" and their possible connections with democracy and the empire or the differences between Athens and other Greek cities. We also need to take into account the dynamics and tensions inherent in Athenian society and the social, political, and economic experiences that stood behind, and interacted with, developments in the cultural sphere. It is no exaggeration to say that, within little more than one generation from the Persian Wars, Athenian society was profoundly transformed. The purpose of this chapter is to outline some of the changes the Athenians witnessed from the late sixth century, focusing mostly on aspects that are not covered in other chapters of this volume. I shall examine in turn the rise and impact of imperial power, including changes in warfare, the impact of democracy, developments in the economic sphere, various aspects of the transformation of Athenian society, and changes in religion.[1]

The Rise and Impact of Imperial Power

Herodotus took it for granted—and found it useful for his interpretative purposes—that Athens and Sparta were the leading Hellenic powers already in the mid-sixth century. For Athens, this assessment is questionable.[2] Information about its history and relations to other poleis before the mid- to late sixth century is spotty and of doubtful reliability.[3] Athens was conspicuously absent among colonizing poleis; hence for a long time land reserves in Attica must have sufficed to accommodate a population that was hardly growing at a much slower rate than elsewhere. Despite scattered references to Athenian involvement in the "First Sacred War" and in wars against Megara, Aegina, and Mytilene, the chronology and nature of which are much debated,[4] the power and willingness or capacity of the polis Athens to act communally toward the outside are largely unknown before the time of the Peisistratids. They—and their opponents—preferred to rely on private military resources, and their foreign policy, like that of many tyrants, was mostly cautious and based on personal connections.[5] By the time the tyranny fell, therefore, Athens probably had never been a major Hellenic power and was not used to acting and thinking as such.

If so, this changed quickly. Kleisthenes reorganized the polis' hoplite army.[6] Soon the board of ten strategoi was established (Aristotle, *Constitution of the Athenians* 22.2). In 506 Athens emerged victorious from a war against Sparta, Thebes, and Chalkis (Herodotus 5.74–77); Athenian citizens were settled on land taken from Chalkis. The continuing threat from Sparta caused the Athenians to seek contacts with Persia; the attempt backfired and led them to support the Ionian Revolt (Her. 5.73, 96–97)—which in turn helped trigger the Persian attack in 490. These Athenian actions, revealing new scope, initiative, and determination, clearly were communal in decision and execution.[7] As Herodotus recognized (5.78), the struggles, successes, and reforms after 510 united the Athenians, enhanced their ability to act as a community, and eventually gave them the courage to resist the Persians at Marathon and to bank all their chances for survival on a newly built fleet at Salamis.

Although the trireme was invented earlier, few Greek poleis had yet acquired a communal war fleet consisting of these expensive vessels. Naval raids and battles were fought mostly with the smaller penteconters and privately owned ships. At Lade in 494 an effort to decide a war in a great naval battle with triremes had disintegrated and sealed the Ionian defeat against Persia (Her. 6.7–17). Whether the Athenians had more than a minimal communal fleet before the mid-480s is debated. In any case, their decision to entrust their fate to naval warfare and to build a fleet of two hundred triremes was daring.[8] The consequences of this decision, from Salamis to the foundation of the Delian League, its successful continuation of the war against the Persians, and its transformation into an Athenian empire, are well known. Here, for the first time, a Greek polis transformed leadership over her allies into direct control and imperial rule. This meant, above all, that the Athenians introduced an amount of military, administrative, and political centralization that was unheard of in the world of Hellenic poleis.[9] This process affected the Athenians massively, both collectively and individually. I mention but a few aspects.[10]

Hegemony and empire were based on Athenian naval power. In fact, naval and imperial power were interconnected: the Delian League provided both the necessary resources to maintain a fleet and the coastal support network that was indispensable to allow this fleet to move freely throughout the Aegean and far beyond, while its existence and the Athenians' determination to use it usually sufficed to keep the empire together. Athens thus continually maintained a military presence in the Aegean and beyond, and relied on an enormous war fleet of about three hundred triremes (mostly its own, partly the allies'). This fact revolutionized warfare in the Hellenic world. Unlike hoplite warfare that was normally conducted in intervals of several years and limited to a few days per campaign, naval actions lasted weeks, sometimes months or years.[11] A small fleet was on constant patrol and training mission—for naval warfare was highly technical and required constant training—and other contingents collected the tribute.[12] Even when the Athenians were not fighting wars against the Persians or Peloponnesians, they were involved in military actions, often of considerable size and duration—in no less than two out of every three years.[13] The navy made it easier to blockade a city and to transport troops and resources; hence the Athenians soon became the foremost Greek experts in siegecraft. After a long hiatus, they reintroduced into Greek warfare the "Homeric" custom of destroying a captured city, killing the males of fighting age, and selling women and children into slavery.[14] Although the hoplite army continued to play a significant role,[15] reliance on naval warfare changed the community's outlook on war. By fortifying the Piraeus and constructing the Long Walls, the Athenians turned their city and harbor into one big fortress and abandoned the traditional ideology of defensive hoplite warfare. Henceforth the countryside was largely yielded, the enemy not decisively confronted on Attic territory.[16]

Naval warfare required huge investments in time, manpower, and money. The construction of a trireme cost roughly one talent, and between one-half and one talent was expended on one month's pay for the crew of two hundred men. Already then war was more expensive than works of peace: the nine-month siege of rebellious Samos cost fourteen hundred talents, the Parthenon with statue twelve hundred to thirteen hundred.[17] The fleet was manned by citizens, especially volunteers of the lower classes (thetes), and by metics (resident foreigners) and mercenaries, in times of severe crisis also by slaves.[18] Hence large numbers of citizens—at least several thousand—were frequently engaged in paid work for the community (below at n.38). As a result, public funds and cash reserves as well as financial planning became very important. Detailed information about the provenance of the enormous sums required to finance fleet and wars is spotty and often debated. But in general terms it is clear that, in varying combinations, funds provided by the allies' tribute and other imperial as well as domestic income, supplemented by contributions from the rich in the form of the trierarchy, normally were more than sufficient. In exceptional cases, loans were taken out from the Goddess' treasure on the Akropolis (which consisted mainly of Athena's quota of one-sixtieth of all tribute income) and from other sacred funds; even more exceptionally, direct taxes were imposed especially on the wealthy citizens.[19]

Naval battles often caused substantial casualties; if unsuccessful, the casualty figures could become astronomical. In a single year, 460/59, one of the ten Athenian tribes (civic subdivisions), Erechtheïs, alone recorded losses of 177 men (roughly 3½–4½ percent of its adult men) who were killed fighting in Cyprus, Egypt, Phoenicia, Halieis, Aegina, and Megara (ML 33). Eight thousand Athenian citizens (one out of five or six adult men!) may have perished in Egypt, at least ten thousand in Sicily, twenty-eight thousand overall in the entire Peloponnesian War.[20]

We are used to thinking of Athens as an enlightened state full of culture and humanity and seeing Sparta as a permanent military camp with *agōgē*, blood soup and all. Both these pictures are true to some extent, but the warmongers sat in Athens, not Sparta. At least before the late fifth century, the Spartans were reluctant to commit themselves to war and especially to long conflicts with incalculable risks. The Spartan hoplite army was formidable but weakened by shrinking citizen numbers.[21] It was Athens that built the most powerful war machine the Greek world had seen and used it permanently and ruthlessly. The Athenian citizens were exposed to a constant barrage of visual and oral expressions of a highly militaristic ideology of war, power, and commitment to service and sacrifice for the polis. Sites, monuments, and rituals reminded them of their city's glorious past and unprecedented power, of their ancestors' heroic accomplishments, and of their obligation to live up to these examples: as Thucydides' Perikles puts it, the citizens' *aretē* culminated in being lovers of their city and willing to die for it.[22]

The empire's administration too absorbed much energy and manpower. Hundreds of officials served abroad in various administrative and military capacities, overseeing allied governments and commanding garrisons. The "scale of this administration" was "not only very large by Greek standards but also . . . relatively larger than the formal administration in the provinces of the Roman empire."[23] Some ten thousand Athenians, mostly thetes, received land allocations on territory confiscated from rebellious allies; some of these stayed in Athens as absentee landlords, but many moved abroad, lived in cleruchies and colonies, and served as members of garrisons.[24] In Athens, the council, assembly, and law courts were occupied increasingly by business connected with the empire.[25] As we shall see, on the economic side as well the empire created numerous opportunities for business and gain, and on the political side it facilitated the realization of full democracy.

The Rise and Impact of Democracy

Recent discussions about the 2,500th anniversary of Kleisthenes' reforms in 508/7 have stimulated much thought about the nature and origins of Athenian democracy.[26] We now understand much better the plurality of factors that made the development of democracy possible precisely in ancient Greece and precisely in Athens. The Greek polis was built on substantial egalitarian foundations in the first place.[27] As a result of a long evolution, advanced decisively in the sixth century by Solon's and Kleisthenes' reforms and the long period of stability provided by Peisistratid tyranny, by the end of the sixth century Athens indeed reached a high level of equality, participation, and integration, involving a large number of citizens.[28] But, although perhaps realized in Athens in exceptionally ingenious and effective ways, this "isonomic" stage of social and institutional development was not unique to Athens. Egalitarian features were widespread through large areas of the Hellenic world in the sixth and fifth centuries.[29]

Kleisthenes' system underwent further changes as a consequence of the Persian Wars and the introduction of naval warfare as a permanent feature. The latter is crucial. Had fighting against the Persians ended in 479, the full democracy familiar from the second half of the fifth century most probably would not have been realized. Three factors were decisive, all connected with the thalassocracy.[30] First, by rowing the fleet, the lower class citizens *permanently* assumed a military role that was crucial for the security and power of their city. Traditionally in the Greek polis socioeconomic, military, and political status were closely linked: the farmers fought in the hoplite army and were involved in communal decision making. The thetes who did not own enough land to qualify as hoplites did not count for much politically either.[31] Their rise to a completely new level of constant military importance thus was bound to improve their social prestige and political standing.[32] Second, in the average Greek polis the political agenda and citizen involvement were limited. As a result of Athens' ascent to "world power," the foreign relations agenda of council and assembly and related business of the law courts multiplied.[33] These institutions, long in existence, thus greatly increased in importance; service in them became more demanding and the decisions to be made more complex, with potentially far-reaching consequences for the entire community. Given the new roles and responsibilities assumed by polis and citizens, the traditional distribution of power and participation could no longer be taken for granted. Hence the question became urgent who really should be in charge in the polis and what role the people should play in the decisions that directly affected their safety and future. Third, the empire generated considerable income. Probably most of Athens' military expenses were covered by outside funding; certainly vast reserves were accumulated, and eventually some money was spent on domestic programs (most famously, buildings on the Akropolis).[34] The polis' budget thus was greatly relieved in some areas, which made it possible to spend in others, and the knowledge that there existed a steady source of sizable income encouraged such spending. This was a crucial condition for the Athenians' decision to introduce pay for juries and eventually for other political offices—an innovation "for which there was no precedent anywhere."[35]

Whatever other pressures were involved, reforms realized in 462 by Ephialtes and supplemented over the next twelve years by several (perhaps Periklean) laws decisively shifted the focus of power to the institutions that represented the entire demos, modified the operation of these institutions, facilitated the political participation of all citizens, and defined more strictly who was to count as a citizen.[36] By the mid-fifth century *dēmokratia* was fully developed—continuing modification and improvement notwithstanding.[37] The citizens, including those of the lower classes, now were in charge of politics: in council and assembly they elected some and controlled all the officials (the principle of accountability applied to all office holders, whether selected by vote or by lot), set policies, and made decisions and supervised their execution; in the proliferating law courts they decided on litigation that was often politically important and involved issues of foreign relations; and in innumerable offices they dealt with the daily affairs of a large, rich, and imperial community.

How did all this affect the individual citizen? According to Aristotle (*Const. of the Athenians* 24.3), "More than twenty thousand men earned their living as a result of the tribute, the taxation and the money the empire brought in." He mentions among these the six thousand jurors; five hundred members of the Boule; seven hundred offices in the city and hundreds abroad; apart from hundreds, if not thousands, of archers, horsemen, guards, hoplites, and rowers. Even if not all these soldiers were citizens and not all those listed were employed full-time, the number of citizens deriving much of their livelihood from communal service—at least ten thousand out of at most fifty to sixty thousand—is astounding.[38] So is the intensity of political participation, whether paid or unpaid. From the time membership in the council was limited to two annual turns (perhaps in 462?), at least every third to fifth—and of those who reached the requisite age of thirty more likely every second—Athenian served at least once in this demanding function. Frequency of and attendance at assembly meetings in the fifth century are debated but it is safe to say that at least two to three thousand and sometimes up to six thousand citizens (naturally, not always the same) spent at least half a day at least thirty times a year in the assembly.[39] If we add the thousands in the *dikastēria,* council, and various offices, the thousands serving semipermanently in military functions, and the many more serving during actual wars, and finally the festivals and rituals that proliferated in the democratic and imperial city (below n.159), we get an intensity of participation in communal life that is unparalleled certainly in the Greek world, probably in world history.[40]

As a consequence, communal and political functions became a dominant part of the citizen's life. His role in politics decisively set him apart from the large number of metics who participated in some religious rituals and were eligible for some service in the army as well, often prospered economically, and were prominent socially. The citizen, in Christian Meier's words, developed a political identity which assumed primary importance in his life and shaped his thinking and behavior.[41] All this was reinforced by the ideology of the democratic city which, partly overlapping with that of the imperial city, emphasized the importance of equality, freedom (including freedom of speech), and service to the community. Participating in government in their polis and through it ruling over the empire, the Athenians enjoyed the unique privilege of belonging to the "greatest and freest city."[42] For large parts of the fifth century they were gripped by a collective sense of pride and accomplishment and a feeling of almost unlimited possibilities; they became political activists and interventionists (*polypragmones*) and this attitude shaped their foreign policy.[43] Tensions and conflicts inevitably resulting from such massive changes are reflected not least on the dramatic stage.[44]

The upper classes too had to adjust.[45] The opportunities they found to exert leadership, gain glory and power, and enrich themselves, legally and illegally, were enormous, without parallel in the Greek world. Aristophanes' plays (especially *Knights*) and the sales of confiscated property of those involved in the scandals of 415 illustrate this vividly. But politics had also become a much more dangerous activity: competition among rivals, the constant scrutiny and surveillance by the democratic bodies, and the demos' propensity for punishing unsuccessful leaders created a "jungle atmosphere" in which the fittest survived and many fell by the wayside; examples abound. Democratic ideology and the need to conform to patterns of behavior that were deemed popular imposed upon the elite major changes in lifestyle, social practice, and self-presentation.[46] No wonder that many withdrew into an "internal exile" and that the "quiet Athenian" (*apragmōn*), though maligned by official ideology, became a phenomenon to be reckoned with. Some prominent Athenians began to conspire against democracy, and this movement grew rapidly as soon as democracy was weakened by the failure of its policies.[47]

The Transformation of the Athenian Economy

We know and think far too little about the economic and social consequences of naval warfare, the empire, and democracy. On the economic side, the obstacles are formidable: "Of all the major aspects of Athenian imperialism the economic is the most elusive."[48] The Greeks were simply not interested in writing about many questions we consider crucial, and important sources of information do not predate the late fifth century. Yet, although the period from 480 to 430 is poorly documented, some basic observations and inferences are possible.[49]

By the late sixth century Athens was still a fairly small city, its Akropolis splendidly adorned in the middle of a still loose conurbation, the Agora laid out only recently as a public square with but few public monuments and buildings.[50] Athens had no permanent army or fleet, much simpler political and administrative structures, and no paid offices; it was an almost completely agrarian state with a relatively small number (hundreds rather than thousands) of professional craftsmen and traders and a relatively small population of metics and slaves.[51]

In the late 480s the Athenians committed vast resources in money and manpower to build, maintain, and operate a large war fleet; the money was provided by a newly discovered silver mine at Laureion.[52] After the Persian Wars, the fleet gradually increased to three hundred units; maintenance and new construction (most likely on average between ten and twenty hulls per year) were financed by public funds and individual contributions: the trierarchy became a method of "taxation in kind," by which wealthy citizens could prove their generosity to the community.[53]

A vast infrastructure needed to be put in place to build and fit out so many ships, to repair and maintain them, to provide harbor and storage facilities to shelter them and keep them dry in the winter, to organize the labor required for all these tasks, to support and house the personnel, and to keep track of everything. Epigraphic and literary sources (mostly of the fourth century) inform us of the administrative arrangements that evolved over time.[54] Robert Garland estimates that the workforce needed to maintain the fourth-century fleet of four hundred hulls amounted to no less than twenty thousand.[55] Much of the raw material for shipbuilding (including timber for hulls, masts, and oars, flax for sail cloth and ropes, iron, copper, and hides) had to be imported, which required not only a highly developed system of trade and transportation but also diplomatic efforts and the determination to invest power, if necessary, to secure sufficient supplies.[56] The processing took place in the Piraeus in and around the ship-yards and in many small shops. A whole industry must have sprung up for this purpose. Hence the continuing needs of the fleet gave a big boost to trade and employment.

On a smaller scale, the same must have been true for meeting the needs of the hoplite army that was on campaign much more frequently than before the Persian Wars. Here too, many of the raw materials needed to be imported. Aristophanes ridicules weapons manufacturers as warmongers and profiteers. Their sizable factories are well documented later in the century, but their profitable business must have picked up decades earlier, in the course attracting businessmen from abroad.[57]

The large workforce employed here probably lived mostly in Athens and the Piraeus. They needed to be housed. Even if most of them lived in modest circumstances,[58] their growing numbers must have given a big boost to the building industry[59] which was kept busy also by public projects in the Piraeus, Athens, and elsewhere.[60] These workers represented a great mass of consumers who supplied themselves through the local markets; hence they contributed further to stimulating trade, agriculture, and manufacture. This process was accelerated even more by the increasing flow of cash from the state coffers to the thousands who served in military and political functions. Eventually, there emerged a vast range of specialized producers and dealers, whom we meet in Aristophanes, as well as a whole new class of wealthy politicians, who had made a fortune in trade and industry, best known among them Kleon "the tanner."[61] The composition of the assembly gradually changed as well: by Xenophon's time, it was largely made up of "fullers and cobblers, builders and smiths, farmers and merchants, and traffickers in the market-place who think of nothing but buying cheap and selling dear" (*Memorabilia* 3.7.6).[62]

Several scholars have discussed the "balance sheet of empire," that is, the advantages the Athenians derived, individually and collectively, from their polis' imperial rule and the price they paid for them.[63] Some of the advantages were mentioned before: the "budget relief" brought about by tribute and other revenues facilitated pay for public office and large-scale public building; opportunities arose for thousands of citizens to earn or supplement their living through paid service to the community;[64] rich and poor alike acquired land on allied territory, individually or in cleruchies and colonies; for many of the estimated ten thousand thetes involved, this entailed promotion to hoplite status.[65] Moreover, naval power allowed Athens to control the sea, to safeguard its own import interests, and to put massive pressure (economic and political) on cities that did not comply with its wishes.[66] Overall, there is no question "about the overwhelming importance of the empire in stimulating economic development."[67]

On this general level, things are clear; specifics are more uncertain. To take as an example the Athenian rowers, their pay hardly seems to have exceeded the subsistence minimum; the same amount was available for less dangerous work on land. Pay alone therefore does not explain sufficiently why service on the fleet was considered attractive enough so as to induce, normally, sufficient numbers of volunteers.[68] Occasional profits from shares of booty may have made a difference.[69] Finley believes that rowers were professionals and did little else.[70] This is difficult to accept. Rather, we should assume that most Athenian thetes had some other source of support, cultivating some land or owning a small shop operated by the family, or working in the dockyards when not at sea.[71] Finley also thinks that the empire so massively and directly profited the poorer half of the Athenian population that they simply accepted the price, the hardships and losses of warfare: war was endemic and generally taken for granted; no change of policy would have brought permanent peace; "Athenian morale remained buoyant to the bitter end, reflecting their calculus of the profits and the losses."[72] This assessment falls seriously short because it does not take into account "the 'benefits' (not unimportant) arising from glory, prestige, the sheer pleasure of power" mentioned by Finley himself. In the case of Athenian imperialism, I suggest, these and similar factors were crucial.[73]

The Athenians were well aware that, due to the empire, their city had become a magnet for people and trade, the Piraeus the economic center of the Aegean and far beyond. Whether or not regular imports of grain to supply the growing population began already in the sixth century, they certainly accelerated toward the middle of the fifth, protected by the polis' rule of the sea, providing opportunities for employment and enrichment to many, and eventually prompting public supervision and legal regulation.[74] The Piraeus, "emporion in the middle of Hellas" (Isokrates 4.42), served both as a gate for imports to and exports from Athens and as entrepōt for exchange among traders from a great number of destinations.[75] As Thucydides has Perikles say, "The greatness of our city brings it about that all the good things from all over the world flow in to us, so that to us it seems just as natural to enjoy foreign goods as our own local products."[76] Markets spread out as well on and around the Agora in Athens.[77] All this may have induced wealthy merchants from abroad to move their business to the Piraeus, and stimulated the development of new forms of banking and financial transactions which eventually resulted in early forms of a veritable "finance industry."[78]

The influx of population to Athens and the Piraeus and the building activity this necessitated resulted in a large-scale expansion and concentration of the separate settlements that originally formed Athens (the city demes of Kleisthenes' system) and in "the explosive growth of Piraeus from a medium-sized village to a huge planned city."[79] These twin cities also accommodated a growing number of visitors: businessmen, "tourists," diplomats, and others who had official dealings with the Athenian authorities or courts.[80] The fact alone that members of "allied" cities were increasingly compelled to stand trial in Athens brought the Athenians multiple benefits: "the 1% tax levied in the Piraeus brings in a greater revenue; individuals who own rooms to let, a carriage, or have a slave for hire make a greater profit; and the heralds make more because of the visits of the allies." We should not forget the taverns and other branches of the "entertainment industry"—prostitutes paid taxes![81] The profits went both to the individual and, via taxes and dues, to the public treasury.

Thucydides insists that before the Peloponnesian War the majority of Athenians still lived in the country (2.14.2, 16). Hence agriculture remained predominant. Although it is unclear whether the emporion in the Piraeus remained separated from domestic exchanges and whether large amounts of agrarian products (especially oil and wine) were exported from Attica,[82] we may assume that many Attic farmers adapted to the new conditions: the security of grain imports may have encouraged the cultivation of oil and wine instead of cereals in hilly areas, and the vicinity of a large urban market prompted those nearby to specialize in vegetables and other garden cultures, all offering bigger profits than traditional ways of farming.[83] Such changes may have coincided with a process that perhaps was about to transform agriculture substantially in large parts of the Hellenic world. Ian Morris tentatively summarizes this process as follows: Beginning in various places at different times, "there may have been a shift toward rural residence on concentrated blocks of land. This would have meant higher yields and greater overall prosperity, but also higher labor inputs and greater risk. Such a pattern of landholding seems to suggest maximizing strategies oriented more toward production for markets than toward peasant subsistence."[84] In Attica such trends might have been especially successful, but lack of extensive surveys and of other supporting evidence recommends caution.

Hence, although neither the entire economy nor the whole population was directly affected by the ongoing changes, these were massive nevertheless. In a process of accelerating interdependence, the rise of imperial power and the influx of imperial revenue helped bring about democracy in its specific Athenian form, pay for military and political service, greatly increased circulation of money, population growth, urbanization, massive increases in jobs, manufacture, building, and market transactions, and new economic opportunities, challenges, and attitudes. For the first time a large proportion of the population lived in truly urban conditions and the nonagrarian sector (trade, manufacture, services) assumed an essential role in a Greek community's economy and absorbed a very considerable portion of its manpower. Also for the first time, a Greek polis developed an almost completely monetized economy and relied on huge resources of annual income and accumulated reserves.[85] The Athenians themselves recognized that their heavy reliance on the labor and initiative of metics and slaves was extraordinary, inseparable from their polis' imperial rule and the demands it imposed on the citizens.[86] Combined with and mutually influencing one another, the broad range of phenomena involved eventually caused the transition from more rudimentary to more advanced forms of economic behavior and interaction. The resulting combination of seemingly incompatible elements ("not only primitive technology, small-scale organization and a general contempt for economic enterprise, but also wide-spread trade, the beginning of banking and economic analysis, and attitudes characterised by contemporary sources as individualistic and mercenary") has proved elusive to modern attempts at categorization.[87]

Trusting in their resources, the Athenians finally took the unprecedented step of largely abandoning Attica to the enemy (n.16), thus dramatically advancing the thrust of this development. For an exceptionally large part of the citizen body pay for public works or service now became the main source of subsistence—with far-reaching consequences.[88] This transformation, though accelerating during the Peloponnesian War and fully visible in the late fifth and fourth centuries, began in the period around the Persian Wars and must have progressed far well before 431.[89]

The Transformation of Athenian Society

Slaves

I touch briefly upon three interconnected points. First, Finley considers it a fact "that social and political progress in the Greek *poleis* was accompanied by the triumph of chattel slavery over other statuses of dependent labour. But it is also a fact that much of the Greek world did not take this step (or did not take it fully)."[90] The elimination among the citizens of status categories that were characterized by social and/or economic dependence—one of Solon's lasting achievements—was made possible by reliance on, and increased the importance of, another form of dependent labor: imported chattel slaves. Since dependent labor was essential in all ancient societies, the citizens' guaranteed freedom thus was based on the slaves' total lack of freedom.[91]

Although the interdependence of the two developments can hardly be doubted, this does not automatically imply that the citizen's *democratic* freedom depended to the same extent on the slave's lack of freedom. According to Geoffrey de Ste. Croix, however, in Athens, "just because it was a democracy and the poorer citizens were to some extent protected against the powerful, the very most had to be made out of the classes below the citizens." Unlike the metic who was free to leave if "milked" too intensively, the slave could be exploited at his master's pleasure. "We need not be surprised, then, if we find a more intense development of slavery at Athens than at most other places in the Greek world . . . This *explains* 'the advance, hand in hand, of freedom and slavery' in the Greek world, noted by Finley . . . but left by him as a kind of paradox."[92] What de Ste. Croix establishes is that democracy, like (but not more than) all other Greek and ancient societies, depended on slave labor. Finley concurs: the evidence, examined without moral, intellectual, or political prejudices, compels us to conclude, "without hesitation, that slavery was a basic element in Greek civilisation." *A,* not *the,* basic element, Finley adds: here analysis should begin not end; it should focus on function, purpose, and cause of the phenomenon.[93] I do not think that this analysis—or that of the further question about the connection between freedom, *democracy,* and slavery—have been completed.[94]

Second, quite probably slavery increased on a massive scale in Athens only after the Persian Wars. The numbers are much debated. No solid evidence is available; the Athenians themselves did not know and their guesses of 150,000 adult male slaves and 400,000 total certainly are far too high. Recently, low estimates of a total of 50,000 and 66,000–93,000 have been proposed.[95] The elite made extensive use of slavery, in agriculture, mining, business, and domestic life, and derived substantial income from it.[96] Such income was used in part for liturgies and other benefaction from which the citizens profited collectively and individually, in part to finance a professional political career. This factor was especially important for the rich "industrialists" who challenged the traditional aristocratic leaders.[97] Slavery, increased massively by wealth derived directly or indirectly from the empire, thus made demographic diversification of democratic leadership possible. Moreover, the extant evidence gives the impression that every citizen who could afford it bought a slave.[98] These slaves too freed their nonelite masters (in nonagrarian production even more than in agriculture) from daily labor and enabled them to make the extraordinary commitment to the public sphere and their function as citizens that democracy demanded. Given the criticism that many citizens did not have the leisure (that is, the economic capacity) to participate in politics (Eur. *Suppl.* 417–22), this seems a crucial factor.[99] Most importantly, the connection between democracy and the citizens' dependence on the labor of slaves (and metics) was clearly recognized already at the time; as a result of this aspect of the "aristocratization" of the demos, the disdain for paid labor, which is visible from the Archaic period, must have increased sharply: any paid labor for any employer other than the state was now considered "unfree" and unworthy of a citizen.[100]

Third, already the contemporaries noticed that such dependence forced the Athenians to give their slaves more independence of movement and enterprise than was usually the case in Greek poleis.[101] There certainly was no lack of exploitation, and the fate of workers in the silver mines or in some factories was not comparable to that of slaves serving the families in their homes, working alongside citizens or metics on public construction crews, or running their own businesses. What matters, though, is that the latter categories were common, essential because of and for the democratic and imperial society, and perceived as giving this society a character that differed markedly from others. Sally Humphreys, I think, has provided the most compelling explanation:

> [Under] the peculiar historical circumstances of urbanisation and Empire, social change and economic development in classical Athens . . . the burden of production fell on slaves; as the organisation of business and production grew more complex and new forms of enterprise developed in which rich citizens would not take an active interest and poor citizens would not accept employment, the conditions of slavery were modified to fill the need for new kinds of labour. But these changes in slavery increased the poorer citizens' anxiety at the blurring of status distinctions between citizen and slave, and intensified the political activity by which they sought to maintain their political and economic identity.[102]

Metics

Athens undoubtedly acquired a sizable population of metics only in the fifth century.[103] True, there is earlier evidence of immigration of foreigners and the need to sort out their status.[104] But the numbers cannot have been very large. By contrast, the economic upswing after the Persian Wars must have attracted large numbers of foreigners. Just how many again is unknown. The numbers probably fluctuated; recent estimates vary from twenty thousand to almost fifty thousand, the great majority of whom must have settled in the Piraeus and in Athens.[105] The metics paid a poll tax; through their economic activities they contributed indirectly to Athens' revenue in taxes and dues; and they were liable to military service. More than five thousand of them may have qualified as hoplites; thousands more helped row the fleet.[106] The metics thus became an essential part of Athenian society and contributed significantly to its security, economic prosperity, and social and religious life. In fact, they were indispensable, as the "Old Oligarch" acknowledges: "The city needs metics because of the multiplicity of her industries and for her fleet." Aristophanes calls them "the bran of the citizens."[107] Yet we wonder whether such a massive influx of foreigners might not also have caused strong reactions on the part of the citizens: anxiety, outbursts of hatred and rejection, comparable to the reactions provoked in recent decades in various European countries by large-scale population movements and heavy concentrations of foreign workers in cities and industrial complexes. Those who assume that the citizenship law of 451/0 was largely motivated by such reactions are perhaps right, and the tradition about a *diapsēphismos* (review of the citizen list) in 446, prompted by a gift of Egyptian grain, seems to confirm the existence of such sentiments.[108]

Thetes

This brings us to the citizens: a big topic, and like the others fraught with uncertainties.[109] I begin with the thetes. Archaeological and literary as well as circumstantial evidence, meager though it is, argues for a rapid increase, during the first half of the fifth century, of the population of Attica in general and of the Piraeus-Athens area in particular, for changes in settlement patterns and for a shift of population from the country to the city. The labor force needed to sustain the economic boom must have consisted, apart from immigrants, mostly of members of the farming population of rural Attica who moved to the city.[110]

By the time of the Persian Wars, there may have been at most 30,000 adult male citizens; fifty years later there were perhaps 50,000, some think even 60,000, among an overall citizen population of between 150,000 and 240,000. No land reserves were left in Attica, and by midcentury, at the latest, large-scale importation of grain became necessary.[111] Large parts of the increasing population thus needed to find other means of supporting themselves in Attica or to emigrate. Both possibilities were available, the latter due to the foundation of colonies and cleruchies. As often, here too the availability of new forms of livelihood actually may have contributed to accelerating population growth.

The result was a process of substantial vertical mobility, in part down, in part up. Those who moved to the urban areas, among them presumably many sons from farming families, swelled the ranks of thetes. Hence the proportion of thetes in the total population increased. This raises the question of what this proportion had been before. Scholars usually assume, over centuries of polis existence, a fairly stable pattern of class distribution in which the hoplite farmers represent "a small sector of the community," the subhoplites or thetes half, perhaps substantially more, of the citizen population.[112] I doubt whether this is correct. In a society consisting overwhelmingly of subsistence farmers, in which few opportunities existed to earn a living outside the agrarian sector, the segment of very small farmers or nonfarmers must have been relatively small. It is these thetes—citizens who mostly lived in the metropolitan area and worked primarily in nonagrarian occupations and largely, directly or indirectly, for the "public sector"—whose share in the citizen body would have grown out of all proportion in the post–Persian Wars period. If correct, this would further help explain the democratic reforms of 462–450. Conversely, many thetes received land in the new cleruchies and were "promoted" into the zeugite (hoplite) class (above at n.65). Within one generation, many thousands of Athenians profoundly changed their work habits and ways of life. Even if they did not permanently migrate to the city, their outlook shifted: besides the traditional rural village mentality and local loyalties, the polis and its policies demanded a rapidly increasing amount of their attention.[113] Again, tensions and conflicts were inevitable.

State Care for War Victims

The imperial democracy clearly perceived its responsibility especially for those citizens who were killed or injured in serving the community, and for their families. Thereby the state took over some functions of the family, which, though conveying public honor, might have caused tensions as well. The main expression of such public care, the public funeral (*patrios nomos*), with funeral oration, games, and hero cult in the public cemetery (*dēmosion sēma*), is well known.[114] Support for the families of the war dead is well-attested but the extant information is unclear enough to have prompted much modern discussion about the date of introduction and the extent of such measures.[115] The custom was firmly established by the late fifth century: "The city will undertake the upbringing of their [the heroes'] children (*paides*) until they grow up, thus conferring a valuable crown on them and on the survivors of conflicts like these. Where the prizes for valour are the greatest, there the men will be the best citizens" (Thuc. 2.46.1, tr. Rhodes 1988); that is, men who know that their families will be cared for even if they die will fight with greater abandon. The same intention is emphasized in an undatable fragment of the comic poet Kratinos (fr. 183 *PCG* = 171 Edmonds 1957–59). In a summary statement, Aristotle (*Const. of the Athenians* 24.3) lists orphans among thousands of persons who received state pay or pensions. Pseudo-Xenophon (*Const. of the Athenians* 3.4) alludes to the responsibility of Athenian courts to decide disputes about the eligibility of orphans.[116]

Conflicting reports date the introduction of state support for war orphans either to the mid-fifth or, as part of Solon's reforms, to the early sixth century. Since the latter attribution occurs only in late sources and questionable claims of Solonian ancestry abound from the fourth century, Solonian authorship of this law has been doubted.[117] Even if it is correct, changing conditions of warfare must have caused as well a change in attitude and increased awareness of communal responsibility for war victims. Hoplite warfare was conducted intermittently by armies consisting of farmers; a social support system, probably sufficient in all but few cases, was provided by the fighters' extended families. By contrast, naval warfare, which involved thousands of lower-class citizens, was likely to produce large numbers of casualties (above at n.20) and potentially left many poor families in desperate conditions. Hence, whatever earlier regulations may have existed, measures introducing or improving support of war orphans became imperative once new emphasis was placed on communal warfare, naval warfare became the rule, and, perhaps, a major naval disaster brought the problem fully to public attention. Ruschenbusch's conjecture—that such a measure was introduced after the Egyptian disaster in 454—thus is attractive.[118] These privileges were extended to the sons (or children) of the Athenian democrats who died in fighting against the Thirty.[119] Upon reaching adulthood the war orphans were honored in a solemn ceremony on the first day of the Great Dionysia: they were equipped at state expense with panoplies, their names and their fathers' names were announced by the heralds, and they were discharged from state care to assume responsibility for their own lives.[120]

Several questions remain. First, we do not know whether the privilege of receiving a panoply was extended to the sons of all war dead or only to those of hoplites. Lacking evidence to the contrary, we have to assume the former but, if so, it bestowed upon the sons of thetes the honor of a rise in status.[121] This would seem easily acceptable in the late fifth and fourth centuries, when status distinctions between zeugites and thetes were blurred in the military and largely ignored in the political spheres, but remarkable if the custom was indeed introduced much earlier.[122] Second, no Athenian source tells us whether the daughters of the war dead were cared for in a similar way. *Paides* and *orphanoi* are ambivalent terms.[123] Regulations in fourth-century Thasos and Rhodes prescribe special privileges and maintenance for parents and children of the war dead: a full panoply worth no less than three minae for boys and a dowry for girls.[124] Because in Athens we know of no general regulation concerning dowries and Plato mentions only boys it is likely that the girls received only the food allowance.[125] Third, support for parents of war heroes, comparable to that provided in Thasos and Rhodes, is mentioned only in Plato's *Menexenos;* in Athens it seems to have been limited to some form of legal protection.[126] Fourth, we do not know the identity of the women (*gynaikes*) for whom Solon's law (n.117) provided a food allowance. If, in analogy to the orphans, they were war widows, it is most remarkable that we hear nothing further about measures supporting them beyond legal protection offered generally to widows who were pregnant at the time of their husbands' deaths.[127] The words Thucydides lets Perikles address to them, interpreted by modern scholars in widely divergent ways, certainly do not contain any promise of tangible material or emotional support.[128] And fifth, what was done for the families of metics, thousands of whom died alongside the citizens? Essentially, it seems, nothing.

Clearly, then, the purpose of these measures, which focused on the upbringing of male war orphans, was to strengthen the morale of the citizens and to raise future soldiers; accordingly, they were limited to citizens.[129] The possibility of sixth-century antecedents notwithstanding, I think they were essentially a consequence of Athens' reliance on naval warfare, the increased frequency of wars, and the massive rise of casualties caused by the polis' imperial rule and its aggressive foreign policy.

Women

The discussion of the status of women in Athens has long been hampered by the bias inherent in male-produced sources and the condition of ancient women as a mute or silenced class; by selective use of evidence, inadequate research strategies, and lack of efforts to differentiate among various categories of women; and by the almost unavoidable intrusion of modern judgments and agendas. Research has been more successful since Sarah Pomeroy and John Gould exposed these methodological problems to open discussion. In addition, the enormous discrepancy between source materials available for Athenian and non-Athenian women (except, in part, for Sparta and Gortyn) makes broad-based comparison almost impossible; moreover, democratic Athens was not a typical Greek polis. It is thus difficult to determine what about the situation of Athenian women was specifically Athenian and, even more specifically, due to democracy. Few scholars have paid precise attention to this problem. Moreover, the parameters of the debate on this question have recently been challenged and redefined.[130] In my present context, however, status and perception remain central.

Several factors determining the status of Athenian women were universal, that is, independent of specific conditions in fifth-century Athens:[131] their legal status as "permanent minors" and their resulting dependence on a *kyrios* as well as their political incapacity (both of which determined their exclusion) and, by contrast, their important role in cult and ritual, their protection by law and custom, and the tendency to keep them separated from nonkin males (all of which attest to their inclusion and the recognition of their importance to society). The explanation for all this lies in the basic facts that, like most premodern societies, the Greeks, while acknowledging as citizens only adult males who met certain conditions of descent and status, were perfectly aware of the crucial role of women in perpetuating the citizen body and transmitting property and legitimacy. Hence even the "charter myth of Athenian patriarchy," although addressing the specific condition of Athenian women, largely explains a situation that applies to women not exclusively in democratic but fairly generally in Greek society.[132] What made the biggest difference within these shared conditions probably was social class—elite women tended to play a more conspicuous and "independent" role than nonelite—and the individual character of those involved.

Nevertheless, the question of whether there was any interaction between democracy and the status of women remains important. One side of the question concerns the problem of whether democracy depended on "an underclass of women," just as it depended on "an underclass of slaves." As Mogens Hansen asserts, "In the agrarian societies of the Mediterranean world, from antiquity till today, much of the work has been left to the women: ploughing seems to have been the only task that was reserved to the men. It may well be thought that it was the work of the women even more than that of the slaves that provided the male citizens of Athens with their opportunity to run the political institutions."[133] This condition, however, even if intensified by the specific conditions prevailing in democratic and imperial Athens, was even less specific to this polis than that of slave labor.

The other problem is whether empire and democracy had any definable impact on the status, judgment, and treatment of women. Pomeroy, continuing a long-standing debate that has always been influenced heavily by current ideology and cultural conditioning, concludes that Athenian women "were forced into obscurity" in the classical period. Usually, "some women—at least those of the upper class—flourished in an aristocratic society while none fared as well under the democracy." She continues,

> The curbing of the aristocrats by the democracy of the fifth century B.C. entailed the repression of all women, but leaned especially heavily on the aristocrats who had the time and the means to make and enjoy displays of wealth. It may also be suggested that after the class stratification that separated individual men according to such criteria as noble descent and wealth was eliminated, the ensuing ideal of equality among male citizens was intolerable. The will to dominate was such that they then had to separate themselves as a group and claim to be superior to all nonmembers: foreigners, slaves, and women.[134]

The former observation probably is valid: while many elite men profited from the new opportunities of gaining distinction, influence, and wealth, elite women were forced to lead a less conspicuous—though hardly less comfortable —life. Pomeroy's latter observation, however, seems less compelling. Here too we should differentiate. The political sphere was always reserved to male citizens. In the social sphere things were more complex. The rise of all male Athenians to equality and shared power in politics and their domination of the public sphere did create a sense of exclusiveness and superiority and a sharper separation of public and private; like all other noncitizens, Athenian women were relegated to the nonpolitical sphere[135] and to powerlessness—but far from completely and not necessarily as the result of the male citizens' urge to dominate and repress the others. In some respects, democracy seems also to have had a broadly liberating and leveling effect. Metics had clearly defined and protected rights as well as obligations and enjoyed vast economic opportunities. Slaves could enjoy a great deal of independence and exploit opportunities unheard of elsewhere.[136] Athenian women, too, played a conspicuous and communally important public role in religion. Democratic Athens was famous for its many festivals and, through its empire, attracted many new cults; quite likely, all this contributed considerably to raising the status and visibility of some if not all women.[137] More specifically, examining three state festivals that largely or entirely excluded men, Lin Foxhall concludes that

> the intensive and critical work which women's festivals of Demeter bound and celebrate is stereotypically men's work. It is as if men's practical activities are ineffectual without the partnership of women's ritual activities . . . [T]hese festivals . . . simultaneously provide arenas in which women may constitute themselves as a distinct social and political group . . . [T]he general unease in the sources about what the girls got up to strongly suggests that women did not necessarily passively accept men's ideas about how they ought to behave . . . [These festivals at which women gathered from all over the city and Attica] must have provided an opportunity for women to socialise and maintain the links with their natal families, especially their mothers and probably also their sisters . . . There was a complex symbolic relationship between the state, the women who constituted it alongside men and the goddesses who carry the *thesmoi*, which, whether they are customs or corn or both, provided the foundations for the civilised *polis*.[138]

Furthermore, though otherwise relegated to the private sphere, an Athenian woman's individual fate was determined much more by personal circumstances than by law. The ideal was often contradicted by reality; movements were restricted, contacts and relations much less. As David Cohen explains plausibly, separation should not be confused with seclusion.[139] In literary sources the husband who speaks least of all to his wife or rudely tells her to shut up when she asks questions about his political opinions stands next to one who diligently consults his wife on issues of family, finances, and politics—although the latter may be a somewhat idealized picture.[140] And finally, the tendency, so prominent in our sources, to keep respectable women secluded is most naturally explained precisely by the women's crucial role as transmitters of legitimacy and property.[141]

Nevertheless, democracy probably *did* influence the Athenian women's situation and lives in several ways that differed perceptibly from other poleis. I mention three (there may be more). First, the fact that the political sphere and service to the polis assumed such a high priority in men's lives and provided them with a new "political identity" (above, at n.41), could not but marginalize women more than was usually the case. According to Jeffrey Henderson's compelling interpretation, the women's plot in Aristophanes' *Lysistrata* intends precisely to overcome the split between the public and private spheres that had emerged as a result of democracy's demands on the male citizens, and to reintegrate *oikos* and polis.[142] Second, the democratic polis clearly encroached upon traditional spheres of women's and family responsibility, most conspicuously through the public burial and heroization of the war dead in the *patrios nomos*.[143] It is difficult not to think that some conflict of this kind was dramatized in the *Antigone*. And third, recognition of and concerns about women's role as transmitters of legitimacy and property certainly were massively enhanced in the mid-fifth century by a measure that indeed was most intimately connected with democracy.

The Athenian citizenship law of 451/0 "turned the Athenian citizen body into a closed corporation, recruited only by descent from citizen father and citizen mother duly pledged." Although much discussed, it remains a puzzle. Aristotle's explanation, "because of the large number of citizens" (*Const. of the Athenians* 26.4), may be a mere guess. In absolute terms, it carries little conviction for the time soon after the Egyptian disaster in 454 or for the law's renewal in 403.[144] In relative terms, with reference to a specific problem that was obvious to contemporaries, it may be more plausible. Alan Boegehold suggests as background a growing number of court cases about inheritance of land—an increasingly scarce and contested commodity—in which juries perhaps tended to decide in favor of sons of Athenian rather than mixed marriages. Other modern explanations too emphasize the presence of large numbers of metics—whose daughters, for example, might have represented unwelcome competition for citizen girls.[145] At any rate, the fact that Athenians of all classes, not just the elite, now got around in the Aegean and that great numbers of foreigners now lived in Attica must have resulted in a substantial increase of mixed marriages; hence many more sons of foreign mothers were presented to demes and phratries, eventually to become citizens. All this may well have prompted negative reactions among citizens. Probably combined with other social, political, and economic factors, such reactions helped form a groundswell of popular opinion to which Perikles responded with his law.[146] In unprecedented ways, it had become important and profitable to be a citizen; hence this status was revalued and considered a prized possession, to be defended against dilution and intrusion.

Once the law was passed, the question of the legitimacy of children assumed much higher importance than before, and this certainly had a negative impact on the citizen women's lives. They were not registered in citizen lists—a strange oversight by the lawgiver—and very rarely introduced to phratry or deme members—perhaps precisely because the rules of decorum prohibited them from being known, in person or by name, by many nonkin males. Proof that one's mother was a citizen therefore was circumstantial: her parents' status, her participation in rituals reserved for *astai,* and her good reputation.[147] Hence avoidance of any spot on her reputation was crucial, which explains increased efforts to prevent her from meeting nonkin males.

Religion

"It is a truism . . . that for the Greeks the city was intimately bound up with the gods." As Christiane Sourvinou-Inwood states, the polis "provided the fundamental framework in which Greek religion operated . . . The *polis* anchored, legitimated, and mediated all religious activity . . . The role of the *polis* in the articulation of Greek religion was matched by the role of religion in the articulation of the *polis*: religion provided the framework and the symbolic focus of the *polis.*" Much "of a group's perception of its own identity is formed through religious acts"; this applies to the polis as a whole and to its subgroups.[148] Given such close interaction between polis, group identity, and religion, we should expect the deep changes experienced by the Athenian polis in the fifth century to be reflected in the forms and intensity of its religious practices, especially in cults, festivals, monuments, and other forms of religious expression and behavior. In the case of democracy, however, this assumption has been called into question. For example, Arnaldo Momigliano observes that "The connection between democracy and religion in the classical world, if it does exist, is not so obvious." Although a recent discussion comes to a similar conclusion, many partial studies and several broad surveys that have recently been written on this issue make it possible to present a more differentiated picture.[149] I shall limit myself to sketching brief answers to three questions: (*a*) What was the impact of democracy on religion? (*b*) What religious changes occurred under the influence of the empire? (*c*) Can we detect reflections in religion of the tensions and anxieties that we should expect to have resulted from the massive and rapid transformation of Athenian society, especially after the Persian Wars, and from the dramatic events, both successes and disasters, that highlight Athens' history in the fifth century?

To begin with democracy, it is clear that the background and origins of much that developed in the fifth century are to be found in the preceding period.[150] But Kleisthenes' reforms in many ways marked new beginnings.[151] In Robert Parker's words, "Attic religion in its familiar shape is a creation of Clisthenes no less than is the democracy."[152] The essential elements are well known. The new civic units, especially the demes and tribes, were also constituted as religious units with their own cults and festivals. Although most of the existing religious structures and offices were left intact (Aristotle, *Const. of the Athenians* 21.6), on the local level of the demes sacrifices and festivals, partly old, mostly new, must have served as important integrative occasions for the entire population. On the tribal level, two of four occasions (besides service in the council and in the tribal regiments of the hoplite army) that united the members, who lived in different parts of Attica, were of a religious nature: the festival of the tribe's eponymous hero at which the tribe conducted its official business, and the main polis festivals, especially the Panathenaia and Great Dionysia. There the demos took on a prominent role, competing for prizes in ten tribal men's and ten boys' choruses (girls and women were conspicuously absent).[153] Tribal identity was also emphasized in the method of financing the choruses and celebrating the victory and perhaps even in the seating arrangements in the theater. "Thus the polis represents itself in its tribal divisions to the god and at the same time to itself."[154] The tribal heroes became intermediaries between citizens and gods; they were represented as such on the Parthenon frieze and received their own monument in the Agora, probably in the Periklean period.[155]

The other most explicitly democratic monument was the statue group, also in the Agora, of the Tyrannicides who received cultic honors at their tombs as well. The political and ideological functions of this monument, like those of monumental buildings, especially the temples—beginning with the Old Temple of Athena on the Akropolis, now dated to the Kleisthenic rather than the Peisistratid period, and culminating, though far from ending, with the Parthenon—are discussed by Tonio Hölscher elsewhere in this volume.[156] Important though these political and ideological aspects are, we should not forget that these were sanctuaries, erected and decorated lavishly by the democratic citizen body in gratitude for the gods' support in past trials and to secure their continuing favor.

Clearly, however, in such cases the connection between religion and democracy is indirect at best (see below, at n.167). Henk Versnel rightly points out that much we should expect to find is in fact absent from the record. He mentions as examples prayers for the democracy and its salvation or restoration, the consultation of oracles on issues of internal politics, or the adaptation of gods, cults, or rituals to specifically democratic, as opposed to "patriotic," needs (except perhaps for the cult of Peitho, Persuasion). Indeed, the extent to which the democracy encroached upon or took over traditional cults is much debated. Michael Jameson argues that the polis essentially reviewed and regulated existing cults only when changes or problems required it.[157] New cults were handled differently: the democratic principles of appointing officials by lot and for a limited time were applied to priesthoods as well—and gradually influenced also traditional cults.[158]

Otherwise, perhaps the most important impact of democracy is reflected in the spectacular increase in religious activities and in overall citizen participation in such activities. Contemporary sources attest, both critically and proudly, to the extraordinary number and lavishness of Athenian festivals.[159] Examining the intersection between and close coordination of the sacred and secular realms in Athenian society, Robert Connor considers it likely

> that one of the ideals that informed Attic democracy was that of achieving a festival society. The linkage is particularly close between the idea of free speech (*parrhēsia*) in festivals and in the conduct of Athenian democracy. But the analogy between the court system as *agōn* and the athletic and other competitions of some Athenian festivals should not be overlooked . . . [If] the political structure of Athens encouraged the growth of civic festivals . . . [and] strongly influenced the form of religious celebration, the reverse may also be true: that certain Athenian festivals ultimately influenced the form of political practice within the city. Some provided an implicit model for what the polis should be.[160]

Increased state sponsorship of rituals and festivals meant more cults, more sacrifices, more public financial involvement, more buildings and committees to manage finances and oversee buildings and activities; it also meant that as members of such committees and as participants in rituals and sacrifices more citizens were involved more frequently and regularly in such activities. Not least, more sacrifices produced more meat: "At the Panathenaia all citizens who marched in the procession received a share in the meat which was first divided up by demes (*IG* II^2 334, 25–27). There was hardly a more democratic feature of the religious life of Classical Athens."[161]

Polytheistic religion in general and Athenian religion in particular were open and in constant flux. New cults were imported and celebrated, some adopted by the polis, others not. Generally, individuals and groups had much freedom in their religious preferences and activities.[162] State interference was rare and limited to special circumstances (see below).

Second, more briefly, let us look at the empire's impact on Athenian religion. This aspect has been thoroughly explored recently by Bernhard Smarczyk.[163] "Athens' self-presentation as the 'mother-city' of the whole empire was a potent imperial fiction." Going back at least to the early sixth century, this ideology was vastly enhanced in the course of the fifth and served as a method to integrate the empire. Colonies and "allies" sent a cow and panoply to the Panathenaia, first fruits to Eleusis and perhaps a phallos to the Dionysia, which became an "imperial" festival especially through the presentation of the tribute and other political celebrations at the opening ceremony.[164] Although the Center of the League was moved from Delos to Athens in 454, at the latest, Delos, the Delian Apollo, and the Delia, allegedly founded by Theseus, a "revamped Ionian festival, not replacing but complementing and overshadowing the Panionia," played a crucial role in Athens' imperial conceptions, not least in reaction to the uses made by Sparta and her allies of religious issues, festivals, and sanctuaries.[165] Whether the Athenians actively promoted the establishment of some of their cults in "allied" cities is debated; that Athenian settlers abroad brought their cults along and in their religious life interacted with native cults as well goes without saying.[166]

Domestically, a clear separation in religious matters between democracy and empire seems more difficult than one might expect. Victory monuments, documenting a close connection of foreign relations and war with religion, were set up in Athens from the late sixth century; Herodotus, however, interpreted such victories as proof of the superiority of democracy.[167] Some scholars think that the Tyrannicides soon received a cult at the place of their deed but that the famous statue group was created much later, celebrating the victory of Marathon which was popularly seen as the second expulsion of the tyrants.[168] Theseus as the hero of Attica's unification was also the hero of its naval power—before he explicitly became the founder of democracy. His increased prominence in many festivals and monuments can be traced confidently to the influence of Kimon, the Athenian Empire builder par excellence who brought Theseus' bones to Athens.[169] As Alan Shapiro observes, the "happy coexistence of Theseus and the

Tyrannicides as joint heroes of the Athenian democracy—indeed the intermingling of their iconographies which many scholars have observed—may reflect the mutual relationship of internal and external affairs under the democracy."[170] This same relationship is visible spectacularly in the festival of the Great Dionysia, a quintessential civic event with strong imperial overtones (mentioned above), and in the sanctuary of Athena on the Akropolis, goddess of Athens *and* the empire—a monument to both democracy and its triumphant policies, with its splendid frieze that can be interpreted both as a civic and imperial celebration.[171]

Athenian religion thus changed greatly under the influence of democracy and empire; or perhaps it is more accurate to say, it developed rapidly and broadly, became more intensive and varied, rather than changing its character. It penetrated every aspect of public life, and since public life was so much more intense and pervasive than before, religion in all its aspects too became a much more pervasive reality in the citizens' lives, on both the local and polis levels. This, of course, says nothing about the depth and intensity or sincerity of religious feelings. Since we know so little about this aspect,[172] an answer to our third question is much more difficult. Were tensions and anxieties brought about by the rapid and profound transformation of the Athenian state and society reflected in religion? Perhaps, but what kind of evidence would reveal this to us? We observe reflections of political events, especially military victories, in religious monuments; the temple of Athena Nike, constructed in the late 420s to celebrate the triumph at Pylos, is a superb example.[173] Conversely, the religious despair and neglect of traditional practices and beliefs caused by the plague of 429–425 is attested by Thucydides and confirmed to some extent by other evidence.[174] The importation of new healing and mystery gods in the years of the Peloponnesian War can be interpreted as a reaction to plague, war, and related pressures.[175] Signs of religious intolerance, culminating in the trial of Sokrates, but intermixed there, as at other occasions, with political motives, appeared in exceptional constellations, representing responses to specific crises.[176]

To some extent, then, as we should expect, Athenian religious life did react to social and political experiences and changes. Where we are able to perceive it, however, the connection seems close and specific, not broad and general. Tensions and anxieties caused by patterns of comprehensive social change—but perhaps even more by protracted war and plague—may have provided added stimuli for the intensification of religious life in democratic and imperial Athens, to some extent in the public sphere, perhaps more markedly in the private realm of the *oikos* which is much more difficult to grasp.[177] On the present state of evidence and research this seems all we can say.

Conclusion

It was the purpose of this chapter to sketch the rapid pace, depth, and pervasiveness of the changes Athenian society underwent in little more than one generation after the Persian Wars. The economy, the composition of the population, and politics and social life were very different in the 430s from what they had been only fifty years earlier. A sense of unlimited opportunities and possibilities pervaded the community, punctured occasionally by major disasters. The whole polis was involved in an exciting, breathtaking adventure. Democracy and its policies and the quest for ever more power even transformed the Athenians' collective character—at least so some contemporary observers thought.[178] But all these changes had their negative sides too, and the disappearance of the old ways must have left many unhappy—not only because those who traditionally counted for little now had a lot to say in politics.

The fundamental transformation of their whole polis must have affected the Athenians deeply and, at times, traumatically; tensions and conflicts must have abounded. Even if, as our sketch of religious developments has shown, it remains difficult to trace these in the extant evidence—except perhaps in drama[179]—it is not implausible to assume that all this had an impact on the arts. The arts in general played a very complex role and served many purposes and needs in the society that developed and used them. Christian Meier suggests that in a long period of rapid development, change and innovation, ever new opportunities and challenges as well as uncertainty, crisis of identity, and anxiety, the Athenians needed their arts.[180] More generally, democracy and the empire, both new phenomena with massive and pervasive impact on Athenian society, created new needs and provoked new reactions that could not but influence developments in the arts in many ways. To what extent and how exactly this may have been the case is the challenge posed to the contributors to this volume.[181]

CHAPTER THREE

Accounting for Culture in Fifth-Century Athens

LISA KALLET

Introduction

The title of this chapter is intended to highlight the twofold nature of my subject, the financing of cultural production in fifth-century Athens and its relationship to democracy and empire. At issue, first, is the practical question of how the Athenians paid for the tremendous cultural output of the fifth century and the role imperial wealth played in this; second, how contemporary Athenians perceived, or accounted for, the connection between public and private expenditure on culture on the one hand and, on the other, the democracy and empire. While scholars have examined various aspects of this subject, interest in economic matters has tended to be both more focused and broader, and has only selectively pertained to the theme of this volume.

Exploration of economic aspects of classical Athens has long focused on the fourth century—of necessity, due to the concentration of evidence in that period—and on two chief concerns: the nuts and bolts of the polis' fiscal condition and the broader question of whether Athens had a primitive (or pre-) economy, embedded in social and political institutions and inseparable from them, or something closer to a modern market economy, only earlier, less developed, and on a much smaller scale.[1] Scholars focusing on the fifth century have mostly been interested in public fiscal issues, especially those arising from the empire, and in the wealth of individuals, some of it accruing from the empire.[2] Another old but recently revived debate is more directly related to the theme of this volume, namely the extent, origin, and use of Athens' reserve, especially as far as tribute and the building program are concerned.[3] I do not propose to undertake a comprehensive examination of expenditure on the arts in Athens; rather I shall concentrate on two areas, the Periklean building program and agonistic liturgies: both should be particularly useful for exploring the link between the arts, democracy, and empire.

Athenian Public Economy in the Mid- to Late Fifth Century

I begin with a brief and selective overview of Athens' fiscal condition in order to place expenditure on culture in its broader context. By the mid-fifth century, Athens, through its naval empire, had accumulated wealth greater than any other polis in the Greek world—a pittance compared with, for example, Persia or Hellenistic kingdoms, but unprecedented for its time. According to Thucydides (2.13), at its height Athens possessed a reserve of ninety-seven hundred talents, which had been reduced by some twenty-three hundred talents by 431 due to the building program and military expenses like the siege of Poteidaia.[4] This extraordinary reserve was the result of a systematic policy of accumulating and centralizing public wealth.[5]

Imperial Revenue

Our principal evidence is twofold: (1) the tribute quota lists recording the tithe, or *aparchē,* dedicated to Athena and starting in 454 (*IG* I[3] 259–90), from which scholars estimate average annual tribute totals paid by Athens' allies of around four hundred talents; (2) Thucydides 2.13, which provides a figure of six hundred talents for annual imperial revenue. Since the best way to understand Thucydides' Greek is that six hundred talents, "the majority of it from tribute," represents the grand total collected annually, some two hundred talents must have come from imperial revenue other than tribute, for example, from mines,[6] rents from sacred land,[7] or officially sanctioned plundering parties.[8] This non-tribute revenue, which leaves no trace in the epigraphic record, could be sizable: Thucydides (4.108.1) notes the Athenians' consternation when Amphipolis was lost in 424, partly because of the revenue it provided, none of which was in the form of tribute. Similarly, Ionia is described, perhaps not without exaggeration, as the "greatest source of revenue" to Athens (Thuc. 3.31.1);[9] since Ionia collectively did not contribute sizable tribute, this reference must also be to non-tribute revenue.[10] Such additional imperial revenue helps explain how the Athenians could have accrued such a large reserve.[11] For it is clear that as a matter of policy the Athenians collected far more revenue from the empire than was needed for immediate military purposes.

Another area of imperial exploitation relevant here is income that wealthy citizens derived from individual land holdings abroad.[12] That this phenomenon was widespread can be inferred from the prohibition against such property holdings in the decree of the Second Athenian League.[13] Evidence of the actual extent of such property is incomplete but suggestive, coming from records of the sale of confiscated property, including land abroad, of those convicted of mutilating the Herms in 415,[14] and from casual references to Athenian-owned foreign property in our sources.[15] Such private income may be an important factor in the willingness of the wealthy to support both the democracy and the empire, for their wealth was directly linked to both; moreover it may be a crucial factor in the apparent absence of indebtedness and liturgy avoidance in the period before the Peloponnesian War. Such individuals will have belonged to the liturgical class, which incurred often considerable expense in performing festival liturgies.

Domestic Revenue

For domestic revenue we have two pieces of evidence, both problematic. First, in Aristophanes' *Wasps,* performed in 422, Bdelykleon instructs his father Philokleon on Athens' total revenue in order to show how little of it the dikasts, or jurors, receive. "First total roughly . . . the tribute that comes in to us from the allied states, and apart from that the taxes, and the many one-per-cents, court fees, mines, markets, harbors, rentals, confiscations. These add up to nearly two thousand talents" (656ff.). It is indeed dangerous to take this list, but especially the total, literally, since it is here in Bdelykleon's interest to emphasize the gap between the total revenue of Athens and the amount that filtered down to Philokleon and his fellow dikasts; exaggeration generally was a favorite tool of comic poets, and it is unlikely that Aristophanes undertook careful research into Athens' revenue and expenditures.[16]

Second, in his *Anabasis* (7.1.27), an early work, Xenophon refers to an annual revenue of "not less than" one thousand talents from both imperial and domestic sources. August Böckh did not believe "that Aristophanes made any gross exaggeration" and therefore trusted him more than Xenophon,[17] and even Alan Sommerstein assumes, on the basis of Xenophon's text, that the total was closer to two thousand than one thousand talents.[18] I disagree; my guess is that, at least up to the beginning of the Peloponnesian War, imperial revenue supplied the bulk, especially since Perikles (Thuc. 2.13.3, above at n.6) explicitly mentions revenue from the empire as six hundred talents a year and then the undefined "other revenue." If domestic revenue had been equal to or larger than tribute one might expect more precision, especially in a context where specific figures added rhetorical force. Conversely, Perikles here might have minimized domestic revenue in order to emphasize the necessity of the empire and the flow of imperial revenue. In any case, given the nature of the comic genre, Xenophon's minimum of one thousand talents probably is closer to the mark.[19]

Regular Expenditures of the Polis

Athens' reserve, around ninety-seven hundred talents at its height (Thuc. 2.13.3)—likely in the mid-fifth century—supplemented by an annual revenue of approximately one thousand talents, was vast by Greek standards. It supported the maintenance of the empire, pay for participation in the democracy and other expenditures, and the extraordinary cultural life of the polis. We would like to know the ratio between public income and expenditures and, for our present purposes, the percentage of annual expenditure on artistic production in comparison with other domestic expenditures. No such comprehensive data survive, however. Scattered inscriptions on stone list isolated expenses, but the Athenians did not record in permanent form cash income; and we have no record of a double-entry accounting procedure recording receipts and expenditures.[20]

Nevertheless, it is possible to reach at least a rough estimate of public expenditures. Military operations would have cost at most six hundred talents annually, assuming two hundred warships and a three-month campaigning season.[21] The average probably was considerably lower but from time to time extraordinary expenditures were incurred on campaigns against recalcitrant allies that could deplete the reserve substantially; for example, the siege of Samos in 441–439 cost over twelve hundred talents, that of Poteidaia (432–430) two thousand talents.[22] For domestic expenditures Böckh estimates for the fourth century about four hundred talents annually,[23] not including large outlays for festivals, buildings, and other extraordinary expenditures, which could bring the total up to one thousand talents.[24] Hansen puts pay for participation in the democracy alone at around one hundred talents in the fourth century.[25] But these figures are high for the fifth century, when the cost of the democracy was considerably lower,[26] and in some cases exaggerated.[27] A ballpark figure might be seventy-five talents for the running of the democracy alone and above three hundred for the total expenditure, not including the cost of operating the fleet in wartime and other extraordinary expenditures.[28]

The percentage of this annual total that was spent on regular festivals is notoriously difficult to determine.[29] For the Dionysia, one recent estimate puts state expenditure at six talents (compared to almost nineteen talents spent by the *chorēgoi,* the individuals who financed dramatic choruses),[30] while another assumes total choregic costs of up to six talents, with the state supplying five talents.[31] Public funds would have paid for most of the remaining costs, including sacrifices, a bronze tripod for the victorious *chorēgos* in the dithyramb competition, prizes for the victorious poets, the procession, and pay for poets and actors.[32] The widely differing estimates of the total cost, and, importantly, of the proportion of private to public moneys, testifies to our general lack of good evidence for Athenian finances. Even if private expenditure outweighed public in dramatic festivals, still, as Böckh commented, "it is easy to conceive that the state expended much money upon the celebration of festivals."[33]

Our sources show indeed that festival expenditure as a whole was notorious: Demosthenes (4.35) claims that the Panathenaia and Dionysia cost more than any naval enterprise; Plutarch (*Moralia* 349a) similarly notes that more money was spent on the theater than on wars undertaken for freedom; and Pseudo-Xenophon, dubbed the "Old Oligarch," comments that Athens held more festivals than the rest of the world.[34] These statements, however exaggerated, reflect a popular perception of heavy expenditure on festivals, especially dramatic performances, but also a willingness to devote public and private money to the cultural life of the city; they also show that such expenditure, like that on public building, could be a heavily contested issue.[35]

Expenditure on the democracy and on the cultural life of the city, then, was considerable; where did the money come from? Objectively, funding for these purposes clearly did not depend on the empire: pay for democratic participation not only survived into the fourth century when Athens had lost both its empire and great wealth, but it was increased and its scope broadened. In the fifth century, rather, the enormous League moneys probably freed the Athenians to use regular domestic revenues to pay for the democracy whereas otherwise they might not have felt able to, despite their ability to do so later.[36]

The more interesting question is how fifth-century Athenians themselves perceived and accounted for their ability to support the democracy. If Aristophanes can be trusted they assumed that pay for certain functions in the democracy came from imperial funds. The best example is the *Wasps*.[37] While the comedy presupposes that Philokleon and his fellow jurors rely on the empire for their pay—their power and livelihood as they see it—imperial revenue in fact was not its source; rather—and recognized in the play—the dikasts receive their pay (*misthos*) from the *kolakretai*, the disbursers of state moneys, not imperial funds.[38] Yet contemporaries could easily blur this distinction since litigation involving Athens' allies, as the *Wasps* attests, was perceived to constitute the lion's share of the courts' business. Most significantly, the general idea that money from the empire was used in domestic areas makes the empire seem necessary not only for the functioning of the democracy but for individual livelihood as well; Philokleon and his cronies see their own individual betterment as coming from the city's *archē*.

We can discern, then, clear perceptions of a symbiotic economic relationship between empire and democracy on both the public and private levels. I shall now explore this relationship in two areas of the cultural realm, the Periklean building program and the festival liturgies, to see how it functioned and was perceived by the Athenians, collectively and individually.

Paying for Culture

Irregular Public Expenditures on Culture: The Periklean Building Program

Gorgias said of Kimon, "he made money to use it and he used it to be honored."[39] Much of what Kimon spent his money on were monuments, both religious and secular.[40] Beginning with Perikles, however, that kind of individual lavish expenditure on public monuments virtually disappeared.[41] The building program initiated by Perikles was funded almost entirely from public moneys: the great bulk was treasure belonging to Athena.[42] While the Parthenon was certainly the most impressive, many other major buildings were erected in the second half of the fifth century in Athens and Attica, among them the Propylaia on the Akropolis, the Hephaisteion, the temple of Poseidon in Sounion, and the Telesterion in Eleusis.[43] The extant building accounts are fragmentary and insufficient to allow an estimate of the total cost which thus must be made by analogy, e.g., with the Asklepieion in Epidauros. Heliodoros' figure of 2,012 talents for the Propylaia alone[44] must be wildly off but is perhaps not far from the cost of the entire program.[45] Stanier's estimate of near five hundred talents for the Parthenon and seven hundred to eight hundred talents for the chryselephantine statue of Athena still seems reasonable.[46]

It is not possible here to treat the financing of the entire program and its relationship to the democracy and empire; for purposes of this discussion I shall focus on the Parthenon, for it relates most significantly to our theme. The chief contributor was Athena, but there were contributions in certain years from other sources: the Hellenotamiai ("treasurers of the Greeks," who received and administered imperial funds) in five of the fifteen years, the *teichopoioi* (officials in charge of maintaining the walls), the *xenodikai* (judges who heard suits against foreigners), the *trieropoioi* (the trireme builders), and the treasurers of Hephaistos in Laureion;[47] some of these officials, including the Hellenotamiai, contributed to the Propylaia as well, though at other times.

Were the supplementary contributions necessary from a financial standpoint? Or did these administrative boards wish to contribute for other reasons? Unfortunately no complete figures are preserved for the contributions of the Hellenotamiai, and what tends to be absent are the crucial beginning numbers that would indicate the general level of contribution. The amounts, however, have been thought to correspond to their contributions to the Propylaia—which were not substantial: only one-sixtieth of a year's tribute, or roughly six talents (assuming an average tribute total of four hundred talents).[48]

It is likely, therefore, that the contributions by the Hellenotamiai and other boards were modest in proportion to the total spent on the temple, and that Athena could easily have funded the project solely from her own treasury, given both the total of the reserve in the mid-fifth century and the fact that while the Parthenon was expensive for a temple, it was not a large burden in the broader context of public expenditure.[49] If their contributions were not financially essential, might these magistracies have wanted to be immortalized by their inscription as contributors to such a magnificent civic project? A more mundane and likely explanation may be that the Hellenotamiai, *xenodikai,* and the others simply had a surplus in certain years which they contributed to the Parthenon and the Propylaia instead of carrying it over to the following year.[50] The irregular appearance of these boards in the accounts supports this, although, given the fragmentary state of the inscriptions, it is possible that they contributed more often. Finally, we do not know whether the decision to contribute lay ultimately with the various boards or depended on an official vote of the demos.[51]

Whatever we are to make of the significance of such contributions, it is important to keep in mind that the amounts are a modest part of the overall cost of the Parthenon and Propylaia. In contrast to the epigraphic evidence, however, Plutarch (*Perikles* 12) implies extensive use of money from the empire on the construction of temples: Perikles' political rival, Thucydides, son of Melesias, supposedly accused Perikles of squandering the allies' money on the building program, "decking the city out like a prostitute with thousand-talent temples." Scholars have argued over the authenticity of this famous anecdote. Although Andrewes dismisses it completely,[52] most accept it in some degree,[53] as I am inclined to, especially since we know that some imperial funds were contributed by the Hellenotamiai. Moreover, as we have seen from the *Wasps,* there was a popular (mis)perception that they were used in other domestic areas. It is highly significant, therefore, both that Thucydides thought he could make political hay over this issue—which reflects a tension about the uses of imperial money (see further below)—and that he remained unsuccessful.

Yet, despite the blatant exaggeration inherent in Thucydides' rhetoric—for example, his reference to "thousand-talent temples"—Plutarch's story has proved irresistible to modern scholars compared with the rather less exciting implications of the Parthenon building accounts. Since Athena's treasury was undeniably the largest contributor to the Parthenon's construction, some scholars theorize that it contained all the surplus of the allies' tribute because the Hellenotamiai routinely deposited two hundred talents (envisioned as the normal annual tribute surplus) there every year.[54] This theory, while possible, rests on insufficient evidence.[55] Moreover, what seems to be at issue in Plutarch is current tribute, not reserve.[56] Furthermore, if all tribute surplus was routinely placed in the treasury of Athena, how would the Hellenotamiai have had any extra to give to the building program and why record this contribution separately?

It is not at all clear, then, that the Parthenon was built chiefly with tribute, although the building accounts confirm that *some* tribute was indeed spent on it. There is still an important question to consider, however: how did the Athenians regard the role of tribute and the empire in the construction of their civic religious monuments? Two relevant points emerge from the preceding discussion: first, Plutarch shows that there were contemporary perceptions that the empire financed the building program, and second, the contributions of the Hellenotamiai to the Parthenon (and Propylaia) were openly advertised, recorded on stone, and set up on the Akropolis for all, Athenians and non-Athenians, to see.

While the epigraphic and literary evidence disagree about the actual amounts of tribute used, they complement one another if we focus on perception and representation. Thucydides' exaggeration and the official response in which the principle of using tribute was accepted, seen both in Plutarch[57] and the inscriptions, reflect, as do plays like the *Wasps,* collective acceptance of the use of allied money on the democracy and on the building program. Far from wishing to downplay or hide such use of allied money, the Athenians openly regarded the functioning of the courts, a cornerstone of democracy, and the building program, the city's most spectacular manifestation of greatness, glory, and the power of the *demos,* as made possible by the empire. Indeed, because of the wealth it generated, the empire was seen as necessary to the functioning of the city's democracy and cultural life.[58]

The building program was a symbol of the city's power through its control over the allies,[59] just as Philokleon in the *Wasps* regards himself as having a stranglehold on the empire. But the connection, economic and otherwise, between empire, democracy, and culture is even more explicit and integral in the case of the Parthenon and the statue of Athena: the Delian League was in a sense refounded as the League of Athena of Athens, no longer that of Apollo of Delos.[60] The allies' mandatory dedication to the goddess, the *aparchē,* was inscribed on stone outside the Parthenon, likely the home of the League's new treasury, a function formerly served by the temple of Apollo—as Thucydides troubles to point out (1.96.1). Athens advertised itself as the mother-city of the empire, its allies therefore as colonists, whose participation in the Panathenaic procession—in which they brought a cow and panoply for their (new but, according to the propaganda, old) patron goddess[61]—reflected their new identity.

Within this climate the contributions of the Hellenotamiai to the Parthenon and even the Propylaia could be seen as unexceptionable,[62] even as a use of Athens' own money, and those who contested the propriety of using tribute were effectively muffled. Yet there was dissent. Although Thucydides was ostracized, he cannot have been alone. The beginning of Xenophon's *Poroi* ("Revenues") contains a tantalizing reference to certain "influential men" who "have said that they know what justice is as well as others" but "because of the poverty of the majority they are forced to be a little unjust with respect to the allies" (1.1). Although likely referring to the period of the Second Athenian League, the comment reveals unease about the domestic use of the allies' wealth that can reasonably be held to apply to fifth-century practice as well.[63] Tension about the empire itself, intimately bound up with the use of its wealth, can also be inferred from a famous comment attributed to Perikles in Thucydides: "The empire you hold is like a tyranny: it may seem wrong to have taken it, but it is certainly dangerous to let it go" (2.63.2).

These allusions in our evidence confirm that Athenian opinion was complex. They raise the possibility of a further issue at work in the Athenians' willingness to acknowledge their use of tribute in a domestic context, namely, conceptions about the appropriate use of excess wealth. This is a typical concern of individuals[64] that would have been applied to the polis once Athens accumulated its enormous public reserve. The major justification for amassing wealth was the maintenance of a naval empire; yet by the mid-fifth century the polis had accumulated a reserve—almost ten thousand talents (Thuc. 2.13.3, discussed above)—that far exceeded its military needs. To be sure, this amount could be whittled away quickly by expenditures on the building program or costly military campaigns; but the latter, like the nearly three-decades-long Peloponnesian War, were unpredictable and do not affect the basic argument that the Athenians had built up a surplus of wealth that was staggering for a Greek polis. I suggest that the demos collectively faced a similar moral difficulty as individuals like Ischomachos (the gentleman estate manager in Xenophon's *Oeconomicus*), who found it necessary to justify the acquisition of surplus household wealth by directing some of it toward the adornment of the polis.[65] Thus, to the community, spending part of its collective wealth on ostentation and magnificent public projects could be a supporting argument for the propriety of its accumulation.

However it justified its lavish spending, the demos as benefactor of Athens' building program was spending in ways similar to the magnificent expenditure, or *megaloprepeia,* of aristocratic individuals. Yet in the case of the latter, such spending could evoke tyranny.[66] Greeks drew a close connection between tyranny and (the expenditure of) wealth;[67] what are the implications and significance of the fact that the demos took on the role of a *megaloprepēs*?

The Demos as Tyrant

Plutarch claims that in response to public concern over the high cost of the building program, Perikles offered to pay for it himself, at which point the people objected strenuously. Impossible as this is factually, it at least suggests what an elite Athenian like Perikles might have done (on a smaller scale) for prestige and, by implication, what power he might have expected to gain from magnificent expenditure.[68] The use of public rather than private funds for such projects marks a fundamental change from the days of Kimon. It is clearly connected with democracy: what is its significance?

While some scholars see this change negatively, as a move to prevent individuals like Kimon from gaining political power through their own expenditure,[69] I suggest a different conception of the new public patronage, one that may seem at first paradoxical. Athenians thought of men like Kimon as patrons of monuments but, as noted above, such magnificent expenditure also conjured up tyranny.[70] Tyrants of course were also known for their impressive buildings.[71] Aristotle describes Kimon as possessing "tyrant-scale property,"[72] and the worry about Alkibiades was that the size of his expenditures pointed toward a bid for tyranny (Thuc. 6.15.4). I suggest that the demos, assuming the role of public benefactor, was acting not simply in an aristocratic way but like a tyrant, and that its control over and magnificent expenditure of wealth provided a crucial demonstration of its power not just abroad, but at home.[73] Perikles, while deflecting the idea that he himself might be a tyrant, was, in effect, elevating the demos to that position, especially through the excessive, extraordinary expenditure of its wealth. Like tyrants, who may have appropriated wealth unjustly but put it to acceptable use in adorning the city, the demos could enhance its power through the skillful use of accumulated wealth.

The metaphor of Athens as a tyrant appears in our evidence mainly in connection with Athens' rule over its allies and has both negative and positive nuances.[74] For example, the famous allusions in Thucydides to Athens as tyrant (2.63.2, 3.37.2) explicitly refer to Athens' *archē,* and the context, if not negative, is one of resigned admission: "Like it or not, we're like a tyranny in our control of our allies." While other contemporary allusions suggest the ambiguity of the metaphor, most striking are passages that cast the position of the tyrant in a favorable light.[75] As Connor observes, "when the word reflects upon the situation of the ruler it is commonly neutral or positive in tone; when it reflects upon the situation of the tyrant's subjects it is commonly hostile in connotation."[76] Hence for the Athenians to think of themselves collectively in the position of a tyrant could be a very positive and empowering notion.[77]

Is the idea of the demos as tyrant at home—as opposed to the polis as tyrant over its allies—attested at all, and is it a positive or negative—or ambiguous—idea? In *Knights* (1111ff.) the metaphor is ambiguous as the chorus sings, "O Demos, your rule is a noble thing, seeing that all men fear you just like a tyrant."[78] This suggests an imperial context but may also apply to the domestic arena, since the chorus continues by alluding to Demos' gullibility in the assembly. At the end of the play, however, Demos is represented as the monarch not only of Greece but "of this land," clothed and perfumed in decidedly undemocratic fashion, emulating eastern luxury (1330ff.).[79] Finally, in the *Wasps*, trying to prove that the jurors' power is not inferior to that of a king, Philokleon asks, "is this not a mighty power that allows us to mock at wealth?"[80] Here the context shifts from the empire to the city: the dikasts' power—which, as the same play makes clear, comes from having an empire—is so great at home that they can be completely unimpressed by others' individual wealth. Why? Because their own collective wealth and power allow them to act without restrictions; as they claim, they cannot be called to account (587).

These passages suggest that the metaphor of tyranny was applied to the demos in its political role at home: like a tyrant in his city, the demos is all-powerful and unaccountable. Its power was perceived as being connected to its wealth; thus when Bdelykleon pokes holes in what he sees as an illusion of power, he argues that Philokleon—and the demos by extension—is not as wealthy, and therefore not as powerful as he thinks.[81]

In conclusion, the demos took over from aristocratic individuals the role of financier or public benefactor in the most visible area of conspicuous consumption and display, the building program. By playing the aristocrat, even the tyrant, the demos demonstrated its extraordinary power, able to do what it wanted with its money and choosing, among other uses, to spend it on magnificent monuments, and to pay itself to be in power. All this shows the demos' remarkable confidence and may have been a factor in its willingness to let liturgists spend as much as they wanted (see below). Moreover, its lavish use of wealth arguably constituted an important part of popular democratic ideology: Athenians, like other Greeks, associated power with wealth and paradoxically found a way to make the average, poor Athenian take on the role of the elite at the same time that they espoused the democratic principle that the poor should enjoy political equality with the rich.

Thus the ambiguous image of Athens the tyrant city as ruler of an empire may have been accompanied by a more positive construction of the demos-as-tyrant spending its wealth on the city. Furthermore, if the city in the form of the collective demos was tyrant, its extraordinary wealth and control over resources would make it difficult for any individual Athenian to threaten this order.[82] Yet individuals continued to spend their money in the cultural sphere; we need now to explore the significance of the festival liturgies in relation to democracy and empire.

Private Spending on Culture: From Largess to Liturgies

In the age of Kimon, we see at work what Connor terms the "politics of largess,"[83] illustrated especially by Kimon himself who was known for his liturgies and buildings and for personal benefactions to his demesmen.[84] Spending "to be honored," as Gorgias put it, however, was a hallowed Greek tradition that did not end with Kimon. Plutarch says that Nikias, who "had excessive wealth, sought by means of this to win the leadership of the people . . . He tried to captivate them by his *chorēgiai* and *gymnasiarchiai,* outdoing all predecessors and contemporaries in costliness and splendor" (Nikias 3). What is the difference? Kimon's spending had an ad hoc, personal quality to it; he bestowed largess perhaps even more on individuals than on the communal group.[85] By contrast, Nikias' liturgical expenditures benefitted the people as a whole.

The question of what precise role liturgical expenditures played in democracy has been answered in widely divergent ways. Some scholars view them as an aristocratic institution at odds with democracy, while others argue that they were integral to democracy. Lauffer thinks that liturgies, causing an overreliance on the elite, were not vital to democracy but in fact weakened it.[86] Similarly, Veyne writes, "We see [in Athens] . . . some features which could open the way to euergetism. And finally, one institution, the liturgy, foreshadows oligarchy: it consecrates the division of the democratic city into poor and rich, and testifies to a euergetic mentality among the rich. Helped by the depoliticization of the mass of citizens, the transition to an oligarchy of euergetistic notables would take place almost automatically."[87]

On the other side, Davies and others argue that liturgies were important to democracy as a highly effective form of taxation, as well as bringing a claim to power through the bond of *charis,* that is, the reciprocal exchange of favors.[88] This twofold aspect of liturgies explains how Athenians could be regarded as generous simply for carrying out a liturgical obligation. Similarly, Finley saw the liturgy system as the "democratic answer" to the need to overcome the disparity between rich and poor, for which rich Athenians were "recompensed by corresponding honours."[89]

The sheer extent of scholarly disagreement on this issue alerts us to its complexity. We need to consider it from the standpoints both of the Athenian demos and the individual liturgist. Christ comments, "the well-being of the Athenian state depended largely on its ability to harness the private resources and energy of the wealthy through . . . liturgies."[90] Does this mean that liturgies were economically necessary in the fifth century? Some of them presumably predate the evolved, and wealthy, democracy—tragic choruses at the Dionysia probably begin about 501 and comedy about 486—and it makes sense to assume that the liturgical system was put in place at a time when Athens had not yet built up its public moneys.[91] If so, at their inception the civic liturgies would have been financially necessary. Yet arguably this was no longer the case by the mid-fifth century, when both the democracy and the empire were fully developed and the city had amassed its reserve and could count on ca. one thousand talents of annual revenue.

In Demosthenes' day, there were apparently nearly 100 agonistic (competitive, i.e., festival) liturgies, increasing to about 120 in a Panathenaic year,[92] chosen in different ways depending on the occasion.[93] Next to the trierarchy, the most expensive of the liturgies, requiring an outlay of one talent during a year, the cost of performing festival liturgies varied, from 300 drachmas for a chorus at the Panathenaia, to 1,600 drachmas for a comic chorus, and up to 3,000 for a tragic chorus.[94] So the festival liturgist was normally looking at an outlay of up to 3,000 drachmas.[95] A conservative estimate puts the average choregic cost at 1,000 drachmas and the collective expenditure of civic liturgists at about sixteen talents a year.[96] Much though this may have been for an individual, the cumulative amount, if expended by the polis, would not have dramatically affected its overall fiscal condition.

If these liturgies were not financially necessary, why did the demos embrace liturgies so enthusiastically that the prevalent attitude apparently was "the more spent the better," and why were liturgists willing to spend lavishly? From the perspective of the demos, or state, extravagance drained individual wealth, easing the disparity between rich and poor, and benefitting the city. Pseudo-Xenophon brings out the point (typically cast in negative terms): "In the case of choral performances, athletic contests, and the command of warships, the demos knows that the wealthy pay while the people are entertained and obey. Therefore the people justifiably take the money (of the rich) so that they have it and the rich become poorer."[97] Aischines, writing in the fourth century, puts it more positively: the liturgist spends his wealth for the people's enjoyment.[98] The demos, then, is seen self-consciously as benefitting from the liturgical system,[99] and indeed demanding that the system be in place.[100]

Lysias 21 provides the best example of someone trying to outdo everyone else in the costliness of liturgies which the speaker lists in great detail: he spent over ten talents on liturgies in the course of several years, including agonistic liturgies, sometimes two in one year, and seven successive trierarchies. He makes clear that he went beyond the call of duty, both in the sheer number and the amounts spent, and that he would not have spent a quarter of what he did if he had limited himself to what the law required.[101] This speech and others suggest that there was no enforced maximum nor, apparently, did this level of spending raise questions about the liturgists' intentions vis-à-vis the democracy; rather, it constituted a "safe" outlet for aristocratic display, even if it aroused envy.[102] A liturgist might enhance his prestige by setting up a monument on which to place the tripod awarded him by the polis, but such prestige was limited and "democratized" by the fact that the monument and tripod celebrated the victor's tribe and included the names not only of the *chorēgos* but of the poet and trainer as well.[103] Moreover, as I suggested above, the city's remarkable public expenditures and the power they gave collectively to the citizen body help explain the demos' relative lack of concern about lavish individual spending, for the demos outspent every individual in magnificence.

The motives for liturgists' generosity were complex. Our sources make clear that they saw their expenditures in both aristocratic and democratic terms.[104] Liturgies provided an avenue for prestige and prominence that kept individuals from becoming invisible in the face of large-scale public expenditure, which brought power to the demos as a whole, just as politically ambitious individuals became *rhētores* (speakers), that is, political leaders, which gave them prominence in Athens' mass democracy. These Athenians expected to convert their generosity to political power, advantage in the courts, or the generalship.[105] But besides their function as an aristocratic measure of value, liturgies were also regarded as an important public service[106] and confirmation of one's civic worth. The speaker of Lysias 21 cites his liturgies as proof that he was a good citizen, and accusing someone of stinginess in this realm was considered a rhetorically effective way of impugning an opponent.[107]

An added incentive, however, was less noble: liturgists could expect tangible gain in return.[108] Lysias (19.57) is explicit about the aim of making money through gifts or bribes while holding the office at which the liturgies had aimed; the speaker refers to "other people" who "spend money in advance [i.e., on liturgies] . . . to obtain a return of twice the amount from the appointments which you consider them to have earned."[109]

Recognition of the complex function of liturgies in fifth-century Athens allows us to discern further links among democracy, empire, and culture. On the simplest level, from the expected conversion of splendid liturgy service to political power and the generalship, festival as well as military liturgies (trierarchies) were clearly perceived as connected to both democracy and empire. Another link operates on a much deeper level. Alkibiades argues that his choregic expenditures, as well as his victories in chariot races, enhanced the perception of his city's power among outsiders.[110] Here, then, a leading Athenian is linking cultural production, Athens' standing as an imperial power, and magnificent performance of civic liturgies specifically with the polis' strength and reputation.

There may be a further link, although not directly mentioned, that is suggested by the apparent absence of liturgy avoidance in the fifth century (at least before the Peloponnesian War) in contrast to its prevalence in the fourth.[111] While this may be due partly to the nature of the extant evidence, it makes sense that this problem is absent in the fifth century, for attitudes toward the polis and the benefits of public service, including the performance of liturgies, clearly changed as a result of the war: fourth-century sources focus on the wastefulness of agonistic liturgies.[112] I would argue that the existence of the empire and the profits wealthy Athenians acquired from it, including ownership of foreign land,[113] helps explain an evident willingness to perform liturgies in the fifth century and, in this and other ways, support a system of governing that had a symbiotic relationship with the empire. Likewise wealth from the empire reasonably accounts for the fact that the Athenians celebrated more festivals than any other Greek polis: they could afford to.

The evidence we have examined firmly supports the "democratic" interpretation of liturgies. The important difference between Kimon's personal benefactions and individual expenditure from Perikles on was therefore that through the liturgical system the latter was increasingly channelled into the institutional structure of democracy, limited in scope, and controlled by the state.[114] As part of Athens' civic religious festivals which were in turn reflective of its *politeia*, their democratic nature was reinforced by the role of the state in the selection of the *chorēgoi*[115] and the use of the lot for the *chorēgos*' selection of pipers.[116]

Viewing liturgies as comfortable in and appropriate to the democratic state does not, however, eliminate their function of demonstrating aristocratic power and worthiness; indeed Athens' democracy, in which the masses were far from "depoliticized," allowed for individuals to stand out as long as they did not threaten the status quo.[117] Moreover, while the liturgical system was adjusted to a democratic context as a regular form of taxation or redistribution of wealth, it was not necessarily regarded as inextricably linked with it. When the 400 put down the democracy in 411, they prohibited public spending on festivals but left the liturgical system in place (which obviously would have been essential to fulfill the community's religious obligations).[118] Only after the democracy had been destroyed in 323, under the regime of Demetrios of Phaleron, were festival liturgies abolished and, interestingly, the demos became the official *chorēgos.*[119]

Conclusion

Perhaps the best representation of the link among democracy, empire, the arts, and finances is the parade of tribute onto the stage at the Great Dionysia, in front of Athenians and foreigners alike;[120] this act symbolizes beautifully the intimate connections between the Athenians' position as ruler of an *archē,* their wealth, and the cultural and political life of the polis. In all the areas explored in this chapter, one common factor is the enhanced power that results from these linkages. We can see how the Parthenon, partly through the role of the Hellenotamiai and tribute in its construction, an ' partly through annual dedications made to Athena and placed in the temple, was as much a monument to and for the entire empire as a product of the democratic polis for the Athenians; and as the Athenians fostered a new religious connection with their allies they also strengthened their power symbolically in the larger Greek world. Moreover, while the polis as "tyrant city" demonstrated its power over the outside world, the demos, through its control of the city's enormous wealth gained largely from the empire, was able to act the role of tyrant at home in constructing splendid buildings and supporting the arts, thus demonstrating its political power in the cultural realm. Finally, I argued that liturgists helped in creating and strengthening a link between culture and the power of the city, and thus implicitly between their private finances, the democracy, arts, and empire. These linkages, some explicit, others more subtle, confirm what has become increasingly obvious in the study of fifth-century Greek history: that it is necessary to examine the intersection of areas of Athenian life that were traditionally seen as having separate and separable histories. This applies to democracy, empire, the arts, and religion, but also the realms of finance and economy.

CHAPTER FOUR

Beyond Democracy and Empire: Athenian Art in Context

IAN MORRIS

Introduction

The art of Athens, the Greek miracle made material: can we really *explain* such a thing in conventional historical terms? Few would deny that democracy and empire transformed Athens in the fifth century, or that cultural forms like Aeschylean tragedy or the public paintings in the Agora were, at least to some extent, meditations on the great changes of these years.[1] But that is not the same as suggesting that we can account for fifth-century Athenian art as a reflection of underlying political, social, or economic forces. Were Zeuxis and Pheidias merely superstructural epiphenomena? What would it profit us to look at the Parthenon and see an unintended consequence of a system of voting or the might of the Athenian fleet?

In some ways, these are odd questions to raise in the 1990s. The last fifteen years have seen the emergence of a "new cultural history" whose practitioners argue that we should abandon such attempts to reduce cultural phenomena to underlying "realities." Political, economic, and social formations, they insist, are themselves discursively constituted, created, and given meaning by knowledgeable actors operating within and manipulating shared but contested systems of expectations. In her introduction to a collection of essays called simply *The New Cultural History*, Lynn Hunt suggests that "Economic and social relations are not prior to or determining of cultural ones; they are themselves fields of cultural practice and cultural production—which cannot be explained deductively by reference to an extracultural dimension of experience."[2] To scholars operating within such a framework, it might seem unrealistic to look for explanations of fifth-century Athenian art in democracy or empire. Far better to think of representations of democracy, empire, and the arts as three discursive fields within which Athenians negotiated their identities.[3]

In this chapter, I draw on some of the new cultural historians' ideas to locate fifth-century Athenian art within a broader cultural context. I suggest that this way of looking at the evidence complicates the relationships between ancient art, politics, and economics, and calls for consideration of patterns and forces transcending the narrowly Athenian scale. My argument rests on two premises, one drawn from the methods of the new cultural history, the other from the study of the classical Greek archaeological record. First, I propose that we can make real progress by breaking down the artificial distinction between "high" and "low" forms of Athenian material culture—that is, between the kinds of artifacts normally studied by classical archaeologists (sculpture, architecture, the best vase painting) and those normally studied by prehistorians (house remains, burials, etc.). For reasons I explain in the following section, I narrow my focus to just one of the principles normally seen as crucial to the success of fifth-century art, austerity, and try to show that this in fact characterized the whole range of Athenian uses of material culture in the early and mid-fifth century.

My second argument broadens the geographical context within which we view this expanded category of Athenian material culture. I suggest that the history of material austerity at Athens is paralleled all over the Greek world. Once we leave Attica, the quantity of archaeological data declines, but there is nonetheless plenty of evidence to show that Athenian behavior was but one local variant on a truly panhellenic pattern. It would take a large book to provide comprehensive documentation; I focus here on three other central Greek poleis (Eretria, Corinth, and Argos; see fig. 1) that parallel the Athenian pattern closely, and then turn to Macedonia, at the fringes of what Athenian writers considered to be the real Greek world. Macedonia defines the spatial limits of this Greek pattern: to some extent the history of its material culture follows the same rhythms as the Aegean world, but (particularly in Upper Macedonia) it gradually fades into more Balkan patterns.

My arguments in this chapter do not explain what happened to Athenian art in the fifth century in the sense of reducing cultural life to logically prior, nondiscursive realities. If anything, they complicate the picture. But this, I suggest, is a necessary step. I am reluctant to follow the new cultural historians in abandoning materialist causality;[4] but before we can even begin to discuss the possibility that politics and imperialism acted as independent factors that shaped artistic activity, we need a proper cultural history, operating at more appropriate sociological and geographical levels. Sculpture, architecture, and vase painting

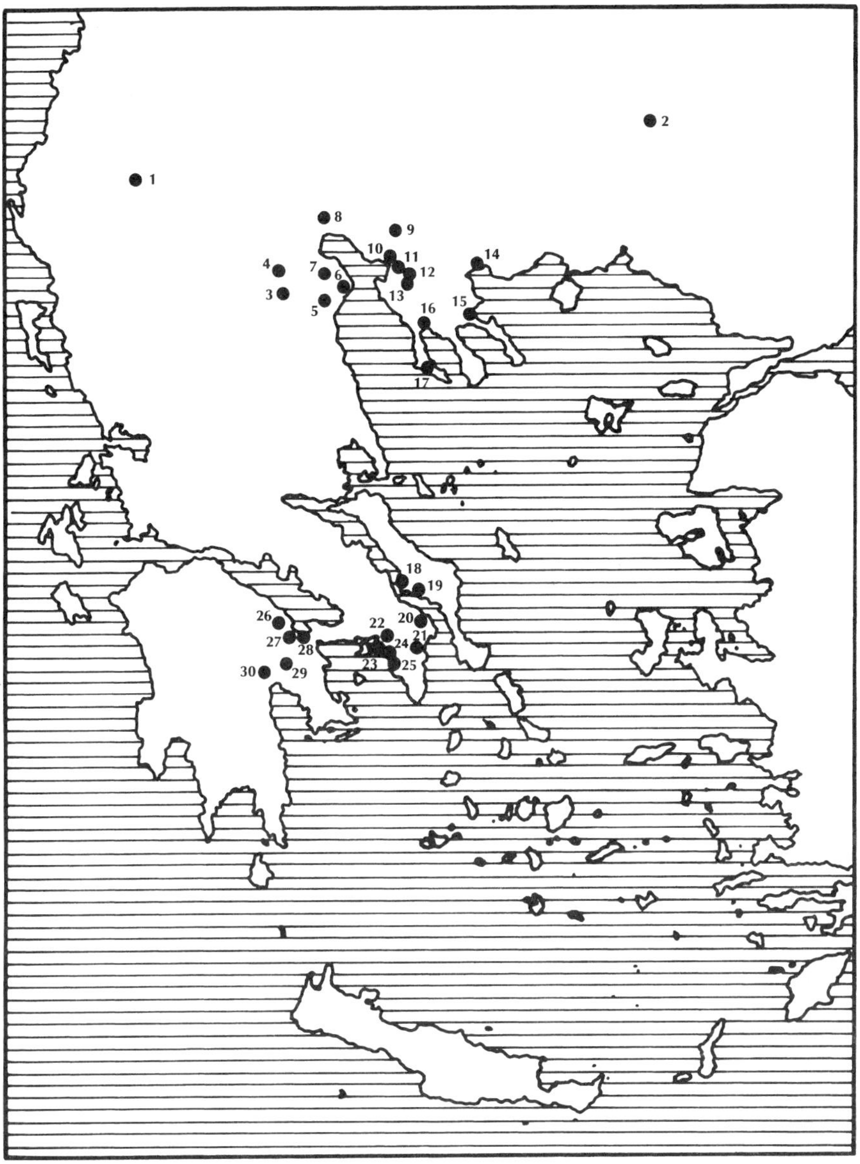

Figure 1 Map of Greece: Sites mentioned in the text. (1) Trebenischte (2) Duvanli (3) Aiani (4) Kozani (5) Sevasti (6) Makriyalos (7) Vergina (8) Pella (9) Derveni (10) Sindos (11) Thessaloniki (12) Thermi (13) Ayia Paraskevi (14) Tragilos (15) Akanthos (16) Olynthus (17) Mende (18) Chalcis (19) Eretria (20) Rhamnous (21) Marathon (22) Athens (23) Piraeus (24) Glyphada (25) Voula (26) Sicyon (27) Lecchaion (28) Corinth (29) Mycenae (30) Argos.

must be examined alongside more mundane artifacts; and we must recognize that we are dealing with a panhellenic cultural system. Only when we have identified what the Athenians had in common with the rest of Greece can we recognize what was peculiar about them, and look for particularly Athenian explanations, whether we expect to find them in political institutions, imperial exploitation, or discursive categories.

In the following sections I justify my methodological assumptions in more detail, briefly review the archaeological evidence from Athens before turning to my four comparative cases and, at the end, discuss some of the inferences we might draw from this material.

Methods

Historians working in modern cultural history have repeatedly found that they begin to make sense of their data only when they abandon the assumption (often supported by the sources themselves) that an elite cultural sphere stood in radical opposition to the practices of the lower orders. To take just two examples, both concerned with the stage, Lawrence Levine transformed understandings of the success of Shakespeare in nineteenth-century America by showing how Elizabethan drama looked to people who had grown up listening to classicizing rhetoric and were steeped in a tradition of blood-and-thunder amateur dramatics; David Cannadine, by contrast, revealed that much of the middle-class appeal of Gilbert and Sullivan's operettas in Britain after 1878 came from a deliberate reaction against lower-class theatrical forms.[5]

Obviously there are limits to the relevance of essays like these for the study of ancient Greek culture. After all, we cannot just go out and find examples of rustic festivals or lower-class drinking songs to provide a fuller context for reading Aeschylus. But the recent turn toward material culture among modern historians perhaps *does* suggest ways to expand our evidence. In a study of French furniture from the seventeenth through the nineteenth centuries, Leora Auslander shows how elite tastes responded to a wide variety of social logics, sometimes distancing the court from popular tastes, and at other times denying any such distinctions.[6] Despite obvious differences, Auslander's book points to one possibility of contextualizing Athenian culture: when we think of Athenian art as but one element within a broader system of objects,[7] the whole wealth of the archaeological record becomes available to us.

In the first great modern work on ancient Greek art, Winckelmann suggested that there were important changes in Athenian styles at the beginning and end of the fifth century: the century began with a shift from the "straight and hard" art of Archaic times toward the "grand and square" idealizing austerity of the Pheidian age, and closed with another shift, toward the "beautiful and flowing" styles of the world of Praxiteles.[8] The terminology has changed, but Winckelmann's scheme, essentially originating with Roman thinkers, has stood the test of time. Almost without exception, scholars continue to identify the fifth century as *the* classical moment in which creativity and restraint were perfectly balanced in dynamic tension, before austerity gave way to display and self-indulgence around 400.[9] I do not dispute these characterizations, but I argue in this chapter that these changes were not restricted to the classes of objects that fascinated Winckelmann. The rise and fall of the "grand and square" arts was in fact part of a larger process affecting every dimension of Athenian material culture.

In order to keep this essay within manageable bounds, I concentrate on a single aspect of the broader material context of classical Athenian art, Winckelmann's principle of fifth-century austerity. I also restrict the context within which I set Athenian "high art" to two categories of material culture, the house and the grave. I choose these for three reasons. First, they were genuinely items of mass culture; second, Athenian writers attach enormous symbolic weight to both the house and the grave;[10] and third, both have left substantial archaeological remains. Just like the public monuments of architecture and sculpture that have dominated art-historical discussions, humble houses and graves saw a shift toward restraint at the beginning of the fifth century, and a reversed shift near the century's end.

This fact adds an interesting new dimension to the study of fifth-century art, but it is nonetheless perfectly compatible with an Athenocentric explanation. We could easily see changes in democratic ideology and/or the winning and losing of an empire as triggering a broad range of cultural transformations. But, as my comparison will show, this pattern was not confined to Athens alone.

Attica may be the most thoroughly explored archaeological zone in the world, and none of my comparative cases can match its richness. At Eretria there were extensive (but poorly documented) excavations in the West Cemetery a century ago. Although Swiss archaeologists have worked since the 1960s in the sanctuary of Apollo, and Greek scholars have carried out important salvage work, our knowledge is patchy. At Corinth, the American School has explored parts of the Agora, the Potters' Quarter, and North Cemetery in detail, but the residential areas and other cemeteries are virtually unknown. At Argos, the French School has studied the Agora since the 1950s, and the Greek Archaeological Service raced against explosive urban growth in the area of the Iron Age cemeteries; but this only touched the edges of the Archaic and classical cemeteries, which remain little known.

Inadequate evidence is of course normal in ancient history. But knowing that we cannot be certain about the overall picture at Argos, Corinth, or Eretria is no reason not to make the most of the evidence we do have. The conclusions we reach are less secure than they would be were our information fuller, but their plausibility must depend on how carefully we make inferences on the basis of the evidence we *do* have. Taken individually, the finds from each of these cities are more frustrating than enlightening. But taken together, they clearly parallel the overall trends at Athens. There was a small increase in funerary spending by the elite at the end of the sixth century, followed by a period of very homogeneous and poor cemeteries through most of the fifth century. Fifth-century houses are everywhere poorly preserved, suggesting that they were often insubstantial. But at Athens and Eretria, the two sites where there has been extensive settlement excavation, grander houses appear in the fourth century.

Macedonia presents different problems. The very richness of finds since the 1960s means that publications tend to be sketchy at best. But the overall pattern is unmistakable. From the tenth century on, the archaeological record in Macedonia is richer than that in central Greece, and the gap widens in the fourth century. But behind the difference in scale we see common trends. In cemeteries, spending declined between 500 and 475, ushering in a period of restraint (by local standards), followed by rapid escalation in lavishness around 350. Typical houses changed little between the sixth century and the fourth, but during the fourth century a new class of spectacular houses appeared, reaching extreme levels of splendor in the homes of the kings.

Athens and Attica

Burial

Athenian adult burials in the seventh and sixth centuries had been grander than was normal in other parts of central Greece.[11] Virtually all known examples were marked by mounds. Spending peaked around 550–525. Grave sculptures became more popular, bronze cinerary urns returned, traces survive of two truly enormous mounds in the Kerameikos, and there was a period of flirtation with rich Lydian grave goods.[12]

But by 500, all this ended. Monuments virtually disappeared.[13] Fifth-century burials were poor and homogeneous. Only six out of almost two thousand graves contained gold,[14] and metal of any kind was rare (table 1). Most burials held a few pots, but rarely with figured scenes. Grave (gr.) 11 on Veikou and Aglavrou Streets, holding thirty-two vases with such decoration, is unique. These vessels were not expensive, but almost all grave vases are plain, black glazed, or decorated only with simple bands or floral patterns.[15]

Period	Pots		Metal	
	x	G	x	G
500–475	3.0	.547	0.1	.927
475–450	2.9	.601	0.5	.965
450–425	2.5	.601	0.3	.920
425–400	4.5	.625	0.2	.883
400–300	1.7	.587	0.5	.805

Table 1 Distribution of pottery and metal offerings in Athenian adult burials.[16]

There was a limited range of grave types. Down to 425, two-thirds of all adults were inhumed in pit graves, with traces of wooden coffins sometimes surviving, and 50–60 percent of children were buried in household pots (usually amphoras). A few sculpted tomb monuments may date as late as the 480s, but overall such markers went out of style after 500. Half a dozen mounds date to the years 500–425, including a sequence of superimposed tumuli and mudbrick tombs in the Kerameikos cemetery and the poorly known "Tomb of Aspasia," a mound reported to be 76 m in diameter (and an improbable 24 m high) covering a cremation in a bronze urn.[17] These monuments look back toward the grave mounds of the sixth century and evoke the world of heroic burial. A cautious estimate suggests that fewer than 5 percent of graves dating 500–425 were linked with mounds, and the true figure may be closer to 1 percent.

A few male burials were in monumental state tombs, the earliest known example being a mound at Marathon in 490. This, like nonstate mounds, archaizes and heroizes, but later state war burials were very different. Starting by 464, the main road through the Kerameikos was lined with state tombs of dressed stone. The earliest definite examples are the simple stelai set up for Pythagoras of Selymbria (c. 450) and a group of Corcyrean ambassadors (432).[18]

Rapid changes occurred in the last quarter of the fifth century. Grave types became much more varied. After 425, no single form accounted for more than 40 percent of burials, and new forms (tile graves and sarcophagi for adults, clay larnakes for children) displaced the older favorites. Grave goods changed little, although metal grave goods were more common in the fourth century than in the fifth, and also rather more widely distributed. Before 425, few graves held any metal; after 400, roughly 20 percent had at least some metal. Two warrior burials—extremely rare at Athens since 700—are known from the fourth century.[19]

The most striking change was the return of large monuments. The Kerameikos cemetery was replanned shortly before 420, and laid out for the "Terrassenanlage," a series of peribolos tombs (groups of graves enclosed by dressed stone walls and often decorated with sculpted monuments). We cannot date changes in other cemeteries so precisely, but everywhere in Attica peribolos tombs appeared between 425 and 400. At Rhamnous, more than twenty elaborate periboloi have been preserved, and even minor sites produce spectacular monuments. At Glyphada (ancient Halai Aixonidai), for instance, the classical cemetery is dominated by a monument almost 7 m square, surrounded by a circular wall 13 m in diameter (fig. 2).[20] This outpouring of wealth transformed the Attic landscape, filling it with family monuments. There must have been thousands of periboloi in Attica by the late fourth century. These tombs took up a lot of space, and even relatively small towns had long rows of imposing stone tombs lining the roads stretching away from them, creating a transitional zone between town and country.

Roughly 10 percent of late fifth- and fourth-century graves are associated with a peribolos tomb, and many more were marked by simple inscribed stone stelai. More than ten thousand tombstones have been published, and it may well be that virtually all fourth-century burials were originally marked in this way.[21]

Athenians were spending tremendous sums on tombs. The simplest stelai cannot have been too expensive, but the tombs of the rich are another matter altogether. According to Lysias (32.21), in 409 one Diogeiton was asked to spend five thousand drachmas on his brother Diodotos' tomb. Apparently, he spent only half this amount, and pocketed the rest. It was in the speaker's interest to exaggerate the cost of the tomb in order to represent Diogeiton as the worst possible scoundrel; but since the speaker also needed to impress the jury with Diodotos' moral excellence, an expenditure of five thousand drachmas for a tomb could hardly strike Athenians as shockingly self-indulgent. Even on a conservative estimate, between 425 and 400 rich Athenians must have spent several hundred talents on tomb building,[22] in years when the state itself went through major financial crises. Spending only escalated in the fourth century. By 349, a speaker ([Demosthenes] 45.79) could claim that his opponent had spent more than two talents on a tomb for another man's wife after he had debauched her. He had every reason to exaggerate, but the archaeological finds confirm that lavishness peaked between 350 and 325.

Family tombs borrowed visual imagery from the state war tombs, and in some cases families even put up their own memorials to members whose bodies lay in state tombs. The most famous but far from unique example is Dexileos who was killed in battle in 394 and buried in a state tomb (part of an inscription recording his name survives) but also commemorated by his family in a nearby monument.[23] Perhaps in response to the increasing assertiveness of family tomb builders, state spending escalated as well. Fourth-century state tombs were much

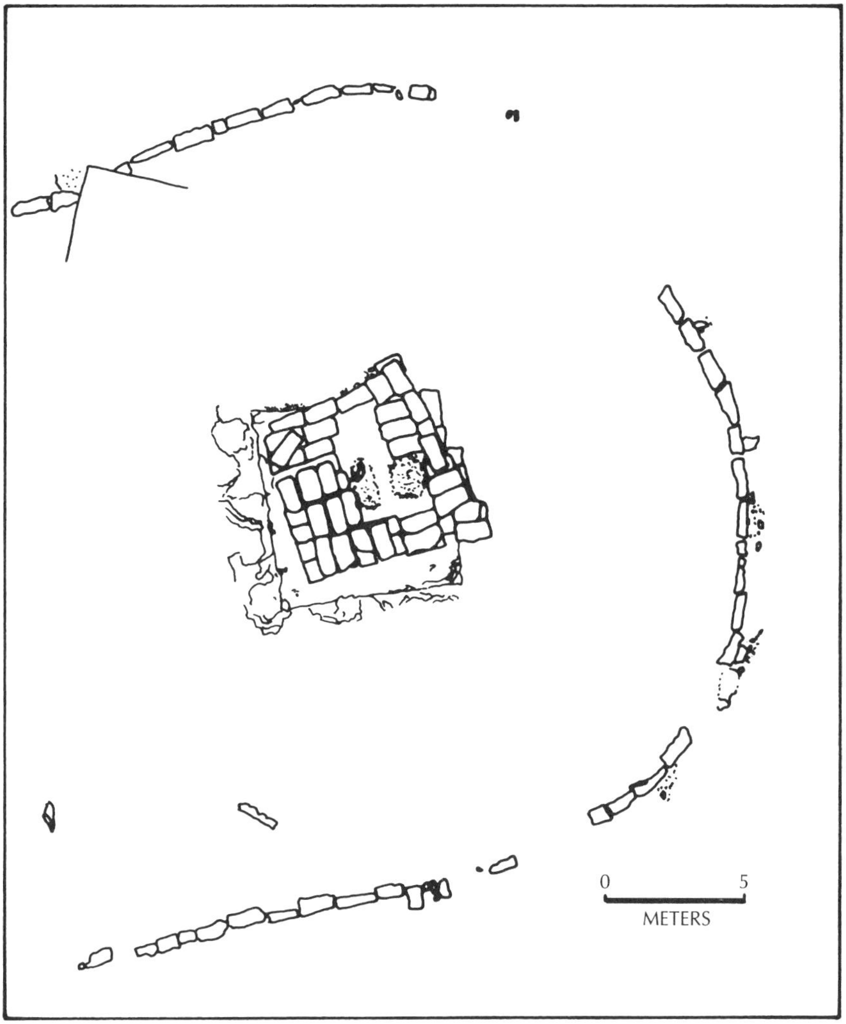

Figure 2 The funerary monument at Ano Glyphada, Attica.

bigger than those of the fifth century, and some simple fifth-century memorials, such as the tombs of Anthemokritos and the Corcyreans, were rebuilt on a grander scale after 400.

Houses

Relatively little fifth-century housing[24] has survived in Attica.[25] Hoepfner and Schwandner suggest that the Piraeus was laid out on a grid in the 470s in a "democratic," egalitarian reorganization of space. So far, the evidence is not strong, al-

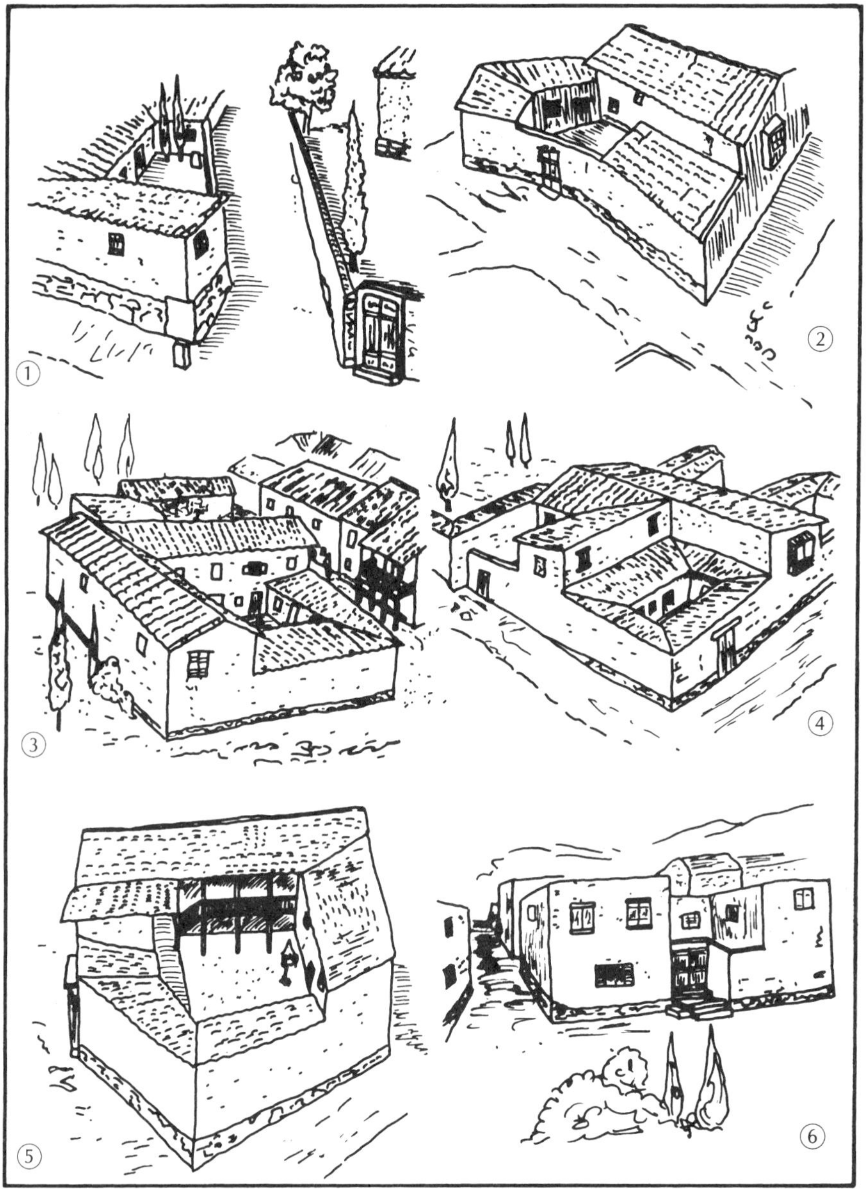

Figure 3 Reconstructions of fourth-century Athenian houses: (1) the "House of Simon", (2) the "House of Mikion and Menon", (3) Agora houses C, D, and L, (4) house on the Areopagos north slope, (5) the "House of the Greek Mosaics", (6) the "Flügelhofhaus" on the Pnyx. Reconstruction by John Ellis Jones.

though the most regularly planned houses at Athens do date to the 450s.[26] Fourth-century houses, by contrast, are common all around Athens and Attica, even though the population was smaller.[27] This may be explained in several ways. Most of the known fifth-century houses continued to be occupied across the fourth; it may be that fourth-century occupants often destroyed all traces of the earlier use of their homes, and that the pattern has little significance. This is not likely because fourth-century occupants normally just laid new floors on top of old ones and built on new rooms, rather than systematically demolishing earlier features. Alternatively, it may be that fifth-century houses were generally not as sturdy as those of the fourth century. Yet in many cases of continued use after 400, there were no significant structural changes, and the older 30–45 cm thick stone foundations with mudbrick walls on them survived across the whole classical period.[28] In the large-scale excavations around the Agora, fifth-century precursors of better-preserved fourth-century houses have often been detected, but in many salvage excavations conducted elsewhere in the city under far from ideal conditions less substantial fifth-century houses may have been overlooked because they are harder to identify. This difference in relative archaeological visibility, if that is the correct interpretation of the evidence, would itself be important, suggesting that fourth-century houses were on the whole more solidly built and presumably more expensive than those of the fifth century.[29] Only the publication of more detailed site reports can resolve this puzzle.

Some fourth-century houses are very imposing (fig. 3). A partially excavated house on Dionysiou Areopagitou Street had foundations 70 cm thick, and the excavators of another, on Amphiktyonos Street, commented on the great size of the building blocks. Most houses at Athens can be excavated only partially but, even so, it is clear that a fourth-century house found on Aristeidou Street and another in the Piraeus were unusually big. Outside Athens, a recently published house at Stephanos, apparently of fourth-century date, had a double internal courtyard.[30]

The Aristeidou Street house and a house on Rovertou Galli Street both had well-finished plaster floors, and a third big house dating to the very end of the fifth century, on Karyatidon Street, had a pebble mosaic floor in one room. This is a new development around 400: four other fourth-century houses have produced even more impressive mosaics (fig. 4), one of them in a bathroom. Paved floors have also been found in two fourth-century houses at Voula, and in the Dema farmhouse.[31] The most elaborate and expensive form of house decoration was probably wall painting; although no examples survive, the earliest anecdote referring to wall painting in Athens tells of Alkibiades trying to force Agatharchos to decorate his house, presumably around 420. Walter-Karydi has collected

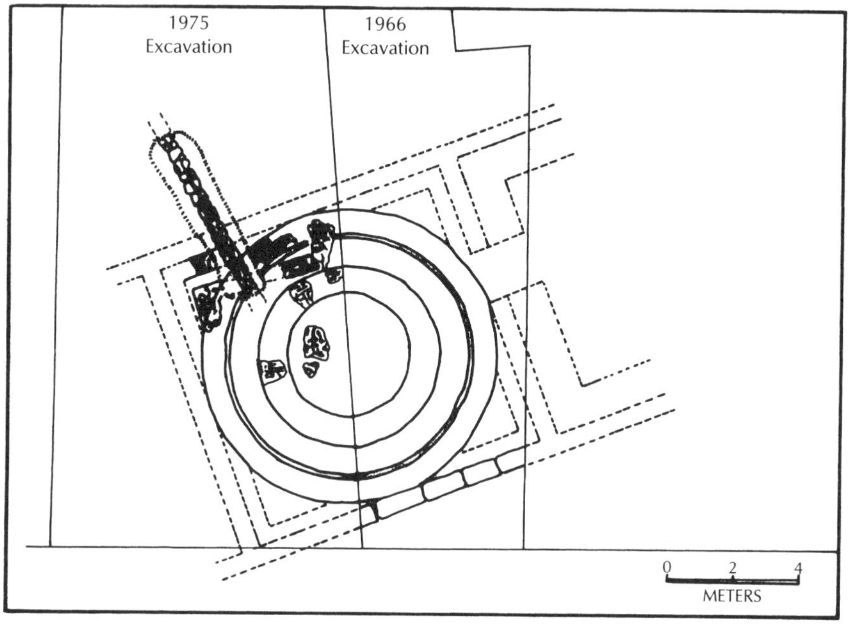

Figure 4 The mosaic from the house on Menandrou Street.

the scattered evidence for wall decoration and the use of textiles and sculpture in houses, showing clearly that these were chiefly fourth-century devices.[32]

Demosthenes (23.207–8, cf. 3.25–26, 13.20) claims that in the fifth century even the houses of great men were very simple, whereas now (in 352) "every man who takes part in public life enjoys such superfluity of wealth that some of them have built private dwelling houses more magnificent than many public buildings." Demosthenes had good tactical reasons to construct a "good-old-days" argument, regardless of accuracy; but the finds suggest that there really was a trend toward more sumptuous elite housing in fourth-century Athens.[33]

Other Central Greek Poleis

Eretria

Burial. The sample of graves is much smaller than at Athens, but the patterns are strikingly similar. Large Archaic and classical cemeteries were excavated between 1886 and 1907 but not well published. The early reports mention some gold ornaments but rarely assign precise dates to them.[34] However, in every case where a valuable object can be dated, it falls at the end of the fifth century or in the fourth. A sarcophagus containing white-ground lekythoi (and therefore likely to date 430–400) found in 1898 held three gold ornaments, while two graves of the end of the fifth century found in 1900 each held gold necklaces. A marble sarcophagus found in 1902, holding a bronze mirror, a gold necklace, and a gold stater of Alexander, can be confidently placed in the late fourth century. More recent work has exposed some one hundred fifth-century graves, all poor, but also a monumental chamber tomb of the early fourth century, fragments of fourth-century grave stelai, and a row of peribolos tombs outside the West Gate, beginning around 400.[35] Finds at nearby Chalkis are even patchier, since the site is buried under a substantial modern city, but they fit the same general pattern. The classical graves are poor, but recent excavations have found a richly furnished fourth-century cremation, and fragments of three fourth-century grave stelai.[36]

Houses. Excavations in the 1970s exposed many areas of housing. As at Athens, only fragments of fifth-century houses have survived, but there are substantial remains from the fourth. This similarity in the finds despite the very different histories of excavation at Athens and Eretria suggests that we are not dealing solely with what archaeologists term post-depositional forces (i.e., destruction or concealment by later building activity, erosion, natural deposition, etc.):[37] fourth-century houses tended to be more substantial than those of the fifth. These late classical houses were often large, and mosaic floors were more common than at Athens. Most spectacular of all are the two so-called palaces, spanning the fourth century, that were excavated near the West Gate, with double peristyle courtyards and elaborate mosaics (fig. 5). The evidence is even clearer than at Athens: there was a huge increase in the luxury of the homes of the rich after 400.[38]

Corinth

Burial. Corinthian graves were simple and poor across the Archaic period, but there was a slight increase in spending in the later sixth century. In the North Cemetery, gr. 206 (c. 550) was an unusual warrior burial, with an iron spearhead; gr. 250 (c. 525) held two gold, two silver, and two bronze ornaments, as well as glass and iron. Around 500, gr. 257 held a silver ring, and gr. 262 even contained some bronze armor. But overall the graves at Corinth remained poor, so much so that another grave of c. 525, holding a pair of bronze tweezers, counts among the richest burials. Grave markers were also rare. North Cemetery gr. 240 (c. 550) had a small gravestone, and a grave at Aetopetra was marked by a marble sphinx.[39]

But even this meager level of display eclipsed anything in the fifth century.

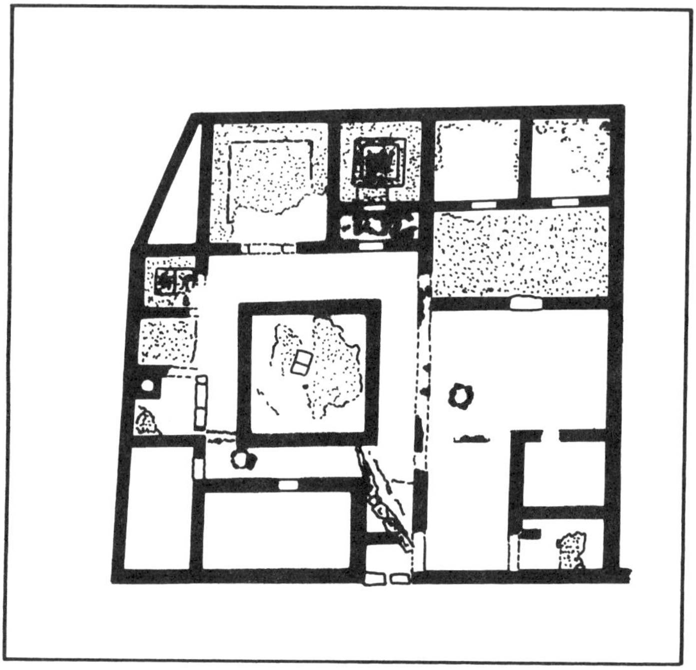

Figure 5 The "House of the Mosaics" at Eretria.

As table 2 shows, the use of grave goods in the North Cemetery was similar to that in Athens. Of course, no two sites are ever exactly the same: both pottery and metal were commoner at Corinth than at Athens, the overall downward trend in the use of pottery at Athens has no parallel at Corinth, and there are more warrior burials before 425 (grs. 262, 366) than after (gr. 419). But the general pattern of restraint is common to both sites, as is the somewhat wider distribution of metal grave goods after 425. Twenty-two percent of the 144 graves dating 500–

Period	Pots		Metal	
	x	G	x	G
500–475	3.4	.389	0.5	.889
475–450	5.3	.464	0.25	.865
450–425	4.0	.285	0.5	.856
425–400	5.8	.331	1.2	.676
400–300	2.7	.366	0.5	.714

Table 2 Distribution of pottery and metal offerings in burials in the North Cemetery at Corinth.[40]

425 contain some metal, as opposed to 41 percent of the 110 graves dating 425–300.[41] The most striking change is in the appearance of precious metals in some fourth-century graves. Lechaion gr. B9 (c. 350–325) contained a silver dagger, and in the damaged cemetery of the end of the fourth century on the north slope of Acrocorinth, gr. 4 contained a pair of gold earrings, gr. 6 a gilt clay necklace, and grs. 10 and 11 each held one silver coin. The ashes of a man were buried at Lefkos Potamos in a bronze hydria adorned with a gilt bronze crown. The only monumental classical tomb, a vaulted chamber, also dates to the fourth century.[42]

Houses. Excavations in the southwest corner of the Agora exposed a group of substantial classical buildings (fig. 6). Buildings I–IV are large, with courtyards and cement floors. Building II also boasted a staircase, and Building IV a small area of mosaic floor. Building I may be late fifth or early fourth century; Buildings II–IV are definitely fourth century. However, it is not clear whether these structures were elaborate residences or public or commercial buildings. The small fifth-century "Pentagonal Building" was probably commercial, and the much larger (15 × 13.3 m) "Punic Amphora Building," built c. 475–450, was almost certainly so. The most interesting of this group of buildings is the "Centaur Bath," built in the last years of the fifth century, with an elaborate figured mosaic. Again, its function is unclear, but it is the most likely candidate for a private residence. Prewar excavations found two more mosaics. One, complete, probably comes from a private house; the other was found in fragments in an early-fourth-century fill, but may date to the end of the fifth century. A sixth- or fifth-century house found before the First World War had no rich features.[43]

Nearby Sikyon has never been systematically explored, but nevertheless it provides a surprising number of houses with mosaic floors, probably dating around the middle of the fourth century. Sikyon may well have been the center of a school of mosaicists in this period.[44]

Argos

Burial. There is some evidence for an increase in grave goods in the last quarter of the sixth century, but as at Corinth, this was subdued. The most impressive burial, Orphanage gr. 4, held thirty-five pots, a clay tripod table, a figurine, and an iron strigil.[45] But, again like Corinth, even this outshines the fifth-century finds. Between 37 and 215 classical graves have been published (the uncertainty concerns more than 175 poorly reported classical and Hellenistic graves at the Gymnasium site, in sector d, and on Menandrou and Polyneikous Streets).[46] Among the closely datable graves, offerings increase after 425 from an

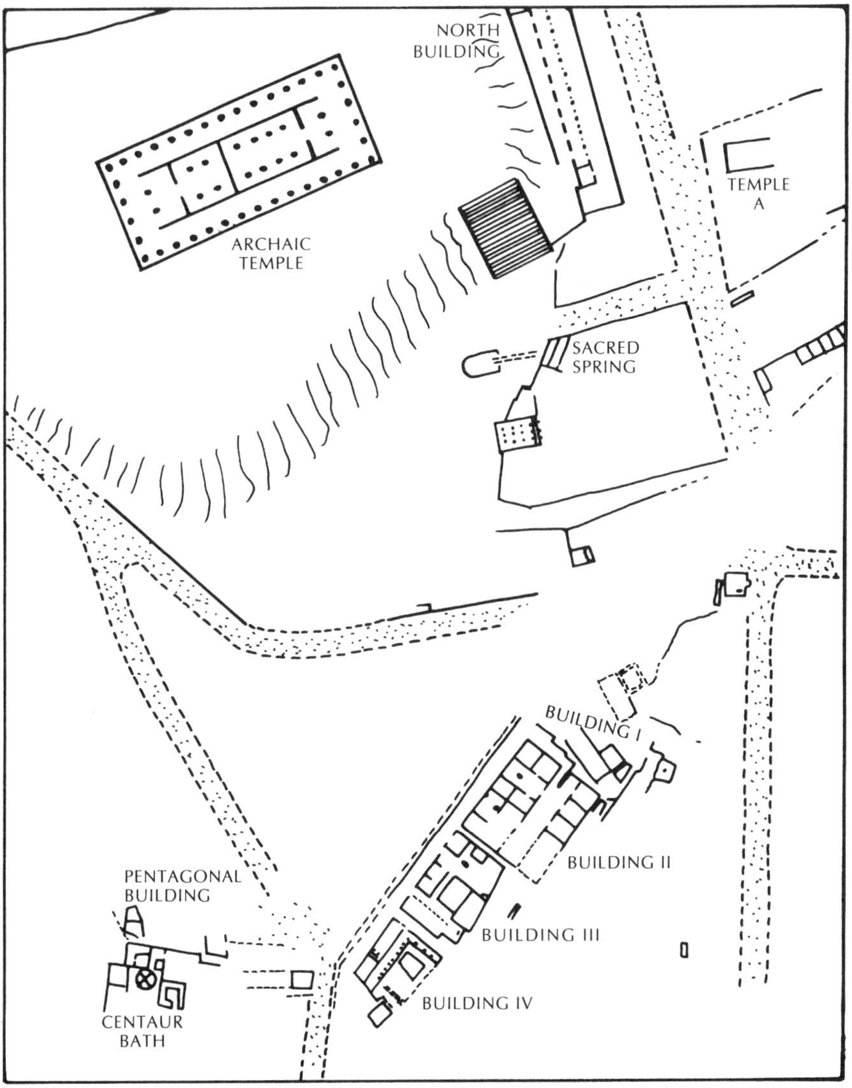

Figure 6 Houses in the Agora of Corinth around 400.

average of 2.5 pots and 0.25 metal objects per burial to 6.8 pots and 5.8 metal objects; but the total of this sample is only sixteen graves.[47] Only one fifth-century grave contained metal, compared to three in the fourth century, including the only object of precious metal, a silver coin from Kourou gr. 7.[48] No monumental tombs are known until the beginning of the Hellenistic period, although the small sample does suggest that sarcophagi were becoming larger in the fourth century. All the graves definitely dated before 425 contained only one skeleton, while those after 425 regularly contained two or three, and Kourou gr. 7 held seven bodies. Recent excavations have discovered five simple gravestones, two belonging to the fifth century, and three to the fourth.[49] The funerary sample from Argos is frustratingly small but consistent with the Athenian pattern.

Houses. Little is known of the classical settlement. Two classical houses have been noted in salvage digs, but in many places around the Agora it is clear that the fifth- and fourth-century settlement levels have been completely destroyed.[50]

Conclusion

Examples could be multiplied,[51] but these three summaries make the most important point. Athens was not alone in going through a phase of restraint in house building and burials in the fifth century, followed by a shift toward greater spending and display in the fourth.

Macedonia

Burial

Around 550, very rich cemeteries appear all over Macedonia and Chalkidike. The best known are the great tumuli of Duvanli and the smaller mounds of Trebenischte on the fringes of Macedonia, covering amazingly rich graves (fig. 7). Women in these cemeteries were normally buried with gold, silver, and bronze jewelry, and men with arms, armor, and sometimes with extraordinary gold-leaf death-masks, strangely reminiscent of those buried in Grave Circle A at Mycenae more than a millennium earlier. Recent excavations at Vergina have discovered yet another set of impressive burials of the late sixth century. The undisturbed gr. L II, from c. 500, contained fourteen solid gold ornaments and many thin gold dress attachments, four silver ornaments, three silver vessels, fifteen bronze vessels, an iron tripod, a stack of iron spits, and numerous smaller objects. Equally rich cemeteries are now known at Aiani and Ayia Paraskevi, and the finds from Sindos are truly breathtaking. Some of the late-sixth-century burials included magnificent gold filigree earrings and necklaces, along with dozens of gold-leaf ornaments and more death-masks (in grs. 20, 56, 62, 67, and 115), and standard equipment of an iron sword and two spears in male graves.[52]

But at all these sites, rich tombs are much less common after 475. At Trebenischte and Sindos, the rich burials of the years 550–475 were followed by a series of poorer graves spanning the fifth and early fourth centuries, with much less gold, silver, weapons, and armor. At Thermi, where the ninety-nine exca-

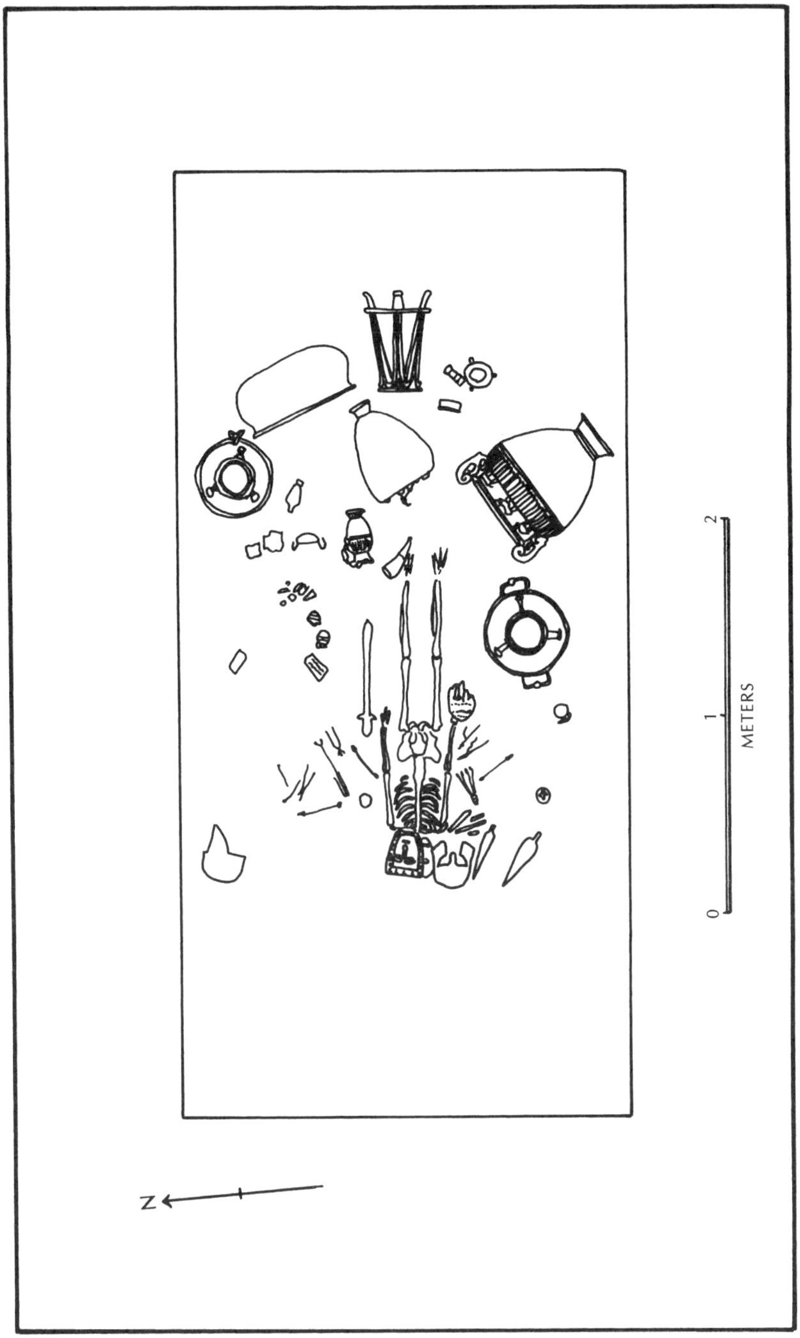

Figure 7 Grave I at Trebenischte.

Period	Total graves	Pots	Iron	Bronze	Silver	Gold
Fifth century	46	4.2	0.7	1.2	0.3	0.3
Fourth century	115	2.3	0.7	2.2	0.4	1.2

Table 3 Mean numbers of offerings in fully published intact Macedonian burials.

vated burials begin shortly before 500 and span the whole fifth century, some 70 percent of the male graves still had weapons, chiefly iron spearheads; but only one helmet and two swords were found. These graves compare poorly with those of the years c. 550–475. Most female graves had bronze, not silver or gold ornaments, and the only two silver coins dated early in the fifth century. At Akanthos, more than five thousand graves have been excavated, many of them fifth century, but the excavators singled out very few for their riches; at Makriyalos (probably ancient Pydna), where dozens more graves have been found, only one contained gold, and even bronze was uncommon.[53]

Only a few graves have been published in enough detail to be quantified in table 3, but even in this small sample we can identify two important patterns. First, as in the central Greek poleis, expensive grave goods (particularly gold) are more common in the fourth century than in the fifth. Classical Macedonia moved to much the same cultural rhythm as the Aegean, albeit with a time lag of a generation in the fifth century, and two in the fourth. But when we compare table 3 to tables 1 and 2, a second important pattern is clear. Macedonian burials were *always* noticeably richer than those in central Greece. Even during the fifth-century period of Macedonian restraint, some of the (by sixth-century standards) poor graves at Sindos included gold (grs. 49, 68, 75, 76, 96, 111, 113), albeit in smaller quantities, and recent work at Vergina has revealed a series of graves filling the gap between the Archaic and Hellenistic cemeteries. South of Macedonian Tomb IV, gr. 1991/1 (c. 450–400), holding just two clay figurines and some glass beads, was much poorer than the late-sixth-century burials described above, or the eight nearby late-fourth-century graves, which contained gold, weapons, and gilt crowns. But the five robbed fifth-century graves[54] found near Rhomaios' Tomb in previous seasons contained fragments of gold, and were probably originally quite rich. Nor were Sindos and Vergina unique in having some rich fifth-century graves: a grave of c. 425 at Thessaloniki contained three outstanding gilt bronze vessels, gold plaques with impressed decoration, and an iron spearhead, and in early-fifth-century cremation grs. 10 and 15 at Pydna the burned bones were buried in bronze cauldrons.[55]

But the richest fifth-century graves come from Upper Macedonia. Some of the tombs of this period at Aiani may be as rich as any from the sixth century.

At nearby Kozani, there is no gold, but four of the eleven published fifth-century graves contain arms or armor, including a unique bronze sword (gr. 17, c. 500–450), and at Perivoli, a fifth-century bronze urn held two enormous iron spear-heads, an iron spear-butt, and an iron sword.[56]

As we move north and west, away from the Aegean world, connections with the polis-pattern weaken. Thessalians followed central Greek practices closely: the Archaic tradition of mounds and chamber tombs broke off by 475, only to revive after 400.[57] The survival of warrior burial in fifth-century Lower Macedonia and the occasional use of gold grave goods would doubtless have struck Athenian observers as barbaric,[58] but overall, the trend was toward elite restraint after 475, in line with Greek practices, albeit after a delay of about a generation. But Upper Macedonia seems to mark the limit of the Aegean world. Here Greek-style funerary customs merged with more typically Balkan practices, including the continuous use of tumulus burial and rich grave goods across the fifth century. Palavestra would link the Upper Macedonian burials not just with Illyria but also with Hallstatt Europe, seeing a "princely" aristocracy defined through shared systems of elite burial stretching most of the way across the continent.[59]

The transformation of Macedonian burial in the fourth century is even more remarkable than what we see in central Greece. Again, Macedonia lagged behind the Aegean, showing little change until the second quarter of the fourth century. Then, however, the Macedonian elite began to divert fabulous amounts of wealth into burial. They regularly constructed mounds 25–30 m in diameter and 5–10 m high, each requiring some two thousand man-days of labor. Dozens of these mounds have been discovered since the 1970s, and Borza observes that new finds are being reported so rapidly that no one can even assemble an up-to-date catalogue.[60] Even relatively minor sites like Kitros and Nikisiani have mounds 50 m in diameter around 350, while at Vergina itself, the Great Mound, probably constructed near the end of the fourth century, was 110 m across, the result of some seventy-five hundred man-days of labor (fig. 8a, 8b). A seemingly endless series of smaller mounds, typically 5–10 m across and 1 or 2 m high, began to spread across the plain around Vergina after c. 325, renewing the Early Iron Age tradition of burial.[61]

The graves that the mounds conceal were equally impressive. Table 3 shows a striking increase in the use of gold and bronze, but understates the real scale of the change. In the fifth century, most gold and silver grave goods were small ornaments, but after 350 they often include complete vessels. Excavators rarely provide information on the weight of the objects, so this is not represented in the table. Further, although there is probably a tendency among excavators not to report poor graves in as much detail as rich ones,[62] this is more than offset by the

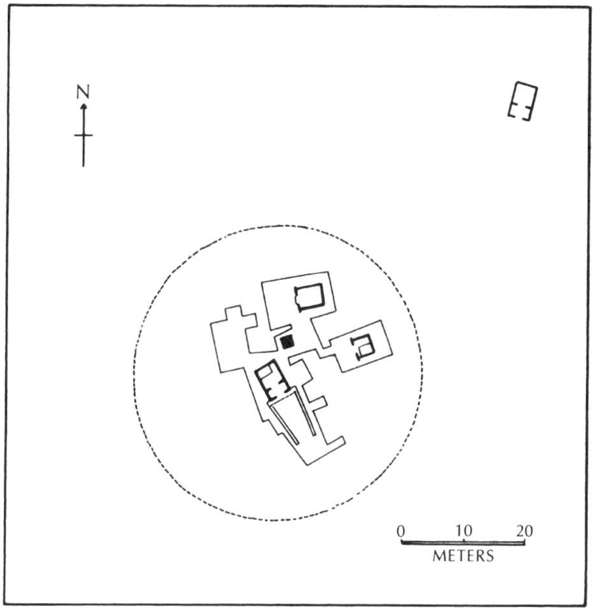

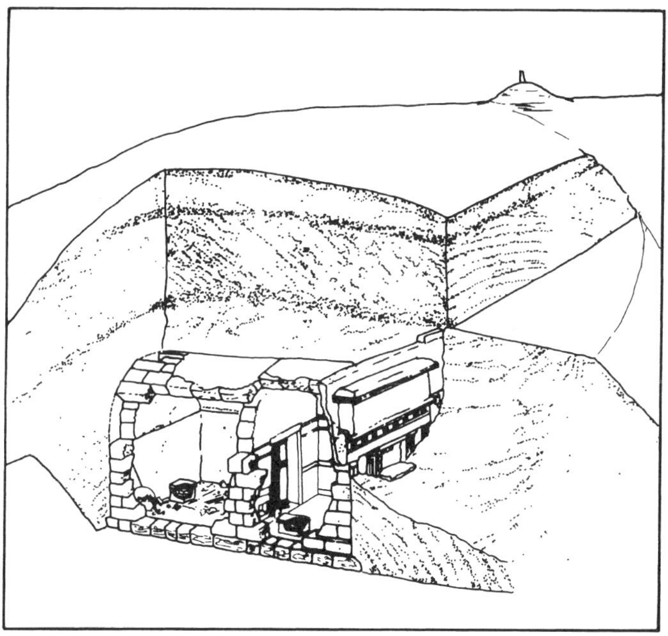

Figure 8a, b The Great Mound at Vergina.

fact that only a handful of the rich burials under tumuli have survived intact.[63] Table 3 includes none of the dozens of robbed graves that reports simply describe as containing fragments of gold, ivory, etc.

A new tomb-type, the barrel-vaulted "Macedonian" tomb, was created around the middle of the century. An enormous cist grave of c. 350 found recently at Pella, measuring 10 × 5 m, may be a transitional type; but by 300 expensive vaulted tombs were common, often decorated with wall paintings. Their characteristic pointed mounds have attracted the attention of robbers for centuries, and few are found intact. But in virtually every case even the robbed chambers are littered with fragments of gold leaf, ivory, glass, silver, and bronze. Nor were Macedonian tombs the only rich burials; one of the most spectacular finds of gold and silver vessels, at Derveni, came from a group of six cist graves. Graves of every kind in the years 350–300 tend to include gilt bronze crowns (and often crowns of thin leaves of pure gold), bronze vessels, weapons, and gold and silver coins. As just one example among hundreds, I cite the fairly typical Sevasti gr. 3, from c. 350. This was a gigantic pit grave, measuring 9 × 5 m, and 4.3 m deep. It was entered by a flight of eleven steps. The body had been cremated and the ashes placed in a bronze urn, which lay on a wooden bier decorated with ivory panels. A second bronze urn stood on an iron tripod, and other bronze vessels, a pair of bronze greaves, and bronze and iron fittings which may have been part of a shield were scattered around the grave. Above the urn were a gold crown and a gilt bronze crown, a gold Illyrian pin, five ivory cubes, iron strigils, and various other small objects.[64]

Houses

Thessaloniki Ano Toumba is the only Macedonian site with a well-stratified sequence of houses from the sixth through the fourth century. There is no clear sign of architectural change here: most of the excavated classical houses were built in the fifth century and remained in use across the fourth. We are therefore forced to compare fifth- and fourth-century houses between sites, rather than within sites; but the contrast between the magnificent late classical houses at Pella and any of the earlier houses from Macedonia leaves no doubt that there was a spectacular increase in spending in the fourth century. The two most famous examples are the House of the Rape of Helen, which covered some 2,350 m^2, and the nearby House of Dionysus, which was even bigger at 3,160 m^2, with two internal peristyle courtyards (fig. 9). Both houses date to the 320s and were adorned with remarkable mosaics, from which they take their names.[65]

The most impressive of all fourth-century dwellings were presumably the royal palaces, where private houses merged with public political buildings. King

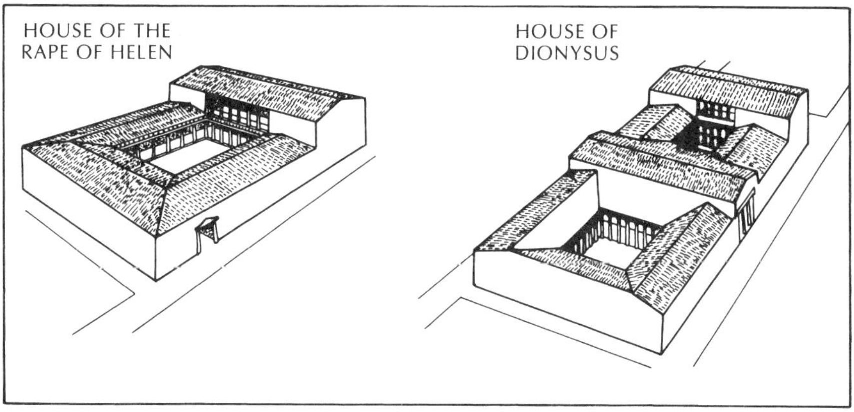

Figure 9 The House of the Rape of Helen and the House of Dionysus at Pella.

Archelaos moved the capital to Pella and built a palace there, decorated by the painter Zeuxis, in the last decade of the fifth century. No trace of this has been found, but the location of the vast late-fourth-century palace is known. Similarly, at Vergina we are ignorant about a fifth-century palace, but a structure covering nearly 10,000 m^2 and probably dating to the late fourth century has been discovered.[66]

Three sites in Chalkidike also show a sharp increase in the scale of domestic architecture in the fourth century. At Olynthos, the "New Town" was apparently laid out early in the fourth century, with large houses, and fifteen mosaic floors. The most spectacular house, the "Villa of Good Fortune" (so-called after the message *agathē tychē* on one of its mosaics) covered more than 400 m^2. No other site is so well known, but at Tragilos, houses I and II, built in the fifth or late sixth century, had a pebble-covered and a paved courtyard respectively, while a fourth-century house had a mosaic floor. At Mende, the only rich house (with a paved courtyard and a bathroom) belonged to the fourth century, and the short stretch of roadway uncovered was first paved at the end of the fifth century.[67]

Conclusion

We see connected cycles of display and restraint in the use of material culture in classical Athens, Euboea, Corinth, Argos, and Macedonia. In each region, a period of restraint in housing and burial in the fifth century was followed by a sharp increase in display in the fourth. There are of course differences among regions: the Macedonians remained attached to great tomb monuments for a generation after these had gone out of style in central Greece, and lagged by even longer before increasing spending in the fourth century; the Sikyonians, apparently, were particularly fond of mosaics; and the Athenians used writing in their fourth-century monuments to the dead much more than other Greeks.[68] These local peculiarities deserve serious study but should be seen for what they are: particular variations on a larger and more important pattern. When we ask why classical Athenian art developed as it did, we cannot limit our field of view to an abstractly conceived category of "high art," nor can we restrict ourselves to purely Athenian explanatory factors. We are dealing with panhellenic patterns of material culture. Any convincing interpretation of Athenian art must take this into account.

We should not limit our questions about events like the mid-fifth-century rebuilding of the Athenian Akropolis or the development of the Agora to asking whether they were democratic statements or masks for imperialism. We must first look at them within a broader Athenian context, coupling communal expenditure with familial restraint; and then we must see them within a broader Greek context. We know much less about the fifth-century Agora of Argos than about that of Athens, but recent excavations show that the Argives too undertook a massive program of civic building in the middle of the century. Around 460, the enormous Hypostyle Building (clearly a public monument, though its exact functions are unclear) was set up in the Agora, followed, about a decade later, by a monument to the Seven Against Thebes, now known, and ingeniously reconstructed, from the scantiest of traces. At about the same time, the Argives built their first monumental theater. Des Courtils connects these projects with the South Portico of the Argive Heraion, also dating around 450, as elements of what he calls a "programme de grands travaux." Within a generation, the Argives further adorned their Agora with a pi-shaped portico, and built the first temple in the Aphrodision sanctuary.[69] Argos had no empire, although its citizens did briefly govern themselves as a democracy, and the excavators have indeed suggested that in both Athens and Argos civic building reflected democratic principles.[70] But the Agora at Corinth, a city which was neither imperialist nor democratic, also shows clear signs of a major public building campaign in the middle and third quarter of the fifth century.[71] Despite all their political differences, what these three poleis (and indeed virtually every region of classical Greece) have in common is their broader pattern of restraint and display in material culture. It is in terms of this that we should try to explain their architectural, sculptural, and painted monuments.

Some of the mechanisms by which this panhellenic system took shape are already well understood. Herman has shown the extent of elite contacts across state boundaries in the fifth and fourth centuries, arguing that the rich constructed a veritable international culture framed in opposition to the local interests of their home states, and I have argued that we can trace the emergence of such a system between the eighth and the sixth centuries. In a more abstract argument, Renfrew has used the distribution of sixth-century kouroi to illustrate his principle of "peer polity interaction," whereby networks of small states develop their institutions through the constant exchange of people and ideas.[72]

But it seems to me that top-down models do not do justice to classical Greek social structures. I have argued elsewhere that the most important sociological and cultural fact of the fifth century, all across Greece, is the strength of the poorer male citizens, and their success in controlling the rich. This is what makes classical Greek civilization unique, and what is most in need of explanation.[73]

Coming up with an adequate model of the relationships between social changes and artistic activity—particularly one that enters into the details of styles, and all the subtle variations between contexts of use—will be a vast undertaking. In this chapter I set myself the much more limited goal of presenting some of the evidence that shows that in looking at the interrelations between democracy, empire, and the arts in fifth-century Athens, we run a serious risk of misunderstanding the scale of the processes we are dealing with and, as a result, of finding answers that can explain only a small part of the phenomenon. Hölscher rightly emphasizes that the quantity and quality of Athenian artistic production went beyond what we see in other poleis. He argues that Athens' previously unparalleled position in the fifth century, charting new waters at the head of an empire, "must have created an ambivalent state of collective psychology, between euphoric assertion and profound self-doubt, in which all themes of social import were discussed, represented, celebrated, and questioned without end."[74] Yet we should also remember that the classical moment of fifth-century Athenian art was thoroughly embedded within far-reaching cultural transformations that collectively constituted a truly panhellenic process. To seek explanations solely in terms of developments peculiar to Athens—whether that means democracy, empire, the machinations of statesmen, or the genius of individual artists—is to miss much of the point.

Appendix 1: Peribolos Tombs in Late-Fifth- and Fourth-Century Attica

To the references in Garland 1982 should be added: Alimos: *AD* 46:2 (1991) 64. Athens: *AD* 19:2 (1964) 61; 21:2 (1966) 65; 27:2 (1972) 68; 28:2 (1973) 33–34; 31:2 (1976) 30, 35; 32:2 (1977) 21, 22, 23; 33:2 (1978) 25–26; 34:2 (1979) 13, 18–20, 33–37; 40:2 (1985) 32; 42:2 (1987) 26; *AAA* 18 (1985) 39–50. Ayia Varvara: *AD* 38:2 (1983) 54–55. Ano Voula: *AD* 29:2 (1973/74) 58–59, 159–60; 31:2

(1976) 42; 34:2 (1979) 78, 79, 81–83, 86. Dionysos: *AD* 38:2 (1983) 59–60; 42:2 (1987) 99. Eleusis: *AD* 30:2 (1975) 42; 31:2 (1976) 57; 38:2 (1983) 30; 44:2 (1989) 27–29, 31–32. Kallithea: *AD* 32:2 (1977) 38; 42:2 (1987) 61. Kaminia: *AD* 42:2 (1987) 58. Keratea: *AD* 46:2 (1991) 66. Legrena: *AD* 34:2 (1979) 88. Marathon: *AD* 38:2 (1983) 61. Moschato: *AD* 44:2 (1989) 54–55. Neo Kosmo: *AD* 39:2 (1984) 10–11. Oropos: *AD* 36:2 (1981) 59–64; 42:2 (1987) 103–4. Pagai: *AD* 30:2 (1975) 37. Pallini: *AD* 38:2 (1983) 59. Pigadakia Voulas: *AD* 40:2 (1985) 62–65. Rhamnous: see n.19 above. Salamis: *AD* 38:2 (1983) 63; 40:2 (1985) 54; 41:2 (1986) 16–18; 43:2 (1988) 75–79. Sounion: *AD* 44:2 (1989) 83–84. Spata: *Praktika* 1982.123–26. Vari: *AD* 29:2 (1973/74) 160–62; 35:2 (1980) 74–75; 38:2 (1983) 53. Voula: *AD* 42:2 (1987) 85; 44:2 (1989) 60–61, 62–64; 45:2 (1990) 73; 46:2 (1991) 59–60.

Appendix 2: Expenditures for Tombs in Late-Fifth- and Fourth-Century Attica

To quantify spending, we need to estimate the number of tombs originally built (which I will call variable *a*) and their typical cost (variable *b*). For *b*, I rely chiefly on the figures in the literary sources, some of which I quote in the text above. A typical peribolos tomb probably cost something like half a talent in the mid-fourth century; a lavish example might cost as much as two talents. Tombs like Harpagos' (Diodorus 17.108.5) were too rare to have a significant impact on the average price. Variable *a* is more difficult to calculate. Roughly 10 percent of excavated fourth-century graves are associated with a peribolos tomb. If we extrapolate this proportion from our excavated sample to the whole number of burials originally made, further assume that, as in the excavated tombs, on average about five people were buried in each tomb, and estimate the total number of Athenians who died between 420 and 320 as roughly 750,000, then a grand total of some fifteen thousand tombs would have been built. (In estimating the number of Athenians to be buried, I draw on Hansen's [1985] population estimates. I include metics in this figure, since Isager & Hansen's [1975.217–19] catalogue of inscribed tombstones includes 450 non-Athenians; but I exclude slaves.)

The figure of fifteen thousand tombs should not be divided evenly over the period 420–320, since before 400 periboloi were still relative novelties; further, the heavy casualties in naval battles in the Peloponnesian War years will have reduced the number of Athenians buried in Attica (though, as Strauss [1986.179–82] shows, these deaths disproportionately affected the poorer citizens, who probably had less access to expensive tombs anyway). The great plague of 430–428 may also have reduced the number of tombs being built, though since it falls at the very beginning of the peribolos-using period, its relevance is unclear.

Finally, both the literary sources and archaeological remains suggest that the late-fifth-century tombs tended to be cheaper than those of the mid-fourth century.

Taking a conservative estimate of average tomb price at half a talent, fifteen thousand tombs spread across roughly one hundred years would require on average seventy-five talents per year. This figure should be weighted, with spending higher after 350 and lower before 400. But even if annual spending was as low as twenty talents in the late fifth century, the richer Athenians would have consumed around four hundred to five hundred talents on tomb building during the Peloponnesian War—enough to have added significantly to their military effort (cf. the figures in Gabrielsen 1994).

The number of estimates piled on top of one another in this calculation forces us to reckon with a significant margin of error. Even if we halve or double the final figures for spending, however, the overall point stands: rich Athenians began to direct very substantial sums into tomb building after 420, just when the polis as a whole began to experience severe financial problems. (On estimated values in quantitative history, see particularly Fogel 1983.)

Appendix 3: Fifth- and Fourth-Century Houses in Attica

Fifth century: Athens: *Hesperia* 20 (1951) 135–288; 23 (1954) 51–55; 28 (1959) 98–103; 38 (1969) 382–94; 42 (1973) 146–56; *Archaeology* 13 (1960) 234–40; *AD* 19:2 (1964) 49; 30:2 (1975) 37; 34:2 (1979) 13–16; 35:2 (1980) 31; 36:2 (1981) 22. Ano Voula: *AD* 29:2 (1973/74) 60–63; 33:2 (1978) 58–59; 44:2 (1989) 74; 45:2 (1990) 74. Dema house: *BSA* 57 (1962) 75–114. Kiteza Kalyvion: *AD* 45:2 (199) 77–78. Lathouriza: *AD* 42:2 (1987) 92–96. Piraeus: *AD* 30:2 (1975) 31–32; 32:2 (1977) 38; 33:2 (1978) 44. Thorikos: *Thorikos* I (1963) 87–104; II (1964) 48–72; III (1965) 57–71; IV (1966/67) 121–34; V (1968) 103–33; VII (1970/71) 39–110; IX (1977/82) 12–62. Voula: *AD* 44:2 (1989) 61–62, 66; 46:2 (1991) 61–62. Zostir: *AE* 1938.1–31.

Fourth century: Athens: Judeich 1931.287–99; *Hesperia* 35 (1966) 51–53; *AD* 16 (1960) 30; 19:2 (1964) 49, 50; 20:2 (1965) 44, 53; 22:2 (1967) 49, 98–100, 112–14; 23:2 (1968) 17; 25:2 (1970) 42; 27:2 (1972) 30, 38, 65, 92–93, 102, 104–5, 114–15, 139; 28:2 (1973) 22, 30, 41; 29:2 (1973/74) 92–95; 30:2 (1975) 17, 18, 24–27; 32:2 (1977) 16, 18; 34:2 (1979) 13–16; 35:2 (1980) 31; 40:2 (1985) 16, 33–34; 43:2 (1988) 29; 45:2 (1990) 43. Academy: *AD* 35:2 (1980) 37–41. Alimos: *AD* 38:2 (1983) 47–48; 44:2 (1989) 56. Ano Voula: *AD* 24:2 (1969) 89; 29:2 (1973/74) 59–60, 108, 158; 40:2 (1985) 57–58, 59–62. Draphi: *BCH* 80 (1956) 246–48; 81 (1957) 515–19; 82 (1958) 680–81. Eleusis: *AD* 45:2 (1990) 54. Lavreotiki: generally, Lohmann 1993. Limani Pasa: *AD* 35:2 (1980) 76. Menidi: *AD* 34:2 (1979)

91–92. Piraeus: *AD* 29:2 (1973/74) 101–2, 103, 146–49, 151, 153–56; 30:2 (1975) 31–33; 31:2 (1976) 47; 32:2 (1977) 38; 33:2 (1978) 44–46; 34:2 (1979) 63–65; 35:2 (1980) 56–63; 36:2 (1981) 46; 38:2 (1983) 43; 39:2 (1984) 26–29; 42:2 (1987) 53–55. Stephanos: *AD* 45:2 (1990) 75–77. Tsepi: *AD* 42:2 (1987) 102. Vari: *BSA* 68 (1973) 355–452; *AD* 36:2 (1981) 53–54. Voula: *AD* 42:2 (1987) 73, 85–86; 44:2 (1989) 69; 45:2 (1990) 70–73.

CHAPTER FIVE

Democracy, Empire, and Art: Toward a Politics of Time and Narrative

ERIC CSAPO AND MARGARET MILLER

Others in this volume consider the connection between Athenian democracy, empire, and individual arts. Here we consider whether democracy and empire worked some fundamental, general change in art. (In this chapter "art" encompasses figural, literary, and dramatic arts.) To this end we will examine an ingredient universal to all art: time or rather time as it is experienced, conceived, and represented, that is, "temporality." All art shapes time, through narrative (or its absence), through the ordering of narrated events, through the choice and treatment of subjects, in the medium and circumstances of performance, or in the manner it interpellates the historical consciousness of its consumers. Here we follow scholarly tradition in observing a significant shift in the dominant temporality of Greek art in the later sixth and fifth centuries.[1]

The terms of our study may seem paradoxical. In Greece the phenomena of democracy and empire are usually construed as primarily or exclusively Athenian. Insofar as the changes we will describe may be characteristic of Greek art in general, does this not invalidate our claim that they are expressions of the ideology of democracy and empire? Not if one allows democracy and empire their full spatial and temporal limits, and especially not if one views history as a process rather than a series of disconnected events.

Classical Athens holds a privileged place in the history of Greek democracy, but Greek democracy is neither exclusively Athenian nor entirely classical. As a *form of government*, democracy—or at least some essential elements of it—was a panhellenic phenomenon of the Archaic through Hellenistic periods. The dearth of historical information about the earliest democracies contributes to the misleading notion that Athenian democracy was unique in every respect. Recent studies affirm the existence of Archaic forerunners of democracy throughout Greece: the latest, by Eric Robinson, concludes that egalitarian ("isonomic") political systems were widespread by the mid-sixth century. More importantly, democratic action was not confined to states with democratic constitutions. Once established as a viable political option, democracy shaped Greek political life, whether it erupted in a coherent political program, or merely influenced local politics as a body of articulate values. As an *ideological system* democratic beliefs and values can be traced well beyond the spatiotemporal limits of democratic government. For example, in a recent study of the development of a concept of a "middling space" in opposition to the elite ideology of Archaic Greece, Ian Morris drew two conclusions that are especially important here: that elements of an egalitarian ideology can be found throughout Greece from the late eighth century onward; and that, by the late sixth century, this ideology grew measurably more egalitarian. The "democratic revolution" in Athens was not, therefore, a freakish creation ex nihilo, but part of a general process, albeit a justly privileged part, not only because of Athens' influence, or because of its active support of democratic factions throughout Greece, but also because Athenian democracy carried the process farther than any other city did and achieved a paradigmatic status as the "most democratic" of democracies.[2]

Empire was also not only an Athenian affair. Inclusive by nature, imperialism and its ideology affect the subjects as much as the imperial city. Expansionist by nature, imperialism and its ideology are also everyone else's affair. In the Archaic period, imperialism broke in upon the Greek world from the East, deeply altering traditional concepts of power, self-sufficiency, and freedom. Imperialism on the part of a Greek state first appears in classical Athens and is an index of a general change in Greek interstate relations, one that Kurt Raaflaub closely associates with the transition from aristocratic to democratic domination. In Homeric times wars between Greek states had a quasi-ritual function, and were generally confined to conflicts between neighboring states, plundering expeditions, and military assistance given by one noble to another. This changed gradually from the seventh century when the developing poleis absorbed neighboring states and sometimes distant territories by integrating them within their own political structures. But even the tyrants sought only limited territorial expansion. The Athenian Empire is the first Greek foreign enterprise that can be characterized as a programmatic pursuit of power for its own sake through unlimited territorial expansion and the subjection of other states. Raaflaub shows that the association between democracy and empire, widely accepted by ancient contemporaries, was in fact systemic. At about the same time as Athens, democratic Syracuse also harbored expansionist ambitions (against all Sicily according to Diodorus 12.30.1), though it was less successful, due in part to Athenian intervention. By the end of the century imperialism became a more general phenomenon: even Sparta, once champion of the status quo, would convert hegemony into empire.[3]

Thus the ideological affiliations of an artifact or art form cannot be fixed merely by calculating the time and place of its production. We are not dealing with a sudden or simple replacement of one ideological system by another, but with a gradual shift from an aristocratic to a democratic dominant. We are dealing, in other words, with two competing ideological systems which eventually became coeval and ubiquitous, though at any place and moment they might differ in their relative degree of ascendancy and their level of articulation. Insofar as we are able to speak at all of aristocratic or democratic lifestyles, cultures, values, or mentalities, we are dealing with class definitions which are by nature oppositional and products of social competition. Some attention has recently been paid to the process by which Greek elites constituted themselves as an aristocracy. Elke Stein-Hölkeskamp, for example, shows that the Greek elites of the eighth century suddenly began to model their lifestyle upon that of the Homeric heroes, thereby initiating a process of self-invention that would reach its culmination in the world of Pindar where gods, heroes, and elites mingled indiscriminately.[4] In the grand scheme of things, it appears that the formation of elite and egalitarian culture was a dialogic process, and that egalitarian values were not formed in response to a preexistent aristocratic ideology, but rather each formed in response to the other. For the purpose of recapturing the artistic dimension of this ongoing ideological debate, the time and place of production matter less than the social and economic context of reception. What makes art democratic or aristocratic is the degree to which it implicitly or explicitly supports the interests of one group over another.

In this chapter we explore the way in which art forms participate in the temporality of social ideologies. After a sketch of earlier approaches to the problem of Archaic and classical Greek temporality, we attempt to reconstruct the different temporalities of the Greek (and principally Athenian) aristocracy and democracy, and then turn to examine the temporality of artistic narrative. We conclude with a comparison of developments in the imperialist democracies of modern Europe. Our sweep is large, and we touch upon many topics; time and space may not always permit the level of detail a specialist might desire.

Times Past

Long ago anthropologists and historians were fascinated to discover that other cultures conceive time differently. Far from the universal absolute or the a priori category imagined by Newton or Kant, time now began to be viewed as relative and culture-specific. Two principal models emerged for organizing and explaining the diversity of time concepts. The first was evolutionary. It attempted to salvage something of absolute time by describing other temporalities as deficient. Concepts of time were arranged in a progressive sequence according to their logical proximity to a "modern scientific" concept of time. The second, constructivist, approach, though not always innocent of evolutionary ideas, tends to embrace relativism, to explain different temporalities by their function within each specific cultural system, and to make cross-cultural comparison, if at all, only at an abstract level of basic social formation (frequently "mode of production"). From this vantage point the dominant modern notion of time as linear, quantitative, and abstract is viewed as an epiphenomenon of the capitalist mode of production and, insofar as we privilege it as objective, a cultural and ideological illusion. From this perspective, "modern" time's modernity is to be understood only in the epochal sense of "modern," rather than in the strict sense of "current," since it is the constructivist view that now dominates the literature, and insofar as "modern" time is also "progressive," this modernity is "modern" as opposed to "postmodern," in the sense that it is the temporality we live with, but no longer believe in. The constructivist critique of evolutionary time nicely illustrates the view that temporal organization is best explained as part of a strategy of social and political domination. Evolutionary concepts served Western imperialism by redistributing the mentalities of coeval societies along a temporal continuum. By converting geographical into temporal distance, and by periodizing and qualifying that distance as "savagery" or "backwardness," evolutionary history legitimized Western domination: westernization was deemed a relatively painless shortcut to an in any case destined state of grace.[5]

Most of the scholarship on ancient Greek temporality can be conveniently divided under the same headings. The evolutionary approach to intellectual history enjoyed high fashion in classical scholarship from about 1930 to 1970, where it came to be known as *Geistesgeschichte* in recognition of its German origin, though its appeal extended to England, Italy, France, and America. A more relativist and constructivist approach to Greek temporality dominates French scholarship from the late 1940s and draws its inspiration from the Durkheim School and from Lévi-Straussian structuralism. For our purposes they may be distinguished not only by their results but by the attitudes to time implicit in the evolutionary and structuralist approaches.

Evolutionists suppose that real time—their time—is unified, abstract, progressive, linear, homogenous, and absolute. With it Greek temporality is contrasted or compared depending on whether Greece serves as a point of departure or as a stepping-stone in the steady march toward contemporary thought. Johannes Fabian refers to evolutionist time as "allochronic," since the goal of the project is to produce a primitive "Other" removed in time from the more fully evolved "I" of the beholder. The earliest treatments of ancient Greek temporality appeared in surveys of Western or global intellectual history by nonclassicists, especially theologians and historians. They tended to telescope antiquity, flatten its contours, and ascribe a single view of time to the Greeks, though often not the same view. Select Greek authors expressing cyclical time theories offered theologians a theoretical "Other" for Judaeo-Christian time which was linear and progressive; "no concept of time" offered some historians a convenient zero-point from which to write the biography of their discipline; qualitative time could be opposed to quantitative time by genealogists of modernity. These clichés can still be found in the nonspecialist literature.[6]

Specialist study of ancient Greek temporality begins with Hermann Fränkel in 1933. His view that "temporal awareness" only appears after Homer, in Solon and Pindar, but is not fully developed until Aeschylus and tragedy, inspired a host of complementary studies, like Jacqueline de Romilly's, which professed to trace the "progressive development [of 'temporal awareness'] from one author to another." Fränkel's views doubtless owe some of their prestige in professional circles to his defense of the ancients, whom the nonspecialists sometimes glibly described in a way one would hesitate to speak of dogs or monkeys, as having "no sense of time." *Geistesgeschichte* at least restricted the apparent primitivity of the Greeks to the "Homeric Age," a convenient zero-point, while locating the discovery of various components of "modern" intellect firmly within Greek antiquity. Its fashion in the 1950s and 1960s is probably to be explained as a professional response to the decentering of the classical curriculum in postcolonial Europe, but arrived ironically at a time when Ernest Gellner proclaimed evolutionism "quite dead in academic philosophy, . . . virtually dead in sociology . . . [and] in formal thought only defended by very occasional biologists and historians." The temporality of the modern Academy had taken a definite turn toward a relativist pluralism, but not proponents of *Geistesgeschichte*, whose temporality was curiously "out of synch," as they defended the classics as originary to Western thought just in time to see Eurocentricity plummet on the Academic Exchange.[7]

The observations of this school are useful, but often vitiated by its temporal assumptions. Evolutionist time is a radically decontextualizing time, erasing much that smacks of social and historical context. The collection and use of data resembles a process of industrial extraction and refinement: fragments of poetry are wrenched from their textual environment, and artifacts from their genres, to be reduced to objective eyewitness accounts of cognitive acts on the part of their authors, then arranged in a sequence, at once "logical" and "chronological," to support the illusion that "Time" was revealing itself bit by bit to the passive eye of chosen serial witnesses, in a tantalizing two-thousand-year striptease. The desired results necessitated such decontextualization. How could one plot the words of Homer, Pindar, and Aeschylus on a straight line except by extracting artifacts from genres? If genre enters the equation, then we find, as in Bakhtin's study, that the Greek romance, the latest literary genre of antiquity, had a time that was ahistorical, nonprocessual, irrational, and in most ways more "primitive" than one finds in early epic, and yet it continued to be used well into the modern era. Even when *Geistesgeschichte* directs its operations at a particular genre, it mistakes the genre's range of temporal expression for a progression within the minds of its authors. Contrast de Romilly's study of time in tragedy with Nicole Loraux's study of temporality in the funeral oration. De Romilly presents the tragedians grappling with the problem of time from one work to another, amassing and sorting their observations like collaborators in a school of experimental chronometry. By contrast, Loraux is fully aware that the funeral speech was a genre engaged in a cultural discourse with specific goals and functions, and as a genre it configured and distorted time to serve these ends. The temporality of the genre, far more than the sum of its practitioners' insights, all but effaces the idiosyncrasies of its authors' perspective: "Despite every effort by the orator every *epitaphios*, even the most resolutely innovatory, presents a model of *timelessness*." Different conceptions of time are revealed not by Homer, Aeschylus, and Herodotus, but by epic, tragedy, and history, because genres have different etiquettes, audiences, and functions. Not Mind, but genre, makes philosophers speak of time absolutely and historians contextually.[8]

Once the door is open to social and historical context, it is no longer possible to compare one author's evocation of time directly with another's. It might seem possible to arrange cognitive acts and individual works in this way, but not full-bodied authors and genres, since the latter respond to a specific public, specific conditions of production, and specific personal and social needs. The error of *Geistesgeschichte* was to suppose that art simply records perceived reality. Aristotle's theory of *mimēsis*, which is (rightly or wrongly) held responsible for this correspondence theory of art, makes it both difficult and unnecessary to distinguish poetry from scientific reports. This valuable distinction is best saved by turning Aristotle on his head, with Brecht, and finding "that the pleasure given by a representation . . . hardly ever depended on the representation's likeness to the thing portrayed."[9] Pleasure often depends more on the artifact's distance from perceived reality, on utopic distortions that reshape nature to the contours of human desire. Art is part, perhaps the most vivid part, of that ideological process that selects, articulates, privileges, and willfully distorts experience when social groups engage in a collective meditation on their distinctive values, their role, and their historic destiny.

The sociological and structuralist approach of the "French School" has few of these faults. At times one can detect some of the influence and evolutionary bias of *Geistesgeschichte,* but the approach to time is generally relativistic, contextualizing, and sensitive to the ideological function of time concepts. From the discussion that follows it will be obvious that we rely heavily on the results of scholars like Louis Gernet, Jean-Pierre Vernant, Pierre Vidal-Naquet, Marcel Detienne, and Nicole Loraux, and so we limit our commentary to the main point of difference between their approaches and ours. The problem lies in the dominant temporality of structuralism which can best be understood as a reaction to the evolutionary approach. In Fabian's words, structuralism attempts to avoid the error of evolutionary temporality "by exorcis[ing] Time from the study of relations between cultures," but also by exorcising time from the study of relations between the structured phases or synchronic systems within an individual culture. By suspending the tumult of history, structuralism can better investigate the internal logic of a cultural system and more readily find it coherent, completely structured, often even totalizing. Structuralism breaks culture down into basic phase-formations and studies each as a meaningful system independent of the others. Since the expulsion of time is the enabling condition of synchronic analysis, one cannot expect time to reappear magically when the synchronic systems are placed in series. What structuralists call diachrony does not constitute history but the juxtaposition of frozen synchronic moments. The more thorough the synchronic analysis, the more each appears a serenely isolated, logically integrated, and seamlessly noncontradictory system, and the more impossible it is to see how change occurs at all or where it would come from since the system leaves no space open from which to budge the inert monads. In Maurice Bloch's words, "if all concepts and categories are determined by the social system a fresh look is impossible since all cognition is already moulded to fit what is to be criticized." Little wonder that structuralist historians, like Foucault, view history as a series of periodized moments organized around epistemic models that can only succeed one another by violent ruptures. But this is to pursue cultural relativism to a fault, substituting lurching discontinuities for the threads of what used to be regarded as an ideally coherent fabric, and leaving no grounds even to assert the self-identity of a single culture in its different phases.[10]

The French School's point of departure is not the opposition between "premodern" and "modern" temporalities, as with *Geistesgeschichte,* but rather between the temporality of "prepolis" and polis. Each is the basic formation behind two distinct social and ideological systems, including two radically different (and in fact opposed) conceptions of time, one basically cyclical and qualitative, and closely connected to the timeless otherworldliness of myth, the other linear and logical and more like modern notions of time. Unlike *Geistesgeschichte,* the French School does generally recognize the coexistence of different temporalities within the same epoch, but generally not within the same formation, since alternative temporalities are located conceptually "outside the polis." It is easy to see how the value-system of the polis is opposed to the value-system of the rural, traditional society that preceded it, or the religious cults that rejected it. But the structuralist concept of culture as total system makes it difficult to conceive of different and competing temporalities within the polis, and hence impossible to see how one temporality comes to replace another, since it allows no "polis"-temporality to appear in the prepolis system. In the extreme case, the structuralist concept of system is so radically overdetermined that there is a tendency to ascribe a certain numinous quality to the polis, as both structuring principle and structured totality, simultaneously a kind of *structura structurans* which creates the social world, and a *structura structurata* which is that world's substance, ultimate signifier and ultimate signified united in a single perfectly self-sufficient, self-referential monad. Here all parts and processes merge in so undifferentiated and homogenous a substance that Loraux can simply equate temporality in the polis with the polis itself: "To study time in the *epitaphioi* amounts, then, to studying the representation that Athens makes of itself, for in order to conceive of time the polis uses no other norm than itself: it is in time, and time is concentrated in it."[11] The problem with reifying the polis as a kind of unmoved mover is that it effaces human agency, which is precisely why we lose sight of the active ingredient of diachronic change: the internal divisions within the citizen body, and their long- and short-term conflicts and struggles over institutions, processes, and ideologies.

Two other studies, independent of these "schools," deserve mention here. One of them neatly poses the question that will occupy us for the rest of this chapter, and the other points to the answer. B. A. van Groningen found that the Greeks had two opposed conceptions of time. In general the Greeks lived "in the grip of the past," but one could distinguish a "mythical" and a "historical" past. Mythical time is heterogenous to and independent of our normal concept of historical sequence; it is a time with a beginning and an end; an imaginary time, differing from the time of experience; an originary time in which the world as we know it came into being for all eternity. Historical time is an uninterrupted chain linking the past with the present, without beginning or end, homogeneous in itself, but an agent of constant change. "What lies at the bottom of this remarkable duality of conception?" van Groningen asked, but in response simply restated the question: "That the Greek distinguished two kinds of past is just a consequence . . . of the fact that he did not look in a one-sided and narrow-minded way at the universe."[12]

Christian Meier makes reference to the emergence in fifth-century Athens of a "political time" which appears to be a consciousness of time predicated upon a faith in the ability of humans to master their destiny through the political process. This is a temporality extrapolated from the experience of collective deliberation and decision making in the democratic assembly and courts. It insists upon a linear logic of cause and effect, and allows for human interventions in the causal chain. It discriminates neatly between past, present, and future, articulating the different moments of democratic procedure (deliberation, decision, and execution) and lending coherence to the belief that knowledge of the conditions that configured the present can inform choices made in the here and now and in turn determine the conditions of the future. Above all it expresses a myth of control centered upon the critical actions of a unique and voluble present.[13]

Van Groningen's recognition of two temporalities anticipates one of our premises. Though long interested in documenting the relativity of concepts of time in different cultures, cultural anthropology has only recently begun to acknowledge what Henry Rutz calls "the probability that disparate times coexist in the *same* social formation." The acknowledgment that a multiplicity of time concepts coexist in a given society has important consequences. Individual temporal experience in any time or place is as various as the contexts and activities of ordinary life, but while few of these experiences of time attain full conscious expression, and even fewer are promoted beyond their proper spheres, only one or two are selected, generalized, and made to represent the abstract category of "time" as a whole: the question is no longer *how* one concept of time *replaces* another, but rather *why* some concepts of time *dominate* others.

Meier's "political time" points us in the direction of the relationship between temporality and power, which distinguishes his from other discussions of Greek time. This conforms to recent anthropological studies of temporality, which treat time not as a disinterested "cultural artifact," but as "an object of power relations," where, according to Rutz, "the shape of time is forged in contests of power," whether these contests are waged internally or externally, in domestic political struggles, or in an imperial system.[14]

Despite our criticisms, we draw heavily upon the observations of these earlier works. We are particularly interested by the general perception (1) that there are two dominant conceptions of time in antiquity, (2) that these two conceptions are mutually contradictory, and (3) that one of these corresponds in some way to a "modern" conception of time. To this we would add some further conclusions that emerge from the discussion so far, namely (4) that the two ways of thinking time in antiquity are opposed both synchronically and diachronically; (5) that concepts of time are social facts and, as such, they are to be evinced mainly through the study of the norms of social discourse rather than individual utterances, that is to say, through speech genres and artistic genres rather than statements and artifacts; and (6) that the time consciousness that became ideologically dominant in classical Athens was "political," both in the general sense that it was related to the formation of the polis, and in the narrower sense that it was a construction of democratic ideology and an active ingredient of democratic hegemony.

If the representation of time has a political dimension, this dimension will not be evinced by the tools of traditional intellectual history, but by the kind of approach that Karl Mannheim ascribes to the "sociology of knowledge," namely: a concentration upon the thought of groups, not isolated individuals, and a concern with thought as a form of collective action by competing groups in concrete situations. In illustrating his approach with a discussion of the crisis of values in classical Athens, Mannheim provides a model that we can apply directly to the problem of the two temporalities. In his view two or more ways of thinking collide openly and more or less consciously in periods of high social mobility. Of social mobility there are two types: vertical movements by which people change social status and learn to see their own society from a new perspective, and horizontal movements through which a people comes into contact with other cultures and sustains the full shock of the relativity of cultural values. Both types of movements are necessary for an ideological upheaval. So long as horizontal movement is unaccompanied by vertical movement "the ways of thinking which are perceived in other groups are regarded as curiosities, errors, ambiguities, or heresies." When this is accompanied by "rapid movement between strata in the sense of social ascent and descent . . . the belief in the general and eternal validity of thought-forms is shaken." While vertical mobility is decisive, horizontal mobility gives a clear articulation to the reasons for disorientation caused by vertical mobility. Moreover, mere vertical mobility is not sufficient but must be accompanied by a shift in power from the previously dominant to the previously subordinate group. "As long as a society is stabilized on the basis of authority, and social prestige is accorded only to the achievements of the upper stratum, this class has little cause to call into question its own social existence and the value of its achievements." In other words, the conditions for a crisis in values are met (*a*) when an aristocratic society gives way to a democratic society, and (*b*) when this vertical displacement is doubled by horizontal displacement, a condition best fulfilled when the society in question confronts other cultures and absorbs other states within its sphere, that is to say, when it engages in an imperialistic enterprise.[15]

Returning to van Groningen's question of how two such contradictory views of time could coexist, our answer is that they coexist because of the emergence of democracy and empire. That the emergent view of time is generally perceived to resemble "modern time" may be explained by the fact that the dominant temporality of the West, since the eighteenth century, is a product of the reemergence of imperialistic democracies from aristocratic domination. The analogy, however, can be deceptive as well as instructive: we will draw attention to an important structural difference. But first let us consider just how the opposed temporalities represent the opposed interests of the Greek aristocracy and demos.

Aristocratic Temporality

Aristocratic time is structured upon the family. The family, hypostasized as "something which has a life and significance of its own," has a quantitatively and qualitatively different time experience from that of the individual.[16] Its time is experienced simultaneously as unity, continuity, and eternal repetition. Plutarch describes the *genos* (family descent group) as a "unity and a continuity . . . dependent on a single point of origin which imbues it with a power and all-pervasive communion. That which is inborn is not separable from its progenitor like an artifact from its creator, for it is created not by him but out of him, so that it contains and carries some part of him in itself" (*On Belated Divine Vengeance* 559c–d). Plutarch's description has two features peculiar to the Greek aristocracy, a fixation upon "a single point of origin" and a stress upon the virtual survival of the past into the present (the point of his argument is that it is right to take vengeance on people for the sins of their ancestors).

Aristocratic ideology not only privileges the past but warps the entire time spectrum in its favor. The Greek aristocracy did so more than most. For entrenched and more developed aristocracies, like the later European or even the Roman, the past is a more historical past for the reason that privilege is regulated by institutional guarantees (charters, grants, and so on). But the credentials of the Greek aristocrat rarely exceeded a dubious genealogy and a hodgepodge of family legends, more likely to be damaged by historical investigation (because usually fictitious). This situation had two consequences. First, the orientation to the past was mythical rather than historical and so had to a greater degree the originary as well as the otherworldly focus characteristic of myth. For this reason aristocratic families had less a history than an origin and less interest in ancestors than in founders of the line. Second, the only means of authentication open to a Greek aristocrat was prestige competition, and so, while oriented to the past like other aristocrats, the Greek felt still more intensely the interdependence of present and past; demonstrative action in the present was the chief means of sustaining the fiction of the past. In this way the aristocracy dreamed the merging of past and present into what has been called a "timeless present," an aristocratic time such as Pindar evokes with his complex chronological layering, his temporal "condensations" and "transgressions," which aim to "break free" from the flow of time and merge the moment of his patron's glory with a permanent supernatural order. And just as past glory lends its numinous power to the present, so present glory empowers the past. Alkibiades is credited with the strange claim that his chariot victories would increase not only his own reputation, but also *the reputation of his ancestors* (Thuc. 6.16.1). It is not hard to see how reputation can be handed down in time, but many have balked at the idea that it may also be handed *back*. In his comment on the passage, A. W. Gomme tried to explain away Alkibiades' reversal of causal time: "he may mean that men felicitate . . . his dead ancestors for what he himself does . . . or that the credit . . . belongs to his ancestors in so far as they enabled him, by accumulating wealth, . . . to do it, or . . . that horse-racing brought renown to his ancestors and brings it to him." But perhaps Alkibiades meant precisely what he said. For the Greek aristocrat, present and past are locked together or, to use Plutarch's phrase, they share "a power and all-pervasive communion." Power is concentrated at either end of the time scale, but time is also collapsed into an abstract featureless continuum: Rosalind Thomas describes the medium of Greek aristocratic family traditions as "a timeless historical vacuum." This temporality also served as a prestige model for nonaristocratic families and guild organizations: the aristocratic practice of naming after a clan-ancestor was widely imitated in the common practice of zigzagging generations by naming grandsons after grandfathers, or reasserting continuity by drawing names from the same root (e.g., *Alk*ibiades from *Alk*maion); trades and even poetic "guilds" organized themselves around mythical ancestors who authenticated them through hereditary powers. This temporality, which scholars have identified as "Greek time," "Archaic time," and "divine time," is all three. It was at once the dominant temporality of the Archaic period and of religious thought in all periods, but functionally and ideologically it was aristocratic time. In an anthropological survey of cultural temporalities, Robert Rotenberg characterizes the temporality of the "Tributary Mode of Production" (in which "a class of nonproducing elites . . . coerce support from producers") by cyclicity as opposed to linearity, particularly as represented in religious calendars or in the definition of persons as "current transformations of their ancestral past." What makes this part of an aristocratic ideology is not that it is an exclusively aristocratic form of thought, but that the aristocracy was its chief beneficiary.[17]

It has often been noted that Greek ideas about time are inextricably linked with other concepts that organize and justify social power. We offer two significant examples of the way the temporality of the aristocratic household structures the crucial concepts of "value" and "knowledge." For the first we refer to the "mythic notion of value" described by Gernet, which attached itself to aristocratic exchange goods: grave gifts, votives, guest gifts, prizes, and choice spoils of war, all forms of acquisition that promoted the merits of the recipient. The value of such objects lay precisely in their capacity to distinguish aristocratic exchange from vulgar commerce, or rather to convert it into a form of anticommerce. The objects of aristocratic exchange were distinguished from such common truck of barter economy as agricultural produce: they were normally of precious metal or semipermanent material, so as to be capable of acquiring a history, and normally luxury artifacts, so as to reflect their owner's worth and individuality. But to distinguish this currency from commerce's standardizing measures of equivalence, ideology made these objects numinous, magical, and otherworldly by giving them pedigrees, typically focussed upon the object's immediate and ultimate origin. Thus in the *Odyssey* (4.613–19), when Menelaos makes Telemachos a gift of his palace's "most valuable treasure," to the description of its precious metals he adds that he received it as a guest gift from the King of Sidon and that it was made by Hephaistos himself.[18]

In the cognitive domain the temporality of the aristocratic household can be seen in the archetypal forms that dominate Archaic thought and some kinds of authoritative discourse in later periods. Archetypes are mental templates or schemata, which belong both to tradition and to the realm of eternal values. As expressed by Ortega y Gasset, "archaic man . . . stepped back a pace before doing anything, like the toreador poising himself for the death-stroke. He sought an example in the past, and into this he slipped as into a diving-bell in order to plunge, at once protected and distorted, into the problems of the present. In this way his life achieved its own expression and meaning."[19]

Archetypal thought embraces what van Groningen calls "the aetiological way of thinking," exemplified by early Ionian science, where to know the "origin," "first cause," or *archē* of something is to know it in all its qualities and determinations. Thus Aristotle defines wisdom as "knowledge about the beginnings and causes of things" (*Metaphysics* 982a1). To such a way of thinking, theology is reduced to theogony, cosmology to cosmogony. The Ionian and Eleatic philosophers, according to van Groningen, "strive after ontological insight, but they do not succeed in detaching themselves from the chronological conception. They seek a *principium* and they formulate an *initium*. They seek the eternal and timeless and they discover the past, the beginning. In this manner the past and the original starting-point express the essence itself; they are nearer to it than the present or the future, so near that they are absorbed by each other." Archetypal thought also embraces "the paradigmatic way of thinking"; as Sophokles says, "a sensible man orients himself to the new by the example of the old" (*Oedipus the King* 915–16). The ancient conservative knew right from wrong through archetypes and paradigms. Archetypal thought compounds essences and origins, and it replicates the aristocratic ideological fusion of quality with pedigree.[20]

Democratic Temporality

In the classical period a "new" and opposite concept of time became dominant. This time is variously named "real time," "linear time," or "rational time." Emergent expressions of this temporality already appear in Archaic lyric and in the early forms of the law courts and assembly which were to become the central organs of Greek democracy. But this temporality is most fully expressed in the art and institutions of classical Athens where its dominance was not only contiguous with the democratic experiment, but also followed its trajectory, emerging in the late sixth century, gaining in the fifth, and losing vigor through the fourth when Athenian democracy grew more moderate and less confrontational, if not less egalitarian.[21] In opposition to the dominant temporality of the Archaic period which privileged the distant past, the new dominant privileged the present. To the Archaic dominant the present continued or repeated the past and was determined by it, but to the new temporality the present was its own moment which could be freed from past determinations by knowledge of historical causality, and this knowledge could be put toward shaping the future. Time became historical. This meant that time could be ordered by logic, reason, and causality, all of which brought it within the compass of human control. By the end of the fifth century, faith in the ability of humans to control their destinies was so great that many moderns mistake it for a general belief in human progress, which (Meier shows) is not the same thing. Above all the late Archaic and classical periods are characterized not by what *Geistesgeschichte* deemed "an awareness of time," but by an obsessive problematization of time, and a "temporalization" of civic discourse as two time-centered value-systems clashed head on.[22]

Like the old, this new dominant temporality was deeply implicated with ideas about value and knowledge. In illustration of the reorientation of concepts of value from the past to the present, one need only point to the fetish for novelty which marks the literary self-portrait of Athens in the late fifth and early fourth centuries, when Thucydides contrasted Athenian "innovationism" with the "backward-looking lifestyle" of the Spartans (1.70.2, 1.71.2). This innovationism is most directly concerned with empire, democracy, and art. Military innovation, especially in naval tactics, was a source of particular pride, putting Athenian self-conceptions at their best advantage against Sparta's plodding traditionalism, since naval action was above all a matter of skill, mobility, and outwitting one's enemy through new and unexpected maneuvers (Thuc. 1.142). An implicit contrast in the military styles of oligarchy and democracy lies behind Plato's praise of the hoplite virtue of "standing one's ground" against naval mobility, versatility, and the creative exploitation of opportunity (*Laws* 706–7). Athenians could be caricatured by the belief that "the State of Athens . . . would not be saved, unless yet another novelty is contrived" (*Assemblywomen* 219–20).[23]

In the political sphere, ancient sources for Athenian innovationism usually take the form of criticism and parody. Thucydides' Kleon chides the demos for being "the best dupes of any new argument, unwilling to follow any course that is tried and true, but slaves to the ever unheard-of, and despisers of the familiar" (3.38.5). Aristophanes' *Assemblywomen* is an extended parody of the Athenian lust for the "bold and innovative." The gynecocracy is approved by the assembly because "this appeared to be the one thing that had never yet been tried in the city before" (456–57). Praxagora's own hesitations about the radical nature of her constitutional reforms are met with a warning: "Just bring forward things that have never been done or said before, for [the demos] hates seeing old stuff too often," and "don't hesitate as far as innovation is concerned, for innovation is the rule here; just forget about the old ways" (578–87). Contemporary rhetoric, especially political rhetoric, placed a high premium on saying something new, and this is frequently reflected in the exhortations of the comic *agōn*. The fact that the sources take the form of criticism or parody reflects the deep division in Athenian ideology about the value of the new or the old. Most particularly, it shows that temporal consciousness had advanced the debate from the utility of old or new particulars to the value of oldness or newness *in itself*. For this reason political philosophers could argue in the abstract whether it is good or bad to alter traditional laws (Arist. *Politics* 1268b26–69a28).[24]

It is rather in the social and artistic sphere that the temporal values of the Athenian democracy are most clearly expressed. Aristophanes in particular makes high comedy of the confrontation of adherents of the new with adherents of the old, in general values, in science and education, and most especially in aesthetic judgment. Yet this same comedian who debunked innovation in general (and in the arts above all) was careful to insist upon the novelty of his own production, as were many artists of the late fifth and early fourth centuries.[25]

In its relation to knowledge, the dominant temporality of the fifth century represented a direct challenge to the authority of tradition. Since time and the world had become historical, so had knowledge and morality: they were no longer finished and immutable codes, but ongoing projects, and the rules of the game were radically different. Experience was no longer sifted through archetypes, nor action fixed by paradigms; in contrast to the timeless otherworldly authority of the Archaic "masters of truth," the sophists challenged and encouraged others to challenge traditional wisdom and morality. Truth entered the public domain and could be constructed from nothing more arcane than empirical data, ordinary sense experience, centered in the here and now and worked by tools no less accessible than logical argument, which at that time was scarcely distinguished from common language itself. In Bakhtinian terms, the monologic and authoritarian epistemology of the Archaic period had yielded to a dialogic and egalitarian form. In this atmosphere men no longer looked through the particular at the universal, nor through the present instant at eternity, but the particularity and individuality of the moment became an object of interest and contemplation. We will refer to this interest in the particular, the individual, and the historic as an interest in "phenotypes," from Greek *phain,* "appear" and "seem," stressing the empirical, sensory, relativistic, and provisional nature of this new epistemology.[26]

Rational, empirical, egalitarian, and dialogic, this new temporality is the temporality of public deliberations, immersed in the present, but inclined toward the immediate future, since the future is shaped by present decisions, and treating the past as a tool for comprehending and manipulating the present. It is the temporality of the chief organs of the democracy, the courts and the assembly, where decision depended upon the authority of the citizen body, but where this authority was expressed as the consensus of an instant, a consensus that was sovereign like the demos itself, was unconstrained (though perhaps swayed) by earlier decisions, and was not binding on future decisions. Laws were no longer customs receding into the mists of time and presumed to originate in divine ordinance, but things that could be created and altered at will and convenience. Gernet's study of legal procedure in the Archaic and classical periods helps illustrate how public control of the decision-making process led to the invention of historical time. Gernet distinguished an Archaic "prelaw," based on magic and ritual, from the legal system of the classical polis. Prelaw ritual was a form of ordeal, an *agōn* in the strict sense, "which enabled decision or confirmation by sending one or both parties to another world where their fates came into play."

The most common ordeal was the oath: a true speech act, not because it bound the oath giver by legal sanction, but because it put the litigant in contact with magico-religious powers that he abused at his peril. In law, however, divine sanction gives way to collective sovereignty and action gives way to investigation. In form still an *agōn,* the trial becomes a trial of words, not of actions. In prelaw there is no inquiry into the history of a case, no attempt made to establish the facts behind rival claims: "the object of the trial is not to establish what we would call a historic truth—the restitution of a past qua past. For the judge, there is nothing but the court drama and it is played in the present; there is no temporal background." Prelaw procedure is a contest of actions in which a timeless present is placed in immediate contact with the eternal and divine sphere. But law is a contest of words and an investigation into the past in aid of a present deliberation to be sanctified and guaranteed by the decision of the community. As such, even in its earliest appearance, law represents a fundamentally egalitarian form, a "laïcisation de la parole."[27]

The new temporality found its most precise designation in the classical concept of *kairos*. In the Archaic period, *kairos* was associated with a critical place or appropriate and just measure, but in the fifth century its meaning became predominantly temporal. It is chiefly associated with contests, the *agōn* form which the classical democracies adapted from athletic to verbal contests. *Kairos* became the fleeting opportunity exploited by a skillful athlete or orator to get the better of his opponent. Opposed to the timeless *aiōn* of religious thought, *kairos* is always oriented toward the concrete, the momentary, and the particular, and always located within the pragmatic realm of human decision and action. "Favorable or unfavorable," says Monique Trédé, "good occasion or danger, this critical hour breaks the continuity of time, and slices through the thread of hours and days: the present *kairos* stands in opposition to the rest of time." By nature it is always something new: Ion's *Hymn to Kairos* calls him "the most recent child of Zeus" (*PMG* 742). *Kairos* is unknown and unpredictable, but the astute athlete, rhetor, or politician will be prepared to seize him when he appears. Detienne and Vernant have shown that *kairos* belongs to the realm of the ambiguous, and in the classical period, to the realm of politics, which is "the world of ambiguity itself." When matters are most uncertain, when they threaten to fall out either way, knowing how to use *kairos* will make the difference between success and defeat. *Kairos* captures the act of decision in the intensity of the briefest possible moment; in some contexts the word means "criterion," "judgment," or the act of decision itself. A semantic fusion of ideas about time and ideas about knowledge (not of permanent and unchanging values, but a "know-how"), *kairos* permits one to triumph over contingency. At its most extreme, *kairos* represents a complete departure from traditional aristocratic morality: morality no longer resides in the acts themselves; right decision no longer springs from timeless knowledge of right and wrong. Morality is a matter of timing; right and wrong depend on the immediate context, on *kairos* itself: "Nothing is absolutely honorable or shameful," says an unnamed tragic poet, "but *kairos* can make the same action shameful or honorable" (*TrGF* II, Adespota F 26).[28]

According to Trédé, the use of the word *kairos* reveals this fusion of ideas about knowledge and ideas about time principally in the fifth century, and at the outside only from the sixth to the fourth. At the end of this period, Lysippos embodied *Kairos* in a bronze statue and personified him as an adolescent precariously balancing on tiptoe on a ball, twisting his agile body to keep on top of the situation, and stressing the instability and instantaneity of the present moment. On the tip of his left index finger he balances a scale. His wings show that he is fleeting, and he has two pairs, upper and lower, to move in either direction. In his right hand he carries a knife, symbol of the atomized moment. Poseidippos saw the significance of a peculiar asymmetry in the statue's hairstyle (*Anthologia Graeca* 16.275.7–10).

> "Your hair, why does it hang over your face?"
> "To be grabbed by any who encounter me."
> "And why is the back of your head bald?"
> "Because once I have run past on my winged feet
> No one will ever grab me from behind no matter how much he yearns to."

What is past is past, what is present is unique and uncertain, what is future depends on how we weigh present opportunity. *Kairos*, "tamer of all" (*Anthologia Graeca* 16.275.2), is the concrete image of the classical faith in the power of humanity to forge its own destiny through right deliberation, to determine the future, free from the determinations of the past.[29]

Narrative Time

Scholars generally recognize a difference in narrative strategies between classical and Archaic painting and sculpture, but not the temporal nature of that difference. A rash of experimentation and innovation in narrative form beginning in the late Archaic period gives evidence of a general temporalization of art. An important development is a new interest in narration through sequential or logical time.

The forms of narrative in the visual arts in the Archaic and classical periods are schematized in figure 1. In the chart movement from left to right shows an

Increasing temporalization →		THROUGH SPATIALIZATION		
↓		single	complex	polyscenic
THROUGH CAUSAL SEQUENCE	noncausal	iconic	synoptic	cyclic
	causal	monoscenic	progressive	phased
		space organizes time	*space corresponds to time*	*time organizes space*

Figure 1 Types of visual narrative in Archaic and classical Greece: Logical relations.

increase in the spatial representation of time, that is, the translation of distinct moments of narrative time into pictorial space. Movement from top to bottom shows an increase in linearity and causality, that is, the placing of narrative moments in temporal sequence; this temporal sequence increasingly implies a relation of cause and effect as we move from left to right in the chart.

"Single" scenes capture a single moment. We call *iconic* forms that others describe as "timeless" because they eternalize the moment (e.g., the kouros, fig. 2). Snodgrass defined *monoscenic* as the portrayal of "one essential and dramatic moment": a "moment" because previous and subsequent action are implicit (the Diskobolos caught midswing, fig. 3; the Doryphoros poised between steps), and "dramatic" because details make explicit logical reference to the previous and/or subsequent action (the flying arrow, fig. 4).[30]

The second column in figure 1, labelled "complex," groups images that imply two or more moments in time. The *synoptic* form brings two or more moments into the same spatial field, conflating essential elements of a story without representation of sequence or cause: on the Boston Circe cup (fig. 5), in defiance of causal logic, Circe (center) offers the magic potion to an already transformed companion of Odysseus, while Odysseus (left) reacts to the news, sword in hand, even as Eurylochos (far right) flees to tell him. Though *progressive* narrative also presents different moments of the story in a single field, it differs from *synoptic* in that it spatializes temporal sequence as linear sequence. From Pausanias' description of Mikon's Marathonomachy (1.15.3), it is clear that as the viewer moved from one side of the painting to the other, the progression of the battle in space corresponded to a progression of the battle in time, so that as one's eye moved across the battlefield it also moved from first engagement to victory

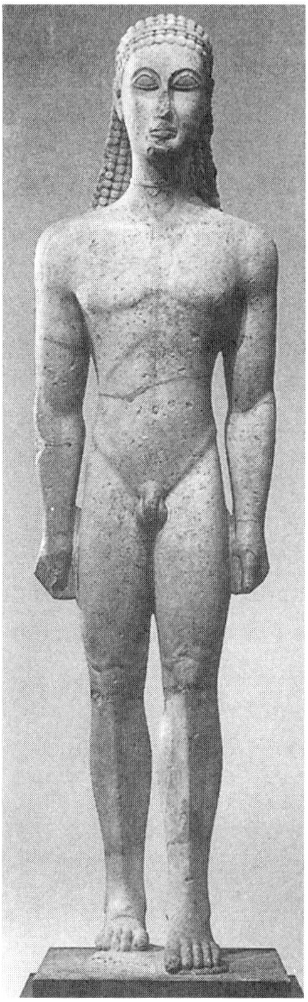

Figure 2 Iconic: Attic "New York" marble kouros, ca. 580. New York, The Metropolitan Museum of Art, Fletcher Fund, 1932, 32.11.1.

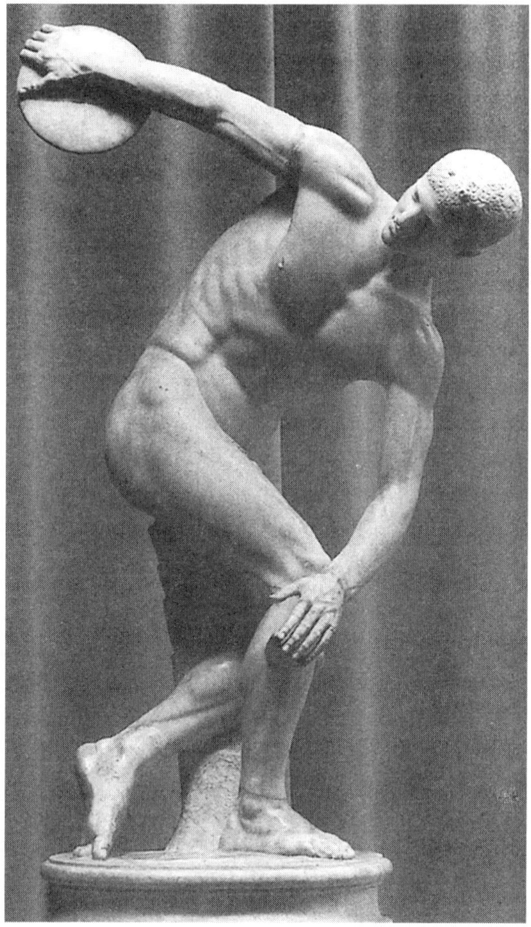

Figure 3 Monoscenic: Roman copy of Myron's Diskobolos, original ca. 460. Rome, Museo Nazionale delle Terme 126371; DAI Rom Inst. Neg. No. 70 2013.

(Harrison's reconstruction: fig. 6); likewise, in the most convincing interpretation, the Parthenon frieze depicts the Panathenaic procession moving from the lower city to the Akropolis in a continuous spatiotemporal progression.[31]

Unlike "complex" narratives, where space corresponds to time, the "polyscenic" narratives of the third column prioritize time such that space is organized temporally. *Cyclic* refers to a series of discrete scenes, each showing an episode in the life of a single character: the deeds of Theseus, for example (fig. 7;

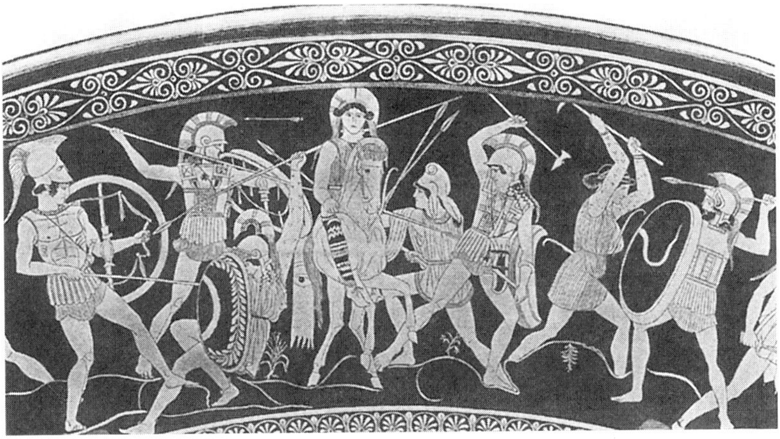

Figure 4 Monoscenic: Attic red-figure calyx-krater, Painter of the Berlin Hydria, Amazonomachy, ca. 460. New York, Metropolitan Museum of Art 07.286.86; Beazley 1963.616.3. After Furtwängler & Reichhold 1904–32, vol.2, pl. 118.

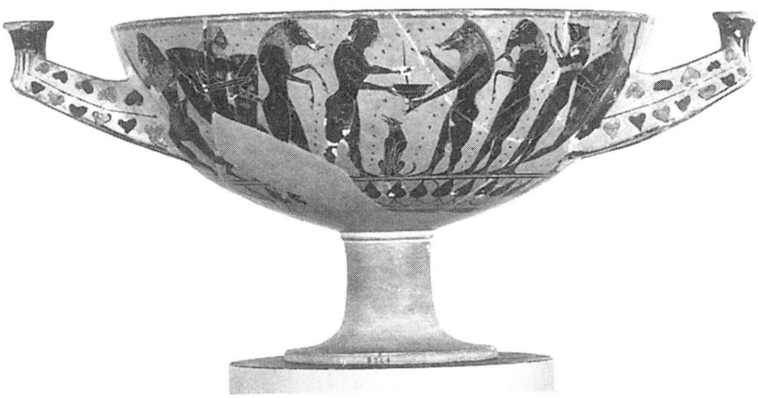

Figure 5 Synoptic: Attic black-figure cup, Painter of the Boston Polyphemus, A: Circe, ca. 550. H. L. Pierce Fund. Courtesy, Museum of Fine Arts, Boston, 99.518; Beazley 1956.198.

note the use of trees as scene dividers). But here, as Dasen observed, the scenes are not organized in narrative sequence. More importantly, they are treated as distinct adventures: only the hero himself governs the logic of combination, and his importance is stressed by the fact that his presence is central to each scene. In *phased* narrative, by contrast, the scenes are both discrete and causally linked: the scenes are selected precisely to encapsulate in their aggregate the entire story

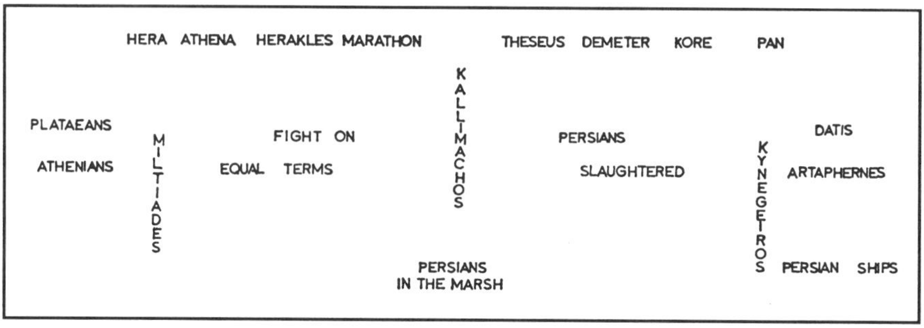

Figure 6 Progressive: Mikon's painting of the battle of Marathon in the Stoa Poikile, Athens, ca. 465. Schematically reconstructed by E. B. Harrison. After *American Journal of Archaeology* 76 (1972) 364, fig. 1 (by permission).

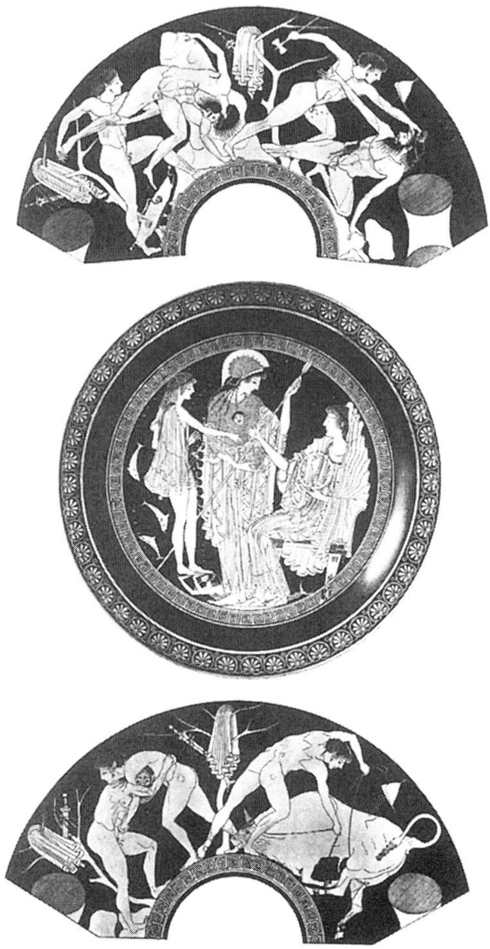

Figure 7 Cyclic: Attic red-figure cup, Onesimos, 500–480, Deeds of Theseus. A: Skiron, Prokrustes; B: Kerkyon, Bull; I: Amphitrite. Paris, Louvre G 104; Beazley 1963.318.1. After Furtwängler & Reichhold 1904–1932, vol. 3, pl. 141; vol. 1, pl. 5.

logic. Thus, the tondo of a cup by Douris (fig. 8) shows Odysseus' offer of the arms of Achilles to Neoptolemos, which presupposes the adjudication of the arms of Achilles to Odysseus on side B, which in turn presupposes the quarrel between Odysseus and Ajax shown on side A. The logical extension along both trajectories of figure 1 is the "continuous" narrative of Hellenistic and Roman art, in which an extended narration is presented in discrete scenes governed by linear and causal sequence rather than the presence of a single hero (e.g., Telephos frieze at Pergamon).[32]

Figure 1 shows the *logical progression* of narrative types, from the kouros' "zero degree" of temporality (that is, by the modern concept of time) to the full three-phased narrative of the arms of Achilles. But something more can be

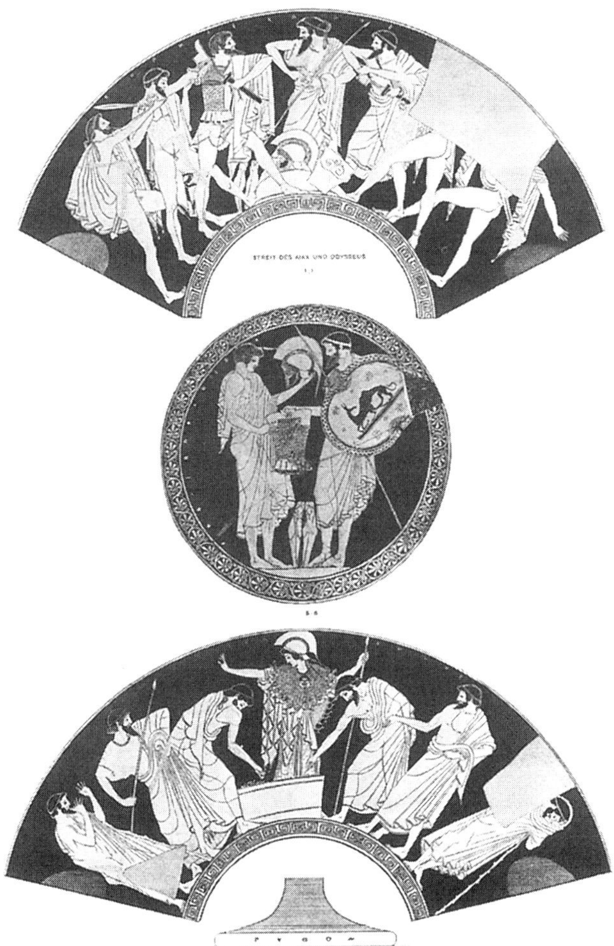

Figure 8 Phased: Attic red-figure cup, Douris, 500–480, Arms of Achilles. A: Ajax and Odysseus quarrel; B: Vote; I: Odysseus gives armor to Neoptolemos. Vienna, Kunsthistorisches Museum 3695; Beazley 1963.429.26. After Furtwängler & Reichhold 1904–32, vol. 1, pl. 54.

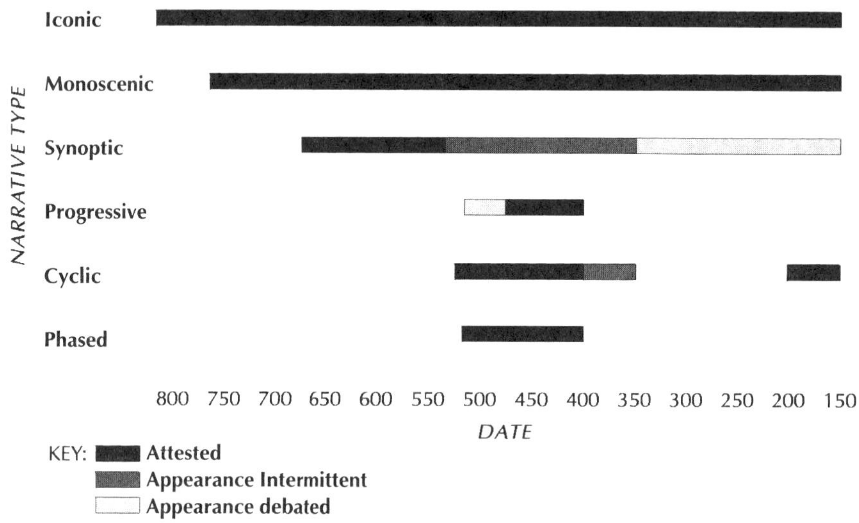

Figure 9 Chronology of appearance of types of visual narrative.

learned from considering the *chronology of use* of these different types of narrative (fig. 9). Both iconic and monoscenic dominated Archaic art from the inception of figural representation and continued to play an important role throughout antiquity. Synoptic, always less frequent, soon followed (or perhaps was present from the beginning). Progressive narrative, comparatively rare, is attested by the second quarter of the fifth century and possibly had already appeared in the late sixth. Cyclic narrative first appeared about 520; while the raw materials (e.g., decorated metopes) had long been available, as were mythic cycles which could serve as a subject (e.g., the labors of Herakles), they were only now combined. Monoscenic forms gained favor over iconic in the classical period, where artists revealed a tendency to select scenes immediately before or after the climactic moment of a story, precisely in order to force the viewer to place the scene within its larger story context.[33] In the fifth century, "phased" narratives appeared for the first time. In other words, the shift from Archaic to classical narrative is characterized by an increased emphasis on linear and causal sequence. But it is a process of accretion: the introduction of new narrative types did not cause the disappearance of preexisting types.

In the late Archaic period Athens also invented tragedy. Tragedy replaced epic as the dominant genre, so much so that Aristotle could make the counterfactual claim that epic disappeared with the advent of tragedy "because its forms were grander and more prestigious" (*Poetics* 1449a6). The genres are so different in their temporality that Goethe and Schiller identified temporality as the chief point of contrast between the two, describing epic as "absolute past" and tragedy as "absolute present." The temporal opposition is pervasive, and can be found in conception, presentation, subject matter, form, and even reception. Detienne and Vernant argue that the epic bard was conceived as never fully present, but a faceless conduit for divine Memory, as if a timeless and otherworldly past spoke through his voice. Gregory Nagy emphasizes the archetypal and originary character of this past. Even when the performance of Greek epic still belonged to a fluid oral tradition, Archaic bards effaced their creative contributions, regarding their changes as no change at all, since they conceived of change as a movement back, in Nagy's words, to the "known, certain, and predictable . . . the traditional, even the archetypal." The conceptual horizon of epic composition and performance is well expressed in Nagy's description of the Archaic *mimēsis* as reenactment rather than copying. Performers did not perform Homer but "became" Homer; the archetype was not remembered but resuscitated. The description is worth quoting as an exemplary articulation of the temporality of the aristocratic household we described above, with its emphasis on the unity, identity, and continuity of the "family" of performers created by the originary bard: "If you re-enact an archetypal action in ritual, it only stands to reason that you have to *imitate* those who re-enacted before you and who served as your *immediate* models. But the *ultimate* model is still the archetypal action or figure that you are re-enacting in ritual which is coextensive with the whole line of imitators who re-enact the way in which this ultimate model acted, each imitating each one's predecessor." From such a conception it is easy to see how epic performance might seem to belong to an "absolute past." Nagy continues: "Implicitly, only the pleasure of exact reperformance, which is supposedly the ongoing achievement of *mimēsis*, is truly lasting, while the pleasure elicited through changes in response to an immediate audience is ephemeral . . . Here the notion of *mimēsis* becomes an implicit promise that no change shall ever occur to accommodate the interests of any local audience in the here and now." Tragedies, by contrast, were new and composed with a single performance in mind. The actors of tragedy turned narrative into an immediate and physical presence. Both genres take their subject from heroic legend, but unlike the distant and valorized past of epic, that of tragedy is an often ill-disguised present unperturbed by glaring anachronism: in the *Bacchae* the chorus hymns Dionysus in accordance with "timeless tradition" (71), while the play presents (and presentifies) him as a new god. But it is form that best expresses the genres' different orientations. Archaic epic is unlimited, both externally, since it is part of an expandable cycle, and internally, since no strict logic of closure determines its beginning or end: an *Achilleis* need not end with Achilles' death; an *Odyssey* may end with a new departure. Its sequence is sooner agglomerative than strictly logical. Tragedy, by contrast, observes narrow temporal and causal constraints, ideally limiting its time frame to the events of a single day. The tragedians insist upon the brevity of the tragic instant: "a single day can ruin or restore all human striving" (Sophokles, *Ajax* 131). The tragic day is not a day in the life, so much as a life packed into a day. The temporal concentration is replicated by the logical development of the plot. The epic poet builds *onto* his narrative, but the tragic poet builds *up*, through a series of moments that are both present in their urgency and set toward the future by premonitions, anticipations, and the momentum of a compulsively linear logic, all leading to a single decisive concentrated moment that will precipitate disaster or avoid it. In reception, epic was thought to be a repository of timeless moral values, whereas some thought tragedy could purvey practical advice of immediate utility to the polis.[34]

Among the many new artistic genres born in the early classical period, it is, paradoxically, history that shows the clearest break with the past. As with tragedy, this is most obvious in subject matter, form, presentation, and function. Near-contemporary life and events, the Persian Wars, and the Persian Empire's history and ethnography dominated the interests of the early Ionian historians. Even when presenting recent history or its remoter background, the contemporary world is often close: Raaflaub shows "a strong tendency on Herodotus' part to transcend . . . the lower chronological limit of his work," whether by drawing explicit connections between Persian War events and those of his time or, like the tragedian, by shaping the past for the eyes of the present, drawing implicit connections with matters of contemporary concern (e.g., the improbable constitutional debate of the Persian grandees). Not distance but immediacy is the mark of the Greek historian. The greater the historian's own immediacy to the events described, the greater his authority. A premium is placed on autopsy and eyewitness reports. Thucydides' history was the first by an active participant, writing "immediately after [the war] erupted" (1.1). Indeed, Thucydides thought history opposed to myth and epic, as present is opposed to past, and logical argument to verbal amusement; history was based on evidence and proofs, legends were "undisprovable . . . , time having robbed them of historical value" (1.21). "Thereafter," says M. I. Finley with some exaggeration, "serious historical writing was about contemporary history." Indeed, Ion of Chios took the next logical step by inventing the genre of "memoirs," and Xenophon's *Anabasis* is virtual autobiography.[35]

The historians directly express the new concern for temporal and causal sequence. Whereas legend and epic were "fully indifferent" to chronology—Anthon's dictionary notes that by traditional genealogy Helen was 94 when her face launched a thousand ships—the historians coordinated genealogies and developed an absolute chronology. Causality too turned from the inscrutable will of the gods to explanations that were (in Finley's words) "human . . . , secular, and, in particular, political." Ionian history, like early tragedy, still overlaps divine with human responsibility, but Thucydides admits only human causality. This turn to the secular enabled historical time. The historians wrote from the conviction that nothing was fixed or permanent and that time was always changing the shape of things. But if events had no natural shape, they had a logical one, upon which depended the utility of the whole historiographical enterprise. In the preface to his *History,* Thucydides opposes his purpose to that of the bard: he promises not entertainment, but utility, on the grounds that an exact knowledge of the past can serve as an aid to discerning the future. Some have distinguished Thucydides' "logical time" from the "historical time" of his predecessors. The *telos* is statecraft, the political helmsmanship that from a sure knowledge of the political process and its historical consequences can guide the state to security and profit. "One of the most remarkable manifestations of the consciousness [of the fifth century]," writes Meier, was the belief that "there is no such thing as chance: chance was an excuse, used by those who were unable to plan properly; or at least good planning made it possible so to calculate chance that it could ultimately be neutralized."[36]

Thucydides' narrative highlights the genre's temporal orientation: it progresses by years and seasons, a graphic representation of linear and irreversible time. This chronological sequencing is doubled by a strict causal sequencing. For the most important events Thucydides shows the political process at work, moving from debate to decision to action. In every case the consequences of action are foreseen within the debate. Like tragedy, history became a pathology of decision. When Thucydides stages a debate, it is designed to give a dramatic immediacy to the issues and to make us feel that the future hangs entirely upon a moment's decision. If special attention is given to the reversal of the decision in the Mytilene debate, it is to make us see how rarely the decisions of a moment are subject to reversal. Like tragedy, Thucydides represents every present moment as determining the future, but some moments stand out as crisis points; these deliberative moments are made fully present to his readers. This, indeed, is the temporality fundamental to the genre of deliberative rhetoric, which creates urgency by warning its audience, like Demosthenes, that "what is done cannot be undone even by immediate measures" (4.14, tr. A. N. W. Saunders).

The arts of the classical period made much of temporal and causal sequence, and the temporal and causal most fully coincide in the notion that present deliberations determine future conditions. Archaic art spoke of a distant and determining past and a distanced, because timeless, present. Classical art fixes upon an immediate present and an immediate future. The present is now its own moment, caused perhaps by past events, but unconstrained by them. The gain is precisely a sense of human liberty and human responsibility. If classical art insisted upon a conjunction of temporal and causal sequence, if tragedy and history dramatized present deliberations and their future consequences, it was to make a theater of self-determination.

Classical art expresses a view of time diametrically opposed to that of Archaic art because the democratic ideology that dominated the classical period had a different conception of human destiny. Men determined history, not history men. Hence time and history were imbued with a new importance, but always with a focus on the present since the choices made at any given moment would shape the course of the future. This orientation toward present time magnified the importance of careful and thorough deliberation. If the Archaic and aristocratic Greek thought of a timeless present oriented toward the distant past, the classical and democratic Greek thought of a "deliberative present" oriented toward the immediate future.

Aristocrats never problematized decision; knowledge of the good was bred in the bone and this knowledge took the form of archetypes of value and paradigms of action.[37] Homer may briefly show us his heroes being "of two minds," but never mulling, regurgitating, or retracting. Sophokles does not even show us this, but only the unwavering intransigence and uncompromising individualism of his aristocratic heroes. But democrats believed that the collective vision had incomparably greater resources of knowledge and skill for making important decisions. Tragedy and history dramatized the partiality of individual perspectives and gave a reassuring sense of the complementarity if not completeness of the deliberative process in debate. When tragedy struck it was never for want of warning, but through a failure to engage in dialogue.

Innovationism marks the "moment" of Greek democracy as a whole: in its first century and a half many artistic genres appeared for the first time and older genres underwent transformation (fig. 10). Like the figural arts, tragedy, and history, many of these genres express the new temporality in their internal organization or in their function: rhetoric, for example, or even dithyramb, which Zimmermann described as the democratic art form par excellence.[38] Space does not allow us to explore these other new genres here. Instead it will be more profitable to look at expressions of the new temporality which cut across all genres and represent changes in the form and content of narrative generally. In particular, we turn our attention to the epistemological values collected under the term "phenotype."

	Innovations	***Transformations***
530–490	Tragedy?	Satyrplay?
	Epinician	
	Ceramic techniques	
	Lunging/falling figures	
	Bouleuterion (profane use of Doric)	Dithyramb
	Civic monument	
490–460	History/Ethnography	Comedy
	Epitaphios Logos	Tropaion
	Theatre building	
	Ekklesiasterion (Pnyx I)	
	Tholos	
	Monumental Painting	
	"Portraiture"	
	Commemorative Monument	
460–430	Rhetoric	Artistic Treatise
	Odeion	
430–400	Mime?	New Dithyramb
	Memoires	Historical Epic
	Political Pamphlet	Private Art
	Dikasterion	Stoa (winged, Π-shape, complex)
	Public Baths	
	Colonnaded tholos?	Propylaia
	Corinthian order	Cuisine
	Peristyle building (Pompeion)	
	Document Relief	
	Perspective painting	
	Chiaroscuro	
	Pebble mosaic	
400–	Philosophical dialogue	Middle and New Comedy

Figure 10 Innovation in and transformation of genres and styles.

In classical art three developments illustrate the new predominance of phenotypal over archetypal thought: individualization, historicization, and fictionalization. The archetypal conception of the human figure was emblematized by the Archaic kouros, long a celebrated problem of interpretation due, significantly, to its lack of individuating characteristics (fig. 2). No consensus was possible so long as scholars asked the question, "WHOM—god, hero, or mortal—does the kouros represent?" since the kouros could in fact stand for all three.

Recent scholarship sooner asks, "WHAT does the kouros represent?" turning its attention from essence to ideological function. But the error of the first question is the key to the second. Something can be learned of Archaic ideology by asking "WHY does the kouros lack individualizing distinctions?" since this lack is not simply due to the ineptitude of primitive art (as *Geistesgeschichte* would have it). It is interesting to note that while the kouros type is almost invariable, a greater degree of individualization appears in lower-status art forms: Archaic grave reliefs differentiate by physique, dress, and attribute to show two (or three?) ages for men; their evocation of aristocratic pursuits reflects a concern to stress status, which the dedicator of a kouros never needed to contest. Votive objects show even banausic labor.[39]

The kouros was the format first used for Archaic athletes (Paus. 8.40.1). By contrast, Myron's early classical Diskobolos was individuated qua athlete (fig. 3). The emergence of individuated sculptural forms may be dated with the aid of the Tyrannicide groups. Whereas the first, by Antenor (ca. 509), was probably a pair of kouroi, the figures of the replacement group (477/6) were distinguished from one another by age and from all other statues by the action for which the men were commemorated (Hölscher, this vol., fig. 1). Tradition held that these were the first official portrait sculptures erected at Athens. Individuation by age in sculpture and vase painting was expanded to include the old, the adolescent, and, by the end of the fifth century, even realistically rendered babies and toddlers.[40]

Vase painting and relief sculpture show a growing interest in individualization by profession from the later sixth century. Tragedy, in addition to the generic citizenry of the chorus, includes low-status minor characters who are identified by profession (heralds, soldiers, farmers, nurses), but only comedy admits free urban professionals (tradesmen, merchants, industrial workers), and perhaps not before the 420s. Individualization by ethnicity first appears in partial form in some sixth-century painting of mythological subjects, but only in the fifth century do accurately depicted foreigners figure prominently, especially Persians battling Greeks, but also Blacks and Thracians. Early tragedy represented Easterners probably in eastern dress. Differentiated speech patterning characterizes foreigners by speech, probably as early as Aeschylus (*Suppliants* 825–902) but is especially pronounced and common in drama and lyric of the late fifth century, notably the foreigners and barbarians of Aristophanes and the Phrygians of Timotheos' *Persians* (*PMG* 791.115–73) and Euripides' *Orestes* (1369–1526). Status group also becomes a significant criterion for distinguishing figures in art and drama: earlier art occasionally opposed free to slave by size and physique, but red figure expands both the means and the frequency of status distinction.[41]

An important aspect of individualization is attention to detail, especially the sort of gratuitous particulars of which Aristotle complains when he distinguishes history from poetry by the different levels at which each seeks to present reality: the historian is concerned to represent particular truths, while the poet's approach is serious and philosophical insofar as the poet attempts, by stripping his models of all that is contingent and idiosyncratic, to represent a universal truth (*Poetics*, chap. 9). Aristotle wishes character to have no more particularity than functionally required by the action. Contingent and inconsequential details do appear in Aeschylus and Sophokles, but they are reserved for plebeian characters like the nurse of *Choephoroi*. Euripides, however, is notorious for a generalized use of "irrelevant distractions." To modern sensibility, it is precisely the gratuitous details of Euripides' late plays that create a sense of realism. George Gellie, for example, awards three dimensions to Electra when she declares she hasn't a thing to wear to the dance; Frederic Will finds the way she clips the tips of her curls "gives Helen reality"; and Charles Garton declares Menelaos' psychology particularly convincing when, upon being asked why he pokes his nose into Agamemnon's affairs, he responds "because the desire itched me."[42] The development of character from Old to New Comedy also reveals a shift from purely functional to empirical models.

Another aspect of the turn from archetype to phenotype is historicization, a turn from the mythical past to contemporary experience. When human figures appear in Archaic painting it is in depictions of myth or ritual (komasts, weddings, funerals). From ca. 530 Attic black-figure painters add quotidian scenes; red-figure painters are drawn to the social life of the elite. The treatment of historical subjects, always rare in the visual arts, begins ca. 490, with the earliest of some twenty Attic vases of Greeks fighting Persians. Almost all subsequent historical artworks deal with Persians. Historical and contemporary references are pervasive in lyric poetry but greatly increase in the wake of the Persian Wars. Phrynichus and Aeschylus wrote tragedies on the Wars. If they did not deal with the Persian Wars, historical art and tragedy addressed oriental history (a Croesus amphora, ca. 490, and possible tragedies on Croesus and Gyges). The Persian Wars and the ethnography of the Persian Empire preoccupied the early Ionian historians. After a hiatus, historical subjects seem to reappear in 430–400: a probable Marathonomachy on the Temple of Athena Nike; a historical epic (the first) by Choirilos of Samos on the "Athenian victory over Xerxes" (Choirilos went on to write epics for Lysander's campaigns); Timotheos' *Persians* celebrating Salamis. The fourth-century historians, Xenophon, Ktesias, Dinon, and Herakleides, revived Persia as a historical and ethnographical subject; two tragedies titled *Themistokles* dealt with the battle of Salamis.[43]

Classical art expresses a third aspect of phenotypal thought in its development of fiction and suspense narrative. Archetypal thought shows a preference for analeptic and proleptic narrative forms; phenotypal thought brought narrative into closer relation with narrated time by ordering events chronologically. Analeptic or retrospective narrative is characteristic of epic, plunking the listener in medias res with explanatory returns backward in time. Proleptic narrative makes events known in advance of their unfolding (a story *a b c* may be narrated *c a b*). The audience of a proleptic narrative does not ask "What will happen next?" but rather "How will it happen?" In narrative terms both prolepsis and analepsis distance the audience from the narrative present, creating a kind of universal time or "omnitemporality" as Gérard Genette calls it. In ideological terms proleptic and analeptic narratives produce a sense of predestination and inevitability, whereas chronological narrative creates suspense, uncertainty, and a greater sense of the importance and immediacy of the narrative present. The opposition, in short, is one of predetermination to self-determination. Proleptic narrative is the dominant mode of most Archaic narrative, but less usual in classical.[44]

Euripides and Agathon were most daring in developing a narrative of intrigue and suspense. Older tragic plots favored traditional renderings of myth, proleptic prologues, elaborate foreshadowing and preparation. Later Euripidean tragedy frequently plays with audience expectations. In *Ion,* for example, Apollo announces his plans through Hermes in the prologue, and almost all of them are frustrated by turns of events the god of prophecy has not foreseen, a point not missed by the sarcastic assessment of Athena ex machina that "Apollo has done a really fine job of everything" (1595). In *Helen* and *Orestes,* Euripides departs boldly from the mythic tradition, showing that Aristotle's prescription that "it is not possible to undo the traditional stories" is conservative wishful thinking (*Poetics* 1453b 22–23). Agathon's *Antheus* was the world's first serious fiction.[45]

Three aspects of the change from archetypal to phenotypal thought have a direct relation to Athenian politics. First, the evidence does not attest to a steady development. Rather, two periods show intense change: ca. 530–460, and 430–400, not coincidentally the periods in which the demos was most self-assertive (from the Kleisthenic to the Ephialtic reforms, and the so-called radical democracy; see fig. 10). The fourth century, by contrast, sooner reverses these trends. The periodicity suggests substantial overlap between the aesthetic response of the Athenian public and the intensity of their partisan feelings.

Secondly, the Persian Wars and the Persian Empire were central to all three facets of phenotypal expression (i.e., individualization, historicization, and fictionalization). Apart from the Tyrannicides, only Persian War leaders received public commemoration in art. The *barbaroi* of art were always people of the Persian Empire. Persian subjects dominated historiography and historical art. Later fifth-century painting fictionalized Persians (e.g., Xenophantos' aryballos, where Persians hunt mythical beasts). The Persian Empire provides the setting for the first ancient novel, Xenophon's *Kyropaideia*.[46]

Yet the continuing appeal of archetypal thought reveals ambivalence toward phenotypy. This is our third point. The demos' interest in contemporary history, while a reaction against the aristocratic obsession with a distant past, was also an attempt to create a new heroic age. In the very act of cutting loose from the mythic past, the demos attached it to a mythicized present. Mikon's Marathonomachy was juxtaposed to an Amazonomachy and an Ilioupersis in the Stoa Poikile.[47] Herodotus' history shows a concern to make the Persian Wars part of a causally linked continuum with the Kadmean, Argonautic, and Trojan cycles. The new Simonides fragment juxtaposes the battle of Plataea and the Trojan War. The mythicization of the Persian Wars explains the unprecedented placement of a historical subject (the battle of Marathon) on the Nike Temple, and the appearance of Salamis in fifth- and fourth-century tragedy. Tragedy and figural arts convert their entire repertoire of historical characters into archetypes: oriental kings to paradigms of tyranny; the Tyrannicides to founding heroes; and the generals of the Persian War to guardian heroes. The democratic imagination converted the killing of Hippias' little brother to the foundation of Athenian democracy: popular drinking songs assure the Tyrannicides of immortal glory and even a place in the isles of the blest with Achilles and Diomedes "because you killed the tyrant and made Athens egalitarian" (*PMG* 893–96). The myth of Marathon also conflated liberation and democracy: it was supposed that the aged Hippias led the Persians to Marathon (Her. 6.102, 6.107), so that the repulse of the barbarian was indistinguishable from the defense of democratic freedom. Indeed Herodotus makes the Tyrannicides serve as mythic paradigms even for Miltiades at Marathon (6.108). In aristocratic circles, according to Thomas, "the democracy . . . promot[ed] the memory of a new kind of family tradition more concerned with the recent past," as great families scrambled to forge links with the new heroic age of the polis. And just as the Homeric orator begins his speech with an appeal to ancestral achievements, and the eulogist with a genealogy, so Perikles began a speech to the Athenian demos with an appeal to ancestors, but with a slight twist: "Our more distant ancestors are worthy of praise, but even more so our fathers [the generation of the Persian Wars], for they acquired, in addition to what they received, the empire we now possess" (Thuc. 2.36.1–2). Even as an appropriation of an aristocratic form, the ancestor worship of the demos, at least in the fifth century, had a significant temporal difference: Perikles' funeral speech perverts even as it appropriates aristocratic time. It is not a continuing past, but a retrograde present, as Loraux shows: "it is to Pericles' contemporaries that the ancestors have handed down the land of Attica, and the fathers did not acquire the empire for themselves, but for their sons, who alone give each reality its full meaning. Thus each period is linked directly to the culmination of the process. Ancestors have rarely been eclipsed to such an extent by their descendants." The same appeals to Marathon and the Persian Wars can be found in the political rhetoric of the fourth century, but the ethos is very different: "The appeal," says Josiah Ober, "is to an essentially reactionary sensibility which regards the past as good, the present as a falling-away from the ideal, and the future as likely to be better only if it recapitulated the past."[48]

Individualization was also the subject of ambivalence. The new categories *did* express a rejection of archetypal forms with their stress upon the human character's continuous and undifferentiated connection with tradition, but not in celebration of the individual for his own sake. Rather the categories of age, gender, class, ethnicity, and profession aimed primarily at a redefinition of the individual as a public persona—not a member of a family tradition, but the embodiment of an *état civil.* This is evident in the employment of particularizing detail, for it is almost always the noncitizen "Other" who is particularized: the foreigner and the slave. The exception to this rule is all too revealing, for individualization also affects the urban poor, creating within the citizen class an "Internal Other." It was the hoplite class that represented the ideological norm of Athenian citizenship: thus in Athenian red figure the heroic Greek fighting the Persian is always a hoplite, never a sailor. Knights alone represent the military on the Parthenon frieze, which has all the rigid blandness of Archaic archetypes. It may be stated as a law that the greater the *ethopoeia,* the further down the social scale the object of imitation. Particularizing detail was trivial and comic.[49]

It is at least questionable whether Euripides' particularism aimed only at comic effect, but by the fourth century the realm of truth and value was once again the realm of archetypes. In generalizing about the difference between poetic and historical truth, Aristotle notoriously excluded from participation in poetic truth both Old Comedy and iambic poets who "deal with particulars" (*Poetics* 1451b14). Enzo Degani explains that "invective poetry, tied as it is to particulars and stuck in the mire of the *hic et nunc,* could not but be an inferior poetry, far from the universal." Despite historicization, contemporary non-mythicized experience could only be a subject for low genres. It remained, in Bakhtin's words, a "reality of a 'lower' order in comparison with the epic past." Agathon's bold experiment with serious fiction was never repeated in antiquity. Erich Auerbach could speak of an ancient rule that "realistic imitation, the description of random everyday life, could only be comic (or at best idyllic)."[50]

Ancient and Modern Temporality

In the first section of this chapter we noted a tendency to equate classical with modern temporality, and indeed the story of fifth-century temporality touches many modern themes: the faith in the present and in novelty; the depreciation of the past and all that is unoriginal; an attitude of mental dexterity free of preformed notions that enables us to adapt most readily to the dizzying pace of cultural change. The widespread belief that classical temporality represented a step toward modernity surely points to some analogy in the ancient and modern constructions of time. But these themes are far less crisp in the age of postmodernity than they once were: for comparanda to classical Athenian temporality we must look to eighteenth- and nineteenth-century Europe. The arts of this period show the same trend to particularism; the use of contemporary subjects and "realistic treatments"; individualization and the portrayal of unique and idiosyncratic aspects of characters, places, and times; the invention and mixing of genres; the avoidance of proleptic narrative; and fictionalization. The novel, the invention and dominant genre of the age, gives these trends their fullest expression. Of all genres the novel is most concerned with time. Its very name indicates a fetish for innovation; its celebrated formlessness advertised an abandonment of genre archetypes; and its fictional realism promised a departure from collective tradition in the name of truth to individual experience. E. M. Forster called the novel a portrait of "life by time" as opposed to the classic genres' "life by values."[51]

The new concern with the present and future, with particulars, and with novelty is oppositional in character, for the neoclassical aesthetic founded literary decorum upon the traditional, the universal, the timeless and true. As its spokesman, the earl of Shaftesbury claimed: "The variety of Nature is such, as to distinguish every thing she forms, by a peculiar original character; which, if strictly observed, will make the subject appear unlike to anything extant in the world besides. But this effect the good poet and painter seek industriously to prevent. They hate minuteness, and are afraid of singularity." By contrast the new mentality saw truth not in the reduction of phenomena to ideas received from the past, but in the immediacy of sensation, and in the belief "that everything that exists is particular." Like the new empirical philosophy, the novel argued, both by its formlessness and by its interest in the details of contemporary experience, that traditional archetypes were cultural illusions actively deleterious to the interests of the individual who paid them homage, and that everyone was free to trust his own knowledge and experience of the world.[52]

The rise of the novel gives a particularly vivid example of the way a genre, in its basic aesthetic organization, can serve as a vehicle of expression for the most fundamental social oppositions. If there is an analogy between the new genres of the classical period and those of modern Europe, it is partly to be explained in terms of a new order confronting an old. However, the analogy is more specific than merely a conscious confrontation of old and new, for which any oppositions might serve. That time itself was chosen as a primary locus of ideological struggle is due to the fact that the opposed ideologies were themselves temporally organized, for the past and present were the respective instruments of aristocratic and democratic thought, since aristocratic ideology was committed to the concept of a fixed and immutable social order and democratic ideology to a social order adjustable to the vicissitudes of history. It is no coincidence therefore that wherever we see democracy emerging from aristocracy we also find a problematization and a sharply divided expression of time.

In studying German conservative thought from 1750 to 1850, Mannheim concluded that "progressives experienced any given present as the beginning of the future, while conservatives experienced the present as the latest phase of the past." Reinhart Koselleck used the term "temporalization" to explain a process whereby the important social concepts of the era came to be colored with nostalgia or expectancy depending on one's political leanings. Leading liberal and revolutionary concepts acquired a marked future orientation, aristocratic and monarchic concepts a marked past orientation, while the concept of time itself acquired a paramount cultural significance. The temporalization Koselleck describes is a distorting and coercive process. It urges, rallies, and sets agendas.[53]

But the temporalization of modern Europe is not a perfect analog for classical Athens. In all the parallel trends in thought and expression, antiquity displays a certain "halfwayness." Greek democracy promoted the phenotype but in the end disprized it as ignoble. By contrast with Archaic art, classical art shows a high degree of individualization, but compared to the "realist" art of nineteenth-century Europe, this individualization seems little more than an extension of the human typology to include a public persona defined by ethnicity, social class, and trade. Beyond that, particularizing detail in art retained a comic quality reserved for the portrayal of foreigners and low-status individuals. History soon turned into a new order of mythology: Marathon ceased to compete with Troy and merely replaced it. Even the rage for the new was exhausted by the fourth century; fifth-century arts became standards of imitation; the aesthetic revolutionaries were converted to dull classics. Bakhtin rightly insisted on the unique temporality of the modern novel despite much study of its anticipation in antiquity. The halfwayness of classical antiquity's modernity is well brought out by Meier's comparison of the temporalization of modern Europe with fifth-century Athens. While he admitted that the transformation of concepts in Athens was comparable in "rapidity, profundity, and momentum," he found that temporalization took place "to only a relatively modest extent." What Meier missed most was a sense of "processual dynamism," a "concept of progress or history" expressed by a programmatic set well beyond the present to an incomparably transformed future. Why is classical Athens at once so near and so far from modernity?[54]

An orientation toward futurity and distant futurity is characteristic of the revolutionary movements studied by Koselleck. But we have argued that classical Athenians fixed their sights on the present and immediate future. By the fourth century, Athenian democrats worked to maintain their democracy, not to extend the process of democratization beyond its present achievements: there reigned what J. K. Davies calls an "ideology of static institutions." Very few shared the aspirations of those who, as Theramenes put it, "would not think democracy right until it was extended to slaves and those so poor that they would betray their country for a drachma" (Xenophon, *Hellenica* 2.3.48). Meier articulates the critical difference between the ancient and modern concepts of progress. Though the sophistic histories of civilization were progressive, they marked the present "as a special level of achievement," and "a limit that was hardly ever transcended." The concept of progress, and of time itself, never became the reified "autodynamic" process it became in the modern era. "Insofar as men thought in temporal terms at all, they were conscious of the progress they themselves had made, not of progress *per se*." The ancient concept of progress is best expressed by the Aristotelian notion that things grow until they attain their *physis* and then stop. For Athenian democracy, the evolutionary clock stopped, but not for the democrats of 1750–1850. The explanation may be that ancient society was structurally incapable of further democratization: Athens had pushed its potential to the limit.[55]

Earlier in this chapter we drew attention to Mannheim's theory that societies experience a conscious confrontation of worldviews when in the context of a democratic regime the citizens encounter a different class consciousness through upward mobility, and at the same time experience the relativity of cultural values through extensive horizontal mobility in the form of contact with different cultures. These conditions were met in classical Athens as in modern Europe. Any comparison of the ideological struggles of these very different eras must take account of the vertical and horizontal hierarchies that gave definition to this ideological split. Though both modern Europe and classical Athens had emergent democracies and extensive empires, there is at least one important structural difference. In Athens there was a closer relation between the horizontal and the vertical displacements of the citizen class. The foreign cultures with which Athens came into contact also provided the slaves on whose labor the economic and political "freedom" of the average Athenian depended. The metic Greeks who made up the rest of the noncitizen population were by and large citizens of the same states that made up Athens' empire. At Athens the hierarchy of the horizontal was closely matched by the hierarchy of the vertical. This was not the case in the modern Western democracies where the domestic proletariat and the colonials were two quite distinct groups.

The ideology of the Athenian demos was therefore fundamentally ambivalent. It both opposed and appropriated aristocratic values. In turning from myth to contemporary history it set about creating for itself a new myth of a heroic age. In individuating the human figure, it created a new archetype of the public persona, and reserved true individuation as the distinguishing mark of the noncitizen and an object of ridicule. By the mid-fifth century the Athenian demos established itself as a birth elite. Its freedom was prized as the basis of its superiority, because it could never really distinguish the concepts of freedom and superiority (cf. Plato, *Gorgias* 452d). The Old Oligarch complained that the demos "wishes to be free and rule others" (Pseudo-Xenophon, *Constitution of the Athenians* 1.8). Loss of empire, on the other hand, as Perikles warned, entailed a loss of freedom (Thuc. 2.63.1). Classical temporality expressed itself best in the treatment of foreign wars, imperial victories, social class, and slavery because the conception of time was inseparable from the conception of power, and power was something one gained necessarily at another's expense. This is a far cry from the universal equality espoused, however hypocritically, by the liberal democrats of the modern era. Both indeed had empires; the great difference was that Europe could afford to aspire to universal democracy at home, while reserving patriarchal control over colonies abroad. But the Athenian demos never aspired to full democracy. It felt its middle position on the social ladder too keenly. Looking up it spoke the language of equality. Looking down at the enormous metic, slave, and subject population at home and abroad, it spoke the language of the elite.[56]

Conclusion

We have attempted to explain the existence of two opposed ideas about time in classical Athens. Our account does not oppose the insights of previous scholarship, at least at the level of detailed analysis, so much as provide a general picture that unites these diverse insights into a systematic whole, located within the discourse of power in democratic and imperial Athens. The term "ideology" has a narrow sense that refers to conscious values related to political aspirations, and a broad sense that includes usually unconscious values related to politics only indirectly, but related nevertheless, since ideology aspires to a total systematization and simplification of the world, though one which it can never achieve. If there is any connection between the overt politics of the imperial democracy of Athens and the arts that flourished under its regime—apart from the direct and deliberate use of art for propagandistic purposes—then it is to be found in the relationship between ideological deep values and aesthetic deep values. A large part of artistic pleasure, we maintain, is simple wish fulfillment, the creation of a utopic image of the world which incorporates group values, while attempting to screen out, bracket, modify, or subsume those competing values that make real life in a divided society so turbulent and complex. Time was the locus of competition between the aristocracy (and other elites who adopted their values) and the demos. Time is also fundamental to all the arts insofar as art is (or implies) narrative. Artistic innovation, the appearance of new genres and styles, and the general process of particularization, historicization, and fictionalization all gave expression to the new democratic temporality. Empire both served as a catalyst for the general crisis of values in the fifth century and was one of the conditions that sharply modified the development of a coherent egalitarian ideology, perhaps thereby contributing in some way to the democracy's final collapse.

CHAPTER SIX

Autochthony and the Visual Arts in Fifth-Century Athens

H. ALAN SHAPIRO

The extraordinary flowering of the visual arts in fifth-century Athens is well attested in surviving examples of architecture, sculpture, and vase painting.[1] Many other monuments are lost to us but can, to some extent, be reconstructed with the help of other sources, such as Roman copies of bronze statues or literary descriptions and reflections in other media of monumental wall painting. The visual arts were undoubtedly pressed into the service of both democracy and empire, to proclaim and inculcate in the citizenry the ideals and values of Athenian society.[2] In this chapter I propose to explore one theme that was central to the ideology of both democracy *and* imperialism—that of autochthony—in some of its manifestations in painting and sculpture. But first, I will present a few brief observations on what types of visual art are characteristic of fifth-century Athens and how these differ from the Archaic period that preceded it.

A crude comparison of the archaeological record for Archaic and classical Athens suggests that there is not so much a steady increase in the rate of production or the quality of the material as a change in the balance of publicly versus privately commissioned or displayed monuments. The Archaic Akropolis, for example, had been marked by a great number of private sculptural dedications, from the Moschophoros and the earliest of the korai, about 570–560, down to the Persian sack of 480.[3] After 480 private dedications do still occur, but rarely in the form of large-scale statuary.[4] Even in cases where we may suspect the influence of private individuals like Perikles, as with the portrait statues of Anakreon and Xanthippos, this may not have been made explicit, in the way that the inscriptions on Archaic statues proudly announced their dedicators.[5] The major dedications of the classical period were those put up by the state, most conspicuously the great bronze Athena, often referred to in modern scholarship (though not in antiquity) as the Promachos and attributed to Pheidias.[6] She commemorated the victory over the Persians, as did so many other public monuments of the middle years of the fifth century.

Similarly, elaborately carved and painted tomb monuments, often bearing epigrams naming the deceased and the family, dotted both the Kerameikos in Athens and cemeteries in outlying parts of Attika throughout the sixth century but ceased to be produced by the early fifth. Whether such a prohibition was actually legislated by the young democracy, to curb aristocratic display, is debated,[7] but this was certainly the effect. By about 470 the state was putting up simple memorials to the war dead in the form of casualty lists inscribed on marble slabs, in a section of the Kerameikos set aside as a *dēmosion sēma*.[8] The demotic nature of these monuments was emphasized by listing the dead according to their tribe and, as far as we can tell, no sculptural decoration was present. When carved gravestones do reappear about 430, this may mean no more than that the long-suppressed need for private memorials became too great after the outbreak of the Peloponnesian War.[9]

Most public architecture in Athens was religious in nature and adhered to certain traditions unaffected by the vicissitudes of war and politics. Thus the Old Temple of Athena on the north side of the Akropolis was built about 570–560, probably on the site of older predecessors.[10] Athena Nike may have received her first shrine at about the same time, on the bastion at the west entrance to the Akropolis.[11] Both sanctuaries were renewed in the later fifth century, as part of Perikles' building program, in the Erechtheion and the Nike Temple. The most conspicuous element of that program, however, the Parthenon, was a different matter. Its predecessor, the uncompleted Older Parthenon begun in the 480s, was, I believe, the first temple on the site and represented a new phenomenon in Athens, the temple as victory monument (in this case for Marathon).[12]

The tradition that the sculptural decoration of Greek temples conveyed deliberate messages is likewise an old one, but the messages themselves keep changing. The earliest pedimental groups from the Old Athena Temple, with their emphasis on the elemental forces of nature and the deeds of Herakles, have only a tenuous link to the goddess and her city.[13] When a replacement pediment in marble was installed by the new democracy at the very end of the sixth century,[14] its Gigantomachy gave pride of place to Athena in one of her greatest victories, one that played a key role in the Panathenaic festival.[15] Perhaps there is a subtle reference in the defeat of the hybristic Giants to the recent overthrow of the tyranny as well. By the time we reach the Parthenon, temple sculpture embodies a whole intricate network of messages, discussed by Tonio Hölscher elsewhere in this volume.

The manufacture of fine-ware pottery in Athens, that is, Attic black- and red-figure, continued uninterrupted from the Archaic into the classical period, along with the export of most of it to the West and elsewhere. Though the vases often reflect ideas circulating throughout Athens in other media, as we shall see later in this chapter, they represent an essentially private art form, with the exception of those dedicated on the Akropolis and in other sanctuaries.[16] Very different are the large-scale frescoes that decorated both shrines (the Theseion and Anakeion) and civic buildings, particularly the Stoa Poikile on the north side of the Agora. Their heyday begins just after the Persian Wars, and they have no counterpart in the Archaic period, for the technique of monumental painting was perfected—probably in the Northeast Peloponnese rather than in Athens—only in the later sixth century.[17] The role of these paintings in shaping popular perceptions of Athens, her history, and her place in the world can hardly be overstated.[18] They include the first large-scale historical narrative in Athenian art, the Marathon Painting in the Stoa Poikile.[19]

In sum, then, the output of art and architecture was already prodigious in Archaic Athens, as it was in other tyrant-ruled Greek cities, such as Corinth or Samos. But it was primarily art commissioned by private initiative, as a form of aristocratic self-representation, and to this extent the democracy must be seen as inhibiting rather than encouraging the public display of art. Where, then, did the democracy find its own expressions in the visual arts? With the exception of those buildings put up in the Agora to house the institutions of government—the Old Bouleuterion, the Tholos, the Royal Stoa—it is not possible to speak of a distinctive architecture of democracy.[20] Nor is it easy to find unambiguous expressions of the democracy in sculpture or painting,[21] at least not before the last two decades of the fifth century, in such monuments as the document reliefs and treasury accounts that personify the Athenian Demos,[22] or the first collective monument of the Eponymous Heroes in the Agora.[23]

If the Agora is the physical setting of democracy, then the Akropolis ought to be the locus of Athens' imperial self-image. Some of the relevant monuments are discussed in this volume by Tonio Hölscher, but what strikes me is how seldom the Akropolis sculpture of the fifth century, both on the buildings and on the ground, refers explicitly to Athens' hegemonic role in the Aegean. With rare exceptions (possibly the friezes of the Nike Temple),[24] the language of the visual arts is still that of myth rather than history, of the heroic past rather than the strife-torn present.[25]

The first concern of the Athenian democracy was to create what Hölscher has called "Identität im Inneren," that is, to represent the Athenians to themselves, to forge an image embodying their own values and ideals. An example of this process is the rapid promotion of the Tyrannicides to the status of founding heroes of the democratic state and, through their physical presence (as statues) in the Agora, as exemplars and role models for the citizenry.[26] It was in this changing context that the notion of Athenian autochthony assumed a new importance from roughly the time of the Persian Wars. I turn now to this theme and its expression in the visual arts.

In order to assess the role and importance of autochthony, it is first necessary to ascertain just what this concept did and did not signify. A recent study of the etymology and usage of the word *autochthon* by Vincent Rosivach concludes that its basic meaning is "always having the same land," that is, "a people which has lived in its homeland since time immemorial."[27] Perhaps the notion incorporates a vague recollection that Athens had escaped the widespread destruction that engulfed much of Greece at the end of the Bronze Age. Rosivach rejects the meaning often found (for example in Liddell, Scott, and Jones) as "sprung from the earth itself" and argues that the story of the earth-born Erichthonios was blended with the tradition of the Athenians as an indigenous people only quite late, in the course of the fifth century.[28] I am inclined to modify this view somewhat, on the basis of the archaeological evidence presented below, but would accept that the fully formed notion of autochthony, such as we find in the tragedians and the orators, was shaped in direct response to the needs of the democracy and the growing importance of Athens in the Delian League.[29]

At the same time, there are clearly several things that autochthony did not mean. It did not mean, for example, that every Athenian family (*genos*) in the fifth century claimed to be descended from a native Athenian hero. On the contrary, no *genos* claimed descent from the true earth-born heroes, Kekrops and Erechtheus. Of the few *genē* that had a genealogy going back to any Bronze Age hero, the best known are probably the Peisistratidai, from Neleus of Pylos, and the Philaidai, from Ajax of Salamis and, before him, Aiakos of Aegina—all non-Athenian heroes who only in historical times, perhaps through the intercession of their supposed descendants, became "honorary Athenians" with the creation of local cults.[30] Thus autochthony also does not mean that the early kings of Athens were all native Athenians, for the family of Kodros and Neleus clearly was not,[31] and even Theseus was born outside Athens, to a foreign (Troizenian) mother and, as he says in Sophocles' *Oedipus at Colonus* (561–66), he felt like a foreigner (*xenos*) in Athens. Finally, autochthony does not even mean that those first Athenians, in the time of Kekrops and Erechtheus, were the first human inhabitants of the land of Attika, for the tradition that non-Greek Pelasgians once lived in Athens was already well known to Herodotus (1.57, 2.51, 6.137). Elsewhere (8.44), Herodotus is aware that before the time of Kekrops (but presumably after that of the Pelasgians) the people later called Athenians were called Kranaoi, after the obscure hero Kranaos (cf. Aeschylus, *Eumenides* 1011).

In the later fifth century we find expressions of a second ideology that seems at first glance almost in conflict with that of autochthony, the image of Athens as a hospitable place of refuge for those forced to leave their own homes. Thus, for example, Theseus agrees to bury the Argive heroes who fell before Thebes,[32] to take in the exiled Oedipus and the Children of Herakles, and Aegeus offers a safe haven to Medea.[33]

But this claim is not at odds with the notion of autochthony; rather it complements it, if we understand autochthony in the other, mythological sense (the one that Rosivach rejects). It referred specifically to the fact that the first true Athenian—Kekrops—and the first king of a united Athenian state—Erechtheus—did not come to Athens from elsewhere, nor did their ancestors (since they had none), but rather they sprang from the very soil of Athens. What autochthony implies, then, is that, in a collective sense, all historical Athenians are descended from the two founding heroes, even if (or perhaps because) no one Athenian family is directly descended from either of them. Autochthony did not by any means make the Athenians unique in all of Greece—the Thebans, for example, had the story of the "sown men" who also sprang from the soil, in the time of Kadmos[34]—but it did set them apart, most notably from the Dorian Peloponnesians (against whom the claim would most often be made), descended from the Herakleidai.[35]

A number of recent discussions have helped to make it clear why the theme of autochthony was so useful both to the democracy and to Athens' imperialist ambitions. On the one hand, autochthony is, like democracy itself, a great leveller.[36] It asserts that every native Athenian is as good as every other, by virtue of their common ancestry going back to Erechtheus, and better than any non-Athenian. This belief in the inherent superiority of the Athenians was also a cornerstone of the democracy, as evident, for example, in Perikles' citizenship law.[37] At the same time, autochthony also implies that the Athenians are an older, purer, and nobler race than other Greeks, and hence natural born leaders of an alliance. They are the chosen people, as it were, favored and protected in their enterprise by the whole host of Olympian gods.

If, as I believe, the claim of autochthony does derive in part from two specific individuals, Kekrops and Erechtheus, then there is some evidence, both textual and archaeological, that this is not simply a construct of the fifth century. First

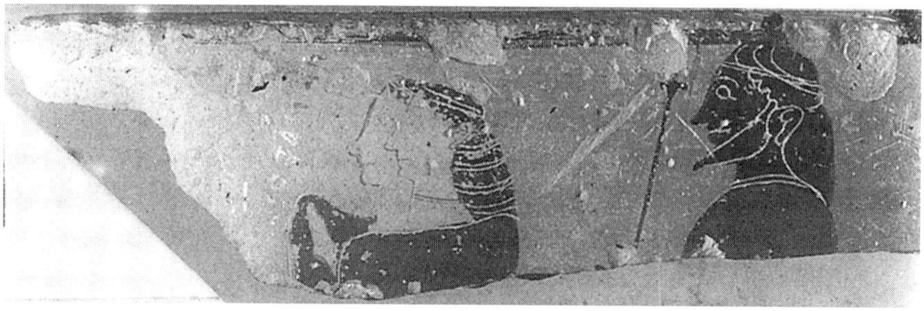

Figure 1 Kekrops and his Daughters. Black-figure fragment from the Akropolis. Athens National Museum, Akropolis 585a. Ca. 580. Photo: German Archaeological Institute, Athens.

there is the well-known passage in the Catalogue of Ships describing Athena's rich temple on the Akropolis, where she has installed Erechtheus (*Iliad* 2.547), and another in the *Odyssey* (7.81) referring to that same temple as "the strong house of Erechtheus." That is to say, the close association of Erechtheus with the Akropolis (where the myth says he was conceived and born) and with Athena as patron goddess of the city is not a later invention, but is, in fact, the very first thing that the literary tradition tells us about Athens. And what of Kekrops and his three daughters who, as nurses of the baby Erichthonios, provide the chief link between the two generations of heroes? There is, to be sure, no mention of them in Homer, but a few pieces of archaeological evidence suggest that they, too, are not inventions of the fifth century.

Some battered fragments by the painter Sophilos belong to what was once a rather splendid big bowl dedicated on the Akropolis in the 570s (fig. 1).[38] We see parts of a procession: two women share a mantle, one labelled Pandrosos; the other must be her sister Aglauros (the third sister, Herse, who has no known cult, seems to be a later invention, a doublet of Pandrosos). The kingly figure with scepter just behind them, as Beazley recognized, should be their father Kekrops.[39] Hermes was also here (only a bit of his Kerykeion survives), and, significantly, Poseidon as well. We shall hear more about his role on the Akropolis later.

Since the narrative context is lost, these fragments can do no more than to reassure us that Kekrops and his daughters were known on the Akropolis by the early sixth century. The sanctuary of Aglauros, now securely located on the eastern slope by a recent epigraphical discovery,[40] was certainly there at the time of the Persian invasion (Her. 8.55) and possibly much earlier.[41] A small poros pediment that may have decorated a treasury building on the Akropolis in the mid-sixth century was named by archaeologists after the olive tree incised on its architectural setting—surely a reference to the sacred olive tree of Athena that was said to grow in the sanctuary of Pandrosos on the north side of the Akropolis (Pausanias 1.26.5). The building represented in this pediment should then be the adjacent "old" temple of Athena (the *archaios naos*) and the women none other than the Daughters of Kekrops.[42]

None of this, of course, proves that the *ideology* of autochthony was current in Athenian thought in the sixth century, only that the heroic and cultic traditions on which the belief in autochthony is in part based were genuinely old and not first created in the fifth century. I think it is important to emphasize this point, since so many other aspects of the early genealogy of Athens do seem to be fifth-century inventions: the figure of Kodros, for example, the Neleid king of Athens who sacrificed himself in battle to save the city and whose son (another Neleus) was said to be oikist of Miletos and other cities in Ionia;[43] or the tradition, first in Euripides, that Ion, son of Erechtheus' daughter Kreousa, was fathered by Apollo in a cave of the Akropolis.[44]

Having satisfied ourselves that Kekrops, his daughters, and Erichthonios/Erechtheus[45] were all well established in Athenian legend and cult in the Archaic period, we may now look at what fifth-century Athenian artists and poets did with them in shaping and promoting the ideology of autochthony.

The visual tradition makes it clear that the central event in the narrative of autochthony is the birth of the baby Erichthonios from the soil of Attika at the very heart of the city, the Akropolis. That this story was in fact the primary vehicle by which Athenian artists and their public could visualize the notion of autochthony is suggested by the chronology of its occurrences in vase painting, first appearing at the time of the Persian Wars and reaching its most intense level of popularity and creativity during the Peloponnesian War years. These scenes have been catalogued and discussed many times, most notably by Uta Kron, and I will not rehearse them all here.[46] But I believe that the *way* the vase painters rendered the story tells us a great deal about how fifth-century Athenians understood it and what was important to them about it.

The birth is not, of course, depicted "clinically" or realistically, but rather in an allegorizing manner that is characteristic of Greek art in the fifth century: the Earth, in the form of the goddess Ge, rises up out of herself carrying the newborn baby and presents it to Athena (figs. 3, 5, 11). The objection of Nicole Loraux that this cannot be the birth,[47] because Erichthonios is too big for a newborn baby, but is instead a representation of the nurturing of the child Erichthonios by Athena, rests on a misunderstanding of the conventions of Greek art.[48] This is what infants look like in vase painting down to the late fifth century; they don't come any smaller than this.[49] When the painters wanted to show the boy

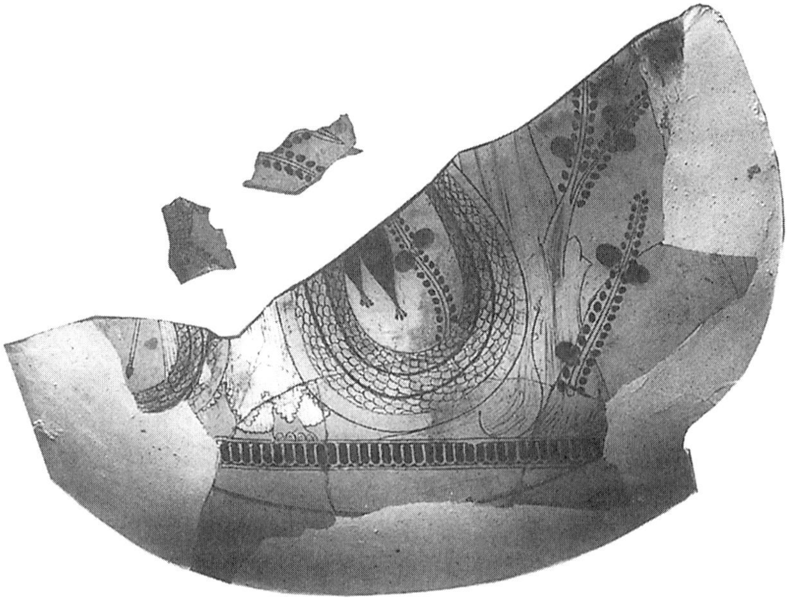

Figure 2 Athena, Erichthonios, and the Snake. White-ground cup from the Akropolis. Athens National Museum, Akropolis 433. 500–490. Photo: German Archaeological Institute, Athens.

Erichthonios in the care of Athena, they had a very different formula for this, as on a white-ground cup dedicated on the Akropolis ca. 490 (fig. 2).[50] Athena, at the left, is recognizable by the tip of the spear she carries; of Erichthonios, at the right, little remains, but enough to make out that he raises his right hand to acknowledge the goddess. The huge snake that winds through the scene is both the protector of Athena's sanctuary and a reminder of Erichthonios' miraculous birth. Only a few years after the date of this cup, the violation of the sanctuary by the Persians and the necessity for the Athenians to desert their own city would be signalled by the departure of the guardian snake from the Akropolis (Her. 8.41; cf. Plutarch, *Themistokles* 10).[51]

In Homer, Erechtheus is said to have been born simply out of the "rich soil" (*zeidōros aroura: Iliad* 2.548). In personifying the Attic soil as they did, the vase painters naturally turned Earth into a motherly, nurturing figure, and the Athenian viewer would automatically have understood her as that same Ge Kourotrophos whose sanctuary was located on the south slope of the Akropolis, near the western entrance (Pausanias 1.22.3). She had close associations in cult with both Athena and the Daughters of Kekrops, all of whom function in this story likewise as *kourotrophoi*.[52]

Athena's receiving of the baby is, as Loraux rightly points out, an official acknowledgment that it is in some sense hers, even if she had earlier rejected the advances of the baby's father, Hephaistos (fig. 7).[53] This in turn implies, as Deborah Boedeker has stressed, that Athena is the true parent of all the Athenians, for they are all descendants of Erechtheus.[54] But they are the descendants of Hephaistos, too, as Aeschylus acknowledges at the beginning of the *Eumenides* (13), and so we see him as the proud father in this peculiarly Greek version of a "holy family" (fig. 3).[55] Once again it is the cult traditions familiar to all Athenians that inform the representations more than the details of the narrative, which

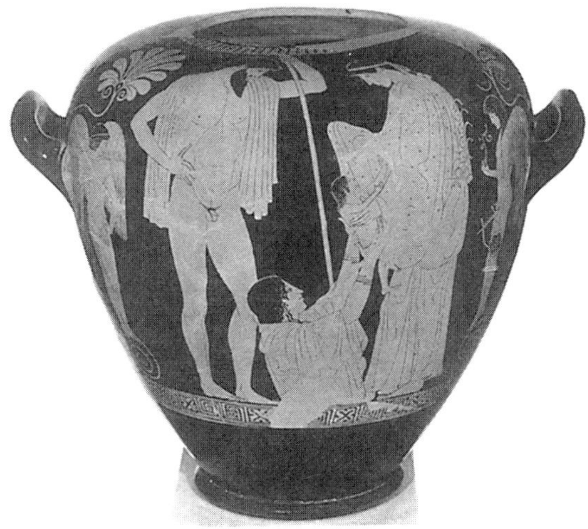

Figure 3 Birth of Erichthonios. Red-figure stamnos, Side A. Antikensammlungen Munich. 2413. Ca. 460. Photo: Museum.

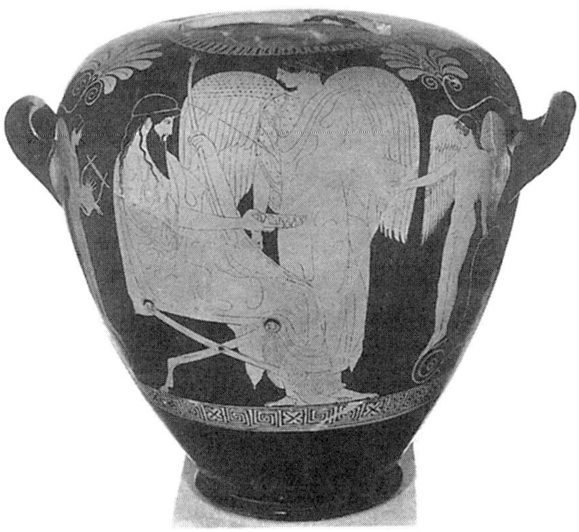

Figure 4 Zeus and Nike. Red-figure stamnos, Side B. Antikensammlungen Munich. Ca. 460. Photo: Museum.

implies a strained relationship between the two divinities. Hephaistos and Athena were in fact closely linked in cult, especially on the Akropolis where, as Ergane, patroness of crafts, she was like a colleague to him,[56] but also above the Agora, where the two were jointly worshipped in the Hephaisteion.[57] Their collaboration on another "earth-born" creation—Pandora—was celebrated on the Akropolis as well, on the base of Pheidias' great statue of Athena for the Parthenon.[58]

These four figures—Athena and Hephaistos, Ge and the baby Erichthonios—thus comprise the essential elements of the story. But it is the additional figures included in the various painted versions, along with the chronological development of the iconography over nearly a century, that enable us better to appreciate some aspects of the larger context in which the Athenians understood it.

Kekrops is present in the earliest surviving depiction, on a lekythos in Palermo dated soon after 500.[59] He promptly disappears from the scene for a long while, then appears again irregularly from the Kodros Painter's cup of the 430s (fig. 5) down to the end of the century. No preserved story recounts the autochthonous birth of Kekrops, but the snaky lower body that marks him whenever he attends the birth of Erichthonios clearly establishes this essential link between the only two genuinely autochthonous heroes. Elsewhere on Attic vases, where Kekrops' autochthony is not of primary importance, he may be shown in fully human form—for example when he witnesses the Rape of Oreithyia by Boreas or his own daughter Herse pursued by Hermes.[60] And certainly he was imagined fully human in his guise as one of the ten Eponymous Heroes, whether in vase painting, on the Parthenon frieze, or in their collective monument in the Agora.[61]

The snaky Kekrops, then, shows his kinship with the earth-born Erichthonios, who will be guarded by snakes in his cradle and, in some later versions, was believed to have taken the form of a snake himself.[62] Though not the biological father, Kekrops is nevertheless seen as a fatherly figure to Erichthonios who, as the grown-up Erechtheus, will be the heir to his throne. Thus autochthony is established early on, if somewhat paradoxically, as something that can be "inherited" from one generation to the next. This seems to be the premise behind the promotion of Ion, a descendant of Erechtheus, to a key role as an ancestor figure of the Athenians.[63]

Kekrops' presence at the birth of Erichthonios also alludes, of course, to the fact that it is his daughters to whom the newborn will next be entrusted. This is made even more explicit when one or more of the Kekropids are themselves witnesses to the birth (figs. 5, 6; cf. fig. 16), or when a single vase shows both the birth and the subsequent episode of Athena punishing the disobedient Kekropids (figs. 9, 10).[64] The front side of this fragmentary pelike of ca. 460 shows Athena having already received the baby from Ge. On the reverse, we can make

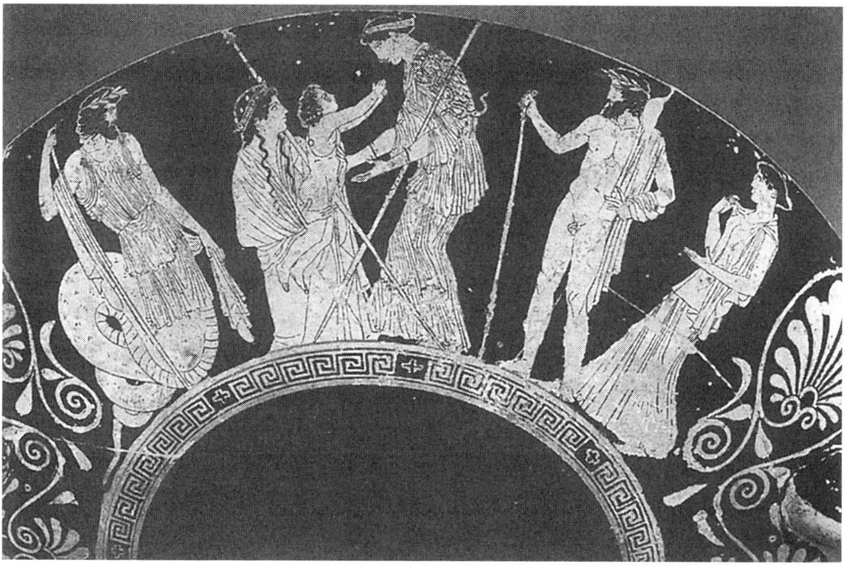

Figure 5 Birth of Erichthonios. Red-figure cup, Side A. Berlin, Antikenmuseum F 2537. 440–430. Photo: Museum (J. Tietz-Glagow).

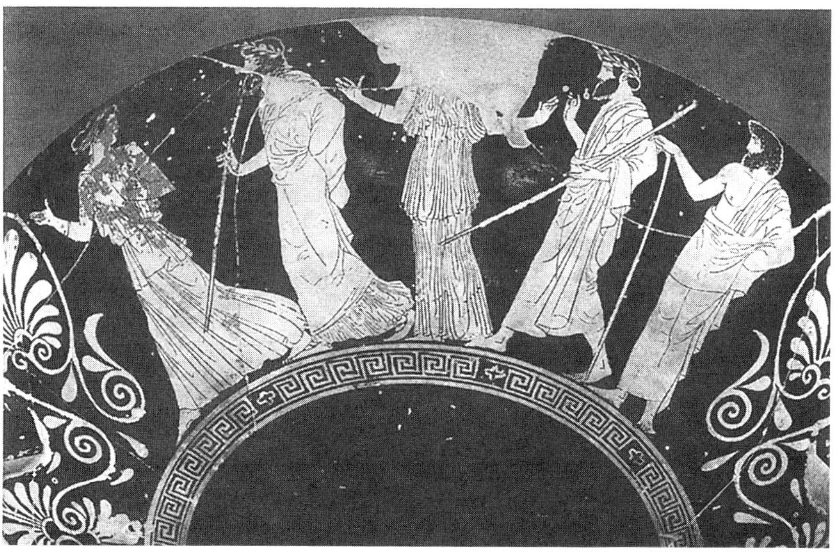

Figure 6 Daughters of Kekrops and Attic kings. Red-figure cup, Side B. Berlin, Antikenmuseum F 2537. 440–430. Photo: Museum (J. Tietz-Glagow).

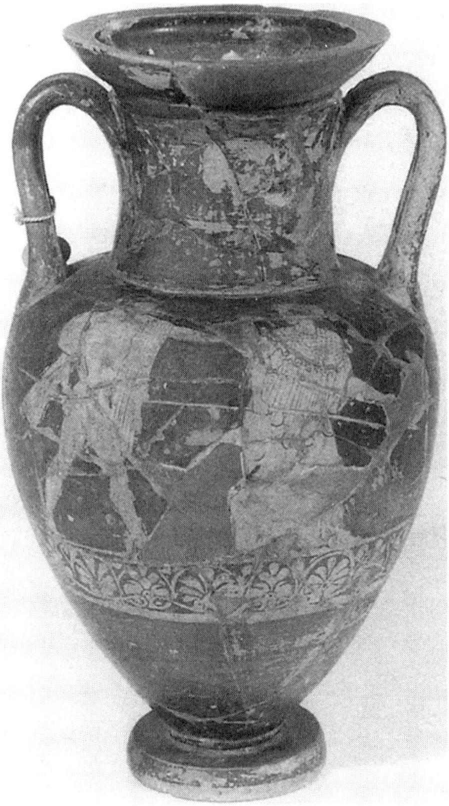

Figure 7 Hephaistos pursuing Athena. Red-figure neck-amphora. Bologna, Museo Civico 158. Ca. 460. Photo: Museum.

out the basket fallen on its side,[65] indicating that it was dropped by the girls fleeing Athena's wrath. The extra female figures at the left and right of the front side (fig. 9) are too fragmentary to identify with certainty, but it is not impossible, as Uta Kron suggests, that these are once again the Kekropids, greeting the birth of the child with a libation (cf. fig. 12).[66]

Nevertheless, what matters most about the Daughters of Kekrops, at least in the fifth century, is not their role as joyous observers or as *kourotrophoi* (though this may once have been true), but rather their disobedience to Athena's command in opening the chest. This was especially relevant in classical times if, as Walter Burkert has shown in a famous article, the story functioned as the *aition* for the initiation ritual of the Arrhēphoroi, young girls in the service of Athena who had to carry a chest down the north slope of the Akropolis without peeking inside.[67]

An early classical hydria, in London (fig. 11), substitutes the figure of Zeus, clutching a large thunderbolt, where we would have expected Hephaistos.[68] His presence, and that of his helper Nike, who brings a garland for the baby, help to

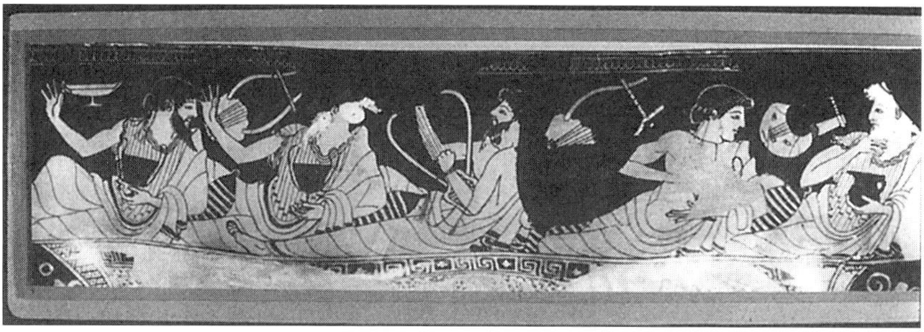

Figure 8 Symposium of Attic kings. Red-figure rhyton. Richmond, Virginia Museum of Fine Arts 79.100. Ca. 480. Photo: Museum.

set this local Athenian event in a more cosmic and Olympian framework. As Athena's father and only parent, Zeus too had an important role on the Akropolis,[69] and Nike's gesture heralds the meaning of the birth for the future glory of Athens. The roles of Zeus and Nike in celebrating the birth are alluded to elsewhere as well, on the reverse of the Munich stamnos (fig. 4) and on the Sotades Painter's rhyton (fig.12), where Nike assists Kekrops in pouring the libation as his daughters bring news of Erichthonios' birth.[70]

The Kodros Painter's Berlin cup (figs. 5, 6) marks the beginning of a new tendency, in the last third of the fifth century, to place the birth of Erichthonios in an even broader political and religious context. As the baby is born on one side (fig. 5), the king he will become, Erechtheus, appears on the other (fig. 6), along with two kings of a later generation, the brothers Aigeus and Pallas.[71] The vase is thus not strictly "logical"; that is, it does not present ten characters who could all have gathered at one time.[72] Rather, its message is a political one: Kekrops and Erichthonios, the autochthonous heroes, found a dynasty that will unite the Athenians, under divine guidance, down through the ages, encompassing many generations of kings. This insistence on the continuity of Athenian kingship, despite the lack of traditional family ties and bloodlines, was first enunciated in the visual arts by the Richmond rhyton (fig. 8) and lies behind the continuous reworking of Attic genealogy throughout the fifth century.

Even more complex than the Kodros Painter's cup is the gathering on the great calyx-krater in Adolphseck, name vase of the Kekrops Painter, of ca. 400 (fig. 13).[73] The libation is once again a central motif, this time performed by both Athena and Kekrops in honor of the baby Erichthonios, who lies concealed in his chest at the foot of Athena's olive tree on the Akropolis. The subsidiary figures, as Erika Simon has shown, are all linked by the cult places they occupied in or near the new temple of Athena that would later bear the name of Erechtheus: Hermes and Hephaistos at the upper right; the Kekropids at the upper left; Zeus seated at

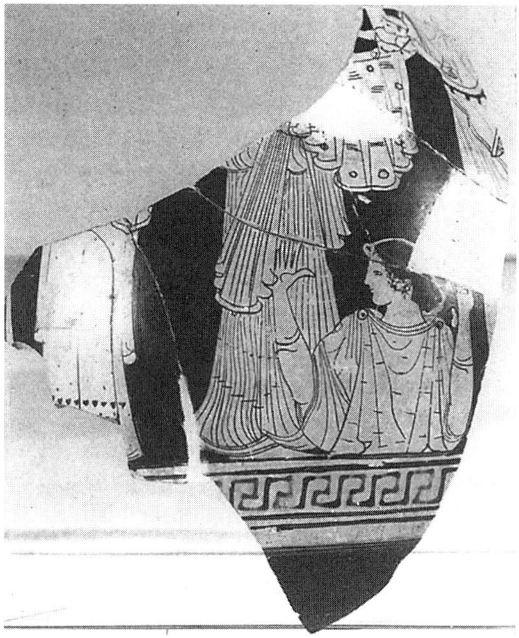

Figure 9 Birth of Erichthonios. Fragmentary red-figure pelike, Side A. Leipzig, Antikenmuseum T 654. Ca. 460. Photo: Museum.

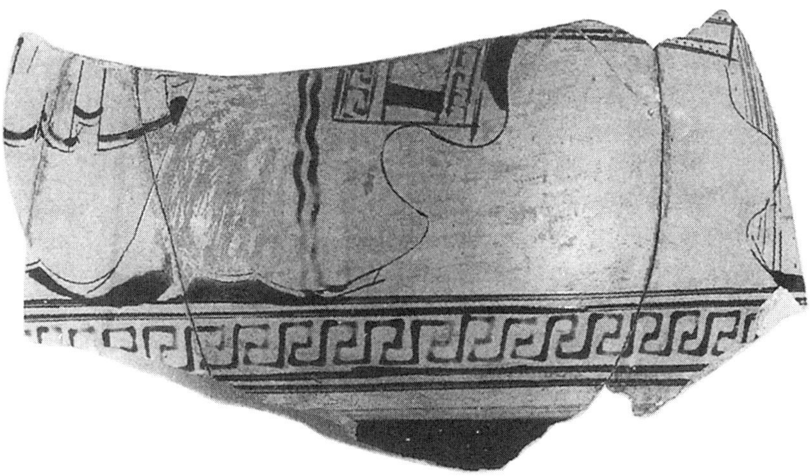

Figure 10 Daughters of Kekrops. Fragmentary red-figure pelike, Side B. Leipzig, Antikenmuseum T 654. Ca. 460. Photo: Museum.

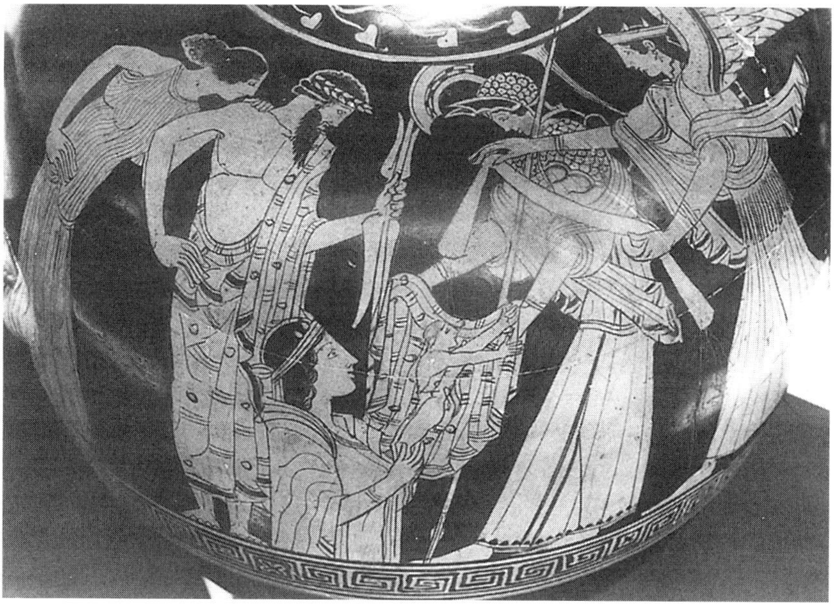

Figure 11 Birth of Erichthonios. Red-figure hydria. London, British Museum E 182. Ca. 460. Photo courtesy Trustees of the British Museum.

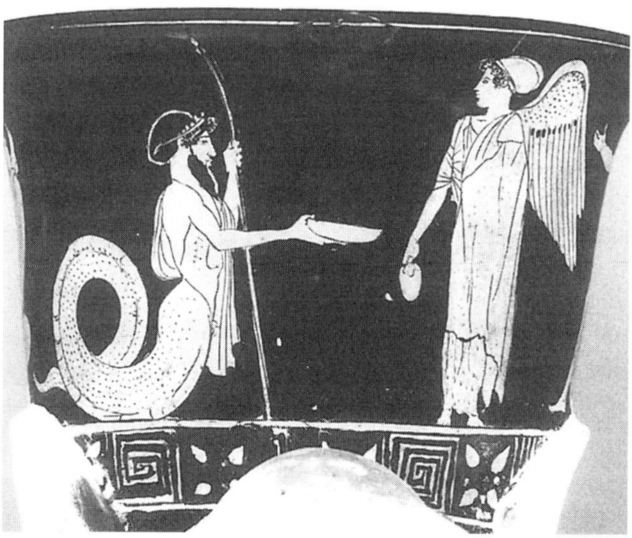

Figure 12 Kekrops and Nike. Red-figure rhyton. London, British Museum E 788. Ca. 450. Photo courtesy Trustees of the British Museum.

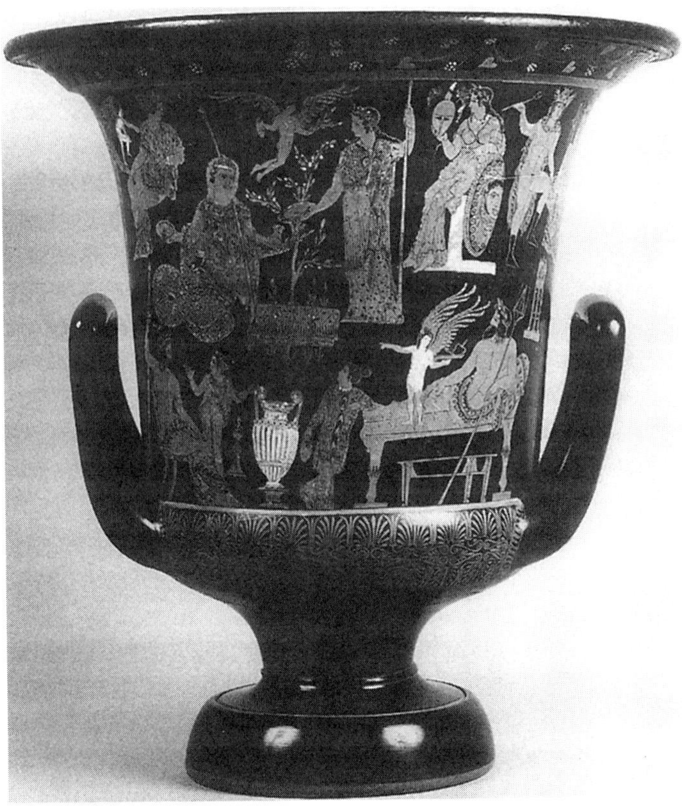

Figure 13 Libation for the birth of Erichthonios. Red-figure calyx-krater. Adolphseck, Schloss Fasanerie 77. Ca. 400. Photo: Hessische Hausstiftung (E. Gutberlet).

the lower left, before a large volute-krater; and Poseidon reclining on a *klinē* at the lower right.[74] Interestingly, this is the first time we find Poseidon in this context, yet his presence here confirms the fact that Erechtheus shared his cult on the Akropolis with Poseidon,[75] a tradition that may already have been known to Homer.[76]

An equally fine calyx-krater of these same years, at the end of the fifth century,[77] adds two new divinities who had not previously figured in the birth of Erichthonios (figs. 14, 15). Aphrodite sits and observes the birth from the lower right, just in front of Zeus. As her scepter suggests, this is the civic goddess Aphrodite, whose cult as Pandemos was located near the entrance to the Akropolis (Pausanias 1.22.3).[78] In a famous choral ode in the *Medea* in praise of Athens, Euripides speaks of this same Aphrodite, "beside the sweetly flowing stream of

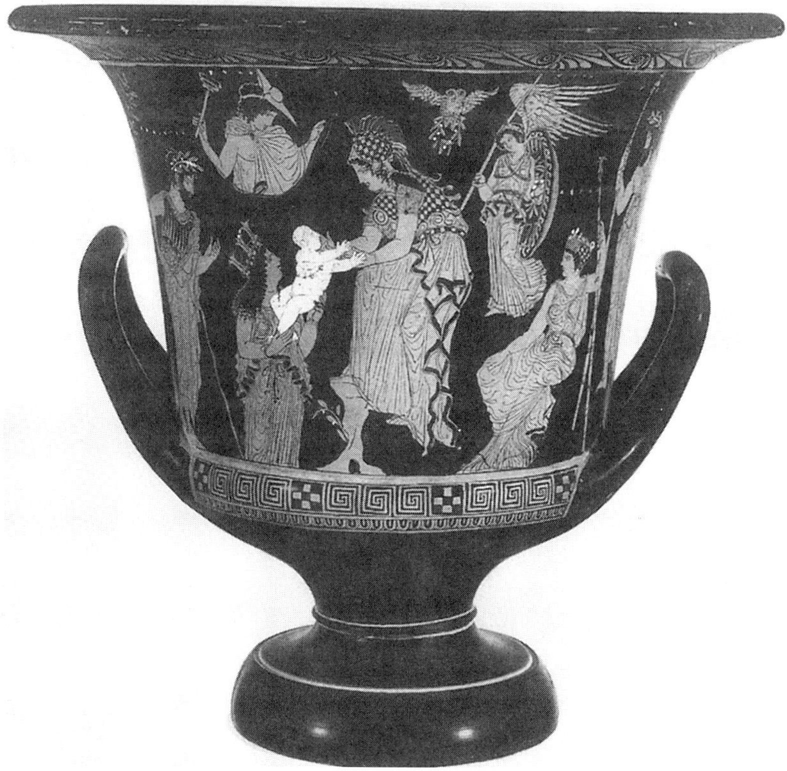

Figure 14 Birth of Erichthonios. Red-figure calyx-krater. Richmond, Virginia Museum of Fine Arts 81.70. Ca. 410–400. Photo: Museum, courtesy of J. H. Oakley.

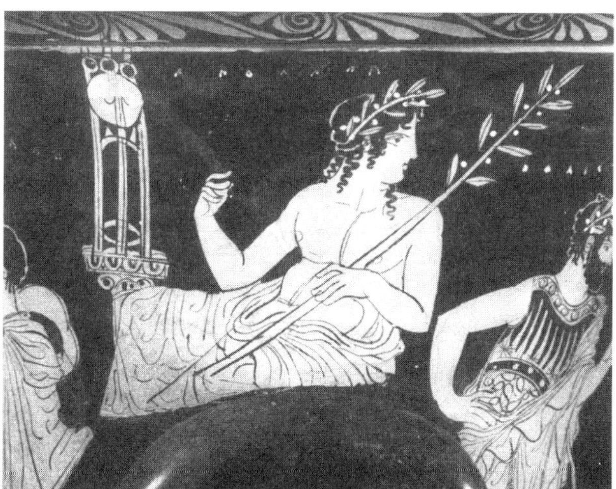

Figure 15 Apollo. Detail of red-figure calyx-krater. Richmond, Virginia Museum of Fine Arts 81.70. Ca. 410–400. Photo: Museum, courtesy of J. H. Oakley.

Kephisos" (835). "Pandemos"—she who unites all the people—originally commemorated Theseus' synoicism of Attika (Paus. 1.22.3), but she is equally appropriate here at the birth of the future king who defines the common identity of all Athenians. Observing the birth from above one handle is Apollo (fig. 15), whose newly created role in the family of Erechtheus had been dramatized in the *Ion* of Euripides just a few years before the date of this krater.[79] The belated entry of Apollo into Athenian royal genealogy came, ironically, at a time when the god's key role as patron of the Delian League had already been superseded by that of Athena as *Reichsgöttin*.[80] Yet in spite of this (or perhaps in compensation for it), Athenian vase iconography of the later fifth century gives an increasingly prominent role to Apollo as the protector and guarantor of *nomos*.[81]

Finally, the circle of the Meidias Painter, which also took up the theme of Erichthonios in the last two decades of the fifth century, exploited yet a different aspect of it. Instead of majestic kraters like the two just discussed (figs. 13–15), the Meidian vases are small, delicate, "feminine" shapes that create what Lucilla Burn has called an "Attic Paradise," an idyllic world of grace and charm sometimes seen as a form of escape from the grim reality of the Peloponnesian War.[82] By setting the birth of Erichthonios within this Attic Paradise, the painters suggest the favor that the gods bestowed on Athens in that distant age. Twice the birth is attended by a host of nymphlike women whose identity is unfortunately withheld from us by the lack of inscriptions (figs. 16, 17).[83] The Cleveland lekythos is unique in several respects: the Kekropids looking down from above, in a shorthand attempt to render the topography of the Akropolis; the figure of Ge, for the first time fully emerged from the ground; and Athena striding vigorously to receive the baby. Not that this is a particularly "motherly" Athena: the elaborate helmet and the prominent Gorgoneion on her aegis, which she usually swings around onto her back (cf. figs. 3, 5, 11) to avoid frightening the baby, make her the most martial Athena we have seen in this context and also hint at the fierce wrath the Kekropids will soon incur. Quite different are the languorous women all about, who could personify the many blessings bestowed by the gods on the newborn and his city.[84]

The third Meidian vase, a lidded pyxis, does label all the figures, though with some surprises.[85] The birth scene, on the lid, includes two personifications otherwise unattested on vases, Basile and Soteria. The scene of Athena chastising the disobedient sisters, on the body, includes a host of ancillary figures, one labelled Basileia. The message seems to be that Erichthonios will carry on the institution of legitimate kingship (*basileia*), which is essential to the preservation (*soteria*) of the Athenian people.[86]

The vases we have just considered, taken together, make it clear that the charter myth of Athenian autochthony enjoyed some currency throughout the fifth century. But if it was as central to the city's self-image as I am suggesting, then we might well have expected to find it more prominently displayed in public places. Some stories associated with the family of Erechtheus found limited use in temple sculpture from the early classical period on—so, for example, Boreas and Oreithyia or Eos and Kephalos as acroteria groups, the latter on the Royal Stoa (Pausanias 1.3.1) or on the Temple of the Athenians on Delos[87]—but to find the birth of Erichthonios in sculpture we must move down to the last years of the fifth century, and even then the picture is uncertain.[88] The best candidates are the base of the cult statue in the Hephaisteion,[89] in the penultimate decade of the century, and the North Frieze of the Erechtheion, not completed until the last decade.[90] Evelyn Harrison has made the intriguing suggestion that the birth of Erichthonios was woven into the Panathenaic peplos around this time, having in mind the tapestry in Ion's tent at Delphi that depicted Kekrops and his Daughters (*Ion* 1163–65).[91]

Since the discovery of the new fragments of Euripides' *Erechtheus* on papyrus in the 1960s, we now have good evidence for an episode from the reign of that king—the war with Eumolpos and the sacrifice of Erechtheus' three daughters to ensure Athenian victory—which, in its political relevance for classical Athens, may have overshadowed the story of his autochthonous birth.[92] Yet autochthony was surely a central motif of the play, as we see in Praxithea's speech on why Athens is worth dying for (fr. 50.7–10):

> We are autochthonous by birth. But other cities,
> scattered randomly by a throw of the dice,
> are immigrant from elsewhere.

But themes do not always move as freely and easily between the stage and the visual arts as we might like to think. So, for example, in spite of Euripides, there is not a single certain representation of Ion in Athenian art.[93] Recently several attempts have been made to see episodes from the story told in the *Erechtheus* on the Parthenon West Pediment and Frieze, but it remains uncertain just how much of the story was current in Athens, or what version of it was being told, when these sculptures were designed in the 430s, more than a decade before the production of Euripides' play.[94] If the *Ion,* in which Euripides essentially rewrote the myth by making Apollo the father of Ion,[95] is any indication, then the story told in the *Erechtheus* is likely to have been heavily rewritten as well. One major change we can detect with some certainty was in turning Eumolpos and his followers into Thracians, for which there is no evidence in the earlier tradition.[96]

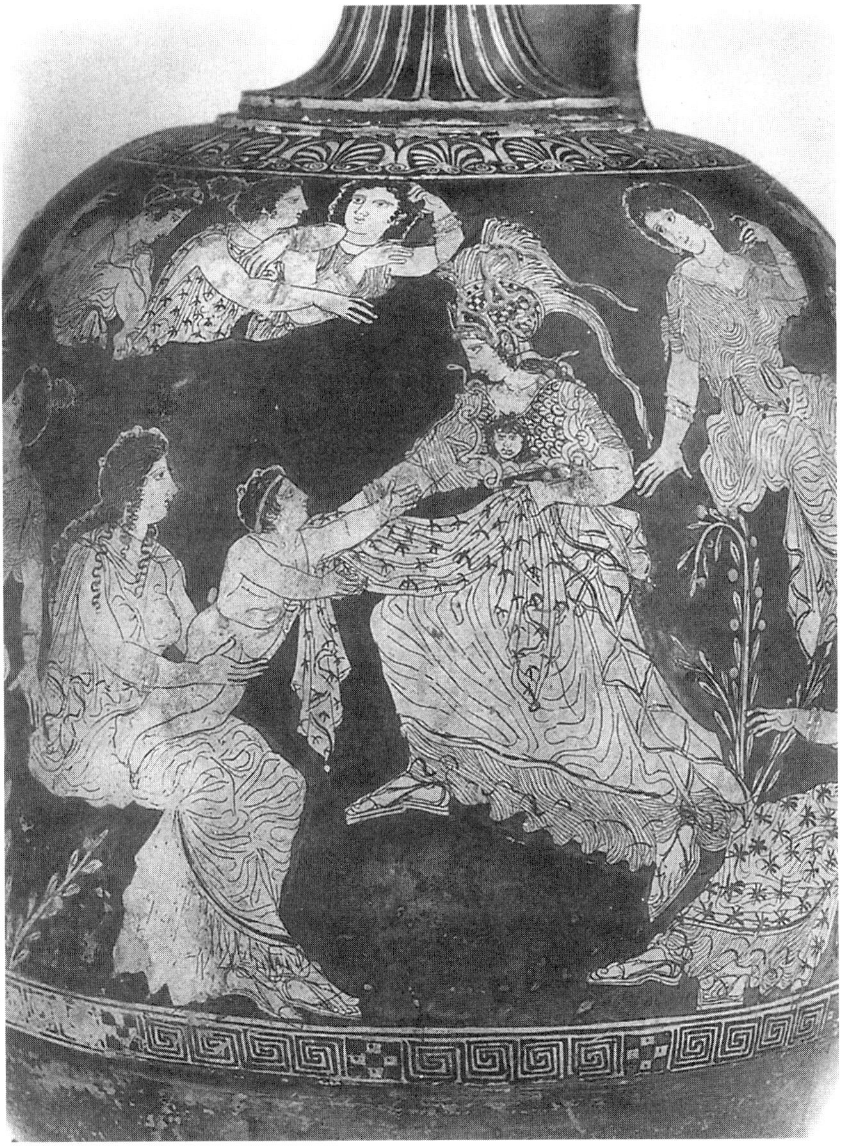

Figure 16 Birth of Erichthonios. Red-figure squat-lekythos. The Cleveland Museum of Art, Purchase, Leonard C. Hanna, Jr. Bequest, 82.142. 420–410. Photo: Museum.

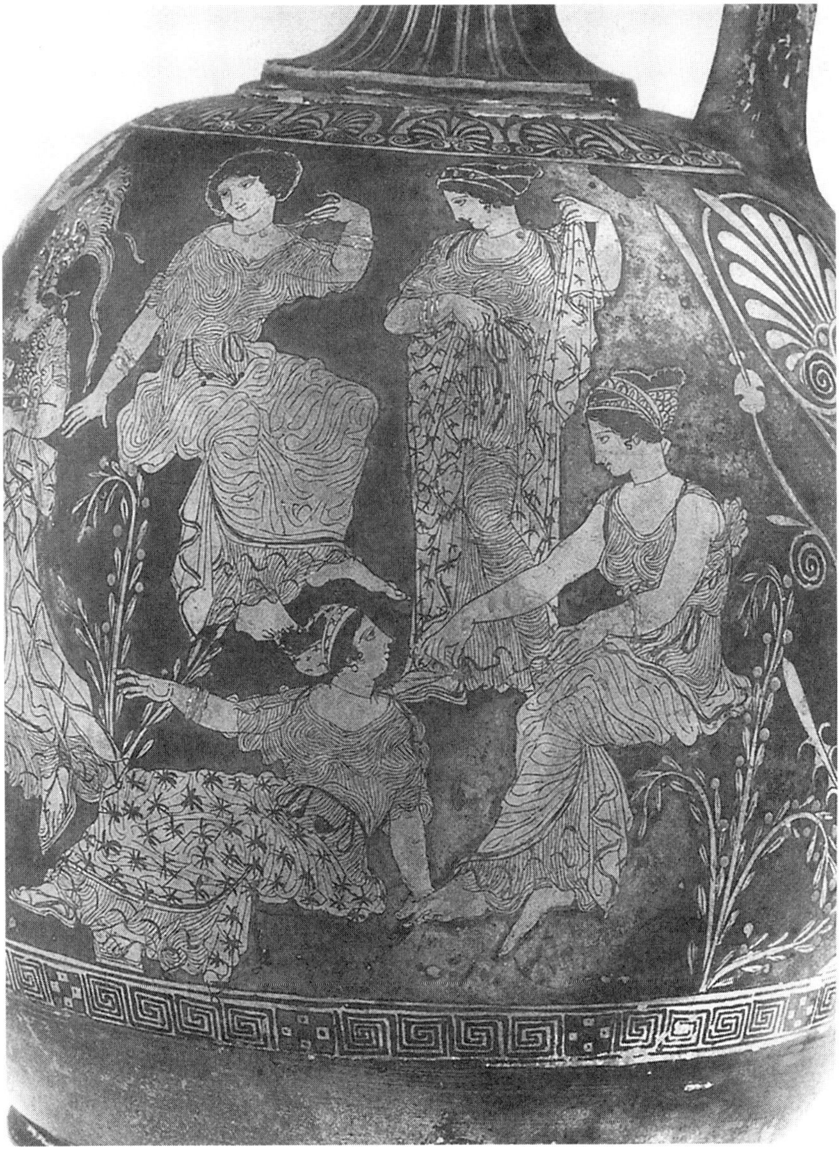

Figure 17 Women attending the birth of Erichthonios. Red-figure squat-lekythos. The Cleveland Museum of Art, Purchase, Leonard C. Hanna, Jr. Bequest, 82.142. 420–410. Photo: Museum.

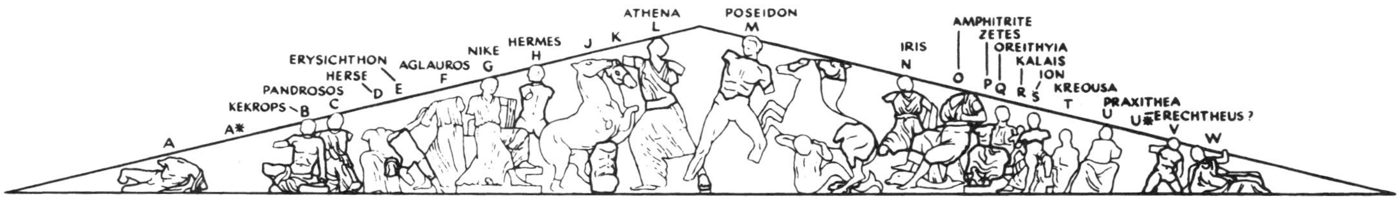

Figure 18 Parthenon West Pediment. Ca. 440. Reconstruction drawing by M. Cox, from Olga Palagia, *The Pediments of the Parthenon*. Leiden: E. J. Brill, 1992, pl. 22.

But even without these arguable theories, the Parthenon does clearly contribute to the continuing Athenian dialogue on autochthony in important ways. We have already noticed how the scene on the base of the Athena Parthenos seems to turn Pandora into another autochthonous Athenian, as Sarah Morris and Jeffrey Hurwit have recently observed.[97] Even more important is the story of the contest of Athena and Poseidon for the patronage of Athens, first attested in the West Pediment (fig. 18). The earliest preserved literary reference to this episode is in Herodotus 8.55, who had no doubt seen the temple when it was new.

The story is set in the age of Kekrops, who in some versions acted as judge of the contest.[98] His role as the first autochthonous hero and king was probably emphasized by the depiction with snaky lower body.[99] Prior to this time, the reign of Kekrops was largely a blank in Athenian tradition; all the interest focussed on his daughters and on the story of Erichthonios. Now that tradition is filled in retrospectively,[100] to show how the new race of Athenians under Kekrops was so favored by the Olympian gods that two of them vied with precious gifts—Athena's olive tree and Poseidon's salt spring[101]—for the privilege of bestowing on the city their name. The contest also becomes, in one version, the *aition* for the rigid patriarchy that underlay Athenian democracy in the fifth century. After all the Athenians had voted strictly along gender lines, the women who gave Athena her narrow victory were stripped of their political rights.[102]

The central group of the Parthenon West Pediment is mostly lost, and only a handful of reflections in the minor arts can give us some idea what it might have looked like.[103] The finest of these is a red-figure hydria of about 400, discovered at Pella in 1980.[104] As expected, Kekrops is the most prominent representative of the Athenians, the monstrous lower body offset by his august white hair and beard. The greatest surprise here (though predicted by Erika Simon)[105] is the magnificent thunderbolt of Zeus crashing down from Olympos, causing all the participants and observers to leap or gesture in amazement. There could be no more potent symbol of the Athenians' self-assurance that their city had been founded with the blessings of the Olympian father, almost as a gift to his favorite daughter.

Of all Athenian heroes, the one who best combines both sides of the national character in this era of democracy and imperialism is clearly Theseus. Though a king, he becomes in tragedy the chief spokesman for Athenian democracy,[106] while his successful defense of Athens against the Amazon invasion, along with his exploits across, and under, the sea, reflect Athens' naval hegemony and military might.[107] From the time of Kleisthenes, Theseus was in every way the perfect Athenian national hero—every way but one, that is. He was, as Sophocles says, a *xenos,* not native born, and his mother was not even Athenian. Under the Citizenship Law of 451/50, he would not have qualified. It was, I would suggest, in part to offset this problem that the story of Erichthonios' autochthonous birth was so vigorously promoted throughout the fifth century.[108] As a culture hero who is, unlike Theseus, a native Athenian, Erechtheus then takes on certain civic roles that had also been associated with Theseus, such as the founding of the Panathenaic Games.[109] At times we seem to glimpse parallels between the two heroes, as when a childlike Theseus is presented to his divine father Poseidon (fig. 19) in much the same manner as Erichthonios is usually presented to Athena.[110] Another kind of parallel is suggested by the companion piece to the Kekrops Painter's name vase (fig. 13), a similar calyx-krater featuring Theseus' triumph over the Marathonian Bull.[111] And it may be that classical art sought to create direct links between Kekrops and Erechtheus and Theseus, for example

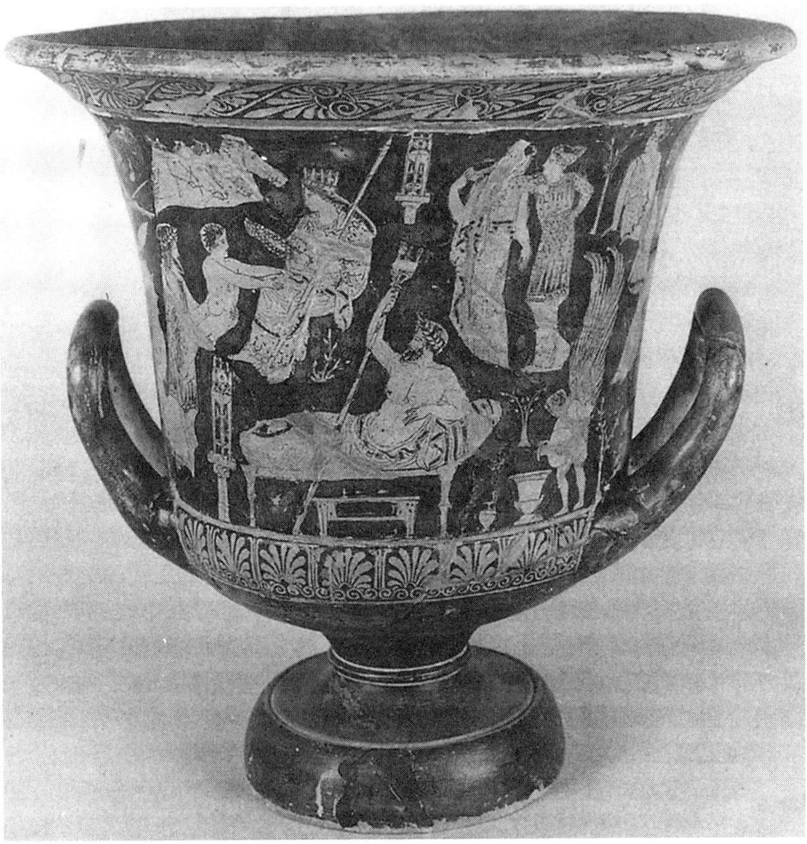

Figure 19 Theseus at the bottom of the sea. Red-figure calyx-krater. Bologna, Museo Civico 303. Ca. 410–400. Photo: Museum.

by having them fight alongside one another in the defense of the Akropolis from the Amazon invasion on the shield of Athena Parthenos, as Evelyn Harrison has proposed.[112]

Later Atthidographers and genealogists contrived to make Theseus a descendant of the family of Erechtheus.[113] But this was not a concern to most fifth-century Athenians, who took such delight in the messy multiplicity of their heroic ancestors that they were still adding new ones in the classical period. Each contributed another dimension to the Athenians' mounting pride in themselves, a pride that seems to have reached a crescendo at the very moment of their most humiliating defeat at the hands of the Spartan foe.

The end of the Peloponnesian War marks the close of a chapter in the development of autochthony as a cornerstone of Athenian ideology, one that was laid at the time of the Persian Wars. But it would be a mistake to regard autochthony as an artificial construct created in the wake of the Persian Wars to serve the needs of democracy or empire. The belief in the autochthony of the Athenian people was inseparably linked to the stories of Kekrops and Erechtheus, which the visual tradition assures us were firmly rooted in Archaic Athens (e.g., figs. 1, 2). The victory over the Persians unleashed a revival of many early Athenian heroes and legends, of which the autochthonous kings are just one prominent example. The manifold ways in which fifth-century Athens drew on the past are explored in detail elsewhere.[114]

Imperial Athens' exploitation of autochthony to create a myth of racial purity and superiority comes uncomfortably close to recent historical experience. But the mitigating influence of a democratic constitution and an open society saved Athens from the excesses to which that ideology might lead. Even at the height of the Empire, autochthony was an essentially benign influence, helping to forge a shared Athenian identity imbued with historical depth and a powerful attachment to the soil, the city, and its spiritual heart, the Akropolis.

CHAPTER SEVEN

Images and Political Identity: The Case of Athens

TONIO HÖLSCHER

Some Generalities

"Democracy, Empire, and the Arts in Fifth-Century Athens": if this title refers to the connection between a specific political and social system and a specific artistic "culture," the problem it poses can be approached from two different points of view. Focusing on fifth-century Athens, we can search for various products and activities of the arts and their functions in this specific polis, thereby envisaging art in relation to a single, limited, and specific political and social system. Or else, focusing on fifth-century arts as such, we can define a broader range of political systems and historical societies within which these arts had their functions, thus seeing political or social systems in relation to a specific artistic culture.

All this would be easy if artistic styles coincided with specific political and social systems. This, however, is an ideal constellation that does not correspond easily with the real conditions of Greek culture. Chronological or regional differences in artistic styles often do not coincide with political changes or differences. Conversely, many artistic phenomena as well as their changes over time are common to all of Greece, independent of specific political systems.

Monolithic concepts of culture tend to construct homogeneous cultural systems, divided into regional units and following each other in clear-cut homogeneous epochs. This approach, based on an a priori assumption, encourages simplistic views of structural unity that ignore or even suppress contradictory factors. A more dynamic and open concept should take into consideration that a society's cultural manifestations and developments are multiple and often conflicting: sectors with long-term traditions, like religion or family structures, may coexist with dynamic ones, like social values or artistic styles, all of these intersecting with political events and changes. This does not mean that individual cultural fields coexist independently, one beside the other; rather, all sectors interact with one another and are connected in the minds of the same people. Among these factors contributing to a society's "cultural makeup," one, such as religion, politics, or private life, may for a time rise to predominance and influence other fields more or less thoroughly, resulting in relatively uniform cultural attitudes. But on the whole, we should envisage complex interactions among various cultural factors, that is, not structural unity but multifactored functional systems. In this sense we may ask whether fifth-century Athens used general forms of contemporary art, adapting them to her specific purposes, or created new forms that can properly be called specifically Athenian, democratic or imperial.

In Greek art, the early fifth century was a period of sudden and radical changes. Within one decade, 490–480,[1] artists created a new image of the human figure and a new concept of the human person that remained influential at least to the beginning of our own century. Some of the most impressive examples of this new art, which we still call "classical," were created in Athens. A few years earlier, this city had begun her revolutionary development toward democracy, and it remained the protagonist of democracy for two centuries. Hence we may reasonably ask whether classical Greek art was democratic art.

At first sight, the answer seems obvious. During this period all major works of art in Athens as elsewhere in Greece were public monuments and had their function in public spaces; moreover, those of Athens were mostly commissioned by the people's Assembly. There seems little doubt, therefore, that democracy was the ultimate cause or at least an important condition of artistic developments. Yet things are more complicated. In fact, the "artistic revolution" of the early fifth century was neither a specifically Athenian nor a specifically democratic revolution.

Generally, our view of fifth-century art is heavily influenced by Athens, not only because the literary sources are much richer and modern research has been much more active there than elsewhere, but also because of all Greek cities Athens had by far the greatest resources to invest in public monuments. This, however, explains primarily quantity, not quality. The question of whether classical art was essentially a creation of democratic Athens prompts us to ask further in what sense it was—or was not—specifically Athenian and democratic.

Without going into details, it is obvious that all essential features of the new formal system—above all the distinction between active and nonactive parts of the human body demonstrating the potential activity of the figure, the austere faces signifying self-control and self-consciousness, the ideological simplicity of clothing and attitudes, and on the whole a new sense of time and space—were adopted immediately in all parts of the Greek and Greek-influenced world, from Xanthos to Motye, from Thessaly to Cyrene, in democratic as well as aristocratic or monarchic states.[2] The leading sculptors of the first generation were Onatas from Aigina, Hageladas from Argos, and Pythagoras from Samos, the latter working mostly in southern Italy. Pheidias of democratic Athens is not more "classical" than Polykleitos from Argos, the first theorist of sculpture, originating from and working for Peloponnesian aristocracies that fostered athletic ideals. Hence the general language of classical art was not tied to specific political conditions. Differences of style certainly existed, depending on collective tastes of individual regions or poleis, or even the preferences of individuals, but these were minor variations. The general "revolution" of the visual arts in the fifth century cannot be explained by the "miracle" of Athenian democracy.[3]

Obviously, this "revolution" is not merely an aesthetic phenomenon but part of a radical change of thought, mentality, and social values all over Greece.[4] The rise of democracy has something to do with this change, although not in the sense of an immediate, straightforward, and exclusive interdependence of the two phenomena. Rather, *isonomia* (political equality) and democracy should be seen as particular aspects of this global change which, however, was far more encompassing than such political manifestations and affected aristocratic and monarchic societies as well.

In order to concentrate on Athens, then, I shall not ask whether and to what extent classical art as such was Athenian, democratic or imperial, but how classical art was used in democratic Athens, and whether in the use of art Athens' specific conditions prompted specific differences from other cities.

Political Monuments: An Introduction

The Athenians made intensive use of images to create and strengthen political and social identity. This function of images developed in principle on two levels. On one, public monuments created political identity; on another, objects of social life, especially equipment of symposia and religious rituals, presented in their images the society's ideal concepts and models. All this, however, was common practice in Greece. But within this framework there developed in Athens, on both levels, some characteristic features that were connected with the specific political and social conditions of this city.

Political monuments are not a new concern of classical archaeology.[5] For more than a century, the iconography and historical circumstances of public monuments as well as their reconstruction have been investigated in Athens and elsewhere.[6] Following an intermediate period of pure art history in the first two generations of this century, scholars began to "rediscover" such monuments in the 1960s, paying special attention to their political and ideological messages and taking into account entire groups of public monuments, such as the votive monuments of the Persian Wars or historical paintings of the classical period.[7] Categories of semiotics were employed moderately, for example, in analyzing the image of Athena Parthenos.[8] The examination of votive practices of poleis, especially in the conflict between Athens and Sparta that resulted in a veritable war of monuments, offered better insight into the functions of political monuments.[9] It represents a significant change of perspective, compared especially with the nineteenth century, that such monuments are not considered merely as material sources left from antiquity but as powerful factors in political conflicts. We should continue in this direction, asking even more comprehensively how monuments were used and how they worked in the reality of public life.

What, then, is the function and meaning of what we call a monument?[10] To begin with, monuments are designed and erected as signs of power and superiority. As such, they are effective factors of public life: not secondary reflections, but primary objects and symbols of political actions and concepts. They may be disputed and even fought over, pushed through against possible resistance, or destroyed by a successful opposition.

Monuments have their place in public space. They mark its public character, claiming it and unfolding their effect in it. They inevitably address the community and, precisely because of their public nature, challenge it, provoking consent or contradiction; they do not allow indifference because recognition automatically means acceptance. They represent the public power of certain persons or ideological concepts. They proclaim a public message and demand its general and collective approval. In this sense monuments represent and create ideological identity; in fact, they are the concrete expression of such identity, be it of a whole community or of groups or individuals within this community, and their destruction signifies the annihilation of that identity. Toward the outside, they fence off their community and turn aggressively against foreign or hostile communities.

The character of monuments is particularly subject to historical change. It is defined by the sector of social life within which a community develops its identity, be it religious, political, economic, cultural, or otherwise. This means that very different objects, such as temples, statues of political heroes, banks, libraries, or sports fields can become monuments of their respective communities.

For all these reasons, it is a fact of considerable historical significance that in Greece from around 500 political monuments became a characteristic feature of major cities and sanctuaries. The centers of public life were now occupied by symbols expressing political claims and by examples of political behavior for citizens to imitate. This suggests that these communities for the first time expressly and consciously developed a political identity—which is obviously connected with the fact that politics constituted a new sphere with its own standards, behavior patterns, and ideals.

Forerunners and Early Forms of Political Monuments

Before the sixth century the Greeks apparently did not know political monuments in the strict sense of the word. Certainly, from the eighth and seventh centuries poleis and tyrants erected public buildings and dedicated votive offerings which all had or could assume a political character. Above all, great temples of polis deities and large areas used as agoras must have strengthened collective identity, as well as expressed it. But all these structures served primarily concrete public or religious functions; none of them had the main purpose of conveying a strictly political message. Even the lavishly decorated treasuries at Delphi, the chest of Kypselos at Olympia, or the throne of Apollo Amyklaios at Sparta do not define explicitly the political identity of their dedicators; their themes remain within the sphere of panhellenic religion and myth, without referring to specific political claims, objectives, merits, or ideals, and thus without defining the specific identity of a polis.

A first step toward political self-representation seems to have been taken with the emergence of the tropaion.[11] From the late eighth century, successful or wealthy warriors after a military victory deposited their arms in one of the great sanctuaries as votive gifts.[12] But only from the middle of the sixth century, written sources inform us of tropaia erected on the battlefield by the victors to mark the place where they had put their enemies to flight. This probably corresponds to the actual development: trophies originated in the sixth century, not primarily as religious offerings to the gods by victorious warriors, but as a monumental, celebratory sign of victory set up collectively by the army on the place of its glorious success. An analogous measure, attested above all in post-Kleisthenic Athens, was the dedication of spectacular pieces of booty in great sanctuaries, resulting in veritable war monuments that referred to specific victories over specific enemies.[13]

At first, trophies, erected on wooden stumps, were obviously not meant for eternity. But as early as the middle of the fifth century, the ephemeral sign of victory changed to a lasting monument: parts of a column and a large ionic capital from about 450 were found on the battlefield of Marathon, presumably crowned by sculptural figures, perhaps a Nike group with a tropaion.[14] This column seems to be the remains of a monument for the famous battle, erected probably under Kimon.

In the decades around 500 several Greek states erected at Delphi and elsewhere large statuary groups that show a new political character.[15] A remarkable example is the monument of Phokis, dedicated around 490 after the famous victory over the Thessalians, and representing Apollo, the strategoi of the cavalry and infantry, the seer Tellias, and the epichoric heroes.[16] This clearly was not only a votive offering to the god but also a proud self-representation of a victorious state, celebrating a decisive political success. Similar monuments are known from cities as different as Tarentum, Phlious, and Apollonia in Epiros.[17]

A new wave of political monuments originated in the Persian Wars,[18] representing many states with testimonies of their glorious deeds both in the panhellenic sanctuaries and in their own cities.

These observations reveal some basic aspects of the origins of political art in Greece. The sphere of politics detached itself more and more from other sectors, gaining increasing autonomy. Public monuments were erected deliberately to present famous achievements most effectively in public spaces. This reflects a society's efforts to develop its identity, decisively and in a very new way, in the public sphere. And such efforts, like the concept of equality appearing in burial customs,[19] were common to states of very different geographical location and political order.

Athens, however, soon became the protagonist in this process. The collective identity of her citizens was concentrated first and most resolutely in the political sphere. The erection of political monuments was prompted by several experiences in different political domains, all enhancing the development of political identity: first, within the community and in opposition to tyranny, the identity of the "isonomic" citizens; then, toward the outside, against the Persians, Athens' identity as the champion of the Greeks; finally, in part against the resistance of her allies, Athens' identity as the dominating force in the Delian League.

Monuments of the Athenian Democracy

The history of Athenian political monuments begins with the statue group of the tyrant-slayers Harmodios and Aristogeiton (fig. 1).[20] This was the first truly political monument in Greece, without any religious function in the sense of cult or votive practice (the Tyrannicides' hero cult was celebrated at their tomb in the Kerameikos cemetery); it was set up in the Agora, in the center of political life, commemorating and celebrating the ideological founders of the new isonomic state. Familiar with the monuments of Washington, Garibaldi, or Bismarck that furnish our modern squares, we find it difficult to appreciate what an unprece-

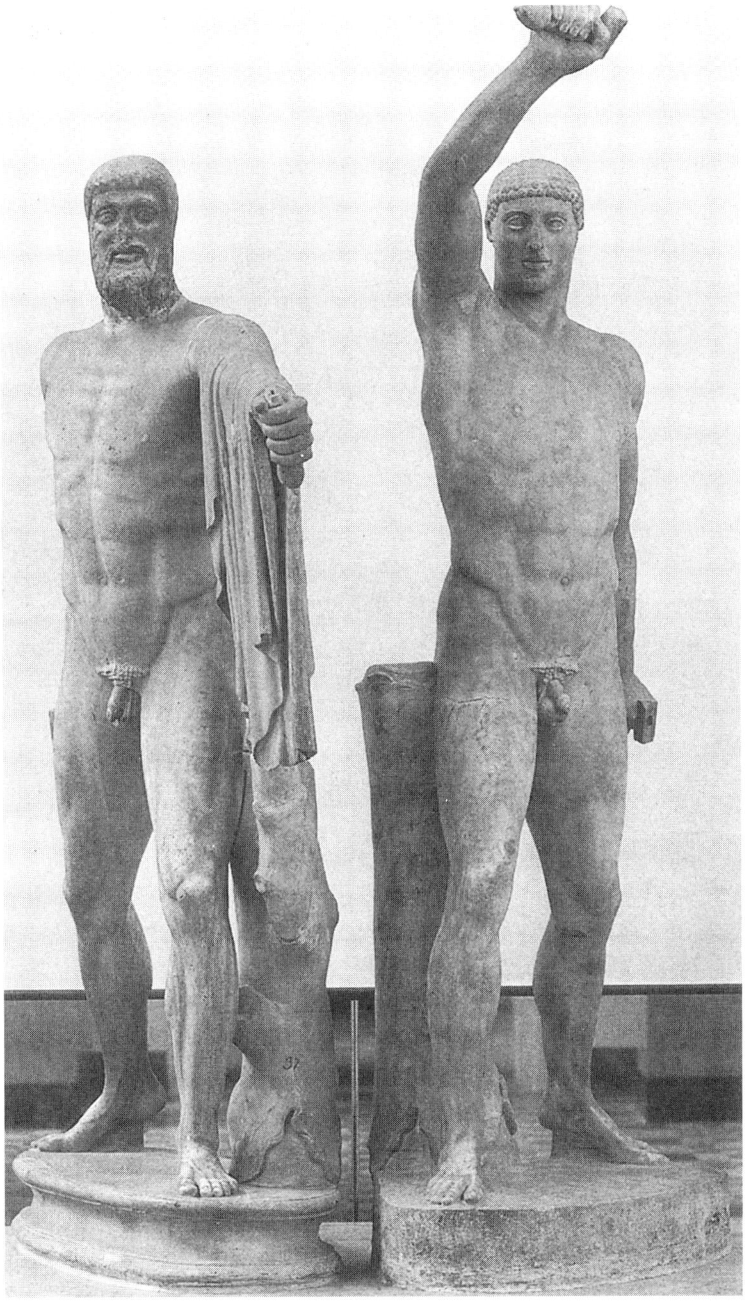

Figure 1 The Tyrant-slayers, Harmodios and Aristogeiton. Naples, Museo Nazionale Archeologico.

dented act the erection of this one was: neither cult statues nor votive dedications to a deity nor sepulchral statues, they did not belong to any traditional category of sculptures. Their meaning is revealed by their placement on the edge of the orchestra, the meeting place of the citizens' Assembly before the construction of the Pnyx.[21] There the tyrant-slayers stood not only as praiseworthy heroes but above all as concrete examples of behavior for the citizens during the *ekklesia* and the *ostrakismos*. Its paraenetic character is particularly evident from the fact that this monument recognizes not a successful achievement but a political attitude. Since the citizens of isonomic Athens developed their identity in opposition to tyranny, Harmodios and Aristogeiton were supposed to encourage them to embrace the ideology of the Tyrannicides!

The setting of a monument is an integral part of its function; hence the location of the tyrant-slayers is a salient and innovative feature, to be explained by the specific situation of isonomic Athens. More precisely, this monument's historical significance is twofold. First, in politics, these images must have served the needs of citizens who, confronted with the new responsibility of taking decisions on their whole political order, may have felt insecure and helpless; lacking adequate preparation, they had to learn new behavior patterns—for which Harmodios and Aristogeiton, protagonists of the new order, provided helpful models. Second, as a testimony of historical structures, this monument appears as the most significant symbol of this very political order. For if it is correct that the state of Kleisthenes, creating a sphere of politics as an almost autonomous domain, was the first political system that did not grow slowly and more or less unconsciously from Archaic times but was constructed almost completely from scratch by a conscious intellectual act, then the setting of a visible symbol in the central public space appears as the clearest indication of this new political consciousness.

The equivalent of the tyrant-slayers on the level of myth was Theseus.[22] His introduction into political art by the early isonomic state was well calculated: while the fame of Harmodios and Aristogeiton probably was mostly limited to Athens, monuments outside Attica evoked the glory of this widely known hero. Precisely in the first years after Kleisthenes a new sequence of Theseus' youthful deeds, equivalent to those of his great model Herakles, appears on Athenian vases (figs. 2a, 2b) and on the Athenian treasury at Delphi.[23] In the present context, two points should be stressed. First, while Herakles, the principal hero of Archaic Athens, represented the panhellenic ideals of the upper class,[24] Theseus was chosen as a patriotic hero. Second, this hero was less an aggressive warrior than a protagonist of the domestic order which in those years seems to have been the main concern of Athenian self-confidence. It was only after the Persian Wars that Theseus changed into a protagonist against foreign aggressors. In the Theseion, the new center of Athenian imperial identity, he was depicted fighting against centaurs and Amazons, assuming a role he allegedly played also at Marathon. A third painting, alluding to Athens' dominion of the sea, showed him recovering Minos' ring from his father Poseidon.[25]

Later, under the full-grown democracy when the realm of political activities

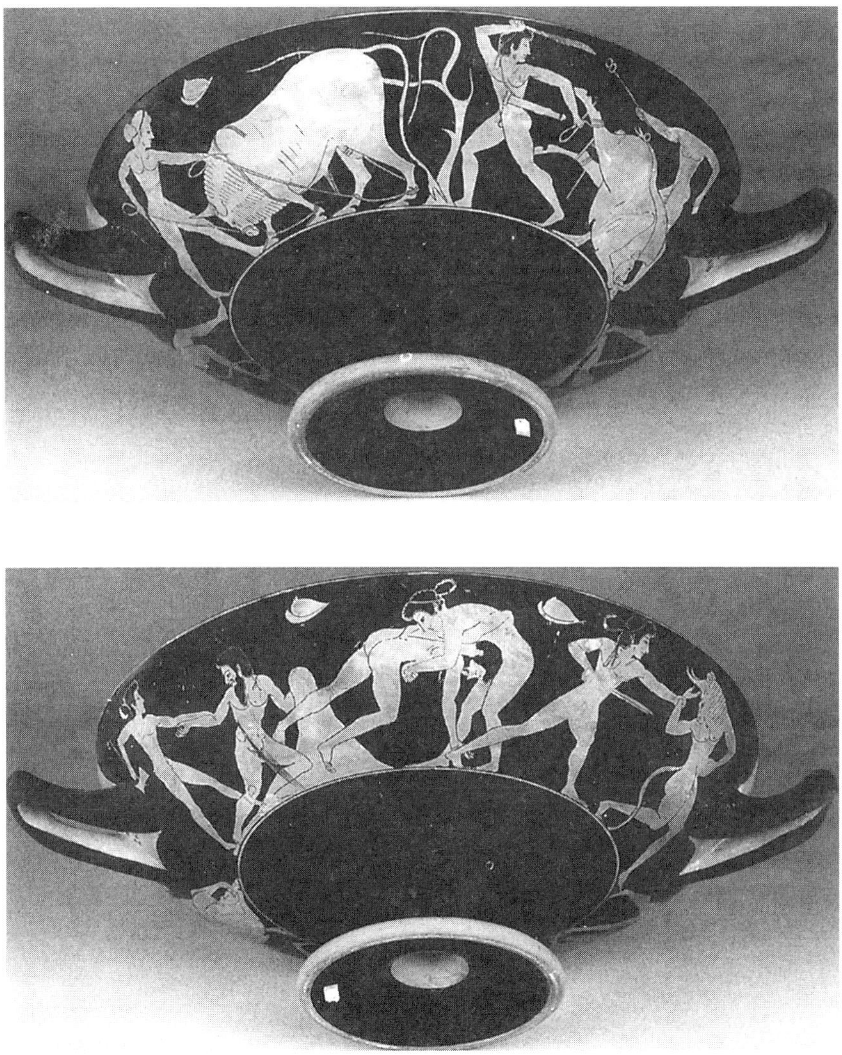

Figures 2a, b Cycle of the deeds of Theseus. Red-figured kylix. London, British Museum.

expanded greatly, there apparently emerged a need for models of broader significance, representing Athenian citizenship as such. This perhaps is the reason for the increasing frequency in vase painting of the Eponymous Heroes of the Athenian tribes.[26] Even in the Agora, the monument of the Tyrant-slayers was supplemented by a nearby statue group representing the Eponymous Heroes, probably erected under Perikles.[27] Like the tyrant-slayers, these statues did not have any religious function—the various tribes attended the cults of their heroes separately in their own districts of the city; rather, as a community of heroes on the Agora, they represented the citizen's community in its political subdivisions. In addition to the initial and individual act of tyrannicide, political identity was thus created by evoking collective consciousness of the polis' political organization. In this case too, in addition to its general significance, the monument served a special function. The pedestal of the Eponymous Heroes was used for putting up public announcements, such as lists of citizens liable to military service, initiatives for new laws, or court cases. The monument's shape fits this function well: a fence of stone beams was installed, certainly not only for the people's comfort while they were reading the announcements (as assumed by some scholars) but primarily to prevent tampering with those texts. In a city that had become far too big for oral transmission of such information, it must have been vital to have a central place for public announcements. It should be no sacrilege against classical art to assume that this was the main reason for erecting this monument: the heroes of the ten tribes stood there as the symbols of the community and its political order, sanctioning its public acts.

The force of collective egalitarianism in the fifth century is demonstrated above all by the disappearance of aristocratic grave sculptures which were so prominent in Archaic Athens. This striking change in burial customs seems to have been misinterpreted by those scholars who connect it with an alleged law, of Kleisthenes or his immediate successors, restricting funerary expenditure.[28] From Cicero we know only of a law "some time after Solon,"[29] and its content is not easily understood as a reference to sculptured grave markers. More importantly, the end of sepulchral sculpture in Attica did not come abruptly, as we should expect in the case of legislation, but gradually: after large numbers of kouroi and stelai on tombs of the late sixth century, scattered latecomers occur until ca. 490–480[30] which can be explained only as a result of collective self-restriction. If so, the importance of the phenomenon becomes even clearer: the end of proud self-assertion on the part of the elite was caused not by a political law, possibly proposed by a particular political group, but by general social self-control.[31]

As a further consequence, this process encouraged the creation of new political spaces.[32] The new Boule of the 500 was given a new Bouleuterion, perhaps the first example of a type that was to become very successful, and, above all, although perhaps somewhat later, the *ekklesia* was transferred to a new meeting place on the Pnyx. Even topographically, the domain of politics now occupied a space of its own.

Monuments of the Persian Wars

In the long run the ideology of *isonomia* and democracy seems to have been an insufficient base for the patriotic self-confidence and political identity of normal Athenian citizens. Not much democracy is visible in Athenian state monuments of the fifth century. The principal idea of the new political order was equality—an ideal that was not easy to swallow for a society as competitive as the elite of Archaic Greece, especially if this meant including the demos. The "agonale Mensch" of Jakob Burckhardt was not well equipped mentally for the egalitarian demands of the new epoch. Therefore, if the citizens had to be equal, at least their state had to be superior to others. Moreover, by strengthening patriotic feelings and turning energies against outside rivals and enemies, interior tensions could be overcome more easily. This seems to be the reason why in Athens, as in other cities, most political monuments celebrate military victories. Obviously this corresponded to the mentality of the majority of Athenian citizens. Some of them might have thought that democracy was the essential basis for such successes, but the glorious results overshadowed this basic structure.

Already the young state of Kleisthenes founded its self-confidence upon a famous military victory over the united forces of Chalkis and Boeotia in 506, celebrating it with a conspicuous votive offering on the Akropolis.[33] This dedication, displaying the chains of the prisoners of war together with a bronze four-horse chariot and a celebratory epigram (fig. 3), was much more than a traditional act of gratitude toward the city's goddess; it was also a spectacular self-assertion of the dedicators. So, contemporaneously with the beginnings of political monuments, votive gifts in the great sanctuaries could assume the character of explicit political manifestations.[34]

The great moment of new political self-confidence and identity were of course the wars against the Persians. The problem that immediately arose in this situation was the emergence of two partly conflicting identities: a panhellenic identity, opposed to the barbarians, and a polis identity, competing with other Greek states. The erection of monuments reflected this development and was part of the process itself.[35]

It is striking how systematic the practice of erecting political monuments became soon after its introduction. Panhellenic solidarity of course had to be

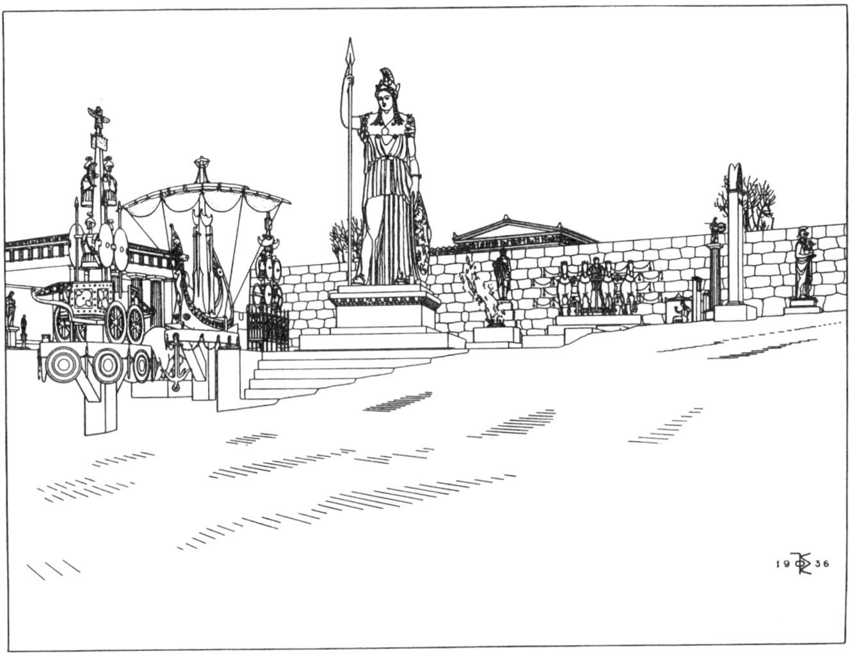

Figure 3 Political monuments of the Athenian Akropolis. Athena Promachos and (background right) victory-quadriga from Chalkis and Boeotia. After G. P. Stevens, *Hesperia* 5 (1936) 494, fig. 44.

demonstrated in places of shared significance. The great monuments of the anti-Persian alliance were thus set up in the three great panhellenic sanctuaries: after the battle of Salamis a statue of Apollo with a ship's acroterion at Delphi, after Plataea the tripod on the serpents' column in the same sanctuary, a colossal statue of Zeus at Olympia, and a statue of Poseidon at the Isthmos.[36] Individual cities, however, chose two different and even opposite places to manifest political identity. Within their own polis they sought to strengthen the patriotic feelings of their citizens; places to set up such monuments were the Agora and the city's main sanctuary. Toward the outside they had to compete with other cities, and since competition presupposes a common place as well as a common public, such monuments were almost all set up in the same panhellenic center, at Delphi. In several cases, this bipolar structure of political representation resulted in double monuments erected at the same time at home and on the stage of panhellenic competition: around 480 the Phokians set up two monuments representing the struggle of Apollo and Herakles over the tripod, one at Delphi, the other in their own sanctuary at Abai;[37] two decades later, the Argives celebrated their victory near Oinoe, together with Athens over Sparta, with large sculptural groups of the Seven against Thebes and the Epigonoi, both at Delphi and in their Agora.[38]

Again, Athens soon became the protagonist in these practices. At home, three public spaces developed into a panorama of glorious military achievements: the Akropolis, the Agora, and the state cemetery of the Kerameikos, i.e., the public spaces of gods, citizens, and the dead.[39] No other polis created so systematically an ideological topography of its political identity, based on the memory of its glorious achievements, almost a public monumental physiognomy directed both toward her own citizens and foreign visitors.

In the Agora, monuments were erected for various battles against the Persians.[40] Some of their epigrams have been preserved, both in literature and on fragments of their pedestals. What the monuments themselves looked like remains obscure; perhaps they consisted of stelai with names of fallen warriors. This would accord with a stele erected in the Agora of Samos after the battle of Lade in 494, containing the names of those who had fought against the Persians.[41]

Better known are the three herms erected after the capture of Eion in 476 for Kimon and the other strategoi, a particularly conspicuous monument (fig. 4).[42] Its character was both religious and political, as in other cases in this early phase of political monuments: the pillar form followed the Archaic tradition of images

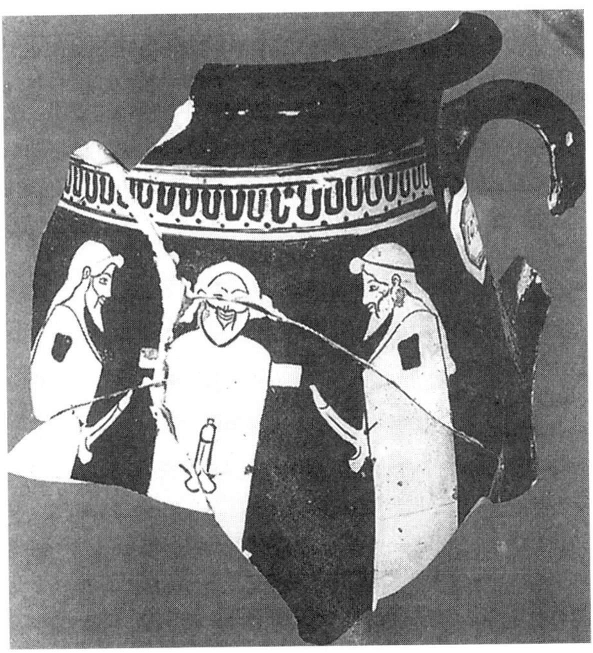

Figure 4 The "Eion Herms." Red-figured pelike. Paris, Musée du Louvre.

of Hermes, while three famous epigrams proclaimed that the Athenians had erected these herms as a political honor to their victorious citizens and generals, and that this monument was intended to inspire the Athenians to endure the hardships of war for the common cause.

These herms were placed in the northwestern corner of the Agora, together with many other, in part older, images of that type, which gave the area the name of "The Herms." This placement offers a key to understanding the significance of the herms.[43] It has been rightly assumed that before the Persian Wars the city wall ran just north of the Agora; hence in Archaic times the most important gateway, the predecessor of the Dipylon and the Sacred Gates, must have been located precisely beyond this northwestern corner.[44] Set up on the borderline between inside and outside, the herms of the Agora therefore protected the community's public space, initially perhaps the whole area of the city, later the political center. This explains how they could become honorary monuments of military victories. It was their old religious function of protection that was now turned in a political sense against a specific external enemy: the Persians were to be expelled concretely and symbolically from Athens' public space.

Later monuments in the Agora prove that the Persian Wars were instrumental in enhancing political and patriotic identity. Three phenomena seem essential here. First, the achievements and glory of contemporary politics were emphasized more and more openly in such monuments. The best example is the famous "Painted Stoa" (Stoa Poikile), erected around 460 by the circle of Kimon and adorned with a great cycle of paintings that combined two great deeds of mythical ancestors with two contemporary Athenian victories: the expulsion of the Amazons by Theseus' Athenians, the fall of Troy with considerable participation of an Athenian contingent, the triumph of Marathon under the leadership of Kimon's father Miltiades, and a battle near Oinoe, where Athens had recently won her first spectacular victory over Sparta.[45]

Second, a new aspect is introduced into political self-representation by the fact that the celebration of the Persian Wars was not confined to the aftermath of the event itself but continued in the Stoa Poikile several decades later. Other Greek states praised their contributions against the "barbarians" in monuments immediately after those battles—but Athens continued this habit over the next generations, thereby creating a sort of historical physiognomy of the city that demonstrated her superiority over her rivals. This attitude resulted from an unparalleled need of legitimation for permanent hegemony; not accidentally, the only possible candidate for a similar perpetuation of the Persian War glory is Sparta.[46]

Third, accordingly, these achievements of the recent past became worthy of memory and took on a dimension of glory comparable to the great deeds of the heroes of myth, as the cycle of paintings in the Stoa Poikile illustrates. This shows a new kind of self-confidence of the present in comparison with the overwhelming mythical past.[47] The discovery of history in classical Greece is a discovery not of the past but the present. A similar sequence of Athenian glorious accomplishments from mythical times to the present day was created in the funeral orations at the state burials in the Kerameikos. Other cities too used their patriotic myths for present-day political aims, but none of them, as far as we know, perhaps again with the exception of Sparta, developed its political identity so decisively as an ideological system of myth, history, and actuality.

This systematic character of patriotic myths is even more evident in two other monuments that were placed not in the Agora but in the second area of political self-representation: on the Akropolis. Already in the 450s the shield of the colossal Athena "Promachos" showed a mythological scene, the battle of Theseus and the Lapiths against the centaurs.[48] Soon afterward the Parthenon was decorated with a comprehensive mythological apparatus, containing the four great myths of Greek self-defense against foreign enemies: giants, centaurs, Amazons, and Troy.[49] The traditional interpretation of these myths sees them as predecessors and metaphors of the Persian Wars. But, without opposing this view, I sense that this program has a much broader meaning: it represents a range of polar oppositions and threats to the Greek way of life that were repelled by Greek, especially Athenian, heroes: blasphemous giants, brutal semimonsters, aggressive females, and Orientals as hybrid cultural antipodes.

Taken together, these myths constitute a manifold, almost complete panorama that defines Greek identity against various opposite worlds. This corresponds to a basic structure of Greek thought that defines values in polar oppositions: kosmos versus chaos, humankind versus animals, men versus women, Greece versus Orient, culture versus primitiveness, self-control versus hybris and brutality, freedom versus slavery.[50] These myths therefore are more than mirrors or metaphors of the Persian Wars: they constitute a cosmic-historical panorama within which these wars receive their interpretation and significance. In developing and using paradigmatic myths in such a global system, Athens probably again was unique.

The Parthenon, of course, covers a much broader range of themes, constituting the most systematic program of Athenian self-presentation, including, besides the defeat of hostile forces, the evocation of the city's own patriotic traditions. Significantly, even in this most complex symbol of Periklean Athens not much stress is placed on democratic values. The pediments show the religious and mythical traditions of the city: the birth of Athena and her contest with Poseidon for Attica, surrounded by local divinities and heroes; and the frieze selectively represents the community of citizens in the Panathenaic procession, with the majority of the participants being noble young men in the functions of horsemen and charioteers.[51] Democracy seems to be more an implicit condition than an explicit theme of Athenian self-confidence.

The third area that developed into a monument of historical self-representation was the state cemetery in the Kerameikos. Beside extensive areas of family graves, from the fifth century a separate political cemetery was reserved for public burials[52]—another symbol that politics had become a domain of its own, an autonomous space in a concrete as well as metaphorical sense. In the course of time the collective graves of the fallen warriors with their lists of names and relief decorations formed a sequence of achievements from the past down to the present, another historical physiognomy, a façade of glory in front of the main entrance to the city.

All three public spaces where the citizens came together for their most important common concerns—in the Agora for political decisions with their fellow citizens, on the Akropolis for religious rites with their goddess, and in the Kerameikos for collective burials with their dead—were adorned with and defined by monuments that were supposed to foster a strong political and patriotic identity in all those who participated in these public manifestations.

At Delphi Athens expressed no less systematically her ambitions toward the other Greek poleis. After Salamis the Athenians built there a wonderful stoa to exhibit the captured ropes of Xerxes' bridge over the Hellespont.[53] After the foundation of the Delian League, they erected a striking monument celebrating the battle of Eurymedon: a bronze palm tree with gilded fruits and a gilded palladion on top.[54] A third Athenian monument at Delphi, right at the entrance of the sanctuary, was even more ambitious. Supposedly made from the booty, it glorified the battle of Marathon, representing the commander Miltiades with Apollo and Athena, the heroes of the ten Attic tribes, and three other Attic heroes, Theseus, Kodros, and supposedly Philaios, the ancestor of Miltiades.[55] In such cases there is almost no difference between a religious votive offering and a political monument. The message of the Athenian votive group in Delphi does not differ fundamentally from that of the Marathon painting on the Athenian Agora or the statues of the Eponymous Heroes in the same place.

As for the impact of such monuments on the Athenian public, the epigrams of the Eion Herms proclaimed the aim to inspire the Athenians, now and in the future, to endure the hardships of war for the common good. The same exemplary character is obvious in the tyrant-slayers' images. This must have been a feature of most political monuments.

On the other hand, such monuments must have been rather challenging for visitors to the Agora.[56] Public images of contemporary fellow citizens were considered an extraordinary honor and looked at with great suspicion. This attitude, which originated in the egalitarian ideology of democracy, is well attested for the fourth century but certainly goes back to the early times of Athenian *isonomia*. The celebratory representation of Miltiades in the Marathon painting is said, although in a later source, to have caused debate and alternative proposals in the Assembly,[57] and Plutarch reports that the proposed award of an honorary wreath to Miltiades was rejected with the argument that the battle had been won by all Athenians.[58] The Eion Herms were praised in the fourth century as examples of good political practice because they celebrated all ten strategoi without naming any of them.[59] And the Tyrannicides, considered the first honorary images set up to contemporaries, were succeeded only in the early fourth century by those of Konon and other politicians.[60] Even then, there existed a law prohibiting honorary statues near these founding heroes of democracy,[61] and a series of rules established a clear hierarchy of such honors.[62] Such rules, supervised by the Assembly, indicate the criteria by which people judged these monuments when visiting the Agora.

Unfortunately, much less is known about the impact of political monuments in panhellenic centers like Delphi. The concentration of most monuments along the sacred way made them conspicuous not only to common visitors but especially to the official delegations of poleis from the whole Greek world who certainly made known in their cities the "messages" they perceived. Public control will have watched suspiciously even votive offerings in those sanctuaries; this may explain why the Pythia forbade Themistokles to dedicate Persian spoils at Delphi.[63]

The Athenian monuments for the Persian Wars testified first and foremost, although implicitly, to Athens' claim to superiority in Greece. This is why in the Stoa Poikile the glorious representation of Marathon was complemented by the Oinoe painting, celebrating a victory over Sparta. Soon such monuments would announce this claim, in surprisingly explicit forms, also to the allies in the Delian League.

Monuments Concerning the Delian League

The first aggressive monument of Periklean policy against Athens' allies was the statue of Athena Lemnia, celebrating the institution of cleruchies (Athenian settlements on confiscated territory) after the departure of new settlers to the island of Lemnos around 450 (fig. 5).[64] This was much more than an ordinary votive offering after a successful undertaking; it was a political monument of consider-

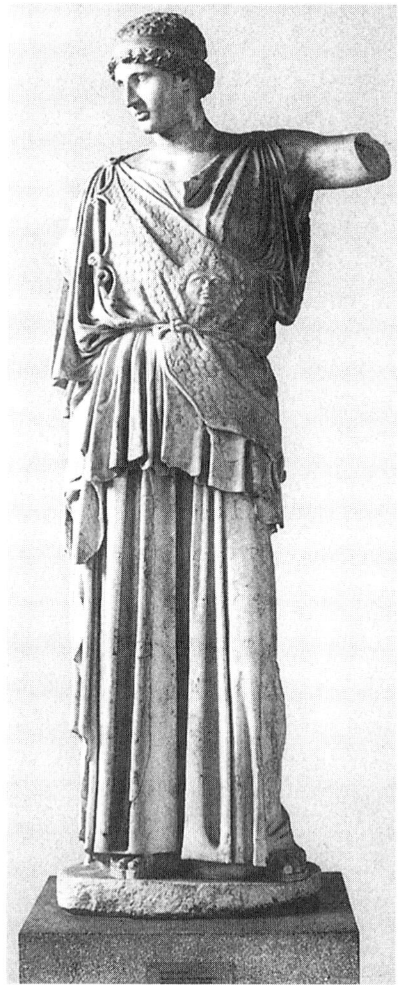

Figure 5 Athena Lemnia. Dresden, Staatliche Kunstsammlungen.

able ambition, larger than life size and executed by the famous Pheidias. Although apparently dedicated by the clerouchs themselves, it was surely not financed by the poor emigrants but by the Athenian state, quite probably at the instigation of Perikles himself.

This highly important monument was placed in an equally important position, at the entrance to the Akropolis, within the Propylaia, to the left. Later the connection with Perikles was stressed by setting up his portrait statue next to it. In the early 440s, at the very time when Perikles proposed the project of a panhellenic congress to discuss the rebuilding of the sanctuaries destroyed by the Persians,[65] the statue of Athena Lemnia as protectress of his imperialistic policy also marked his new emphasis on the Akropolis and the start of his building program to embellish the sanctuary.

At the same time, outside the Akropolis he gave another signal of his building plans, through the statue of Hermes Propylaios, created by Alkamenes (fig. 6).[66] Rightly dated to the 440s, it must originally have been made for the Old Propylaia.

Hermes Propylaios and Athena Lemnia marked the occupation of the Akropolis by Perikles: Hermes outside defining the religious sphere, Athena inside emphasizing its political character and making clear that the building program was inseparably connected with Athens' domination of the Delian League. The representatives of the allies, who had to come to Athens every fourth year to participate in the celebration of the Panathenaia, entered the Akropolis under the eyes of this Athena. Surely they will have reported to their fellow citizens how openly Athens proclaimed her imperialist ambitions.

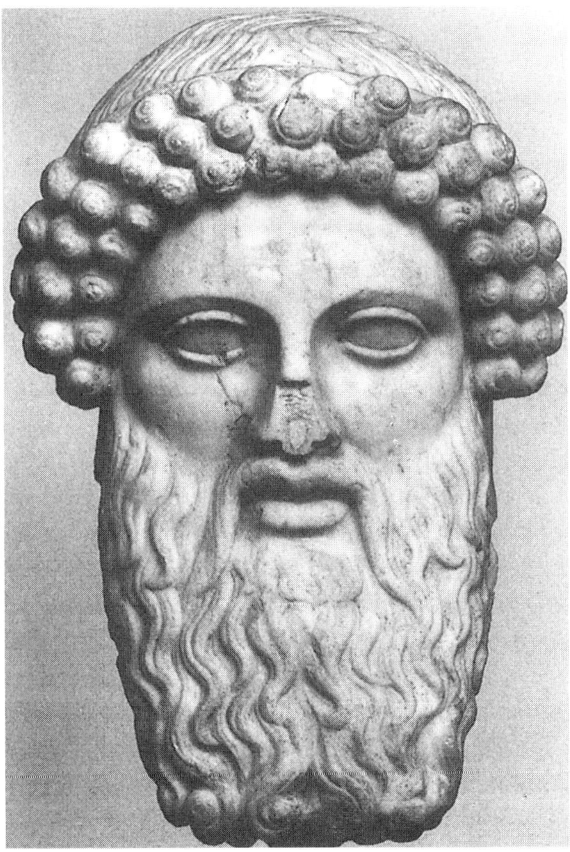

Figure 6 Hermes Propylaios of Alkamenes. Munich, Glyptothek.

Soon afterward an allied state documented its suppression by Athens with a monument on its own territory. In the Heraion of Samos the most important votive monument of the fifth century was a group by Myron, showing Herakles' introduction into Olympus.[67] The curved pedestal supported three over-life-size figures: Zeus standing in the middle, Athena on one side, both turning to Herakles coming from the other. The group has been interpreted convincingly as a monument celebrating Athens' victory over the Samian revolt in 440, commissioned probably not by Athens, for it was not usual to dedicate monuments in the sanctuaries of other cities, but by the pro-Athenian party of Samos which thereby openly proclaimed its political allegiance. In this monument the Samian Hera did not appear at all but the goddess of Athens played a prominent role: its message was unmistakable.

Other cities avoided open conflict with Athens. At Ephesos, in the sanctuary of Artemis, a monument was erected in these same years, the early 430s, perhaps as a direct answer to the statuary group in neighboring Samos: the famous Amazons, made by Polykleitos, Pheidias, Kresilas, and some other sculptor(s) (fig. 7).[68] These Amazons did not represent dreadful oriental enemies, as in Athens,

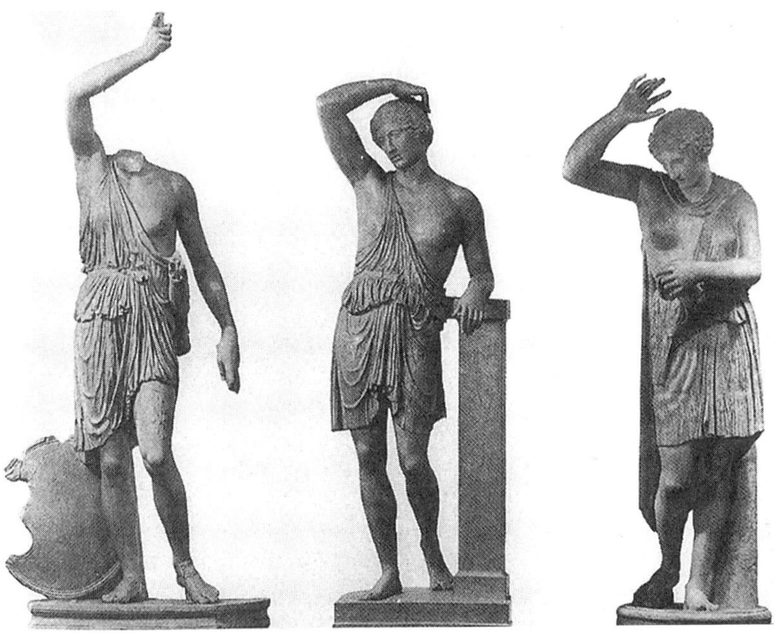

Figure 7 The Ephesian Amazons. "Amazon Mattei": Tivoli, Villa Adriana; "Amazon Sciarra": Berlin, Staatliche Museen; "Amazon Sosikles": Rome, Museo Capitolino.

but highly venerable figures, symbolizing the city's own traditions and identity.[69] Having found asylum in Ephesos, they testified to the age and the protective force of the sanctuary of Artemis. The date of the sculptural group has tentatively been connected with the dedication of the temple, 120 years after its foundation.[70] However this may be, the Ephesian and Samian monuments, dedicated around the same time, reflect two possible political attitudes toward Athens. While the Samian group expresses submission, the Ephesian Amazons represent an act of self-assertion against overpowering Athens: the Ephesians claimed to possess a sanctuary with a myth at least as old and venerable as that with which arrogant Athens dominated the scene. They even challenged Athens, where artists from all over Greece were attracted by the allies' money that financed Perikles' buildings,[71] by inviting to Ephesos the most famous sculptors of the age: not only Pheidias from Athens but also his great rival Polykleitos. So at least once the Ephesians demonstrated that Athens, acting as the center of the world, was not that unique!

Even this impressive monument, however, could not really compete with Athens, where the most ambitious temple project since Archaic times, the Parthenon, was almost complete, and the unprecedented chryselephantine statue of Athena Parthenos was dedicated in 438. A year later, the rebuilding of the entrance of the Akropolis was initiated with the new Propylaia of Mnesikles, followed by the temple of Athena Nike, the figural decoration of which reflects the atmosphere of the great victories of the middle 420s.[72] Proof that this temple was planned together with the Propylaia has at last freed us from the old controversy about its initiators. The building indeed was part of Perikles' program, and even if the figural decorations were created only after his death they could not stand in complete opposition to the original concept.[73]

The Nike temple's decoration follows but extends the program of the Parthenon. The eastern pediment showed the fight between the gods and the giants, the western pediment another mythical battle, perhaps against the Amazons.[74] In any case, these must have been selections from the myths of the Parthenon that recorded the victories of the Greek, especially the Athenian, kosmos over threatening enemies. The middle acroterion on the roof, known from an inscription, represented the fight of Bellerophon against the Chimaira.[75] This too is a Greek hero's victory over a dangerous foreign monster, emphasizing again, though with a different accentuation, the classical confrontation between Greek ideals and the menace from opposite, outside forces.

The friezes illustrate historical themes:[76] on the south side fights against the Persians, probably not a specific battle but the Persian Wars as a whole (fig. 8); on the western and northern sides Athens' fights against contemporary Greek ene-

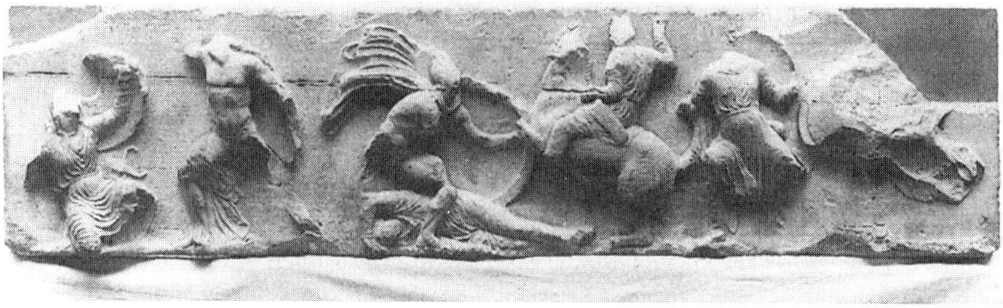

Figure 8 Greeks fighting Persians. South Frieze of the temple of Athena Nike in Athens. Athens, Akropolis Museum.

mies in the decades after the Persian Wars, perhaps differentiated between Peloponnesians and central Greeks. The themes of the Parthenon were thus taken up but continued into recent historical times, creating a mythical-historical sequence as in the cycle of the Stoa Poikile and in the funeral orations. In allegorical form, the same theme is developed on the parapet.[77] Relief decoration, turned toward the outside, facing the city, repeated the same motives on all three major sides: Athena seated on a rock, surrounded by Nikai celebrating victories (figs. 9a, 9b). The Nikai are setting up tropaia, decorating them with Greek and oriental armor; they glorify victories against the Persians as well as against Greek enemies, as represented in the fighting scenes on the friezes; other Nikai are sacrificing bulls—according to one recent interpretation, at the festival of the Oschophoria; in my own opinion, more likely in an ad hoc victory celebration, typical after successful battles. This crowd of attractive girls celebrating victories seems to illustrate most suggestively the high spirits prevailing in Athens in these years.

An important point in this context is picture-language. These are not realistic scenes of a sacrifice, not only because it is executed by divine girls but also because the erection of tropaia and the offering of sacrifices could not have taken place at the same time. Nevertheless, they are drawn together effectively in this composition, just as the multiplication of the Nikai represents the great number of Athenian victories. Similarly, on a contemporary vase a victorious musician is surrounded by four Nikai who, according to their inscriptions, indicate his successes in various competitions.[78] Art has here created a new "conceptual" picture-language for celebratory messages of which there are further examples in this period: personifications of poleis and other political entities, and of abstract political notions; allegorical motives, such as handshakes between deities representing treaties between specific poleis; or state deities conferring honorary crowns to men of merit.[79] The emergence of such a political picture-language

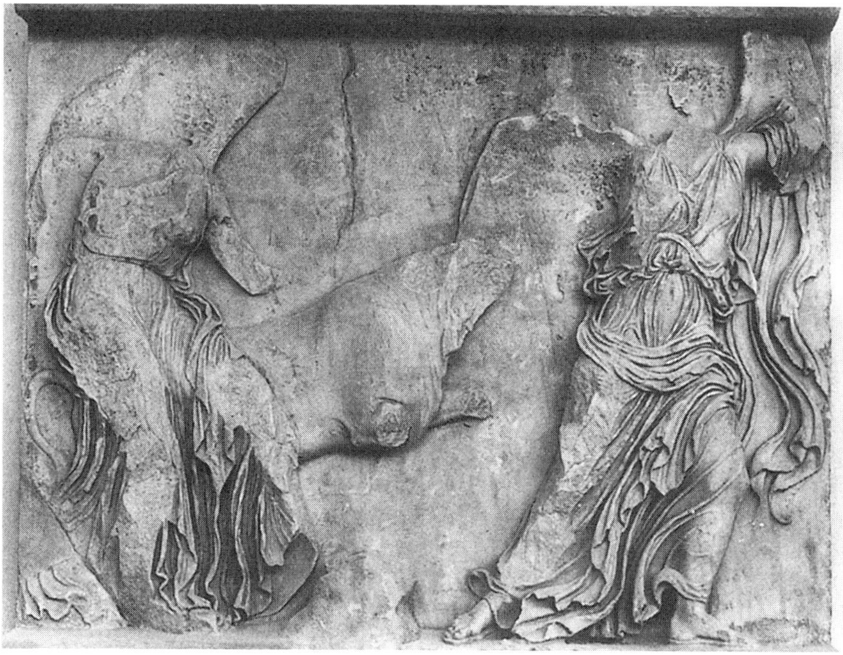

Figure 9a Nikai with bull. Parapet of the temple of Athena Nike in Athens. Athens, Akropolis Museum.

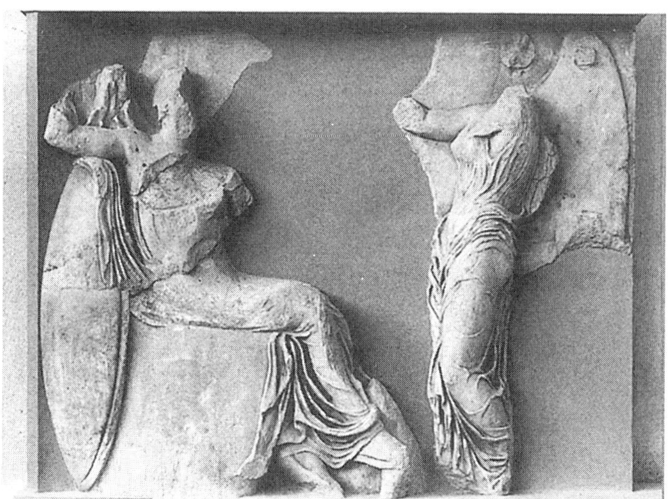

Figure 9b Athena and Nike, decorating a tropaion. Parapet of the temple of Athena Nike in Athens. Athens, Akropolis Museum.

with special iconographic motifs and a specific compositional syntax is closely related to the creation of political monuments in this period. An architectural equivalent to this ideological "hymn to Athenian superiority" is the Stoa of Zeus Eleutherios in the Agora, built in these same years and pronouncing the claim of "liberty" in the center of the "freest of all Greek cities"—with a similar whirling Nike on the roof.[80]

On the Nike parapet elements of this picture-language are adopted for the most euphoric victory celebration in classical Greek art. Here we sense almost physically the effusive atmosphere and the enthusiastic optimism that so often dominated politics in Athens. Moreover, this euphoric state of mind seems to have been infectious. We find the same high-spirited style in a contemporary monument, the famous Nike on an eagle, on top of a 9 m-high pillar, set up in Olympia by Athenian allies, the Messenians and Naupaktians, to celebrate the victory over Sparta near Sphakteria in 425 (fig. 10).[81]

All this originated in but was not bound to Athenian conditions. After the Peloponnesian War victorious Sparta gave a harsh response to the monuments of the defeated Delian League. At Sparta, the commander Lysander dedicated two Nikai on eagles, thus outdoing the monument at Olympia;[82] at Amyklai, among other votive offerings a tripod was erected that was supported by a figure of Sparta, thus making use of the new picture-language of state personifications;[83] and at Delphi, Lysander surpassed the Athenian ex-voto representing Miltiades between Apollo, Athena, and Athenian heroes by a much larger monument showing himself between the gods and heroes of Sparta, accompanied by twenty-eight commanders of the allied fleet.[84]

In Athens the soldiers of the allied Spartan army who had fallen in 403 against Thrasyboulos were even buried in the state cemetery of the Kerameikos, the heart of Athenian patriotism. No wonder that Thrasyboulos, after recovering from this defeat, reacted by erecting a huge trophy beside this document of Athens' humiliation.[85]

Vase Painting

Beside the public sphere of political monuments with their explicit messages there was, at least equally important, the whole sphere of social, religious, moral, and mental values and attitudes. The richest source—and far from sufficiently exploited—among the visual arts for such phenomena is vase painting: preserved in tens of thousands of specimens and therefore accessible by statistical methods, it offers an incomparable repertoire of themes and is rather precisely datable. A systematic investigation of Athenian vases could result in a complex history of Athenian social mentality, as it developed from decade to decade. In

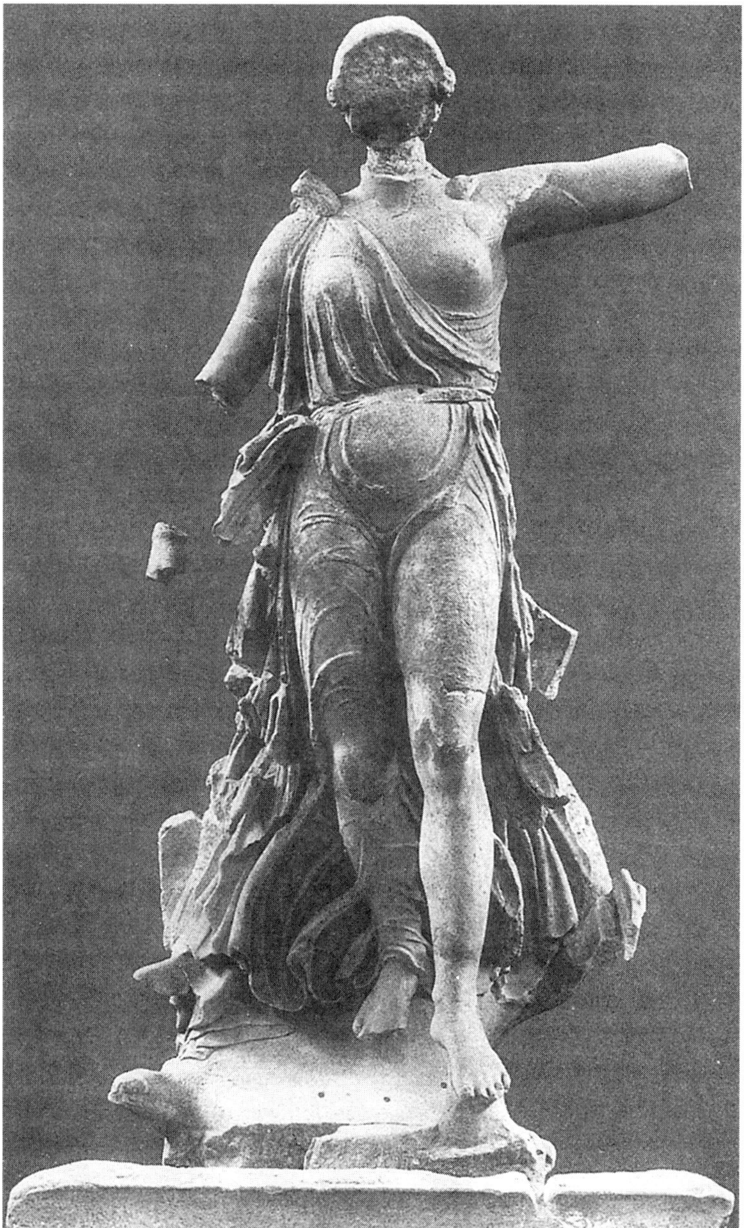

Figure 10 The Nike of the Messenians and Naupaktians. Olympia, Museum.

accordance with their functions, Athenian vases were not a medium for political messages but emphasized more personal themes. Yet they mirror not only individual interests of vase painters and the purchasers of their products but also the themes of social discourse during the important occasions when they were used, especially the symposium.

Vases with figural representations cover a much wider range of themes than public monuments, and are of a different character. This becomes particularly evident when vase painting chooses the same subjects as monumental art. Systematic investigations of this phenomenon are almost completely lacking, but some examples may demonstrate the nature of this discourse within the private sphere.[86]

The experience of the Persian Wars prompted various reactions that were expressed on different occasions, and therefore in different kinds of works of art. While Aeschylus emphasized in his *Persians* the religious and moral aspects of this conflict, and the mural painting in the Stoa Poikile praised the exemplary bravery of the Athenians and their protagonists, vases show more personal attitudes (fig. 11).[87] Beside heroic encounters, there appear extremely negative depictions, the most disgusting on an oinochoe where a Greek with an erect penis, held in his hand like a pistol, approaches a man in oriental costume who offers himself for the sexual act.[88] Such scenes did not occur in dramatic performances nor in public monuments, but we can imagine that people who had appreciated the "official" view in the theater and on the Agora could make quite different statements in the evening during the symposium. Mentalities change according to occasions.

Different attitudes are also reflected in myths. The painting of the fall of Troy in the Stoa Poikile stressed the moral implications of the victory of Greeks over mythical Orientals, while the Vivenzio hydria, painted immediately after the sack of Athens in 480, evidently expresses compassion with the conquered city through its mourning women (figs. 12a, 12b).[89] And while on public monuments the Persians for centuries remained the exemplary enemies of the Greeks, vase paintings of real and mythical Persians show a radical change of attitude from an extremely negative to an almost utopian image of otherness in the late fifth century.[90]

In this sense painted vases were, beyond the realm of politics, an effective medium of a discourse on complex themes of collective relevance. However, although produced for a long time exclusively in Athens, they are not exclusively Athenian phenomena, for they were traded and appreciated all over the ancient world, especially by the Etruscans with their very different political and social

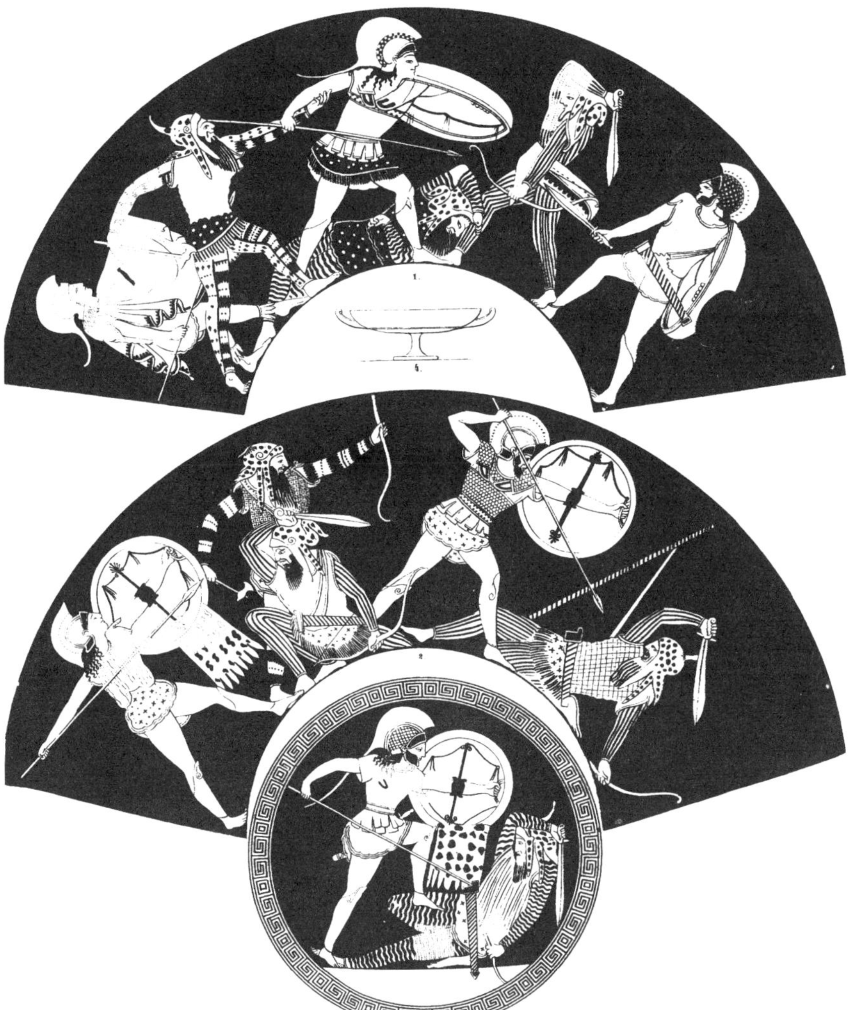

Figure 11 Greeks fighting Persians. Red-figured kylix of the Painter of the Paris Gigantomachy. Rome, Market (Basseggio).

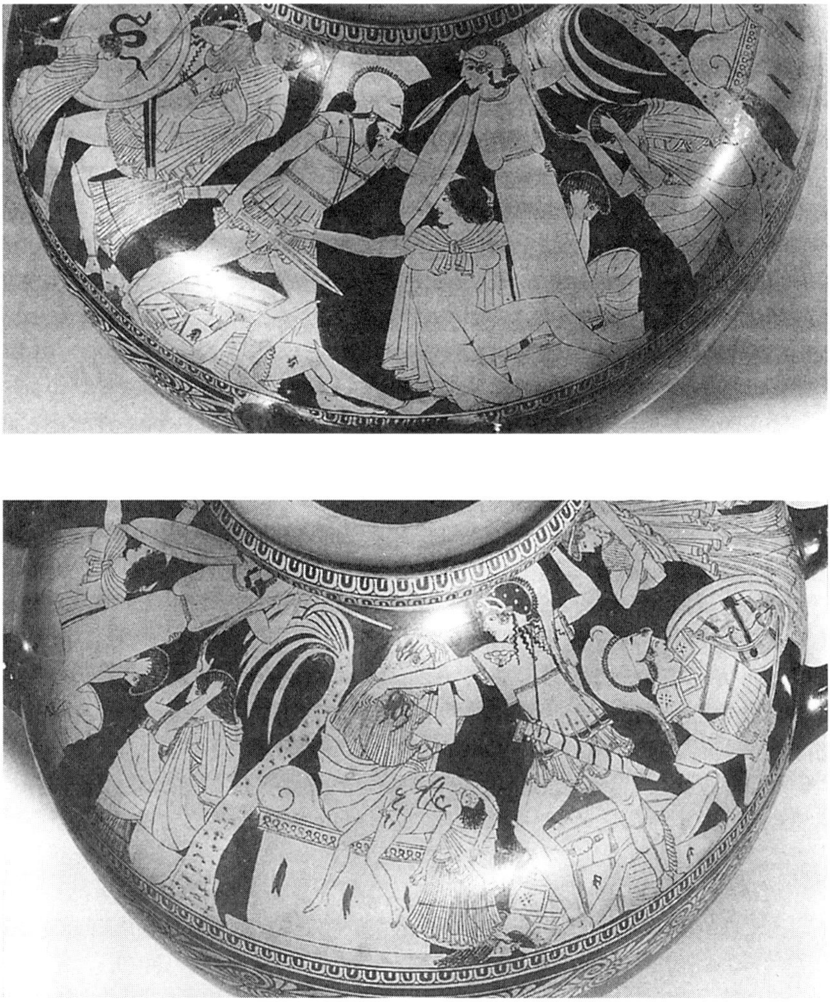

Figures 12a, b Iliupersis. Red-figured hydria of the Kleophrades-Painter. Naples, Museo Nazionale Archeologico.

structure. Even so, it was certainly not by chance that this lively discourse of images originated in Athens.

Conclusion

Was all the art discussed in this chapter specifically Athenian, imperial or democratic? And if so, in what sense? The answer depends on whether we focus on Athens and its monuments or on political art as such.

Political monuments were confined neither to Athens nor to isonomic or democratic states at all. Political identity, the general theme of such monuments, was expressed from the early fifth century by states with various constitutions. They followed in principle the same practices and spoke the same language.

The phenomenon of political monuments is closely connected with basic features and attitudes of classical art, culture, and mentality. I can sketch this here only with some short remarks. Explicit identity was an important new concern of this epoch. It appears on various levels: as individual identity in realistic portraits as well as personal behavior, e.g., of Themistokles who "always wanted to behave in his own way";[91] as polis identity in public monuments; as Hellenic identity against the "barbarians" in many manifestations, both iconic and literary.

All this goes together with the basic feature of classical sculpture: the contraposition of active versus nonactive parts of the human body, indicating a change of the entire "system" and the whole concept of man and nature; it aimed primarily at showing explicitly the body's own forces, especially a figure's ability to stand upright and move by its own energy, and implied connotations like self-determination and responsibility. At the basis of this attitude stood the radically new mentality expressed by Xenophanes:[92] not the gods have given all things to men, but men themselves have found everything in the course of time. Although at first sight such phenomena seem to go well together with democracy, they are attested in states of very different character. It was a broad change of cultural patterns that formed the basis of the Athenian development toward democracy but was not bound to these specific political tendencies and ultimately affected all kinds of society in Greece.

Within this general frame, Athens was a special case. Political monuments, secular as well as religious, were used here in an explicit and systematic way to create political identity. This practice is attested from the beginning of the Kleisthenic order and is essentially connected with it. Some monuments, above all the group of the tyrant-slayers, stress the values of *isonomia* and democracy and show to what extent politics had become the focus of the citizen community.

Yet such monuments are remarkably rare. Much more emphasis is given to Athens' glory in the Persian Wars and its predominance in Greece. Political mythology too concentrates on these themes. The Athenians' collective identity was composed of various elements. Among these, *isonomia,* with its egalitarian demands, was of course an indispensable basis of the citizens' political role and thus of civic identity, but it was a concept of potential rights, of necessary conditions, more than of positive achievements. In the foreground of Athenian pride and self-assertion stood those concrete heroic accomplishments in war that accorded so well with the traditional agonistic values. Since the principal aim of political monuments was to ensure the identification of the citizens not with the underlying principles but with the most acknowledged aspects of their state, military superiority as guarantor of public and private prosperity proved more attractive.

Most elements of political art, iconographic motifs as well as components of picture-language, are not exclusively Athenian. But in many respects Athens appears to have played a leading part. Political monuments in the public space of an agora are known from various sites, but the Athenian tyrant-slayers are apparently the first and certainly the most programmatic example. Monumental victory memorials made from war booty were dedicated in sanctuaries by various states, but none as spectacular and specifically commemorative as the Athenian dedications from Chalkis on the Akropolis and from the Persians at Delphi. From the Archaic period, many cities connected myths and contemporary history to express political claims, but fifth-century Athens used this combination to create particularly complex and global concepts. Public spaces were laid out and differentiated everywhere in Greece from the origin of poleis, but democratic Athens created a particularly complex public topography. State burials were conferred to single persons in various poleis, but the concentration of collective and individual graves in the Athenian state cemetery, forming a façade of glory, a historical physiognomy of the city, at its main entrance, was unique in Greece. Monumental works of art were used everywhere in Greece to adorn public areas and buildings, but the Athenians adopted art in uniquely systematic and ambitious ways to define the specific character of public spaces. As a result, by monumentalizing and perpetuating with works of art the glory of her great citizens and their famous achievements, Athens gradually developed into a monument of her own historical identity.

Athens' only possible rival in this respect may have been Sparta. Pausanias' description gives an impression of Sparta's complex and ambitious historical topography, focused also on the city's glory in the Persian Wars.[93] Critical investigation is needed to make clear to what extent these sites were authentic testimonies of classical Sparta rather than retrospective glorifications by later centuries. But, Thucydides' comment on the modest appearance of late-fifth-century Sparta notwithstanding,[94] many of these memorial sites—less magnificent than their Athenian counterparts but effective places of memory —may well testify to Sparta's political identity as the great rival of classical Athens.

Since most Athenian political monuments seem to have been stimulated less by democracy than by empire, the need for legitimation must have been particularly strong in the latter sphere. This must be the reason why Sparta in this respect appears as Athens' only possible rival.

Ultimately, in all these manifestations a psychological factor must have been at work. The sheer quantity and the ambitious scale of artistic achievements in Athens should not only be explained by a surplus of financial resources—which of course was an indispensable factor—but also understood as a qualitative feature. Clearly, the citizens of Athens, more than those of other cities, felt an unprecedented need to create political identity by way of public monuments. Moreover, they surrounded themselves in their private sphere, especially in the form of painted vases, with an immensely rich discourse of themes related to their social, religious, moral, and mental values. I suggest that such artistic intensity was a result of the "adventure" on which Athenian society had embarked in the fifth century.[95] Their path led them, almost irresistibly, into a political order without precedent and into dominion over an empire of incomparable extension; theirs was a balancing act without net that must have created an ambivalent state of collective psychology, between euphoric self-assertion and profound self-doubt, in which all themes of social import were discussed, represented, celebrated, and questioned without end. In this psychological sense, the background to Athenian art of the fifth century was not so much democracy or empire as such but the intense and risky character of Athenian politics in this age of unprecedented opportunity, accomplishment, and challenge.

CHAPTER EIGHT

Presenting the Past in Fifth-Century Athens

DEBORAH BOEDEKER

The innovations of fifth-century Athens are rightly famous.[1] Not only did a single city-state develop rapidly into a major center of military, commercial, and cultural importance, but classical Athens was the only Greek polis to acquire an "empire" (widespread military and political dominance over other Greek cities, which were even required to pay tribute), and the first society we know of to grant full political rights to so wide a range of citizens.

Athens was also a city particularly rich in large-scale public sculpture and painting,[2] especially in its many temples and sanctuaries, and in elaborate poetic performances, most of all in its several yearly dramatic festivals. The city's remarkable political and military achievements, however, are seldom directly reflected in its visual and verbal arts. Instead, public Athenian art in the fifth century strongly tends to focus on legendary deeds set in the distant past. In addition to this "ancient history," a few memorable events from the late sixth or fifth century also become the subject of tragedy, wall painting, architectural or free-standing sculpture; some of these are regularly mentioned in official funeral orations as well. Until late in the fifth century, however, even these historical events are presented as almost timeless and unconnected; unlike some other Greek cities, Athens seems to produce no continuous narrative of past events until Thucydides.

This chapter will first survey how several fifth-century art forms (most of which are treated in greater detail elsewhere in this volume) present great moments in the city's past, sometimes juxtaposing heroic myths with recent achievements. Then I will consider the paradox that historiography itself develops relatively late in a city so rich in memorials of its great past deeds, offering as partial explanation the argument that the city uses its "past" in public art in ways directly at odds with practices of fifth-century narrative historiography.

I

Like other monumental arts in Athens, architectural sculpture in the fifth century privileges the mythical past. Favorite themes include adventures of Theseus, the national hero, especially his battle with the Amazons, which appears on a number of monuments inside and outside the city. This motif was depicted on metopes of the Athenian treasury at Delphi perhaps as early as about 510;[3] it appeared also on the pediment of the temple of Apollo Daphnephoros at Eretria on the island of Euboia, which was probably built a few years later under Athenian influence (in this period Athenians and Eretrians were allied against Euboian Chalkis, and they fought together against the Persians at Sardis in 498). Two generations later, the Amazonomachy was a prominent motif in the Parthenon decorations as well, both on the west metopes and on the colossal shield of Pheidias' statue of Athena inside the temple;[4] at roughly the same time, it was depicted on the West frieze of the Hephaisteion above the Agora.

Also found in fifth-century architectural sculpture are scenes from the Trojan War, the Gigantomachy, the battle of Lapiths and Centaurs, and other heroic tales. Depictions of such panhellenic myths occur frequently in early-fifth-century vase paintings too. (Later in the century, as Lucilla Burn notes, Athenian art shows a heightened interest in less widely known Attic myths and rituals.)[5] These mythical scenes have long been assumed to reflect in some way the contemporary military and political situation, but just how specifically they do so is a matter of controversy. A recent book by David Francis proposes a number of very precise historical references in such mythical scenes, many of which require significant down-dating from the dates art historians have ascribed to the images. For example, Francis argues that the Amazonomachy on the pediment of the Apollo temple at Eretria (mentioned above) alluded to the battle at Ephesos (498), where the Persians caught up with and defeated the Athenians and Eretrians who had just attacked Sardis; Francis suggests—particularly if the pediment showed any Greek victims of the Amazons—that it even referred specifically to the death of the Eretrian commander Eualkides.[6]

Interpretations of mythological scenes at this level of detail would no doubt differ widely, and few scholars agree with Francis that the references were ever intended to be so specific.[7] Tonio Hölscher interprets the mythical scenes much more generally as expressions of broad cultural oppositions (e.g., order versus chaos).[8] David Castriota argues that they convey the current ethos of the city.

After the Persian sack of Athens in 480, for example, Athenian images of the sack of Troy empathetically show Trojan victims of atrocities committed by the (Greek) despoilers, but later images focus on the restrained behavior of most Greeks in their war against the barbarians, even judging and punishing fellow-Greek perpetrators of war crimes.[9] To put it in simplest terms, as Athens' military power grew, its perspective on ancient victims and victors changed.

Similarly, it has been shown that myths about Theseus increase in popularity and develop different emphases as the empire grows. The story of "the ring of Minos"—in which Theseus boldly confronts a villainous Minos on the way to Crete, is challenged to prove his descent from Poseidon, and eventually is warmly recognized and honored by Poseidon's wife Amphitrite—becomes more prominent as Athens' dominance of the Aegean increases, as we can see in the Theseion decorations, in vase paintings, and in the vivid narrative of Bacchylides' third dithyramb (fr. 17).[10] The Amazonomachy myth develops as well, to suggest fundamental opposition between free and rational Greeks on the one hand and threatening eastern barbarians on the other.[11]

In the 420s, several subjects from recent history suddenly appear on architectural sculptures in the manner of the well-established "legendary" scenes. On the little temple of Nike, built at the entrance to the Akropolis, the South frieze shows Greeks fighting Persians, and two other friezes (North and West) apparently show Greeks fighting Greeks. The South frieze is variously interpreted as the battle of Marathon, Plataea, or a generic reference to the Persian Wars; the North and West friezes may refer to the war with Sparta that had begun in earnest some years before, although it has been argued that these friezes depict the Persian Wars (allied Greeks fighting medizing Greeks at Plataea), or even refer to Greeks fighting Trojans in the Trojan War.[12]

Mythological or historical images in fifth-century Athens include also free-standing anthropomorphic statues in bronze and marble, ranging from quite small to over life size. These were commonly dedicated on the Akropolis of Archaic and classical (and later) Athens as elsewhere in the Greek world. Many of these images represented gods, as is clear from their attributes (e.g., Athena's helmet, Apollo's bow). Others—the famous archaic kouroi and korai—are more controversial; they may also be gods (in many cases the hands have fallen off, and with them perhaps the identifying attributes),[13] but have also been interpreted as representations of the dedicators, members of their families, or idealized representations of their social type. Easier to identify are statues from the same period that represent athletes, such as heavily-armed racers (*hoplitodromoi*), presumably dedicated as thank offerings for victories in the games held at the Panathenaia or other festivals. Such images recall the odes composed for winning athletes by epinician poets, where a medium (choral lyric) associated with mythical narratives is used to celebrate a contemporary success in the games. With these statues, then, we seem to have commemoration, if not of "history" in the usual sense, at least of specific deeds, rather than the timeless representations of immortal gods (however time-bound and specific may have been the occasions for their dedication).[14]

Like the reliefs on the Nike temple, at least one group of free-standing sculptures—the famous statues of the Tyrannicides—specifically recalls recent events. This pair of monumental bronzes was erected not on the Akropolis but in the Agora, a space especially associated with political activities.[15] The statues represented the lovers Harmodios and Aristogeiton, who killed Hipparchos, brother of Hippias the tyrant, in 514, a few years before Hippias was expelled. The monument known to us in Roman copies (see Hölscher, this vol., fig. 1) probably replicates not the original statues erected in the late sixth century, soon after the fall of the Peisistratid tyranny, but the replacement pair by the sculptors Kritios and Nesiotes, dedicated a few years after the Persian Wars: the originals were said to have been carried off by the Persians when Xerxes sacked Athens in 480. The Tyrannicide statues are not static figures like kouroi but rather, like the dedicatory statues of victorious athletes, are memorialized in the process of carrying out their significant deed. Weapons in hand, they stride forward resolutely, in a pose that became characteristic of "antityrannical" action.[16]

By the late fifth century, statues of historical figures (often identified by inscriptions on their bases) were being dedicated on the Akropolis.[17] These include not only priestesses and other officials but the sixth-century poet Anakreon and Perikles himself. From the later fourth century on, statues of prominent citizens were erected in the Agora as well. This public commemoration of historical individuals signals an important change in Athenian memorial practice, one that corresponds to the more "democratic" sense of time proposed by Csapo and Miller in this volume.[18]

Like architectural and free-standing sculpture, wall paintings also occasionally portrayed historical figures and events. Large paintings on panels or plaques decorated a few temples (e.g., a Poseidon temple at Isthmia) as early as the mid-seventh century, but in Athens, monumental painting was introduced for a brief period after the Persian Wars, in new sanctuaries and public buildings.[19] Like architectural sculpture, these paintings generally portrayed heroic deeds set in the distant past; even some of the same motifs are used. The second-century C.E. travel writer Pausanias, for example, describes murals from the classical period in several Athenian cult places including the Theseion (a shrine built to house the bones of Theseus after Kimon recovered them from the island of Skyros in the 470s), where he saw paintings of Amazons attacking Athens, Lapiths fighting Centaurs at the wedding of Theseus' friend Peirithoos, and the confrontation of Theseus with Minos on the way to Crete (1.17.2–3).[20]

Around 460 the famous Stoa Poikile or "Painted Portico," a public space overlooking the political center of the city, was constructed just north of the Agora. According to Pausanias' description (1.15.1–3), wall paintings of the Amazonomachy and the sack of Troy (two of the best-attested mythical scenes in Athens) were displayed in the Stoa,[21] but along with them was depicted an event that had taken place less than thirty years earlier, the battle of Marathon, with Miltiades figuring prominently in it. No doubt the influence of Kimon (Miltiades' son) was at work in this glorification of the commander,[22] yet the fourth-century orator Aischines presents the portrayal of Miltiades as the result of a public decision, maintaining that the Athenian demos allowed him "to be depicted in front exhorting the soldiers" (*Against Ktesiphon* 186).[23]

Also shown in the Stoa, according to Pausanias, was a battle fought between Athenians and Spartans at Argive Oinoe; this might represent an event even more recent than the battle of Marathon. The rather shadowy battle of Oinoe, not mentioned by Thucydides or other historians, probably took place in the 460s, with Argives and Athenians fighting Spartans in a preliminary to the first Peloponnesian War.[24] Lillian Jeffery objects that the commemoration of a recent battle of Greeks against Greeks would have been "an abnormal action for this period," and suggests that the "Oinoe" painting did indeed commemorate the battle of that name, but with a painting from saga—perhaps the Athenians fighting Thebans on behalf of the Argive warriors who were refused burial when they fell attacking Thebes.[25] Francis and Vickers, for their part, argue that the "Oinoe" Pausanias saw in the painting was not Argive, but a village of the same name near Marathon, so that the picture showed a preliminary stage of the battle of Marathon.[26] Even if the Oinoe painting was not what Pausanias says it was, however, the Marathon painting alone indicates that both "ancient" and fairly recent battles were depicted on the walls of the portico—as is likely for the Nike temple too, almost four decades later.

This juxtaposition of legendary and recent events parallels the patterns well known from epinician odes performed for athletic champions.[27] Since the earliest victory odes known to us date from shortly before the time of the Persian Wars, it is possible that the past/present juxtapositions in those poems influenced the similar structure in the visual representations. But I think it more likely that they come from a common impetus, a way of seeing the present as analogous to the past, that was heightened by the experience of the Persian Wars—events the Greeks in general perceived to be of "heroic" quality.

Explicit comparison between past and present heroism is also attested in the famous "Eion poem," a set of epigrams inscribed in about 475 on three herms in the Agora.[28] One of these epigrams bases its praise of contemporary Athenian military achievements, the victorious siege against the Persians at Eion, on the (rather weak) Homeric praise of Athenian performance at Troy:

> Once from this city Menestheus with the sons of Atreus
> went as leader to the holy plain of Troy;
> Homer once said that, of the stout-corseleted Danaans
> he was outstanding as marshal in battle.[29]
> So it is not unseemly that Athenians be called
> marshals in war and manliness.
> (Poem A, Aischines, *Against Ktesiphon* 183)

We now have evidence that this process of mythologization started to take place—and not just in Athens—immediately after the battles themselves. A recently published fragment of an elegiac poem by Simonides on the battle of Plataea explicitly draws a comparison between the fame of Homeric heroes who fought at Troy and that of the Greeks who fought the Persians at Plataea.[30] This fragment suggests that the analogy with the Trojan War was drawn very soon after Xerxes' invasion, and that it was not restricted to Athens (as it is in the Eion poem). The Plataea elegy is clearly directed toward praise of Spartans (as well as other Greeks, who are mentioned in other fragments of the poem),[31] which reminds us that Athens was not unique, just more prolific, in using the heroic past to represent, and even to shape, its civic identity.[32]

Heroic past deeds also form part of the conventional subject matter of public speeches in classical Athens. The funeral orations, presented each year when the war dead were officially commemorated and laid to rest, made use of an idealized Athenian past, citing especially the help given to the Heraklids, burial provided for the Seven against Thebes, and above all the city's role in the Persian Wars, as grand analogues for the current military deaths. This subject has been richly discussed recently, especially in Nicole Loraux's influential book *The Invention of Athens,* which shows how the *epitaphioi* promote the notion of a city that commands and deserves the full dedication of its inhabitants.[33]

The Athenian past plays a role in forensic speeches as well. Rosalind Thomas has shown how traditions about patriotic forebears are used by defendants in court, presenting ancestral deeds in ways that tend to conform with "official" Athenian history and democratic ideology (for example, *everyone's* ancestors were staunchly antityrannical). These family traditions sometimes contain detectable historical gaps and errors, but they also can preserve more specific kinds of information (e.g., who was associated with which victory) than do the more "official" funeral orations. Nevertheless, being oriented toward rhetorical success rather than factual accuracy, both kinds of speeches tend to situate historical deeds in a kind of "timeless historical vacuum."[34]

Tragedy, the fifth-century Athenian genre par excellence, of course deals, with few exceptions, with myths set in the distant past.[35] Implied parallels between present and past nevertheless appear in many tragedies whose bold anachronisms, whether unconscious or intentional, are another way of grounding contemporary Athenian ideals and institutions in ancient parallels—as if the issues, and the city itself, never changed in essence. But changes are perceptible over time in tragedy's representation of the past, reflecting developments in Athens' view of itself and its role in the Hellenic world. An example of this is found in the framing of questions about who should make political decisions in the *Suppliants* plays of Aeschylus and Euripides. In both dramas, the king of a Greek city in the "heroic age" insists on applying democratic principles when a decision must be made about whether or not to risk citizens' lives by taking up the cause of a weaker party.

In Aeschylus' play, produced probably in the late 460s, the debate is staged in a foreign city, Argos, which serves as a kind of mirror in which contemporary Athens can examine questions facing it at an early stage of its democracy and "protectionist" empire. Euripides' play, however—performed around 422, near the end of the Archidamian War, when Athens' empire was hated as tyrannical and was under attack by the Peloponnesians—significantly sets the scene for democratic apologia and protective heroism in Attika itself, when Theseus was king, as if to show Athenians and their visiting allies alike the just and benevolent motives behind Athenian military interventions.[36]

Like some architectural sculptures and wall paintings, the few dramas that deal with recent events take as their subject matter Greek struggles with Persians.[37] Herodotus records the well-known incident of the fine levied against the early-fifth-century dramatist Phrynichos for disturbing the audience with his all-too-moving drama on the *Capture of Miletus* (Her. 6.21), in which Athens itself was closely involved.[38] We know less about Phrynichos' *Phoenician Women,* but in Aeschylus' *Persians* (472) it is possible to see how freely and selectively tragedy can treat historical events—in this case the battle of Salamis, brilliantly presented as if from the Persian perspective. Here, even more than in the Eion or Plataea poems, we see the Persian Wars being mythologized.

Besides tragedies set in the recent past, those few that are set in Athens may be presumed to have had a special resonance with their Athenian audience. In

Aeschylus' *Oresteia* trilogy (458) the action moves from Argos to Delphi to Athens, where the cycle of vengeance is finally broken. In a bold innovation, the *Eumenides* makes the story of Orestes' crime and eventual acquittal into a kind of Athenian suppliant drama: the matricide, pursued by Furies, seeks and gains the support of Athens' patron goddess in her citadel. Even the dire Furies are in the end transformed and given a home and homage in the city. Several extant tragedies focussing on Athens were, like Euripides' *Suppliants,* produced during the Peloponnesian War. They can be described either as suppliant dramas, presenting the city as a courageous protector of the oppressed (e.g., Euripides' *Herakleidai,* Sophokles' *Oidipous at Kolonos*), or dramas of autochthony (Euripides' *Ion*), which suggest Athens' intrinsic right to its own territory and its superiority over other Greeks, who are by comparison interlopers in their own lands.[39] Whatever their "distance" or "nearness" to Athens, however, tragedies use past events to dramatize contemporary concerns.

II

Now it is obvious that representations of recent historical events did not begin in Greece (much earlier precedents are attested, for example, in Egypt), and Greek representations of historical events did not begin in Athens.[40] According to Herodotus (4.88), the engineer Mandrokles of Samos commissioned a large painting and dedicated it in the great sanctuary of Hera on Samos, commemorating his successful construction of a pontoon bridge over the Bosporos. The painting showed King Darius, who had ordered the bridge to be built, seated on a throne, watching his army cross over into Skythia. Tonio Hölscher suggests that Mandrokles' painting was inspired by Achaemenid monuments featuring the Great King with lines of marching soldiers.[41] Unlike the Athenian monuments, such a painting marks the accomplishment of an individual rather than a city (even though the dedicatory inscription on the painting declares that the deed won "glory [*kydos*] for the Samians").

It is also clear that Athens was by no means unique in commemorating the Persian Wars.[42] We have epigrams (some of them certainly authentic)[43] from many Greek cities celebrating the victory and commemorating the war dead, as well as dedications of spoils or works paid for by spoils, especially in the great Panhellenic sanctuaries.[44] But only in Athens, it appears, were scenes related to the Persian Wars depicted visually—on vase paintings as well as in monumental art.[45] Moreover, this practice continued long after the battles were over, as we have seen, in the Stoa Poikile and the Nike temple frieze. Similarly, the annual funeral orations and even Athenian policy speeches to other Greeks (discussed below) continued for many decades to highlight Athens' role at Marathon and Salamis.

Margaret Miller and Eric Csapo postulate in this volume that among historical representations, apart from the Tyrannicides, *only* figures or events associated with the Persian Wars were depicted in the narrative art of classical Athens. An exception to this rule might be the battle of Oinoe (discussed above), if this battle really took place and if it was really depicted in the Stoa Poikile.[46] Another exception could be the West and North friezes of the Nike temple, which may show Athenians fighting other Greeks in the Peloponnesian rather than the Persian War.[47] It is significant, however, that even though Greek poleis had been warring against each other for centuries, visual narratives of Greeks fighting Greeks did not in the end prove as compelling as showing Greeks against "others," whether Trojans, Amazons, or Persians. The same tendency holds for the funeral orations, which emphasize that Athenians have given their lives for the freedom of Greeks, whether fighting against barbarian or Hellenic oppressors.[48] The overthrow of the Peisistratids (which came to symbolize the beginning of the democracy) and the defeat of the Persians (the starting point and justification of the Athenian empire) succeeded in entering the mythology and iconography of Athens in ways that were virtually closed to other deeds of recent history. Given the radical novelty and importance of democracy and empire for Athens, it is fitting that the city should commemorate these events in particular.

The city's great achievements against the Persians "went down in history" largely through a process of implied analogy to the mythical past. As has been abundantly demonstrated, Athenian narrative art in this period—both visual and verbal—sets up many parallels between ancient and recent events—or makes both ancient and recent events embody the same large structures of opposition, such as order versus chaos, Greek versus barbarian, male versus female.[49] The parallels are often left to the audience to discover, especially on the visual monuments. A representation of an ancient battle like the Amazons' attack on Athens might encourage viewers to draw an analogy with recent events like the sack of Athens by the Persians, and to recognize their underlying conceptual similarity.[50] Occasionally, however, the relationship is fairly explicit, as with the Stoa Poikile paintings, the Eion poem, or Simonides' newly discovered elegy on the battle of Plataea (mentioned above), which overtly compares the fame of those who fought at Troy with those who fought the Persians at Plataea.[51] These more explicit parallels make it all the more likely that we are correct in looking for contemporary references in ancient depictions of heroic myth.

There is an extraordinary self-confidence in these parallels, as Hölscher rightly points out.[52] The Athenian attitude reflected here contrasts sharply with the common view expressed in earlier epic and elegy that the past was greater than the present—expressed for example by the narrator of the *Iliad,* singing of men who could hurl stones that two men of his own time could not lift (5.302–304); in Hesiod's myth of the races of men, degenerating from the Golden to the Iron Race of his own time (*Works and Days* 109–201); or in an elegy of Mimnermos (14.1–4W) that looks back to an earlier hero (unnamed in the fragment) for a model to imitate:

> Not such [as yours] were *his* strength and bravery,
> as I have heard from older men who saw him
> on the plain of Hermos with his spear routing the Lydian
> cavalry's thick ranks . . . (tr. Martin West, adapted)

Athens' construction of a heroic past analogous to the contemporary city raises the question of historical distortion, if not outright propagandistic "rewriting" of the past. David Castriota summarizes a widespread view of scholars about one aspect of fifth-century uses of the past, in what he calls "the manipulation of myths." He finds raw invention in all the heroic themes we have been looking at: "The Centauromachy had been made to erupt en masse at the wedding itself; a wholly new invasion of Greece had been manufactured for the Amazons; while the epic of the Seven acquired a sequel in which the Athenians now took center stage."[53] David Francis similarly discusses conscious invention and manipulation of myths, and Robert Parker refers to the "invention of tradition" in the same sense.[54]

We should be careful, however, not to apply too readily what Ian Morris has dubbed the "propaganda fallacy,"[55] as if policymakers took a conscious decision to distort facts and deceive a naive audience. Instead, it is more helpful to focus on an interpretive community (in Stanley Fish's formulation, which Castriota himself also uses) that could both produce and "read" the images; to this community the heroizing images were probably both relevant and credible. In a sense, myths exist only to be "manipulated" for contemporary purposes. Prior to the ideal of scientific historiography, what other reason could there be for preserving stories and images of bygone times?[56] Jack Goody and Ian Watt's explanation of the "homeostasis" maintained by oral traditions still provides a useful model for this phenomenon: only that portion of the tradition is preserved which still speaks to the present situation; it is constantly reshaped—often unconsciously—to conform to present realities; otherwise it disappears.[57] In any event, the system of representation in Athens is not prepackaged, watertight, or strictly regulated by an Archon for Propaganda.

It was natural for Athens to look "backward" for laudable models of behavior. In the period we are considering, the city was going through enormous changes,[58] which must have provoked some level of anxiety.[59] At the same time Athens, like the rest of Greece, was very much "in the grip of the past."[60] Its most prestigious models of behavior were preserved in heroic traditions attributed to the daughters of Memory, its landscape littered with places that echoed with some memorial of past deeds. The point is obvious but bears repeating: for such a community, which deems the future hidden but the past luminously visible, it is essential—inevitable—to find continuities, analogies, foreshadowings that connect present with past, whether in events (barbarian attempts on the home citadel), civic attributes (protecting the weak), or policies (leadership of Ionians). This is especially true if the community has in some ways made a major, visible break with the past, as Athens did through its democracy.[61]

Thus Athens constructs and uses a past that will provide a foundation for its radically innovative present. Some elements of this past, such as autochthony and tyrannicide, especially support democratic aspects of the present; more of them connect with imperial policies—not so much Athenian hegemony per se, but protection of suppliants, leadership against barbarians, genealogical and other relationships with Ionians.[62] Hölscher thinks the empire was more problematic for Athenians than was the democracy, hence more often "justified" by monuments.[63] This may have been the case, but I would propose an additional reason, related to the genre or mode of representation, for the disparity in frequency of their visual representations.[64] As we have seen, Athens preferred to allude to its recent achievements with mythical parallels rather than show them directly, but—in contrast to myths of conflict, for example—there were few existing myths that would evoke democracy as such.[65] Apart from the story of the tyrannicide, democracy was not a very dramatic iconographic theme. By the fourth century (when, in line with Hölscher's thesis, democracy was more overtly challenged within Athens), abstractions such as Demokratia or Demos would begin to appear on monuments; before this time visual art preferred narrative rather than allegorical subjects. In contrast to figural arts, tragedy, with a very different set of generic possibilities, does sometimes develop the "democratic" themes of Athenian kinship (*Ion*), trial by jury (*Eumenides*), and the right of the demos to decide on war (the *Suppliants* of Aeschylus and Euripides).

Athenian use of the past to suit the needs of the present develops in several stages within the early fifth century. At first, as in the Eion epigrams and the Stoa Poikile, "ancient" events are invoked as parallels to the city's role in the Persian Wars. But soon, the Persian Wars themselves (especially the battles of Marathon and Salamis) are added to the catalogue of more remote events, and are used to justify Athens' hegemony.[66] This rhetorical ploy appears in Herodotus' account of the battle of Plataea, when Athenians argue (perhaps anachronistically) that they deserve a place of honor in the battle line because of their traditional bravery in the time of the Heraklids, the Seven against Thebes, and the Amazons—but especially because of their recent actions at Marathon (9.27).[67] In Thucydides as well, the Athenians argue in their speech ascribed to 432 at Sparta that they deserve their empire because of their leading contributions to Greek liberty during the Persian Wars (1.73–74).[68]

The tyrannicide may also have played a paradigmatic role. The pair of statues, at least, came to evoke liberation not just from the Peisistratids, and perhaps not only in Athens. As is well known, Harmodios' active, slashing stance and Aristogeiton's noble, level-eyed pose are replicated in architectural sculptures of Theseus, the archetypal antityrannical Athenian hero, on a west metope showing the Centauromachy on the Hephaisteion in the Agora. Farther afield, there is perhaps a reflection of Harmodios' vigorous pose in a similar figure on the west pediment of Zeus' great temple at Olympia (another Centauromachy).[69]

Funeral orations of course also draw analogies between the deeds of contemporary Athens and those of legendary times. Since this genre probably became established in the 460s, it may have helped to fix the pattern, at least in verbal genres.[70] Similar analogies are found in vase paintings as well.[71] As François Lissarrague has pointed out, vase painters use the same configurations for paintings of Homeric heroes as for sixth- or fifth-century Athenian hoplites, in scenes such as leave-taking, arming, or heroic return from battle (dead or alive).[72] The democratic fighter is shown in a heroic configuration, as was his predecessor under the tyrants.[73]

At least in vase painting, then, the tendency to present contemporary *aretē* in terms of an ancient model did not begin with the democracy but predated it. The democracy exploited this process in many different genres and with many themes, however, emphasizing the bravery not just of individual heroes like Theseus, but of groups of anonymous warriors as well. At times these anonymous Athenians of the past are even evoked with the first person plural: according to the Athenians debating about their position at Plataea, "we " rescued the Herakleidai, buried the companions of Polyneikes at Eleusis, and drove off the Amazons (Her. 9.27.2–4). Past and present Athenians become virtually indistinguishable.

III

It is paradoxical that, despite all the attention it paid to "history," not to mention its great resources and attraction for creative individuals, Athens did not play a more prominent role in the beginnings of historiography. The cliché maintains that history is written by the winners, and Athens certainly belonged in that category for most of the fifth century. Yet prose historiography originated in Ionia, beginning in the late sixth century, and was slow in spreading to Athens.[74]

Consensus still rightly grants to Herodotus the title "father of history"—and Herodotus was not an Athenian. Christian Meier, among others, believes nonetheless that Athenian democracy had a great influence on Herodotus: its lively, debate-oriented political and judicial systems would have encouraged the historian to think in terms of an open-ended, contingent history of events with a plurality of actors, rather than a unitary view of events controlled by a single king or god, moving toward a fixed end.[75]

Meier's position is illuminating, yet I find it significant that Herodotus was an outside observer of Athens rather than a native or even adopted Athenian. He says positive things about democratic Athens, such as how after the reforms of Kleisthenes the city's new equality made it stronger than before (5.78). He insists that an allegedly unwilling audience accept the centrality of Athens' role in the Persian Wars (7.139). But he describes flaws as well, such as the tendency of the demos to be fooled by clever rhetoric (5.97). Even granting that all these Herodotean statements derive from Athenian traditions or "informants," it must be admitted that he paid heed to a wide range of voices in presenting the city's deeds and fortunes.

Some scholars maintain that prose histories of Athens must have predated the account of Thucydides. Lionel Pearson, for example, would date the Attic history of Hellanikos of Lesbos to the time of Perikles, and even suggests that Perikles encouraged Hellanikos to compile that work.[76] More recently, Gianfranco Maddoli has argued that there was a written account of Peisistratos' famous trick—when the ousted tyrant reentered Athens with a tall young woman, dressed as Athena, driving his chariot—dating to the early fifth century and used independently by Herodotus and Aristotle; but the evidence for this is slight.[77]

The current state of our knowledge suggests rather that the ten books of Pherekydes' genealogies, dating perhaps to the 460s, are the closest thing to prose "history" produced in Athens before the late fifth century. Pherekydes' annotated family trees bear little relation to a plausible history of events. Even so, they were surely important for stabilizing and promulgating the ancestral catalogues of the great families of Athens, finding a primogenitor for numerous institutions and policies,[78] and helping to confirm the antiquity and continuity of Athens itself—thus providing a bridge between family pride and civic ideals.[79] Pherekydes' role in paving the way for historiography is thus not negligible: his work developed the attempt to systematize Attic mythology that Martin West finds adumbrated already in the Hesiodic *Catalogue*.[80]

It is likely too that these long lists of generations, quite independent of their accuracy, are related to the development of a more abstract sense of history in early-fifth-century Athens and elsewhere.[81] Certain disconnected events, such as the birth of Erichthonius, Theseus' exploits, and the Trojan War, were well attested on the far end of the historical spectrum, while the Tyrannicides and the Persian Wars were conspicuous on the near end. The resulting very imperfectly balanced Athenian "history" resembles the situation typical in predominantly oral cultures, which has been described as an "hourglass" structure, or one with a "floating gap" in the middle:[82] there are stories about distant origins, and memories of recent events, but little in between. Pherekydes' genealogies helped to fill in the gap.

It appears though that before Thucydides there is no Athenian author who purports to reconstruct and narrate a relatively continuous, plausible, contingent history of events. Thucydides of course deals primarily with quite recent history: the Peloponnesian War. Although a native and well-connected Athenian, he presents himself emphatically as an "objective" observer, even an exile (5.26.5). His home city is anything but the object of uncritical praise.[83] And it is not coincidental that, unlike tragedy, monumental sculpture and painting, andfuneral orations, Thucydides' history is not publicly sponsored.

Thucydides freely criticizes popular, heroized versions of the recent past. Not for him, he declares, the stories that please an audience for the moment; he will construct an enduring treasure based not on popular traditions, which are mostly inaccurate, but on his own observations and magisterial judgment (1.20–21). Probably Thucydides' best-known refutation of a pleasing story is his repeated deconstruction of the Tyrannicide myth: Hipparchos was not even tyrant when he was murdered by Harmodios and Aristogeiton, and the act was not motivated by politics but by injured family pride and jealous love (1.20, 6.53–59). The contrast between this attitude and that implied in the Tyrannicide statues could hardly be starker. As Josiah Ober has recently written: "By showing that Hipparchos was a minor figure, Thucydides undermines a foundation myth of the democracy and so robs popular rule of a 'usable' aspect of the polis' past history... [Thucydides] will present facts that have been 'tested' and so are more reliable than the hodgepodge of erroneous beliefs that constitute democratic knowledge and underlie Athens' civic ideology."[84]

In a city where civic identity was constantly in search of support, and where (as Robert Connor reminds us)[85] myths, rituals, and images were an essential part of constructing that identity, Thucydides' critical attitude toward Athenian history would hardly be perceived by the demos as a useful civic goal. The comparison with Sokrates' contemporary criticism of democratic political ideals and institutions, and with Sokrates' eventual trial and execution by the city,[86] is obvious and instructive. In Athens, the critical writing of history, like the rhetoric of dissent in other areas, developed when the democracy, no longer enjoying its old success, came under attack from within and without. Herodotus and Thucydides alike used this genre to judge and criticize, and to privilege change, not continuity.

IV

How fifth-century Athens uses the past in its public visual and verbal art may help explain why historiography is not a well-represented genre. The past deeds displayed in public sculpture and painting, and implied in tragedy and other poetic forms, are discontinuous, virtually "timeless," and surely used to suggest analogies among different events. Narrative historiography, however, presents a series of events in a fixed sequence—logical rather than analogical—where this event *follows* that, and therefore somehow *comes from* that. The very structure of traditional verbal narrative sets up a *post hoc ergo propter hoc* view of events.[87] This linear narrative history emphasizes changes,[88] which makes the past bear a very different relationship to the present than does "analogical" history, which emphasizes continuities.[89] From this standpoint, chronological or causal relation of events to each other is of slight importance; what matters is the highly charged representation of what it is to be Hellenic, Athenian, heroic.

In a virtual reversal of the separate-but-parallel events painted in the Stoa Poikile or the "timeless" praise of democracy declaimed by Euripides' Theseus (*Suppliants* 403–8, 426–41), the first paragraphs of Herodotus' *Histories* present formerly independent stories as part of a connected history: the rapes of Io, Europa, Medea, and Helen become steps in an escalating sequence of abductions of women between Europe and Asia, which lead first to the Trojan and ultimately to the Persian Wars. Herodotus concludes (1.4.3–4), "The Persians say that they themselves made no account of the women carried off from Asia but that the Hellenes, for the sake of a Lacedaemonian woman, gathered a great force, went to Asia, and destroyed the power of Priam. From then on, the Persians always considered Hellas as hostile to them." Herodotus' Persians here construct linear history from elements of separate myths, in an account that serves as prelude to the *Histories*' main subject, the intercontinental conflicts of the fifth century.

Another example of the difference between "timeless" and "historical" uses of the past can be found in one of the first historical monuments of post-Peisistratid Athens, a bronze chariot dedicated to Athena and prominently placed at the entrance to the Akropolis. On its base was an inscription in elegiacs, recorded by Herodotus (5.77.4–78) and confirmed by archaeological evidence, proudly celebrating a double victory over Thebans and Chalkidians in 506, soon after Kleisthenes' reforms.[90]

> The sons of the Athenians with deeds of war
> conquered the nations of Boiotia and Chalkis;
> they quenched their hybris with grim iron chains
> and dedicated these horses, a tithe of the spoils, to Athena.

In describing the dedication, Herodotus remarks (5.78) that this victory proved how much more effectively a city fights under *isēgoria* than tyranny. The inscription itself, however, says nothing about the politics of the victors; it simply refers to them as "sons of the Athenians," a Homeric-sounding tag that tends to associate the Athenian hoplites with traditional epic valor. But for Herodotus, or perhaps his Athenian informants, the chariot dedication marks a political shift as well as a military victory. The historian's emphasis is here on the effects of political change, whereas the original dedicators, as far as we can tell, were more interested in characterizing their victory as an example of timeless *aretē*.

In its great age of innovation and empire, the Athenian demos had no desire for the kind of interconnected and changing past described by the new historians. The monumental genres that had their roots in predemocratic, Peisistratean times worked well to establish civic identity for the new democracy by drawing on cultural memories old and newer, passing over the disjunctures—the facts of change—for democracy and empire alike, and highlighting (only) glorious moments—sack of Troy, fall of the tyranny, defeat of Amazons or Persians.[91] In addition to their superbly developed technical skills and the special cachet of close association with the gods (the Dionysia festival for tragedy, and the sanctuaries where monumental art was most often displayed), these genres had distinct advantages:

1. They were *public* enough to reach the populace and its visitors en masse, far more so than the long and complex prose works of the historians. By midcentury, they were also public in the sense of being financed by and accountable to the democracy.
2. Based on generally *familiar* stories, monumental art had the ring of authenticity and antiquity. With so much that was novel in Athens, it would have been reassuring to see current policies and achievements reflected in images of traditional heroism. This would imply that not everything had changed—or indeed, that nothing had changed: the city of autochthonous equals was doing what she always had done.

3. The monuments were *malleable* enough to permit interpretations that could change with time and circumstances, as we have just considered in connection with the bronze chariot, a victory dedication that Herodotus could describe as a monument to *isēgoria*. In democratic Athens it may have proved beneficial to have not one single voice to decide for all in all circumstances what "really" happened, but the possibility of different voices (in Mikhail Bakhtin's dialogic model) which could be perpetuated in competing traditions. From this perspective the sometimes frustrating ambiguity of much Athenian art may be easier to understand.[92] Ambiguity not only accommodates the similarities in separate events, but also allows a scene to be interpreted differently on different occasions.

So too, some traditions are preserved that glorify not the polis as a whole but certain elements within it (especially elite families), as long as they do not conflict too strongly with the dominant traditions. Kimon's brilliant foregrounding of Theseus, his own Vorgänger but also the Father of his Country, provides an example of this. But the democracy was evidently wary of versions that conflicted too strongly with an important tradition. Such a conflict can be detected, for example, in the debate about who was really responsible for the expulsion of the tyrants. Some Athenians argued that the Peisistratids had been overthrown not by the slaying of Hipparchos by Harmodios and Aristogeiton (a deed that simply embittered Hipparchos' brother the tyrant Hippias), but instead by the persistence of the Alkmaeonids, a powerful family exiled by the Peisistratids. The Alkmaeonids, according to this version, vehemently opposed the tyranny, and eventually, by bribing Apollo's Pythia at Delphi, they convinced the Spartans to help them drive the tyrants out of Athens.

This version of the story is reported by Herodotus (5.62–63), who makes us well aware that the Alkmaeonids were controversial figures in Athens; no doubt they were criticized by factions that preferred the Harmodios-Aristogeiton version of the story. Herodotus finally comes down firmly on the side of the Alkmaeonids: "by their contrivance the Peisistratids were driven out of the tyranny, and therefore they are the ones who freed Athens far more than Harmodios and Aristogeiton, as I judge it" (Her. 6.123.1–2). Thucydides too, as mentioned before, criticized the Athenians for their credulity and lack of accuracy in the widespread popular accounts of the assassination of Hipparchos; he goes to great lengths to correct the version promulgated by the Tyrannicide statues, emphasizing in particular that the motives of Harmodios and Aristogeiton were primarily personal rather than political, and that in fact it was Spartan intervention rather than the murder of Hipparchos that ended the tyranny (6.52–59).

The Tyrannicides prevailed in public monuments, but the existence of regulations protecting them from slander indicate a certain measure of opposition to what they represent.[93] Konrad Kinzl even suggests that the Tyrannicides' heroic gesture was parodied on a red-figured wine bowl painted about 470, showing a drunken pair striking the familiar pose.[94]

But the historian can take a perspective even broader than this "pro and con" level, as we see in Thucydides' well-known complaints about Athenian misinformation. He criticizes not the Tyrannicides or their detractors, but the Athenians who perpetuate a foolish tradition about the Tyrannicides, and so in an even larger sense, the process by which this "information" is perpetuated. The historian makes it his job not just to determine as well as he can what happened, but to critique the sources that try to tell him what happened.

Narrative history, as we see it in Herodotus and Thucydides, is clearly a genre in which the author's reasoning voice counts for a great deal. Active authorial judgments stand in contrast to the more silent genres of monumental painting or sculpture, for example, which only show and do not tell, and even to tragedy, where only characters and chorus have voices, not the dramatist. Prose historiography, on the other hand, is an authorial and judgmental genre, critical both of its sources and its actors. When dealing with the great icons of cultural memory, the narrative historian does not just perpetuate but contextualizes and evaluates. Indeed it seems that this critical spirit is at the heart of the enterprise.

Democratic Athens worked hard to shape a useful past, deliberately making little distinction in its monumental arts between mythical stories and events such as the fall of the tyranny or the victories at Marathon and Salamis. It was critics and outsiders who first attempted to write a continuous, plausible historical narrative; Herodotus and Thucydides connected Athens' present more causally, and sometimes more ironically, to its past. Herodotus for example lets us glimpse the Greeks who were allies in the Persian Wars becoming mortal enemies in the later fifth century (6.98.2); and in Thucydides' history, the city that prides itself on being the liberator of Hellas becomes an admitted tyrant city over other Greeks (2.63.2, 3.37.2).[95] For the development of civic identity in a diverse and potentially divided citizen body, many voices might be permitted, but not that of the authorial observer, the historian doing what linear narrative does best: showing not a timeless world full of paradigms and analogies, but rather a time-bound picture of development, inconsistency, and change.

CHAPTER NINE

The Sophists in Athens

Robert W. Wallace

Consensus Views, and Questions

The term "sophist" is commonly used to refer to a group of intellectuals who worked and taught, in Athens and elsewhere, during the second half of the fifth century. The principal sophists include Protagoras of Abdera, Gorgias of Leontinoi, Prodikos of Keos, Hippias of Elis, Thrasymachos of Chalkedon, and Antiphon the Athenian. A number of less conspicuous figures are also associated with the movement, such as the Athenian Kallikles and the Chian brothers Euthydemos and Dionysodoros. How far the Athenians Damon, Kritias, and Sokrates should be considered sophists is more controversial. The sophists are typically described as travelling "wisdom professors" for hire, especially in the techniques of rhetoric. Although there is no evidence that they regarded themselves as a group and only Protagoras is said to have called himself a sophist (Plato, *Protagoras* 317b), ever since the fourth century the sophists have been sharply distinguished from the philosophers who preceded and came after them. Following Plato (*Hippias maior* 281c–d) it is generally agreed that, beginning around 450 (Protagoras is almost always regarded as the first of them), the sophists represented a fundamentally new type. "Never before had such teachers been seen, never such teaching."[1] For Plato and his followers, ancient and modern, three of the principal characteristics that set the sophists apart from earlier philosophers were their technical and political orientations, and their rejection of positive doctrine. Earlier philosophers developed theories on physical and metaphysical matters, in search of the truth. The sophists, it is commonly stated, were centrally occupied with teaching rhetoric, the techniques of exposition rather than positive doctrine, especially to those who sought careers in public life. Plato's Gorgias proclaims that rhetoric "brings freedom to mankind in general and to each man dominion over others in his own country . . . Possessed of such power you will make the doctor and the trainer your slaves, and your businessman will prove to be making money not for himself but for another, for you who can speak and persuade multitudes" (*Gorgias* 452d–e). As "the most obvious observation," Martin Ostwald writes, "all sophists were primarily concerned with rhetoric and argumentation."[2] In the fifth and fourth centuries this characteristic was often reported in negative terms, as making the wrong or false seem right or true, to make "the worse *logos* seem the better." According to Aristotle (*Rhetoric* 1402a), Protagoras taught his students how to "make the lesser argument the stronger . . . wherefore men were justly disgusted with his promise; for it is a lie, not a true but an apparent probability." Aristophanes' *Clouds* (889–1113) portrays a debate between "Just Logos" and "Unjust Logos" in which the latter is victorious. The sophists' typical clients were young men who wanted to think smart, talk smart, and win success in the democracy.

The sophists, notoriously, also accepted pay for their teaching. In Plato's *Protagoras* (349a; see also *Hippias maior* 282d), Sokrates states that Protagoras "set up as a teacher of culture and virtue" and was "the first to claim payment for this service." Elsewhere (*Sophistes* 231d) Plato defines the sophist as "a paid hunter of the young and the wealthy." We hear of a number of fees: for example, Prodikos' "fifty-drachma lecture course" (Plato, *Cratylus* 384b). Xenophon (*Memorabilia* 1.6.13) states that "those who sell [wisdom] to anyone for money are called sophists." Aristotle characterizes as a sophist one who conducts arguments for the sake of publicity and financial gain (*Sophistical Refutations* 171b 22–30). They are "just like prostitutes" (ibid. 165a 21).

Finally, since antiquity it has also been standard to link the sophists with Athens—"the very town hall of wisdom in Greece," as Plato's Hippias remarks (*Protagoras* 337d)—and with Athens' democracy. Since "it is clear that Athens . . . in the second half of the fifth century B.C. was the real centre of the sophistic movement," G. B. Kerferd states, "it would seem probable that without Athens the movement would hardly have come into existence at all."[3] In Aristotle's assessment, which has been widely influential, Athens emerged as the center of sophistic philosophy as a consequence both of its rise to imperial power and of its democratic form of government. The Persians' defeat gave the demos confidence, the empire gave them resources, and the expansion of the democracy meant that political success required persuasive skill in the assembly and jury courts.[4] "As resources increased," Aristotle writes, "men had more leisure and acquired a loftier pride in standards of *aretē*; and both before and after the Persian Wars, in which their success had increased their self-confidence, they fastened eagerly upon learning of every kind, pursuing all without distinction" (*Politics* 1341a 28–32). Also contributing to the sophists' rise were the democratic ideologies of egalitarianism and of personal freedom, especially freedom of speech (*parrhēsia* and *isēgoria*). These encouraged philosophical and intellectual speculation, as well as open political discussion. As Reimar Müller remarks, "There can be no doubt that the sophistic movement as such, without the notion of democracy, is unthinkable."[5]

There is much truth in these consensus views of the sophists. The preceding summary also shows how many of these standard opinions began in Plato's dialogues. That Plato and his followers were hostile witnesses may encourage us to raise questions about these figures and test the philosopher's opinions about them in the light of a broader evaluation of the extant data. How new and revolutionary were the sophists? How far did they form a coherent group? How closely were they linked to democracy? And how far have Athenocentric sources colored our perceptions of them? In particular, to what extent did Plato (and perhaps others of his generation) apply more generally a title perhaps used only by one philosopher of the preceding generation, as it were tarring many others with the same brush because of his distaste for contemporary trends in philosophical analysis? How far did Plato focus his hostility on those philosophers who lived close to him in time and whom he had therefore directly to oppose, obscuring their relationship to earlier Greek philosophy and culture? And finally, how far is the perception of the sophists' link to Athens' democracy a consequence of the Athenian origin of most sources about them?

In the following pages I shall argue that "the sophists" represent not so distinct and coherent a movement as Plato and some modern scholars have supposed, and that they continued and emerged out of much older traditions. In fifth-century texts the distinction between sophist and philosopher was not made. Virtually all the various characteristics of their teaching and careers are attested earlier than 450, and not in narrow association with Athens. These characteristics developed not simply as a result of or always in conjunction with democracy—though they certainly flourished under open democratic systems—but also for internal philosophical reasons. Even during the second half of the fifth century, most of those whom we regularly call sophists spent most of their time outside Athens. Philosophical inquiry occurred widely in the Greek world, and found an audience in many places. In the years before 430 some of the sophists proved useful in democratic Athens, and for various reasons were a positive force in the democracy. After 430, intellectual and philosophical developments as well as political and social change lent a darker and more pessimistic color to philosophical analysis. During this period, most sophists in Athens worked outside the sphere of politics.

Philosophy after 450 B.C.

As Kerferd observes, "too much attention has been given in the past to attempts to arrive at general characterisations of the sophists and the sophistic movement."[6] Although some philosophers of this period shared certain traits, there were also significant differences among them.

First, our sense of the term "sophist" can be traced back to the fourth century. It is unclear if sophists other than Protagoras called themselves *sophistai,* or sought to distinguish themselves from the philosophers or theoreticians who came before them. Furthermore, in adopting that title Protagoras was taking for himself a traditional and venerable epithet, "expert in wisdom." Does the name *sophistēs* indicate "revolutionary intent," knowledge with a purpose, to make use of in the community?[7] *Sophos,* "wise man," denotes not a profession but a state of mind, and *-ēs* may well denote an action word. However, as Kerferd shows, the term *sophistēs* is nonetheless an ancient one, for poets and others.[8] Although for simplicity I continue to use it, Plato and others have made the term "sophist"—the "s-word"— inescapably pejorative, and a replacement should probably be found.

Second, the sophists often traveled, teaching by lecture and private seminar and occasionally also by public speech or *epideixis,* as Gorgias did at Olympia (DK 82 B7–8a). However, the fact of travel is surely irrelevant to a philosopher's identification as "sophist." Travel brought wealth and fame. Also, sea travel was comparatively easy, and most sophists came from port towns where, as F. Braudel demonstrates, access to the sea meant access to wide areas of knowledge.[9] Although (for reasons we shall consider) after 450 probably most intellectuals were happy to visit Athens, and although we have at any rate no evidence that the Athenians Damon, Antiphon, Sokrates, and Kritias travelled elsewhere to study or teach, our Athenocentric evidence makes it easy to exaggerate Athens' monopoly on these persons' attention.

Third, the sophists were often paid, though other philosophers of the period were paid as well, such as Parmenides' student Zeno, who received one hundred minai from Kallias (Plato[?], *I Alcibiades* 49a).[10] Furthermore, although his testimony may be biased, Isokrates states that some of "the so-called sophists" lived "in poor, others in moderate circumstances" (15.155). Sokrates, who fits most of the standard characteristics of sophist,[11] did not take pay. Some considered teaching for pay a critical issue because men might be constrained to teach anyone with sufficient money, regardless of personal character (see, e.g., Xenophon,

Memorabilia 1.2.6–8, 6.5, 6.13). The anecdote is apropos that when Isokrates opened his school in Chios and "saw the tuition fees counted out, he burst into tears and said, 'Now I recognize that I have sold myself to these people'" ([Plutarch], *Lives of the Ten Orators* 837b). For this very reason working for pay was often perceived as discreditable in antiquity. However, we need not believe that the sophists themselves felt constrained to teach all comers. As Kerferd suggests, the primary reason for this objection to the sophists is that those whom "the best people" considered unworthy might receive instruction in the techniques of governing.[12]

Fourth, as for the content of their teaching, an interest in rhetoric was common but not universal.[13] Although both Prodikos and Hippias were interested in language and both were capable of producing elaborate speeches, neither is associated with the teaching of rhetoric. Damon worked not in rhetoric but in the equivalent ways of using music. The sophists also worked on quite different topics, and often had quite different philosophical perspectives. Richard Bett has recently argued that at best only Protagoras can properly be called a relativist in "the strong philosophical sense" of that term, that is, in denying the possibility of objective judgment.[14] Many sophists retained a strong interest in the physical world and cosmology. In Aristophanes' *Clouds* (359–60), the Clouds say that they are prepared to listen only to Prodikos "of the current *meteorosophistai* (cosmologic sophists)." Sokrates, we are told, spent his last hour discussing the structure of the earth (Plato, *Phaedo* 108d2–113c8). Hippias and Antiphon both worked in the field of mathematics. Prodikos did specialized work on language, for example on synonyms. Conversely, during this same period Demokritos, who is not normally considered a sophist, wrote works such as *Correct Language and Glosses, On Rhythms and Harmony,* and *On Euphonious and Harsh-Sounding Letters.*

Those called sophists by Plato had perhaps three central points in common. First, all of them appear to have been critical of, or at any rate avoided, transcendental religion and the metaphysical: they focussed primarily on humanity, *to anthrōpinon* in Thucydidean terms. Their refusal to teach these materials in a positive way was new, and perhaps the major reason why Plato found them so offensive. (This was surely one of Plato's primary criteria for labelling sophists, and one reason why for example Demokritos is not so labelled.) This development was a consequence largely of the broader evolution of Greek religion and philosophy. By 450, in the face of numerous competing explanations of metaphysical phenomena and the mounting evidence of comparative religion, it had become clear to many intellectuals that what a person accepted as religion or positive philosophy was only what he had been convinced to believe.[15] Hence, in part, arose the science of rhetoric, the art of convincing others. From a second perspective, reflecting on humanity was of course not new—this had always been a principal topic of Greek poetry—and after 450 B.C., others who are not considered sophists also studied these questions. Demokritos wrote on ethics, in favor of pleasure but with moderation and wisdom (DK 68 B189, 191, 207, 224, 231); he also wrote on law, and in support of democracy (B251, cf. 255). As A. W. H. Adkins remarks, "The atomist Democritus may be broadly classed with the sophists when he is concerned with ethical topics."[16]

Second, the sophists' work often had a technical element. This is reflected in the complaint of Plato's Protagoras that "the other sophists . . . treat their pupils badly. These young men, who have deliberately turned their backs on *technai*, they take and plunge into *technai* again, teaching them arithmetic and astronomy and geometry and music" (*Protagoras* 318d–e). It is noteworthy, however, that at least in Plato Protagoras—the archetypical sophist—pours scorn on this technical orientation. Plato's Sokrates describes Damon's work on poetic meter in sarcastic terms, implying that it was overly technical (*Republic* 399e–400b).

A third basic trait shared by the sophists is that, unlike most earlier philosophers (although probably not the Pythagoreans), they studied different aspects of human culture by means of empirical research.[17] As J. de Romilly writes, since the sophists could accept nothing a priori, "the only sure criterion was immediate concrete human experience."[18] Again, however, this is also a wider phenomenon of the period, visible, for example, in the medical research associated with the Hippocratic authors who made close observation, not abstract reasoning, the basis of their theories.[19]

Sophists before 450

If certain intellectuals after 450 shared a number of principal perspectives, many of the ideas that are associated with these men are also attested in the decades before 450. The inadequate sources for this period, and Plato's resolute separation of "the sophists" from earlier philosophers who were not so immediately his rivals, supply two reasons for the relative neglect of this material. As we have seen, Plato's Protagoras complains that "the other sophists" teach their students "arithmetic and astronomy and geometry and music" (*Protagoras* 318d–e). These of course are also philosophical topics of periods before 450. It is generally agreed that the scepticism often associated with the sophistic movement originated in the early fifth century in the Eleatic school of Parmenides (born ca. 515: Plato, *Parmenides* 127b). For example, Parmenides called cosmology "deceptive," *apatēlos:* the senses could not themselves ascertain reality, but only an image or appearance (28 B8: 52). Gorgias, it is thought, derived his scepticism from Parmenides, then developed it further. The early to mid-fifth century Sicilians Tisias and Korax—if Korax, "Crow," is a historical person—developed the study of rhetoric, for example by means of the *eikos* (probability) argument.[20] Around the year 500 Xenophanes (fr. 2 West) sang that a city gains much less from athletic prowess than from such *sophiē* as "increases its *eunomiē*" and "makes its treasure house fat." Emerging out of an antiaristocratic tradition stressing communal good over individual achievement, this is also the kind of statement we might otherwise attribute to an early sophist, with its emphasis on practical political wisdom and benefit to the polis. Much of what is typically called sophistic thought after 450 developed out of earlier work and was not in itself revolutionary.

As culture figures also, the sophists continued patterns of preceding generations. Experts in wisdom, sometimes expressly called *sophistai,* had long been known in Greece as the principal educators of the community and its political leaders. As Kerferd has demonstrated, the old term *sophistēs* denoted "those who in one way or another function as the sages, the exponents of knowledge in early communities."[21] In calling himself *sophistēs,* Plato's Protagoras expressly states that he is not setting himself off from those who came before him (*Protagoras* 316d–317c). Early on, Greek *sophistai,* "experts in wisdom," were poets whose public role was as educators of the upper classes, privately or in the symposion, and also of the polis, down through Aristophanes and the time when poetry was supplanted by prose as the most serious medium of discourse.[22] As far as the "education" of the polis is concerned, this is not the place to rehearse in detail the impressive evidence for the remarkable phenomenon of popular "high culture" which is clearly attested from the sixth century. The openness and curiosity of the Athenian populace are already visible in the sixth-century dramatic festivals, where year by year farmers and craftsmen confronted the hardest issues facing the polis. The evidence steadily increases that from this period the demos was increasingly open to what had been elite culture, including education and intellectual innovation.[23] As Marcel Detienne points out, the relativity of truth emerged for example in debates on the meanings of oracles during the Persian War period; relativity rather than a quest for the absolute was implicit in the assembly formula *edoxe tōi dēmōi,* "it seemed best to the people." Antilogies were the norm in Greek assemblies and courtroom *agōnes.*[24] Jean-Pierre Vernant has traced the origins of Greek philosophy itself to the public debates, over elections and other community decisions, that were characteristic of Greek poleis from the seventh century onward. Was this a product of the emergence of democracy during the sixth century? Or rather, was democracy itself—self-government by the demos—a further example of these same attitudes?[25] It is important to note that in their poetry these earlier poets were not only giving political advice: indeed, Greek cultural history of the fifth and fourth centuries generally is marked by a progressive degree of specialization, which was uncharacteristic of earlier periods.[26] But political education was one of the poets' prime functions. Among elites, poets such as Theognis and Solon addressed young men such as Kyrnos (certainly not a *pais*) to transform them into *kaloikagathoi* and leaders of their communities.

These poets often travelled—Pindar, Simonides, Bakchylides, and also Aeschylus (to Sicily), and they were well paid for their work.[27] Like Solon, Theognis, Pindar, and the Attic dramatists, they often gave direct political advice to the community. This role is reflected in a series of musical legends. Thus, for example, according to the early-fifth-century Athenian poet Pratinas, Thaletas saved Sparta from a plague by means of his music ([Plutarch], *De musica* 1146b). Terpander, we are told, by his songs "established *homonoia* among the Spartans" (Aristides, *Or.* 46.189 = II p.253.4ff. Dindorf = Gostoli T20). When during the fifth century prose and logical analysis replaced poetry and poetic inspiration as the fundamental means of thought and communication,[28] poets were replaced by—or, in essence, I believe, grew into—the persons we call sophists, and the central importance of poetry faded. In their performances to the demos in oratorical displays, and also privately in teaching wisdom to the community's elite, the sophists directly continued the tradition of earlier poets, as among other points Gorgias' poetical style of rhetoric indicates. We mostly view the sophists through the eyes of Plato, as something new and evil. But those who called themselves sophists wished to associate themselves with an older typology, experts in wisdom as Solon and others had been. The issue of pay arose in the later fifth century only because for the first time nonnobles were prominent in politics, and conservatives such as Plato and Aristotle felt that teaching the art of politics to such men was improper.

For the elite, the figure of community and symposion poet was joined with a second typology, of the wise counsellor to political leaders. According to Herodotus (8.57–58), Mnesiphilos of Phrearrhioi suggested to Themistokles the strategy at Salamis. Plutarch says of Mnesiphilos that "he was not a *rhētor* nor a physical scientist, but a cultivator of what was then called *sophia*, although it was only political cleverness and practical sagacity" (*Themistokles* 2.6). In Xenophon (*Memorabilia* 4.2.2) someone asks Sokrates, "was it by constant association with some wise man or by natural ability that Themistokles stood out among his fellow-citizens" as a leader? Sokrates replies that it would be absurd to suppose that leadership could arise of its own accord. Leaders require practical advice from competent *didaskaloi*. It is not so important whether these specific reports are historically accurate. Rather, they are based on and indicate an early type, fulfilling one role that the sophists had later. Hence, as a cultural and educational phenomenon the sophists were not new.

Support for this reconstruction is provided by various ancient sources. Explicit statements regarding early sophists are of uncertain value, both because their historical reliability is questionable and because their sense of the word "sophist" is unknown. For example, in *Meno* 91e Plato's Sokrates tells Anytos that there were many other sophists besides Protagoras, "some before his time and some still alive." According to [Plutarch] (*Lives of the Ten Orators* 832c), Antiphon, born around 480, was a pupil of his father Sophilos, here also called a sophist. When Herodotus (1.29) says that at the time of Kroisos, all the *sophistai* of Greece including Solon came to Sardis, now at its height because of Kroisos' great fortune, his intended meaning of the word is uncertain.

With several other individuals, however, we are on safer ground. Thus in both ideas and career it has long been suggested that Simonides "anticipated" the sophists. Born in 556 on Keos near Attika, he led a wandering life, travelling to Athens under Hipparchos, though he left when the tyranny fell. He again lived in Athens during the Persian Wars, and was associated with the politician Themistokles, possibly even attacking one of Themistokles' enemies in his poetry. Although Simonides was also capable of quite traditional work (as in the new Plataea elegy),[29] Lesky observes that "the prominence of the human element in his choral poetry is one of the features [that look forward to the sophistic movement]. In the scolion for Skopas and the protest against Kleoboulos we detect a penchant towards a critical approach which sets up the results of individual reasoning against traditional ideas." Detienne points out that Simonides can set up *doxa* (appearance) in opposition to the *alētheia* (truth) of the poets.[30] According to an anecdote in Cicero (*De natura deorum* 1.60), when questioned by Hiero about the nature of the gods, "he asked for longer and longer periods to consider his answer; at last he said that the question became the more obscure the more he thought about it." This of course resembles the opening sentence of Protagoras' *On the Gods* (DK 80 B4). Lesky states, "In his scheme of values, so far as we know it, [Simonides] expressed a realistic sense of the immediate actuality of life . . . His powers of memory were renowned, and he is said to have devised a system of training the memory—a faculty on which Hippias of Elis so prided himself."[31] Simonides is also said to have been interested in orthography and, notoriously, in money.[32] A dictum indicates reflection on the relationship between the different arts: poetry is spoken painting, painting is silent poetry (Plutarch, *Glory of the Athenians* 3). We may compare Gorgias, that poetry is speech in meter (DK 82 B11.9).

A second set of examples concerns music research in the early fifth century, for which Athens seems to have been a center. The first of these music researchers was Lasos of Hermione, a complex and remarkable figure. Born in the 540s, he came to Athens under the tyranny (most famously, Herodotus 7.6 says he caught Onomakritos inserting a prophesy into the oracles of Musaios), but stayed on under the post-Kleisthenic democracy. According to the *Suda* (*s.v.*), he introduced the annual dithyrambic contests, dated 509 or 508 by the *Marmor Parium*. He wrote hymns and dithyrambs in a new style. According to [Plutarch] (*De musica* 1141c), "by altering the rhythms of the movement of the dithyramb and by pursuing the example of the multiplicity of notes of the *auloi* and so making use of more notes, widely scattered about, he transformed the music that existed before him." According to Aristotle, when asked what was the most important thing, Lasos said "experience" (*Chreiai* fr.1 Rose). Hence we find in Lasos innovations in instrumentation and musical experimentation, which he presumably carried out also in public performances. He was empirical, and a theoretician. According to Aristoxenos (*Elements of Harmonics* 1.3), he argued that a note had breadth. He may have invented the musical *harmonia,* a word not attested in its technical musical sense before him, replacing the older musical *nomos.* He experimented with sounds, filling vessels with different amounts of liquid and striking them like a glass harmonica (Theon of Smyrna 59.4–21). The *Suda* says he was the first to write a book about music. Most famously he avoided the letter *s,* on the grounds of euphony (Athenaeus 455b–d). He was profoundly different from the Pythagoreans, in that he showed no interest in the cosmic or abstract qualities of music.

According to Plato (?) (*I Alcibiades* 118c) and possibly Aristotle (cf. Plutarch, *Perikles* 4), Perikles' two music teachers were Damon and the Athenian Pythokleides. Although the scholiast on *I Alcibiades* 118c calls Pythokleides a *didaskalos* of *semnē mousikē* (solemn music), he was no mere *kitharistēs,* and Perikles no mere schoolboy. The same scholiast calls Pythokleides a Pythagorean. According to [Plutarch] (*De musica* 1136d), he invented the Mixolydian type of *harmonia,* itself a genre possibly invented by Lasos as I have noted. In my book on Damon I shall set out the evidence that Pythokleides was a figure of the earlier fifth century. Pythokleides was a music theoretician and a teacher of one young member of Athens' wealthy elite. Again, therefore, theoretician-teachers of young adults were not altogether new after 450.

The last of Athens' early musical theoreticians is Lamprokles, identified by Aristophanes (*Clouds* 967) and his scholiast as a figure of the Marathonian period. According to the passage of the *De musica* just quoted, "Lamprokles the Athenian, realizing that the disjunction in this *harmonia* is not where almost everyone supposed it to be, but at the top of its range, gave it the form of the series from *paramesē* to *hypatē hypatōn*" (two notes on the Greek enharmonic scale).

What consequences does this material have for our conception of the sophists in democratic Athens? As I have indicated, it is the standard view that starting with Protagoras around 450, the sophists were a revolutionary phenomenon, linked with the empire and the democracy. It now appears that this consensus view should be modified. Intellectuals had been coming to Athens at least since the time of the Peisistratids, to serve as wise counsellors and advisers to political leaders such as Hipparchos, Themistokles, and the young Perikles. The work of these figures included analyses of music that parallel the research of the sophists Hippias in music and Prodikos in language during the later fifth century. In addition, although we associate the later fifth-century sophists with Athens and certainly these sophists did come to Athens, like the Archaic poets they were in fact a panhellenic phenomenon. It is notorious that none of the "major" sophists —only Damon of Oa, Antiphon of Rhamnous, Kritias, and Sokrates—were Athenians. In Plato Protagoras is represented as having recently arrived in Athens from abroad (*Protagoras* 309d3), and reference is made to a previous visit to Athens a few years earlier (310e5). Where had he been in the meantime? When not in Athens, these travelling wisdom experts must have been plying their trade and performing elsewhere in the Greek world, as Pindar and Bakchylides had done. Born ca. 480, Gorgias first came to Athens in 427 when he was over fifty. Isokrates (15.155) mentions that "he spent his time in Thessaly" and made his money there. Where, also, had these philosophers learned their stuff? Protagoras came from Abdera, Gorgias from Leontinoi, Prodikos from the island of Keos, Hippias from Elis, Thrasymachos from Chalkedon in Bithynia, and the brothers Euthydemos and Dionysodoros from Chios, all as adults. So far as I have determined, no one has investigated in detail the implications of these remarkable data, that those philosophical developments that we call the sophistic movement not only began much earlier than 450 but were widespread in the Greek world. Just as other aspects of culture were not limited to Athens but are visible—if no longer so conspicuous—elsewhere in Greece,[33] so too highly sophisticated intellectual work, including philosophy, was pervasive among elite groups in Greece, and in cities that were not democratic.[34] In Plato's *Hippias maior* (282d–e) Hippias claims, "If you knew how much money I have made, you would be amazed. I won't mention the rest, but once, when I went to Sicily, although Protagoras was staying there and had a great reputation and was the older, I, who was much younger, made in a very short time more than one hundred and fifty minas [two and a half talents!], and in one small place, Inykon [location unknown!], more than twenty minas." Whether this testimonial is entirely serious is uncertain. The phenomenon itself, although almost completely obscured by our Athenocentric sources, cannot be doubted.

Sophists in Athens, after 450

Just as *sophistai* are said to have gone to Sardis in the 550s and Aeschylus and Pindar had visited the palaces of wealthy rulers, so after 450 philosophers came to Athens at least partly because of the riches that poured into that city as a consequence of the empire. They found a city profoundly stimulated by its newfound power and influence, and remarkably open to what they had to say. Democratic Athens did not create the sophistic movement, but certainly welcomed it, elite and demos alike. For the elite, of course, the uses of rhetorical training in the democracy were of considerable interest. But ordinary citizens also were excited by these figures, as, most famously, the reception they accorded Gorgias indicates (Diodorus Siculus 12.53.3). The Athenians generally were conscious of the opportunities now opening to master all kinds of technical and scientific problems. In *Antigone,* Sophokles' Chorus sang to them that man possesses skills (*technai*) exceeding all expectation, *huper elpid'* (362). In Thucydides (1.71.3) the Corinthians state that in politics as in any other *technē* the new must drive out the old. Bernard Knox ably demonstrated from Sophokles' *Oedipus Tyrannus* that intelligence was a quality prized above all by the Athenians.[35] *Philosophoumen aneu malakias,* Thucydides' Perikles told the gathered demos (2.40.1): "we are lovers of wisdom without loss of manliness." As Thucydides' Kleon remarks (3.38.5), "simply overcome by the pleasure of listening," the Athenians in assembly "are like an audience sitting at the feet of sophists."

It is commonly said that there were two periods or two generations of sophists. I agree, but I propose to modify the standard view of this. In the early period, down to about 430, the sophists were actively involved with the democracy, and on the whole they were a benevolent force, working for the good of society. Two main reasons for this were that Athens' upper-class leaders, who traditionally had such advisers, were not yet alienated from the democracy, and that these years were a period largely free of disillusionment, and marked by optimism. After 430, by contrast, the sophists were less involved with Athenian politics, and they were a more negative intellectual force in the democracy. Three main reasons for this are that the traditional elite (the sophists' clientele) was now largely alienated from politics; the war and the plague had put enormous strain on the citizen body; and third—no less important—various philosophical positions associated with the early sophists perhaps inevitably developed over time into more extreme and even offensive formulations, as philosophers sought fame (or notoriety) by ever bolder intellectual innovations. We may compare the history of contemporary painting and photography.

Of the early group of sophists, Protagoras both defended democracy and seems generally to have wished to improve people's lives, to "make men good citizens" (Plato, *Protagoras* 319a). In one of antiquity's few theoretical justifications of democracy (in *Protagoras* 323–25), Plato's Protagoras states that since to some degree all men share political wisdom, respect for others, moderation, and a sense of justice, all therefore should have a voice in polis government. And if (as he thought) each person must determine for himself what is real (DK 80 A1), this puts a premium on every person's judgment and hence supports democracy and egalitarianism.[36] Protagoras aimed, it appears, to form a governing class capable of directing an egalitarian democracy by means of rhetoric, thus enabling politicians to dominate the city through intelligence. In *Theaetetus* (166d) Plato's Sokrates explains Protagoras' concept of relativism and remarks, "by a *sophos* he means a man who can change any one of us, when what is bad appears and is to him, and make what is good appear and be to him." If a sick man says that his food tastes bitter, it is no good trying to convince him otherwise. What is needed is to make the sick man healthy. A little later (in *Theaetetus* 167a) Sokrates has Protagoras remark that the sophists make all people better by *logoi*. Their aim is not just to help the leaders. Again in Plato (*Protagoras* 316c, 318a) Protagoras says that his conversation will improve his students every day. The picture from these testimonies is of a positive-thinking, democratically oriented, basically cheerful theoretician who sought to improve community life.

A second figure of Athens' earlier sophistic period was Damon, born about 500 and active probably till the end of the century. Damon combined the elements of wise political counsellor, a concern for shaping the polis, and a traditional Athenian interest in music theory. As political adviser, Damon counselled Perikles to introduce jury pay in the 460s, formulating the slogan "to give the people their own" (Aristotle, *Constitution of the Athenians* 27.4). Both provision and slogan are democratic. Although Damon was later ostracized, according to Polykrates in 392 he was not voted out for "trying to destroy the demos" (see Libanius, *Declamation* 1.157), the traditional justification for ostracism. As was typical of the sophists, some of Damon's research was purely scientific. Thus he first named, described, and categorized the different *harmoniai,* quite possibly creating the categories of hyper and hypo (as in hyper-Phrygian). He did the same with poetic meter (Plato, *Republic* 399–400). Beyond this technical work, a principal focus of his research concerned the social and political consequences of music, through what came to be called the ethos theory. He studied the effects of different types of music on individual behavior and character. Perikles' interest in this research, presumably in order to influence the demos in ways similar to the contemporary science of rhetoric, may well have led to Damon's ostracism. It appears that Gorgias's theories on the psychological consequences of language (which he called a drug: DK 82 B11.14) were based on Damon's earlier musical research. The same is true of observations regarding the consequences for human character of geography and climate in the Hippocratic *Airs Waters Places* (see, e.g., 12, 16, 23).

A third case of positive-minded, egalitarian applied research in Athens before 430 is more controversial. However, our results so far may help solve the well-known problem of "one or two Antiphons," sophist and rhetor. The sophist Antiphon is often regarded as "having preached a thorough-going left-wing egalitarianism"[37] by stressing that there is no natural distinction between Greek and barbarian, or between well born and low born (DK 80 B44b, from *Truth*). "We give reverence and respect to the children of noble fathers: we neither revere nor respect the offspring of a humble house. In this we have barbarised ourselves." The historical difficulty with this conception of Antiphon is that by 411 *an* Antiphon, an able speechwriter, is known as a passionate conservative and oligarch (Thuc. 8.68.1). Furthermore, in *On Concord* (DK 87 B61) Antiphon *the sophist* writes, "There is nothing worse for men than lack of rule. With this in mind men of old accustomed children to being ruled and to do what they are told so that when they became men they should not become confused in a great change." This passage seems to echo the conservative Athenian political view that Athens needed to return to a form of government based on the model of an old-fashioned, paternalist household, the *patrios politeia* or *patrios dioikēsis,* which is first attested in politics in 411, just when Antiphon the rhetor became most prominent (Aristotle, *Constitution of the Athenians* 29.3).[38] To be sure, as H. D. Rankin points out, B44b could reflect not so much democratic sentiment as Antiphon's awareness of "the deficiencies of the traditional aristocracy, with whom, after all, as an oligarch and politician he has to do business day by day."[39] It should also be noted that elsewhere in *Truth* Antiphon argues that because laws do not accord with nature, it is in a person's best interest to ignore them when he can get away with it: a position rather similar to those of the extremists and pessimists, Kallikles in Plato's *Gorgias* and Thrasymachos in the *Republic* (see below). Although there are many reasons to identify the two Antiphons, their apparently contrasting politics have been the principal reason for distinguishing them.[40] If, however, the sophistic movement underwent a general shift from positive-democratic to negative, pessimistic, and antidemocratic after 430, a change in Antiphon's orientation might be explained.

A second, striking testimonial about Antiphon should also be noted. According to [Plutarch] (*Lives of the Ten Orators* 833c–d), before he turned to speech writing Antiphon "invented a method of curing distress, just as physicians have a treatment for those who are ill. At Corinth, fitting up a room near the marketplace, he wrote on the door that he could cure by words those who were in distress; and by asking questions and finding out the causes of their condition he consoled those in trouble." Admittedly, the source for this early effort at psychiatry is late and of uncertain value. However, a number of scholars have shown how well this report parallels other elements of sophistic research.[41] Just as Damon by music and Gorgias by rhetoric—as if by "a drug"—sought to affect emotions and character, so Antiphon may have attempted to help people through personal interrogations. Plato's Protagoras remarks (*Theaetetus* 167a), "in education a change has to be effected from the worse condition to the better; only, whereas the physician produces a change by means of drugs, the sophist does it by *logoi*." For other examples of applied theorizing in a positive and constructive way during this period, Hippodamos redesigned the Piraeus and Protagoras may have composed a law code for Thurioi. The positive and optimistic spirit of intellectual work during this period shines through in a contemporary dedication: "It is a noble thing for wise men to be wise (*sophizesthai*) through *technē*, for he who possesses *technē* will have a better life" (*IG* I^3 766).

The democratic leader Perikles himself constitutes the primary example of the association of elite politicians with sophistic research before 430. Kerferd has assigned particular responsibility to Perikles for promoting the sophistic movement, linking that statesman with Damon, Anaxagoras, Zeno, Herodotus, Pheidias, and Sophokles.[42] According to Plutarch (*Perikles* 36.2), philosophical meetings were held at Perikles' house. Also, the mother of Kallias son of Hipponikos, who (we are told) spent more on sophists than all other Athenians put together, had been Perikles' first wife. Philip Stadter has challenged this picture, in part with good reason. Pheidias was not a sophist or intellectual; too much has been made of the story that Perikles discussed with Protagoras a legal case involving a javelin (a legal topos, as Stadter points out); also, the state of Perikles' relations with Sophokles was certainly questionable.[43]

On the other hand, we cannot doubt Perikles' close intellectual associations with Damon, Pythokleides, and Anaxagoras. These are attested by a number of good fifth- and fourth-century sources.[44] In addition, the most pronounced characteristic of Perikles that emerges from Thucydides' portrait is his confidence in intelligence.

Perikles' interest in philosophy was apparently both intellectual and practical. In *Phaedrus* (269e–270a), in an argument that success in any field requires innate capacity, knowledge, and practice, Plato's Sokrates claims that Perikles acquired from Anaxagoras the mental elevation and finished execution needed for success in rhetoric. "By enriching himself with high speculation and coming to recognize the nature of wisdom and thought—on which topics of course Anaxagoras was always discoursing—Perikles drew from that source and applied to the art of rhetoric what was advantageous to it." Thucydides said that Perikles was *legein te kai prassein dunatōtatos* (1.139.4), "most skilled at both speaking and taking action," which again emphasizes the practical. Anaxagoras was probably in Athens between 480 and 450, rather than later.[45] Hence, Perikles' association with him should be dated to the period before Protagoras.

This combination of abstract thought and practical utility is also apparent in Perikles' association with Damon. As I have indicated, Damon's major interest was the effect of different rhythms and *harmoniai* on human character, emotion, and action. Perikles' interest in the social and political utility of music is suggested by his construction of a public music hall, the Odeion, probably in 446, his reorganization of the musical aspects of the Panathenaic festival, and his personal selection of the musicians for the initial competition (Plutarch, *Perikles* 13). Olympiodoros remarks that "there are songs that harmonize the citizens, songs which Perikles learned from Damon and through which Perikles harmonized the city" (*In Plat. Alcibiad. comm.* 138.4–11). Although it is most uncertain what Olympiodoros actually knew (and his statement is in any case highly idealizing), his words would nonetheless reflect an important aspect of Perikles' interest in applied theoretical research.

Beginning with Thucydides (2.65) it is standard to see a sharp transition in Athenian politics after the Periklean period, to a new age of demagogues, "living off the law courts and the assemblies" (Isokrates 8.130).[46] Although many of the characteristics of politics during this period developed out of Periklean antecedents, no longer were age, military ability, or blue-blooded lineage required for political success. The primary necessity was rhetorical skill. It is therefore paradoxical that the post-Periklean years were marked by a reaction against the sophists and against intellectual activity, especially on the part of democratic politicians. Although the sources for this development are almost all hostile to these politicians, their combined testimony is nonetheless impressive.

The best known of these "new politicians" is Kleon. Kleon's father had been *chorēgos* in 460/59 and hence his family was wealthy, but it was not noble. Kleon's anti-intellectualism is portrayed especially by Thucydides. In 3.37 Kleon argues that ignorance combined with *sōphrosynē* (moderation) is more beneficial than adroitness combined with license, and that men who are "baser" (*phauloteroi*) are generally more successful at governing cities than the more intelligent. The latter wish to appear wiser than the law and to get the best of it in the assembly, by fine displays of intelligence. This, he says, causes cities disaster. By contrast, those who distrust their own intelligence and consider themselves more ignorant than the laws and less capable of finding fault with those who speak well, but are judges on equal terms rather than competitors—such men, he states, for the most part prosper.

A similar attitude is reflected in Aristophanes, against Kleon and, even more strikingly, against the *Knights*' other politician the "Sausage Seller." In *Knights* (188–92), when told that he will be the greatest man in the city, the Sausage Seller replies, "But my good man, I don't know anything about *mousikē*, except the alphabet, and that just barely." The response to this is: "That is your only drawback, that you know it, even 'just barely.' The *dēmagōgia* is no longer for a cultured or well-behaved man, but for the ignorant and the obnoxious."

A similar attitude is attested for another democratic politician, Anytos. Plato (*Meno* 90a) describes Anytos' father as a self-made man: he left his son a tannery and a shoemaker's business. When with typical irony Sokrates defends the sophists, Anytos remarks that people must be mad to pay money to sophists or let their children study with them—cities should not even let them in! "I've never in my life had anything to do with a single one of them, nor would I hear of any of my family doing so" (*Meno* 92a–b). According to Xenophon (*Apology* 29–32), Sokrates publicly berated Anytos for bringing up his son in the tannery trade. "At one time I had a brief association with the son of Anytos, and I thought him not lacking in firmness of soul; and so I predict that he will not continue in the servile occupation that his father has provided for him. Rather, through want of a worthy adviser (*spoudaios epimeletēs*) he will fall into some disgraceful propensity and will surely go far in the career of vice."

Except for the ambiguous Alkibiades (see n.50 below), among democratic politicians only one or two minor or doubtful exceptions to this phenomenon of anti-intellectualism are attested. Euathlos is said to have been a pupil of Protagoras (and later was involved in litigation with him over his fee: Diogenes Laërtius 9.56). Secondly, according to a joke in Aristophanes (*Clouds* 876), Sokrates received a talent for teaching Hyperbolos to speak. As Robert Connor points out, democratic politicians are not included in the groups gathered to hear the sophists in Plato's dialogues, and Old Comedy almost never attacks democratic politicians for their intellectual activities.[47] Although a more conservative democratic politician, Nikias shared this lack of interest in intellectual matters.

By contrast, after 430 the elite upper classes retained their interest in intellectual matters, as appears in the scenes in Plato's dialogues, but increasingly withdrew from politics.[48] In [Plato] (*Axiochus* 368d–369b) Axiochos remarks,

"I've had enough of the public platform." In Xenophon (*Memorabilia* 3.7.1–2) Sokrates says that Charmides is quite capable of serving in politics but is unwilling to do so. Ian Morris mentions the reappearance of private memorials from around 430, which may reflect the phenomenon of upper-class withdrawal from the public community.[49] Why did this occur? In *Knights* and also in Thucydides' Mytilenian debate, the conclusion drawn is that only a hyper-Kleon (such as the Sausage Seller) can defeat Kleon.[50] Euripides' Ion remarks, "If I make an effort to be in the first rank of the city and to be somebody, we'll be hated by those of no ability. For superiority always rankles. But the upper classes (*chrēstoi*) and those who are capable of being *sophoi*, who keep quiet and do not hasten into public life, will treat me as a laughing stock and a fool if I don't mind my own business in a city filled with fear" (*Ion* 595–601, dated between 412 and 408). In 428, Euripides' Hippolytos remarks (*Hippolytus* 986–89):

> I am unpolished in speaking to the mob (*ochlos*),
> although among my age-group and among the *oligoi* I am rather *sophos*.
> That is as it should be. Those who are base (*phauloi*)
> among the *sophoi* are rather *mousikoi* in speaking before the mob (*ochlos*).

How do we explain the rejection of intellectual activity by democratic politicians? One reason is surely related to their lower social and economic status. In the later fifth century Eupolis remarked (*Demes* fr. 117): "Once upon a time our city's generals came from the best families, first by wealth and first by birth. We used to pray to them as if they were gods—and so they were, and we prospered. But now we go on campaign at random, electing as our generals—garbage."[51] These men were not a part of the sophisticated world in which the sophists moved, and they had limited experience with the educational resources of the elite classes: symposia, *hetaireiai,* and wise counsellors. On the contrary, they were suspicious of these, as undemocratic. According to Plutarch (*Moralia* 806f), Kleon deliberately rejected his *philoi.*

At the same time, we must ask why their scorn of intellectual matters was successful with the demos. The attacks against ignorant "new politicians" in Old Comedy presuppose that the demos did not generally regard a good education as problematic. According to its third *Hypothesis,* Aristophanes' *Frogs* was restaged because of the wisdom of its *parabasis,* which lamented Athens' neglect of its "better" citizens, "modest (*sōphronas*), nobly born (*eugeneis*), just and gentlemanly (*kalous kagathous*), educated well on the wrestling ground and in dancing and music" (*Frogs* 727–30). We have noted the marked intellectual excitement of the demos' reaction to Gorgias, and (that very same year) Thucydides' Kleon's description of the people in assembly as "slaves of the ever unheard-of, and despisers of the familiar" (3.38.5).

Athens' new politicians succeeded in discrediting the sophists, I believe, primarily because sophistic philosophy had become more extreme after 430, and also less sympathetic to the interests of the democracy. From the 420s onward, increasing popular scorn is attested against philosophers for their *adoleschia* (idle prattling) and *leptologia* (subtle quibbling) and their immoral rhetoric. In *Clouds* 359, of 423, Sokrates is called "high priest of the most hair-splitting twaddle." A fragment of Aristophanes (506 Kassel-Austin) states, "a book has ruined this man, or Prodikos has, or at any rate one of the idle prattlers [*adoleschoi*]."[52] Isokrates (11 [*Busiris*] 48–49) says that philosophy is hated because its practitioners defend shameful causes. Kallikles in Plato's *Gorgias* (482cff.) defends the use of power for private ends, as does Thrasymachos in book one of the *Republic*. Plato's Kallikles states, "nature itself proclaims the fact that it is just for the better man to have the advantage over the worse, and the stronger over the weaker" (*Gorgias* 483d). In the *Republic* (338c), Thrasymachos also defends the proposition that justice is the interest of the stronger. Although the dramatic dates of Plato's dialogues are sometimes unreliable, the *Republic* is possibly set ca. 420.[53] Kallikles' dates are unknown and Plato's evidence for the dramatic date of the *Gorgias* is contradictory, but the setting of that dialogue must in any case belong to the post-430 period: Gorgias himself first visited Athens in 427. Also symptomatic of these developments is the debased moral tone of Thucydides' fictional Melian Dialogue of 416 (5.85–111). The Melians argue for their lives on the basis of justice, the gods, blood relations, and the power of shame. The Athenians counter with expediency, self-interest, and superior power. "The strong do what they can, and the weak suffer what they must" (5.89).

The explanation for this negative intellectual development may partly lie in an intellectual momentum within the sophistic movement itself, as newer philosophers had to carve out ever more extreme positions for themselves, which simultaneously attracted members of the embittered and increasingly antidemocratic elite, such as Kritias and the Old Oligarch. Thucydides' political cynicism and hostility to democracy are another example of this. Many philosophers withdrew from politics and civic activity. After returning from his ostracism in the late 430s, Damon continued research and teaching, but there is no evidence for any further association with politics.

The negativism of newer sophistic theorizing, and the increasing aversion to democracy by Athens' elite, culminated in what Forrest calls "the bloody lunacy of 411," the oligarchic revolution shaped in part by political theorizing.[54] Intellectuals had ceased to operate in public and retreated into now politicized *hetai-*

reiai. Out of power, Athens' elite turned first to fantasies, and then to the reality, of polis revolution. Hence, so far from fostering the democracy, the later sophists were in opposition to it. From the intellectual's perspective, the culmination of this destructive alliance between sophists and antidemocratic members of the upper classes was the ban on the teaching of rhetoric which the elite—Athens' Thirty tyrants—imposed in 404 (Xenophon, *Memorabilia* 1.2.31).

Conclusion

Three standard conceptions of the sophists, that they were closely linked with Athens and democracy, that they were a new intellectual and social phenomenon, and that they were a coherent philosophical movement, are thus seen to be in some measure distortions shaped by the limitations of extant evidence. This evidence is chiefly Athenian, mostly from periods after 450 B.C., and it is largely focussed on certain controversial aspects especially of the later sophists' work in ethics and rhetoric. Plato grew up in this later sophistic climate, and fought against it with all the skill of his formidable intellect. He himself was not concerned with the historical antecedents to these developments, or with aspects of the sophists' work that he did not immediately need to oppose. It is clear how persuasive and also how misleading he has been in regard to these figures. Aelius Aristeides wrote, "Plato seems somehow to be always reviling the term 'sophist,' he seems the one who has especially attacked that term. The reason for this is his contempt for the masses and for those of his profession" (*Or*. 3.681 = *Or*. 46 [II 407 Dindorf]).

In this chapter I have endeavored to fit the sophists more broadly into three historical contexts: the wider Greek world before 450, Athens after 450, and Athens after 430. I have argued that those philosophers who came after 450 should not be so sharply distinguished from philosophers (and poets) who came before and that, by contrast, from 430 marked new trends appear, as a result of both political and intellectual developments. Before 430, the sophists were a positive force for Athens' democracy. Afterward, they helped to destroy it.

CHAPTER TEN

The Constraints of Democracy and the Rise of the Art of Rhetoric

HARVEY YUNIS

The most important recent scholarship on Greek rhetoric has focused on the role of theory as the essential component in rhetorical art. The insights that have accrued, outlined in section 1 of the chapter, fundamentally alter the traditional view of rhetoric in fifth-century Athens. But the emphasis on theory inevitably provokes another look at practice, which is the purpose of the rest of this chapter. In section 2 I will reexamine the view that prior to the articulation of rhetoric as a coherent discipline, the political conditions of Athenian democracy stimulated both rhetorical practice and the development of the discipline. In section 3 I will argue that literary innovations in formal modes of argument around the end of the fifth century helped transform practical political rhetoric into fully self-conscious, theoretically based rhetorical art. Thucydides is the key figure; in his work rhetoric began to attain an independent, disciplinary identity by distancing itself from Athenian democracy.

The Fifth Century: No Rhetorical Theory and No Discipline of Rhetoric

To consider fifth-century rhetoric is to peer into the darkness before the dawn. With a dazzling suddenness, rhetoric achieved its first prime in fourth-century Greece; there for the first time one encounters both an abundance of rhetorical masterpieces and original works of rhetorical theory. Born in the fifth century, Isokrates produced his large corpus of polished speeches in the fourth and solidified the young tradition of written artistic prose. The fourth-century Athenian orators were engaged legal and political advocates; by the end of the century, their preserved speeches were being transformed into literary models for education and scholarship throughout the Hellenistic world. About one quarter into the fourth century, Plato outlined in the *Phaedrus* for the first time what a systematic theory of rhetoric might look like; by the beginning of the last quarter of the century, Aristotle had completed his *Rhetoric,* the first and still the most challenging systematic work of rhetorical theory. The fourth century also produced the *Rhetoric to Alexander,* of unknown authorship but plausibly attributed to Anaximenes of Lampsakos. This work, which contains practical advice for constructing effective speeches, is the only document to survive classical Greece that warrants the designation of rhetorical handbook.[1]

From the fourth century on, one can, without great difficulty and largely on the basis of primary sources, survey the long development of rhetoric into a complex, systematic discipline embracing theory and practice. Already by the time of Aristotle's student Theophrastus, rhetoric was a field in which there existed recognized experts and formal disciplinary studies. The two monumental rhetorical works of classical Rome, Cicero's *De oratore* and Quintilian's *Institutio oratoria,* reveal a discipline so highly evolved that mastering just the basics required extensive study. In the course of time ancient rhetoric divided itself into subdisciplines concerning argument, arrangement, narration, style (itself further divided into diction, tropes, figures of thought, figures of speech), memory, and delivery, to name only the most important ones. To maintain its status as a discipline, rhetoric acquired schools, teachers, and students, treatises, handbooks, and models. It established connections with and divisions from other disciplines and activities, including law, politics, imperial bureaucracy, religion, philosophy, psychology, education, drama, literature, composition, and the graphic and plastic arts. Throughout the development of rhetoric, theory and practice were joint endeavors and mutually reinforcing.[2]

As a mature discipline, rhetoric is a purely formal art. It assumes as its generating principle that communication contains two distinct parts, the message and the medium through which the message is conveyed. The medium is entirely neutral with regard to the content of the message, but it greatly affects how the message is received. The latter fact supplies the art of rhetoric with its task and its domain: to manipulate the resources of language—spoken, written, gestural—in order to convey a particular message to a particular audience as effectively as possible. Rhetoric is thus not a fine art, like music or painting, but aims at utility: the art of the art of rhetoric concerns the manipulation of linguistic resources and the use of the art of rhetoric emerges whenever it matters that some message, regardless of its truth, beauty, or advantage, be presented to a particular audience as forcefully as possible. Thus neither the art nor the use is peculiar to democracy or to any other political system; and politics in general, though it offers a highly charged setting, does not begin to exhaust the occasions for which rhetoric is appropriate. Historically rhetoric has been developed and utilized as much for religious and literary purposes as for political ones.[3]

One need not be a rhetorician to manipulate basic features of language as these affect communication. All of us, not least children, daily shape our discourse to ensure that our messages are received by our interlocutors as we wish them to be. Literary characters created by acknowledged artists impress with their eloquence; consider Homer's Achilles or Euripides' Hecuba. Such instances provide the student of rhetoric with material for study; none presupposes a developed discipline of rhetoric, which should be distinguished from both natural eloquence and poetic artistry. Rhetoric turns the natural talent for or poetic uses of linguistic manipulation into a systematic, consciously deployed discipline aiming specifically at persuasion, so that, for example, a complex message ("we are right to pursue democracy, because it is the most equitable and most effective form of government"), an unendurable message ("we have been all but destroyed, but we must go on and fight, even though defeat is inevitable"), or one that nonbelievers might find improbable ("God sacrificed his only Son so that we may have eternal life") has a good chance of being accepted precisely when it matters that it be accepted. Rhetoric supplies by systematic, rational means, and therefore puts in our power that eloquence which the gods supply according to their whim.[4]

The historian of rhetoric encounters none of these disciplinary assumptions, institutions, and habits in fifth-century Athens. In place of the familiar prose rhetorical genres of the fourth and later centuries, the fifth century reveals innovation and experimentation in various genres of prose and verse. In place of disciplinary coherence and identity, the fifth century produced a diversity of approaches to language, speech, and persuasion. Even the Greek word *rhētorikē,* the original word for rhetoric, occurs for the first time in the extant literature in Plato's *Gorgias,* a work of the early fourth century. Now a good deal of the earlier literature in which the word *rhētorikē* might have occurred has not survived; and the way Socrates first mentions "what is called *rhētorikē*" suggests some currency (448D). Yet *rhētorikē* is properly an adjective of a type common in Plato and rare before the fourth century. Grammatically, it implies the noun *technē* as its complement—hence the full expression *rhētorikē technē,* or art of rhetoric. In the *Gorgias,* Plato wants to deny that sophistic teaching has the coherence, purpose, and effectiveness of a proper scientific discipline; he does so by arguing that *rhētorikē* is not, in his sense, a *technē.* Because it suggests *technē,* or disciplinary status, in its very formation, *rhētorikē* allows Plato to interrogate sophistic teaching within his conceptual scheme. Even if Plato did not coin the word himself, it probably originated in the Socratic circle and its usage was largely confined to Socrates' followers and their successors.[5]

There is a further difficulty in studying fifth-century rhetoric. Virtually all the evidence regarding fifth-century rhetorical theory stems from the fourth century, specifically from Plato and Aristotle, who were the first historians of rhetoric and certainly had access to much fifth-century material that is now lost. Plato's treatment of Gorgias is the earliest instance in which the sophist is explicitly regarded as a teacher of and expert in the art of rhetoric (esp. *Gorgias* 448D–452A). In the *Phaedrus* (266D–267D), while criticizing earlier, botched attempts at rhetoric, Plato offers what amounts to a catalogue of famous fifth-century sophists—Theodoros, Euenos, Teisias, Gorgias, Prodikos, Hippias, Polos, Likymnios, Protagoras, and Thrasymachos—all of whom are credited with writing documents, known as arts (*technai*), that concerned various features of discourse and linguistic usage. This single passage, short on details and shot through with irony, has borne the brunt of scholarly investigation into fifth-century rhetorical theory.[6] Aristotle's "Collection of Arts" (*technōn synagōgē*), known to us chiefly from brief references to it by Cicero, presumably assembled information from and about fifth- and fourth-century written arts. After this "Collection" was completed, any remnants of fifth-century arts still extant at the end of the fourth century were doomed to oblivion. All later ancient sources on early Greek rhetoric derive both their basic information and their frame of reference from Plato and Aristotle; no later ancient source unambiguously had direct access to a fifth-century art of rhetoric.[7]

The fact that none of the sophistic arts of rhetoric has survived and that reports about them are meager, confused, and uninformed has not prevented virtually all modern histories of rhetoric from adopting some version of the fourth-century Platonic-Aristotelian account and presenting the sophists as the founders of the discipline.[8] Here is an area in which scholarship runs up against the limits of the evidence. This is nowhere more evident than in the case of the two Syracusans, Korax and Teisias, whom the ancient doxography exalted as authors of the first rhetorical treatises and the joint founders of the discipline. It is hard to see why modern scholars followed the ancients on this point. Korax and Teisias are patently so mysterious to all the ancient sources who speak of them, including Plato and Aristotle, and so convenient as figureheads for ancient disciplinary historians dependent on the notion of disciplinary "founder" (*prōtos heuretēs*) that we must admit our complete ignorance regarding any contribution to rhetoric they may have made.[9]

As a result of Thomas Cole's book of 1991, *The Origins of Rhetoric in Ancient Greece*, fifth-century rhetoric now faces a full-blown existential crisis. In opposition to the testimony of Plato and Aristotle and to more than two millennia of consistent interpretation, Cole has argued that rhetoric was invented not by the sophists of the fifth century, but by the fourth-century philosophers themselves. The rhetoric whose origins Cole seeks is rhetoric in the purely formal, apolitical sense that supplied the mature discipline with its subject matter.[10] Well aware of the exploration of verbal resources undertaken by sophists and other late-fifth-century writers and aware too of the innovative features of this activity, Cole perceived that the fifth-century figures did not attain two insights that underlie the mature discipline of rhetoric: they did not posit form and content as the abstract, exhaustive constituents of communication; and they did not view the manipulation of verbal resources as a systematic tool for tailoring discourse to all specific communicational goals.[11] Indeed, they were not in a position to do so: Plato and Aristotle utilized opportunities for linguistic analysis made available by the advent of prose texts composed for reading, a cultural trend to which the late-fifth-century figures contributed but that became consequential only around the beginning of the fourth century. Cole has done more than devise a new set of concepts for familiar phenomena. The historical fact that the disciplinary institutions and assumptions of rhetoric can be traced back to the fourth century but are apparently absent from the fifth has now been tied to specific developments in literary and intellectual culture that occurred in the fourth century.[12]

Cole's insight (though he does not put it this way) is to insist on the status of rhetoric as an art, or *technē*, in the developed, fourth-century sense of the term. Cole argues that the *technē* texts attributed to fifth-century sophists must have been practice and demonstration texts, devoid of systematic theory; Gorgias' preserved speeches and Antiphon's tetralogies are prime examples. Cole concedes that precept may have been implied and supplemental oral instruction may have been available.[13] But without a conceptual apparatus for rhetorical analysis, sophistic *technē* was essentially empirical and did not include explicit standards of theoretical knowledge, objective expertise, and reliable success. Otherwise, it would make no sense for Plato and Aristotle to explain (at great length) what such things are and to criticize the sophists (vehemently) for failing to perceive them. From the perspective of Plato and Aristotle, sophistic *technē*, as the inherited dominant model, had to be refuted if a superior, true notion of *technē* was to be substituted—hence the inclination of Plato and Aristotle to treat the sophists as forerunners in *technē*, though especially inept ones. Yet that contingency should not compel *us* to grant to sophistic *technē* the attributes that were inaugurated by Plato and Aristotle, that distinguish Platonic-Aristotelian *technē*, and that were adopted by the artistic and scientific disciplines that subsequently evolved. Only since Plato has rhetoric been fully a discipline, that is, a *technē* in the sense that European culture accepted as definitive: a systematic useful practice that, like medicine, is supported by an appropriate body of theory and cannot be properly pursued in the absence of that theory.[14]

The Rhetorical Situation of Fifth-Century Athenian Democracy and the Practice of Political Rhetoric

Rhetorical theory and the mature discipline of rhetoric are indeed creations of the fourth century, but by themselves they do not account for the early development of Greek rhetoric. Hence Cole's argument needs to be revised. Consider first the corpus of Athenian oratory. Though nearly all the speeches of the corpus stem from the fourth century, only those of Isokrates, who saw himself as a philosopher, reflect fourth-century theoretical debates on rhetoric.[15] One of the best of the orators, Lysias, was writing and publishing speeches well before Plato was seriously thinking about rhetoric. Demosthenes was young enough to come under Plato's influence and may conceivably have received some influence directly or indirectly from the philosopher. But Demosthenes learned his craft mainly in a nonphilosophical tradition, namely, from previous and contemporary practicing *rhētores,* from studying Thucydides, and from his own attention to the demands of his task.[16] Now Plato's treatment of Lysias in the *Phaedrus* indicates clearly enough *his* readiness to dismiss Lysias as a rhetorician; and aside from the fact that Plato indulges in caricature, one may, perhaps, concede that his attack on Lysias' deficiencies in rhetorical theory hits home. Yet Lysias' undeniable artistry should not, and clearly will not, be dismissed on that account.[17] The brilliance of Demosthenes' art is equally plain, and a similar point can be made in regard to other, lesser but still significant, Athenian orators.

Athenian oratory operated strictly within a small, well-defined set of legal and political situations and aimed only at certain types of legal and political objectives. So the corpus of Athenian oratory does not in itself imply the existence of the mature discipline of rhetoric with its theoretical components and universal aspirations. The corpus does indicate, however, that within these limitations the speaker's message and its linguistic form were functionally independent and could be artistically manipulated for the sake of persuasion without the benefit of an accompanying theory of communication. To restrict rhetoric just to the status of self-conscious scientific discipline, as Cole's view requires, ignores this fact. Indeed, Cole virtually ignores Lysias, Demosthenes, and the other orators, and thus he departs from the disciplinary tradition whose theoretical basis he seeks to elucidate; that tradition consistently recognized Lysias and Demosthenes as masters. In spite of the insight that Cole brings to the study of Greek rhetoric, his account, like that of the ancient doxographers, is limited by the impulse to seek the disciplinary founder. Plato and Aristotle contributed more to the growth of rhetoric than did Protagoras and Gorgias, and certainly more than did the mysterious Korax and Teisias; but rhetoric, not unlike other disciplines, sprang from intellectual and social roots that are too complex for any one or two individuals, no matter their genius, to be regarded as the sole cause of the new phenomenon.

The fact that most fourth-century Athenian oratory was produced out of actual political and legal contests and without the benefit of disciplinary study suggests the other main factor in the growth of rhetoric, Athenian democratic politics. Plato substantiates this notion himself: his interest in rhetoric stems directly from his critique of democratic discourse and of sophistic influence on that discourse. When he used the word *rhētorikē,* he intended a connotation that was obvious then but is no longer so. *Rhētorikē technē,* translated above as the "art of rhetoric," more properly means the "*rhētōr*'s art," which is indeed Plato's usage in the *Gorgias.*[18] Literally the word *rhētōr* means "speaker," but in Athens it was a political word, designating a citizen who volunteered to address the assembly either to move a proposal or to contribute to the debate. The term was also used more loosely to designate those notable citizens who regularly or frequently moved proposals or participated in debates, and thus repeatedly put themselves in the public eye as political leaders; thus *rhētōr* also means "politician."[19] In the present case, etymology reveals meaning: behind the art of rhetoric as it was ultimately fashioned lies the art of being a politician, that is, of being a politician specifically as politicians functioned in Athenian democracy. Unlike Greek theory of *technē,* democratic politics attained its distinctive form by the mid-fifth century, when, after decades, even centuries, of development, the popular assembly and courts achieved institutional supremacy in the Athenian polis.[20]

Without apparently intending it, the Athenians instituted a striking "rhetorical situation" as a result of the way they implemented their democracy. To grant all citizens an equal share in official decisions, those decisions had to be communal ones rendered by equal votes. In the absence of any effective technology for transmitting information to large numbers of people, direct, spoken language uttered in the presence of the community was the only way to engineer group deliberations and decisions. The entire citizen body was indeed too large and disparate to assemble. But through continual open access in the assembly and systematic lotteries to enroll panels of judges in the courts, large bodies of anonymous, randomly chosen citizens gathered together regularly to render official decisions. The number of participants in these institutions was too large—from several hundred in a small legal case to several thousand in the assembly—to permit anything like orderly discussion among the entire group; but it was not too large to preclude individual citizens from addressing the group directly in turn. There was no constitutional, religious, or professional authority that the demos was obliged to recognize; that would weaken the absolute political power the demos jealously guarded. Rather, persuasion was built into the system: in the assembly individual citizens volunteered to engage in open, competitive debate before the voting, sovereign audience; in court litigants were compelled to speak for themselves before the same audience. Verbal combat in the assembly and courts could be intense: personal fortunes, political careers, lives, or the welfare of the community often hung in the balance.[21]

To arrange matters this way answered contemporary democratic requirements. But a new and huge burden was thereby placed on public discourse: communication under these circumstances had to be rendered effective. The burden made itself felt over time and provoked reactions that led gradually but inexorably to rhetoric.

The Athenians of the first half of the fifth century, those who collectively were responsible for the developed democratic institutions, may not have been aware of a burden on public discourse at all. Amateurism, a hallmark of Athenian democracy throughout, was especially pronounced at the beginning. Although politicians fought for supremacy, leadership and political debate remained centered in the traditional aristocratic elite. The elite's inherited conventions of discourse, supplemented by raw talent and experience, seem largely to have sufficed. The evidence is extremely sparse, but the few surviving notices for this period indicate a solemn acceptance of weighty, though not overwhelming, demands on public discourse. In Aeschylus' *Suppliants* (produced in 463), King Pelasgos refers to the popular assembly a decision crucially affecting the welfare of the community; the plot hinges on the outcome. As a result of the king's "verbal turns addressed to the demos" (*dēmēgorous strophas*, 623), the people's decision is successful: they both advance their communal welfare and receive Zeus' sanction. The *Eumenides* (produced in 458) demonstrates the justice and political utility of trial by debate between opposed parties with the people as judge. In the final scene Athena saves Athens from the Furies' wrath by skillfully persuading them to accept a place in the Athenian community. Aeschylus emphasizes the hazards and difficulties of the enterprise, but he portrays the "new" system optimistically as the foundation of the state, approved by the Olympian gods.[22]

As the fifth century progressed, the Athenian Empire and its attendant military commitments grew enormously in size and complexity; at home the Athenians continued to fine-tune the democracy and embarked on ambitious public expenditures. Competition among politicians was exacerbated by the entry of men from outside the aristocracy. With increased demands for reliable expertise and information and for effective, timely decisions, the burdens on public discourse multiplied.[23] By the end of the fifth century, the trials of governing themselves and ruling an empire, while fighting an extended and ultimately disastrous war, rendered Aeschylean optimism obsolete and made evident the obstacles to effective mass communication. Athenian drama during the last quarter of the fifth century, both tragedy and comedy, reflects this plight. Recall, for instance, Aristophanes' *Knights* (produced in 424), a vicious, transparent parody of deliberation in the assembly in which political discourse is derided as unrelieved shameless pandering. In Euripides' *Suppliants* (produced in the 420s), the Theban herald condemns democracy for demagogy, the moblike behavior of the political audience, rhetorical deception and manipulation, and the inability of the demos to understand political speeches; but he does not leave the scene without an answer from Theseus, the Athenian hero and democracy's defender (399–455). If the basic problems of democratic deliberation had not been obvious already, the Athenian public was certainly made aware of them.[24]

Where so much daily depended on competitive speechmaking before mass audiences of average, anonymous citizens; where such audiences possessed unlimited political power; where access was open and professionalism discouraged; where political authority was continually subject to legitimate challenge; where there was a long tradition of the spoken word used for public and artistic purposes; where, further, linguistic innovation was rife and the scientific investigation of language was underway; and where, finally, politicians and litigants had such enormous incentive to find the best way of putting their case and the need for efficient public communication was becoming distressingly obvious—here the conditions that would favor the development of rhetoric were all in place. This was a new situation. Though public eloquence had been prized and attained by poets such as Solon and Pindar and used by them for social purposes, for the first time Athenian democracy made persuasive speaking into a critical necessity for both leading figures and average citizens in order to perform their normal recurring tasks.[25] Eloquence was now ripe to be cultivated as an art, useful for everyone, at least with regard to law and politics. So, for example, in Aristophanes' *Clouds* (produced in 423), when Strepsiades can see no way to pay his debts and knows he must face his creditors in court, where we would ask, do you know a good lawyer? he says "I want to learn to speak" (239), looking to the learned, unmistakably sophistic Socrates as the one to teach him.

To understand better what lay behind Strepsiades' impulse, consider a small but important feature of Plato's argument against both Gorgias and Protagoras. In the dialogue named for him, Gorgias defines the rhetoric he claims to teach as "the ability to persuade by speech the judges in court, the councilmen in the council, the assemblymen in the assembly, and those in any other gathering which is a political gathering," thus specifying the political institutions of a democratic polis like Athens (*Gorgias* 452DE). In the rest of the dialogue, by casting rhetoric as the vicious imitator of political science, Plato targets specifically the manipulation of political discourse. In the dialogue named for him, Protagoras claims to teach the "political *technē*" that confers on the recipient "effective deliberation (*euboulia*) . . . in the affairs of the polis, so that one might speak and act most powerfully in the affairs of the polis" (*Protagoras* 318E–319A).

Thus for both Gorgias and Protagoras, as Plato portrays them, rhetoric is clearly a *political* activity, the utility of which derives from its application in precisely the sort of political circumstances that distinguish Athenian democracy. On this point at least Plato's account of Gorgias and Protagoras must be accurate. In both dialogues his main concern is to challenge the *qualifications* of Gorgias and Protagoras to offer instruction on political matters. When he attributes to them the claim that they teach the manipulation of political discourse, he is merely establishing a premise for the main argument, a premise that is both necessary and meant to strike the reader as a valid, noncontroversial description of their activity. Since it serves his interests to be accurate on this point, regardless of the merits of his critique of the sophists, we ought to assume he has not misrepresented his target.[26]

Given the available evidence, we can have only an imperfect notion of the content of sophistic political instruction. One passage in Aristotle has been taken to imply that sophistic instruction was restricted to judicial rhetoric (*Rhetoric* 1354B25–28). But other and better evidence, from Thucydides, Plato, Aristotle, the *Rhetoric to Alexander*, and elsewhere, shows that sophistic instruction concerned the assembly as well as the law court.[27] Sophistic instruction probably extended over both the form *and* the substance of political and legal speeches: for instance, concrete matters requiring expertise, such as finance, warfare, diplomacy, law, and so on; the procedures and conventions of addressing the assembly or a court, in which memory and delivery could be important; and memorable commonplaces, especially for use in preambles.[28] Arrangement—what a speaker says first, what second, what in conclusion, and so forth—was a feature of sophistic instruction that especially piqued Plato and Aristotle.[29] Among the few surviving sophistic texts, Gorgias' *Helen* and *Palamedes* demonstrate numerous formal techniques, especially argument from probability. On the other hand, Dionysios of Halikarnassos (*Demosthenes* 3) quotes from a demonstration speech by Thrasymachos that concerns a substantial political idea, namely, concord in the assembly (*homonoia*). Unfortunately the quotation breaks off too soon for us to see what Thrasymachos made of it.

We have little idea how far and in what ways sophistic instruction affected real political discourse in the fifth century. Most of the surviving late-fifth-century literature stems from acknowledged artists such as Euripides, Aristophanes, and Thucydides, who present the most concentrated display of formal properties of language and discourse from this period.[30] Usually it is assumed that these artists were influenced by the sophists, which may be a naive simplification. Sophisticated artists are in any event unlikely to reflect the ordinary level of political discourse. Few Athenian litigants, even those able to hire *logographoi* (speechwriters), will have sounded as polished as Lysias, the best *logographos,* enabled his wealthy clients to sound. Perikles maintained a reputation as a powerful speaker in the years after his death. But we have access only to the Thucydidean version of Periklean rhetoric, which need bear little relation to the original; and the late reports asserting a close connection between Perikles and Protagoras (especially in Plutarch's *Perikles*) are most likely inventions. Andokides' speeches, the earliest surviving examples of actual political rhetoric, are relatively artless; he was clearly not interested in sophistic technique.[31]

On the other hand, both Thucydides and Plato castigate politicians whose excessive displays of flashy speaking threatened to turn debate in the assembly into an epideictic contest. Antiphon, an expert in formal argumentation and spoken of by Plato as a teacher of rhetoric, was active as a speechwriter and political advisor. So it is likely that daring individuals experimented by including artistic innovations in actual political discourse.[32] Yet politicians and litigants normally strove to conceal art rather than draw attention to it; and a truly flamboyant, Gorgianic style would be grossly out of place in the assembly or courts and defeat the speaker's attempt to inspire trust.[33] By the mid to late fourth century, when politicians such as Demosthenes and Aischines were active, Athenian political discourse had clearly integrated considerable rhetorical skill with effective political and legal knowledge. However, by that time knowledge and expertise in both rhetoric and politics had increased dramatically in comparison with the late fifth century.

To attempt to catalogue further elements of fifth-century sophistic political/rhetorical instruction would quickly bring us up against the limits of the evidence. But it would also mislead. The term *sophist* is a loose one; and the fifth-century figures who today are customarily accounted sophists were a diverse group of itinerant polymaths, responding to the demands of their various audiences and clientele.[34] It is evident that certain sophists, principally Gorgias and

Protagoras, recognized the rhetorical features of Athenian democracy and taught prosperous, ambitious citizens how to manipulate them. A similar but less intense rhetorical situation must have existed in the other democratic poleis of the Greek world, indeed in all poleis where mass deliberative institutions enjoyed some power, even if such poleis were less than fully democratic. Sophists no doubt found audiences interested in their verbal skills elsewhere in Greece. Yet Isokrates' famous boast of Athenian supremacy in rhetoric is a fair one (15.295–96). As the largest, busiest, and most innovative polis of the Greek world, Athens pursued rhetoric more intensely, with greater rewards, and at a higher level of proficiency than was done anywhere else. Sophists, both Athenian and non-Athenian, contributed to rhetorical pursuits in Athens, but Athenian democratic politics provided the impetus.

Even when rhetoric achieved fully independent disciplinary status in the fourth century, its roots in the rhetorical situation of Athenian democracy remained evident. Plato's universal *technē* of discourse proposed in the *Phaedrus* incorporated both sophistic achievements and his own critique of Athenian political discourse delivered in the *Gorgias.*[35] Aristotle's *Rhetoric,* like the rhetoric outlined in the *Phaedrus,* is not limited to politics; it is applicable to any situation where persuasion by rhetorical argument is desirable. Yet the *Rhetoric* repeatedly focuses on the political and legal situations that are typical of a classical democratic polis. Examples and advice are often directed to the demands of contemporary Athenian civic discourse. And Aristotle's enormously influential classification of three genres of rhetoric, deliberative, judicial, and epideictic, is drawn straight from the institutions of the polis. The usefulness of that classification endured but never suited later rhetoric so well as it did its original milieu.[36]

Antithetical Argument and the Growth of Literary Rhetoric

To illustrate the transition from the political, sophistic stage of rhetorical practice to the postpolitical, literary stage of rhetorical art, a concrete example is in order. Antithetical argument is unusual in that sufficient evidence exists to observe its evolution from actual political polemic, to sophistic demonstration, and finally in Thucydides, with evident rhetorical purpose, to a literary format for artistic expression and instruction. (The story could be carried further into Platonic dialectic, but that would go well beyond the bounds of this chapter.) What I am calling antithetical argument is referred to by several names, among them *antilogiai* ("antilogy" or "opposed arguments"), *ton hēttō logon kreittō poiein* ("to make the weaker argument the stronger"), *in utramque partem disputare* ("to argue on either side" of a question); and it covers a group of different but related phenomena. The basic idea is debate, pro and contra, a pair of arguments that directly oppose one another, regardless of the origin and purpose of the arguments and the nature and outcome of the opposition.[37]

First of all, antithetical argument drove democratic politics. In the courts prosecutor and defendant, usually speaking directly against each other, were compelled to present antithetical arguments. In the assembly and council, without the simple structure of prosecution and defense debate could twist and turn with several speakers representing different views. But even in those institutions the issue always came down to voting for or against a particular proposal or between two alternative proposals; so participants were pushed toward advocating and adopting one or the other of two antithetical positions.[38] To consider complex matters in terms of antithetical positions is clearly a way of simplifying them, which was necessary if the citizen body en masse was to grasp the issues and decide policy cogently. In practical politics antithetical argument necessarily leads to a decision for one side or the other, whereby the necessary business of issuing judgments, creating policy, and confirming or discarding a leader is achieved. The intensity of antithetical debate fueled political rivalries which in turn risked warping the process of formulating policy. But in the eyes of the demos that was a tolerable sacrifice for the sake of more important goals, namely, maintaining open debate and overseeing the competition among leading politicians.[39]

Later doxographers viewed Protagoras as the originator of antithetical argument, yet nothing of his work in this format survives; and as a formal mode of argument, antithesis goes back to the earlier history of reasoning in Greek philosophy. Fifth-century sophists embraced the form, developing antithetical argument into vigorous freestanding compositions. The extant examples include a report of Prodikos' discourse on Heracles' choice between virtue and vice; the *Double Arguments* (*dissoi logoi*) of unknown authorship and written in Doric; Antisthenes' *Ajax* and *Odysseus* on the contest for Achilles' armor; and Antiphon's three tetralogies, each of which consists of two pairs of opposed judicial speeches. The contest between the Stronger and Weaker Arguments in Aristophanes' *Clouds* is a parody of this sophistic format (112–15, 889–1114). A further set of sophistic documents forms a closely related category. In Gorgias' *Helen* and *Palamedes,* the speaker advocates one side of a famous debate in which an opposing argument must be presupposed. The antithetical implications were realized when a response was provoked; Alkidamas' *Odysseus,* for example, in prosecution of Palamedes, responds to Gorgias' *Palamedes,* which defended the accused.[40]

All these speeches demonstrate a technique that was especially pertinent to agonistic political and legal debate. For any question on which people can differ (which in the eyes of sophists meant virtually all questions), an endless stream of argument can be generated not merely by a vicious circle of affirmation and denial, but by an increasingly complex and imaginative elaboration of facts, interpretations, and likelihoods. If the debate were stopped at any point, the last word would seem decisive; but debate could always be renewed, allowing the opponent to respond with a new and apparently more decisive argument. With his usual irony, Plato recalled the sophistic antithetical arguments concerning a case of assault (*Phaedr.* 273BC, tr. Rowe): "If a weak but brave man beats up a strong coward and steals his cloak or something else of his, and is taken to court for it, then neither party should speak the truth; the coward should say that he wasn't beaten up by the brave man single-handed, while the other man should establish that they were on their own together, and should resort to the well known argument, 'how could a man like me have assaulted a man like him?' The coward will certainly not admit his cowardice, but will try to invent some other lie and so perhaps offer an opening for his opponent to refute him."[41]

Antiphon's tetralogies demonstrate precisely this technique on a large scale and with reference to the conventions of an Athenian court. Like the case of assault recalled by Plato, the first tetralogy operates through increasingly elaborate probability arguments regarding the facts in a dispute (esp. 2.2.3, 6). But sophistic antithetical argument was hardly restricted to probabilities: in Antiphon's second and third tetralogies, the facts are known but their interpretation is disputed; other paired arguments exhibit moral, aesthetic, and psychological debate.[42] Regardless of the topic, the sophist's antithetical argument constituted a paradigm that the individual was meant to adapt for his own ends; this is the premise of Strepsiades' original intention (defeating creditors in court) and the ultimate use of Pheidippides' sophistic instruction (justifying assault of his father).[43] Antiphon's speeches from actual lawsuits exemplify this kind of adaptation. In the speech *Against the Stepmother* the speaker uses a standard argument against one who rejects examination of a slave by torture: having refused to allow such an examination, the opponent must be hiding the facts (1.8). A standard counterargument occurs in the speech *On the Murder of Herodes:* testimony obtained under torture is untrustworthy because the slave's natural desire to end the torture will lead him to say whatever the torturer wants to hear (5.31–32).[44] Not only do the sophistic paired arguments differ from actual politics in lacking a mechanism for attaining a decision and thus settling the debate; they even amplify the agonistic features of democratic politics: none envisions the possibility of an analysis, synthesis, or other abstract process that might resolve or even weaken the fundamental opposition. The pro and contra of sophistic antithetical argument remain adversaries locked in the pursuit of victory.

Artists traditionally enjoy the prerogative, and certainly have the habit, of appropriating material from any source and using it for their own purposes. Antithetical argument underwent a transformation when literary artists aloof from practical politics incorporated it into larger, complex works. In the *agōnes* (set verbal contests) of Euripidean tragedy and the antilogies of Thucydides, certain characteristics of style, argument, and arrangement replicate the antithetical discourses of politics and the sophists. But the similarities hardly extend further. While maintaining the form, both Euripides and Thucydides sublimate raw antithetical argument by modifying the polemical drive for victory into an expressive function. What was originally a weapon of agonistic debate passes into a resource for persuasion in a variety of literary contexts, that is, a rhetorical device adaptable to the author's purpose. In Euripides' case, the methodical oppositions of antithetical discourse allowed the dramatist to sharpen the conflict, reveal character, and vary the pace of the action; the *agōnes* take their place among the range of dramatic devices that contribute to the total theatrical effect.[45] Thucydides' antilogies also constitute episodes in the progress of a large, complex narrative; and the historian exploited dramatic advantages not entirely unlike those that are evident in the Euripidean *agōnes* fashioned for the stage. Yet Thucydides' use of antilogy warrants a closer look here because it contributed directly to the rise of the new literary rhetoric of the fourth century.[46]

Thucydides' antilogies represent critical debates that occurred during the course of the Peloponnesian War and that are important for the reader to understand; hence their inclusion in the narrative. Yet the antilogies plainly do not portray in historically accurate detail how the debates proceeded and the decisions were made. The literary artifice is so conspicuous and the web of verbal and conceptual alignment between speeches so dense that it would be perverse to view these antilogies as anything but Thucydidean compositions.[47] There is no reason to infer that Thucydides' artistic representations are necessarily false ones: the antilogical structure crystallizes the debates, which may have been long and meandering, into their essential components. Yet the rhetorical objective is superimposed, so to speak, on the historical: the antilogies presume as their audience not those who originally heard the debate, but Thucydides' reader, the student of his didactic work of interpretive history. The success and significance of any of the antithetical speeches in the text depend not on whether that speech represents the winning side in the debate, but on whether it makes the best possible case for its side.[48] Of course for historical reasons we need to know and are clearly informed that, for instance, Kleon's bid to annihilate Mytilene failed in the actual debate in the Athenian assembly. Yet that fact does not affect our appreciation of Kleon's argument and our interest in the way in which the argument is put. And our main interest in Diodotos' winning speech lies in its peculiar argument, not in the fact that it won. So too the reader is likely to register the harsh fate suffered by the Plataeans, who lost their lives in a debate the outcome of which was determined in advance. But the reader's attention is engaged by the language and arguments through which the Plataeans attempt to extricate themselves from this situation. Their failure to do so does not diminish Thucydides' rhetorical achievement at all. Thucydides did not compose his elaborate speeches merely to record winners and losers or to report the main points raised by each side.[49]

Thucydides' use of antilogy has a literary function above and beyond his characters' need to be persuasive in the assemblies he describes. Unlike sophistic antilogies, those of Thucydides do not advance an endless spiral of opposing arguments and do not supply the weapons for agonistic debate; and while the original audience may have faced a specific either/or choice (for example, destroy all the Mytilenians or just the guilty ones), Thucydides' audience—the reader—faces no choices at all. Rather, the systematic interconnections between the speeches of a Thucydidean antilogy provide the reader with a basis for apprehending complex equations of political life.[50] The Mytilene debate, for instance, poses the dilemma faced by an imperial power between ruling harshly or with restraint; the problem was a real one, and Thucydides' version of the debate makes evident—again, to the reader—the real advantages and drawbacks of each side. Further, by inserting antilogies periodically throughout the work, Thucydides established connections between the individual instances and highlighted the recurring features of political debate. This was possible neither in sophistic antilogies, which are isolated literary units, nor in Euripidean *agōnes,* which occur only once in a play. Consider the expansive argument on retribution and calculation that evolves in a verbal, conceptual, and historical dialectic through three antilogies: the Mytilenaean debate, the "trial" of the Plataeans, and the Melian dialogue. The argument on balances of power initiated in the antilogies of Book I resurfaces with a twist when the Athenians attempt to justify their invasion of Sicily in the debate in Kamarina in Book VI.

Thucydides was able to develop antilogy into a flexible tool of expression and instruction because written prose compositions destined for a reading public had become a viable mode of publication toward the end of the fifth century. For political discourse, the consequences were enormous. Traditional discourse within the democratic institutions was necessarily constrained by the conditions in which it was issued and received: time was limited; complexity and subtlety were useless or undesirable; immediate events defined the parameters of debate; other speakers competed for attention; and above all public attitudes and habits could force the *rhētōr* to pander. Written texts published outside the political forums did not, indeed, have an immediate impact on policy; throughout the classical period the Athenians continued to make all their policy decisions on the basis of the live debate that occurred in the decision-making institutions. But the "best possible case," as rhetoricians think of their goal, became a thoroughly different matter once it was extrapolated from the political institutions and pursued with artistic freedom in a work of literature.[51] Thucydides' blunt arguments on the tyranny of the empire or the stupidity of the demos, matters that even Aristophanes approached gingerly, or his unorthodox arguments on retributive punishment (in Diodotos' speech) would be scarcely conceivable in an actual assembly. The diction and style of his speeches, often so dense as to border on the incomprehensible if delivered in the hubbub of an actual assembly, were designed to provoke careful reading and reflection.[52]

In the development of rhetoric Thucydides is an intermediary figure, connected both to the political world of the fifth century and to the literary world of the fourth; he belongs entirely to neither. On Cole's account, in which Plato's theoretical approach to persuasion inaugurates a new era, an intermediate position is impossible. Placing Thucydides squarely with the sophists on the far side of the Platonic divide before rhetoric, Cole sees fit to characterize Thucydides' text as a sophistic demonstration text on a grand scale for one reason: there is no evidence (in his view) that Thucydides possessed the means or the inclination to analyze what made any of his speeches good or bad.[53] It is true that Thucydides' antilogies offer no formal resolution, synthesis, or final authoritative analysis; indeed, it would be wrong to view Thucydides as a student of disciplinary rhetoric.[54] Yet even without a conceptual apparatus to analyze language such as that developed by Plato and Aristotle, Thucydides constitutes a crucial stage in the emergence of rhetoric. While indelibly representing the underlying rhetorical pressures of the democratic polis, he manipulated the formal properties of language and argument, for the first time, over an impressive range of issues and in pursuit of the best possible case, an abstract category of linguistic thinking that Thucydides evidently employed even if he failed to formulate it clearly.[55]

Cole's account of Thucydides not only fails to register the qualitative differences in linguistic and argumentative artistry between Thucydides and the sophistic antilogies, but it also ignores the connection between Thucydides and the various fourth-century political prose writers. Like Thucydides, theorists such as Plato and Isokrates, logographers such as Lysias, and ultimately politicians such as Demosthenes all composed literary political speeches that circulated outside the political institutions while artistically representing live political speech.[56] The distinction between practical political rhetoric and artistic literary rhetoric is not hard and fast, but it is nonetheless real; and as a tool of analysis, it is invaluable for scrutinizing the emergence of rhetorical art in classical Athens.[57] Clearly the orators and prose writers of fourth-century Athens added literary refinements and generally pursued rhetorical devices and techniques that were utterly foreign, and perhaps inconceivable, to Thucydides. But they were emulating the historian when they used the conventions of literature, rather than those of actual politics, to address a notional political audience and thereby avoid the severe encumbrances of actual democratic political discourse. It is fourth-century Athens that saw the phenomenal rise of political discourse addressed to readers, for whom judgment on the questions at stake was achieved by a dynamic entirely different from that found in an actual court or assembly. Although the ultimate sources are numerous and scattered, the trend takes characteristic shape in Thucydides and leads directly to the theoretically based, practical discipline that extended the lessons of persuasive speaking from Athenian democratic politics to the multitude of human endeavors.

CHAPTER ELEVEN

Democracy and Sokratic-Platonic Philosophy

CHRISTOPHER ROWE

This chapter deals almost exclusively with Plato: a brief section is devoted to Sokrates, but for reasons stated there (at n.22) I consider only the character called "Sokrates" as he appears in some of Plato's dialogues, without making any claims about his relationship to the historical figure. In my view, it is only with Sokrates and Plato that we can discover and describe any significant interaction between democratic politics and philosophy in the fifth century.[1] Even Plato perhaps hardly scrapes in, since most if not all of his writing belongs to the fourth century. But any licence involved in including him may surely be readily granted. If the subject is the influence of democracy on the development of philosophy—and since that of philosophy on democracy is either minimal or zero, that surely is the proper subject for now[2]—then Plato must be the main character in the story, not only because of his pivotal position in the emergence of philosophy as a distinct activity in itself,[3] but also because of the importance of political thinking in his writing as a whole.

It might be thought that room should be found in the present discussion for other, indubitably fifth-century, figures. Thus Cynthia Farrar, protesting against the identification of political thinking with "abstract" political theory, finds some of the origins of democratic thinking in the "reflections on the self and the community"[4] of Protagoras, Thucydides, and Demokritos, at least the last of whom would certainly count as "philosophical" on the standard reckoning.[5] But even if we can establish what is authentically Demokritean among the "fragments," Demokritos was not an Athenian, and presumably not reflecting on

Athenian political forms and institutions; as for Protagoras, at least most of the material that might have been interesting for our present purposes is available only in the form in which Plato has constructed, or reconstructed, it for him, and may accordingly be legitimately treated in the context of the discussion of Plato himself.

We should clearly be sympathetic to Farrar's resistance to the idea that there was no such thing as an "articulated democratic theory"[6] in the fifth century, and that everyone at Athens was too busy doing and participating to think about what they were doing. It is barely conceivable that any democracy, including the Athenian, however we define it and at whatever date we suppose it to have begun, should have functioned independently of any sort of theory of what it was about. Such a theory might not have been "well articulated,"[7] beyond, that is, what might have been reflected in the writing of a Protagoras, or a Demokritos; it might have been only indistinctly recognized by the citizens at large. But it is hard to see how, without *some* sort of general perception of it, what we, at least, consistently refer to as "democracy" could have lasted as long as it did at Athens, changing from "moderate" to "radical" or "extreme," perhaps, and maybe back again.[8] In fact, as Kurt Raaflaub and others have pointed out, there is rather good evidence for such a "general perception" of democracy in fifth-century Athens: in the historians, in tragedy and comedy, and in the orators.[9] However, these writers will not play a direct role in the present chapter, which is exclusively concerned with the two dominant and homegrown representatives of philosophy at Athens, Sokrates and Plato.

In the first section, I shall conclude by suggesting ways democracy and democratic values may themselves be seen as a major factor in the development of Sokratic-Platonic philosophy as a whole. In the second section, I shall discuss briefly Plato's response to the rhetorical and sophistic traditions. Then, in the third and final section, I shall attempt to show that so far from representing the polar opposite of the democratic ideal, as for example the *Republic* might lead us (and has traditionally led us) to suppose, Platonic political thinking is not only based on a continuing reflection on the nature and problems of democracy and of mass-rule, but ultimately shares—albeit mostly in a form that some (more "extreme"?) democrats would have found unacceptable—some of the fundamental premises on which it claimed to be built. One of my central theses (though I can give only a sketch of an argument for it) will be that it is the *Politicus* and the *Laws*, rather than—as is usually supposed—the *Republic*, that provide us with the clearest picture of his political ideals, and of the shape of his proposals for reform. Plato's best city, in short, is not one ruled by a remote class of philosopher-rulers, but one in which the citizens rule, and are ruled by, each other, according to a rational system of law and on the basis of a set of common beliefs. According to his own classification, this will constitute a case of rule by many, for which the only title available is "democracy" (see especially *Politicus* 291E–292A). At the same time, it fits remarkably well with the Athenians' own idealized constructions of the system under which they lived. If Magnesia represents a *mixed* constitution, the base of the mix is provided by democracy.[10] What Plato is looking for, in the absence of the expert knowledge of ruling, is a means of establishing the principle of self-rule by the citizens which avoids the excesses of current forms of "rule by (the) many."[11] That will perhaps immediately suggest that I am viewing Plato from an Aristotelian standpoint; if so, I make no apology for that, for I believe that Aristotle's solutions are largely built on Plato's. I shall turn to the Aristotelian connection shortly.

The form of government in question would obviously entail the abolition of a number of the central perceived features of fifth-century Athenian democracy.[12] The most important of these features, which would apparently be lost in an Athens reformed on Platonic lines, would be the right of all adult male Athenians in possession of full citizen status to participate in political decision making, and to sit in the popular courts;[13] there would also be severe limits on the citizens' ability to "live as they please." Yet, on the other hand, there was no period in which all Athenian citizens automatically shared identical political rights.[14] One could also point out, in legalistic fashion, that in a Platonic Athens there would in fact be no citizens who were deprived of participation, insofar as anyone not allowed to participate would thereby cease to be a citizen. Such considerations would hardly, of course, have convinced any contemporary, or fifth-century, democrat. Nor does Plato himself ever call the (Platonically) best city a democracy; the closest he comes to it is in his suggestion at *Laws* 693D that democracy will form one element in the mixture represented by Magnesia. Yet he is ready to accept that the appropriate mixture, or some approximation to it, might come about even from a democracy (710E).[15] And again, whatever anyone else might have thought about what Plato proposes, and whatever reservations he himself might have had about calling it a "democracy," he does not seem to have any clear alternative term available.[16] It would be a very different kind of democracy from any ordinary ones, which he continues to write off as *stasiōteiai* rather than *politeiai;* nevertheless it is—as I shall argue—more like a democracy than anything else. If the restrictiveness of the criteria for citizenship, and especially the exclusion of anyone involved in productive work, seems to make this an unlikely and implausible claim, I would stress the importance of recognizing that on Plato's own account even Magnesia represents only a model, to which we must come as close as possible (*Laws* 739E). Quite how we are to do this, we are not told—and this, I take it, is what Aristotle has primarily in mind when he says that "most of those who have declared their views on the subject of constitutions . . . fail when it comes to questions of what is practically useful" (*Politics* IV.1, 1288B 35–37).

Aristotle fills the gap with something that under some descriptions looks distinctly like Magnesia, but under others is adapted to existing conditions under oligarchies and democracies: the "polity" or (as I prefer to translate it) "citizen-state,"[17] in which sometimes citizenship is represented as limited to those wealthy enough to bear heavy arms, but which is more often described as a compromise between oligarchy and democracy.[18] The orators had used the term *politeia* to signify nontyrannical regimes in which the citizens ruled themselves freely and autonomously. In such cases the category "polity" would refer either exclusively or primarily to democracy; having—like Plato—proposed to regard democracy itself as a kind of tyranny, and true monarchy and aristocracy as unlikely events, Aristotle now arrogates the term ("polity") for a kind of limited mass-rule, which he sees as the only context in which the idea of "ruling and being ruled"—i.e., rotation of office among all the citizens, which he takes to be both a mark of democracy, and essentially democratic[19]—is practicable and realizable without bad consequences. He thus underlines the difference between his "best practicable" state and democracy, while at the same time clearly indicating its connections with it, not just through the term "polity" itself (if I am right about the connections of that with its sense of "free government," as used by the orators), but by the parallel treatment of this novel form of constitution as itself in one way or another a mixture of oligarchy and democracy, avoiding the extremes of both. The thinking behind Magnesia in Plato's *Laws,* and behind its close relation, the city that is implicitly sketched in the *Politicus,* has its roots —so I claim—in a similar set of considerations. The crucial question, again, is about the kind of government that is appropriate in the absence of any individual or set of individuals with the special qualifications to justify giving power exclusively to them—in a situation, that is, in which either everyone or a large body of people has similar claims. The issue for both Plato and Aristotle is to organize the self-rule that this situation seems to require without permitting the excesses of rule by, and for, the demos, i.e., *dēmokratia* as a form of partisan rule. This is what I set out to show in the third section of this chapter. I shall conclude that while the standard description of Plato, and of Aristotle, as fundamentally antidemocratic is in some important respects true,[20] their relationship with democracy was a highly complex one, which cannot be reduced —as it has sometimes notoriously been, in Plato's case[21]—to one of simple opposition.[22]

Sokrates and Democracy

In this short section "Sokrates" will stand for the character called Sokrates in those dialogues normally classified as "early" and "early-middle" (or "transitional"),[23] that is, the so-called Sokratic dialogues. Whether, and to what extent, these really show us the ideas and arguments of the historical Sokrates is much debated,[24] and it is probably in principle undecidable; but even if their "Sokrates," like that of other ("later") dialogues, is a fiction, the story is more detailed and philosophically interesting than anything we are likely to be able to piece together from the non-Platonic evidence. As I shall argue, it also represents a central and enduring moment in Plato's own political argument. Whatever parts of it we may finally want to attribute to the real Sokrates, it is embedded in, and fundamental to, the larger project that finds its expression in the *Republic, Politicus,* and *Laws.*

Sokrates (or "Sokrates") believes that "man is rational and is misled only by intellectual errors," with the consequence that "people can be reformed through the use of logical persuasion, rational arguments alone";[25] he is also (perhaps) an egalitarian, at least in an intellectual sense: everyone, at least in principle, is capable of being persuaded of the truth, or at any rate everyone (else) is equally ignorant. The "truth" in question is moral or ethical truth, and Sokrates (so Plato's story goes) spent his time trying to persuade his fellow citizens to look for it. This he did by talking to people individually. At first sight, such an approach looks supremely apolitical, and all the more so when he himself contrasts it with advising the city in the assembly, which he says he has never done (*Apology* 31C). Yet this very passage suggests that conversing with individuals is an alternative route to the same goal, of persuading the *city,* that is, the citizens at large, to refocus their concerns. He also appears to be committed to the idea that the city would, ideally, be run by those who possessed the knowledge he himself is looking for (though he never finds it), because the most important decisions to be taken are always moral or ethical ones. This emerges most clearly from his encounter with Protagoras in the *Protagoras,* when he implicitly criticizes the democratic practice of looking to experts in order to decide less important matters like construction or shipbuilding, but allowing anyone to contribute on "matters concerned with the government of the city" (*tōn tēs poleōs dioikēseōs,* 319C8–D1), which require the virtues appropriate to a citizen (319A 4–5).[26]

To ask whether Plato's Sokrates is a democrat or an antidemocrat is perhaps not a useful question.[27] He is an otherwise loyal member of the citizen community who nevertheless has some fundamental criticisms to make of the system under which he lives—and the system is such as to permit him to do that.[28] (Much the same might well have been true of Plato, but we know far too little about him to tell.) The real significance of Sokrates' criticisms of democracy is not that they allow us to attach some convenient label to him but rather—or so I suggest—that they give sense to, or provide the context for, his philosophical activity. He is usually credited with an ethical theory, of striking complexity and with few if any antecedents.[29] But Plato repeatedly locates it in a political setting. It is the politicians—the *politikoi,* or so-called experts in statesmanship—who are the first people Sokrates goes to in the search he is made to report, in the *Apology,* for someone wiser than himself (21B–C): before the poets, and before the craftsmen, with whom the politicians are later paired (23E). It is of course the craftsmen, not the poets, who turn out to know *something,* if not the right things, but it is the politicians who have the reputation for being wise, or clever. Then we may think of the famous passage in the *Gorgias,* which pictures Sokrates—of all people—as "one of the few Athenians, not to say the only one, to engage in the true political art and . . . [to do] politics," [30] and the implicit suggestion in the *Politicus* (299B–D) that in a "well-governed" city people like him would have to be executed or exiled for looking for the truth, and so daring to appear "wiser than the laws." Then again, there is the *Protagoras,* where the ignorant Sokrates wins out over someone who explicitly claims to teach political knowledge and democratic virtue.

Whatever may have been true of the historical Sokrates, it looks as if Plato wants to present *his* Sokrates as someone who, if he does not actually possess the kind of knowledge that politicians need (and pretend to have already), is in the best position to find it. From this perspective, it is tempting to see Sokratic philosophizing, at any rate in its constructed Platonic version, as a direct response to the values of democratic politics. True, any private citizen making important choices or decisions may implicitly be claiming to know about "the good, the fine and the just"—the very things that are consistently described in the dialogues as "most important and valuable" (*Politicus* 285E 4, with, e.g., *Phaedrus* 276A ff., 277E–278A), and about which knowledge is said to be most elusive; but it is in the political sphere that questions about such things either ought to or actually do arise in their broadest form, and where people are bound to claim expertise, or some kind of authority, if they are to stand any chance of persuading their audience. To such people, Plato opposes the figure of the philosopher as (Sokratic) *searcher* for knowledge—a figure that seems to me, in the final analysis, the key element in the argument of Plato's political dialogues as a whole. Something of the flavor of the idea in question is conveyed in Xenophon's wry remark (*Memorabilia* I.1.10) that Sokrates "was usually talking, and it was allowed for anyone who wanted to listen." The democratic idea is turned on its head: in the assembly, everyone has the right to speak, whereas elsewhere in the city everyone has the right to *listen* to Sokrates—and the implication is that they would be better off if they did so.[31]

Plato on Orators and Sophists

But, as it happens, everyone *may* speak, whether or not (on Plato's terms) they have anything useful to contribute.[32] The ability to speak persuasively is at a premium. Plato's most characteristic way of treating contemporary oratory is to see it, as he does in the *Gorgias*, as a form of *kolakeia*, "pandering." The *Menexenos*, in its parody of a funeral speech, gives a concrete example of the way the sophist or the political orator takes on the color of his audience,[33] telling them just what they want to hear, whether it is true or not (the "dead man gets a fine and costly funeral, although he may have been poor," says Sokrates, "and an elaborate speech is made over him by a wise man who has long ago prepared what he has to say, although he who is praised may not have been good for much" [234c2–6, tr. Jowett]).[34] Protagoras' Great Speech also no doubt tips, ultimately, into a similar category, insofar as it fails in its purpose as an *apologia* for democracy. According to the myth of the *Menexenos*, democracy is "really an aristocracy [or government of the best] which has the approval of the many" (238D1–2), where the necessary quality of the many derives from the soil of Attica; Protagoras simply makes virtues, or the capacity for them, somehow natural to human beings. On such a basis, of course, the orator's going along with his audience would cease to be a bad thing. But in fact, on Plato's account, the special capacity of rhetoric consists precisely in feeding people's illusions about themselves: "they praise ourselves also who are still alive, until I feel quite elevated . . . and all in a moment I imagine myself to have become a greater and nobler and finer man than I was before" (*Menexenos* 235A5–B2).

This all looks much like the same point as before, about the need for real as opposed to merely apparent knowledge. But Plato has another, quite different, accusation to make against oratory and those who teach it: that the orator typically dupes his audience, and manipulates it to his own ends. One of the classic texts is of course the *Gorgias*. The scene is set by Gorgias himself, and his praise of the power of oratory; Polos and Kallikles then show the possible consequences of such power, in the hands of individuals who neither know nor care about the truth. According to Kallikles, real virtue means committing so-called crimes with impunity; the laws are framed by the majority merely to make up for their individual weakness. Thrasymachos, in *Republic* I, takes a similar position, except that he extends Kallikles' theory about legislation to cover laws under all sorts of constitutions: "each form of government enacts the laws with a view to its own advantage, a democracy democratic laws and tyranny autocratic and the others likewise" (338E 1–3, tr. Shorey). The moral drawn is that if the laws are there to maintain others' advantage, it will be mere simplemindedness to submit to them, and a sign of weakness not to turn to "the most consummate form of injustice," namely tyranny, and achieve domination for oneself (344A). Thrasymachos does not here make the connection with rhetoric that is made explicitly in the *Gorgias,* but his position is clearly in line with Gorgias' claim there that rhetoric "brings freedom [i.e., presumably, from restraint and control] to mankind in general and to each man dominion over others in his own country" (452D 5–8, tr. Woodhead). He immediately explains this in terms of "the power to convince by your words the judges in court, the councilmen in Council, the people in the Assembly," and so on; in other words, the power he gives is to be put to legitimate use within society. But the examples of Polos and Kallikles are there to remind us that no such restriction will follow automatically.

This view of the orator, as manipulator, is in the end complementary to the view of him as a pander: it is by being persuasive that the speaker gets his own way, and the easiest means of persuading an audience is to tell them what they want to hear. Of course, not everyone who learns to speak does so with Kallikles' motivation. Plato's point is surely the more moderate one, that the danger of a Kallikles is always there, in a society that—in principle if not in fact—allows any decision to depend on who happens to have spoken most persuasively at the time. On Protagoras' account (that is, the one Plato attributes to him in the *Protagoras*) either no such danger exists, or else the institutions of democracy and the character of the citizens are already strong enough to withstand it. "Aspasia" in the *Menexenos,* and her models in Lysias and Thucydides, say much the same. Plato disagrees: such a view is at best complacent, at worst absurd. He himself responds with a basket of arguments, first to establish the superiority of the philosophical life over the life devoted to the pursuit of power (which, in the absence of knowledge about how to *use* the power, must be self-defeating); and second, to establish, in a somewhat different form, what Protagoras (or "Protagoras") merely asserted, that virtue is natural to us rather than the mere product of convention. Simultaneously, he proposes that a new kind of city, with fundamentally different laws, based on philosophical insight, will be needed to make that virtue in the citizens a reality.[35]

Democracy and Plato's "Best Constitution"

There is, then, a sense in which Plato's own project overlaps with that of the democrats; it is just that he thinks democracy ill equipped to achieve what (in some moods) it thinks it has already achieved. "Democratic wisdom"[36] needs to be replaced by its philosophical counterpart, and there is also a requirement for a new rhetoric, which takes its orders and its material from a philosophical, rationally based statesmanship. Both the new rhetoric and the new *politikē technē* would be the product of inquiry of the sort recommended and exemplified by Sokrates—which is also the unifying bond between the apparently solitary option of the philosophical life on the one hand and Plato's endorsement of the shared life of the citizen on the other.

Large parts of this picture would be compatible with what is still the usually accepted account of Platonic political thinking. On this account, the optimism of the *Republic,* with its autocratic philosopher-rulers, gives way gradually to a grudging acceptance[37] of the need for a return to constitutional rule, of a sort that owes much to an Athenian democratic model.[38] But this sort of interpretation, though widespread, is neither necessary nor universal. So Richard Stalley writes: "We have seen that, according to the *Laws,* neither the direct rule of philosopher-kings nor community of property are possible among men as they actually are. Thus the ideal state of the *Republic* could never in practice be attainable. This may mean that Plato has changed his mind in the direction of greater realism, but it is equally possible that the *Republic* and the *Laws* represent different kinds of ideal."[39]

If there is a single key question in this whole area, it is about the nature of Utopias in general, and of Plato's in particular. The most important recent work here is probably that of André Laks. Building on his insights, I think we can establish three preliminary points: first, that the political constructions of both the *Republic* and the *Laws* are Utopias; second, that they are Utopias in the sense that they are neither realized now (they are literally nowhere), nor realizable, as such, in the future; and third, that they are nevertheless "possible," in the special sense that it is possible (so Plato claims) to *approximate* to them.[40] It is important to Sokrates/Plato that he should not merely be thought to be a dreamer. For this, it is necessary only that the projects described not be *fantastic,* or simply *absurd,* like the constructions of the comic poets; this is the burden of the treatment of women in the first part of Book V. It is plainly not necessary, on the other hand, for him to be committed to saying that they can be fully completed in practice.

Here we need to look at Plato's text, and what he actually has his characters say about the cities of the *Republic* and the *Laws.* First, the *Republic:* in two places especially, at 499 and 502, he has Sokrates insist that the city he describes is possible; on the other hand, he also makes him say that "perhaps there is a pattern of [the city whose establishment we have described] laid up in heaven for him who wishes to contemplate it and so beholding to constitute himself its citizen. But it makes no difference whether it exists now [Glaukon has just said that it "is to be found nowhere on earth"] *or ever will come into being*" (592B 2–4, tr. Shorey).

What the combination of these passages seems to suggest, so far, is that Kallipolis is at best a theoretical possibility, and that (as Aristotle would have put it) nothing is being proposed the conditions for which simply could not obtain. The crucial passage, however, is the one at 471E ff., a passage introduced by Glaukon's proposal, "let us at once proceed to try to convince ourselves of just this, that it is possible and how it is possible, dismissing everything else." The main part of Sokrates' response is to offer the general principle that nothing can be executed quite as it is described: "Is it possible for anything to be done just as it is spoken? Is it not rather in the nature of things that action comes less close to truth than utterances, even if some disagree on that point? . . . Don't force me to assert that things must come into existence in practice exactly as we sketched them in the argument; but if we are able to find out how a city would be organized as closely as possible to what we said, allow that we have found that these things are possible, as you ordered us" (473A 1–B 1).[41] Sokrates goes on to make his notorious proposal for the unification of political power with philosophy, and then argues at length for its practicability. But it is something far less ambitious than the rule of a class of ideal philosopher-kings that seems to be recognized as the best that is even conceivable under existing conditions (499B–D).[42] As to what kind of city would be the best approximation to the one described, the *Republic* is silent. The most that we are told is its institutions will be rationally defensible, in terms of "possibility," and useful in the sense of contributing to its overall ends. We are also given some examples of such institutions, as in the case of the treatment of women and children. But again, we are not told, in the *Republic,* how and to what degree these institutions could *in practice* be realized.[43]

The *Laws,* at 739, implicitly recognizes this. A complete "community" of women, children, and property—the ideal, limiting case described in the *Republic*—is identified as belonging to a *paradeigma politeias,* a *paradeigma* directly contrasted with the *politeia* currently being described. This latter constitution is said to come as close to the first as is possible in a city of men, as opposed to gods, or sons of gods (as the members of the first would need to be). But in case we should suppose that there is now a straight equivalence between "possible" and "practicable," there is also mention of a *third* city: "of the third, under heaven's favor, we will treat hereafter," says the Athenian, though it is not clear that they ever do, or that, if they had, there would not turn out to be a fourth, and a fifth . . . But this is only consistent with that general principle Sokrates enunciated in the *Republic,* that it is always easier to talk about something than to put it into effect.[44]

If this is right, then Plato's "best practicable" state will be closer to Magnesia than to the city of the *Republic.*[45] In particular, there will be no direct rule by philosopher-kings, a point that seems specifically confirmed by *Laws* IV (711D–712A) and IX (875A–E): the idea of a single individual being able to combine incorruptible wisdom with absolute power, suggests the Athenian, either belongs to the realm of myth, or would require someone with actually superhuman powers. But that—on my view—was always Plato's position. Two considerations support this claim. First, the argument in the *Republic* for the installation of philosophers as rulers depends on their possessing complete knowledge, at any rate of all subjects relevant to ruling (they are to rule because they have knowledge rather than mere belief; any incompleteness in their knowledge will render it insecure, and so apparently indistinguishable from belief). However, the conception of the philosopher that otherwise predominates in the *Republic,* through the figure of Sokrates himself, is that of the philosopher as *searching* for wisdom, not actually possessing it. The *Phaedrus* (278D), too, tells us explicitly that the description *sophos* belongs properly only to gods, and that men are rather (at best) *philo-sophoi;* and the Athenian in the *Laws* is apparently in agreement.[46] Second, when the city of the *Republic* is introduced as the starting point of the *Timaeus-Critias*—and we are, surely, meant to suppose that it *is* the city of the *Republic*—the one central feature of it that is missing is that of the philosopher-kings. In this respect, and in others, the "ancient Athens" of the *Timaeus-Critias* resembles Magnesia. There are rulers, certainly,[47] but it is not specified that these are a class apart; on the other hand, the twenty thousand "guardians" (soldiers) are very much apart from the remaining part of the citizen body, living separately on the Akropolis, with the craftsmen and farmers living on the slopes below (*Critias* 112A–B). All of this might, of course, be determined simply by the requirements of the story, in which soldiers, not philosophers, are to play the leading role. But that in itself suggests something important about the philosopher-rulers. They were needed, in the *Republic,* primarily and in the first instance, in order to *bring about* the right kind of city;[48] in ancient Athens, that role is performed by the gods themselves (*Critias* 109D). What is needed subsequent to the foundation of the city is some permanent "element having the same conception of its constitution that you the lawgiver had in framing its laws" (*Republic* 497D). In the context of the *Republic* itself, it is natural to identify this with the philosopher-rulers themselves; but as soon as we begin talking about *approximations,* it can be provided for in different ways, as indeed it is in the *Laws,* in the shape of the Nocturnal Council.

Even if I had not signalled it at the beginning, it should by now be easy enough to guess the general direction of my argument. This is to suggest that underlying both the *Republic* and the *Laws*—and also the *Politicus*—there is a single preferred model for constitutions, with the essential features (1) that its laws and institutions are rationally based (and that there is a part of the population, however small, that can understand the reasonings of the original lawgivers); (2) that it promotes the common good of all the citizens, which consists of a life informed by virtue, if not necessarily by knowledge; (3) that such a life, for all the citizens, includes ruling as well as being ruled; and (4) that anyone prevented from living such a life, by their occupation and/or their character and temperament, is excluded from full membership of that community. It seems clear to me that this model, when all four features are taken in combination, has considerably more in common with the democratic idea than it has with oligarchy, or with the usual varieties of autocracy (though it has certain features that we, and Plato, might want to treat as "autocratic"), and certainly more than it has with the sort of autocracy—of the intellect—with which Plato is usually associated. The most fundamental of the four features is the first (the requirement for laws and institutions that are as rational as possible), insofar as the remaining three both can be and actually are derived rationally, argumentatively, from a variety of premises. There is of course nothing democratic about the requirement of rationality, and indeed Plato typically treats actual democracies as representing nearly the least rational of all types of political organization. Nevertheless, as we have seen, he also allows for the possibility that even a democracy ("of a certain sort," *Laws* 710E) might evolve into a different, and better, kind of state—one that has acquired the right kind of legislation, and therefore, to one degree or another, the other features of the model; furthermore these features have their direct analogues in Athens' own idealized depictions of itself,[49] if not in real fifth-century (and fourth-century) Athenian democracy. Plato's "best constitution,"[50] in fact, bids fair to be a paradigm of what democracy should have been but in his view was not: in the words of Sokrates in the *Menexenos,* "an aristocracy . . . which has the approval of the many."[51]

Plato himself, when describing the constitution of Magnesia as partly "democratic," is referring primarily to its identification of a shared goal for the community: "There are two matrices, as we may call them, of constitutions from which all others may truly be said to be derived; the proper name of the one is monarchy, of the other democracy . . . [I]t is indispensably necessary that there should be both ingredients where there is to be the combination of liberty [freedom] and amity with wisdom" (693D 2–E 1, tr. Taylor). For Plato, of course (or rather the Athenian, but it seems right to suppose that the Athenian is speaking for him), wisdom is what justifies, or would justify, autocratic control; what he is saying is that in the right kind of state *wise* control will be combined with freedom. What kind of freedom? Not, clearly, freedom to do what one likes, if we go by the general description of Magnesia (although the citizens might all be of a reliable sort, still they need to be restrained by law, or the persuasive power of the lawgiver). Rather, it is freedom *from*—from, specifically, control by factional elements. The Magnesians will be "slaves" (willing slaves) to the law, but at the same time free from despotism of the kind Plato associates with actual constitutions.[52] But this is surely closely related to that freedom that the democrats value so highly—autonomy, freedom from being ruled by others, and freedom from tyranny.[53] The difference is that Plato sees democracy itself—if that is rule by the demos—as a form of the same tyranny.

A final point: There is a widely accepted view, to which I referred earlier,[54] that the *Laws* is to a considerable extent modelled on Athenian democratic laws and institutions—which would make Magnesia even closer to democracy than I am alleging. If what this view literally says is true, as in some sense it surely is, it is as well to be clear that Plato cannot be accepting those laws and institutions *because they are Athenian,* belonging to a past and better Athens. He accepts them because they are rationally justifiable and useful; as he suggests, good laws may come from anywhere.[55] In this sense, that Magnesia shares any feature with any actual city or constitution is purely coincidental. Plato does not begin from any attachment to a particular location or time: Sparta, Crete, or the Athens of Marathon.[56] He simply praises them, and draws from them, to the extent that they exemplify institutions and practices that he thinks he has independent reasons for accepting. The *Laws,* in particular, gives no grounds for supposing any reconciliation to Athenian democracy as such,[57] of whatever period. Plato's model is a *politeia* that he can only sketch in words, or as belonging to a mythical past, even though aspects of it may have been realized here and there. It will also, of course, fall outside his sixfold (or fivefold) classification of constitutions, as he means it to do. But if one had to locate it in relation to that classification, there would be no option but to associate it with the better kind of democracy. It is, to borrow Gill's term, a kind of "hoplite democracy";[58] and I hope that I have presented sufficient argument to suggest that that is not too much of a contradiction in terms. Our own ideal of an "educated democracy," if it could be realized, might even fit—at a stretch—as a kind of approximation to this Platonic paradigm; and the education we might have in mind would, I hope, have something in common with the Sokratic idea of intellectual progress that, despite all appearances, underlies all Plato's thinking.

CHAPTER TWELVE

Attic Old Comedy, Frank Speech, and Democracy

JEFFREY HENDERSON

Drama and oratory, organic elements of the Athenian democracy, were Athens' most politically engaged forms of speech and also its principal voices. Members of the sovereign demos, numbering at most fifty thousand male citizens, composed some 1,250 tragedies (equal to about 180 volumes of Oxford Classical Texts) and 650 comedies (115 volumes), together with countless speeches in assembly and courts; subtract these, and little Athenian literature would remain.[1] This chapter surveys the complementary roles of comedy and oratory[2] by examining the two central and related principles that set the rules for public speech and so enabled democracy to function in the first place: *isēgoria,* the right of every citizen to offer advice, and *parrhēsia,* the right of every citizen to voice frank criticism. I will suggest that the ideological alignment and structural complementarity of oratory and comedy in voicing criticism and advice to civic audiences support the classical understanding of comedy as essentially democratic and politically engaged, as against the modern tendency to see comedy as detached, innocuous, and essentially apolitical.

First, I will give an overview of the ideology and practice of frank speech in the democracy, leaving drama temporarily out of the picture.

Frank Speech in Ideology and Practice

In the course of the fifth century, executive power was taken over by the demos. Eligible citizens in good standing enjoyed political equality (*isonomia*) and, by the right to address the assembly (*isēgoria*), equal access to political power. Thus this *dēmokratia* sought to channel the power and privileges of its elites to the benefit of all the citizens, and also to protect its nonelite citizens from political dependency and from certain forms of social and economic exploitation. The watchword was "freedom" (*eleutheria*) as opposed to "tyranny."[3]

Isēgoria was a defining characteristic of democracy (e.g., Plato, *Republic* 557b), especially Athenian democracy (e.g., Plato, *Gorgias* 461e). Every assembly began with the herald's question, "Who wishes to speak?" Whether *isēgoria* was customary or recently introduced as a legal right,[4] certainly "assembly-based politicking was intermittently possible long before the fifth century."[5] Homer's Thersites takes us back to the Archaic period: Odysseus punished him for his speech, but no one prevented him from speaking. But *isēgoria* came into its own with full *dēmokratia,* to which it was essential. By giving every citizen the opportunity to demonstrate, and to be rewarded for, his excellence in counsel,[6] *isēgoria* promoted a politically vigilant and active citizenry, broadened the range of classes and groups from which leaders could emerge, and put all leaders more firmly under the demos' control. The process was well underway in the 440s; by the 420s the "new politicians" were appealing directly to the demos, the assembly having achieved full control of state affairs "with a minimum of restraint by Boule or officials."[7]

Aligned with the right to speak up was the right to speak frankly (*parrhēsia*), that is, to advise, criticize, admonish, or abuse anyone, individual or collective, by telling the truth as one saw it.[8] *Parrhēsia* was both ideologically and procedurally essential in maintaining the integrity of the democratic system, so much so that it could be considered not merely a citizen's right but his moral obligation.[9] *Parrhēsia* safeguarded equal treatment across class lines[10] and so distinguished democratic citizens from the slaves or subjects of other systems, particularly Sparta, thus bolstering the central concepts of *eleutheria* and civic equality.[11] In 411 the oligarchs suppressed free speech (Thucydides 8.66.1), as the Thirty would later ban the teaching of rhetoric (Xenophon, *Memorabilia* 1.2.31). As a "privilege of the bema" (Demosthenes 7.1), *parrhēsia* served as a check against bad judgment by encouraging the kind of spirited debate that the demos needed in order to choose the best proposals in an assembly or the better case in a law court.[12]

Speakers in assembly and law courts were therefore allowed wide latitude to criticize an opponent's arguments, to question his motives and even his character, and also to criticize the demos for bad judgment. Being free to speak frankly, speakers need not flatter the voters on the one hand[13] or seek to intimidate opponents on the other,[14] and bribe takers could be said to have "sold their *parrhēsia*" (Deinarchos, *Against Aristogeiton* 1). For the mass of citizens who listened, judged, and voted, *parrhēsia* fostered a critical attitude and a sense of intellectual autonomy, and so became the frontline defense against flattery, bullying, corruption, deception, or incompetence on the part of the speakers. *Parrhēsia* also allowed any member of the demos, be he as inconsequential as Thersites, publicly to expose the misbehavior, dishonesty, bad counsel, or incompetence of anyone, however powerful, who threatened the integrity or well-being of the community.[15] The openness and frankness of the democracy were even invoked as contributing to its military prowess.[16]

But the political arena thus far described was only a subset of a broader democratic *culture*. Citizenship and its exercise had become central to every Athenian's identity and, for ordinary citizens, crucial to their sense of personal dignity and safety. Fifth-century Athenian democracy was both a political system for the demos and a way of life for everyone. A member of the demos took his democratic freedoms with him when he stepped out of the public spheres, and much the same ideals of personal freedom, though not of political equality, were shared by the members of his private world of household and family, including the freedom of frank speech.[17]

In personal relationships *parrhēsia* was "a privilege openly granted to *philoi* to rebuke, and to enemies to attack each other's faults" (Isokrates 2.3, cf. 2.28). *Parrhēsia* also licensed the sort of forthright speech and personal abuse, both jocular and aggressive, that were endemic to the marketplace, to symposia, and to komastic and festive contexts, especially the cults of Dionysos and Demeter, where both sexes participated in ritual flyting.[18] In these contexts, too, there was the *parrhēsia* of intellectuality, skepticism, and irreverence[19] enjoyed by sophists, scientists, and philosophers. In the world of the *oikos*, a citizen woman was ideally expected to defer to men, but to *deny* her the right of *parrhēsia* could be portrayed as both unreasonable and undemocratic,[20] to say nothing of the power she might exercise by virtue of her dowry: according to the comic poet Alexis, married men "have sold off their *parrhēsia* to live as slaves to women" (150.1–3).[21] What is more, it was a truism that even Athenian metics and slaves enjoyed greater liberties than citizens of nondemocratic states,[22] the Athenians considering it prudent to grant even subordinates a degree of *parrhēsia*.[23]

So much for the democratic ideology of *isēgoria* and *parrhēsia*. In reality, however, free speech was not unlimited. There was no provision either in private or in public life either for intellectual freedom or for protected speech. The right to speak frankly did not guarantee a tolerant reception of offensive views, for there were in practice distinct limits to free speech in terms of particular categories of persons and types of speech, and these limits were both legal and practical.

First, only the adult male sons of two citizen parents could belong to the demos and thus participate in political life. And even a member of the demos could lose his right of *isēgoria* if anyone could convince the demos that he was guilty of one of the *aporrhēta* (unspeakable things), that is, of being a public debtor, a parent abuser, an evader of military service, a shield thrower, an inheritance squanderer, or a prostitute,[24] or indeed of posing any comparable threat to the integrity of the democratic process. Conversely, although citizens were free to abuse one another publicly in virtually any terms they liked, no one could falsely charge a fellow member of the demos with any of the *aporrhēta*, for that would unfairly silence a potential contributor to the democracy and so threaten the integrity of the system. False charges in these categories were actionable slander and were therefore constrained.[25]

Then there were practical deterrents to the exercise of *isēgoria* and *parrhēsia*. Their exercise was the highest form of participation in democratic politics, and success could win a man praise, admiration, power, and wealth.[26] But in practice, speaking was not for the many; it required at least some oratorical skill, experience, expertise, leisure, and preferably wealth and/or family.[27] The ordinary citizen, the modern-day Thersites, did occasionally rise to speak (Isokrates 12.248), but habitual speakers belonged to a very small minority of ambitious men, all wealthy and most wellborn, who constituted a political "class" or "elite."[28] But not all such men would want to enter the fray, preferring to be quietists or nonparticipators (*apragmones*). After 429 the number of such quietists seems to have been substantial; Alkibiades and Kritias were the only remaining "wellborn" politicians still competing for leadership.[29] For speaking up, especially speaking up frankly, took a good deal of courage: one risked not only his political standing but his social position and personal life as well, since these were now open to competitive scrutiny and legal accountability.[30]

Every assembly began with a curse against any who would deceive the demos (Demosth. 19.70; Deinarchos 2.16), and any speech could be punished if it led to bad consequences to the community, even if the assembly had initially agreed with it.[31] Speakers often appealed to *parrhēsia* to show that they intended to speak truthfully and in the demos' interests, not their own.[32] A speaker might also make a fool of himself or offend the people, who were not particularly fond of criticism, tolerant of antidemocratic sentiment, or open-minded about unpopular opinions, which they typically greeted with heckling and interruptions.[33] And one's opponents might well resort to intimidation, as "new politicians" like Kleon were said to do,[34] including the sort of abusive *parrhēsia* that not everyone had the stomach to respond to in kind. Men of conservative, upper-class breeding were particularly loathe to resort to violent, blaming, or shameless speech, which was traditionally associated with the lower classes and which is constantly condemned by critics of radical democracy like Thucydides, Isokrates, the philosophers, and the Old Oligarch.[35] What for the democratic masses was admirable and entertaining *parrhēsia* was for Pindar *panglōssia* (babbling, *Olymp.* 2.87), for *aidōs* (respect for others), dignity, *sōphrosynē* (moderation), and good manners were traditional aristocratic virtues.[36] In aristocratic society, public praise for one's fellows was the rule, blame being reserved only for enemies; under the rules of democratic discourse, the speaker's job was not to praise but to warn, criticize, or blame his fellow citizens, praise being reserved solely for the demos.[37]

In the political arena, then, *isēgoria* and *parrhēsia* seem to have been largely the prerogative of a small class of wealthy activists who knew the ropes in assembly and courtroom and were prepared to risk the possible consequences. In pursuit of their ambitions, these men were granted very wide latitude in advising the demos and abusing their rivals, so long as nothing they said impeded the workings of democracy or challenged its justification.

But that does not mean that for everyone else *parrhēsia* was unlimited. In his Funeral Oration Perikles does claim that whereas public life (*ta dēmosia*) was regulated by fear (*deos*) of officeholders and the laws, private life was free and self-regulated, being left to the informal jurisdiction of the "unwritten laws," that is, social custom (Thuc. 2.37.2–3).[38] And normally that seems to have been the case. But the demos had the power, legally or by special decree, to forbid or punish any speech it deemed harmful to the polis whether or not covered by statutory law and regardless of context, and any citizen in good standing had the right to call for such sanctions. And the demos regularly used this power: against Sokrates for his private conversations;[39] against sophists like Anaxagoras and Damon for their teaching;[40] against Diagoras of Melos for his book;[41] against Alkibiades and his friends for profanation of the Mysteries in their own homes;[42] and, as we will see, against dramatists for their plays. None of these targets ever appealed to the right of *parrhēsia* to excuse their offensive speech, because protected speech and intellectual freedom were not concepts covered by *parrhēsia*.

So it was that the demos encouraged free speech but forced critical voices to express themselves in terms of its own hegemonic discourse and under its own rules of engagement. The democracy sanctioned free speech not to protect the individual but to promote and safeguard the interests of the demos, and through it, the collective well-being of the polis.

It is apparent that in this system there were major rifts between ideology and reality that are germane to our subject and that were identified by critics of the democracy already in the fifth century. Ideally, the right of *isēgoria* enabled any member of the demos to express an opinion or to challenge one. But in reality the ordinary Athenian was seldom in a position to do so; for the most part he could only vote on the choices given him by elite speakers. Ideally, the right of *parrhēsia* empowered the sort of leaders who could educate the demos and lead it in making wise decisions. But in reality, under the conditions of democratic competition, politicians could often get farther by flattering the demos, by catering to its whims and prejudices, than by telling it the truth. Aggravating this problem was the tendency of open competition to generate in politicians and litigators a rhetorical prowess that could disguise dishonesty, incompetence, bad judgment, and self- rather than public-interestedness, and so corrupt the deliberative and judicial processes.[43] Finally, for the majority of the population—women, children, metics, and slaves—there was no outlet at all for the public expression of opinion or complaint; these residents could only be represented publicly by members of the demos, but even so the protocols of public discourse blocked much of their worlds from significant attention, especially the women's world.

Thus far we have omitted drama, after oratory the second most productive category of Athenian speech. Does the picture change when we include it?

Drama and Frank Speech

For Plato, Athenian drama and oratory were not merely *the* representative expressions of democratic culture but were also closely related: both, he claimed, were forms of civic rhetoric that were integral to democratic culture and served to maintain popular control. Nor was Plato making a surprising equation. Old Comedy in particular impressed contemporaries by its topical outspokenness: "shameless" speech and action, criticism and advice on current issues, and—especially impressive—explicit and sometimes fierce abuse of contemporary individuals, usually by name and even by physical caricature; Aristoph. *Knights* 230–32 shows that such portraiture (in this case of Kleon) was not exceptional.

The comic poets themselves, like their hero(in)es, claim to be distinct from the politicians and litigators whom they routinely criticize, but at the same time they regard themselves as genuinely political voices: like other speakers, they consistently claim to benefit the polis by giving it good, honest advice and by attacking those who would harm it, and like other speakers they express concern about the potential risks of their outspokenness, namely offending the demos and provoking retaliatory attacks. Contemporary witnesses like the Old Oligarch (Pseudo-Xenophon, *Const. of the Athenians* 2.18) and Plato agree, though they doubted that either orators or poets, mere caterers to the sovereign masses, could ever save the demos from itself. As Isokrates said to the assemblymen, "I know that it is hazardous to oppose your views, and that though this is a democracy, there is no *parrhēsia* except here for those [speakers] who are the most thoughtless and who give you no thought, and in the theater for the producers of comedy" (8.14).

Since Hellenistic times, however, the accuracy of this picture has been questioned, and so a brief history of the main controversies is in order.[44]

Hellenistic scholars, who were most interested in comic abuse of individuals, wondered how mere poets could get away with outrageous attacks on powerful people. So they introduced a distinction between comic and forensic abuse: the democracy needed a way to expose delinquents who escaped exposure in assembly or law court and found one in the comic festival. In support of their theory they postulated a legal "license" that protected comic poets from retaliation. They were, however, aware of instances of retaliation by individuals against comic poets and restraints on comic speech imposed by the demos. To explain these, they assumed that the license had at some point been "repealed" because the poets began to attack "good people" or because the delinquents managed to silence the poets.

Since Müller-Strübing's book, *Aristophanes und die historische Kritik* (1873), this view has been largely jettisoned. Modern scholars find it difficult to imagine any close conjunction of religion, art, humor, and politics and thus tend to see Athenian comedy as essentially detached, nonpolitical, and therefore without any actual or intended impact on the "real" world. This model, like the Hellenistic one, accepts the notion of comic outrageousness and also explains it by postulating a special "license," but this time, it was a license *not* to be taken seriously. This model deals with the attested retaliations and restraints against comic poets either by denying their historicity or by considering them to be insignificant anomalies.[45] It also assumes that comic poets were essentially entertainers and had no discernible political leanings or overt agenda.[46]

Common to both the Hellenistic and the modern models, then, is the theory that comic speech was somehow uniquely exempt from the standards and sanctions that otherwise applied to public speech. But this theory is based on a misunderstanding of those standards and sanctions.

The Hellenistic theory of a legal exemption is clearly anachronistic, and not merely because differential subjection to the laws would be fundamentally undemocratic. In fifth-century Athens, by contrast with a Hellenistic monarchy, the patronage of the demos was all a poet, or anyone else, would ever need for the exercise of *parrhēsia,* nor would the demos have needed to protect itself from delinquents by granting comic poets, or anyone else, immunity from its own control; as we have seen, the denunciation of delinquents to the demos was a privilege of *parrhēsia* that was available to any citizen. And so we never hear of such an exemption, nor does any comic poet ever appeal to or suggest the desirability of one. The legal record of comedy is in fact one of restraints imposed rather than exemptions repealed.

The Old Oligarch observed that in the case of comedy the democrats "do not allow ridicule and abuse of the demos, to avoid being criticised themselves, but in the case of individuals they encourage anyone who wishes, in the sure knowledge that the individual ridiculed is not as a rule one of the demos or the masses but someone rich, well born or powerful. Very few of the poor and the demotic are ridiculed, and these only if they make a nuisance of themselves or seek to have more than the demos" (Pseudo-Xenophon, *Const. of the Athenians* 2.18). Here the writer (1) aligns comedy with the self-interest of the demos (encouragement of attacks on the elite) and (2) challenges democratic claims of full *parrhēsia* (restraint of attacks on the demos).[47] His analysis squares well with our evidence. Let us take point (1) first.

Two decrees limiting comic outspokenness are well attested. The terms of the decree of Morychides, which lasted from 440/39–437/6,[48] are unknown, but since it was in effect during Athens' support of Miletos in her war against Samos, it is plausible to suppose that the intention was to prevent the inflammation of partisan violence, particularly in the presence of foreign allies at the Dionysia: a goal fully in line with the standard limits of *parrhēsia*.[49] It may be significant that the Lenaian comic competition, which foreigners did not attend, was instituted c. 440, and that comedy seems to have turned "political" around this time—a development perhaps related to other manifestations of growing popular sovereignty: the first prosecutions of intellectuals like Damon and Anaxagoras, and the prohibition of personal glorification on public monuments.[50]

The existence of a second decree is properly inferred from a complaint by the comic poet Phrynichos in his *Monotropos* of 415 (fr. 27 = Schol. *Birds* 1297): "[Syrakosios] deprived me of those I wanted to ridicule."[51] That the decree limited comic reference by name to any of the some sixty-five men denounced in the scandal of the Mysteries in 415 may be inferred from the actual avoidance of such references in comedies produced between 415 and 411.[52] Some deny the decree's historicity by arguing that it would have been pointless: certainly the demos, having condemned the parodists, would hardly have wanted to spare them comic ridicule.[53] But the decree does make sense in terms of the rules of *parrhēsia* as they pertained to slander, if it was an element in the settlement of the crisis of 415 designed to protect the *innocent* against damaging accusations.[54] Recall that personal accusations were forbidden if (and only if) they unfairly compromised the political standing of a member of the demos. In other words, Syrakosios will have proposed adding accusations of involvement in the profanation of the Mysteries to the list of *aporrhēta*. Like the decree of Morychides,

Syrakosios' decree may well have covered public speech in general, not comedy in particular, but the fact that comedy was included demonstrates its lack of formal exemption from the rules regulating public speech. Several other references in comedy, to politicians hostile to comic poets (Eupolis, *Demes*, fr. 99.29) and to proposals for the reduction of their stipends (Aristoph. *Frogs* 367, Plato com. fr. 141), are not spelled out but likely point in the same direction: restraint of speech that could be portrayed as harmful to the demos' interests.

Individuals could also harass comic poets for harming the demos. Kleon denounced Aristophanes to the Council by *eisangelia* in 426, claiming that in his play *Babylonians* the poet had spoken ill of the polis in the presence of foreigners, had ridiculed the polis and committed hybris against the demos.[55] If any formal exemption existed Aristophanes surely would have invoked it in his defense, but instead he argues that he is innocent of the charges and undeserving of the demos' wrath, since it was not the polis or the demos that he had attacked but rather deceptive politicians (*Acharnians* 366–84, 497–506, 628–64). In the event, Kleon's prosecution failed, and very likely on that defense. As has been suggested, this case could indeed have been the one alluded to by the Old Oligarch when he claimed that elite individuals were fair game for comic ridicule, but not the demos.[56] In *Knights* (424) Aristophanes is careful to portray the demos affectionately, as a fine sovereign temporarily enthralled by an evil slave-demagogue. Indeed there is no sign that any comic poet ever expressed sympathy with any antidemocratic view.[57]

This brings us to the Old Oligarch's second claim, that the democracy encouraged ridicule of elite individuals. It seems a fair claim, for comedy is indeed full of such ridicule. By "encourage" the Old Oligarch may mean (1) that the archon, in granting a chorus, might prefer such plays, or (2) that such plays did well in competition, or (3) that, as Hellenistic theory held, comic ridicule was somehow immune from the laws about slander because the demos enjoyed attacks on their betters. (1) and (2) are plausible enough. The choice of plays for competition was the archon's alone (Kratinos fr. 17); when Plato recommends that the archon be empowered to force conditions on playwrights (*Laws* 817d) he may be recommending a novelty, but Aristophanes' cryptic references to help from influential friends in getting his plays produced may point to some sort of negotiations with the archon.[58] As an officeholder the archon was accountable for his choices and so would try to choose plays with likely popular appeal. Aristophanes had spectacular popular success with his early plays, which featured what he boasted were unprecedentedly bold attacks on Kleon and other "deceivers of the demos," so evidently the people did enjoy this sort of ridicule.[59] But was it formally licensed?

There is no evidence that any comic poet was ever sued under the slander laws, but that does not necessarily imply a special exemption. Such suits were in any case rare, and in the only one that survives the plaintiff feels obliged to apologize for resorting to the law to redress an insult (Lysias 10.1–2). As we have observed, personal abuse was a standard feature of Athenian public life and was actively "encouraged" because it was considered to play an important role in protecting the demos from harmful individuals. The demos was prepared to punish abuse only if it unfairly threatened the capacity of a member of the demos to participate; otherwise the laws afforded no protection to an individual's reputation. As Robert Wallace puts it, "The Athenians seem to have regarded verbal abuse as an aspect of personal freedom that should be answered not in court, but in kind."[60] In this respect there is no essential difference between comic poets and orators: every comic charge against individuals can be paralleled, in substance if not always in tone, in the orators.[61]

In a few cases orators and comic poets alike make accusations that involve the *aporrhēta* and would thus appear to be actionable at law. But in each case it is clear that the charge was arguably true, or reflected shared belief, or was otherwise unlikely to provoke a retaliatory *dikē*. Aristophanes, for example, ridicules both Perikles and Kleon after their deaths, but only on political grounds that at the time many would have agreed with. In five plays he refers to Kleonymos as a shield thrower, but this may be true: apparently Kleonymos had run with the rest in the Athenian retreat at Delion, and "it was his bad luck that his fatness made him conspicuous."[62] Knowing what Kleonymos' defense would be, no one would have cared to prosecute him or the poet who ridiculed him.[63] A similar situation apparently allowed Aischines to get away with accusing Demosthenes of fleeing in the Athenian retreat at Chaironeia (*Against Ktesiphon passim*). Finally, we find accusations of servile origins. But in each testable case, in comedy at least, the individual so accused was born near enough to 451 that such charges were both plausible and unlikely to have surprised the victim.[64]

Nevertheless, the comic poets, like the orators, generally avoided the *aporrhēta:* there is no personal ridicule of acting magistrates or generals (though these may be ridiculed as a class),[65] no accusations of murder, parent abuse, aspirations to tyranny, *asebeia*. We find other areas of self-restraint as well: popular figures like athletes are never ridiculed, nor is anyone's unmarried daughter; other female relatives are named only under certain strict rules that apply also in the orators.[66] In addition, comic poets sometimes contrive to avoid explicitly naming their victims: Aristophanes in *Knights,* for example, never says that Paphlagon represents Kleon, just as Hermippos in *Moirai* and Kratinos in *Dionysalexandros* had not said that their mythological characters represented Perikles.[67] And in the plays of 411, under highly unstable political conditions, Aristophanes virtually avoids personal ridicule altogether and explicitly attributes this to self-restraint (*Lysistrata* 1043–49; *Thesmophoriazousai* 962–64).

Evidently then, orators and comic poets alike felt free to abuse elite individuals, avoiding only those charges that were likely to be actionable or that might displease the demos in assembly, law court, or theater—which amounted to the same thing: exactly as the Old Oligarch charged. If there were any special exemptions, then they applied to *all* public speech, not only comedy. The exemption theory is thus based on an anachronistic understanding of Athenian slander laws that fails to account for the full consequences of *dēmokratia*. The only alternative explanation of the facts is that virtually all public abuse was mere entertainment, perhaps because it had been so debased by the comic example that no one (any longer) took it seriously.[68]

This brings us to the modern theory that postulates a comic exemption that was not legally but "culturally" sanctioned: comedy had to do with art, humor, and festival; these were somehow detached from the real world and so were unable to have any serious impact on it; therefore comic poets were free to say anything they wanted without fear that it would be taken seriously.[69]

Does the fact that comic speech was humorous entitle us to assume that it was innocuous, that is, that a charge made by a comic poet was less potent than the same charge made by an orator? Comedy did employ a register of "shameful speech" (*aischrologia*) containing the sort of obscenity and crude mockery of the high by the low that speakers in formal social, deliberative, or judicial contexts did not normally use. And this *aischrologia* was certainly festive: it appears publicly only in the cults of Demeter and Dionysos, it was traditionally "iambic,"[70] and it was an element of the inversion of hierarchies and rupture of polite norms that characterize carnivalesque celebrations everywhere. But it is clear that noncomic speakers avoided such speech-registers not because they were illegal or ineffective but because they were vulgar and undignified.[71] Thus, for example, Lysias: "Is this not the man who commits such offenses against the gods that it is shameful (*aischron*) for the rest of us even to mention them, though you hear of them from the comic poets every year?" (fr. 53 Thalheim). By the same token, comic poets were not constrained to keep to this register: *aischrologia* is notably absent in passages intended to sound earnest, for example in parabases, where poets and chorus leaders typically advise and admonish the spectators.[72]

In the end *aischrologia* is a specimen of Athenian popular culture that the demos had reserved for itself and that was yet another aspect of the people's assertion of popular control: the outrageous comic figure could say (usually to a big shot) what the ordinary man would like to hear said but probably never would, at least not in these particular words. But then again, the use of vulgar and violent speech-registers by "new politicians" like Kleon was, as Aristophanes and Thucydides saw, an important component of the new populism that after Perikles' death fundamentally altered the traditional decorum of public speech. A case, perhaps, of life imitating the festival.[73] It is intriguing that in the fourth century *aischrologia* is much less prominent in comedy, and that personal abuse also tapers off in comedy[74] but not in oratory. I would attribute these trends to the increasingly international and less parochial character of comedy, while oratory remained a feature of Athenian democratic life.

Over and above the particular issue of *aischrologia,* however, the idea that humor is incompatible with the expression of political or otherwise consequential speech fails to take into account its abundant presence not only in classical oratory and rhetorical theory but also in classical Greek culture generally.[75] In the area of criticism and blame, the categories of speech especially protected by *parrhēsia,* public derision was a potent enough weapon as to be routinely equated with hybris; Aristotle lists it together with assault, murder, and robbery as an act of violence.[76] The honor-sensitive Greeks were much less inclined to laugh off public criticism than we more sportsmanlike moderns, so that when Plato would ban all *kakēgoria* from his ideal polis, he is careful to include comic and iambic ridicule "with or without animus" (*Laws* 935d3–e6). In view of Greek attitudes toward public ridicule, a blanket exemption for comic poets on the grounds that they were mere humorists is most improbable. Nothing prevents us from assuming instead that so long as vulgar humor did not violate the rules of *parrhēsia* the people saw no reason to restrain it.

Finally, the idea that the dramatic festivals were detached because they were festive ignores their demonstrably civic character.[77] And this holds both for the festivals themselves and for the dramas produced in them. To be sure, comedy did retain primeval carnivalesque and poetic traditions, but the poets never appeal to them as protection, nor were they confining. Otherwise Menander would be as outspoken as Aristophanes, and comedy would not have developed as rapidly as it did throughout the democratic era, in tune with contemporary events and personalities. The comic poets often boast of their originality in areas that include social and political novelty,[78] and they freely adapted and augmented traditional material to suit their audiences. Like other public voices, comic poets were members of a tiny elite who competed for a civic distinction that was determined and awarded by the demos. And like other competitors they frequently champion their own excellence and criticize their poetic rivals.[79] But they did not confine their topicality to artistic competition, as we might expect if comedy was a detached activity. The close historical synchrony of democracy and political comedy, as festive competition and as genre, cannot be coincidental. For poets and spectators alike, drama was not an escape or a time-out from democratic life but a form of participation in it.

The Comic Contribution

As institutions the Athenian theatrical festivals were primarily civic: patriotic showcases sponsored and administered by the demos and funded on a grand scale by its wealthiest liturgists, the *chorēgoi,* who, along with poets selected by the appropriate officeholder, competed for prizes and civic prestige.[80] The dancers, numbering some 1,165 per festival, could be compelled to perform and were exempted from military service to do so. Attendance was considered a right and privilege of Athenian citizenship, and front-row seating (*prohedria*) a reward that the demos bestowed upon its most distinguished citizens and guests. That attendance was regarded as a form of democratic participation is further indicated by the spectator fund (*theōrikon*) that had been established by the fourth century, perhaps as early as the Periklean period, to enable even the poorest citizens to attend,[81] just as in the 420s citizens began to be compensated for jury service and in the 390s for attendance at assemblies.[82]

Historically, too, drama and democracy were closely related. Although the dramatic genres had ancient roots, their fifth-century forms were the product of festivals revamped for, and possibly created by, the emerging democracy, and they developed in step with democratic institutions.[83] Significantly, both *chorēgia* and *theōrikon* were abolished by the oligarchy of 322–317. The history of comedy reveals an especially close synchrony with the history of democracy at Athens, and perhaps elsewhere too.[84] Comedy became part of the Dionysia in the reform year 487/6, when archons were first allotted and could be drawn from the second as well as the first census class, and when ostracism was introduced.[85] Comedy's most intensely political phase coincided with the era of full popular sovereignty (the ascendancy of Perikles and the Peloponnesian War); this phase tapered off after the reforms of 403, disappeared entirely during the oligarchic period of 322–307 (the era of the entirely apolitical "New Comedy"), but reappeared during two democratic restorations.[86] Contrast the contemporary West Greek court-comedy of Epicharmos and Sophron, which was entirely apolitical. Conversely, writers critical of democracy (for example, Plato) are notoriously hostile toward all comic festivity and explicitly link it to democratic practice.

The dramatic performances themselves resembled legal trials and assembly meetings:[87] played before a mass audience containing the demos, present as host, bestower of civic honors, regulator, and notional audience; when performers speak of or to the audience they almost always address it as the demos or some subset of it.[88] The audience responded to the discourse of individuals in situations requiring mediation of conflicting social values and the resolution of personal conflicts.[89] Like courtroom and assembly speeches, the plays were written by elite citizens[90] who had chosen to compete by applying to the relevant archon, who were competing for a victory determined by the audience's response, and who were therefore constrained to consider (Plato thought, cater to) its opinions and attitudes. Not surprisingly, the discourse of drama largely reflected contemporary Athenian issues and concerns.

But the dramatists did more than reflect contemporary Athenian life. Like all Greek poets before them, and like orators too, the dramatists were expected also to inform, to instruct, and within certain bounds even to castigate their audiences.[91] Like law courts and assemblies, the dramatic festival exemplified, and devoted much of its attention to, the dissonance between the two major themes of democratic ideology, egalitarianism and elitism.[92] And like law courts and assemblies, civic theater served to temper the understanding, the critical capacity, and the confidence of a citizenry now fully in charge of its own destiny. Like any other organ of the democracy, civic theater was predicated on the theory of the ultimate wisdom, and trainability in wisdom, of the demos. Thus it could not but serve and strengthen the sovereignty of democratic ideology. That is why critics like Plato attacked it in the same terms as they did rhetoric.

Thus far we have looked at the dramatic festivals as civic occasions. But their distinctness from other venues of civic discourse is equally significant. The theater, which accommodated at least seventeen thousand spectators, concentrated much more of the Attic populace in one place at the same time than any other public event; the assembly could house only six thousand. And the dramatic festivals were not exclusive; we hear of no attempt to restrict attendance by any class of residents or even foreigners.[93] Alongside the demos sat as many of those people who were otherwise debarred from civic assemblies as could get seats: women,[94] children, even slaves, metics (who could even perform at the Lenaia), and visiting foreigners.[95] Moreover, all these categories of people, normally invisible from the vantage point of civic assemblies, were standard characters in drama. As for the poets, they were elite competitors in a democratically organized contest, but unlike purely civic speakers, who could appeal only to democratic laws and procedures, the poets could appeal to much older cultic and poetic traditions, and to a more universal ethical code.

Thus the dramatic festivals were supracivic: public meetings that encompassed the whole of society, not just its political subset. The concerns expressed in the dramas included but significantly transcended the set of problems specific to the executive worlds of law court and assembly, for they treated the ethics of family and private life, the lives of people as individuals as opposed to civic categories, the very discontinuity between the political and the larger society, and the wider world beyond Athens. And so drama became the principal communal outlet for portraying the polis in all its diversity and social hierarchies, and for reconsidering traditions and norms, airing concerns, examining problems, and testing solutions that affected the democratic culture as a whole but that had no other public outlet. As theatergoers, people debarred from all other venues of civic discourse could here experience the role of democratic audience. Community knowledge, from popular gossip to the concerns of the political class, could be aired and diffused. And people whose suggestions, concerns, or complaints had not been, or could not be, presented to the executive demos might expect them to be raised by one of the poets, not least the comic poets. Such people would include civic minorities like the "quiet" members of the elite and the "little people" who were rarely able to attend civic meetings, let alone likely to rise in the assembly or to litigate, such as farmers from distant demes, or the very poor. In these ways the dramatic festivals served to mend, or at least to paper over, some of the rifts in the body politic outlined earlier. Dramatic *parrhēsia* served as everyone's *parrhēsia.*

Indeed, the heroes and other sympathetic characters of Old Comedy exclusively represent such "little" or "quiet" people and offer the polis advice and criticism exclusively on their behalf.[96] It is significant that comic hero(in)es are always fictitious creations, whereas their opponents represent real individuals and groups holding power or celebrity in the polis. The comic vantage point is essentially idiotic (in the Athenian sense), that of the ordinary citizen looking into the arena of civic power and faulting those who dominate it, while they themselves, as the Old Oligarch noted, are spared. The illusion of demotic righteousness versus elite chicanery is reinforced by comic avoidance of praise: all good ideas come from comic hero(in)es, even when in actual life they could be attributed to actual people, for example the Peace of Nikias of 421, celebrated in Aristophanes' *Peace* without mention of Nikias. In fact, only nine men are praised in all of comedy, all of them either deceased or politically inactive.

Comic hero(in)es thus gave the majority of spectators vicarious pleasure in the triumph of the insignificant over the great, or the politically excluded over the political class; their complaints might serve as a safety valve for unofficial discontent before it became politically or socially disruptive. In short, by frankly criticizing the powerful, the comic hero(ine) did what *isēgoria* and *parrhēsia* ideally allowed but could not fully provide for. In the democracy, Thersites stood up again in the avatar of the comic poet, but this time no Odysseus could punish him—that was now the people's prerogative.[97]

The comic poets did differ, then, from other public speakers in the *scope* of their criticism and advice: since their audience was more inclusive, they could address social, moral, and intellectual concerns unlikely to be raised in strictly deliberative and legal contexts, and they often did so in uncompromisingly idealistic ways: the greed of the rich, for example, or the arrogance of celebrities, the misbehavior of women and young men, the bizarre ideas of the sophists. But even here the comic poets took a democratic line: such misbehavior is the fault not of ordinary, decent people but rather of aberrant individual(ist)s—wastrels like Kallias, irresponsible tragic poets like Euripides, dangerous intellectuals like Sokrates. By calling attention to such problems comedy supplemented the police functions of assembly and court, using negative publicity as a substitute for legal sanctions. But that does not mean the targets of such negative publicity could afford simply to laugh it off: under the democracy leadership required dignity and was easily undermined by popular suspicions, and even private misbehavior could become the basis for legal action if someone could show that it harmed the polis—as happened in the case of Sokrates who, according to Plato, blamed his prosecution on popular prejudices originally created by comedy.[98] It was the potential for such impact on the real world that kept comic speech from ever being exempted from the rules governing *parrhēsia.*

But the comic poets did not confine themselves to griping on behalf of the *homunculi.* Being citizens as well as poets, they often had their own axes to grind, and they expected to have an impact beyond the festival. When Aristophanes claims that his plays serve only the public interest and not his own (e.g., *Wasps* 1023–28), he is, like an orator, defending himself against plausible suspicions to the contrary, and probably disingenuously. When the demos officially crowned and commended Aristophanes for the advice he offered in the parabasis of *Frogs* (686–705) and decreed a reperformance of the play, there is good reason to suspect a political motivation and a behind-the-scenes quid pro quo deal with the enemies of Kleophon.[99] It is not unlikely that Hermippos' attack of 430 on Perikles' war policy in his play *Moirai* (cf. fr. 47) was politically motivated as well.[100]

Now the comic poet as axe grinder is incompatible with the frequently expressed view that comic ridicule indiscriminately targeted all celebrities, joked only about what was universally considered humorous, and was therefore all in fun. But that view is in fact mistaken. Aristophanes (and also, as far as we can tell, his comic rivals) reveals a consistent bias toward a more conservative practice of democracy than was the rule during the war years. He consistently singles out radical leaders from Perikles and Kleon onward for ridicule, criticism, and unfavorable comparison with the leaders of an idealized past democracy, while entirely sparing men of conservative bent, even if they were "new politicians"

(Nikias is a case in point).[101] He also consistently champions countrymen over townsmen, calls for a negotiated peace with Sparta, urges panhellenic cooperation, denounces musical and intellectual novelty, and warns of structural and procedural threats to democracy, especially the tendency of the demos to be gullible in the face of self-styled "people's watchdogs" like Kleon. This comic *tendenz* was at odds with majority views of the day and more often than not jibes with the *tendenz* of Thucydides and other conservative critics. Apparently the comic poets, like other members of the traditional elite, were disturbed by their class' loss of political ascendency, especially after 429,[102] and used the comic stage to affix blame for what they saw (not unjustifiably) as a decline from the greatness won by the previous two generations.

But how could comic poets have gotten away with grinding that particular axe before a popular audience? Was the audience composed largely of disgruntled conservatives?[103] Unlikely: many of the comedies presuppose a representative audience, and Plato refers to its composition as "the many who are senseless" as opposed to the "few" who are "sensible" or "wise" (*Symposium* 194b). Were the comic poets hostile to the democracy and out to attack it through its leaders?[104] Hardly: apart from the intrinsic unlikelihood that competitors for popular favor would willfully counter the audience's predilections, the right of *parrhēsia* did not protect speech that would disturb or destabilize the democracy; no politician or any other public voice in fifth-century Athens took an "antidemocratic" line. So the best explanation for the comic poets' conservative appeals is that they still retained some power: by urging rejection of radical novelties, the poets were trying to recall the demos to its past greatness in a period of political transition and evident decline, when the demos too must have been a bit nervous, for all its support of a Kleon.

Comic poets, no less than orators, felt free to criticize the demos and its various subsets, e.g., assemblies and juries, but were always careful to blame the demos' shortcomings (and Athens' decline) on particular leaders or on a dominant class of untrustworthy politicians.[105] They seem to have taken the same line about the empire, criticizing Athenian leaders for mismanagement and corruption but never questioning its justification.[106] Thus they warn the demos against the flattery and dishonesty of its leaders, exhort it to reclaim its own rightful sovereignty, and urge it to choose better leaders. They urge the polis to reclaim the strength and success that characterized the democracy in earlier eras. And they offer advice on important current issues. What they do not do is offer illegal advice, question the right of the demos to full sovereignty, or suggest any changes in the rules of democracy, and in this they both parallel the orators and stand in stark contrast to private critics like Thucydides and the philosophers.

If comic treatment of the new leaders sounds snobbish, recall that these were the first ordinary men to achieve ascendancy and had to prove themselves up to the job as elite men did not; in their attacks the comic poets were playing on what must have been real suspicion, perhaps born of envy, as the Old Oligarch implies; Plato (*Lysis* 215d) and Aristotle (*Rhetoric* 1386b) point out that we feel envy especially of an equal. When Aristophanes vilifies Kleon for being a tanner he is not slamming ordinary people but rather tanners who aspire to elite status, just as ridicule of Hitler as a paperhanger was no slam against paperhangers.

Did the comic poets, then, have a political impact? We may infer so from the decrees and prosecutions occasionally brought against them and from cases such as Aristophanes' crowning and Sokrates' prosecution. But precise impact is seldom measurable and often problematic. *Clouds,* for example, was a failure but permanently stigmatized its victim, while *Knights* won first prize but did not stop Kleon's election as general a few weeks later. This sort of ambiguity need not be resolved in an either/or fashion. After all, the poets were contributing to debates and divisions of opinion that were yet unresolved, however self-evident their outcomes may seem to us in long retrospect. Aristophanes' ongoing plea for a negotiated peace may have been a minority view at the time, but it was not a view entertained solely by Aristophanes nor an issue that was ever finally decided.[107] People regarded the threat posed by Sokrates differently after the war than they had in 423. As for Kleon, the people's discrepant responses in the theater and in the assembly may well reflect real ambivalence. As assemblymen the people wanted Kleon, and after Pylos they could hardly deny him a command; but as citizens they may have felt unhappy about giving him so much power.[108] Comedy then counts as an expression of such political complexities.

Conclusion

The Athenians considered frank speech essential to the proper functioning of their democracy. Drama (particularly topical comedy) and oratory were the principal outlets for frank speech; both flourished and withered in tandem with the democratic institutions that fostered them. Their modes of frankness were essentially identical and were governed by the same basic rule: all speech was allowed as long as it did not threaten the democracy or impede its processes. Topical comedy differed from oratory primarily in its more representative audience, the festive/poetic nature of its competitions, the free range of its subject matter, and its service as a voice for people otherwise lacking an outlet for public self-expression. Transcending the exclusivity of oratorical audiences and unbounded by the practical constraints of deliberative debate, comedy could engage in a kind of experimental politics whose scope was as broad, and whose outcome as open, as poet and spectators cared to make them. In the end, even fantastic, impractical, idealistic, or unpersuasive criticisms could have their impact: their very enunciation expanded the ground in which public debate was possible and change for the better conceivable.[109] Such interventions are essential to any democracy, but the price is the protection of frank speech, however outrageous it may sometimes be.

CHAPTER THIRTEEN

Tragedy and Politics

SUZANNE SAÏD

The aim of this chapter is, first, to describe briefly the institutional background of tragic performances, which was closely related to the civic life of Athens, then to summarize the ancient testimonia on the political nature of Greek tragedy, before giving a survey of recent scholarly approaches to this topic. As a test case, I shall analyze the tensions between *oikos* and polis and the change from Aeschylus, who is mostly interested in the community, to Euripides, who brings the family into focus, in some of the plays centered on the war against Thebes as well as its aftermath—that is, Aeschylus' *Seven*, Sophocles' *Antigone*, and Euripides' *Suppliants* and *Phoenician Women*.

The Institutional Background

"Tragedy is transparently more 'democratic' as an art form . . . than both the epic and the various other kinds of choral or individual lyric, or iambic, that we know of."[1] This statement is readily acceptable, for the tragic poets were living in democratic Athens and their work was primarily addressed to a democratic audience. Moreover, dramatic performances were firmly located within the framework of a civic festival that was perhaps established only after the fall of the tyranny[2] and certainly reached its definitive form under the democracy.

In fact, the State was heavily involved in the dramatic performances.[3] It assumed responsibility for procuring and paying the actors. It appointed, among the well-off citizens, the *chorēgoi* who paid for training and outfitting the chorus.[4] At some point, it established a festival fund (*theōrikon*) to give poorer citizens an equal opportunity to attend the theater.[5] Its highest magistrates played a conspicuous role in the City Dionysia: the eponymous archon designated the poets who were awarded a chorus and the ten strategoi offered a libation before the competition.[6] The citizens participated as performers—the chorus members had to be citizens and the authors, at least during the fifth century, were mostly Athenians[7]—and, in large numbers, as audience.[8] Moreover, "seating arrangements . . . reflected Athens' most important political and social divisions."[9] The privilege called *proedria* (front seating) was granted to various officials, foreign dignitaries, or public benefactors; permanent sections of the theater were reserved for the young men on military service. It has also been suggested that the seating was tribal, but the evidence for this is poor.[10] In typically democratic procedure, the judges were selected by lot from a list of possible candidates submitted by each tribe and approved by the Council,[11] and at the end of the competition an assembly judging the performance of the festival was held in the theater.

The tragic performances were preceded by ceremonies closely linked to civic ideology.[12] Honors awarded to meritorious citizens and foreigners were proclaimed in the theater in order to stimulate the audience's communal spirit.[13] As a demonstration of the power of Athens and the price to be paid for it, the allies' annual tribute was displayed in the orchestra, and the war orphans raised at public expense were paraded in the panoplies given them by the polis.[14]

Besides, there were strong analogies between tragedy and politics. They took place in the same or identical settings.[15] Early on, tragedies were performed in the Agora, the site of political and judicial activity; at almost the same time, the political and theatrical activities were moved to two different locations—the Pnyx and the theater of Dionysus—which, however, were organized in the same way. Moreover, the theater of Dionysus was still used for exceptional public meetings in the fourth century,[16] and in other Greek cities the theater served as the regular meeting place.[17]

Evidently tragic performances were considered political activities. During the Great Dionysia there were no political meetings, which suggests that attendance at tragedy was equivalent to attendance at assembly, and the members of the chorus were granted an exemption from military service.

Tragedy and Politics: Ancient Testimonia

Aristophanes' *Frogs* strongly underlines the political role of tragic performances.[18] In this play, the tragic poet who "teaches" the chorus (*chorodidaskalos*) is also considered a "teacher" of politics (954–55, 1019, 1026, 1035, 1054–57)—undoubtedly a conception of sophistic origin. The content of such tragic teaching is often left vague and does not distinguish morals from politics: the poets teach what is "good" and "useful" to the city and aim at its preservation by "giving good advice" and "improving" the citizens (686, 1008–9, 1035, 1054–57, 1420–21).

When it is more clearly spelled out, this tragic didacticism becomes somewhat contradictory. Aristophanes sometimes seems to validate in advance modern scholarly attempts to find topical allusions in Greek tragedy by assimilating this genre to comedy and by asking the tragedians to give advice, in a veiled and metaphorical way, on day-to-day politics and politicians such as Alkibiades (1422–29). Elsewhere he seems to support critics who interpret Aeschylean tragedy as a validation of the existing order and an inculcation of political virtues: by emotional appeals and portraying heroic characters, Aristophanes' Aeschylus claims to teach respect for hierarchy and magistrates (1071–72) and to inspire martial courage and patriotism (1019–20, 1026–28). Conversely, his Euripides, who boasts of making the Athenians intellectually more acute and better managers of their households (954–55, 973–75), appeals rather to those who think that tragedy questions civic ideology.

Plato's criticism of tragedy and of its "leader" (*hēgemōn*) Homer also establishes a strong link between tragedy and democratic Athens.[19] By describing tragedy as a kind of "public speech" (*dēmēgoria*)[20] and by establishing a close analogy between the poet and the demagogue who both try to "please" (*charizesthai*) their patron, the Athenian Demos, by echoing his opinions, even when they are wrong,[21] Plato clearly implies that tragedy fully endorses civic ideology. Worse, it is plain democratic propaganda, for the tragic poets are prone to celebrate Athenian democracy and harshly criticize its enemies.[22]

The historians and orators provide supplementary evidence. Herodotus (6.21.2) tells us that the Athenians fined Phrynichos for staging the *Capture of Miletos* and "reminding them of their own pains" (*oikēia kaka*),[23] suggesting that tragedy could be perceived as a political manifesto. In *On the False Embassy* (246–48), Demosthenes finds Kreon's words in the introductory speech of *Antigone* "useful and noble." Similarly, in *Against Leokrates* (100), Lycurgus lavishes praise on Euripides for dramatizing, in his *Erechtheus*, an example of heroic sacrifice and patriotism. Later authors such as Aristotle (*Poetics* 1450b7–8; *Nicom. Ethics* 1093a27–b11) or Dio Chrysostom (52.11, 14) emphasize the "political" character of the speeches of fifth-century tragedy, and the way in which Lucian (*Anacharsis* 22) and Plutarch (*Solon* 29)—with total disregard for chronology—have Solon, the early-sixth-century legislator, praise or blame the "teaching" of tragedy also indicates that, during the Empire, the political influence of Greek tragedy was still recognized.

Tragedy and Politics: A Survey of Modern Opinions

Examination of the relations between Greek tragedy and politics[24] has long been vitiated by the modern opposition between "art," understood as "art for art's sake," and political commitment. Whereas vigorous champions of the "committed theater" wanted to banish from their vocabulary the word "art,"[25] their adversaries believed that political messages could be conveyed only at the expense of the artistic form. One had to be either a poet or a politician, and critics intent on praising tragedy as the supreme art denied it any political value. Hence there developed a clear-cut opposition between those who, like D. Conacher, did not think "that tragedy had much to do with politics" and those who, like G. Forrest, "did not believe that it had to do with much else."[26] Straight refusal of the political dimension of tragedy has almost disappeared, however,[27] and most scholars, whatever their national or political background, now agree on its political character[28]—as is amply attested by recent titles, such as *Polis und Tragödie, La polis e il suo teatro, Greek Tragedy and Political Theory,* or *Die politische Kunst der griechischen Tragödie.*[29] In short, Greek tragedies are now "perceived and interpreted as important manifestations of political thought."[30] But, with few earlier exceptions,[31] this consensus has emerged only in the last two decades. Previously, scholars were more cautious and limited the political aspect by qualifying with "political" an "interpretation" or "background" or a few "plays" among the works of Euripides.[32]

The current broad consensus on the political nature of tragedy disappears, however, as soon as one tries to explicate one's definition of "politics" and "political." Do we mean, as Dover and Dodds did in discussing the *Oresteia,* "political comments on the events of the writer's time,"[33] or do we say, following Macleod's superb comments on the same play, that a play is political "in the sense that it is concerned with human beings in a *polis*"?[34] A survey of the different approaches taken to the question of tragedy and politics reveals a gradual shift from the first and narrow to the second and broader meaning.

Tragedy as a "Reflection" of Contemporary Events

Many scholars writing in the 1950s or 1960s considered tragedy a "reflection" or a "mirror" of the period and its spirit.[35] Some historians even thought it possible, rather naively, to use tragedy as a kind of raw material from which to extract hard "facts," whereas many literary critics were content with fixing the dates of otherwise undatable plays by relating them to historical events. The only problem was to spot the allusions to *contemporary* events in *mythical* plays, for allusions are by definition allusive, if not elusive.

The representatives of the so-called *méthode* or *interprétation historique* were looking for "les inconséquences de toute espèce, les remarques déplacées, les idées inattendues" which may represent "les traces fragmentaires d'une pensée profonde." They were thus interested mostly in lines and episodes they perceived as out of place and untragic, supposedly inserted by the poet for the sole purpose of conveying a political message to his fellow citizens.[36]

This type of search for political allusions, notoriously fraught with dangers, has been subjected to devastating criticism by G. Zuntz.[37] To prove that the "allusions" found by previous scholars in Euripides' plays were mostly imaginary, he showed that these passages are not superfluous, but "serve a definite purpose within the context of the play."[38] Similarly, C. Macleod demonstrated that some crucial passages in the *Eumenides*, contrary to E. R. Dodds' view, need not be topical references inserted into the play by the poet himself but are "part of a coherent artistic design."[39]

Several scholars, following the ancient scholiast who identified the mob orator of *Orestes* 903–6 with the demagogue Kleophon, have attempted to uncover contemporary politicians behind tragic-mythical figures—reaching widely differing results. In the *Seven*, Eteokles has been successively identified as Perikles and his arch-adversary Kimon,[40] the Zeus tyrant of the *Prometheus Bound* as Hippias, Xerxes, or Hieron, that is, any available tyrant inside and outside the Greek world.[41] This method is now thoroughly discredited; even those who still see analogies between tragic heroes and historical characters refrain from overemphasizing the similarities.[42]

Others have attempted to recognize in tragic heroes a condensation of the Athenian collective character. According to B. Knox, basic patterns in Sophocles' *Oedipus Rex* suggest "a comparison not to any individual Athenian, but to Athens itself" and C. Meier regards "the passionate impetuous conduct of Apollo and above all, of Prometheus as a reflection of the spirit of Athens."[43]

Finally, many have found in tragedies veritable "running commentaries on contemporary events"[44]—although they could not agree on *which* events. For example, the Danaids' request for Argos' help in Aeschylus' *Suppliants* has been interpreted as an allusion to every possible call for help before 463 (the probable date of the play): 471 when Argos sheltered the ostracized Themistokles, 499 when Aristagoras asked for Athenian support of the Ionians, or even 510 when Plataea requested Athenian aid against Thebes.[45]

By now, this "historical method" fortunately has few supporters.[46] It is generally recognized that it is impossible to prove conclusively that a given passage alludes to a specific contemporary event or character, not least because of the lacunae in our knowledge of fifth-century history and the uncertain dates of many plays.[47] More importantly, tragedy does not "reflect" society: "elle n'est pas un miroir direct du social et du politique, elle est un miroir brisé."[48] Nor, in contrast to comedy, is tragedy topical (which precludes any allusion to particular events or characters)—an idea already well expressed by Aristotle in the *Poetics*

(1451a36–b10). In sum, tragedy's concern with the polis "does not necessarily involve any direct reference to the immediate politicking of the Athenian audience at any one particular time."[49] J. Redfield even turns the historical method upside down by subordinating the use of historical details to the demands of the mythical plot: if the hero of the *Oedipus Rex* is like Perikles, it is "not because Sophocles intended a point about Pericles, but rather . . . because he relied on his audience's understanding of Pericles to create for them a believable Oedipus."[50]

Tragedy as a "Reflection" of Current Politics

According to a different approach, tragedy, by dramatizing the main political problems of the day, mirrors contemporary Athenian political experience. Therefore the mythical characters are equated not with individual politicians but with contemporary political types. In the *Philoktetes,* Odysseus is assumed to represent the unscrupulous politician and Philoktetes the citizen disillusioned by the failure of attempts to reform democracy, and in the *Orestes,* as E. Hall suggests, "several characters are conceived according to a political character typology with powerful current valency."[51] Others claim that tragedy reflects contemporary debates also echoed in Thucydides and Aristophanes. Euripides' *Suppliants,* like the chorus of *Knights* (579–80) and Thucydides (5.16.1), has been taken as evidence of "a debate concerning an Athenian commitment to decisive action outside Athenian boundaries," around 424–421,[52] and *Phoenician Women,* probably performed 411–409,[53] as highlighting the harmful effects of ambition (*philotimia*) and civil strife (*stasis*) on the whole polis.[54]

Tragedy as Committed Theater

Expanding on this view of tragedy as "a means of expressing political thoughts,"[55] some scholars think that the stage served as a platform from which the tragic poet presented to the audience his own opinion on contemporary political issues.[56] This approach is especially tempting for a play dealing with historical events, such as Aeschylus' *Persians*—which, however, has lent itself to so many contrasting interpretations that one has every reason to be sceptical. For a majority it is intended to remind the Athenians of Themistokles' genius and to be a subtle rebuke for their ingratitude.[57] Others interpret it as a plea for reconciliation between Persians and Greeks[58] or a warning against Themistokles' policy and naval hegemony.[59] If the play conveys a definite message, it is not expressed unambiguously.

The case is even more difficult with plays that are based on myth—as the *Eumenides* demonstrates abundantly. Although the historical background is well known and the link to political events such as Athens' Argive alliance and

Ephialtes' reforms seems inescapable, there exists no consensus on the play's political content. Many portray Aeschylus as a conservative looking back with regret on the curtailment of the powers of the Areopagus.[60] Others consider the poet a committed democrat who supported Ephialtes' reforms and favored the Argive alliance.[61] Yet others, more cautious or aware of the ambiguous political language of the play, disagree with both interpretations, either admitting their inability to reach a definite conclusion[62] or embracing a third view, that "Aeschylus was neither justifying the recent reforms nor grumbling about them"[63] but advocated a middle course, pleading for reconciliation between contending parties.[64] It thus seems safe to conclude that Aeschylus took no side in the *Eumenides* and, more generally, that in fifth-century Athens tragedies "transcended factional groupings."[65]

Tragedy as Propaganda for Athens

Yet tragedy, sponsored by the Athenian polis, was not beyond nationalistic propaganda. Like the funeral orations, it often presented its audiences with an idealized picture of Athens.[66] Aeschylus' *Persians,* emphasizing Salamis over Plataea, can be read as glorification of an Athenian victory.[67] The *Eumenides* fashions in mythical Athens the image of civilizing power and an ideal city, free from factional strife and successful in external wars, while guaranteeing justice internally.[68] As Froma Zeitlin puts it well, "within the theater, Athens is not a tragic place. Rather it is the scene . . . where reconciliation and transformation are made possible."[69] Athenian kings, such as Demophon and Theseus, too, behaving like democratic leaders and contrasting sharply with the notoriously bad rulers of other tragic cities, represent "the Athenian self-image at its finest."[70] Conversely, tragedy often projects onto Athens' adversaries, Sparta and especially Thebes, a reverse image of Athenian virtues.[71]

Tragedy as Political Thought

The simplistic view of tragedy as "reflecting" historical facts or propaganda has given way to one that sees it as "reflection" and "important manifestation of political thought."[72] C. Meier and C. Farrar devote whole chapters to tragedy in their analyses of Greek political thinking and J. P. Euben argues for "the continuities between Greek tragedy and classical political theory."[73] Everyone agrees that "problems of public life" and relations among citizens and between citizens and noncitizens are among the major themes of tragedy,[74] and many scholars have systematically explored the function and use in tragedy of political terms and themes such as tyranny, city-state, freedom, barbarian, or war.[75] More specifically, tragic poets explored the problems of decision making and leadership, which were crucial for a society of free individuals. They created complex figures of leaders "who resist straightforward classifications"[76] (Agamemnon in *Agamemnon,* Kreon in *Antigone,* Oedipus in *Oedipus Rex*), skteched ideal portraits of—not necessarily Athenian—good kings (Dareios in *Persians,* Eteokles in the first part of *Seven,* Pelasgos in *Suppliants*),[77] and contrasted these with young and rash new leaders (Xerxes in *Persians,* Zeus in *Prometheus Bound*), mere usurpers (Aigisthos and Lykos), or despicable demagogues like Odysseus.[78] They also depicted ideal citizens (the Theban warriors in the *Seven* or the farmer in Euripides' *Elektra*).

Although tragedy may thus appear as "a democratic paideia complete in itself,"[79] the content of such education and the relationship between tragedy and civic ideology are envisioned in various ways. Describing tragic teaching "with an unhelpful degree of generality,"[80] some assume that it informed "political wisdom," "inculcated civic virtue," or "enhanced the audience's capacity to act with foresight and judge with insight."[81] Others simply juxtapose conflicting definitions of tragic discourse. When Euben says, for example, that tragedy helped "define, sustain and question democratic culture,"[82] he lumps together three different ways of understanding the political role of tragedy.

Tragedy Endorses Athenian Civic Ideology. In the view of Italian Marxists, writing in the 1970s–1980s, and some German or American scholars who, later and independently, reached the same conclusions, tragedy as a "vero e proprio apparato ideologico di stato" validates the political and social order.[83] Politically, it "reinforces notions important to the Athenian community," "promotes the principles of democracy," and "suggests remedies against factions."[84] Socially, tragedy "validates the social order" and maintains "the cohesion of the community" by "the creation of an area of consensus."[85] The blessing of the Chorus in *Eumenides,* disparaging factionalism and advocating "a spirit of love towards the common weal" (985), is thus interpreted as emphasizing the "idea that the members of the different classes should be united by friendship."[86] More specifically, tragedy is seen as confirming sociopolitical roles and the distribution of power in the polis. For example, in an article which is influenced by the works of J. Ober and L. Kurke but ignores the Italian School, M. Griffith proposes "a way of looking at Athenian tragedy in general as an exercise, on the part of rulers and ruled, in mutual mystification and *reassurance* about the exercise of democratic power" (my emphasis).[87]

To achieve this purpose, tragedy integrates "the consolidated system of opinions,"[88] mostly through *gnomai* echoing the basic tenets of civic ideology, or, like the funeral oration, advocates the values of democracy by presenting the triumph of those who fought for freedom against hubristic adversaries (*Persians, Seven*) or risked their lives for the sake of principles (*Heraclidae, Suppliants*). More frequently, political meaning is conveyed through negative examples. In *Antigone*, "Sophocles teaches his audience a general truth about the terrible consequences of suppression of free speech," while *Phoenician Women* addresses the problem of individual ambition and the catastrophic consequences of factionalism, both of obvious importance to the democratic polis.[89]

All this is well known. But there are more subtle ways by which tragedy consolidates democracy. The dialogue on stage formulates concerns and conflicting interests or ideologies of various groups in the community. By "negotiating" between them, it represents and synthesizes the dialectic of the ongoing political process.[90] By expressing what was usually excluded from public speech and giving a voice to those who were deprived of it, tragedy may have played a regulating role and helped prevent any dangerous return of the repressed.[91] Eliciting from the audience collective identification with the experiences of a "collective actor," tragedy created a theatrical community which in turn strengthened the civic community.[92] Because tragedy derives its characters and plot from the world of legend and blends themes of traditional moral poetry with contemporary political concerns, it was able to present "a scheme of values retaining the glamour of the past, yet accessible and appropriate to the present" and to "reconcile traditional aristocratic values with the democratic order."[93]

Tragedy "Constructs" Athenian Civic Ideology. Some historians think that tragedy did not only reflect democratic ideology and culture but played a decisive role in creating it, thus contributing as much as the funeral oration to the "invention of Athens." It "shaped the mental infrastructure of the Athenian citizens" and provided them with "a model for thinking about what has really happened."[94] As C. Meier demonstrates, Aeschylus helped to develop the new concept of collective decision making by interaction between leader and assembly (*Suppliants*) or through a committee (the Areopagus in *Eumenides*).[95] In the *Oresteia* and *Prometheus* he explored the questions of legitimacy and permanence of a new regime. Adapting to politics a lesson taught by Hesiod on a religious level (*Theogony*),[96] he demonstrated that reconciliation is necessary and possible even between bitter enemies and that, in order to survive, a political system must embrace all, respect old values, and integrate those who represent them.[97]

Tragedy Questions Athenian Civic Ideology. Nowadays, however, scholars are mostly interested in the role of tragedy as questioning democratic ideology.

J.-P. Vernant and other members of the French school (P. Vidal-Naquet, N. Loraux) and their followers in England (S. Goldhill, N. Croally) or in the United States (C. Segal, F. Zeitlin) insist that tragedy "calls the normative codes and the familiar institutions into question," "problematizes the assumptions of the values of the civic discourse . . . and investigates the possible conflict in the system of belief."[98] But there are some interesting nuances. Whereas Vernant pays much attention to the "tensions" built into the structure of tragedy and to the contradictions between the values of the inherited culture (*mythe*) and the new social order (*actualité*),[99] others emphasize the limits of such questioning and are more interested in synchrony and performance. Thus Goldhill focuses on the preplay ceremonies and tries to demonstrate that the tragic text "questions and sets at risk the direct assertations of ideology that the preplay ceremonials seem to proclaim,"[100] while R. Osborne asserts that "tragedy (because it is performed during a competitive festival) seems to invite competitive views of the city."[101] Recent books and articles indicate that these assumptions are now shared by a vast majority of scholars and are in danger of becoming "a disabling cliché."[102]

A Tentative Appraisal. These opposite views of Greek tragedy as endorsement or criticism of civic ideology are both globally wrong and partially correct. They are wrong because it is difficult to fit Aeschylus into the role of a radical challenger of democratic values. In his short discussion of *Persians,* Goldhill, far from demonstrating that this play questions democratic ideology (which had hardly had time to develop by 472 anyway), shows only that, during the exchange between Atossa and the messenger, "the Athenians are praised through a series of oppositions which relate closely to the sense of Athenian ideology."[103] D. Rosenbloom argues more plausibly for the possibility that the same play may challenge Athenian imperialist ideology.[104]

Conversely, it seems impossible to find a validation of the existing social and political order in Euripides' tragedies. *Hecuba* and *Trojan Women* destroy the glamor of imperialism and war.[105] *Orestes* and *Iphigeneia at Aulis* expose the corruption of the demos and the failure of democratic institutions and question one of the basic distinctions of civic ideology by problematizing the category of the barbarian, that is, one of the very categories "invented" by tragedy.[106] Even in *Suppliants* which, like Aeschylus' *Eleusinians,* exploits a patriotic myth and a favorite topos of the funeral oration, Euripides gives voice to the antidemocratic ideology of the "quiet" Athenian and reveals the shallowness of the self-congratulatory elements embedded in the festival itself.[107]

A Case Study: The Relations between *Oikos* and Polis in the Theban Plays

I begin by sketching briefly the complex relations between *oikos* (in itself a multifaceted reality)[108] and polis in fifth-century Athens. Some scholars think that the city, according to Aristotle "a community of citizens with regard to the constitution," ignored the *oikos*.[109] Others, also relying on Aristotle, believe the household remained a fundamental building block of democratic Athens.[110] In fact, in the areas of property holding and citizenship, political and domestic roles were intertwined: the polis depended on the *oikos*, because "membership in an Attic *oikos* was a *sine qua non* for Athenian citizenship,"[111] but it restricted its autonomy by regulating marriages and prohibiting exogamy. Sometimes polis and *oikos* maintained separate spheres of activity; occasionally their demands clashed violently.[112]

Because tragedy "interpenetrates polis and oikos in multiple ways not only by using plots about mythical ruling families whose actions have political as well as domestic significance, but also by breaking down the boundaries between public and private speech and action,"[113] it can serve as a magnifying glass for analyzing the interplay between family and city and the tensions between civic duty and loyalty to kin. Actually, political crisis may result from conflicts within the ruling family. Conversely, decisions taken in the public sphere or conflicting political loyalties may affect private lives and family relationships. Aeschylus focuses decidedly on the polis. Euripides, questioning the hierarchic relation between the two spheres, shifts his attention to the *oikos;* as usual, Sophocles is more difficult to place.

Aeschylus' Seven against Thebes

Aeschylus' *Seven* is mostly concerned with the polis. This is suggested by vocabulary—occurrences of "polis" (74) outnumber by far those of "*oikos*" (1), "*domos*" (13), and "*dōma*" (5)—and staging: no royal house is in the background and the scenic space is clearly identified with the city and city walls. Moreover, characters and Chorus are all Theban. Throughout the first part of the play, which opens with a public speech of the Theban ruler to his "fellow citizens of Kadmos" (1), the only focus is the city that is surrounded by an enemy army eager to destroy and burn it. Accordingly, Eteokles is defined only by his relationship to the polis: he is the helmsman controlling the tiller (2–3, 63) who prays and acts on behalf of the city (71). The "houses" which usually are the Thebans' homes or the temples of their gods[114] are but a part of the city, sharing its fate for better or worse.[115]

The city is not only closely associated with the *oikos* and its members; it also appropriates the vocabulary of the household. The Thebans are a family with mythical ancestors: Kypris-Aphrodite is their *promator* and Ares their "father-in-law" (136, 140). Like the Athenians, they are autochthonous: the Earth is the "mother" and "nurse" of all citizens (16–19). The defense of the city therefore is a filial duty: Melanippus "will ward off the enemy spear from the mother who gave him birth" (416, cf. 477), and even the "metic" Parthenopaios will "repay his debt of nurture" (537–38) to his adoptive mother, while Polyneikes is assimilated to the "bad" son who sins against "the ancestral polis and the gods of the *genos*," wants to "dry up the maternal spring," and injures his "fatherland" (582, 585, 668).

With two exceptions (71, 203), the royal household does not appear until the play has run more than half its course. With the introduction of Polyneikes (576), Eteokles who so far has dissociated himself from his family begins to name his father (655, 695, 711) and brother (674) and emphasize the link with his brother (702–4) by using the first person plural that associated him with his fellow citizens in the first part of the play (4, 194, 516, 621). From now on the brothers are twins, always alluded to by dual and not distinguished at all by the Chorus (827, 845, 875, 901–2), except in the closing scene which is generally considered spurious.[116]

In contrast to the metaphorical family of the polis, the real family of the Labdakidai is characterized by perverted relationships: a father (Laios) killed by the son (Oedipus) he exposed (752), a father (Oedipus) cursing his sons out of anger at their *trophē* ("origin" or "nurture"),[117] and two brothers alike in "wrath" (676–77) who fight over patrimony and are not deterred by the pollution of fratricide from killing each other.[118] The *genos* finally collapses: assisted by a "house-destroying" and "race-destroying" Erinys (720, 1054), the brothers, dying "without offspring" (828), achieve the sacking of their own house (875–99).

Moreover, beginning with Laios, this maddened family threatens the community's very existence. The king was offered a choice between survival of polis and survival of family when Apollo told him that by dying without issue he would keep the city safe. Laios, however, "overmastered by the ill counsels of his near ones,"[119] disregarded this warning and begot a son (742–57).[120] The curse of Oedipus that his sons should divide their inheritance sword in hand also jeopardizes the city's existence; for, like the house, the city is part of the patrimony.

Eventually, this connection between the fate of the city and that of its ruling house is broken. As the drama emphasizes repeatedly, the woes of the royal household (740, 853, 994) stand in stark contrast to the salvation of the polis which survives the fall of its hero-leader (793–99, 804, 816), a conclusion foreshadowed by Eteokles' prayer, "Do not utterly uproot the city at least (*polin ge*) in total destruction by enemy-sack" (71): the limiting *ge* suggests a possible distinction between the city which may be saved and the house which is to be destroyed.

Many scholars have recognized as the basic pattern of the play the "entanglement and disentanglement of house and city" and rightly explained it by "the constitutional reforms of Kleisthenes whose result was to disembarass the political life of the city-state from the dangerous influence of the *genē*, the clans."[121] But they have not seen that this positive outcome is possible because Aeschylus carefully separates the city of Kadmos and its inhabitants, the Kadmeians,[122] from the royal family of Laios (691) and Oedipus (654, 801, 833, 1055), which has no connection whatsoever with Kadmos. This separation, which amounts to the negation of family ties between citizens and leaders, explains why the Kadmeians are spared by the gods whose anger is directed only at a maddened *genos*.

Sophocles' Antigone

Sophocles, as usual, is more problematic. Of course, *Antigone* contains echoes of the *Seven*, but the context is quite different. The discourse of the earlier play here becomes one character's opinion—and a questionable one. In *Antigone*, as in the *Seven*, Polyneikes comes to destroy the fatherland and the ancestral gods, burn their temples, and "scatter" their land and *nomoi* (199–201, 284–87). But these are the words of Kreon who attempts to justify his refusal to bury a traitor. The Chorus also remind us of Aeschylus when they speak of a "house" shaken by an *atē* sent by the gods and overburdened by woes from old, and of a *genos* doomed and hated by the gods (583–603). But in *Antigone*, this explanation of the fate of the heroine is not validated by the plot. Far from being the victim of a family curse, Antigone is *autonomos* (821) when she decides to remain loyal to her brother.

The exclusive concern for the polis characteristic of the *Seven* is lacking in *Antigone* and, at first sight, one is tempted to follow Hegel and read this play as a document of the conflict between *oikos* and polis, pitting Antigone's exclusive devotion to the family against Kreon's one-sided commitment to the city.[123] The beginning of the play seems to underline this basic pattern by putting *oikos* and polis side by side: Antigone addresses her sister in front of the house and stresses the importance of family ties (esp. 1); then Kreon argues with a group of citizens (162). Yet an analysis of the two main characters demonstrates that such a clear-cut opposition is highly misleading.

Through much of the play, Kreon appears to represent the interests and "voice of the polis."[124] His introductory speech, quoted approvingly by Demosthenes (19.247), echoes many democratic topoi.[125] Denying the existence of tensions between family and community, Kreon posits that they always have the same interests[126] and are both threatened by money and anarchy (296–97, 672–74). He keeps repeating that he will never sacrifice the interests of the polis to a *philos* (friend or relative) or befriend anyone hostile to the land (182–90). He "adopts the polis as the touchstone of worth" and condemns as "bad" those rulers who do not make right decisions or those citizens who betray the city or disobey its rulers.[127] Judging the sons of Oedipus according to their behavior toward the city, he honors its defender and denies burial to the traitor (192–210).[128] When convicting Antigone, he is anxious to protect the city from pollution by not killing but entombing her alive with a little food (774–76). Moreover, at least Ismene thinks that Kreon's decision is in agreement with the law of the city and the will of the citizens (59–60, 79),[129] which the Chorus, standing behind Kreon to the last moment, seems to confirm.

Kreon's case, however, is more complex. This champion of the polis inherited his power "through those very family ties for which he shows so little respect."[130] Despite his denial of the claims of kinship he demands, as a father, unquestioning loyalty from his son (639–44). While pretending to value the city greatly, he instills fear in his fellow citizens[131] and behaves like a despot, "confusing his position as *kyrios* of his oikos with his political position as a king."[132] In the scene with Haimon, he calls for uncritical obedience, pays no attention to public opinion, and considers the city his personal property which he rules to his own advantage (666–67, 734–38). Moreover, it soon emerges that he lacks the citizens' support: already in the first episode he suspects that some people disagree with him (289–90); his dialogue with Haimon amply confirms this suspicion (692–700, 733), and in the final scenes Kreon, who professed the well-being of the community as his priority, ends up inflicting a plague on his own city (1015, 1141) and provokes hostility in other cities (1080), while his violation of burial rites results in the destruction of his own *oikos* and the deaths of his son and wife.

Antigone's loyalty obviously lies with the blood ties;[133] her relation to the city is less clear. She herself wavers, stressing that the citizens covertly support her (502–5) but also echoing Ismene and recognizing at the end that she has violated the will of the polis (907 echoing 79). If it is uncertain, therefore, whether her mention of the city in her farewell lamentation (842–43) represents an appeal or a repudiation, Haimon's speech demonstrates that the citizens in fact approve of her behavior: they bewail Antigone and regard her deed as most glorious (692–700). Indeed, Antigone's championing of unwritten laws reflects a popular topos of funeral orations.[134]

The conclusion of the play is therefore paradoxical. Antigone, who chose the interests of the house, did "what was the best for the polis," and Kreon, who posed as "the devoted champion of the polis," destroyed his own house and "sowed the seeds of future disaster for Thebes."[135]

Euripides' Suppliants

The *Suppliants* is perhaps Euripides' most overtly "political play."[136] Its protagonists, Theseus and Adrastos, are rulers of poleis. It begins with one city's (Argos') request for aid to another (Athens) and ends with the promise of a perpetual alliance between them. Yet, by focusing on the sorrows of a Chorus of mothers, it pays equal, if not more, attention to the family. It is thus tempting to read this tragedy as a foil to Aeschylus' *Eleusinians,* a play that, like the *Seven,* was mostly concerned with the city.[137] Actually, except for Theseus, Adrastos, and the Theban herald, all characters are driven primarily by familial motives: they are mothers (Aithra and the Chorus), wives (Evadne), fathers (Iphis), sons (the secondary Chorus). Filial devotion decisively influences the play's major political decision, Athens' resolution to help Argos even at the cost of war against Thebes, when Theseus, who initially rejects Adrastos' request to recover the Argive dead, yields to the arguments of his mother, Aithra, who herself is deeply moved by the Argive mothers' appeal (343–45, 361–64).[138] Finally, Adrastos transforms the funeral oration, which usually exalts Athens' interventionist policy for the sake of justice, into an indirect rebuke of activism and a disconcerting praise of a new and private model of virtue.[139]

The dramatic structure interweaves polis with *oikos* in a revealing way. The prologue and parodos stage a mother supplicated by mothers. The following episode opposes Theseus and Adrastos, "the glorious king of the Athenians" (113) and the humiliated king of Argos, but ends with an appeal of a mother (Aithra) to her son (Theseus). The brief first stasimon merges private grief with politics. The second episode, featuring a debate between Theseus and a Theban herald and a comparison between democracy and tyranny, is devoted exclusively to political themes. Concern for the polis also dominates the third stasimon, which contrasts fear and hope, and the beginning of the third episode, with a long report on the victorious battle at Thebes. In his response, however, Adrastos strikes a new note: his condemnation of the folly of war serves as a transition to the second part of the play that focuses on the private grief of the household. When juxtaposing private grief and public salvation, Aeschylus lets the Chorus of the *Seven* emphasize the city but the Chorus of the *Suppliants* stress their private loss: "some things are well but others grievous; for the city and the generals there is renown and military glory, but for me it is bitter to see the spent limbs of my children, to gaze upon the greatest sorrow of all" (778–85). The fourth episode strikes a balance between the political (Adrastos' funeral oration) and the domestic (the first kommos and the outburst of the Chorus' grief). The fifth episode is completely devoted to the sufferings of a single family, with the tragedy of Evadne, the wife who wants to die with her husband, and the mourning of her father, deprived of his son (1036–37, 1092–93) and ruined by the suicide of his daughter (1074–76, 1094–1106).[140] The final kommos with the shared laments of the mothers and children of the dead continues the theme of family, whereas the epilogue, with Athena's speech, is decidedly political.

By involving three poleis (Athens, Argos, and Thebes), the play gives a complex picture of the relations between *oikos* and polis. In Athens, city and leaders are in permanent agreement (349–50, 393–94); the members of the ruling family, Aithra and Theseus, not only enjoy harmonious relations but always identify their own interests with those of the community[141] and do not permit family concerns to endanger the prosperity of the State. Nor, significantly, are Theseus' political decisions influenced by family ties with foreigners, although the Chorus remind him of such ties and the ensuing obligation to help his blood relatives (263–64).[142] In this city, even the women, who are usually driven exclusively by family loyalties, echo the voice of the polis and endorse Athens' policy of activism (320–27).

By contrast, the tyrannical city, exemplified by Thebes, is racked by permanent conflict between the interests of the ruler and those of the private households. The tyrant prevents the citizens from increasing the wealth of their *oikos*—which would only promote his welfare anyway—and from bringing up properly their daughters, who are destined to serve his pleasures (450–54).

Argos best illustrates the tensions between the interests of rulers and polis. The latter has been ruined by a "bitter marriage" (833) that connected the royal family with a polluted *genos* and introduced to Argos the calamitous Erinys of Oedipus (222–28, 835–36, 1078–79). The city was forced into a disastrous war against Thebes because Adrastos wanted to "please" his two sons-in-law, both foreigners, and help one of them, Polyneikes, to claim his share of Oedipus' inheritance (13–16, 131–36, 152–54). Soon there will be new dangers and wars because the sons of the Seven, the Epigonoi, are ready to "avenge" their fathers, doing for them what Adrastos did for Polyneikes and becoming "bitter" for the Thebans.[143]

Euripides' Phoenician Women

From W. Riemschneider to J. de Romilly scholars have paid much attention to the polis motif in *Phoenician Women*. E. Rawson has rightly shown, however, that "the main preoccupation of the play is the investigation of the various relationships, right and wrong, to one's family and one's country."[144] I suggest that this play, which concerns three families (the Houses of Oedipus, Kreon, and Adrastos) and two cities (Thebes and Argos), is also, like Aeschylus' *Seven,* an investigation of the various relationships between family/*oikos* and country/polis. While Aeschylus focused on the city, Euripides here emphasizes the *oikos.*

This is clearly demonstrated by changes in setting and cast. The scenic space is no longer the civic space but defined by a *skēnē* representing the palace of Oedipus. The Chorus' Theban women, closely involved with the city, have been replaced by foreign (Phoenician) women who are connected to the heroes by family ties.[145] Moreover, the main characters, except for Teiresias, are close relatives and the play's episodes are linked together by Jocasta, who exemplifies the wondrous power of mother-love, and by her brother Kreon, a devoted father.

The structure of the play is no less revealing. This play begins not with a ruler addressing his fellow citizens, but with a monologue of a mother. Instead of a dialogue, in the *Seven,* between the king and a Theban spy returning from the Argive army, we have here a dialogue, on the roof of the palace, between Antigone, "the scion who brings glory to the house for [her] father" (88), and a servant; again, Euripides shifts the emphasis to the family. Of course, Antigone worries, as did the Chorus of the *Seven,* for the safety of Thebes and prays for the destruction of its enemies (114–16, 151–53, 179–92). But she also proves "a creature of family ties,"[146] seeing in Tydeus not an enemy, but "the man married to Polyneikes' bride's very own sister" (135–37) and eagerly looking for her brother. The parodos is only partly (239–60) devoted to the war and siege of Thebes. The first episode juxtaposes family and polis: it features first the reunion of a mother with her son, then a political debate between two brothers, with their mother as arbitrator, but ends by focusing on the family ties, when Polyneikes requests to see father and sisters (615–17). Even in the second episode, when Eteokles deliberates with Kreon on the defense of the city, he also consults the "brother of his mother Jocasta" about family affairs (690–93) and makes provisions for various family members in the case of his death (757–63). In the third episode, the dialogue between Teiresias and Kreon is first dominated by the salvation of Thebes, but public concerns quickly yield to those of the family, before Menoikeus decides to give his life for the city. Significantly, in the fourth episode, following the death of Menoikeus and the Theban victory, Jocasta asks the messenger first about her son, then about the city, whereas in the *Seven* the messenger, addressing Theban women, had first emphasized the city's liberation. After a lengthy description of the threat posed by the Argives for the city's survival (1090–1198) the announcement of the duel between the brothers and the attempt of their mother and sister to prevent it again shift attention to the family,[147] whose ruin totally dominates the exodos and obliterates the salvation of the city.[148]

Before investigating the tensions between family and city in this play, it may be useful to look at those passages that suggest a community of interests and a harmonious relationship between them. According to the Chorus, the visitation of the Sphinx was a plague for both: she brought woes to the "fatherland" and filled the "houses" with mourning (1030–35). Jocasta envisions a city that shares the joys and sorrows of the ruling house: in better days it would have celebrated Polyneikes' wedding (347–49) and is now, together with his *philoi,* longing for him (320–21). She postulates that family and city are equally ruined by ambition (531–33) and strengthened by equality (536–37). Even Polyneikes is convinced that the demands of family and city can be harmonized: by reconciling her sons, Jocasta would put an end to the private and public woes (435–37). Menoikeus dies for the sake of city and family: he does not want to "betray his father, his brother and his city" (1003–4).

Yet dynastic and public interests are often incompatible. The treatment of Apollo's oracle to Laios is instructive. In the *Seven* Laios had to choose between the survival of his family and the salvation of his city. In *Phoenician Women,* asking for "a shared possession of male children *for the house*" (15–16), he receives an imperative answer which concerns only the household: "Don't sow the furrow from which children are born against the gods' will. For, if you have a child, your issue will kill you and *the whole house* will make its way through blood" (17–20). Yet his procreating a son, while ensuring the family's continuity, has damaging public consequences for Thebes as well. According to Teiresias, "This land has long been sick," since Laios fathered a child against the gods' will (865–66) and Oedipus, whose birth was "unlawful" (380), polluted the city (1050) by killing his father and marrying his mother "for ill" (381). His curse upon his sons "that they should share the *house* by whetted sword" specifically concerns the *oikos* (68–69, cf. 327–29, 352, 379), but Teiresias, who fears that the city may be caught in the destruction of Oedipus' sons, clearly says that the two brothers should have been expelled, "since they are possessed and will ruin the city" (884–88). As the vocabulary, moving freely from house to kingship, underscores,[149] the strife between Oedipus' sons inevitably affects both city and family (811–13): they fight for their share of house *and* land, and Polyneikes is attacking his "nearest kin" (434) *and* his "fatherland."[150] Thus, when Eteokles is confronted with a decisive choice by Jocasta (560), this choice does not, as Laios' in the *Seven,* pit family against city, but private ambition (tyranny) against the good of the country (saving the polis).

As in the *Seven,* here too the fate of Thebes is finally disentangled from that of Oedipus' family, but in a very different way. The connection between the two is not broken *after* the duel of the two brothers, by the destruction of the royal dynasty (the two brothers die without offspring), but before it. In the third episode, Teiresias' prophecy, a turning point in the action,[151] separates the fate of the brothers from that of the city: the brothers' deaths are inevitable; the latter will escape destruction if Menoikeus is sacrificed, since the death of the last descendant of the Spartoi will assuage the wrath of Ares against Kadmos (931–51). In fact, the messenger clearly presents the Argives' defeat and the deaths of their leaders as a consequence of the self-sacrifice of Menoikeus (1090–1199). Hence the duel of the brothers, framed by Menoikeus' death and a second battle also won by the Thebans (because of a "forethought" of unclear origin, 1466), becomes a mere parenthesis and does not affect the issue of the war.[152]

As the Menoikeus episode shows, the salvation of Thebes is put at risk no less by Kreon's family interests. Initially, Kreon, like Oedipus in *Oedipus Rex,* is eager to learn "what action would be more likely to save the city" (864, 898) and is ready to do anything "to save [his] ancestral country" (900). But when Teiresias tells him that he must "kill his son Menoikeus for the sake of his fatherland" (913–14) and he has to choose between "much ill for him" and "great safety for the city" (917–18, 951–52), like Laios in the *Seven,* he bids farewell to the city (919) and refuses to kill his son and give him to the city (964), thus depriving Thebes of its chance of salvation (993). The end of the play suggests a damaging overlap between the family's and city's interests by associating closely the bequest of Thebes to Kreon and the betrothal of Antigone to his son (1586–88). Moreover, the new ruler's decision to expel Oedipus and forbid the burial of Polyneikes does not seem to be dictated by concern for the public good but by family reasons. Kreon indeed justifies Oedipus' exile by referring to Teiresias' pronouncement "that the city would never prosper as long as [he] lived in the land" (1590–91). But this is either "an unconscious misinterpretation" or "a cynical manipulation" of the words of Teiresias (886–87)[153] which only concern "the offspring of Oedipus" and do not include Oedipus himself. Kreon's decisions to cast the corpse of Polyneikes beyond the border and to impose the death penalty on the burier (1628–30), although justified with Polyneikes' attack on the city (1652) and presented as the will of the city (1668),[154] are in fact the consequence of Eteokles' hatred of his brother: they echo precisely the earlier instructions he gave Kreon and the city at the end of the second episode (774–77, 1646).

The story of Argos provides another illustration of the dichotomy between dynasty and city interests. Because of the baneful betrothal of Adrastos' daughter to Polyneikes and the "foolish favor" granted by the king to his son-in-law

(77–78, 426–29, 569, 578–82), when he swore to restore him to his fatherland, the city waged a disastrous war against Thebes.

Yet in *Phoenician Women,* as opposed to the *Seven,* the complex interplay between city and family cannot be subsumed under a simple formula. If the family more often than not endangers the city, the city may also ruin the family. Jocasta interprets the death of Menoikeus as the result of the strife between her sons and the indirect consequence of her marriage (1204–6). In fact, however, this death is the price to be paid for the mere existence of the city. For the foundation of Thebes, celebrated in the first stasimon, followed upon the murder of a dragon born from the Earth and Ares and the sowing of its teeth by Kadmos with the support of Athena (657–65, 1062–64). Because of the ancient wrath of Ares and Earth against the murderer, Kadmos, blood must be repaid by blood (931–41). Similarly, the marriage and death of Jocasta, which are often closely linked to the arrival of the Sphinx,[155] are presented as the price to be paid for the welfare of the city. Here, too, private grief balances public good, which perhaps explains why this episode is associated in the third stasimon with the sacrifice of Menoikeus.

Accordingly, the "fatherland" no longer appears as "an extension of the family" or as the perfect family contrasting with the cursed family of the Labdakidai.[156] Like Jocasta, Earth also gave birth to children who killed each other, and the mutual slaughter of the Spartoi (670–75, 818–21, 939–40) not only provides "a mythical prototype for the coming fratricide"[157] but also casts an ambiguous light on autochthony. For Earth is both the "fatherland" that "it is inevitable for all men to love" (358–59), the "dearest thing to mortals" (406), and the mother of monsters such as the "earth-born" dragon (931, 935) and the Sphinx (1019–20), and her goodwill must be bought by the blood of her own sons: the victim must be a descendant on both sides of the earth-born Spartoi. The metaphorical family of the polis thus turns out to be as bloodthirsty as the real one. This may serve as a corrective to a one-sided political interpretation. The play that through the words of Menoikeus offers the clearest lesson of unselfish patriotism is not blind to the magnitude of the sufferings inflicted on the citizens.

Tragedy and Civic Ideology: From Approval to Questioning

From Aeschylus to Sophocles and Euripides, the relations between city and family, public and private duties have become more problematic. "*Seven against Thebes* shows a community threatened by male dynastic strife"[158] and does not lay on the polis any responsibility for the family sufferings. In Sophocles' *Antigone,* although, at the very end, "the unwritten laws, the interests of the gods of the dead and the interests of the family prove . . . to coincide with the interests of the city,"[159] the case for the polis becomes more questionable. Euripides still more complexifies the picture in the plays centered on the war against Thebes and its aftermath. In the *Suppliants* Argos exemplifies the ruin of the *oikos* by the polis and its wars but, at least in Athens, there is no discrepancy between family and city interests. In *Phoenician Women*, however, there is no room anymore for a well-regulated city-state where *oikos* and polis could cooperate harmoniously. The play's focus alternates between the ruin of the fatherland by family interests and individual ambitions on the one hand and, on the other, the sorrows brought upon the family by a war waged by the city. Euripides goes so far as to suggest that the mere existence or survival of the city has to be paid for by the destruction of its members. Unquestionably, it is the bitter experiences of the Athenians of the late fifth century that lie behind this new awareness.

CHAPTER FOURTEEN

The Panathenaic Procession: Athens' Participatory Democracy on Display?

Lisa Maurizio

Introduction

The Panathenaia was a state festival celebrated in honor of Athena, Athens' patron divinity.[1] It took place over a period of roughly a week and included musical and athletic contests, sacrifices, a boat regatta, a procession, an all-night revelry, a torch race, and, most importantly, a dedication of a garment to Athena. The Panathenaia has been called the "most political" of Athens' festivals and has been treated as distinctly democratic or populist.[2] This modern assessment echoes that of the Athenians themselves, who saw the Panathenaia as the event that occasioned the defeat of the tyrants and the birth of democracy.[3] And indeed, the festival is exceptional for its inclusiveness—which many scholars have read as an expression of a specifically democratic impulse. Jenifer Neils' recent comment is representative of this reading of the democratic and civic aspects of the Panathenaia. "In its inclusiveness, it exemplified the city's participatory democracy; in its contests it demonstrated the competitive spirit of its people; with its prizes it displayed the skills of its artisans and the wealth of its produce; and above all it celebrated Athena as the divine protectress of a glorious city."[4]

While Neils is no doubt correct in identifying many of the festival's politically inclusive features, her analysis is too simple a summation of the ways in which the Panathenaia and Athens' civic life intersected.[5] In particular, Neils assumes that the Panathenaia "exemplified" or "displayed" the nature of Athens as a democratic city—that is, that the Panathenaia did not so much contribute to the civic life of Athens as simply reflect its political and social structures and values. In this respect, her comments are typical of scholarly opinion on the ways Athenian democracy influenced the city's religious life. Certain religious practices such as the cult of the Tyrannicides and the myths and rituals associated with Theseus, for example, rightly have been treated as symptomatic of Athens' developing democracy. Yet, not all religious practices in Athens were so obviously politically motivated.[6] The Panathenaia, in particular, existed long before democracy took root in Athens, and we might wonder to what degree it really became a specifically democratic festival in the fifth and fourth centuries, as Neils implies. Conversely, we may ask whether the festival, particularly its traditional elements that persisted over a long period, contributed to or even challenged Athenian democratic values.

In this chapter, then, I will examine Athens' most political festival, the Panathenaia, and thereby explore the relationship between Athens' democracy and Athens' religious practices. In particular, the procession, which will be the focus of this study, was the most inclusive event of the festival because elite and nonelite citizens marched, as did noncitizens: women, resident aliens (metics), and freed slaves.[7] Was this inclusiveness an expression of Athens' participatory democracy? Or did the participation of a broad spectrum of Athenian residents in the Panathenaic procession, a predemocratic and traditional feature of the Panathenaia, challenge political definitions of the Athenian community that carefully demarcated citizens from noncitizens? In narrowing the question of how Athenian democracy may have influenced or co-opted traditional religious practices to an examination of one feature of one festival, I hope to suggest the complexity of the issue at hand, namely the interplay between classical Athens' political and religious spheres. More importantly, this analysis of the Panathenaic procession should demonstrate that any analysis that sees religion, or religious activities such as a festival, as a mere reflection of politics will necessarily be incomplete and never capture the vitality of Athens' civic life which was shaped by the interplay of both its religious and political commitments.

The Panathenaic Procession

The Panathenaic procession, like the Panathenaic musical and athletic contests, had its own rules about who was permitted to march and how the marchers were to conduct themselves. The self-presentation of all participants was determined by the order in which they marched and items they wore or carried. These two parameters, order and items, partly registered the marchers' social status and partly reorganized them under Athena's aegis into a hierarchical order that did not necessarily reflect current political and social hierarchies of male over female, elite over nonelite, citizen over metic.

Athenian citizens who marched were distinguished by various male civic identities: magistrates, cavalry men, heavily armed soldiers (hoplites), military recruits (ephebes). Demesmen, a category that would have included all economic classes of citizens, also marched; a late-fourth-century inscription records them as recipients of meat from Panathenaic sacrifices.[8] All citizens with more clearly marked processional roles than simply "demesman," though, would have come largely from the upper half of Athenian society. Among the noncitizens with clearly marked roles, there were Athenian girls, young women and wives as sacrificial ministrants, all from elite families,[9] and metics. While there is no evidence about the selection or background of these metics, they had to be able to afford appropriate costumes, and thus they probably were wealthy. Missing from the well-marked procession of armed citizens were the thetes, members of the lowest economic class. These citizens were often rowers on Athens' fleet, light-armed soldiers, or archers, and they were increasingly responsible for Athens' military might. Even if included among the demesmen, they were noticeably absent from the procession proper.[10] So were Athenian females from nonelite families. To say that the Panathenaia was inclusive, then, obscures the distinctions that its processional order made between nonelite citizens, who could only march among the demesmen, and elite citizens, who could both occupy clearly marked processional roles and march among the demesmen and who, curiously, were accompanied in the procession proper by noncitizens, i.e., females and metics.

The sequence of these participants in the Panathenaic procession no doubt varied over the years. Certain general features, however, would have remained constant. Those carrying items used in the sacrifice preceded all others and the cavalry consistently seems to be last in the procession proper. The latter's order can be approximated from three types of sources: literary descriptions of processional orders, which are likely to have been analogous to the Panathenaia;[11] scattered literary testimonia about Panathenaic marchers,[12] although these seldom provide information about the placement of marchers; and the Parthenon frieze (fig. 1). Of these, the frieze offers the most impressive evidence for the order of marchers, despite scholarly questions about whether the Parthenon frieze represents the Panathenaic procession.[13] In my opinion, for example, John Kroll's treatment of these questions illustrates well why and how the frieze can indeed impart useful information about the procession's order.[14]

That the frieze represents the Panathenaic procession has been questioned because it does not depict the marchers mentioned in some late and scattered literary sources.[15] While it is doubtful whether such late sources are valid for the interpretation of a fifth-century monument, this line of inquiry raises an issue

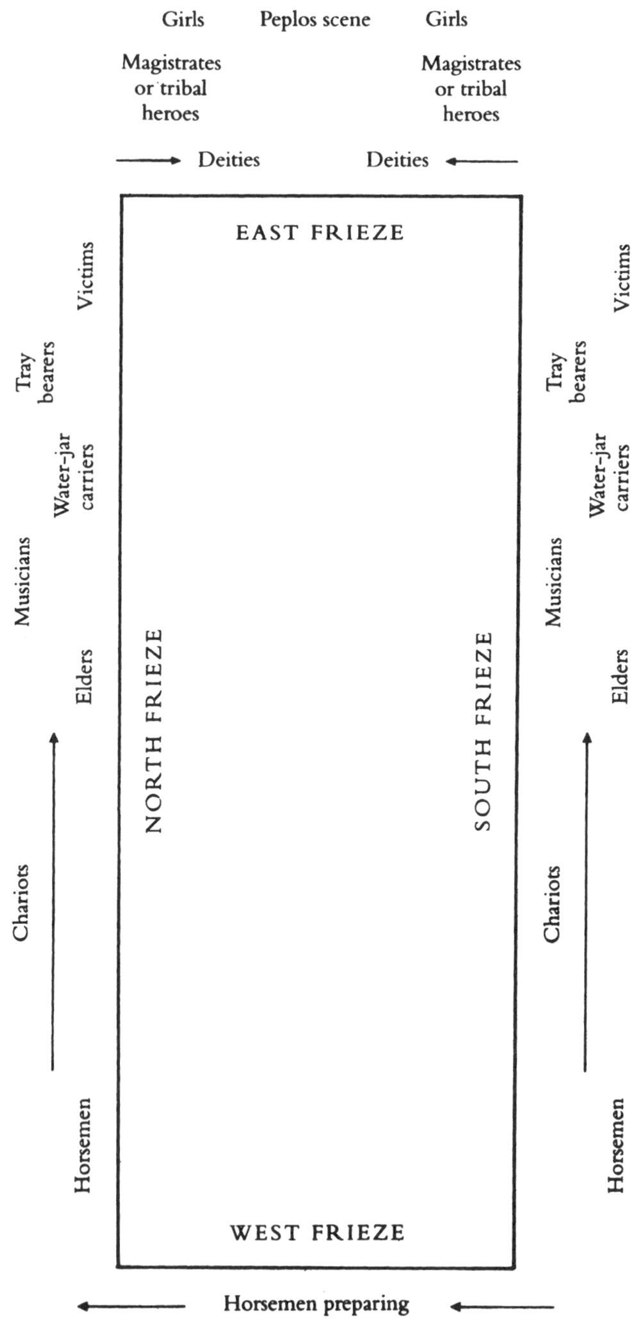

Figure 1 Plan of the Parthenon frieze. Jenkins 1994.82, fig. 12b. Copyright the Trustees of the British Museum, British Museum Press.

worth considering: the preponderance of horsemen who dominate the west, north, and south sides of the frieze. Horsemen and charioteers certainly did participate in the procession, but why do they appear on the frieze in such abundance and to the exclusion of hoplites and Athenian demesmen, who no doubt were more numerous both in the procession and the city?[16] The explanation lies in the significance of horses in classical Athens. Although hoplites massively outnumbered cavalry in the Athenian military, soldiers were often represented as horsemen on individual funerary monuments. Public grave monuments also overrepresent cavalry while denying horses to defeated enemies.[17] Yet traditionally horses were the privilege of the aristocracy; even when the state funded the maintenance of horses for its newly formed cavalry, equestrian pursuits maintained their aristocratic associations.[18] Thus, while horsemen are typical of Ionic friezes, and in this respect the Parthenon is predictable,[19] the horsemen on the Parthenon are not simply decorative or representational.

In part, their significance is indicated by the nudity of some horsemen on the frieze. While competitors in athletic contests may have competed without clothes, neither soldiers nor marchers performed their duties nude. Larissa Bonfante has argued that nudity was a "costume" in classical Athens, where "it comes to mean something special. No longer does it mean vulnerability; it means, on the contrary, the readiness to stand up and fight even though one knew one was vulnerable . . . The relation of this manly nudity to the nudity of the gods is also crucial: the gods could be nude because they relied on themselves."[20] The horsemen of the Parthenon frieze, both nude and clothed, then, might be understood as representing all citizen marchers, demesmen, hoplites, and cavalry, in strikingly heroic guise. Whether this particular construction of the demos can be read as its own appropriation of elite prerogatives or as the elite's success in setting itself as the benchmark for manly and civic courage and divine favor may be disputed.[21] What is clear is that the frieze does not represent the Panathenaic procession with photographic likeness. Nonetheless, it agrees in general outline with the literary, epigraphical, and iconographical evidence about the order of marchers.

Unlike the frieze, however, this evidence is not from the fifth and fourth centuries, when Athens' democracy was at its height, and this again causes interpretative problems. It is difficult to determine to what degree our literary sources—grammarians and scholiasts (commentators) writing many centuries later—describe the Panathenaic procession of the classical age. An early representation of the Panathenaic procession on a cup from the beginning of the sixth century may provide some clues.[22] It includes only basket-bearers (*kanēphoroi*), musicians, branch-bearers (*thallophoroi*), hoplites, and cavalry, suggesting that the early procession included only sacrificial ministrants and the population under arms, that is, fewer groups than were in the procession later on. In this early, predemocratic procession there are, for example, no tray-bearers or stool-bearers. In the later procession, metics performed these duties. Since the institution of *metoikia* which formalized the status of resident aliens was legally established not before Kleisthenes' reforms, positions occupied by metics were most likely created sometime after these reforms.[23] The absence of female basket-bearers (*kanēphoroi*) and weavers (*ergastinai*) on the cup is also notable: both groups of females were no doubt included in the early procession because dedications of robes to goddesses were typically the responsibility of women.[24] Thus, this representation is no more a "photograph" of the early Panathenaic procession than the frieze of the fifth-century version. If it is representative at all, it suggests, nevertheless, that the earlier procession, although structured by the threefold division evidenced for the later procession by the frieze and other sources, had fewer dignitaries and specialized roles than its later counterpart. The following list of marchers, although derived from late and scattered literary sources, can thus be understood as representing the Panathenaic procession of the fifth and fourth centuries, that is, at the height of its formalization.

Procession proper:[25] (1) basket-bearers (*kanēphoroi*): Athenian girls,[26] (2) parasol-bearers (*skiadēphoroi*): metic girls,[27] (3) stool-bearers (*diphrophoroi*): metic girls,[28] (4) weavers (*ergastinai*): Athenian girls or wives,[29] (5) carriers of sacred objects (*arrhēphoroi*): Athenian girls,[30] (6) animals for sacrifice, (7) tray-bearers (*skaphēphoroi*): metic men,[31] (8) water-bearers (*hydriaphoroi*): metic girls,[32] (9) musicians,[33] (10) boys with a decorated branch known as an *eiresionē*, (11) branch-bearers (*thallophoroi*): Athenian men or women, (12) officials, (13) representatives of other cities, (14) victors in contests, (15) ephebes, (16) hoplites, (17) charioteers (*apobatai*), (18) cavalry. End of procession proper: (19) citizens (demesmen), (20) noncitizens and freed slaves (with oak branches).[34]

Assuming that the center of the east frieze, on either side of the gods, is the front of the procession, and following the north frieze to the west, its processional order is as follows: (1) girl with peplos (cloth) (*arrhēphoros*): E 35, (2) females with sacred furniture (*diphrophoroi*):[35] E 31–32, (3) females handing over box (*kanēphoroi*): E 16, 17, 50–51, 53–54, (4) females with incense burners (*thymiatēria*): E 57, 12–15, (5) females with pitchers (*choes*): E 7–11, 58–59, (6) females with offering bowls (*phialai*): E 2–6, 55, 56?, 60–63. North side moving westerly: (7) young boys with cows and sheep: N 1–12, (8) men carrying trays (*skaphēphoroi*): N 13–15, (9) men carrying water pitchers (*hydriaphoroi*): N 16–19, (10) flute players: N 20–23, (11) kithara players: N 24–27, (12) older bearded men (*thallophoroi*): N 28–41, (13) men facing west (magistrates): N 42–43, (14) charioteers (*apobatai*): N 44–68, (15) man facing west (marshal): N 69, (16) *apobatai*: N 70–74, (17) horsemen: N 75–135 (N 136: young boy), (18) man (marshal): W 1, (19) horsemen: W 2–30.

In two places these lists do not overlap. First, as discussed above, the hoplites and demesmen are absent—or represented as horsemen—on the frieze. Also absent are athletic victors, allies, slaves, as well as parasol- and stool-bearers, two duties performed by the wives and daughters of metics.[36] Second, the water-bearers on the frieze are male, rather than female, as the literary sources would lead us to expect.[37] The branch-bearers, if the older men on the north are identified as such,[38] are also male, though there is some evidence that old women also performed this duty.[39] These omissions suggest that the frieze gives a highly stylized version of the Panathenaic procession. Just as the hurly-burly of the procession is replaced by the assured muscularity of the horsemen and the dignity of the other marchers, only Athenians, and perhaps only elite Athenians, are present on the frieze. The possible change in gender that the frieze performs on the water- and branch-bearers bespeaks another aspect of the frieze's representational strategies. By making these figures male, the frieze draws a marked and spectacular contrast between the east and its other sides, for the east, which represents the front of the procession, becomes the only side that includes females.

On this point the literary evidence for the Panathenaic procession agrees with the frieze: Athenian females, usually attended by female metics, were at the front of the procession. As sacrificial ministrants, they reached the Acropolis and partook of the sacrifice in a way that the majority of marchers, mostly male, did not. Next in line were the metics, and not far behind them the magistrates and the branch-bearers (*thallophoroi*), men too old to bear arms. It seems that the procession proper created, and the frieze highlights, an opposition between the arms-bearing citizens on the one hand, and noncitizens, mostly female, on the other. Moreover, the procession, and the frieze even more so, makes an equation in which the female is associated more closely with the divine and accorded a certain honor for this capacity, even though the males at the rear by their sheer number and gaudy display also qualify for honor in the procession's dynamic unfolding.

It is a priori likely that the front of the procession was its most prestigious part. Based on a survey of Greek processions, Arthur Leacock confirms this[40] and, in the case of the Panathenaia, a practical consideration lends further support.[41] The Acropolis was the *sanctum sanctorum,* and the procession moved toward this holy center, reversing the movement of those the city sent out of its bounds as unwanted: ritual scapegoats (*pharmakoi*), the ostracized, exiles, murderers. The high prestige of the front of the procession was enhanced even more by its proximity to the sacred sphere and the goddess Athena herself. On a religious axis, then, those who marched in the front of the procession could attain the greatest status.

Those who entered the procession with the greatest social status, however, came at the end: the cavalry who did not walk like the other marchers but rode their horses and thereby dramatically marked the close of the procession proper. On a civic axis, then, these riders had an honorific place comparable with those in the front. The procession, it seems, accommodated both males and females and celebrated their different contributions to the city: in the former case, their military power necessary for the protection of the city, and in the latter, their religiosity and fertility[42] necessary for the city's continuance and security. Each therefore occupied a position that, in the procession's logic, was prestigious. Between these two poles, I suspect, was a modulated drop in status, impossible to capture or delineate from the fragmentary nature of our evidence. Finally, behind the cavalry and the charioteers, came the demesmen.[43] The Panathenaic processional order did not create a hierarchy between male and female, between the relative values of the respective civic and religious duties of each that it helped represent and establish. Instead, it created a space in which these marchers, as well as those between them, could display themselves and claim public recognition and honor for their contributions to the city in a way unparalleled in other public events—unparalleled because males and females were on display at the same time and in the same public place. In sum, then, the order of the Panathenaic procession in part registered the amount of status and honor one had before entering the procession and in part determined the amount of honor one could attain.

In addition to marchers' place in the procession, costume and items also registered and bestowed honor upon their holders. Certain items, such as the sacrificial knife and barley in the basket-bearer's basket, were used in the sacrifice that followed the procession. So too was the water in the water pitchers carried by the water-bearers and the honeycombs and cakes in the trays of the metics, typically offered to chthonic deities, here perhaps to Ge Kourotrophos who was honored alongside Athena.[44] Since music would have accompanied the sacrifices, musical instruments too had a functional value. Other items, such as stools, parasols, branches, had no functional value in the sacrifice.[45] This distinction—between items used in the sacrifice and those that were not—is important but does not illuminate how such items defined their carriers or the value and meaning attached to them. For this purpose, one must look to a broader social context outside the sacrifice.

In the front and back of the Panathenaic procession, items carried or worn were of high value. The importance attached, for example, to the *kanēphoroi* and their baskets filled with sacrificial knife and barley[46] is documented by an inscription that includes basket-bearers among those select few who receive a reserved share of sacrificial meat.[47] The relative values of hoplite armor, horses, and chariots, used by Athenian citizens at the back of the procession, obviously are unambiguously great as well. It is uncertain whether the weavers of Athena's peplos (*ergastinai*), who are variously identified as young or married women, and carriers of sacred things (*arrhēphoroi*), young girls who helped weave the peplos, carried anything in the procession. In a few inscriptions honoring weavers (*ergastinai*), they request permission to dedicate an offering bowl (*phialē*).[48] Since many young women on the frieze carry such a *phialē*, perhaps they might be identified as weavers. The *arrhēphoroi* may simply have assisted in escorting Athena's garment.

The items carried by metics also marked their bearers. Female metics carried stools and umbrellas for Athenian basket-bearers. Both of these items were associated with Eastern luxury, and in classical Athens they were carried by slaves for wealthy Athenians.[49] Thus, these items, normally used to mark a class difference, here mark the difference between citizen and metic and implicitly link metic with slave.[50] Female metics also carried water jugs, while male metics carried trays (*skaphai*). The value attached to these items, and hence their bearers, was contested. In Aelian and New Comedy the term *skaphai*, by which metics were known, appears to be an insult.[51] Hesychius, however, writes that the purpose of this function was that by "partaking in sacrifices, they may be included as to be of good will."[52] Hesychius' emphasis on "goodwill" recalls the ending of Aeschylus' *Oresteia*. After the Erinyes are persuaded to dwell in Athens and receive purple robes, they are enjoined to be of "goodwill."[53] Since male metics wore purple robes during processions,[54] the Erinyes, in accepting and donning purple robes, symbolically become resident aliens in Athens. Their accommodation in Athens is presented as a boon by Aeschylus, who emphasizes the honors the Erinyes will receive.[55] This suggests that it was likewise perceived as an honor for the metics to be included in the procession. This notion is reinforced by the fact that ephebes, young Athenians being prepared for their military and civic duties, also wore purple robes during processions.[56]

These divergent sentiments about metic participation in the Panathenaic procession, i.e., as both an honor and a disgrace,[57] perhaps reflect historical evolution, but it may be that the Athenians always viewed the inclusion of metics in this and other processions with ambivalence. For, if metics were included in the procession proper in order to demonstrate their incorporation in the Athenian community, their very participation distinguished them positively from onlookers and demesmen, even if their items had low or servile connotations. Could their participation be distinguished clearly from that of citizens? Or did they too become invested with the legitimate authority to worship Athena before and even on behalf of the Athenians? Did their derision in comedy mask this fact? The conflicting responses the inclusion of metics provoked may have been exacerbated if metics performed their duty with aplomb and treated their participation as an honor.

Such divergent interpretations of the role of metics were in some ways matched by those attached to the branches carried by Athenian citizens. While Xenophon writes that branches were carried by older men chosen for their beauty and hence were a sign of honor, in Aristophanes this function is soundly abused, according to the scholia, because it marked the person as feeble, good only for sweeping the roads.[58]

What is clear in all this is that the same item or ritual behavior could have multiple meanings in different contexts and among different groups. A fragment of the comic poet Alexis, ridiculing the distribution of awards to elites during the Panathenaia for their benefactions to the city, underscores such multiplicity of meanings:[59] fishmongers promise to install at the next Panathenaia in the fish market a statue of one Kallimedon with a crayfish in his hand because his prodigious love of fish has sustained their business. While some Athenians, especially among the elite and wealthy, profited from such awards and might endorse their value and social significance, those from other social groups might cast a more skeptical eye on this practice.

To conclude, as the examples discussed above suggest, although high value was attached to some items carried by elite Athenians, the marchers in the center of the procession bore objects of ambiguous value. Conflicting interpretations and sarcastic comments indicate that there was a general awareness of, though not necessarily a general consensus on, the significance of ritual behavior. In the next two sections I shall offer more detailed analyses of the meaning of such processional display and a consideration of the ways its well-ordered inclusiveness may have reflected Athens' participatory democracy or, conversely, challenged it.

Integration and Celebration

In François de Polignac's analysis, the Panathenaic procession was unique, for unlike most Archaic Greek processions which moved from the center to the periphery of a city and functioned to demonstrate the extent of a city's territory, the Panathenaic procession moved from the Kerameikos to the Acropolis, that is, from periphery to center.[60] As de Polignac puts it, "the whole society solemnly marched before itself in a ceremony that manifested its own particular concept of its constitution and its space."[61]

Indeed, civic processions are often understood as a form of self-representation in which a polity attempts to describe and celebrate its political system, social or religious groups, or important civic members.[62] Yet, such attempts at self-representation, or perhaps rather self-understanding, are not fully realistic: like works of art, they may highlight certain elements and ignore others to create an idealizing or even utopian image, representing society not as it is but as certain members would like it to be. The best and most esteemed members of a community, dressed in their finest clothing and exhibiting distinctive traits, may be displayed prominently, while those from lower stations may be relegated to the margins, if included at all. Such an idealized image may serve the interests of those who have the economic or political power to prescribe the form of the procession; it may ignore social ills and dissension, promoting the status quo in the service of those who benefit from it. In the case of the Panathenaia, therefore, when we ask how, if at all, the procession exemplifies Athens' constitution, that is, its participatory democracy, we must remember that the procession is not a "photograph" of Athens' community. Like the Parthenon frieze, it may emphasize the role of certain members and ignore others in order to create, in the interest of the elite, an idealized image.[63]

What image of Athens was displayed in the Panathenaic procession? In the procession proper, almost all the marchers carried something as they marched. W. R. Connor argues that the procession "sends important messages about how members of its society *should* participate in it and relate to one another. It reinforces a system of social values by representing its participants primarily as contributors."[64] In this view, the Panathenaia reinforced the notion that Athens was a society that relied on and rewarded its members' participation in and contribution to the community. The procession, therefore, can be seen as inculcating civic responsibilities in a broad spectrum of Athens' residents and honoring all of them for their performance of these duties. In short, the festival integrated everyone and their contributions in a celebration of Athena's city.

Yet, the procession represents the Athenian community quite differently from the democracy. Just as the frieze favors the cavalry and ignores the hoplites, the procession featured both but ignored the thetes. As said before, the thetes, although certainly more important to Athens' continued military success than the cavalry who seem to dominate the procession, most likely marched, if at all, among the demesmen who followed the procession proper. Thus, their contribution to the city was deliberately occluded. In this respect, the procession clearly did not represent the political reality of Athenian society, but instead gave a distorted view of it.

One reason for this "distortion" may be found in the difficulty the thetes presented in terms of the order of the procession. As citizens of a democracy that valued the principle of equality, the thetes in theory were equal to the horsemen and hoplites. Nonetheless, the ideal of citizen-soldier was based on the figure of the hoplite who confronted the enemy head-on, not on the oarsman who rowed in the bowels of a trireme, as many thetes did. This hoplite ideal was matched by the romance the Athenians had with equestrian pursuits as markers of manly virtue. Moreover, both hoplites and cavalrymen belonged to higher economic classes than thetes, and exercised considerable power in the city, despite Athens' egalitarian ideals.[65] Therefore, to place the thetes in an equal or inferior position in the procession would have been tantamount to sacrificing either heroic ideals or egalitarian principles. To avoid this dilemma, the thetes were not included in the procession proper at all.

The metics in the procession, both men and women, represent another distortion. It obviously was in the best interest of the city to encourage all its members, however marginal politically, to contribute freely to the community, each according to his/her ability, and for this reason to promote the inclusion of metics in the procession. However, in displaying their contributions and providing them with an opportunity to earn honor, the procession contradicted the democracy. For the inclusion of those who were not part of Athens' political community implicitly raised questions about their "proper" place within the city's political life—just as the exclusion of thetes avoided a similar dilemma.

That females, who were noncitizens, marched in the procession proper is also a distortion of sorts, for in the democratic city women typically did not share public places with male citizens. Clothing, items, and positions define women as highly honored members of the procession. Their contributions to the community, particularly their economic service of weaving evident in the dedication of Athena's robe, are displayed and celebrated. How are we to evaluate their inclusion? Clearly, this religious representation of Athens in which women occupy a prominent position is not simply a reversal of the political hierarchy of male over female or a form of tokenism.[66] Rather, it reflects a comprehensive view of the city that derives its power from Athena's authority and from the force of a long-standing tradition. The Panathenaia does not represent the democracy's exclusion of women and emphasis on the male citizen body, nor did it change to accommodate such a view. Moreover, the presence of women should not be read as a mere holdover that had lost its meaning. Since the Panathenaia did evolve, and since the vitality and significance of the procession could not be fully controlled or limited to certain marchers, the women's esteemed positions allowed them to gain honors comparable to those of other marchers.

The position of metics in the procession is unlike that of either the thetes or the women. Noncitizens but permanent members of the community, they paid taxes, served in Athens' military forces, and performed liturgies. Were they to be esteemed as valuable members of Athens, perhaps even getting close to the rights of citizenship, or was their lower status to be permanent and emphasized as such? Their processional roles registered this very ambiguity. Their purple robes, shared with the ephebes who were on the brink of becoming full citizens, and their positions in the procession proper suggest an honored station, fitting for potential citizens or citizens in spirit. Yet the items they carried had servile connotations and implied that, much like slaves, the metics were far removed from the ranks of citizens. Such contradictions reflect ambiguity and questions in Athens' ongoing debate about the definition of citizenship in a democratic community.

While the role of females and thetes, reflecting a distortion of the status quo, argues against reading the procession simply as a reflection of Athens' participatory democracy, the ambiguous position of the metics signals the complex reality that stands behind the seamless unity of the procession and suggests that the procession was an occasion when the relationship between participation in Athens' civic and religious life and citizenship was put on display and questioned. Whether this question was implicit or explicit, that is, whether Athenian residents perceived the questions raised by the prominent or ambiguous positions of noncitizens, depends on the degree to which participating in a procession and thereby gaining public recognition and honor were valuable assets—ones that noncitizens could deploy and citizens could accept in the community's discourse about citizenship.

Honor and Civic Identity

Nicole Loraux enigmatically describes the Panathenaia as "the competition between the *apobatai*, the *kanēphoroi*, and the *thallophoria* [*sic*]."[67] Her choice of the word "competition" recalls an early description of the whole Panathenaic program, presumably including the procession as "a competition (*agōn*) for the grey-eyed maiden."[68] Since *agōn* in its early stages referred to an assembly of the people and only later to athletic competitions, these two types of gatherings may have had more in common than initially appears.[69] That is, all public gatherings, especially those in a festival setting, may have been perceived as inherently competitive. Thus, while the Panathenaic procession did not have a mechanism by which performances could be formally judged, it was a competition for honor among some of Athens' residents. More specifically, by such competition I mean the engagement on the part of a marcher in the procession's logic of distributing prestige to those who display their devotion to Athena and Athens by marching with a particular item and in a particular place in the procession. While this competition was less dramatic and regulated than musical and athletic contests, it represented nonetheless, on the part of individual marchers, an assertion of and bid for communal recognition and honor. Just as athletes competed for honor and acclaim in addition to an amphora of sacred olive oil, participants in the procession marched to make a public statement about their place and importance in Athena's city as well as to worship Athena. Such individual bids for recognition and prestige, although potentially divisive, were tolerated because they were harnessed to wider community interests in the worship of Athena.[70] Thus, in addition to celebrating and integrating the members of the Athenian community and their contributions, the Panathenaic procession paradoxically was also a site for competitive public displays among its marchers. In this respect, it was not unlike other areas of Athenian civic life.

Athenian social relations were essentially competitive, for individuals "defined themselves through a politics of reputation."[71] Elites dominated this competition because their wealth enabled them to compete for honor in athletic contests, liturgies, and spontaneous benefactions given to the city.[72] Since the city benefitted from such competitive activities, nonelites encouraged them and often took part in them, as recipients of elite largess and as judging audience.[73] While there is an obvious difference between the role of performer and judge, Athenian competition nonetheless established an "equality of honor" in which, in principle, all citizens could take part.[74] For example, while elite citizens sponsored tragic choruses, nonelite citizens, chosen by lot, voted on these choral performances and thereby bestowed honor upon the elite person whose chorus was judged best.[75] More pointedly, in the assembly, competition among elites for leadership meant that they vied to serve the interests of nonelites rather than those of their own class. Thus, the competitive behavior of elites, whether in the theater, war, or assembly, was seen to be tied to and regulated by the wider interests of the city.[76]

Love of honor, or *philotimia*, was the impetus behind such competitive social relations and a pivotal trait for defining membership in the Athenian polity. In Xenophon's words, "*Philotimia* is not bred in unreasoning beasts or all human beings. Indeed those in whom there is a love of honor and praise differ most from beasts and are considered not merely human beings but men."[77] Xenophon conflates social death (not having the inclination or capacity to compete) with a symbolic degradation. In his reasoning, *philotimia* simultaneously distinguishes human beings from beasts and men from mere human beings, that is, Athenian citizens from noncitizens who were precluded, in theory, from competing for honor. As several inscriptions record, the Panathenaic procession was a site for the display of *philotimia*.[78] One would think, therefore, that the Panathenaic procession portrayed a community engaged in a competition for honor and that this community consisted only of Athenian, if not elite, citizens.

Surprisingly, however, as we have seen, this was not the case. In contrast to the courts and assembly, the Panathenaic procession included both metics and women, that is, noncitizens, and some of these nonelites as well. The procession thus created a unique social practice in which competitive participation and identity in the Athenian community were negotiated among a broader spectrum of constituents than simply citizens. As observed before, it did not merely replicate competitive displays among citizens in more overtly political institutions and did not reproduce Athens' participatory democracy. Rather, it was a counterpoint to democratic notions of identity.[79]

To what degree, if at all, did Panathenaic marchers consciously participate in this public discourse about honor and exclusion or inclusion in Athens' community? This question may seem dangerously speculative insofar as it attempts to capture the intentions of the persons involved, a goal that, in the case of authors, literary criticism has revealed as problematic. We can, nonetheless, conceive of a ritual actor as a " 'horizon' of expectations," that is, subject to a historically shaped set of expectations, of ways of reasoning and behaving that are common to his/her society and can be reconstructed.[80]

Orations, philosophical dialogues, and essays from the fourth century suggest that participants in processions defined themselves through such public displays, and that these "definitions" were significant because they had consequences beyond the festival. In an extreme case, Demosthenes recalls the death sentence one Ktesikles received for profaning the festival by marching while drunk and carrying a leather lash which he used to whip a personal enemy.[81] More generally, orators criticize their opponents for breaches of decorum during a procession. Demosthenes chastises Meidias for riding a horse he did not own when as cavalry commander he marshalled a procession.[82] This office was particularly important for elites, as witnessed by Xenophon's treatises *On Horsemanship* and *The Cavalry Commander*, which provide extensive instructions on how to march properly on horseback.[83] Similarly, Aeschines and Demosthenes debate in their speeches *On The Embassy* whether Epikrates had marched properly at the Dionysia. Demosthenes castigates Epikrates for not wearing a mask in the procession, while Aeschines stoutly denies the charge and its implications.[84]

Costume as much as decorum was a part of the display. Demosthenes, for example, accuses Meidias of destroying the golden cloak and crown Demosthenes had commissioned a smithy to make for his participation in the procession at the Dionysia.[85] It is significant not only that Demosthenes had this expensive costume made but that he could plausibly accuse Meidias of destroying it as a way of diminishing Demosthenes' status. Similarly, Isokrates in the *Areopagiticus* chastises his contemporaries for appearing in processions in gold-spangled cloaks, despite living the rest of the year in the garments of the impoverished. His comments are part of a broader critique of the decline of values in Athens that has reduced processions in honor of the gods from acts of civic piety to occasions for personal display and rivalry.[86] It is clear, then, that for the Athenian citizens participating in a procession was an opportunity to see and be seen and that they took displays and the judging of displays seriously. Hence Sokrates' ambiguous comment at the opening of the *Republic:* the procession of the citizens was fine, but that of the Thracians no worse.[87] Processions defined their marchers in ways both great and small; participating thus was a serious matter, not only because it was part of cult and worship but also because it played an important role in defining community members, both during and after the festival.

In a telling vignette from Lysias, for example, Agoratos, accused of murder, attempts to march in a procession of armed men from the Piraeus to the Acropolis.[88] Aisimos, the armed men's leader, forcefully removes Agoratos from the ranks, shouting, "Go to hell. A murderer like you ought not to join in the procession to Athena." True, this procession took place during a crisis, but the cultural logic of Lysias' speech nonetheless makes clear that Agoratos' crime and his relationship to the polis were reflected in his ouster from this procession, and that this act sealed his identity as an outcast.[89] The depiction of the Panathenaic procession at the end of Aeschylus' *Oresteia* also suggests that participating in a procession could have longer-lasting consequences.[90] When the Erinyes accept Athena's offer to reside in Athens, their change of residence and identity is dramatically marked by their receiving new purple robes, typically worn by metics during processions, and fully realized when they display their new costumes on the imaginary streets of Athens during their final march on stage, a march that has been compared to the Panathenaia.[91] Their new identity and power are thus valorized, and a new politico-religious order is brought into being, through the material representation of its existence.[92]

Marching, in whatever guise, then, was a means by which one could assert one's identity and earn honor (or opprobrium) and have that identity legitimated by the community at large, even after the festival ended.[93] Because the procession instituted and communicated to society at large an honorific role for its marchers as the community's representatives and designated worshippers of Athena, these marchers acquired honor and prestige.[94] Reasonably, they used their marching subsequently as proof of their elevated status. In conclusion, the Panathenaia and other public festivals shaped ritual actors to expect and aim for honor through ritual acts that were at once both devotional acts by which gods were worshipped and competitive acts by which individuals tried to improve their standing before the social group.[95]

The Honor of All Athena's Worshippers

It is not difficult to imagine that cavalrymen, magistrates, ephebes, or hoplites, that is, male citizens such as Demosthenes, Meidias, or Agoratos, used processions as vehicles for self-presentation and the acquisition of honor. We might wonder, though, whether Athenian females and metics, as noncitizens, did so too. To what degree did they deploy the ceremonial idiom of the procession, their items and clothing, to gain honor? Did they, by marching, implicitly make a claim that they too were members of Athens' community of lovers of honor? If so, did the participation of noncitizens implicitly challenge their exclusion from the ranks of citizens?

Both females, who were part of the Panathenaia before the establishment of democracy, and metics, who became part of it during the democracy, had limited opportunities for manipulating the procession to their own ends.[96] Since, most likely, they could not choose the ritual item they carried or their place in the procession, their individual bids for prestige were limited and they could not fully control their own representation. This does not mean, however, that noncitizen marchers had no capacity or imagination to use the Panathenaia to their own ends. Once given a toehold in the procession proper, we can infer that noncitizens were as fully engaged as male citizens in public competitions for honor. Anthropologist A. W. Geertz describes cultural invention as "the creative interaction between paradigm and agent, where the agent continuously reworks pieces of the cultural repertoire in order to construct, adjust, and reconstruct interpretations of experience. The term 'invention' also implies replication and representation. It implies the living into reality of what is perceived about reality."[97] Panathenaic performances were the "living into reality" of what marchers perceived about their experiences and their role and identity in the city. The views of women and metics of their place in the city probably differed greatly from those of Athenian citizens. We can imagine that their marching was subject to various interpretations, and one of these was that they marched to assert their importance to Athens and win honor for themselves, their families, and their wider social groups.

If, for example, the women of Aristophanes' *Lysistrata* offer to donate rich mantles of wool, cloaks, ties, and gold jewelry to the girl—whosoever's daughter she may be—who is chosen as a basket-bearer,[98] they clearly understand, or so Aristophanes implies, the importance of costume for young basket-bearers. Sumptuary laws limiting women's display at rituals and threatening penalties for the violation of certain dress codes also indicate that women were usually engaged in dressing and presenting themselves beautifully, and that they were aware to some extent of the social and religious implications of their ritual acts.[99] Such legislation also suggests that women's clothing, jewelry, and carriages, apparently censured for social, not economic, reasons, were perceived as a symbolic and competitive assertion of status.[100] Numerous stories in which female marchers are pursued by male onlookers, moreover, indicate that Panathenaic marching was a coming-of-age ritual in which young (elite) women announced their eligibility for marriage.[101] This perhaps explains their persistent presence in the procession, from long before and throughout democracy. Their marching had many purposes, both symbolic and practical, and these purposes, like the clothes they wore to fulfill them, suggest that Athenian females were aware that, in presenting themselves well, they and their families might gain honor and prestige and thereby increase their status.

Four inscriptions honor young girls who marched in the Panathenaia for their *philotimia*.[102] These inscriptions specify as a reward only the right to dedicate an offering bowl (*phialē*) and to have their names inscribed on a votive. However, in another inscription, the Delphians inform the Athenians who have performed a Pythian procession to Delphi that, because the priestess of Athena, Chrysis, daughter of Niketes, led the procession appropriately, she and her family will receive from the Delphians *proxenia*, the right to consult the oracle, safe conduct, freedom from taxes, and a front seat at the contests held by the city.[103] Although this is a late inscription and does not pertain to the Panathenaia, it suggests that marching with decorum could result in honor and, in turn, in economic and political gain.

Although no evidence hints at the conscious engagement of metics in the Panathenaic procession in which they too wore special cloaks and carried special items,[104] there is no reason to assume that they were unaware of the possibilities involved. Their participation may have been dismissed, for example, by those who saw a joke in the term "trays" (*skaphai*). Conversely, it may have earned them respect among others, and perhaps this is what the joke served to mask: that noncitizens, like citizens, could and did participate in competitions for honor in religious festivals and that they could and did present themselves as lovers of honor and lovers of Athena and Athens.

Inscriptions also commend the *philotimia* of metics. As David Whitehead demonstrates, from the mid-fourth century, the *philotimia* of non-Athenian benefactors of the city was regularly acknowledged in inscriptions, rewarding them with the right to be taxed on the same basis as citizens (*isoteleia*) and to own property in Athens (*enktēsis*), if not with citizenship.[105] Such rewards in the fourth century were, of course, a result of the crises of 411 and 403, during which the definition of citizenship fluctuated, and of the growing nonlanded wealth of noncitizens on which the city increasingly depended. I suggest that the capacity of metics to use their wealth to gain citizenship was enhanced at least in part by the fact that, for more than a century before the first attested citizenship awards,[106] they had been marching in the Panathenaia and thus competing with citizens in contests of honor, implicitly claiming membership in Athens' political community. In other words, eventually metics could be perceived as not having bought citizenship in Athens but as having earned it through their contributions to and participation in Athens' social, military, and religious life. If so, this confirms the Panathenaia's capacity to shape the discourse about citizen identity by displaying its participants' honor and contributions to the city's religious life. In short, the procession offered a material representation of a "religious status" which differed from political or economic status and could influence these other criteria for defining membership in the Athenian community.

Conclusion

Religious status, belonging to a religious community by virtue of performing certain religious acts, or, in de Polignac's terms, "religious citizenship" in Athens represented an axis for defining community that did not necessarily coincide with or reflect political citizenship. Religious citizenship, materially reflected in the solemn pathways that developing Greek cities created between their centers and an extra-urban or suburban sanctuary, were, in de Polignac's argument, a model for social integration around which cities formed. Reversing the usual order between religion and politics, de Polignac argues that the formation of the Greek city-state followed upon religious practices: "the *polis* constituted a formal expression of a religious cohesion."[107] These early processions, crucial for the development of the city-state, typically included all the residents of a given territory, not only armed men, but also women, elders, and children, that is, they embraced all those as well who may not have had any political role in the governing of the territory and would, in the case of Athens, eventually become noncitizens or "passive citizens."[108] While the Panathenaia differed in essential ways from these early processions, it nonetheless similarly instantiated a vision of community in which political participation, that is, the capacity to judge (in the courts) and rule (in the assembly),[109] was not a defining criterion for membership. In this light, the eventual inclusion of the metics in the procession was in keeping with its original all-inclusive function.

From before the democracy, in the seventh and sixth centuries, and during the democracy in the fifth and fourth centuries, then, the Panathenaic procession persisted as a form of ritual that defined the Athenian community as a collection of individuals who dwelt in the same land and worshipped the same goddess. In other words, it realized religious citizenship, and this religious citizenship did not change as the political definition of citizenship in democratic Athens evolved. In fact, it increasingly diverged from political citizenship because it continued to embrace passive citizens, i.e., those who did not participate in ruling and judging, such as the metics. The Panathenaia's inclusiveness, then, was decidedly not the result of a democratic impulse but, rather, it was typical of Archaic processions, wherein all residents of a territory marched in a display of social solidarity marshalled in honor of a goddess. Moreover, the Panathenaic procession remained a model for community inclusiveness that could be imitated by political action, as the enfranchisement of some metics in the fourth century shows. Thus, the procession created a world, albeit temporary, whose parameters differed from political institutions in which honor and membership were monopolized by male citizens. More importantly, it could even challenge the strictly political parameters of the debate over identity and inclusion within the Athenian community as all participants displayed their notion of and claims to status and identity.

This is not to say that the Panathenaic procession was impervious to the democracy that grew up around it or, more accurately, that it did not intersect with its political and social setting during the fifth and fourth centuries. Of course it did. As I have argued, the Panathenaic procession was a site where Athens' residents could compete, as well as be joined, in their shared attempts to honor Athena. In other words, the procession could integrate all members of the city, in a manner akin to other democratic institutions. Thus, the Panathenaic procession assumed a functional role in the democracy, as did the courts, assemblies, theater, and war, as its procession was shaped by its participants, mostly elite, into a vehicle for gaining status while worshipping Athena on behalf of the community, not only themselves.

The procession, and hence the festival, thus were not simply inclusive, nor simply contestatory or competitive. Rather, the procession presented two visions of Athens simultaneously: in one, Athens was an inclusive community of religious identity; in the other, Athens appeared as an exclusive community of political identity. Each vision challenged the other, and the simultaneous presentation of both exposed the tensions between these different modes of individual and communal self-definition. The democracy therefore did not completely subsume and reshape Athenian religious life. While it influenced some aspects of the community's festivals, its religious practices, particularly those that predated the development of democracy, often retained their integrity and earlier function. If so, the vitality of Athens' democracy and hence its civic community during the fifth and fourth centuries did not only or perhaps even mainly rest on the consonance between its religious and political spheres, but on their differences, which encouraged debate about the very definition of community.

CHAPTER FIFTEEN

Reflections and Conclusions: Democracy, Empire, and the Arts in Fifth-Century Athens

DEBORAH BOEDEKER AND KURT A. RAAFLAUB

No single answer has emerged to the questions posed in the introduction to this volume. Rather, the preceding chapters present evidence and arguments for many different kinds of interaction among democracy, empire, and the arts in fifth-century Athens, as well as differing perspectives on how unique classical Athens was in respect to its arts. This diversity is instructive and salutary; it helps us avoid unsupported generalizations about the flourishing of creative arts in a democratic society, or the assumption of one-way influence, for example, from economic and political conditions to the arts. In this chapter, reflecting on our collaborators' papers individually and as a whole, we try to synthesize various findings, point out areas where further study is especially needed, and draw conclusions—tentative and partial though they be.

Not Only at Athens

As stated in chapter 1, even though our questions focus on Athens, this volume seeks to avoid a narrow and unexamined Athenocentrism. In precisely that area, several papers pose a major challenge to approaches that have traditionally been applied to these issues. Indeed, Ian Morris argues that, especially if we break down "the artificial distinction between 'high' and 'low' forms of Athenian material culture," there is much evidence "to show that Athenian behavior was but one local variant on a truly panhellenic pattern."[1] Morris demonstrates this by selecting two exemplary sets of evidence, burials and houses, tracing the pattern of restraint that appears in Athens by about 500 and disappears again by ca. 425, and showing that a similar pattern emerges from the archaeological record of other poleis and regions in the center and at the periphery of the Hellenic world. The same pattern is visible in the disappearance and reappearance of funeral monuments in Attic cemeteries.[2] Moreover, just as in Athens, the archaeological records of other poleis, which were not all democratic and certainly not masters of an empire, often reveal major communal buildings and monuments around the mid-fifth century. If these are actually panhellenic or even more general phenomena we will surely fail in trying to explain them through specifically Athenian experiences. Morris concludes that we should not limit our questions about Athenian phenomena "to asking whether they were democratic statements or masks for imperialism. We must first look at them within a broader Athenian context, coupling communal expenditure with familial restraint, and then we must see them within a broader Greek context."[3] It is the emerging widespread pattern that needs explanation. Colin Renfrew's model of "peer polity interaction" (mutual influences among similar communities) and Gabriel Herman's demonstration that a wide network of contacts among elites continued to exist, despite their communities' focus on local interests, may contribute importantly to such an explanation.[4]

Morris rightly cautions us against assuming Athenian uniqueness too easily, and he reminds us how much more we need to know about developments elsewhere in order to draw a more complete comparison: here lies one of the challenges this volume poses to future research. Indeed, whatever its differences from other places in Greece, Athens certainly was and remained a Hellenic polis. The developments in the arts that it fostered were based on a broad foundation of panhellenic cultural values and norms that had come about and continued to evolve by the mechanisms of exchange among elites and others. The rapid dissemination throughout the Greek world of the "artistic revolution" of the early fifth century[5] shows that Athens continued to be influenced by such developments, just as developments within Athens influenced other cities. This is valid for expressions of "high" and "low" culture and for elites and commoners alike, as Morris illustrates.

In their chapter, Eric Csapo and Margaret Miller likewise transcend Athenocentrism by proposing that a new, more democratic "temporality" emerged in fifth-century Greek art; similarly, Tonio Hölscher describes panhellenic developments in sculpture. Both these chapters suggest, however, that the quantity and pace of such developments was especially great at Athens. Other contributors make clear as well that panhellenic phenomena only partially explain the specific development of the arts in fifth-century Athens. Admittedly, the differences concern mostly "high" art, but even this was directed toward and supported by the entire citizen body of the polis through its officials and the decisions made by its Assembly. Needless to say, in focusing on "high" art we pass no value judgment: we do not consider that temple sculptures, tragedy, and philosophy are worth consideration while houses and burials are not. We do think, though, that for the specific questions posed in this volume, comparative evidence from houses or burials illuminates only part of the picture; it remains essential to consider the conditions created by empire, democracy, and their combined impact on Athenian society if we are to understand the flourishing of so many arts in this city.

The differences between, say, Argos or Corinth (two of the examples studied by Morris) and Athens in the speed and scope of artistic development and achievement are, we believe, not just a consequence of greater or lesser intensity, larger or smaller material resources. Morris shows that in some respects—especially an initial decline of individual aristocratic display paralleled by increases in communal display, and a later reversal of this trend—developments in all these poleis fit a similar pattern; yet in other ways, as will be discussed below, they do not. The Athenian artistic experience both resembled and diverged from that of other poleis, and it did so, we suggest, because fifth-century Athenian society both shared many structures and values with the rest of the Greek world and also lived through unprecedented, extraordinary, and unique experiences (see further below, at nn.77ff.).

A related challenge to Athenocentrism, perhaps more familiar, is forcefully presented by Robert Wallace. Granted, Athens was arguably the prime cultural center of Greece,[6] but most of the great artists and intellectuals who helped the city establish this reputation were foreigners, coming from a wide range of poleis around the Aegean and in Magna Graecia or Sicily. In fact, apart from the dramatic poets and vase painters, relatively few leading fifth-century specialists in architecture, sculpture, monumental painting, rhetoric, historiography, science, philosophy, and what is commonly called the "sophistic movement" were Athenians. They came to Athens, attracted by the city's wealth and power and the wide range of public and private patronage they could expect there. But they worked elsewhere as well and formed an international community of skilled men, experts (*sophoi, sophistai*)—more accomplished, we would add, but quite comparable to the *dēmiourgoi* of Homer's time—continuing patterns, as Wallace emphasizes, that are visible among the poets of the Archaic and early classical period.[7]

Focusing more specifically on the role of the sophists in Athens, Wallace emphasizes that these travelling teachers did not represent a distinct and coherent movement, their activities emerged from and continued much older traditions, they did not all primarily teach oratory, and they were not narrowly associated with Athens or its democracy. Most of these men apparently did not learn their trade in Athens; they brought it there and found an eager clientele, but they had acquired their skills in other cities and spent much time travelling, performing, and teaching elsewhere.[8] This is well known but its implications have not been considered sufficiently: there must have existed all over the Greek world an audience eager to hear the sophists, patronize them, and learn from them. If so, and no valid argument seems to contradict it, it seems difficult to maintain, as has so often been done, that Athens and its democracy "produced" the sophistic movement or that this movement would have been impossible without the democracy.[9] Our knowledge of political life in most other Greek poleis is so limited that it is difficult to assess with any degree of confidence why (if this is the right way of putting the question) an otherwise unremarkable polis like Leontinoi produced a Gorgias, or Abdera a Protagoras, or why the skills of these and other men were in such high demand in so many places. We do not know precisely how these cities compared to Athens politically, but the conclusion is almost inevitable that, for example, rhetorical skills to persuade others were increasingly important almost everywhere and therefore that collective decision making in sufficiently large assemblies and/or jury courts was widespread at the time.[10]

Athens, then, was unique less in principle than in the number of opportunities and the level of patronage it was able to offer, and perhaps also because one could expect to find there an extraordinary level of receptivity to, even enthusiasm for, cultural innovation, a greater number of colleagues, and an especially intense and stimulating intellectual climate.[11] Nevertheless, we think, higher degrees of intensity, exchange, and opportunity in Athens may eventually have triggered a change in the quality and purpose of the sophists' endeavor; Harvey Yunis' argument on the rise of the art of rhetoric, for example, supports this possibility. In this respect, as we will argue below, specific conditions in fifth-century Athens may indeed have been crucial for further developments.

The Almighty Drachma?

Wallace's conclusions also lead us to consider just why Athens became a magnet for out-of-towners like the sophists, as well as other leading artists and intellectuals of the time. As Garry Wills wrote in his review of the "Greek Miracle" exhibition, "Admittedly, Athens had more artistic activity than any other city of the fifth century, but this was not because it was a democratic city. It hired artists from all over . . . because it was an *imperial* city, with the huge funds collected from its subjects in the Delian League."[12] Similarly, John Davies has suggested that the unparalleled mass of surviving materials from fifth-century Athens can be explained by "a major historical fact, the concentration of talents and resources at Athens." He continues, "Attracted by public patronage offered by the Athenian musical festivals, by commission for temple decorations or works of art, or by the private patronage and social lionizing offered by wealthy Athenian aristocrats, the previously scattered Greek intellectual aristocracy of painters, performing artists, writers, teachers, and philosophers began increasingly to use Athens as a *pied-à-terre* . . . Patronage costs money. The money was there. If the documentation about fifth-century Athens leaves any one overall impression, it is that of a concentration of monetary resources, in both public and private hands, previously unheard of in Greece."[13]

This is certainly correct but, in our view, wealth is an enabling condition, a necessary but not a sufficient cause; in itself it explains quantitative but not qualitative change. Davies' picture of a city that, like the tyrants of old, bought the best talent available on the panhellenic market takes into account neither the possibility that such concentration of talents in many arts might have deeply affected the arts themselves, nor that these arts might have served specific collective needs of this particular society. Yet this city was a democracy, to some extent from the reforms of Kleisthenes in 508/7 and fully from Ephialtes' reforms in 462.[14] In fifth-century Athens *public* sponsorship of artistic talent was *democratic* sponsorship. This fact should not simply be ignored—and it is intriguing in itself. After all, throughout history, it has been monarchs or wealthy aristocrats, whether religious or secular, who had both the money and good reasons to indulge in such costly endeavors as patronizing the arts.[15] Why would the Athenian citizens have been interested in assuming this habit? What was in it for them?

Part of the explanation must lie in the fact, illuminated by Lisa Kallet's chapter, that most of the citizens were not spending their own money and that art, at least compared with war, was relatively inexpensive. For example, the siege of Poteidaia in 432–430 cost about two thousand talents, as much as Parthenon, Propylaia, and the gold-ivory statue of Athena Parthenos together.[16] The total public outlay for one of the most important and splendid annual festivals, the Great Dionysia, probably amounted to less than 1 percent of Athens' annual state income. Even so, this was not an insignificant sum, and Kallet points out that contemporaries considered the total of public festival expenses very high.[17] The total spent on public buildings over the years certainly amounted to many thousands of talents. Yet the money to cover such expenses did not come out of the average citizen's pocket but, in various combinations, from domestic revenue, from indirect taxes levied on the rich (the liturgies, a unique blend of honor and obligation), and from imperial tribute.[18] Moreover, as the "Old Oligarch" comments cynically, in the festivals and competitions as in the preparation of warships the rich paid and the poor profited (Pseudo-Xenophon, *Constitution of the Athenians* 1.13).

But availability of other people's money does not explain the democracy's decision to spend it on public arts. Two factors seem crucial here. For the most part, such patronage was intended, directly or indirectly, for religious purposes, especially the construction and decoration of sanctuaries and the splendid performance of rituals and festivals. The religious component is important; we will return to it later. On the other hand, as Kallet explains, by financing visual and performing arts, the demos assumed a role previously played by wealthy individuals—aristocrats and tyrants. Troubling ambiguities were connected with the unprecedented accumulation of public wealth; spending part of this wealth for ostentatious public projects imitated proper individual behavior and supported the propriety of owning such wealth. The change from private funding for large public projects, still typical in Kimon's time, to exclusively public funding, normal from the period of Perikles' leadership, was part of the conscious realization of full democracy: the individual was prevented from acquiring too much power, while the demos' "control over and magnificent expenditure of wealth provided a crucial demonstration of its power not just abroad, but at home."[19] Conversely, in performing liturgies, the individual was allowed to excel in aristocratic display and thereby to gain honor, because this form of spending for the community demonstrated good citizenship and was tied into the institutional structure of democracy, limited in scope, and controlled by the state.

Nonetheless, we should add, the role the elite was able to play here was but a shadow of earlier splendor. The long process by which the demos assumed control over the arts exacted a heavy price. As Hölscher has noted elsewhere, "Entire categories of private and public art were suppressed. The brilliant Attic funeral art, statues, reliefs, painting, which had occupied a leading position in Greece, came to an end, perhaps by law, perhaps by social pressure. The genre of private dedicatory reliefs was largely interrupted as well. And the splendid archaic statues on the Akropolis seem to end after 480 too, apparently . . . because the customs of dedicating votive gifts were changing entirely. One should not forget this when discussing the topic of 'democracy and culture'."[20]

Eventually, Kallet continues, "because of the wealth it generated, the empire was seen as necessary to the functioning of the city's democracy and cultural life."[21] In public spending, we conclude, empire and democracy were inextricably intertwined, just as the power—and liberty—of the demos in democracy and the empire were inseparably connected.[22] Celebrations of Athens' power and great accomplishments in war through public display at festivals, in public buildings and monuments, or in their pictorial programs thus were at the same time celebrations of democracy.[23] The link between empire, the arts, and democracy was demonstrated most obviously in the presentation of the allies' tribute on stage at the first day of the Dionysia, as part of a series of ceremonies with great significance for the democracy.[24] Festivals and temples, most of all the Parthenon, were as much demonstrations for the entire empire as productions of the democratic polis for its citizens.[25]

Democracy in Art

Under the specific conditions prevailing in Athens, then, it was possible to glorify the democracy through the display of the city's economic and imperial power. As David Castriota has suggested, the Athenians may have been accustomed, through long cultural training, to "see the celebration of the Athenian constitution as an integral function of victory monuments commemorating a heroized conception of the Athenian national character."[26] This provides one explanation for the vast preponderance, in public pictorial programs, of martial themes: mythical victories of Greeks (and their gods) over non-Greeks, such as Giants, Centaurs, Amazons, and Trojans, as well as soon-mythologized historical victories over the Persians for which the Athenians claimed the lion's share of merit, and eventually even victories over other Greeks. Additional explanations of this phenomenon are not lacking. The citizens of a polis that was almost constantly involved in warfare and repeatedly faced major challenges by large parts of the Hellenic world must have felt a particular need to reaffirm their collective superiority. This need was enhanced by the levelling effect of the ideal of democratic equality and by the fact that past victories over external enemies, on behalf of all Hellenes or of those especially in need of help, served as primary justification for Athenian hegemony and imperial rule. In this respect, the pictorial programs and the funeral orations closely paralleled each other. Domestically, the focus of patriotic sentiments and energies on outside enemies helped overcome tensions and conflicts.[27] And finally, just as it was more conventional and easier (as well as more "heroic") to represent hoplites (heavily armed infantry) and horsemen rather than sailors (below, n.35), so too it must have been easier to represent martial and imperial values than democratic ones.

One of these martial themes, the Gigantomachy, made its first monumental appearance in Athens in the marble pediments installed as replacements for older ones in the Old Athena Temple in the last decade of the sixth century; it probably simply celebrated Athena's greatest victory that played a crucial role in the Panathenaic festival—and perhaps conveyed as well a "subtle reference" to the recent overthrow of the tyranny.[28] In Shapiro's view, the "Older Parthenon," begun but not completed in the 480s, was the first temple built as a communal victory monument (for Marathon).[29] The pictorial program intended for it is unknown. All the post–Persian War sanctuaries and many other monuments, culminating in but not ending with the Parthenon, featured scenes from wars between Athenians or Hellenes and non-Hellenes. The mythical predecessors could easily be perceived as metaphors of the Persian War victories, which quickly assumed mythical significance themselves.[30] But, according to Hölscher, their meaning was broader: this pictorial program "represents a range of polar oppositions and threats to the Greek way of life that were repelled by Greek, especially Athenian, heroes: blasphemous giants, brutal semimonsters, aggressive females, and Orientals as hybrid cultural antipodes. Taken together, these myths constitute a manifold, almost complete panorama that defines Greek identity against various opposite worlds."[31] This corresponds to a traditional pattern of thought defining values in polar oppositions, and it has a distant forerunner in Odysseus' confrontation with a range of societies that all represent some form of opposite to Hellenic polis society as it was evolving in the eighth century.[32] But, as Hölscher concludes, "in developing and using paradigmatic myths in such a global system, Athens probably . . . was unique."[33]

Nonetheless, the apparent absence of specifically democratic themes in Athenian art has puzzled scholars. As Hölscher puts it, "Not much democracy is visible in Athenian state monuments of the fifth century."[34] Indeed, as has often been observed, unambiguous representations of democracy and various related ideas and attitudes occur only from the very end of the fifth century, reflected in the sudden appearance of personifications.[35] A cult of Demokratia perhaps existed since the restoration of democracy in 403, and a statue group on the tomb of Kritias supposedly showed Oligarchia tormenting Demokratia with a burning torch; soon thereafter a trireme was named Demokratia. Later in the fourth century a statue of Demokratia stood in the Agora, Theseus flanked by Demokratia and Demos featured in a famous painting by Euphranor in the Stoa of Zeus Eleutherios, and Demokratia is shown crowning Demos (the only extant representation of this kind) in a relief of 337/6.[36] On present evidence, then, it seems safe to conclude that Demokratia herself came to be personified as a result of the bitter experiences of the second oligarchic coup of 404/3 and that before then there was no need for such tangible reaffirmation of the precise constitutional concept.[37] If so, we should not be surprised to find none of the primary democratic values—such as *isonomia, isēgoria, parrhēsia,* or *eleutheria*—personified in the fifth century either. Conversely, in the fourth century warships were called Eleutheria and Parrhesia.[38] We should not overlook, as is often done, however, that another concept crucial to democracy, that of the sovereign Demos, which easily could and for a long time probably did represent the constitution as well, was personified much earlier, perhaps already in the context of the Ephialtic-Periklean reforms of 462–450. This concept is attested in the cult of Demos and the Nymphs (ca. 450), drama (Aristophanes' *Knights* of 424), and a picture of the famous and influential painter Parrhasios which perhaps dates as early as the Peloponnesian War.[39]

Our knowledge of fifth-century personifications comes mostly from paintings, described by later authors or surviving on vases. Alan Shapiro likewise uses primarily vase paintings in sketching the complex evolution of the concept of autochthony ("always having the same land," or even "born of the land itself," which was conflated with the legend of the earth-born Erichthonios, later king Erechtheus), as it appears on vases from the Persian Wars to the end of the century. Shapiro interprets autochthony as a concept that "was . . . useful both to the democracy and to Athens' imperialist ambitions. On the one hand, autochthony is, like democracy itself, a great leveller. It asserts that every native Athenian is as good as every other, by virtue of their common ancestry going back to Erechtheus, and better than any non-Athenian. This belief in the inherent superiority of the Athenians was also a cornerstone of the democracy, as evident, for example, in Perikles' citizenship law. At the same time, autochthony also implies that the Athenians are an older, purer, and nobler race than other Greeks, . . . favored and protected in their enterprise by the whole host of Olympian gods."[40]

The roots of this concept lie in the stories of the first two Attic kings, Kekrops and Erechtheus, which are well attested in the Archaic period. It became prominent and was elaborated upon when the Delian League was established with Athens at its head in the aftermath of the Persian Wars, and even more so in the period of the Peloponnesian War, when both the notion of autochthony itself—in stark contrast to the traditions about the immigration of the Dorians—and the mythical favors bestowed on Athens by the Olympians helped strengthen the patriotism and self-confidence of a community under great stress. In ways that shifted with circumstances and needs, Shapiro concludes, autochthony helped "to forge a shared Athenian identity imbued with historical depth and a powerful attachment to the soil, the city, and its spiritual heart, the Akropolis."[41]

Shapiro makes the intriguing suggestion that the myth of the earth-born Erichthonios assumed added significance to balance one flaw of Theseus, Athens' national hero, who was not born in Athens and whose mother was not Athenian. Otherwise, Theseus too served both the purposes of domestic and imperial ideology, his myth evolving as needs arose.[42] New depictions of his youthful deeds on vases and on the Athenian Treasury at Delphi reflect his immensely increased prominence in the two decades after Kleisthenes' reforms. Hölscher suggests that, in contrast to Herakles, the principal hero of Archaic Athens who "represented the panhellenic ideals of the upper class, Theseus was chosen as a patriotic hero" who "was less an aggressive warrior than a protagonist of the domestic order . . . It was only after the Persian Wars that Theseus changed into a protagonist against foreign aggressors."[43] Later in the century, precisely when democracy came under increasing pressure, Theseus appeared as its founder and protector, acting, though king, as ideal leader of the people (*prostatēs tou dēmou*) in Euripides' *Suppliants*.

The expression of democratic values, however, was not limited to vase paintings. The public cemetery in the Kerameikos with its long line of collective public burials of each year's war dead, each featuring simple stelai with the names of the heroes, arranged according to tribes, and a praise epigram, served as a powerful reminder of all citizens' equality and *aretē*.[44] Through public buildings and spaces designated for political purposes, democracy dominated the political topography of the city. Hölscher demonstrates how the "civic presence" intended and realized by Kleisthenes' reforms of 508/7 developed into a complex and all-pervasive habit of "civic communication" which is visible especially in the reorganization of public space, in the appearance and use of public monuments, and in the use and adaptation of myths where public concerns assumed priority over private ones.[45] The public space created in the Agora—itself proof that high priority was attributed to public affairs—was politicized and became multifunctional. From the late sixth century, it brought together every day hundreds if not thousands of citizens for public business in the Assembly, law court (*hēliaia*), the office of the Archon Basileus in the Stoa Basileios, the Council in the Bouleuterion, festivals, performances and competitions, or simply the daily market. The square's capacity was soon overtaxed and specific public functions were moved elsewhere: the Assembly to the Pnyx, and the theater performances to the sanctuary of Dionysos on the south slope of the Akropolis.[46] The city thus received a "functional topography" that reflected the changed needs of a society in which public life and institutions assumed a massively increased importance. The new relations among citizens are expressed neatly in the change from the round orchestra on the Agora, where the elite leaders stood in the middle, as they had done for centuries, surrounded by their follower groups and the other citizens,[47] to the Pnyx, where the speakers on a raised platform (*bēma*) had to justify their proposals to the collectivity of self-confident citizens judging their performance and deciding on the issues.[48]

Moreover, although not *in persona*, democracy was celebrated prominently in three important monuments. As a famous drinking song (*skolion*) illustrates, the statue group of Harmodios and Aristogeiton, heroizing those who supposedly had liberated Athens from tyranny, could, by implication, symbolize the establishment of *isonomia* (political equality, an initially aristocratic concept that was probably appropriated by the Kleisthenic order) and even the foundation of democracy.[49] Whatever the historical realities, emphasized in the context of late-fifth-century polemics by Herodotus and Thucydides,[50] there is little doubt that popular imagination eventually celebrated the Tyrannicides as heroes of democracy. As "freedom fighters" par excellence, they embodied a crucial communal value and met a deep social and emotional need. Hölscher suggests that, placed in the Agora where the Assembly met (before the creation of a new Assembly place on the Pnyx), they represented "concrete examples of behavior for the citizens," especially since their monument recognized "not a successful achievement but a political attitude. Since the citizens of isonomic Athens developed their identity in opposition to tyranny, Harmodios and Aristogeiton were supposed to encourage them to embrace the ideology of the Tyrannicides."[51]

Probably in the time of Perikles, this statue group was joined in the Agora by the monument of the Eponymous Heroes (who had given the ten tribes their names). They represented the community in its unity based on civic subdivisions and, guarding the official proclamations posted on their pedestal, they sanctioned its public acts.[52]

The third monument of democracy is the Parthenon frieze, complex and much debated as to function and meaning. In her contribution to this volume, Lisa Maurizio accepts the interpretation of the frieze as representing the Panathenaic procession, though in a highly stylized version. Moreover, as is generally true of processions, that of the Panathenaia too was not a realistic reflection of the Athenian community; it emphasized certain members and ignored others in order to create an idealized image that served partly the interests of the dominating elite, partly those of the entire polis. This festival existed long before democracy was fully developed in Athens; it is questionable, therefore, whether it ever became, as many scholars think, fully inclusive and distinctly democratic. Rather, it offers an excellent opportunity to examine, in an especially important example where the complex interplay between religion, society, and politics must have constantly been at work, the question of how democracy may have continued or changed traditional religious practices.

Scholars have found the preponderance of horsemen and charioteers particularly puzzling: after all, the frieze was commissioned at the height of naval democracy. The fact that many of these figures are naked, Maurizio suggests, perhaps offers a solution: they may represent in heroic guise all citizens serving in the community's armed forces—hoplites and even thetes (lower-class citizens, who generally rowed the fleet), as much as cavalry.[53] This might mitigate the otherwise surprising absence from the procession of the thetes, a large and communally indispensable part of the citizen body; thetes may have marched among the demesmen, but at the end of the procession they would have been hardly distinguishable from the onlookers. From another perspective, the "ennobling" of all citizens in the frieze may thus provide an example of the coexistence of democratic and aristocratic ideologies that is pointed out in Csapo and Miller's chapter.

The procession contradicted other firmly established civic roles as well. It accommodated both males and females and celebrated their different contributions to the city, thus overcoming hierarchies and tensions that were valid in other spheres of public and private life. The participation of metics (resident aliens) stressed their inclusion among the community's members and Athena's worshippers, while items they wore and bore marked them to some extent as outsiders, thus reflecting the ambiguity of their status. The procession was at the same time an eminent civic event and a site where the established relationship between participation in Athens' civic and religious life on one hand and, on the other, membership in the citizen body was put on display and challenged. Here the competition for honor and prestige, normally restricted to citizens if not elite citizens, was open to nonelite persons and noncitizens. As Maurizio sees it, the Panathenaic procession thus "assumed a functional role in the democracy, as did the courts, assemblies, theater, and war." The procession, and hence the festival, "were not simply inclusive, nor simply contestatory or competitive. Rather, the procession presented two visions of Athens simultaneously: in one, Athens was an inclusive community of religious identity; in the other, Athens appeared as an exclusive community of political identity. Each vision challenged the other."[54]

This may be true of Athens' religious life as a whole. Democracy—and the city's imperial role—certainly influenced many aspects, but others retained their older functions. If so, Maurizio concludes, "the vitality of Athens' democracy and hence its civic community" perhaps rested less on "the consonance between its religious and political spheres" than on "their differences, which encouraged debate about the very definition of community."[55] We think that such productive tensions between traditional and innovative patterns—one more static and rooted in structures of the polis dating from the Archaic period and broadly valid, despite variations, throughout the Hellenic world, the other more dynamic and influenced by recent sociopolitical developments more specifically limited to Athens—may well offer a useful explanatory model for some of the principal questions addressed in this volume.[56]

Overall, then, the democracy *was* present in the city's architectural and figural landscape, as it was in rhetoric and drama.

Democratic Discourse in the Theater

Choral poetry and other forms of performance and ritual behavior out of which Attic drama developed were rooted firmly in Archaic panhellenic traditions. Why and how they evolved into the specific forms of drama cultivated in fifth-century Athens is much debated but not important here. It is significant, however, that the rise of drama was paralleled in Athens, in contrast to the rest of Greece, by a decrease in the production and prestige of epic and lyric poetry.[57] The early stages of tragedy and comedy certainly predated the emergence of democracy. Tragedy was integrated into the festival of the City Dionysia under the Peisistratids or, according to a recent suggestion, only after Kleisthenes;[58] comedy became part of this festival only in the 480s. Dramatic performances in both categories were competitive, supervised by the highest officials and the Assembly, and financed by public funds and contributions of wealthy citizens through liturgies. By the mid-fifth century the opening ceremony of the Dionysia, preceding the performance of the first set of tragedies, was a distinctly political event, filled with civic and symbolic significance.[59] Tragic and comic plays thus were at the center of one of the premier religious and civic occasions of the year, staged in front of huge crowds. Various forms of drama were performed in other Greek cities as well, but the prominence and artistic brilliance of drama in Athens were unique.

Although not all comic poets focused on political themes and lampooned politicians, the most famous ones did. "Old Comedy," which reached its climax with Aristophanes and his rivals in the last third of the fifth century, was intimately tied to the democratic experience: as Jeffrey Henderson says in his chapter, its "most intensely political phase coincided with the era of full popular sovereignty (the ascendancy of Perikles and the Peloponnesian War); this phase tapered off" after 403. Comedy's connection with democracy was not only thematic but functional. As Henderson explains, comedy shared with oratory the central principles of free speech (*isēgoria, parrhēsia*) "that set the rules for public speech and so enabled democracy to function in the first place." He argues "that the ideological alignment and structural complementarity of oratory and comedy in voicing criticism and advice to civic audiences support the classical understanding of comedy as essentially democratic and politically engaged, as against the modern tendency to see comedy as detached, innocuous, and essentially apolitical." Comedy—and tragedy—was an important part of civic instruction, again closely related to oratory. Like "law courts and assemblies, civic theater served to temper the understanding, the critical capacity, and the confidence of a citizenry now fully in charge of its own destiny. Like any other organ of the democracy, civic theater was predicated on the theory of the ultimate wisdom, and trainability in wisdom, of the demos. Thus it could not but serve and strengthen the sovereignty of democratic ideology."[60]

But theater, Henderson emphasizes, was also very different from other forms of civic discourse. It admitted much larger audiences than Assembly or law courts, and was open to all members of society, not just the citizens. The same variety of persons was represented on stage, and the issues that were dramatized covered all concerns and aspects of life in the community. And so, to some extent comparable to the Panathenaic procession analyzed by Lisa Maurizio, "drama became the principal communal outlet for portraying the polis in all its diversity and social hierarchies; for reconsidering traditions and norms, airing concerns, examining problems, and testing solutions that affected the democratic culture as a whole but that had no other public outlet."[61]

Much of this is true for tragedy as well. That tragedy served an important communal function and was in essential ways political and engaged theater as well is by now generally accepted. As Suzanne Saïd argues, however, in a broad survey of modern opinions on this question,[62] no agreement has yet been reached on precisely what this means. Some things are clear, though. First, since tragedy was part of the Dionysia throughout the formative period of the democracy, it assumed its political role early on; not accidentally, Aeschylus, arguably the most profoundly political of the great poets, created his plays early in this period. Second, as Henderson's and Saïd's essays show, comedy and tragedy differ greatly in the nature of their political engagement. The latter was rarely involved in issues of everyday politics but mirrors no less intensely the conflicts and concerns that troubled the community. Saïd illustrates this with one example, the relations between *oikos* and polis in some of the Theban plays of all three tragedians, thereby documenting how tragedy "can serve as a magnifying glass for analyzing the interplay between family and city and the tensions between civic duty and loyalty to kin,"[63] and how the poets' changing emphasis in dramatizing such interaction reflects shifts in the social and political experiences of the polis. Third, even more than comedy, tragedy lost most of its political function and impetus at the end of the fifth century, with Athens' defeat in the Peloponnesian War and subsequent changes in its democracy.[64]

Whether or not this marks the beginning of a "more mature," moderate, or complete democracy, characterized by the rule of law rather than the demos,[65] the "depoliticization" of drama accompanying this change serves as powerful testimony to the immediacy and intensity of fifth-century democracy, which apparently needed and fostered highly political forms of drama. The system of "agonistic liturgies" supporting the performance of drama (as well as other performances at various festivals) was put in place before the impact of the wealth flowing in from the empire was felt in Athens.[66] Although such wealth may have prompted individual liturgists to sponsor performances more generously than they might otherwise have done, in the development of Attic drama both as an art form and as civic-political theater the influence of the empire clearly seems secondary to that of the democracy. Even so, issues related to Athens' hegemony can be perceived in many tragedies, from Aeschylus' *Persians* to Euripides' *Ion* to Sophokles' *Oidipous at Kolonos*.[67]

Democratic Temporality

So far we have looked for democratic values mostly as found in the *contents* of Athenian figural, verbal, or festival production. Eric Csapo and Margaret Miller focus not on the subject matter of art but on its ideology, and not on one art form but on an attribute attested in many: temporality—by which they mean "time as it is experienced, conceived, and represented." Temporality, they argue, is conditioned by many factors; it does not progress in evolutionary fashion from a "primitive" to a "scientific" understanding of time, but changes with political and social structures.

Csapo and Miller discern "a significant shift in the dominant temporality of Greek art in the later sixth and fifth centuries," which they attribute to precisely those changes in mentality which made democracy and empire possible.[68] They argue that in the fifth century a new democratic temporality comes to coexist with the older, aristocratic temporality that privileges the past, looking to it for paradigms of behavior and value. Democratic time focuses on the present moment—especially the temporal rhythm of political activity: deliberation, decision, and action—and its effect on the near future, giving special prominence to the concept of *kairos*.[69] Csapo and Miller maintain that the shift in temporality was significantly tempered by the fact of empire, which served both as a catalyst for the development of new "democratic" values and as a break on their development, since it gave Athenians a stake in retaining or resuscitating elitist, authoritarian, and hegemonic forms of thought despite the egalitarian discourse they developed for domestic use. The new temporality was not strictly limited to Athens: first, many parts of Greece were to some extent egalitarian (or "democratic" in a very broad definition of the term, such as that used by Morris in this volume as well) by the late sixth century; and second, the conditions of empire affect not only the ruler but the ruled, and (since empires are acquisitive) even those who might be ruled.[70] Athens was nevertheless the foremost exponent of the new ideology. In the fifth century, as Athens changed from a predominantly aristocratic to a predominantly democratic culture, its art reflected that change, for "[a]rt is part . . . of that ideological process that selects, articulates, privileges, and willfully distorts experience when social groups engage in a collective meditation on their distinctive values, their role, and their historic destiny."[71]

Aristocratic time did not disappear with the emergence of democratic time; both orientations are evident in fifth-century Athenian art, reflecting the ambivalence of the Athenian demos itself, who "both opposed and appropriated aristocratic values . . . [T]he Athenian demos never aspired to full democracy. It felt its middle position on the social ladder too keenly. Looking up it spoke the language of equality. Looking down at the enormous metic, slave, and subject population at home and abroad, it spoke the language of the elite."[72] Such ambivalence is well attested in the strong orientation toward heroic past deeds that, as Deborah Boedeker's chapter reminds us, characterized most genres of classical Athenian public art, whereby present achievements over opponents are represented in terms of (constructed) past glories. Paradoxically, then, the "aristocratic" *subject matter* of architectural sculpture, tragedy, and monumental painting, glorifying a timeless past, was often expressed via a democratic *temporality* emphasizing the present narrative moment as critical time.

Democratic Oratory and Rhetoric

Changes in genres not overtly sponsored by the demos reflect the influence of democracy and empire as well, although sometimes in ways different from the monumental arts.[73] In the period we are considering, oratory, important as it was in public life, was only beginning to become a "professional" genre. As Harvey Yunis puts it at the beginning of his chapter, "To consider fifth-century rhetoric is to peer into the darkness before the dawn." The fourth century produced the masterpieces of practical oratory that served as models for posterity, and original works of rhetorical theory. Thomas Cole has argued, and Yunis confirms, that often-accepted traditions about the origins of rhetoric in Sicily or in sophistic circles must be abandoned. Whatever the groundwork the sophists laid, "Only since Plato has rhetoric been fully a discipline, that is, a *technē* in the sense that European culture accepted as definitive: a systematic useful practice that, like medicine, is supported by an appropriate body of theory and cannot be properly pursued in the absence of that theory."[74]

Yunis describes the specific "rhetorical situation" that prevailed in democratic Athens and the specific development of practical oratory that prompted Plato's reaction and the creation of rhetoric.[75] Oratory, long "amateurish" and embedded in aristocratic education, became more competitive and was put under great pressure as demands for expert leadership and persuasive speech rapidly increased along with the crucial role of mass assemblies passing large numbers of diverse decisions and grappling with ever more complex issues. To some extent, similar challenges existed in all poleis where decisions were made in sizable deliberative assemblies or public law courts—hence the multitude of experts in oratory descending on Athens from many directions, and the interest in such expertise in many poleis, discussed in Wallace's chapter. But, Yunis says, "As the largest, busiest, and most innovative polis of the Greek world, Athens pursued rhetoric more intensely, with greater rewards, and at a higher level of proficiency than was done anywhere else. Sophists, both Athenian and non-Athenian, contributed to rhetorical pursuits in Athens, but Athenian democratic politics provided the impetus."[76]

Oratory was the vehicle that made or broke policies, careers, lives; it became permanently an essential tool for politics and leadership. This explains three important features: first, the enormous qualitative development of practical oratory, culminating in the great orators and leaders of the mid- and late fourth century who, naturally, were all Athenians; second, the pervasive influence of rhetoric on various literary genres, especially drama, historiography (explored in the case of Thucydides in the last section of Yunis' chapter), and philosophy—all genres advanced decisively, if not created, in Athens and by Athenians; and third, Sokrates' and Plato's strong reaction against the general application to politics and communal leadership of a powerful skill that lacked ethical foundations and theoretical penetration. The result was the creation, out of practical oratory and its literary adaptation, of rhetoric as an art and discipline. According to Yunis, Plato's "interest in rhetoric stems directly from his critique of democratic discourse and of sophistic influence on that discourse." Here, then, we find a massive acceleration of and innovation in cultural development under conditions that originated in a broad panhellenic stratum but changed rapidly because of uniquely Athenian circumstances.

From Quantitative to Qualitative Difference: The Fusion Effect

This observation prompts us to consider more generally the effects of such massive acceleration. The production of art and architecture in sixth-century Athens was already "prodigious," to use Shapiro's word. But in this Athens was not different from other poleis ruled by tyrants, especially Corinth and Samos. The advent of isonomic and later democratic structures and values, suppressing elite display, initially even had a retarding effect.[77] Nor was the often-discussed "artistic revolution" of the early fifth century a specifically Athenian, let alone democratic, phenomenon. Rather, this "revolution" should be seen as part of that comprehensive change of social values, thought, and mentality, emphasized in this volume by Morris and by Csapo and Miller, that was going on throughout the Hellenic world and beyond and affected all types of society. Of this pattern the changes happening in Athens were but one particular aspect.[78]

In some—though certainly not all—respects, however, after the Persian Wars and especially after the mid-fifth century, Athens' situation and experiences diverged rapidly from those of the rest of Greece. The sheer quantity of monuments eventually adorning the city must have been overwhelming and certainly had no parallel elsewhere in Greece. More than that: it was work of the highest quality, produced by the premier artists, Athenian and non-Athenian, who, while working on the same or parallel projects, must have stimulated and driven each other to new heights of imagination and accomplishment. In its concentration and cumulative effect and the uses made of it, the art produced in Athens marked a massive advance beyond what had been usual before and was usual elsewhere.

We cite but a few examples. Large-scale mural paintings in a technique perfected only in the late sixth century, probably in the Peloponnese, were deployed in several shrines and public buildings of Kimonian Athens; the concentration of such paintings probably was unique, the effect most impressive: the "role of these paintings in shaping popular perceptions of Athens, her history, and her place in the world can hardly be overstated."[79] From about 500, many Greek states with different constitutions set up political monuments in their agoras and shrines and in panhellenic sanctuaries, especially Delphi. "Athens, however, soon became the protagonist in this process. The collective identity of her citizens was concentrated first and most resolutely in the political sphere." In the aftermath of the Persian Wars, the Hellenic alliance set up victory dedications in the panhellenic sanctuaries, and many participating communities celebrated their accomplishment there and at home with special monuments, later doing the same for victories in inner-Greek wars. "Again, Athens soon became the protagonist in these practices."[80]

In certain respects, we find, thanks to its administrative, political, and commercial importance, Athens came to resemble a panhellenic center itself. Well-chosen monuments could help the city show itself favorably to its large audience of visitors, and unlike at Delphi or Olympia, there would be no rivals to erect competing memorials. We have already mentioned how artists used paradigmatic myth and history to demonstrate Athens' superiority and her unique achievement in preserving Hellenism from barbaric onslaught.[81] Accordingly, the Akropolis, the Agora, and the state cemetery of the Kerameikos developed into what Hölscher describes as "a panorama of glorious military achievements," a systematically created "ideological topography" of the community's political identity. "Monumental works of art were used everywhere in Greece to adorn public areas and buildings, but the Athenians adopted art in uniquely systematic and ambitious ways to define the specific character of public spaces. As a result, by monumentalizing and perpetuating with works of art the glory of her great citizens and their famous achievements, Athens gradually developed into a monument of her own historical identity."[82]

We have paid so much attention to monumental arts because they help us grasp the nature of the specific "Athenian connection" in the complex interplay between democracy, empire, and the arts. What made this connection so powerful was a unique combination of several factors, each potent in its own right: an exceptional concentration of financial resources on both the private and public levels, an exceptional range and intensity of needs prompted by both the democracy and the empire—needs caused by different challenges and thus affecting each discipline in different ways, and needs located more deeply in Athenian society as a whole (below, at nn.91ff.)—and an exceptional concentration of talent. Specialists in many disciplines, able and willing to meet those needs, responded to the new challenges and, in competition with one another, raised the level of their art to new heights, reaching into new dimensions, and thus achieving a qualitative transformation of their discipline. Except perhaps for drama and vase painting (which evolved in very particular ways in Athens from the sixth century on, although they originated in a much broader context as well), this development was rooted in a widespread panhellenic culture. At the end, due to the cumulative effect of these factors, interacting with one another and depending on a uniquely Athenian constellation, the arts had been transformed, in almost every discipline and as a whole, into something qualitatively different. Of course, Athens was not thereby propelled out of its Hellenic context, and intercommunication and cross-fertilization with other centers continued throughout, but, overall, at the end of the century something decisive had happened with the arts that did and could only happen in, and because of, this large imperial and democratic polis.[83]

Critical Reactions to Democracy and Empire: The Arts of Prose

Monumental and performance arts, then, developed hand in hand with Athens' ideology and public life. Other kinds of discourse, however, developed in part as more individualistic and critical responses to the democracy and empire. Wallace argues, for example, that although the sophists contributed positively to

Athenian public life earlier in the fifth century, after about 430 they tended to remove themselves and grew highly critical of the democracy, eventually even contributing to its destruction.[84] Other critical genres, for which we have more direct evidence, include especially the newer and more "private" arts conducted in literary prose: philosophy and historiography.

Philosophers, in the sense defined in this volume by Christopher Rowe, were those who were "engaged systematically in the disinterested search for knowledge"; this definition excludes the sophists but includes the Presocratics.[85] The latter again were a panhellenic phenomenon, though concentrated especially in Ionia and Magna Graecia; none was born in Athens. Anaxagoras of Klazomenai, known not least for his connection with Perikles, was the first to settle there. By and large, they were interested more in *physis* and *kosmos* (nature and the world as a whole) than in human society and its problems. The focus on ethics, politics, and the good of the community, characteristic of Sokrates' and Plato's philosophy, is due less to presocratic philosophical than to sophistic theoretical thinking and the practical experiences of life in an intensely democratic polis. "If the subject is the influence of democracy on the development of philosophy," says Rowe, "then Plato must be the main character in the story, not only because of his pivotal position in the emergence of philosophy as a distinct activity in itself, but also because of the importance of political thinking in his writing."[86] Rowe, interested in how "democracy and democratic values may themselves be seen as a major factor in the development of Sokratic-Platonic philosophy as a whole," argues that "so far from representing the polar opposite of the democratic ideal, as for example the *Republic* might lead us . . . to suppose, Platonic political thinking is not only based on a continuing reflection on the nature and problems of democracy and of mass-rule, but ultimately shares . . . some of the fundamental premises on which it claimed to be built." Plato's best city, as we grasp it in the *Laws* and *Politicus,* is one "in which the citizens rule, and are ruled by, each other, according to a rational system of law and on the basis of a set of common beliefs." This is a form of "democracy" that, despite major differences, corresponds with essential elements of "the Athenians' own *idealized* constructions of the system under which they lived." The main problem for Plato—as for Aristotle—was to organize self-rule "without permitting the excesses of rule by, and for, the demos, i.e., *dēmokratia* as a form of partisan rule."[87]

Rowe concludes that, "while the standard description of Plato, and of Aristotle, as fundamentally antidemocratic is in some important respects true, their relationship with democracy was a highly complex one, which cannot be reduced . . . to one of simple opposition."[88] To the extent, then, that thinking about and consequently constructing a community based on justice and the common good was central to the philosophy of Sokrates and Plato, the experience of Athenian democracy was an indispensable condition in the development of philosophy. Again, a broadly based phenomenon, initially even without specific connections to Athens, was raised to a new level of complexity, achievement, and influence under the impact of circumstances that prevailed uniquely at Athens.

Fifth-century historiography is another literary genre that was stimulated by but critical of democracy and empire. Deborah Boedeker's chapter emphasizes that this genre developed outside of Athens. Moreover, in spite of Athens' frequent foregrounding of its great deeds in both the distant past and the more recent Persian Wars, it is significant—and far from coincidental—that, unlike monumental sculpture and painting, funeral orations, tragedy, and other genres that used the past as their subject matter, Thucydides' history was not publicly sponsored. "Thucydides freely criticizes popular, heroized versions of the recent past . . . Democratic Athens worked hard to shape a useful past, deliberately making little distinction in its monumental arts between mythical stories and events such as the fall of the tyranny or the victories at Marathon and Salamis. It was critics and outsiders who first attempted to write a continuous, plausible historical narrative; Herodotus and Thucydides connected Athens' present more causally, and sometimes more ironically, to its past."[89]

The non-Athenian Herodotus and the Athenian strategos-turned-exile Thucydides in their different ways produced narratives that were almost the antithesis of the "timeless" Athenian myth-historical monuments, which used great moments from the heroic past as analogues to present events and conditions. Both these historians took it upon themselves to treat the past authorially, which included critically judging the very traditions that were their sources. Like philosophy, historiography was stimulated by the experience and observation of democracy, but developed a critical (not exclusively negative) attitude toward it. "In Athens, the critical writing of history, like the rhetoric of dissent in other areas, developed when the democracy, no longer enjoying its old success, came under attack from within and without. Herodotus and Thucydides alike used this genre to judge and criticize, and to privilege change, not continuity."[90]

Cui Bono: Why the Arts in a Democracy?

This brings us back to a central question. On the surface, at least, the role of the empire in the process we are analyzing seems clear enough: it provided both ideological motives and financial means for encouraging public arts. But why democracy? Why did a major upswing in certain artistic and intellectual developments take place precisely in a democratic polis? If it is true that important developments happen because there is both an opportunity and a need for them to happen, what was the need? Why did democracy, or rather, why did the democratic citizens collectively need these arts? Is there a connection between developments in the arts and the fact that democracy was a new, even "revolutionary" system—at least insofar as in Athens all adult male citizens shared political power and responsibility to an extent that far surpassed anything ever experienced before?

Earlier in this chapter we sketched two important aspects of the relationship between democracy and the arts in the public arena. First, in patronizing the arts the demos collectively assumed a role that was played previously and continued to be played elsewhere by individuals (aristocrats and tyrants), and through the display of wealth in decorated buildings and monuments, the demos collectively demonstrated its power, within both the polis itself and the empire, to citizens, subjects, and the world at large. Second, many of the buildings and monuments showing off the community's wealth and advertising its great accomplishments in war had a religious purpose. So too, of course, did the festivals with their processions, contests, and poetic performances sponsored by the community and by individuals for the community. That Athens boasted more festival days and had a richer and more diverse religious life and topography than any other Greek polis seems to us symptomatic.

A third factor emerges in Tonio Hölscher's conclusion that in all these artistic manifestations "a psychological factor must have been at work." He suggests that they were the result of the "adventure" on which Athenian society had embarked in the fifth century, creating a political order without precedent and an empire of unique extension in the Greek world. Theirs "was a balancing act without net that must have created an ambivalent state of collective psychology, between euphoric self-assertion and profound self-doubt, in which all themes of social import were discussed, represented, celebrated, and questioned without end. In this psychological sense, the background to Athenian art of the fifth century was not so much democracy or empire as such but the intense and risky character of Athenian politics in this age of unprecedented opportunity, accomplishment, and challenge."[91]

Hölscher reaches his conclusion by analyzing monuments, buildings, and images. Christian Meier has argued for a similar view, trying to explain the political role of tragedy.[92] More recently, Meier broadened the scope of his inquiry, suggesting that the "Athenian democracy needed the art that was produced in it and for it." The swift rise of Athens to world power and the concomitant profound and rapid transformation of all aspects of Athenian society provoked in the citizens pride and self-confidence as well as uncertainty, anxiety, and tensions. Traditional values and structures were no longer valid; new ones were not easily found. In this situation an urgent need for orientation was met especially by the ability of tragic theater to dramatize the essential concerns confronting the citizen body. The same may be true for other forms of art as well. "I propose that it was precisely the extraordinary possibilities, problems and dangers, necessarily connected with imperial rule, democracy and Athens' transformation, that most intensely fertilized and propelled as well the culture of this city and of all of Greece . . . Where politics is so central, where the various spheres and subspheres of life are hardly separated from each other . . . political developments that disturb and deeply change everything cannot be worked through—except in the various spheres of culture." According to Meier, such culture includes drama, other performances and rituals at festivals, buildings, sculpture, historiography, sophistic thinking, rhetoric, science, and medicine.[93]

While agreeing with much in Meier's argument, we would differentiate more than he does: rather than a need for "culture" as such, we see a need for *specific* disciplines in specific contexts. First, not all the arts mentioned by Meier (particularly science and medicine) are equally well represented in fifth-century Athens, the period of our concern here. Second, different cultural forms responded to different needs: for example, some were important for representing or justifying the Athenians' claim to superiority over other Greeks, others for exploring certain problems faced by the city, still others for gaining the gods' support.

The suggestions of Hölscher and Meier are valuable in part for indicating a direction to explore further. Those who work on and think about fifth-century Athens usually are not sufficiently aware of the fundamental transformation the Athenian community experienced in the fifth century. To elucidate this aspect, Kurt Raaflaub in his contribution to this volume sketches, to the extent permitted by the poor condition of sources, the changes that happened in Athens, especially between the Persian and Peloponnesian Wars, in the political, military, economic, social, and religious spheres. These changes, triggered largely by the rise of imperial power and the influx of imperial revenue, were rapid and pervasive, and they interacted with one another; they affected all sectors of society and all aspects of private and communal life, and they confronted most Athenians with new and hitherto unfamiliar conditions and challenges. They "helped bring about democracy in its specific Athenian form, pay for military and political service, greatly increased circulation of money, population growth, urbanization, massive increases in jobs, manufacture, building, and market transactions, and new economic opportunities, challenges and attitudes. For the first time a large proportion of the population lived in truly urban conditions and the nonagrarian sector (trade, manufacture, services) assumed an essential role in a Greek community's economy."[94]

That in such circumstances there was, as Meier says, a deep need for orientation and support is entirely plausible. Such need is visible particularly in tragedy—explored frequently with good results by Meier himself and others, as discussed in Saïd's chapter. It may be reflected in other categories of the arts as well but there it is much more difficult to identify as a moving force; alternative, more specific explanations may be readily at hand. Caution seems advisable especially since in two areas where we should expect such needs to have left a clear imprint on the evidence, such traces are, in fact, rather elusive.

One of these areas is classical art. Having sketched the political, military, and psychological upheaval of the Peloponnesian War period, and the shattering of Athenian self-confidence as a result of crisis, infighting, and defeat, Pollitt asks, "What kind of art would one expect to see produced during such an era? By analogy with other troubled periods, the late Roman Empire, for example, or Italy after the sack of Rome in 1527, one might naturally predict that there would be at least some traces of an agonized, tortured, insecure art, expressing the anxieties of the age. But the late fifth century confounds one's expectations. What actually appeared was a style which increasingly stressed grace, softness, the elegant flourish, the mastery of manner."[95]

The other area where we might expect reflections of anxiety and a need for support naturally is religion. Two aspects stand out among religious developments in fifth-century Athens: the introduction of many new cults and a general intensification of public religious life, including an increasing number of more elaborate and splendid festivals, more and grander construction for religious purposes, and broader participation in religious affairs on the part of citizens and noncitizens alike.[96] All these changes can be explained largely and perhaps sufficiently by the wealth and success of a community that reached the pinnacle of power, and by the agonies and changing fortunes of a long and ultimately disastrous war. In other words, every single religious change may have been caused by a specific political, social, or military experience for which the community felt a need to thank the gods and/or secure their continuing or increased support. The search for a general "religious crisis" toward the end of the fifth century has not yielded compelling results.[97] Things might look different if we were able to scrutinize private religion and individual religious habits to any helpful degree. As things stand, however, the factors emphasized by Meier and Hölscher should perhaps not be considered more than plausible added stimuli that helped intensify ongoing processes.

Conclusion

In sum, we suggest, triumph alternating with uncertainty, boosted by unprecedented wealth and power, compelled the highly politicized Athenian citizens collectively to boast of their achievements and to implore the gods to support their city on its ride through uncharted waters. Hence the importation of new cults and the increasing number and splendor of their festivals, the high priority accorded to poetic performances embedded in these festivals, the self-conscious probing of political and social issues in the theater, the increasing variety of splendidly decorated monuments and sanctuaries. Hence too the demos' willingness to exploit for the advancement of these very purposes the opportunities offered by the unprecedented influx of resources into the community and to spend some of their wealth on elaborate sanctuaries and festivals, commissioning an unparalleled series of great projects and paying famous artists for executing them in spectacular ways, as well as bestowing high honors and rewards to the victors in their poetic competitions.

By contrast, the intensification of political life in democracy greatly stimulated as well the development of non-publicly sponsored arts and intellectual life in general, rapidly propelling, for example, advances in rhetoric and political theory. Some of the negative aspects of democratic politics—foremost among these precisely the impact of rhetoric and demagoguery or the intimate connection between democracy and imperialism—were reflected upon critically by contemporary thinkers and helped provoke the emergence of critical disciplines, such as an art and theory of rhetoric, political philosophy, and narrative historiography.

If on the one hand a strong case can be made for close connections among democracy, empire, and the development of the arts in fifth-century Athens, on the other hand the picture resulting from our shared investigations appears much more complex and differentiated than it was often seen in the past. In fact, it does not seem possible to find a single, let alone a simple, answer that covers all aspects and disciplines involved. Overall, under the specific conditions prevailing in this city many categories of the arts developed rapidly and far beyond what occurred elsewhere—in scope, intensity, sheer quantity, intellectual acumen and refinement, and the uses made of such art. Yet this did not happen at the same time in all disciplines—the rise of tragedy began early, that of history, philosophy, and rhetoric late in the century. Nor did it happen in the same way and involve the same constituencies. Improvements in the skills and techniques of oratory, although necessitated by the conditions of democratic politics and depending for their success entirely on the demos' reactions, were important primarily for the elite leaders (and were paid for by those individuals, not the whole polis). The literary application of rhetorical patterns and the invention of a theory of rhetoric concerned elite authors and thinkers. The critical discussions reflected in philosophy, political theory, and history, although in essential ways prompted by experiences connected with the principles and discourse of democracy and empire, likewise remained private rather than public and the domain of intellectuals, affecting mostly the Athenian elite and watched by the demos with a mixture of reactions, ranging from admiration to amusement, apprehension, and, for special reasons in a few cases (such as that of Damon), hostility.[98] A direct connection with mass democracy seems more obvious in the cases of the visual arts, buildings, and monuments on the one hand, and tragedy, comedy, and the festival culture on the other, which were all patronized by the demos. Moreover, some disciplines were more specifically Athenian than others: most tragedians were Athenians, most sophists were not. Undeniably, many non-Athenians contributed decisively to the development of the arts in Athens; conversely, many of those who worked in Athens, whether Athenian or not, also practiced their art in other places and left magnificent examples of their achievements elsewhere—we think of the sophists, Athenian tragedians who were invited to perform their plays at the courts of kings and tyrants, Polygnotos' paintings at the Lesche of the Knidians in Delphi, Pheidias' cult statue of Zeus in Olympia, or the assemblage of leading sculptors who created the famous group of Amazons in Ephesos.[99]

All this was not simply the consequence of a unique concentration of material resources—although money was an indispensable contributing factor—and thus not merely one of the benefits of empire. As many essays in this volume suggest, it was as much or more a consequence of specific conditions and policies created by the democracy. The crucial "difference" of Athens lies not in various individual achievements or in the artistic advancement of any one discipline. It lies rather in the comprehensive and rapid development of various disciplines, in the interaction among a multitude of great artists and intellectuals, and, as a result, in a broad qualitative change and advance into new dimensions of artistic and intellectual endeavor.[100] Once underway, these processes converged, developed their own dynamics, and affected one another, resulting in the great variety, astonishing density, and remarkable quality of accomplishments that set standards for and influenced further developments in all the disciplines involved for future centuries and very different political circumstances.

ENDNOTES

Chapter 1 Notes

1. For helpful comments we thank the other contributors, especially Eric Csapo and Margaret Miller, Christopher Rowe, Suzanne Saïd, and Harvey Yunis. We add here our most sincere thanks to Paul Cartledge for detailed comments on the entire volume, and to an anonymous reader for valuable observations. All dates are B.C.E.
2. At least to a considerable extent. In other respects, the Athenian system was much more democratic than any of its modern counterparts. For discussion, see, e.g., Hansen 1989; Dunn 1992.239–66; 1996; Bleicken 1994.423–34; several contributions in Ober & Hedrick 1996; Strauss 1997. On the development of democracy, Raaflaub, this vol., with bibliog.
3. For discussion, see Finley 1978; 1982.41–42; Schuller 1974.2–7, 197–99; Raaflaub 1996a.274–76, with bibliog.
4. Unity of democracy: Bleicken 1987; for discussion, see Rhodes 1980; Ostwald 1986; Sealey 1987; Ober 1989.95–103; Hansen 1991, chap. 13; Bleicken 1994, chap. 12; Eder 1995a, 1997. For the period of transition: Strauss 1986; Munn 1999. Recent discussions of fourth-century Athens: Eder 1995b; Schwenk 1997. See also this vol., chap. 15, text at nn. 64–66.
5. E.g., Pseudo-Xenophon, *Constitution of the Athenians* 1.2; Plato, *Laws* 706c–707a, emphasizing the connection between naval power, involvement of the masses of lower-class citizens, and democracy. On the causal level, establishing that democracy was made possible or necessary by the empire, the connection was made later, probably by Aristotle (*Const. of the Athenians* 22.3, 24, 27.1; *Politics* 1304a21–22; see Ceccarelli 1993; Raaflaub 1994. Fourth-century focus on culture: see below, at n.18.
6. Immerwahr 1960.
7. Hornblower 1987.30–33. Most critics take Her. 1.59.6 (*kosmeōn*) as referring to administration, not buildings; but see Thuc. 6.54.5, which seems to echo Herodotus.
8. Hornblower 1991.35, cf. 33–34.
9. Festivals: see, e.g., Pseudo-Xenophon, *Constitution of the Athenians* 2.9, 3.2, 3.8; Aristophanes, *Clouds* 298–313; Isokrates 4.43; Mikalson 1975. For private pleasures, see Rusten 1989 on Thuc. 2.38.1. This contrasts sharply with the Corinthians' criticism of 1.70.8.
10. See Aristophanes, *Frogs* 408–9; Henderson 1987a.xxxi–xxxii.
11. See Gomme, Dover, & Andrewes 1945–81.1:120–21. For Sparta: Rhodes 1988 ad loc.
12. Gomme, Dover, & Andrewes 1945–81.1:119–20.

13. Rusten 1989.153, accepted by Hornblower 1991.304. We confess to feeling uncomfortable with this interpretation. So does Lisa Kallet, who in a lecture on "Demos Tyrannos and Economic Patronage" (March 28, 1998, at UCLA, to be published in *Popular Tyranny*, ed. Kathryn Morgan) suggests "that we might read this passage (and in a sense the Funeral Oration as a whole) as contesting the notion of the demos as tyrant through its tyrant-scale expenditure. The odd combination in the phrase, which rather paradoxically takes the line that the Athenians' magnificence is moderate, makes sense if the point is implicitly to contest a current conception about excessive magnificence. It reads nicely as well as an implicit response to the criticism lodged in Plut. *Perikles* 12." On this interpretation, an implicit allusion to the buildings on the Akropolis appears more likely.
14. Kakridis 1961.48. For *sophia* see, e.g., Herodotus 1.60.3; Euripides, *Medea* 828–29; Plato, *Apology* 29d. Again, what is remarkable is precisely the *omission* of any substantive allusion to cultural achievements especially in choral odes that praise Athens, such as *Medea* 824–68 or Sophokles, *Oedipus at Colonus* 668–719.
15. That they are undying, everlasting (*aïdia*) recalls the "undying glory" (*kleos aphthiton* or *athanaton*) promised by a Homer or Simonides (on which see Boedeker 1998.234) in the kind of poetic memorial that Perikles explicitly rejects here.
16. Most conspicuously in a passage where Thucydides echoes and opposes Herodotus: "I have dwelt upon the greatness of Athens" because of the *aretē* of these men and because, unlike in many other cases, their deeds (*erga*) are equal to their fame (42.1–2; see Hornblower 1991 ad loc. and Macleod 1983.151–52, whence the tr. of 43.3). It is the deeds of men, not monuments, that justify extensive historical coverage. Castriota 1997.200 suggests that 2.43.1 ("You must yourselves realize the power of Athens, and feed your eyes upon her from day to day, till love of her fills your hearts," tr. Crawley, rev. Strassler) alludes to the monuments.
17. See Gomme, Dover, & Andrewes 1945–81.1:1–28, esp. 25–26. For another important area largely ignored by Thucydides, see this vol., ch. 2, n.172. At the very least, Thucydides has interpreted his task (to discuss the *tropoi* supporting power) narrowly, again consciously ignoring *opsis* (above, at n.8). Interestingly, the tyrants are praised for having "adorned the city beautifully" (6.54.6).
18. On Athens' contribution to the provision of food for the Hellenes, see 4.28–33 and Buchner 1958.47. The idea occurs as well in Plato, *Menexenos* 238b, also a pseudo–Funeral Oration, but not in Lysias' version (*Or.* 2). Isokrates' mention of *hēdonē* seems unique.
19. Buchner 1958.52–53.
20. See Buchner 1958.53–65; Eucken 1983, esp. chap. 4 (on Isokrates' philosophy); Too 1995 (on rhetoric). On Thuc. 2.41.1: Hornblower 1991 ad loc. On the reality of such claims: Harding 1986.
21. Isokrates 7 (*Areopagitikos*). 66; cf. 15 (*Antidosis*). 234 (Perikles). Cf., on the demolition of the dockyards, Lysias 12.99.

22. Meier 1996.205.
23. Plutarch, *Perikles* 12–14; cf. the comments by Ameling 1985; Stadter 1989 ad loc. (ibid. 144 on Plutarch's perspective); Kallet, this vol., text at nn.51–52.
24. Above n.5.
25. Esp. 1009–10, 1030ff., 1054ff., 1419ff.,1482ff., 1500ff.
26. Meier 1993b; specifically on democracy: Raaflaub 1989; on the empire: Rosenbloom 1995; Mills 1997.
27. Homer: Kennedy 1963.35–39; sophists: Wallace, this vol.; Gorgias: Plato, *Gorgias* 452d–e, 456a–c.
28. See esp. Yunis 1996; Halliwell 1997; Buxton 1982.
29. Miller 1929–32.1:42 (whence the tr.). *Pankalos* is an emendation, thus not entirely certain; but it is perhaps no less significant that the *neōrion* is mentioned before the Parthenon, and that the Piraeus appears just as beautiful as the latter.
30. Sallust, *Catiline* 1–3; *Jugurthine War* 2–4; Cicero, *Pro Murena* 9.22–13.29.
31. Buitron-Oliver 1992; see especially the statements by Greek Prime Minister Constantin Mitsotakis, U.S. President George Bush, the foreword by the directors of the museums involved, and the introduction by Nicholas Gage. For a critical comment, see, e.g., Wills 1992.
32. Rhetoric and "sophistic movement": see the beginning of Wallace's chapter in this volume; for discussion, see Kennedy 1963.28–35; Bleicken 1994.389–91; Yunis 1996, chap. 1. Political theory: Farrar 1988. Historiography: Meier 1973, 1987b; cf. Ostwald 1992.329–30.
33. Webster 1973.259.
34. Ibid. 259–60, 265. The other part of responsibility lies with the rich cultural tradition of Archaic Greece on the foundation of which the Athenian achievement was built (ibid. 265–73).
35. E.g., Francis 1990; Castriota 1992.
36. Pollitt 1972, chap. 3 (cit. 63–64, 98); for criticism, see Hallett 1986.73–75. See also Borbein 1989; 1995, esp. 435–37.
37. On the Third Greece see Gehrke 1986; on *ethnos* and ethnicity, Morgan 1991; Hall 1995, 1997; McInerney forthcoming.
38. Equality: Morris 1996; Raaflaub 1996b. Democracy outside Athens: O'Neil 1995; Robinson 1997. For shared ideas in "democratic" Aeschylus and "aristocratic" Pindar, see Kurke 1997.
39. Hoepfner & Schwandner 1994 (doubts were expressed by C. Meier already in the preface of the first edition in 1986, ixff.); for discussion: Schuller, Hoepfner, & Schwandner 1989. Hoepfner & Schwandner now suggest "dass eine Förderung der Schicksalsgemeinschaft Polis durch eine weitgehende Gleichheit der Lebensumstände angestrebt wurde" (1994.xi).
40. See M. Sakellariou's "Discours d'ouverture," in Sakellariou 1996. 9–12, at p. 9.
41. Ibid. 9–11.

42. We thank Professor Sakellariou for his generosity in making a copy available to us soon after the volume's publication.
43. See above, text at n.4.

Chapter 2 Notes

1. No modern comprehensive and well-documented study currently exists on this topic. Welwei 1992 and Starr 1977, 1986 end around 500; Fornara & Samons 1991, Meier 1993a focus on political developments. On economy and society, French 1964, though partly outdated and often speculative, remains useful; Frost 1976; Humphreys 1978, chap. 6; Davies 1992a; 1992b; and 1993, chap. 6 all offer stimulating but brief sketches. Pritchard 1994 should be used with caution. I claim no originality but merely intend to provide background information that will illuminate a series of aspects essential to this volume's enterprise. I thank D. Boedeker, W. Eder, L. Kallet, M. Ostwald, R. Simms, R. Stroud, and S. Todd for valuable suggestions.
2. Herodotus 1.56; Asheri 1988.297; Raaflaub 1988.213, with n.73.
3. Snodgrass 1982a; Andrewes 1982; Welwei 1992.
4. Andrewes 1982.372–75; Frost 1984; Figueira 1991.132–42; 1993, chaps. 2–3; Welwei 1992.146–50, 206–14. On the First Sacred War, Tausend 1992.34–47, 161–66. On misinterpretations of Solon's "Salamis-Elegy," Lefkowitz 1981.40; Raaflaub 1996b.1037–38.
5. Bibliog. in Raaflaub 1990.523–24.
6. Siewert 1982.
7. Meier 1990b.80–81; Fornara & Samons 1991.103.
8. Amit 1965; Haas 1985; Gabrielsen 1985; 1994.19–26; Wallinga 1993. Among others, Jordan 1975.5–16, Ostwald 1995b, and Thomas Martin (in an unpublished lecture) argue for a substantial fleet in sixth-century Athens.
9. Uniqueness: Raaflaub 1990.519–31; 1994.116–18. Empire: Meiggs 1972; Schuller 1974; Steinbrecher 1985; Fornara & Samons 1991, chap. 3; Rhodes 1992b. On the term "empire," Finley 1978; 1982.41–42; Schuller 1974.2–7, 197–99.
10. Space restrictions force me, here and elsewhere, to focus on the main points, often ignoring finer distinctions and changes over time.
11. Hanson 1995.369–75; forthcoming; Strauss 1996. Coastal support network: Gabrielsen 1994.6.
12. Plutarch, *Perikles* 11.4, with Meiggs 1972.427; Stadter 1989.137; Schmitz 1988.29–33.
13. Garlan 1975.15.
14. Ducrey 1968; Karavites 1982; Rosivach 1998.
15. Ridley 1979; Hanson 1995, chap. 8; 1996.
16. Thuc. 1.143.5, 2.62.2–3; Pseudo-Xenophon, *Constitution of the Athenians* 2.14–16; Frisch 1942.63–87; Starr 1979b; Ober forthcoming; but see Ober 1985b; Spence 1990. On the (limited) economic impact, Foxhall 1993, with bibliog.
17. Pay: Thuc. 3.17.3, 6.8.1; Schmitz 1988.25–33; Gabrielsen 1994.110–14. Trireme:

Böckh 1840.196–210; Gabrielsen 1994.139–42. Samos: Thuc. 1.117.3; *IG* I^3 363; cf. Thuc. 2.70 on the siege of Poteidaia. Parthenon: Thuc. 2.13.3, with Hornblower 1991 ad loc.; Kallet, this vol..

18. Amit 1965.26–27, 30–49; Jordan 1975.101–3, 153–270; Rosivach 1985; Gabrielsen 1994.105–10. Metics: Whitehead 1977.84–86. Slaves: Welwei 1974.65–104.
19. Thuc. 2.13.3–5 with Kallet-Marx 1993a.96–107 and Gomme, Dover, & Andrewes 1945–81.2:16–33; Aristophanes, *Wasps* 656ff.; Xenophon, *Anabasis* 7.1.27; see Schmitz 1988.17–37; Gabrielsen 1994.114–18; Kallet, this vol.. Trierarchy: Jordan 1975.61–94; Gabrielsen 1994, pts. 1–2. Taxes: Thomsen 1964.
20. Ruschenbusch 1979.153–56; Strauss 1986.179–82; Hansen 1988.14–28.
21. Cartledge 1979, chaps. 11–12; Powell 1988, chap. 4; Hodkinson 1993; Thommen 1996. *Agōgē:* Kennell 1995.
22. Thuc. 2.43.1; Raaflaub 1994.112, 129–30. Ideology: Hall 1993a; Raaflaub 1998. Lovers: Monoson 1994a.
23. Finley 1982.46.
24. Officials: Meiggs 1972.205–19; Schuller 1974.32–48, 156–64. Arist. *Const. of the Athenians* 24.3: seven hundred, perhaps too high: Balcer 1976, but see Meiggs 1972.215. Land allocations: n.65.
25. See n.33.
26. E.g., Euben, Wallach, & Ober 1994; Ober & Hedrick 1996; Morris & Raaflaub 1997.
27. Polis: Morris 1996; Raaflaub 1996b, 1997b; Sallares 1991.406.
28. Solon: Wallace 1997; Raaflaub 1996c. Tyranny: Stahl 1987; Eder 1988, 1992. Kleisthenes: Meier 1990b, chap. 4; Ober 1993a, 1997; Raaflaub 1995, 1997a; Loraux 1996. See generally Meier 1978; Lotze 1983.
29. Morris 1996, this vol. See also O'Neil 1995; Cartledge 1996; Robinson 1997.
30. Jochen Martin 1974; Fornara & Samons 1991, chap. 2; Rhodes 1992a; Raaflaub 1995, 1997a, 1997b; and see now Lotze 1997.
31. So too Hanson 1995.411.
32. So too Bleicken 1994.52, while1995 focuses too narrowly on the Persian Wars.
33. Ruschenbusch 1978.67–95; 1979.15–17; Schuller 1984.88–90.
34. Reserves: above n.19. Buildings: Plut. *Perikles* 12, with Stadter 1989. Ruschenbusch 1979.157–65; Kallet, this vol..
35. Finley 1982.48–51, 58 (cit.); 1973.172–74. See Arist. *Const. of the Athenians* 27.3–4, with Rhodes 1981 ad loc.; Schmitz 1988.57–70; Fornara & Samons 1991.67–74; Rhodes 1992a.75–76; Podes 1992, 1994; Markle 1985; Todd 1990.
36. Arist. *Const. of the Athenians* 25–27, with the comments by Rhodes 1981; Chambers 1990. Further, e.g., Ostwald 1986.28–83; Meier 1987a; Jones 1987; Fornara & Samons 1991.58–75; Rhodes 1992a.67–77; Bleicken 1994.44–46; Raaflaub 1995.36–46, with bibliog.; 1997a, 1997c.
37. On the latter, Eder 1995a, 1997.
38. Rhodes 1981 and Chambers 1990 on Arist. *Const. of the Athenians* 24.3; Hansen 1980; Schmitz 1988.16–57. Seven hundred offices, see n.24 above.

39. In the fourth century forty assembly meetings were scheduled each year; the fifth-century number is unknown. Generally, though, much of what Hansen 1987 describes must apply to the fifth century as well.
40. Sparta's regulated society of professional citizens is a special case. Athens: Thuc. 2.40.2; Jones 1957.99–133; Sinclair 1988; Hansen 1985.51–64; cf. id. 1988.25: to run all the institutions according to the rules "requires a minimum of ca. 25,000 citizens." Critics who look only at attendance in the assembly thus miss an entire dimension. Given the fact—common until very recently—that active citizenship and participation in politics was limited to men, only male citizens are considered here. Women: below at n.130.
41. Meier 1990b.140–54. Metics: below at n.103. For a contrasting view, especially concerning citizens living far from Athens, see Jones forthcoming.
42. Thuc. 6.89.6 (cit.); Raaflaub 1985.233–48. Freedom: Raaflaub 1985, chap. 6; Hansen 1989, 1996a; Equality: Raaflaub 1996b; Cartledge 1996; Roberts 1996. Freedom of speech: Raaflaub 1980; cf. Wallace 1994a, 1994b, 1996; Henderson, this vol.
43. See Thuc. 1.70; Raaflaub 1994 (107–8 on *polypragmosynē*); cf. Meier 1990b, chap. 8.
44. E.g., *Antigone,* with Meier 1993b.187–203; *Lysistrata,* with Henderson 1980. Generally, Meier 1993b, chap. 2; 1996; Griffith 1995; Goff 1995; Easterling 1997; Pelling 1997; Saïd, this vol.
45. Donlan 1980, chaps. 4–5; Stein-Hölkeskamp 1989.205–30; Ober 1989; Eder 1997.
46. Connor 1971. Dangers: Knox 1985. Enrichment: below n.65; Raaflaub 1994.133 with more bibliog. in n.69. Property sales: ML 79; Kallet, this vol., at n.13.
47. Thuc. 2.40.2 (on *apragmōn*); Carter 1986; Wolff 1979; Ostwald 1986, chaps. 7, 9.
48. Meiggs 1972.255; cf. Humphreys 1978.143.
49. On Athens, esp. French 1964; Humphreys 1978.136–58; Casson 1984; Kallet-Marx 1993a, this vol.; Davies 1993, chap. 6; see also Strauss 1986, chap. 2. On the Greek economy in the fifth century, Hasebroek 1928; Bolkestein 1958; Michell 1957; Hopper 1979; Davies 1992a, 1992b; Lawall 1995. On ancient economy: Finley 1973 (1985); Morris 1994a. On the early fourth century: Ober 1985a, chap. 1. See also Millett 1993.
50. Camp 1986.35–57; 1994; Boardman 1988.415–19; Shear 1994.
51. Demography: next section. Beginnings of economic change in the sixth century: Starr 1977, 1982. Fleet: above at n.8. Craftsmen: n.60. Trade through foreign middle men: Muhly 1992.13.
52. Her. 7.144.1; Arist. *Const. of the Athenians* 22.7. Number of ships: Wallinga 1993.148–57; Gabrielsen 1994.28–30.
53. Trierarchy and financing: n.19; on liturgies also Kallet, this vol.. Three hundred ships: Thuc. 2.13.8. New construction: Gabrielsen 1994.131–36.
54. Jordan 1975, pt. I. On the harbors and shipsheds: Garland 1987.72–100; Blackman 1968.
55. Garland 1987.68.

56. Pseudo-Xenophon, *Const. of the Athenians* 2.11–12; Morrison & Coates 1986, chap. 10; Meiggs 1982, chap. 5; Finley 1982.53–57.
57. E.g., Lysias' father Kephalos from Syracuse (Lys. 12.4). Manufacturers: e.g., Aristoph. *Peace* 447–48, 545–49, 1210–64; Lys. 12.19; cf. Ehrenberg 1951.123–24.
58. French 1964.157–60.
59. Wycherley 1992; Davies 1992b.298–99; 1993.99.
60. Boersma 1970, chaps. 5–6; Davies 1993.96. On the relatively small numbers of workers employed in trades on which we have information, see Cook 1959; Webster 1972, chap. 1 (pottery); Burford 1972.61–64, 78–80; Schmitz 1988.70–75 (temple construction).
61. Aristophanes: Ehrenberg 1951, chap. 13; Politicians: Connor 1971.151–58.
62. But see Bleicken 1994.162–63, 502–3; Kluwe 1976–77.
63. Meiggs 1972, chap. 14; Finley 1982, chap. 3; Schmitz 1988, pt. I.
64. See nn.24, 34, 35, 38.
65. Jones 1957.7, 167–77; Brunt 1966; Meiggs 1972.260–62; Gauthier 1973; Finley 1982.51–53; Schmitz 1988.79–115; Figueira 1991, chap. 2.
66. Hasebroek 1928; Finley 1982.53–57.
67. Humphreys 1978.137; cf. Schmitz 1988.116–25.
68. Schmitz 1988.19–97.
69. Sealey 1966; more cautious: Jackson 1969; Finley 1982.50; Kallet-Marx 1993a.52–53.
70. Finley 1982.58, cf. 51, referring to de Ste. Croix 1972.394–96.
71. Schmitz 1988.25–33, 38–44. For comparison, Jones 1957.80–81.
72. Finley 1982.59–60.
73. Ibid. 57. See now Meier 1990a.586–605; Raaflaub 1994.130–46.
74. Import, post–Persian War period: Garnsey 1985; 1988, chaps. 7–8; sixth century, at the latest: e.g., Starr 1977.156; on the difference in assumptions: Morris 1994a.361. Grain trade: Hopper 1979, chap. 3. Supervision: Arist. *Const. of the Athenians* 43.4 (with Xen. *Memorabilia* 3.6.13), 51.3–4; Kohns 1964; MacDowell 1978.156–58. The imports were probably balanced mostly by the export of silver: French 1964.113–14, 123; Finley 1973.132–34.
75. French 1964.117–19; Garland 1987.27, 83–95. Emporion: Vélissaropoulos 1977; Bresson & Rouillard 1993; esp. Bresson 1993.
76. Thuc. 2.38.2, tr. R. Warner; cf. Pseudo-Xen. *Const. of the Athenians* 2.7, 11–13; Aristoph. *Knights* 168–75; Hermippos, *Phormophoroi*, fr. 63 *PCG*. See Braund 1994; Miller 1997.
77. Wycherley 1978, chap. 3; 1957, chap. 4.
78. Merchants: French 1964.117, 126 (see n.57 above). Banking: Millett 1983, 1991; Cohen 1992.
79. Davies 1993.99; Garland 1987.58: certainly "above the 30,000 mark." The expansion of Piraeus prompted the appointment of a city planner, Hippodamos of Miletus (Boersma 1970.46–50; Hoepfner & Schwandner 1994.22–50).

80. Finley 1973.134.
81. Cit.: Pseudo-Xen. *Const. of the Athenians* 1.17, tr. Moore; see Frisch 1942.227. Trial in Athens: Schuller 1974.48–54. Prostitutes: Halperin 1990.3–4.
82. French 1964.123–24.
83. French 1964.128–34; Hanson 1995.375–79.
84. Morris 1994a.362–65 (cit. 364).
85. Schmitz 1988.8–16; Kallet (-Marx) 1993a and this vol. Archaic Corinth had progressed farthest in this direction: Salmon 1984, esp. chaps. 10–11.
86. Pseudo-Xen. *Const. of the Athenians* 1.10–12; Humphreys 1978.147–48.
87. Humphreys 1978.136–58 (cit. 137); Austin & Vidal-Naquet 1977.3–16; Nippel 1982; Morris 1994a; Meikle 1995; Lawall 1995. See at n.78.
88. Nippel 1982.23–24; Humphreys 1978.147: "This opportunity of state service . . . effectively blocked any possibility of a development of free wage labour in Athens just when expansion of the city population and economy was at its height." On free labor, see Garnsey 1980 (esp. Garlan 1980); Meier 1983/84; Descat 1986; Mrozek 1989.
89. But see Meiggs 1972.263, 267; Humphreys 1978.143. Pseudo-Xenophon, dated usually to the 420s but perhaps writing earlier, attests that by then many of the essential features were deeply entrenched; Perikles' war strategy presupposes the same.
90. Finley 1982.149. See generally ibid., chaps. 6–9; id. 1980, chaps. 1–2; Garlan 1988.39–40.
91. Finley 1982.128–31, 114–15; cf. Austin & Vidal-Naquet 1977.18–19; Raaflaub 1985.54–62, esp. 60.
92. De Ste. Croix 1981.141 (his emphasis).
93. Finley 1982, chap. 6, esp. 111–15 (cit. 111).
94. See Wood 1988, chaps. 2–3 and esp. Cartledge 1993, chap. 6; R. Osborne 1995.34–39; Strauss 1997.146–47 (rightly arguing against Patterson 1991, pt. 2), 150–51.
95. Hypereides, fr. 33 Sauppe = 29 Kenyon; Ktesikles, *FGrH* 245 F1, cited by Hansen 1988.11–12, who offers the higher estimate, Osborne 1987a.46 the lower. See also Gomme 1933.20–24; Gomme & Hopper 1970.862 (110,000 in 431); Sallares 1991.50–60.
96. Jameson 1977; de Ste. Croix 1981; Wood 1988, chap. 2; Garlan 1988.60–69; R. Osborne 1995.30–34.
97. Above, at n.61. See generally Davies 1981.
98. Wood 1988.173–80; R. Osborne 1995.28–30.
99. Jameson 1977, esp. 125, 140; R. Osborne 1995.35; *contra:* Wood 1988, chap. 2.
100. Connection: Pseudo-Xen. *Const. of the Athenians* 1.11–12; cf., conversely, Nikolaos of Damascus, *FGrH* 90 F58; Herakleides Lembos, *On Constitutions* 20 (Dilts 1971) on the tyrant Periander's prohibition of slave ownership by citizens; see Busolt 1893.646, with n.2. Unfree labor: e.g., Xen. *Memorabilia* 2.8; Raaflaub 1983.531–32. On disdain for paid labor, see Vernant 1965; Aymard 1967.316–33, and the bibliog. cited in n.88 above.

101. Pseudo-Xen. *Const. of the Athenians* 1.10–12; Dem. 9.3; Plato, *Republic* 563B.
102. Humphreys 1978.156.
103. Whitehead 1977, 1986b. It is hardly accidental that the issue is prominent in Aeschylus' *Suppliants* of 463 (e.g., 609, 963–64); see Bakewell 1997; cf. Sealey 1983: 116–20. Generally on foreigners: Baslez 1984; Vatin 1984; Whitehead 1984; Lonis 1988–92; Takabatake 1988; Cartledge 1993, chap. 5.
104. Plut. *Solon* 24.4; Arist. *Const. of the Athenians* 13.5, 21; *Politics* 1275b32–37. See Rhodes 1981.188, 249, 255–56; Manville 1990.173–209. Foreigners among potters: Boardman 1975.9–10.
105. Osborne 1987a.46; Garland 1987.58–61; Hansen 1988.10–11; Davies 1993.91–93. See also Whitehead 1977.148–51; Duncan-Jones 1980; Thür 1989.
106. Hoplites: esp. Thuc. 2.31.2, with Gomme 1933.5; Duncan-Jones 1980; Hansen 1988.25, n.13. Fleet: Thuc. 1.143.1.
107. Pseudo-Xen. *Const. of the Athenians* 1.12, with 1.10; Aristoph. *Acharnians* 507–8. More testimonia in Whitehead 1977.34–68. For discussion see also Hansen 1991.116–20; Strauss 1997.149–50. Religious life: Maurizio, this vol.
108. Schol. Aristoph. *Wasps* 718 = Philochoros, *FGrH* 328 F119; Plut. *Perikles* 37.4, with Stadter 1989.336–39. Citizenship law: below at n.144.
109. I omit discussion of the elite; see Arnheim 1977, chaps. 5–6; Donlan 1980, chaps. 4–5; Ober 1989; Stein-Hölkeskamp 1989.205–30.
110. Frost 1976.70–71; Davies 1992b.296–99. Agricultural changes as part of the explanation: Morris 1994a.364.
111. Above at n.74. Numbers of citizens: Beloch 1886, chap. 3; Gomme 1933; Ruschenbusch 1979.133–52; Patterson 1981.40–81; Hansen 1988.7–28; French 1993. See also Osborne 1985; Hansen 1985; Sallares 1991, chap. 2. Sallares 1996.1222 suggests "multiplication by four to account for women and children." Thirty thousand: Her. 5.97.2, a "conventional estimate" (How & Wells 1912.2:.57). At Marathon the Athenians fielded nine thousand hoplites, at Plataea eight thousand (Beloch 1886.60); given the proportion of thetes before the Persian Wars (below), these figures point to an overall number below thirty thousand.
112. E.g., Snodgrass 1980.107 (cit.); Starr 1982.423; Hanson 1995.411.
113. Frost 1976.72; Davies 1992b.291–302; Hanson 1995, chap. 9. Importance of village life in Attica: Thuc. 2.16; Osborne 1985, chap. 2 and *passim;* 1987a.128–32; Wood 1988.100–110. See also Jones forthcoming.
114. Thuc. 2.34; Stupperich 1977; Clairmont 1983; Loraux 1986.
115. Stupperich 1977.239–43; den Boer 1979.34–50; Pomeroy 1982; Weiler 1988. Hands 1968 is too general.
116. See also *IG* I^3 6, C 38–42, cf. *SEG* 10.6, 121–25; Arist. *Const. of the Athenians* 56.6–7; Xen. *Poroi* 2.7; Plato, *Menexenos* 248E; discussion: Stroud 1971.289–90.
117. Fifth century: Arist. *Politics* 1268a8–11; cf. Rhodes 1981.308–9. Solon: Diogenes Laertios 1.55; cf. Stroud 1971.288; Ruschenbusch 1966.43–44; 1979.81. A law concerning war veterans is also dated to the sixth century: Peisistratos supposedly gen-

eralized an *ad personam* measure of Solon (Plut. *Solon* 31.3–4); cf. Lysias 24.26; Jacoby, comm. on *FGrH* 328 F197 (pt. IIIb, 1:562–64); Ruschenbusch 1979.81; Manfredini & Piccirilli 1977.278 (all arguing for Periklean origin); Stroud 1971.288, n.17; Dillon 1995. Moreover, late lexicographers mention a Solonian law that introduced food contributions for women and orphans: Harpokration, Suda *s.v. sitos:* Photios 514.6 = T10, F54 Ruschenbusch 1966: specific mention of the *axōn* seems to confirm authenticity. Lacey 1968.88–90 interprets this law more broadly. Diodorus 12.15 attributes comparable measures to Charondas of Katane.

118. Ruschenbusch 1979.81. (Increased concern with communal warfare is reflected also in the introduction of the *patrios nomos* soon after the Persian Wars: n.113.) The daily rate in the fifth century probably was one obol (lines 9–10 of the Theozotides decree [n.119]; see Stroud 1971.287), equal to that received by war invalids (Lysias 24.26).
119. Thus the decree proposed by Theozotides in 403/2: Stroud 1971; *SEG* 28.46.
120. Loraux 1986.26–27; Pickard-Cambridge 1968 (1988).59, with nn.1–2; Goldhill 1990.107–14. See esp. Lysias, *Ag. Theozotides,* fr. b (Stroud 1971.297–99); Plato, *Menexenos* 248e–249c; Isokrates 8.82; Aischines 3.154.
121. Stupperich 1977.240; den Boer 1979.43; Loraux 1986.27.
122. Raaflaub 1996b.157.
123. Pomeroy 1982.125–26.
124. Pomeroy 1982.116–19.
125. Plato, *Menexenos* 248d–249b. The silence of Aischines 3.258 is especially significant. See also Weiler 1988.24.
126. *Menexenos* 248e–249c. Similarly, the *epitaphioi* of Lysias (2.75) and Demosthenes (60.32, 35–36) mention moral rather than material support.
127. E.g., Aischines 1.28; see Just 1989.30. Lysias 2.75 remains vague.
128. Thuc. 2.45.2; see recently Kallet-Marx 1993b. On widows in general, see Weiler 1988; Günther 1993.
129. The debate about the Theozotides decree illustrates this point: Stroud 1971.297–301. See Goldhill 1990.118–23 (1987.71–75) on a critical reaction to this ideology in Sophokles' *Philoktetes.*
130. On the latter, see Katz 1992. Just 1989 provides a good discussion of the issues relevant here. See generally Pomeroy 1975; Gould 1980; recently Wood 1988.115–20; Cohen 1991; Cartledge 1993, chap. 4; Fantham et al. 1994, chap. 3; Blundell 1995, chap. 3; Hawley & Levick 1995; Pomeroy 1997; Katz 1997; Strauss 1997.147–49, 151–53. Further bibliog. in Pomeroy 1984.
131. For specific differences, most conspicuous in Sparta, see Cartledge 1981; Kunstler 1986; Dettenhofer 1993, 1995; Fantham et al. 1994, chap. 2. See also Pomeroy 1982.118–19.
132. Tyrrell 1984.28–31; Vidal-Naquet 1986.205–23; Patterson 1986, esp. 57–62.
133. Hansen 1991.318; "underclass": R. Osborne 1995.38. Generally on women's work: Scheidel 1990, 1995–96.

134. Pomeroy 1975.78; cf. Keuls 1985. On the historiography of this debate and its ideological background, see Katz 1992.
135. Fantham et al. 1994.75; cf. generally Halperin 1990; Winkler 1990c.
136. Metics: above at n.107; slaves: above at n.101.
137. Festivals and cults: next section. Recent discussions of women in religion: Detienne 1989; Winkler 1990b; Bruit Zaidman 1992; Kron 1992, 1996; Osborne 1993b; Foxhall 1995; Simms 1998; see also Maurizio, this vol. An extreme case is "maenadism" (Henrichs 1978; Bremmer 1984). For correspondences on the deme level: Whitehead 1986a, chap. 7; Jones forthcoming, chap. 4. Another much debated question is whether women were present in the theater: see recently Henderson 1991b; Csapo & Slater 1995.286–87; Goldhill 1994.
138. Foxhall 1995.106, 108.
139. Cohen 1989.
140. Xen. *Oeconomicus* 3.10–11; Aristoph. *Lysistrata* 507–14 vs. [Dem.] 59.110–11; cf. Lacey 1968.173–74; Fantham et al. 1994.101–2, 112–13. See also Henderson, this vol.
141. Harrison 1968–71.1:122–49; de Ste. Croix 1970; Schaps 1979; Foxhall 1989.
142. Henderson 1980; cf. Konstan 1993 and, more generally, Saïd, this vol.
143. Thuc. 2.34; cf. Sourvinou-Inwood 1995b.191–95; Garland 1985.89–93; Parker 1996.131–40; and n.114 above.
144. Moreover, it is contradicted by Arist. *Politics* 3.1278a.26–34, and by *Const of the Athenians* 26.1 which emphasizes heavy losses in previous years (but see Rhodes 1981.326–28; Chambers 1990.262–63). Cit.: Davies 1993.221.
145. Boegehold 1994; Pomeroy 1982.128–29; Sealey 1987.23–25; see Patterson 1981. Conversely, as Lisa Kallet suggested to me, sons of wealthy metics may have been attractive matches for citizen daughters. Ruschenbusch 1979.83–87 assumes that most metics were "Gastarbeiter" and lived in Athens without families; hence, in his view, the problem was that too many Athenian women married foreign men, especially in periods after massive losses of Athenian men (such as were sustained in Egypt in 454).
146. See, e.g., Pomeroy 1975.65–70; Whitehead 1977.147–51; Patterson 1981; Rhodes 1981.331–34; Stadter 1989.333–35; Fornara & Samons 1991.74–75; Rhodes 1992a.76–77; Davies 1992b.299; see also Connor 1994. Humphreys 1974, Walter 1993.209, and Martin 1990.227 stress various political concerns that possibly played a role. Following Plut. *Perikles* 37.3–4, who connects the citizenship law with the *diapsēphismos* of 445/4, many scholars see one of the main purposes of the law in limiting the economic benefits of empire to a tightly circumscribed citizen body: e.g., Bleicken 1994.346–47. Gschnitzer 1981.122–23 plausibly stresses the combination of various factors.
147. Scafuro 1994, discussing plentiful fourth-century evidence. On the obscurity of women: Pomeroy 1995; 1997.72–82; Schaps 1977.
148. Kearns 1985.192; Sourvinou-Inwood 1990 (cit. 295, 297, 322); cf. Bruit Zaidman & Schmitt Pantel 1992a.

149. Versnel 1995 (370–83 on the fifth century); Parker 1996; Jameson 1997; cf. Burkert 1992a; Starr 1979a. Momigliano: cited by Versnel 1995.367, who agrees (369).
150. Parker 1996, chap. 6; cf. Davies 1988.
151. For various aspects of the following, see Kearns 1985; Whitehead 1986a, chap. 7; Lambert 1993, chaps. 6, 8; Shapiro 1994b; Neils 1994; Burkert 1996; Parker 1996, chap. 7; Jones forthcoming, all with sources and bibliography.
152. Parker 1996.102.
153. See, e.g., Pseudo-Xenophon, *Const. of the Athenians* 1.13; Pickard-Cambridge 1968 (1988).75. Absence of female choruses: Burkert 1996.60; Parker 1996.80. Generally: Aristotle, *Const. of the Athenians* 60.1; Shapiro 1992a; Neils 1994; Boegehold 1996.
154. Burkert 1996.60.
155. On the latter, Hölscher, this vol., with bibliog.
156. Tyrannicides: Hölscher, this vol.; Shapiro 1994b.124; Castriota 1997. Old Athena temple: Childs 1994. Other temples and monuments: Hölscher, this vol.; Grütter 1997.
157. On the latter, Jameson 1997.179–82; cf., e.g., Hedrick 1990. On missing aspects: Versnel 1995.370–80.
158. Aleshire 1994.
159. Pseudo-Xenophon, *Const. of the Athenians* 2.9, 3.2, 3.8; Aristophanes, *Clouds* 298–313; Isokrates 4.43; Mikalson 1975.
160. Connor 1996.87, 89; cf. id. 1988. See also Giovannini 1991; Maurizio, this vol. On *parrhēsia*, see Henderson, this vol.
161. Jameson 1997.176–79 (cit. 178).
162. Versnel 1990.102–23; 1995.383–84; Garland 1992; Auffarth 1995; Parker 1996, chap. 9; Jameson 1997.184–87. See id. 171–73 on private cult groups.
163. Smarczyk 1990; cf. Hornblower 1992; Parker 1996.142–51; Shapiro 1996a.
164. Mother-city: Parker 1996.143 (cit.); cf. Schuller 1974.112–17; Smarczyk 1990, pt. II. Gifts: e.g., ML 49 = Fornara 1983a, no.100.11–13. Dionysia: Goldhill 1990; Smarczyk 1990.155–67 (cf. 167–298 on other festivals); Versnel 1995.376–80.
165. Hornblower 1992, esp. 182–83, 186–97 (cit. 196); cf. Shapiro 1996a and, on the role of Theseus in imperial ideology, e.g., Tausend 1989; Calame 1990 (2d ed. 1996, with Garland 1997); Walker 1995; Parker 1996.149–51; Mills 1997.
166. Smarczyk 1990.58–153; Parker 1996.144–49. Id. 1994 on Athenians abroad.
167. Her. 5.78; Boedeker, this vol., at n.90. See chap. 15 below, text at n.27. On the monuments, Hölscher, this vol.
168. Her. 6.109; cf. Shapiro 1994b.124, with bibliog.
169. For documentation, see Boedeker, this vol.; Shapiro 1994b. See also n.165.
170. Shapiro 1994b.125; cf. Versnel 1995.380–83.
171. Metzler 1988 (esp. 132 with references to Persian models); Osborne 1994b; Shapiro 1996b; Maurizio, this vol.; cf. Smarczyk 1990.31–57, 298–317; Goldhill 1990.
172. Due, in part, to the fact that Thucydides largely ignores religion: Hornblower 1992; but see Jordan 1986; Price 1999.

173. Hölscher, this vol., with bibliog.
174. Thuc. 2.52–53; Mikalson 1984. See also Thucydides' remarks on the breakdown of civic and religious norms in the civil war on Corcyra (3.81–84, esp. 82.3), with Kearns 1995.521.
175. See n.162.
176. On the trial of Sokrates, see recently Connor 1991; Hansen 1996b; Parker 1996, chap. 10; Jameson 1997.189–91. The scandals of 415 offer another example where religious and political aspects were intermixed: Furley 1996; Munn 1999.
177. See Starr 1979.17–22, referring to Nilsson 1940.87–90, who emphasizes the increasing separation of state religion from the individual citizen's religious concerns. See generally also Mikalson 1983.
178. Raaflaub 1989.51–52; 1994.
179. E.g., Humphreys 1978.136–58; Meier 1993a, chaps. 7–8; 1993b; see the end of Hölscher's contribution to this volume, and above n.44.
180. Meier 1993b, 1996.
181. For further discussion, see Boedeker & Raaflaub, this vol, chap. 15.

Chapter 3 Notes

I thank the editors and participants in the colloquium for helpful comments. All dates are B.C.

1. Böckh 1842 is magisterial and still widely used. The earlier "primitivist" versus "modernist" debate (see Finley 1979) has been transformed since Weber (1958, 1976) into one between "substantivists" and "formalists." See, for opposing views, Millett 1991; Cohen 1992; cf. also Burke 1992; Morris 1994a (with a survey of the "state of the Athenian economy").
2. Meritt, Wade-Gery, & McGregor 1939–53, vol. 3; Davies 1971, 1981; Meiggs 1972; Finley 1982.41–61 provide basic studies of the evidence. Cf. Nixon & Price 1990.
3. Kallet-Marx 1989; Giovannini 1990, 1997; Samons 1993.
4. I accept Thucydides' amount against that of the scholiast on Aristophanes, *Wealth* 1193 (6000 talents), for both methodological and substantive reasons: see Kallet-Marx 1993a.101–3; cf. Meritt, Wade-Gery, & McGregor 1939–53.3:118–132.
5. Athens first departed from the normal practice of redistributing surplus (e.g., Her. 3.57.2 on Siphnos) in the 480s when the proceeds of a new silver mine were used for the construction of a fleet (Her. 7.144.1; cf. Plutarch, *Themistokles* 4.1–2; Nepos, *Themistokles* 2). See Ostwald 1995b on the development of the idea of "public wealth" in contrast to private expenditures for public purposes.
6. E.g., Thasos (Thuc. 1.101.3); Amphipolis (inferred from its location, with Thuc. 4.108.1).
7. E.g., Lesbos (Thuc. 3.50.1); Aigina (*IG* IV 29); Euboia (*IG* I^3 418).
8. This seems the most likely interpretation of *argyrologoi nēes,* "money-collecting ships" (Thuc. 2.69, 4.50, 4.75); Kallet-Marx 1993a.160–64; similarly Böckh 1842.585–86.

9. The context is rhetorical, an attempt to persuade a Spartan commander to instigate revolts from Athens.
10. See Kallet-Marx 1993a.139–43. I leave aside the controversial "Papyrus Decree" (which, as restored, earmarks 5000 talents of tribute to be placed in the treasury of Athena for the building program) because it does not constitute a certain or near-certain piece of evidence; see Kallet-Marx 1989.254–56; Giovannini 1990.
11. Since it was an aim of the Delian League to accumulate a surplus, a *periousia chrēmatōn* (Kallet-Marx 1993a.52–56), this is not an unlikely or unforeseen development that we should treat skeptically.
12. As opposed to cleruchies or colonies, participation in which enabled poorer Athenians to increase their wealth and status: see Jones 1957.7, 167–77.
13. Tod 1946–48, no.123.35ff.
14. Pritchett 1953/1956, 1961.
15. E.g., Pseudo-Xenophon, *Constitution of the Athenians* 1.19; Andokides 3.36; Xenophon, *Symposium* 4.31; *Memorabilia* 2.8.1; cf. *IG* I^3 118.18–22; Gauthier 1973.
16. I plan to examine elsewhere what basic level of knowledge Aristophanes assumed in his audience.
17. Böckh 1842.434.
18. Sommerstein 1983.198.
19. For Xenophon's interest in the city's finances, see his *Poroi,* "Revenues."
20. On Greek accounting, see de Ste. Croix 1956; Macve 1985. That the Athenians kept track of the income-expenditure ratio at least in wartime can be inferred from Thucydides 7.28.4.
21. At a rate of pay of one drachma per day for a crew of 200; see Gabrielsen 1994.110–14.
22. *IG* I^3 363; Thuc. 2.70.2.
23. Including pay for the assembly, courts, and Council of 500 (including the higher pay for *prytaneis,* the rotating standing committee of the Council; Rhodes 1972.13), officials, the *synēgoroi* ("public advocates," probably at least ten in the fifth century, receiving a drachma a day [Aristoph. *Wasps* 691] or one-half talent each year [cf. also Aristoph. *Acharnians* 715; *Wasps* 482, with MacDowell 1971, at line 482]), ambassadors (two or three drachmas a day, Aristoph. *Acharnians* 65), various other publicly funded individuals (for example, poets, citharists, and physicians) and public expenditure on festivals.
24. Böckh 1842.252ff.
25. Hansen 1991.315–16.
26. For example, pay for attending assembly (*ekklesiastikon*) and theater (*theōrikon*) did not yet exist and members of the Boule probably were not paid the fourth-century rate of five obols a day. Evidence connecting the *theōrikon* with Perikles (Plutarch, *Perikles* 9; Ulpian on Demosth. 1.1) is not sound; cf. Buchanan 1962; Hansen 1991.315–16.
27. Böckh (1842.236) bases his estimate of the annual cost of jurors (150 talents), normally credited to Perikles (Podes 1994), on Aristophanes (*Wasps* 660ff., with schol.)

and assumes regular pay for 6000 jurors; but not all of these sat every day and the poet's figures in this section are greatly exaggerated (above at n.16). Boegehold 1991.172 (cf. 1995.30), more realistically if perhaps overcautiously, estimates the total at 30 talents a year.

28. Böckh, however, includes the cost of the upkeep of the military (naval, cavalry, hoplite, archers) in his estimate of 400 talents.
29. For irregular expenditures, most notably the Periklean building program, see below at p. 48ff.
30. Csapo & Slater 1995.141, based, for private expenditure, on Lysias 21 which is probably exaggerated and unusual (below at n.101).
31. Baldry 1971.33.
32. Sacrifices could be especially costly: Jameson 1988; in the mid-fourth century Lykourgos regulated the cost of cattle for the Lesser Panathenaia at 41 minai, or 4,100 drachmas (*IG* II[2] 334.16ff.), two-thirds of a talent; *IG* I[3] 375.6–7 records 5,114 drachmas *es tēn hekatombēn* at the Panathenaia. The value of prizes for musicians and athletes performing in the Panathenaia, recorded in *Syll.*[3] 1055, exceeded one talent. Plutarch (*Moralia* 842a) mentions Lykourgos' regulation that choral prize winners at the festival of Poseidon in the Piraeus should receive 1,000, 800, and 600 drachmas respectively; cf. Böckh 1842.212–14; Parke 1977.35ff.; Flickinger 1936.268–70. Pay for poets is inferred from Aristoph. *Frogs* 367, with schol. See in general Pickard-Cambridge 1968 (1988).77–78, 90 and Böckh 1842.209–12. *IG* I[3] 370.66–67 lists nine talents which the Hellenotamiai borrowed from the treasurers of Athena in 415 to give to the *athlothetai,* the board administering the (Great) Panathenaia for that festival; cf. *IG* I[3] 375.4 (six talents) and 378, fr. c, line 14; see Davison 1958.29–33; Lewis 1959.246; Böckh 1842.215.
33. Böckh 1842.215, illuminating for its presumption that we cannot determine total state expenditure specifically or precisely. Baldry 1971.33 notes Böckh's estimate (unknown to me) of total state expenditure for festivals of between 25 and 30 talents annually.
34. Pseudo-Xenophon, *Const. of the Athenians* 3.2; cf. 1.13; Aristoph. *Clouds* 300ff.
35. See further below. Obviously difficulties in meeting the costs could result in dissent or unease about the lavishness, as is, not unexpectedly, attested in the fourth century. Evidence from the fifth century seems problematic. During the Peloponnesian War the program of the Dionysia was shortened (Allen 1938, though explanations other than financial worry are possible), and in 415, for example, funds for the Panathenaia had to be borrowed from the state (*IG* I[3] 370.66–67; Lewis 1959.246–47). But whether that is a sign of financial distress is unclear, for in a number of instances money was borrowed from the sacred treasuries when the state was fiscally strong (see, e.g., Wade-Gery 1930.38); hence, in contrast to modern states, the Athenians may have perceived borrowing as a normal means of financing; cf. Migeotte 1984.357.
36. This issue has engendered much discussion; see, among others, Gomme 1951; Jones 1957.5–10; Finley 1973.48–50; 1982.41–61; Ober 1989.23–24.

37. For discussion, see Kallet-Marx 1994.246–47. Most striking perhaps is the placement of all sorts of thoroughly domestic items under the rubric "what Philokleon gets from the empire," lines 577ff.; cf. Pseudo-Xenophon, *Const. of the Athenians* 1.16–17; Arist. *Const. of the Athenians* 24 for the connection.
38. Aristoph. *Wasps* 695, 724; cf. *Birds* 1541, with schol.; Rhodes 1972.102. Only the scholion to Aristoph. *Wasps* 684 mentions tribute as a source. See also Kallet-Marx 1994.247, n.62. The *kolakretai* disappeared as a board after 411 (Ferguson 1932.3); their duties henceforth were apparently divided between the Hellenotamiai and the Tamiai of Athena; but we do not know who paid the *dikastikos misthos* after 411; Ferguson 1932.136, n.1; Meritt, Wade-Gery, & McGregor 1939–53.3:364; cf. Aristoph. *Frogs* 1463–66.
39. Plut. *Kimon* 10.
40. For a list, see Judeich 1931.73–74; also index II.2.9 of Hill 1951. Cf. Plut. *Themistokles* 22 (for Themistokles' construction of the temple of Artemis); Frost 1980.184–85.
41. One famous exception is the offer (apparently refused) by Perikles' family to fund a springhouse, *IG* I^3 49.13–14; see Davies 1981.91–92 for the few other fifth-century exceptions.
42. The amounts of a few private contributions to the building program are not preserved; e.g., *IG* I^3 445.299–300. Listed last, they would have been minor, but they are nevertheless intriguing.
43. See Boersma 1970.65–82; Schmitz 1988.70–73.
44. Harpokration, *s.v. propylaia tauta*.
45. Cavaignac 1908.103.
46. Stanier 1953.
47. *IG* I^3 439, lines 73, 76, 77; 440, line 127; 444, line 249; 445, line 294.
48. Dinsmoor 1913.64–65; 1921. These contributions appear in the first four years of construction (*IG* I^3 462–66), in addition to unknown amounts from the field in 435/4, 434/3, and 433/2, entered separately. The amounts contributed to the Propylaia are equivalent to the *aparchē* dedicated to Athena annually by the allies but cannot be *the aparchē* itself since we have the record of that payment in the tribute quota lists for the relevant years.
49. Burford 1965.26.
50. If so, this perhaps militates against the idea that the Hellenotamiai handed over annually to Athena's treasurers a fixed tribute surplus. If they had extra in a given year beyond the 200–talent surplus (on the theory of Stevenson below at n.54) why not have deposited this as well in the treasury of Athena?
51. Kluwe 1984.11 thinks the latter but certainty seems impossible.
52. Andrewes 1978.
53. See the partial list in Kallet-Marx 1989.260, n.25.
54. The theory was first proposed by Stevenson 1924.
55. Kallet-Marx 1989; cf. Giovannini 1990; for a recent examination supporting the view that tribute was part of the treasury of Athena, see Samons 1993.
56. Plut. *Perikles* 12.2 and 14.1; Mattingly 1961.165, n.75.

57. Plutarch reports Perikles as responding that the Athenians "did not owe the allies an account of (how they spent) their money as long as they fought the war for them and kept the barbarians at bay" (*Perikles* 12.3). One may doubt (as I do) that these were Perikles' exact words but the facts (discussed above) support the general point of the remark.
58. Cf. also Kallet-Marx 1994.239–43, 246–51.
59. See, e.g., Schuller 1974.70–72; 1984.21–23; Eddy 1977.107–11; Raubitschek 1984.19.
60. Cf. also Parker 1987 on the Athenians' cultivation of the myth of Ion to promote the idea that Athens (and therefore Athena) was the founder of the Ionians; also relevant is the exportation of Athena Polias (as Athena *Athenōn medeousa*) in the empire; see Barron 1964, 1983; Meiggs 1972.291–305; Schuller 1974.112–17; Sherwin-White 1978.37–38; Shipley 1987.114–16; Smarczyk 1990, *passim;* Parker 1994, 1996.
61. *IG* I^3 34.41–42; 46.15–17; 71.56–58; schol. to Aristoph. *Clouds* 386; cf. now Smarczyk 1990.525–92 on the date of this practice.
62. Smarczyk 1990.660–65.
63. The assumption that at issue was the domestic use of allied wealth is based on the purpose of *Poroi* to reveal how Athens could create enough domestic revenue to render it unnecessary to take it from others.
64. See Dover 1974.175–77.
65. Xen. *Oeconomicus* 11.9–10; cf. Arist. *Nik. Eth.* 1122b 19–23a 4 on expenditure designating *megaloprepeia,* "magnificence."
66. As Kurke observes (1991.176), "from the point of view of the city, excessive *megaloprepeia* seems to presage tyranny"; cf. her discussion of *megaloprepeia* pertaining to Athenians, 176–82; but cf. von Reden 1995.85 on Aristotle's view of the *megaloprepes.* Alkibiades provides the best example of public unease over excessive *megaloprepeia:* Thuc. 6.15; cf. also Plut. *Themistokles* 22, linking Themistokles' building of the temple of Artemis in Melite with his ostracism.
67. E.g., Archilochus 19 West; Thuc. 1.13; see Kurke 1991.195–224.
68. Plut. *Perikles* 14.1–2. The story is "financially impossible" (Davies 1971.459, n.1) and may be misplaced, relating instead to Perikles' offer to pay for the springhouse (*IG* I^3 49); see Mattingly 1961.164; Meritt & Wade-Gery 1963.106–7.
69. E.g., Roberts 1986.
70. Cf. Kurke 1991, esp. 177–82, and n.66 above for the case of Themistokles.
71. On the ambitious programs of the Peisistratids, see Boersma 1970.11–27; Shear 1978; Camp 1986.42; 1994; Shapiro 1989.5–8; for tyrants in general, Andreades 1933.116–18. Schuller 1978 suggests that building and tyranny were close associates; *contra*: Tuplin 1985.364.
72. *Const. of the Athenians* 27.3: *tyrannikē ousia.*
73. Perikles: e.g., Kratinos, fr. 258 Kassel & Austin; Plut. *Perikles* 16, 39; see Schwarze 1971.11, n.13 and *passim.* I explore in a forthcoming study the seemingly paradoxical relationship between the interpretation advanced here and concurrent negative assessments of tyrants.

74. Connor 1977; Schuller 1978; Raaflaub 1979; Tuplin 1985; Giorgini 1993.229–33.
75. E.g., Aristoph. *Knights* 1111ff.; Soph. *Oedipus Rex* 383; Eur. *Phoenician Women* 506.
76. Connor 1977.102; Raaflaub, in a forthcoming paper, "Stick and Glue: the Function of Tyranny in Fifth-Century Athenian Democracy," contests Connor's thesis as it applies to fifth-century Athens.
77. This does not mean that the notion of the demos as tyrant could not have negative connotations, only that the nuances of and associations with the word *tyrant* suggest that, depending on the context, the metaphor could be read both positively and negatively.
78. Lines 1111–14: *kalēn g'echeis archēn . . . hōsper andra tyrannon.*
79. Cf. also, e.g., Xenophanes fr. 3; Asius fr. 13 (Kinkel); see Donlan 1980.53ff.; Geddes 1987; Kurke 1992.
80. Line 575 (*megalē archē*).
81. In extreme form the problem of the demos' unaccountability presented itself in the famous Arginusai trial: Xenophon, *Hellenika* 1.7.12–13; cf. Ostwald 1986.444. A further connection between demos and tyranny links the tyrants' practice of taxation with democratic pay. In Xenophon's *Symposion* (4.32; cf. Gray 1992.73) one character explains why he is better off poor than wealthy: "now I am like a tyrant, whereas before I was a slave; then I had to pay up to the demos; now the city takes on the expense of supporting me." I take this as a reference to pay for, e.g., jury duty, as suggested by the previous sentence: "People now actually rise from their seats in deference to me, and rich men obsequiously give me the right of way on the street" (4.31; cf. Pseudo-Xenophon, *Const. of the Athenians* 1.18). As Tuplin (1985.352) notes, "the idea of tyrants being supported by city-taxation is evidently banal enough to provide a simile for the use of public revenue to sustain the poorer classes." That tyrants, like poor Athenians in hostile views, were thought of as taking a free ride is a premise of, e.g., *Wasps* 498ff.
82. Significantly, the exception, Alkibiades, was perceived as threatening because of his expenditures, not on building, but on chariot racing and on his lifestyle generally.
83. Connor 1971.21.
84. See Sinclair 1988.35–36, with sources; list in Judeich 1931.73–74.
85. On Theopompos, *FGrH* 115 F89, who implies that Kimon's opening up of his estates and the like benefitted all citizens, see Connor 1968.30–31. Theopompos thus "blurs the distinction between Kimon and Perikles as that between local dynast and national politician" (Davies 1971.311); on Cimon's generosity cf. also Schmitt Pantel 1992b.180–86.
86. Lauffer 1974.148; cf. Davies 1981.88–89.
87. Veyne 1990.71. Cf. also Roberts 1986, who sees liturgies as an aristocratic anomaly in the democracy.
88. Davies 1971.xvii; 1981.92–105. Cf. also von Reden 1995.84–85. On *charis* and politics, see Meier 1985.
89. Finley 1973.152.
90. Christ 1990.147.

91. Arist. *Poetics* 1449b 1 asserts that comic *chorēgiai* were late and volunteers initially supplied the choruses.
92. Davies 1967, not including the numerous festival liturgies on the deme level; on deme liturgies, see Whitehead 1986a.150–52.
93. See Davies 1967.
94. See the list and discussion in Davies 1971.xxi–xxii.
95. Scholars disagree on the size of the liturgical class: Davies (1971.xviiff.; 1981.15–28) thinks that even in the fifth century it comprised only about 300 men, the wealthiest of the wealthy, whereas Rhodes 1982 argues for up to 1200. If limits existed in the fifth century (below n.101) the pool may have been larger than Davies suggests. In any case, according to Arist. *Const. of the Athenians* 56.3, no man was obliged to perform the same liturgy more than once, which makes even more extraordinary the performance of eight *chorēgiai* in nine years by the speaker of Lys. 21.
96. Roberts 1984.45.
97. Pseudo-Xenophon, *Const. of the Athenians* 1.13, implying not only practical benefits to the people but also a symbolically important social/economic equalizing effect. This relates to the suggestion made above (n.81) about a similar effect of pay for offices; meager as the pay was, it enhanced the demos' means and allowed them to partake in an area that traditionally connoted wealth and privilege (Markle 1985). Similarly, their public spending made them feel wealthy.
98. Aischin. 1.11.
99. Cf. also Pseudo-Xenophon, *Const. of the Athenians* 1.13.
100. That liturgies were considered compulsory is clear from our sources, e.g., Xenophon, *Oeconomicus* 2.5–6; cf. Csapo & Slater 1995.140. See also Gabrielsen 1987 on the *antidosis* procedure as a means of sociopolitical control exercised by the demos over the elite.
101. Lysias 21.5 (*kata ta gegrammena en tōi nomōi*), suggesting that there were limits, just not adhered to: Rhodes 1982.2; *contra* Davies 1981.15–28.
102. As Thucydides has Alkibiades claim, 6.16.3. By contrast, Kurke 1991.176–77 sees a potential tyrant even in a lavish liturgist. If Alkibiades' *chorēgiai* (Thuc. 6.16.3) troubled his contemporaries in the same way that his Olympic victories and "other expenses" (6.15.3) did, it was because he appeared to spend beyond his means. Alkibiades clearly was exceptional; Nikias' lavish liturgical spending caused no problems.
103. Pickard-Cambridge 1968 (1988).77–78, with sources. For Nikias' tripod, see Plato, *Gorgias* 472a; the monument ascribed to him by Plut. *Nik.* 3 was likely set up by a later Nikias; see Dinsmoor 1910; for Kimon, Matthaiou 1994.183–88. Cf. also Humphreys 1978.69–70 on the diminution of prestige in the performance of liturgies as compared with extra-democratic aristocratic display.
104. Modern discussion is extensive; cf., among others, Adkins 1960.202–5, 211–14; 1972.121–25; Lauffer 1974; Humphreys 1978.69–70; Gernet 1981.282–87; Davies 1981; Whitehead 1983; Ober 1989.199–247; Kurke 1991.168–76.

105. Alkibiades, e.g., justified his worthiness to lead the Sicilian expedition partly by his *chorēgiai:* Thuc. 6.16.3; Kurke 1991.172–75.
106. Pickard-Cambridge 1968 (1988).89.
107. E.g., Lysias 21.1–5; Demosthenes 21.156; Isaios 5.36, 7.38.
108. Cf. Antiphon 6; Millett 1991.85–86; corruption: Harvey 1985.
109. For the financial benefits one might expect from holding various offices, the example of Demosthenes is illustrative, though possibly extreme; see Davies 1971.3597.XXI; cf. 1981.67. The expectation of a financial return may also explain why individuals were able to take out nonproductive loans: otherwise it is hard to see why someone would lend money to a liturgist, knowing that with fixed assets the likelihood of repayment would be small, given the natural reluctance of an individual to deplete his estate by selling off property; Millett 1991.74, 85.
110. Thuc. 6.16.3.
111. On liturgy avoidance see Christ 1990; Gabrielsen 1986.
112. In Lykourgos (*Leokrates* 139–40), *charis* is earned by trierarchies or building walls: "These are services to the state: they affect the welfare of you all and prove the loyalty of the donors, while the others [sc. liturgies] are evidence of nothing but the wealth of those who have spent the money"; cf. also Arist. *Politics* 1309a 17ff.
113. See above, p. 12, and Finley 1982.
114. See Humphreys 1978.219. This was not a consistent and tidy development. A crucial exception was Alkibiades. As has become clear, his gifts (*epidoseis*) to the people of Athens as a whole (Plut. *Alkibiades* 10; cf. Migeotte 1992.10–11; Kuenzi 1923.8–9 doubts the authenticity of the anecdote) could arguably be seen as "democratic" but his excessive expenditures suggested that something more was afoot than pride and honor for the city, or just political influence in the democracy: despite his attempts to link it to the city (Thuc. 6.16.2), it was a vestige of the old-style, predemocratic aristocratic expenditure and evoked tyranny (Kurke 1991.173–76, 177–82); it therefore fell outside the democratic matrix within which such expenditure was acceptable.
115. Arist. *Const. of the Athenians* 56.3; cf. Sourvinou-Inwood 1994.272; Goldhill 1994.368. That metics could be festival liturgists as well suggests that we should examine liturgies not so much from a democratic perspective as from that of the polis more broadly conceived; see Whitehead 1977.80–81, who also cites Katayama 1970.
116. Dem. 21.13–14.
117. Thuc. 6.15; cf. 2.37.1, where Perikles formulates the principle of aristocratic excellence within the democracy. The exception that proves the rule again is Alkibiades.
118. The Panathenaia, however, was not celebrated in that year; Ferguson 1932.76.
119. *IG* II^2 3073ff. An official, an *agōnothetēs,* was appointed to administer the festival; he was expected to incur considerable expense of his own; cf. Pickard-Cambridge 1968 (1988).91–92.
120. Isokrates 8.82, with Raubitschek 1941; cf. Goldhill 1990.101–4.

Chapter 4 Notes

I thank the participants in the colloquium for their valuable comments on the first version of this chapter, and particularly Deborah Boedeker, Kurt Raaflaub, and Stella Miller for their consistently constructive criticisms of subsequent drafts. In this chapter I refer to many brief preliminary reports in archaeological journals. To keep the bibliography manageable, I depart from the practice in the rest of this volume and cite these reports in the notes only, by journal title rather than by author's name. I use the following abbreviations:

AA	*Archäologischer Anzeiger*
AAA	*Athens Annals of Archaeology*
AD	*Arkhaiologikon Deltion*
AE	*Arkhaiologiki Ephemeris*
AEMTh	*To Arkhaiologiko Ergo sti Makedonia kai Thraki*
AJA	*American Journal of Archaeology*
AM	*Athenische Mitteilungen*
AntK	*Antike Kunst*
AR	*Archaeological Reports* (supplement to *JHS*)
BCH	*Bulletin de correspondance hellénique*
BSA	*Annual of the British School at Athens*
JHS	*Journal of Hellenic Studies*
ÖJh	*Österreichische Jahreshefte*
Praktika	*Praktika tis en Athinais Arkhaiologikis Etaireias*
RA	*Revue archéologique*

1. Macleod 1982 stresses Aeschylus' autonomy from political forces. On cultural forms, see the chapters in this volume by Hölscher, Boedeker, Saïd, and others, on great changes that of Raaflaub.
2. Stedman Jones 1983, Chartier 1988, and Hunt 1989 are among the clearest expositions. Quotation from Hunt 1989.7.
3. See, in different ways, Rosenbloom 1995; Dougherty 1996; Kurke 1997.
4. For reasons I discuss in Morris 1994b.
5. Levine 1991; Cannadine 1994.
6. Auslander 1996.
7. A phrase favored by Baudrillard (1968), an important theorist for the new historians of material culture.
8. Winckelmann [1764] 1880, illuminated by Potts 1994.
9. All dates are B.C. Ancient views of these changes: Pollitt 1965.55–124. For criticisms of this model, see Vickers & Gill 1994.
10. On burial as one of the defining characteristics of civilization, see, e.g., Herodotus 3.38; on the house as a central metaphor for the structure of the good society for many Athenian writers, see Cohen 1991.70–97.

11. For fuller references, see I. Morris 1987.222–33; 1992.108–44; 1994b; Houby-Nielsen 1992, 1995.
12. Bronze urns: *AD* 25:2 (1970) 126–27; 42:2 (1987) 67; *AAA* 7 (1974) 224. Mounds: Kübler 1976.5–21; Knigge 1976. Herodotus (6.103) says that large mounds continued at least until the 520s. Lydian goods: Houby-Nielsen 1995.166–69.
13. Art historians generally link this to a law restricting funerary expenditure, mentioned by Cicero (*Laws* 2.64–65), although the dates suggested for the law vary from the 530s (e.g., Richter 1961.38–39) to the 470s (Clairmont 1970.11–12). For my own views on this problem, see Morris 1992/93.38–43; cf. Hölscher, this vol., at n.28.
14. Kerameikos grs. hS 24, 35 (*AM* 81 [1966] 99, 92–93), C 261 (Kübler 1976.81–82); Veikou and Aglavrou Sts. gr. 3 (*AD* 25:2 [1970] 44); Virginia Benaki St. gr. 9 (*AD* 23:2 [1968] 46).
15. Veikou and Aglavrou Sts. gr. 11, *AD* 25:2 (1970) 47–49. On prices, see Vickers & Gill 1994.85–88. Grave pots: I. Morris 1992.108–18. More figured pots have been found in a single dump from a public building in the Agora (Oakley & Rotroff 1992) than in all the Athenian graves combined.
16. *x* is the arithmetic mean. *G* is Gini's coefficient of inequality, measured on a scale from 0 to 1. The closer the *G* score is to 0, the more evenly distributed the offerings are between graves; the closer *G* is to 1, the more unequally the grave goods are concentrated (see further I. Morris 1992. 138–39).
17. *JHS* 36 (1916) 258; 46 (1926) 253–57. Urn illustrated in Williams & Ogden 1994.58.
18. Marathon: Whitley 1994; other state tombs: Stupperich 1977; Clairmont 1983; Knigge 1988. A mound of stones on Salamis, 20 m in diameter, may be a polyandrion from 480: *AD* 22:2 (1967) 145–46; 35:2 (1980) 91; 36:2 (1981) 64–65.
19. Madytou St., *AD* 27:2 (1972) 68–70; Olymbiou St. gr. 2, *AD* 29:2 (1973/74) 134.
20. Terrassenanlage: *AM* 91 (1976) 37; Kovacscovics 1990.6. Rhamnous: annual reports in *Praktika*, most years, 1975–92. Glyphada monument: *AD* 25:2 (1970) 123–26; 29:2 (1973/74) 55–58; cemetery: *AD* 27:2 (1972) 159–61; 34:2 (1979) 72–76; other monuments at the site: *Praktika* 1919.32–46; *AD* 11 (1927/28) 44; 35:2 (1980) 73; 39:2 (1984) 33–34.
21. On the peribolos tombs, see Humphreys 1980; for some disagreements, Morris 1994b.76–83. The only general review is Garland 1982; additional references here in App. 1. Grave stones: Nielsen et al. 1989; Meyer 1993.
22. See App. 2.
23. Dexileos: Ensoli 1987. Lysias 23 offers another example. Other state tombs: n.17 above.
24. For the older finds, see Jones 1975; for the more recent, Walter-Karydi 1994; Nevett forthcoming.
25. See App. 3.
26. Hoepfner & Schwandner 1994: 22–50; for discussion, Schuller, Hoepfner, & Schwandner 1989. Regular houses: *Hesperia* 28 (1959) 98–103. *AD* 44:2 (1989) 62 describes House B at Voula, dating to the end of the fifth century, as "Hippodamian."

27. See App. 3; virtually all the fifth-century houses listed there were occupied across the fourth century, but were often enlarged. For fourth-century houses, see also App. 3. Population: Hansen 1985.
28. For an exception, see *Hesperia* 20 (1951) 209–15.
29. The substantial rock-cut houses from southwest Athens reported in *AM* 85/86 (1971) 109–24 unfortunately cannot be dated accurately.
30. Dionysiou Areopagitou St.: *AD* 27:2 (1972) 104–5. Amphiktyonos St.: *AD* 19:2 (1964) 50. Aristeidou St.: *AD* 16 (1960) 30. Piraeus: *AD* 29:2 (1973/74) 103. Stephanos: see App. 3.
31. Rovertou Galli St.: *AD* 22:2 (1967) 112–14. Mosaics: Karyatidon St.: *AD* 19:2 (1964) 49. Menandrou St.: *AD* 22:2 (1967) 98–100; 30:2 (1975) 24–27. Dörpfeld's "House of the Greek Mosaics": *AM* 19 (1894) 508; *Hesperia* 35 (1966) 51–53. House northeast of the Areopagus: *Hesperia* 42 (1973) 146–56. Bathroom on Voulis and Apollonos Sts.: *AD* 34:2 (1979) 28–30. General discussions in Robertson 1965, 1982; Salzmann 1982; Walter-Karydi 1994.45–46. Paved floors: *AD* 24:2 (1969) 89, House B; 33:2 (1978) 58. Dema house: *BSA* 57 (1962) 75–114.
32. Alkibiades: [Andokides] 4.17; Demosthenes 21.147; Plutarch, *Alkibiades* 16. [Andokides'] *Against Alkibiades*, of unknown authorship and probably an exercise rather than a public speech, most likely dates to the early fourth century. The dramatic date should be 417. Robertson (1982.241) argues that the episode occurred during Alkibiades' return to Athens in 407/6, and that Alkibiades took the idea from Archelaos' palace at Pella; but this piles up conjectures unnecessarily. On decoration, Walter-Karydi 1994.32–52.
33. See Walter-Karydi 1994.9–11, 55–62.
34. *Praktika* 1886.57–58; 1891.35–36. A pair of Eretrian gold earrings in the British Museum, from 420–400, probably also came from a grave (Williams & Ogden 1994.56–57; cf. *AM* 38 [1913] 296–319).
35. *Praktika* 1898.98; 1900.53–56; 1902.65. Poor graves: *AD* 16 (1960) 150; 23:2 (1968) 230; 27:2 (1972) 355–57; 31:2 (1976) 135; 35:2 (1980) 227; 36:1 (1981) 58–81; *AAA* 7 (1974) 229–48; 9 (1976) 197–212; 13 (1980) 32; 14 (1981) 132; 18 (1985) 106. Chamber tomb: *AD* 20:3 (1965) 270–73. Stelai and periboloi: *AD* 18:2 (1963) 124; *AAA* 18 (1985) 106–14; Auberson & Schefold 1973.95–97.
36. *Praktika* 1900.63–64; 1902.61–63; *AD* 27:1 (1972) 170–84. Rich cremation: *AAA* 19 (1986) 30. Stelai: *AD* 25:1 (1970) 26–28; 31:2 (1976) 147.
37. See Schiffer 1987 for detailed discussion.
38. Fifth-century houses: *AD* 20:2 (1965) 259; 23:2 (1968) 253; 27:2 (1972) 349; 28:2 (1973) 302. Big houses: *AD* 27:2 (1972) 343–44; 30:2 (1975) 161–63; 31:2 (1976) 131–33. Mosaic floors: *AD* 17:2 (1961/62) 152; 30:2 (1975) 156; 31:2 (1976) 131; 32:2 (1977) 102; 33:2 (1978) 127; Ducrey, Metzger, & Reber 1993. "Palaces": *AA* 1977.164–79; 1988.653–66; *AntK* 22 (1979) 3–13; 32 (1989) 3–7. House IV: *AntK* 33 (1990) 111–14; 34 (1991) 133–36; 35 (1992) 123–28; 36 (1993) 126–29. At Chalkis, only a few rooms from one classical house have been published (*AD* 42:2 [1987] 207).

39. North Cemetery: Palmer 1964. Tweezers: *AD* 36:2 (1981) 90. Aetopetra: *AAA* 6 (1973) 181–88; *AD* 29:2 (1973/74) 200.
40. See n.16.
41. Counting the North Cemetery, Lechaion (*Hesperia* 37 [1968] 354–68), Acrocorinth (*Hesperia* 31 [1962] 118–20), Lefkos Potamos (*AD* 30:2 [1975] 59), and Kritika (*AD* 22:2 [1967] 169). The graves at Ayioi Theodoroi (*AD* 17:2 [1961/62] 52), Monastiri (*JHS* 86 [1936] 144), Kenchreai (*AD* 31:2 [1976] 64–65), and Sikyon (*AD* 22:2 [1967] 164–66; 31:2 [1976] 65) are not published well enough to be used here.
42. Carpenter & Bon 1936.297–301; *Hesperia* 31 (1962) 133, n.125.
43. Buildings I–IV: *Hesperia* 22 (1953) 131–40 (= Building III); 41 (1972) 151–74; 42 (1973) 19–27; 48 (1979) 125–36. Pentagonal Building: *Hesperia* 44 (1975) 7; 45 (1976) 108. Punic Amphora Building: *Hesperia* 47 (1978) 15–20; 48 (1979) 107–24; 49 (1980) 108–11. Centaur Bath: *Hesperia* 45 (1976) 109–15; 46 (1977) 45–52; 60 (1991) 3–11. Earlier mosaic finds: *AJA* 23 (1929) 526–28; 41 (1937) 546–47. House: *Praktika* 1892.125–32.
44. Mosaics: *Praktika* 1935.82–83; 1938.123; 1941.59–60; *AD* 21:2 (1966) 124; 22:2 (1967) 165; *AA* 1979.290–306. Dates: Robertson 1982.247. Mosaic school: Robertson 1965.85; 1982.245.
45. *AD* 24:2 (1969) 106–10; 27:2 (1972) 202–3; 28:2 (1973) 121; 46:2 (1991) 94. Orphanage gr. 4: *AD* 40:1 (1985) 178–93.
46. Gymnasium: *AD* 21:2 (1966) 128–30; 22:2 (1967) 172; 25:2 (1970) 155; 26:2 (1971) 78–79. Sector d: *BCH* 91 (1967) 820. Menandrou and Polyneikous Sts.: *AD* 46:2 (1991) 93–95.
47. Sector d gr. 228: *BCH* 91 (1967) 820. Deiras: *BCH* 94 (1970) 437–531. Theater: *BCH* 113 (1989) 721. Korinthou St.: *AD* 16 (1960) 93. Kourou plot: *AD* 18:2 (1963) 60–63. Stasinopoulou: *AD* 26:2 (1971) 78. Charadros river: *AD* 28:2 (1973) 123. Pondiki gr. 1: *AD* 28:2 (1973) 123–25. I do not include the poorly dated graves in the Raptis plot (*AD* 16 [1960] 93), the river Xerias (*AD* 21:2 [1966] 125–26), and the Boukara plot (*AD* 28:2 [1973] 126–27).
48. Fifth century: Korinthou St. (one iron pin). Fourth century: Deiras gr. 4 (two iron strigils, two bronze ornaments); Pondiki gr. 1 (one bronze coin, one iron strigil); Kourou gr. 7 (one silver coin). Boukara grs. 2–4, containing four bronzes and one glass bead, sound exactly like fourth-century burials, but the report does not date them precisely.
49. *AD* 23:2 (1968) 128–30; *AAA* 4 (1971) 92–99; *BCH* 102 (1978) 791.
50. Houses: *AD* 24:2 (1969) 108–10, building a; 25:2 (1970) 155; 46:2 (1991) 88. Fifth-century hearth: *BCH* 107 (1983) 839. Floors: *BCH* 80 (1956) 366; 92 (1968) 1020–21; 95 (1971) 740. Layers destroyed: *BCH* 94 (1970) 766; 95 (1971) 749; 96 (1972) 178–80.
51. The only significant exception to the pattern is Aigina. Here, rock-cut chamber tombs became popular around 550, usually holding two or three burials. A few tombs date to the fourth century (e.g., *AD* 32:2 [1977] 43), but most go out of use by 400. Hundreds have been found, almost always robbed. Large cemeteries of pit

graves also begin by 450. They continue into the fourth century, and at least one fourth-century sarcophagus is known (*AA* 1938.33–34). Chamber tombs: Welter 1938.51–57; *AA* 1928.612; 1930.128–29; 1931.275; 1938.496–524; and annual reports in *AD*, most years, 1964–90. Pit graves: *AD* 21:2 (1966) 100; 34:2 (1979) 69; 36:2 (1981) 67; 42:2 (1987) 68; 44:2 (1989) 86; 45:2 (1990) 81.

52. Trebenischte: Filow 1927; *ÖJh* 27 (1931) 1–42; 28 (1933) 164–86; *AA* 1933.459–82; *RA* 1934.26–38. Duvanli: Filow 1934. Sindos: Vokotopoulou et al. 1985. Bouzek & Ondrejová (1988) compare these three sites. Vergina: *Praktika* 1987.126–46; 1988.99–107; *AEMTh* 1 (1987) 81–91; 2 (1988) 1–4. Aiani: *AD* 42:3 (1987) 424–25; 43:3 (1988) 398–401; *AEMTh* 2 (1988) 19–25; 4 (1990) 46–50. Ayia Paraskevi: *AD* 36:3 (1981) 300; 37:3 (1982) 282–83; 38:3 (1983) 269–70; 39:2 (1984) 216–17; 40:2 (1985) 235; 41:2 (1986) 138–39. There are other rich burials, often of warriors, dating 550–475 at Aphytis (*AD* 34:1 [1979] 70–84), Eion (*AD* 39:2 [1979] 275–76), Galipsos (*AD* 27:3 [1972] 525–27), Kouphalia (*AD* 40:2 [1985] 235), Nea Syllata (*AAA* 14 [1981] 246–50), and Tragilos (*AD* 26:3 [1971] 417–18; 33:3 [1978] 297–99).
53. Sindos: *AD* 35:3 (1980) 368; 43:3 (1988) 360; *AEMTh* 2 (1988) 286–88. Thermi: *AD* 43:3 (1988) 359; *AEMTh* 2 (1988) 283–86. Akanthos (modern Ierissos): annual reports in *AD*, most years, 1971–88. Pydna (modern Makriyalos): *AD* 39:2 (1984) 219; 41:2 (1986) 143–44; 42:3 (1987) 364; 43:3 (1988) 365; *AEMTh* 3 (1989) 155–63; 4 (1990) 241–46; 5 (1991) 171–73. More recent excavations have found more fifth-century gold, some of it illustrated in *Pydna*. Exhibition Catalogue (Athens 1996; I thank Stella Miller for this reference). Cf. Epanomi: *AD* 41:2 (1986) 138; Kitros: *AD* 38:3 (1983) 274, 276; Nea Kallikrateia: *AD* 35:3 (1980) 424; 36:3 (1981) 345; Peristeron: *AD* 30:3 (1975) 247; Polychrono: *AD* 42:3 (1987) 369–70; 43:3 (1988) 364; *AEMTh* 3 (1989) 395–97; Polyrrachon: *AD* 29:4 (1973/74) 720–21; Poliyiros: *AD* 43:3 (1988) 361; Poteidaia: *AD* 29:4 (1973/74) 677; 42:3 (1987) 367; *AAA* 7 (1974) 190–98; Skione: *AD* 39:2 (1984) 226; Veryi: *AD* 22:3 (1967) 425–26.
54. Gr. K3 actually contained the skeletons of two robbers killed in the collapse of the tomb (*AEMTh* 4 [1990] 36).
55. Vergina: *Praktika* 1989.184–98; 1990.181–84; 1991.189–92; *AEMTh* 3 (1989) 1–12; 4 (1990) 35–44; 5 (1991) 23–30. Thessaloniki: *AD* 20:3 (1965) 411; cf. 32:3 (1977) 197. Pydna: *AEMTh* 1 (1987) 210; 5 (1991) 173.
56. Aiani: *AD* 42:3 (1987) 424–25; 43:3 (1988) 398–401; *AEMTh* 3 (1989) 48–51; 4 (1990) 75–92. Kozani: *Praktika* 1934.83; 1950.281–92; 1958.98–100; *AE* 1948/49.85–111. Perivoli: *AD* 20:3 (1965) 438. Cf. gold grave goods at Sianisti: *Praktika* 1934.75–76.
57. End of Thessalian Archaic burial: Ayios Yeoryios Larisis: *AAA* 11 (1978) 156–82; *AD* 38:2 (1983) 208–11; 39:2 (1984) 150–51; 42:2 (1987) 274–76. Iolkos: *Praktika* 1915.158–59. Krannon: *AD* 16 (1960) 179–81; 25:3 (1970) 279–82; 27:3 (1972) 416; 44:2 (1989) 231–33, the latest report suggesting that graves were dug into the mound throughout the fifth century. New pattern in fourth century: Pherai: *Prak-*

tika 1907.147–58; 1915.164. Demetrias: *Praktika* 1915.182–87; 1920.24–25. Pharsalos: *Praktika* 1951.157–63; 1952.185–203; 1953.127; 1954.153–59; 1955.140–46. Krannon: *AD* 16 (1960) 175–82. Yeraki Ayias: *AD* 28:3 (1973) 329–32. Goritsa: *BCH* 55 (1931) 487–91; *AD* 29:3 (1973/74) 550–59. Omolion: *AD* 17:2 (1961/62) 176–78; Miller 1979.

58. See, e.g., Thucydides 1.6, 2.95–101.
59. See, e.g., *Iliria* 1 (1971) 348–60; *Les Illyriens et la genèse des Albanais* (Tirana 1971); Gergova 1993. On Hallstatt links, Palavestra 1994.
60. Borza 1990.267.
61. Kitros: *AD* 38:3 (1983) 274; 39:2 (1984) 220–22; 43:3 (1988) 365–66. Nikisiani: Lazarides et al. 1992. Cf. Phoinix (*AEMTh* 1 [1987] 261–64; *AD* 42:3 [1988] 358), Pydna (*AEMTh* 4 [1991] 146–49), and Rachona (*AEMTh* 1 [1987] 147–59) for other large mounds, c. 350–325. Great Mound: Andronikos 1984. There has been much debate over the exact date of the mound and the identity of its occupants, well summarized in Borza 1990.256–66. Main cemetery: *AD* 17:1 (1961/62) 218–88; 18:3 (1963) 217–32; 25:3 (1970) 395–96; Andronikos 1969.
62. For poorer fourth-century graves, see Akanthos: *AAA* 11 (1978) 5–31; Sarandovryses: *AD* 35:3 (1980) 408–9; Veroia: *AD* 29:4 (1973/74) 714–17; 36:3 (1981) 322–24; 37:3 (1982) 300–301.
63. The extraordinary gold of the "Ganymede Group," said to have come from a grave of c. 300 at Thessaloniki, illustrates the splendor of some of these tombs (Williams & Ogden 1994.74–79).
64. Macedonian tombs: see Miller 1982; Andronikos 1987. One tomb, at Katerini, may date before 350 (*AAA* 13 [1980] 198–209). Pella: *AR* 1994/95.47. Derveni: *AD* 18:3 (1963) 193–96. Sevasti gr. 3: *AD* 41:2 (1986) 144–45; *AEMTh* 1 (1987) 210–13.
65. Makaronas & Yiouri 1989.
66. Pella: Papakonstandinou-Diamandourou 1971; Petsas 1978; *AEMTh* 1 (1987) 119–36; 2 (1988) 101–12; 3 (1989) 59–70. Vergina: Andronikos et al. 1961; Andronikos 1984.38–46.
67. Thessaloniki: *AD* 40:2 (1985) 233–35; 41:2 (1986) 134–35; *AEMTh* 1 (1987) 235–45; 2 (1988) 243–55; 3 (1989) 215–25; 4 (1990) 298–314; 5 (1991) 191–207. Olynthos: Robinson & Graham 1938 (mosaics listed on 290); Robinson 1946; *AEMTh* 3 (1989) 339–50. Tragilos: *AD* 26:3 (1971) 417; 27:4 (1972) 532; 28:3 (1973) 452–54; cf. 40:2 (1985) 271. Mende: *AD* 41:2 (1986) 147–48; 42:3 (1987) 368–69; *AEMTh* 2 (1988) 331–45; 3 (1989) 410. At Abdera in Thrace, there is also a shift toward more elaborate houses in the fourth century: *Praktika* 1956.139; 1989.227–32; *AJA* 76 (1972) 295–301.
68. Explored most recently by Meyer 1993.
69. Generally on the Argive building program: Des Courtils 1992 ("programme": 244–47). Hypostyle building: Bommelaer & Des Courtils 1994. Theater: Moretti 1993.30–32. Seven Against Thebes monument: Pariente 1992. Pi-shaped portico: *BCH* 110 (1986) 763; 111 (1987) 590–91. Aphrodision temple: *BCH* 92 (1968)

1027–30; 93 (1969) 1003; 97 (1973) 476–81; 98 (1974) 759–63; 99 (1975) 696–99.

70. Des Courtils 1992.250–51; Bommelaer & Des Courtils 1994.47.
71. The new buildings in the Agora around 450 include the North Stoa and Painted Building, and outside the Agora, the New Temple at Isthmia and the Long Walls to Lecchaion. Later in the fifth century, the North Building and colonnade, possibly the theater, and the Centaur Bath (which may not have been public) were built, and the wall around the Potters' Quarter rebuilt. Around this time, the race track and wrestling area were laid out (see Salmon 1984.180–84 and n.41 above for full references).
72. Herman 1987; Morris 1996; Renfrew 1986.
73. I. Morris 1987; 1992.108–55; 1996; 1997b; 1997c; in preparation. Small 1997 suggests a very different approach to the tensions between elite panhellenism and lower-class localism; I respond in Morris 1997a.
74. Hölscher, this vol., at end of chap.

Chapter 5 Notes

1. All dates are B.C.E. except those to the eighteenth, nineteenth, and twentieth centuries.
2. Early democracies: Robinson 1997; O'Neil 1973; 1995.21–26; but see Raaflaub, this vol. Origins of democratic ideology: Morris 1996; Raaflaub 1996b.
3. Archaic warfare: Raaflaub 1985.82–92; 1990.516–31; 1994.127, with bibliog. Imperialism and democracy: Raaflaub 1994 (not discussing Western Greeks).
4. Stein-Hölkeskamp 1989.15–56.
5. For the socioeconomic roots of modern Western temporality: Thompson 1967; Zerubavel 1982; Le Goff 1989.29–57; Rotenberg 1992; P. Osborne 1995.34. For conflicts arising from the imposition of capitalist time-discipline in contemporary non-Western cultures, see, e.g., Burman 1981; Smith 1982; Cooper 1992. Evolutionist temporality is studied by Fabian 1983, *passim;* cf. P. Osborne 1995.15–18. The contemporary postmodern is characterized precisely by its rejection of modernist progressive time: see Vattimo 1988, esp. 95–107.
6. For the temporality of the evolutionary approach, see Fabian 1983, *passim.* Much of the nonclassicist literature is surveyed by Momigliano 1966; Starr 1966. Some of the greatest sins are committed by the periodizing tendencies of the recent constructivist rage for genealogies of modernity: see the comments of Golden & Toohey 1997.1–15, and Toohey 1997 on Foucault's modern time.
7. Evolutionary theories of time (*Geistesgeschichte*): Fränkel 1960.1–22; Onians 1954.411–15; Treu 1955, 1965; Accame 1961; Degani 1961; Thornton 1962; de Romilly 1968. Quotations: de Romilly 1968.2; Gellner 1964.11.
8. Bakhtin 1981; de Romilly 1968; Loraux 1986.143–44 and 129 (quotation).
9. Brecht 1964.182.
10. The French School: Gernet 1982b.121–56; Vidal-Naquet 1983.69–94; Vernant 1988.107–52, 1989.232–33; Detienne 1967; Loraux 1986. Trédé 1992 is also much

influenced by de Romilly. Vidal-Naquet is closest to the synchronic conception of van Groningen in opposing a "divine" to a "human" time; cf. Meritt 1928; Mikalson 1975. On structuralist temporality, see Bloch 1977 (quotation: 281); Fabian 1983.38–52; R. Osborne 1995.27–28.

11. Loraux 1986.119.
12. Van Groningen 1953.93–108 (quotations: 107).
13. Meier 1980.420–21; 1990b.218.
14. Rutz 1992.2; the basic study of the heterogeneity of social time is Gurvitch 1963.326–430; 1964.
15. Mannheim 1936, esp. 1–8 (quotations: 6, 7). Unfortunately, Mannheim's theory of ideology fails precisely in its grasp of the power-function of ideas. See Eagleton 1991.109.
16. Philippson 1944.7; van Groningen 1953.81.
17. Gomme, Dover, & Andrewes 1945–81.4:246. On family tradition and genealogy: Thomas 1989, esp. 95–195 (quotation: 117); note also 107: "The recent past was . . . neglected . . . The Greek aristocrat derived more prestige from his legendary past"; 159: "Most aristocratic traditions probably knew only of the recent generations of the family and the distant legendary generation." Timeless present: van Groningen 1953.69, with references. Time in Pindar: see esp. Hurst 1983, 1985 (whence the terms). Alkibiades: for the same sentiment, cf. Thuc. 2.11.9 (the Spartan king Archidamos); Lykourgos, *Against Leokrates* 110 (ancestral glory of the Athenian demos; cf. Lysias 2.69). It is an exaggerated form of "the victor granting glory to his parents" (Hesiod, *Theogony* 438). Trade organization: Burkert 1992b.43–46. Poetic "guilds": Nagy 1990.22–23. Tributary Mode: Rotenberg 1992.24–27 (quotations: 24, 27). Zigzagging time through naming is discussed by Leach 1961.131.
18. Gernet 1968 (1982a).120–79. Such mystifying distinctions were necessary precisely because the aristocracy took an aggressive role in the development of Archaic trade: see Stein-Hölkeskamp 1989.76–81.
19. Ortega y Gasset cited (by name only) by Mann 1937.34, whence Kerényi 1940.22–23; Jung & Kerényi 1969.4.
20. Van Groningen 1953.26, 63, 85 (quotations: 76, 31).
21. For the temporality of Archaic lyric, see esp. Fränkel 1960.1–22; 1973.133–40; Detienne 1967.81, 93–94; Vernant 1988.128–29; 1989.223–24. On fourth-century democracy: the usual view, that Athenian democracy became less democratic both in structure and in practice (argued, e.g., by Hansen 1991), has been challenged by Eder 1995a, and by others in Eder 1995b, *passim*. But the contributors to Eder 1995b also generally agree that Athenian society was less polarized in the fourth century.
22. Meier 1975; 1990b.181–206.
23. On the Athenian fetish for novelty, see especially Meier 1990b.193–204; de Romilly 1956. Military innovations: e.g., Thuc. 6.18.6–7, 6.36.3, 8.96.5 (beginning perhaps with the "mad" but successful running charge at Marathon so prominent in

Herodotus' account [6.112]). For Spartan conservatism in literature and music: Plato, *Hippias Maior* 285d–e; Timotheos, *Persians* (*PMG* fr. 791.206–12 [with Zimmermann 1992.124, n.19]); Cicero, *Laws* 2.39; Plutarch, *Agis* 10.6; *Spartan Customs* 17; *Progress in Virtue (Quomodo in virtute)* 84a; *Spartan Sayings* 220c; Pausanias 3.12.9–10; Athenaeus 632–33, 628b, 636e; Clement of Alexandria, *Stromateis* 1.308; Boethius, *Institutio musica* 1.1 (containing the "Spartan decree"); see also the discussions by Marzi 1988 (with the comments by A. Cassio in Gentili & Prestagostini 1988.286); Gostoli 1988; Csapo forthcoming. On Plato's treatment of the navy in *Laws*, cf. Strauss 1996.318–19.

24. For innovationism in the political theater, see Meier 1990b.194–96. Rhetorical appeals to novelty: e.g., Xenophon, *Memorabilia* 4.4.6; Theophrastus, *Characters* 8.2–3, and, in comedy, Aristoph. *Wasps* 527–28; *Clouds* 1031, 1397; *Birds* 256–57.
25. For old vs. new in Aristophanes, see especially *Clouds* 398, 479–80, 821, 896, 914, 929, 935–1023, 1356–79, 1421–29, 1468. Aristophanes on his own novelty: *Clouds* 547; *Wasps* 57–63, 66, 1044, 1536; *Lysistrata* 1217, with schol.; *Frogs* 1–20. Zimmermann 1993.270 refers to this as the "Aristophanic paradox," but it was probably common to most comic poets; cf. Pherekrates, *PCG* F 84; Lysippos, *PCG* F 4; Metagenes, *PCG* F 15; Xenarchos, *PCG* F 7. Other culture heroes boasting of their innovativeness: Hippias, in Xenophon, *Memorabilia* 4.4.7; Timotheos, *PMG* 791.202; cf. Isokrates, *Antidosis* 82; Theophrastus, *Characters* 1–3; and the complaint that there is no room for innovation in epic by Choirilos of Samos (*Supp. Hell.* 317). In this context note McDermott 1989, who argues that Euripides calls attention to his innovations by the use of the adjective *kainos*. Hölscher 1974 studies the novelty requirement in the arts in the late fifth century.
26. Cf. Detienne 1967, esp. 81; Bakhtin 1981, esp. 30. For ancient empiricism: Fränkel 1973.325–98.
27. Gernet 1982b.7–119 (quotations: 95, 131–32, 110).
28. Agonistic culture: Burckhardt 1963.53–56; Poliakoff 1987.104–15. Verbal *agōn* in general: Froleyks 1973; in sophistic: Buchheim 1986.12–18. *Kairos:* Trédé 1992, esp. 45–73 (quotation: 48), 191–244; Buchheim 1986.82–85, 97–99; Detienne & Vernant 1974; van Groningen 1953.2; Detienne 1967.119–23 (quotation: 119).
29. Trédé 1992.51–52, 69–70, 76–80. Lysippos' statue: Overbeck 1868, nos.1463–67; Stewart 1978.163–67 (copies referred to in n.3 and illustrated in fig. 1 and ill. 1).
30. Iconic: our term, in response to Meyboom 1978.57 (though we reject his claim that a scene shows narrative only if it signifies to a viewer not previously cognizant of the story). Timeless quality of the kouros*:* Brommer 1969.16; a smiting god, scribe, horseman, *korē*, or sphinx could equally be cited. Monoscenic: Snodgrass 1982b.5 (quotation); Weitzmann 1947.14–17 (term), also called "isolated" (Wickhoff 1895.9), "closed" (Himmelmann 1967.13–15, 28–29); Moret 1984.57–58. From the early classical period, many "single" standing figures could be described as monoscenic as they indicate action: Brommer 1969.10–13.
31. Synoptic: Hemelrijk 1970 (term), also known as "complementary" (Wickhoff

1895.8–9), "completive" (Robert 1919 *passim*; cf. 1881.14–20), and "simultaneous" (Weitzmann 1947.13–14; Himmelmann 1967.6–11; Snodgrass 1982b.10–23; Boardman 1990.59 [dates start to eighth century]). Progressive: Harrison 1972 (from Weitzmann 1947.12); cf. Neils 1995.434–36. Marathonomachy: Hölscher 1973.62–68, 78–84. Parthenon: Hanfmann 1957.76; Boardman 1990.59; Stewart 1990.156 (though stressing space, not time; with references); see also Maurizio, this vol.

32. Cyclic: Robert 1881.46; Hanfmann 1957.73 (defines); Weitzmann 1947.22–23; Meyboom 1978.71; Dasen 1983.64 (contrast the Olympia metopes). We might include here the new episodic treatment of the scenes of the sack of Troy. Phased (a kind of "protocontinuous"; see Froning 1988): examples in Robert 1881.29–30; Meyboom 1978.62; Shapiro 1994a.28–37. Other experiments: Shapiro 1992b; Hurwit 1985.172–74; Steiner 1993. Continuous: Wickhoff 1895.9; Meyboom 1978.64–67; Brilliant 1984; Snodgrass 1987.142–46; Boardman 1990.59–61.
33. Brommer 1969.18–27; see also Moret 1984.57–61.
34. *Synkrisis:* Goethe & Schiller 1953.249. Concept of *mimesis* governing the epic tradition: Nagy 1996.2–23 (quotation), 55–56, 60–61; cf. Nagy 1990.373–74. Medium: Nagy 1990.52–81 (55: "ideology of fixity"); Detienne 1967; Vernant 1988.109–36; Rösler 1980a.289–93. Subject matter, in general: Vernant & Vidal-Naquet 1972.13–17; anachronism: Easterling 1985, 1994; Croally 1994.207–34; Neumann 1995; cf. Zeitlin 1994.144–45. Form: de Romilly 1968; Vidal-Naquet 1983.76–77; Lanza 1988.26–27; Henrichs 1994–95.72, n.73. Reception: Taplin 1983; for the "teachings" of comedy, cf. Bremer 1993.127–34; Carey 1994.
35. Ionian historians: Moggi 1972, 1977; Drews 1973. The importance of the contemporary in Herodotus' *Histories*: Raaflaub 1987 (quotation: 230). For historical vs. mythical time in Herodotus, see Vidal-Naquet 1983.81. Thucydides quotation based on Crawley's translation; Finley 1975.31.
36. Epic chronology: Fränkel 1960.1 (whence the "fully indifferent"); van Groningen 1953.96–97. Historical chronologies: den Boer 1967; Finley 1975.14–18. Causality: Finley 1975.30. Utility of history: see esp. Meier 1987b; Raaflaub 1987 (both primarily concerned with Herodotus); Trédé 1992.205–30. Thucydides against epic: Thuc. 1.22, cf. 3.82; Vidal-Naquet 1983.83. Thucydides' "logical time": de Romilly 1956; Meyerson 1956.340; Vidal-Naquet 1983.83 (after Goldschmidt 1970.13–21); Vernant 1988.53. Final quotation: Meier 1990b.198. See also Boedeker, this vol.
37. This follows from the self-definition of the Greek aristocrat himself, nicely summed up in an illuminating unpublished lecture by W. J. Slater: "What is an aristocrat is a question that only, so far as I see, has an answer after about 520. An aristocrat is someone who knows *ta kala* and is capable of realizing *ta kala*."
38. Zimmermann 1992.35–38.
39. Kouros interpretations: e.g., Ducat 1976; Freyer-Schauenburg 1974.8–10; Ridgway 1977.49–59; 1990; Lullies 1979.16; Kyrieleis 1986.35–41; ideological structures: Zinserling 1975; Stewart 1986; 1990.109–10; Steuernagel 1991; Metzler 1992; cf.

Schneider 1975 on korai. Occasional exceptions to the rule of invariability: the late bearded kouros, ca. 500 (Akropolis Mus. 621; Brouskari 1974, fig. 180), the Moschophoros. Stelai: Schmaltz 1983.160, 167–70; Richter 1961. Votives: e.g., Penteskouphia plaques; cf. Geagan 1970.

40. Kouroi as athletes: Sinn 1989, with references; Pausanias' is an Olympic victor of the mid-sixth century. First Tyrannicides: Robertson, cited by Ridgway 1970.82, n.2; Dörig 1969 associates the Webb head. Second Tyrannicides: Brunnsåker 1971. But see Hölscher, this vol. First official portrait tradition: Demosth. 20.70; Pliny, *Natural History* 34.17. Toddlers: Shapiro, this vol.

41. Iconographic interest in professions: e.g., potter on votive relief, Athens, Akropolis Mus. 1332, 510 (Brouskari 1974, fig. 251); cobbler's shop and forge on unattributed Attic black-fig. amphora, 520–510, Boston MFA 01.8035; cf. Tanagra terracottas: Higgins 1986.84–90. In ethnicity, sixth century: Scythians (problematic; see Raeck 1981.10–66; Pinney 1983); Memnon (by means of companion only): London 1849.5–18.10 (B209), Attic black-fig. amphora, ca. 540, Exekias (Beazley 1956.144.8); cf. Miller forthcoming, chap. 6. In fifth century: Mikon's Marathonomachy (Hölscher 1973.78–84), also vases (Raeck 1981 for Persians, Blacks, and Thracians). Linguistic characterization of barbarians: in tragedy, Hall 1989.117–21; in comedy, Friedrich 1918; del Grande 1936.135–40; Dover 1976.359–62; Long 1986.133–37; in Euripides' *Orestes* and Timotheos' *Persians*, Porter 1994.204–7. It is interesting to note that linguistic characterization by social status remains fairly rudimentary in Old Comedy (basically concerned with the contrast of free and slave, educated and uneducated, and urban and rural), as Dover 1976.362–71 shows; in New Comedy, by contrast, characterization of social status by language can be quite sophisticated (and adds a particular concern to distinguish the leisure-class elite from the working classes and the urban poor): see esp. Sandbach 1970. Status distinction in vase painting, sixth century: Himmelmann 1971 (earlier, by scale and physique); Boardman 1974.212; 1975.221 (by profession, late sixth/early fifth); Boardman 1975.218–19, 220 (by elite activity, late sixth/early fifth). In fifth century: McNiven 1995 (esp. physique); Miller 1997.153–215 (by dress, activity); e.g., also Berlin 2294, red-fig. cup, ca. 480, Foundry Painter, Beazley 1963.400.1 (by scale, stance, dress); Boston MFA 10.185, red-fig. pelike, side A, ca. 460, Pan Painter, Beazley 1963.550.1 (by dress).

42. Zeitlin 1970.646 ("irrelevant distractions"); Gellie 1963.253; Will 1960.340; Garton 1957.253. For production of "reality effects" through contingent particulars in modern realist fiction, see Barthes 1984.167–74.

43. Elite in red fig.: cf. Boardman 1975.218–19, 220 (especially Pioneers and late Archaic painters). Historical art: Hölscher 1973; Schauenburg 1975, both with references. Croesus: Attic red-fig. belly amphora, Louvre G 197, Myson, ca. 490 (Beazley 1963.238.1). Nike Temple south frieze: Harrison 1972; cf. Hölscher, this vol. Lyric: Boedeker, this vol. and 1995.

44. Genette 1972.79, 115; Rimmon-Kenan 1983.43–48.

45. Increase of suspense narrative in tragedy: noticed already by Lessing 1769, §48–49. See Petersen 1915, esp. 423–24; Arnott 1973; Hamilton 1978; Segal 1992; on *Orestes,* Porter 1994.208–13. Birth of fiction: Rösler 1980a, who sees it as a moment in the history of technology (literacy), which, to our minds, puts the emphasis in the wrong place. Fourth-century tragedy continued to depart from traditional myth: Wallace 1995.208.
46. Persian war heroes commemorated: Breckenridge 1968.86–90. Xenophantos' aryballos: St. Petersburg St. 1790, Beazley 1963.1407.1.
47. It is uncertain whether the scene at Oenoe painted in the Stoa Poikile refers to a historical or a mythical battle: see Jeffery 1965; Francis & Vickers 1985; Castriota 1992.78–79; Hölscher, this vol.; Boedeker, this vol.
48. Simonides: Boedeker 1995, 1996. Quotations: Thomas 1989.108; Loraux 1986.122; Ober 1989.320.
49. On the ideological exclusion of the thetic class: Raaflaub 1994.140–44. For Greeks fighting Persians in Athenian art: Miller forthcoming, chap. 6. Parthenon frieze: Maurizio, this vol.; Spivey 1996.144–48 (recent summary of problems of interpretation).
50. Degani 1993.4; Bakhtin 1981.19; Auerbach 1968.38–39.
51. See in general Watt 1960; Bakhtin 1981.3–40, 84–258; Sartre 1948.112–18, 132–37. The visual arts were a primary locus for the debate on particularism: see esp. Carr 1980.376 (cf. Mitchell 1986.107). On proleptic narrative: van Groningen 1953.42; Genette 1972.105, cf. 231. Abandonment of genre archetypes: Sartre 1948.132; Williams 1977.180–82; Mitchell 1986.109–12. Novelistic time-consciousness: Watt 1960.21–25; Bakhtin 1981.3–40, 84–258; Forster 1927, esp. 28–42 (quotation: 28); Muir 1957.62–87; Mendilow 1972; Tobin 1978; Kort 1985.
52. Shaftesbury's *Essay on Freedom of Wit* (1709) and Berkeley's *Philonous* (1713), cited by Watt 1960.15.
53. Mannheim 1927.98–99; Koselleck 1979.
54. Fourth-century "classicism": see most recently Seidensticker 1995.195–97. References: Bakhtin 1981, esp. 104, 110, 132; Meier 1975; 1990b.157–85. Quotations: Meier 1990b.159, 180, 181.
55. Koselleck 1979; Davies 1995.35; Meier 1990b.240, 205. On "modern" temporality, see esp. Vattimo 1988.
56. Democracy's heroic age: Ober 1989.263–64. Slaves and metics: Raaflaub, this vol. Democracy as birth elite: Ober 1989.81, 259–66. On the close connection in thought between freedom and rule over others (cf. Thuc. 3.45.6): Raaflaub 1985.233–48; de Romilly 1947.74–75.

Chapter 6 Notes

1. A few recent surveys: for architecture, Rhodes 1995; for sculpture, Stewart 1990, chaps. 11–14; for vase painting, M. Robertson 1992.
2. The fullest recent exposition of this approach to Athenian classical art is that of Cas-

triota 1992. Knell 1990 also explores this issue, specifically in relation to temple sculpture.

3. The epigraphical evidence for these dedications is collected by Raubitschek 1949. For the surviving sculpture see Payne & Young 1936; Brouskari 1974.
4. Typical of the early classical period is the under life-size marble Athena (77 cm) dedicated by Angelitos: Ridgway 1970.29–31 and pl. 39.
5. The portraits of Xanthippos and Anakreon were seen by Pausanias (1.25.1) near one another on the Akropolis, though if he saw an inscription naming the sculptor or the dedicator, he does not mention them. For the suggestion that Perikles and his circle were directly responsible for these dedications, see Hafner 1956.2–3; Hölscher 1988.379. If Perikles could not advertise his role in setting up honorary portraits, including that of his own father, then this was no doubt for the same reason that Hölscher (1988.380) adduces to explain why the statue of Perikles himself was set up at some distance from that of Xanthippos: to avoid the impression of a family dynasty, which would have been politically unacceptable in democratic Athens.
6. Pausanias 1.28. Cf. Gauer 1968b.103–5; Höcker & Schneider 1993.58–60. See also Kallet, this vol.
7. On the end of elaborate grave monuments in Attika shortly after 490, see Hölscher, this vol.; Morris 1992/93.38–44. I agree with Hölscher's view that the phenomenon can be better explained as a response to social pressure to limit ostentatious display under the democracy than as the result of a sumptuary law, for which the evidence is weak.
8. Clairmont 1983.13. The site has still not been precisely identified: cf. Knigge 1988.11, 158–59. For the casualty lists see Bradeen 1964.
9. See Clairmont 1986; Mikalson 1984.
10. See Shapiro 1989.21–24. For the seventh-century predecessor, see Nylander 1962.
11. Mark 1993.21–35.
12. The earlier view, fully argued by Dinsmoor 1947, that a large early Archaic temple (the "Hekatompedon") stood on the site of the later Parthenon, has now been revived by Greek archaeologists working on the restoration of the Akropolis: cf. *Bulletin de correspondance hellénique* 118 (1994) 698–99. It seems to me that the archaeological evidence is still not sufficient to allow certainty one way or another.
13. These poros pediments are conveniently surveyed by Boardman 1978.153–55 and figs. 190–98. Cf. Knell 1990.1–9.
14. For the dating of this pediment in the last decade of the sixth century, see, e.g., Childs 1994. The earlier dating of ca. 520 has again been revived by Knell 1990.39–42; Croissant 1993.
15. See Pinney 1988.
16. Those dedicated on the Akropolis are catalogued by Graef & Langlotz 1925–33. Other sanctuaries yielding large amounts of Attic pottery include Eleusis and Brauron.
17. See Pemberton 1988.

18. The most recent detailed examinations of these paintings include Castriota 1992, chaps. 2–3; Stähler 1992.31–52.
19. See Hölscher 1973.50–68.
20. For recent discussions of the reshaping of the Agora with the advent of the democracy, see von Steuben 1989; Hölscher 1991; Hoepfner 1994; Shear 1994; Miller 1995.
21. Vase painting, in particular, could be expected to reflect democratic institutions, if at all, only indirectly, in mythological guise. For one example, the adaptation of voting practices of the early democracy to the episode of the Arms of Achilles, see Spivey 1994.
22. For the personification of the Athenian demos on document reliefs of the late fifth century, see Lawton 1993; Tzachou-Alexandri 1993; and Meyer 1988.190–94 and *passim*. For the well-known relief in the Louvre containing the accounts of the Treasurers of Athena for 410/09 and a figure who may be Demos, see Kron 1976.209–10. For "political personifications" (e.g., Eunomia) in late-fifth-century vase painting see Metzler 1980; Shapiro 1993.79–85 and *passim*.
23. Thompson & Wycherley 1972.40; Mattusch 1994.
24. Cf. Stähler 1992.75–84; Harrison 1997. Perhaps the most explicit monument of the Athenian Empire is the Athena Lemnia, which celebrated Perikles' policy of establishing cleruchies of Athenian citizens throughout the Aegean. See Hölscher 1988.381.
25. Another exception is, of course, the Parthenon frieze, which I would describe as showing the "mythic present," i.e., a real-life event (the Panathenaic procession) in an idealized form and without any explicit reference to a specific historical period. See in particular the discussion of the frieze, and the values it expresses, by Harrison 1989.49–55, who comments that a "contradiction between democracy and imperialism did not exist in ancient Athens" (55). Cf. below n.94 and Maurizio, this vol.
26. See Taylor 1991; Hölscher 1991.371 and this vol.
27. Rosivach 1987.297, 301. For the occurrences of the word in fifth-century literature, see also Montanari 1981.3–35. He suggests that the first occurrence is in Aeschylus, *Agamemnon* 536, but the title of a work by Pherekydes, *Autochthones* (*FGrH* 3 T2) may well be earlier. Also, while neither the Aeschylean passage nor any of the nine occurrences in Herodotus refer to the Athenians, Pherekydes, who was known for his Athenian genealogies, could well have used the word in an Athenian context.
28. Rosivach 1987.301. Cf. S. Morris 1992.329 for the interesting suggestion that the theme of autochthony was particularly stressed after 480 as a form of compensation for the psychological trauma caused by the evacuation of the city in that year.
29. For the motif of autochthony in Athenian literature, see esp. Montanari 1981; Loraux 1993. Cf. also Loraux 1979; 1986.148–51. Montanari 1981.54–57 argues that the crucial period in the formation of the ideology of autochthony was before the Persian Wars, in the time of the Kleisthenic reforms.
30. For the genealogies, see Shapiro 1983 (Peisistratidai); Thomas 1989.161–73 (Philaidai).

31. See Prinz 1979.325–30.
32. In the *Suppliants* of Euripides. The same story had been staged earlier, in Aeschylus' *Eleusinioi:* Rosivach 1987.304.
33. For the latter story, as portrayed in Euripides' *Medea*, see Sfyroeras 1995. For a more "historical" example of this tradition, see Her. 6.90 on the Athenians giving refuge at Sounion to a group of Aeginetans around the time of the Persian Wars.
34. See Vian 1963. Luginbühl 1992.100–129 surveys the Greek myths of autochthony.
35. The contrast between Athenians and Spartans may not have been made explicit until the fourth century (e.g., Isokrates 4.63), but is probably implicit in texts from the time of the Peloponnesian War, such as the speech of Praxithea cited below at n.92. Thucydides does not use the word *autochthōn.*
36. See Connor 1994.
37. See recently Boegehold 1994. On autochthony and superiority, see Rosivach 1987.302. The earliest expression of this idea is in Her. 7.161.3, supposedly in 480.
38. Akropolis 585a+b; Beazley 1956.40, nos.17, 18; Bakir 1981.26, figs. 17–19 and pls. 35, 36. Figure 1 here is 585a.
39. Beazley 1956.40. For the attribution of the two fragments to the same vase, not recognized by Beazley, see Bakir 1981.26. On Aglauros, Pandrosos, and Herse, see Boedeker 1984, chap. 5.
40. Dontas 1983.
41. Cf. the story in Polyainos 1.21.2, that Peisistratos, when he disarmed the Athenians, had their weapons brought into the Aglaureion. For the variant traditions see Shear 1994.227 and n.9. Another black-figure fragment of the early sixth century found on the Akropolis may be inscribed with the name of Aglauros: Graef & Langlotz 1925–33, vol.1, pl. 48, no.780.
42. Kiilerich 1989. For fuller discussion of the cults and imagery of the Daughters of Kekrops, see Shapiro 1995b.
43. See Brommer 1957.161.
44. See below at n.95.
45. I use the two names, following the convention that Erichthonios designates the newborn child and little boy (and is first attested on the Kodros Painter's cup of the 430s, fig. 5), while Erechtheus refers to the king. See Kron 1976.37–38; Parker 1987.200–210; and Mikalson 1976.141–42, who shows that the name Erichthonios was probably not well established until well into the fourth century.
46. Kron 1976.55–64. Cf. also Kron in *LIMC* I, *s.v.* Aglauros, Herse, Pandrosos, 283–98; *LIMC* IV, *s.v.* Erechtheus, 923–51; and *LIMC* VI, *s.v.* Kekrops, 1084–91. Other surveys and discussions of the iconography of the birth of Erichthonios may be found in Bérard 1974.34–38; Brulé 1987.18–58; Cook 1940.181–88; Loeb 1979.165–84; Metzger 1976; Reeder 1995.250–66. On the sources and interpretation of the myth, see Powell 1906 and, recently, Baudy 1992.
47. Loraux 1993.62.
48. See also Brulé 1987.56.

49. For some examples of the earliest realistic-looking babies, in the last quarter of the fifth century, see, e.g., Lezzi-Hafter 1988, pl. 157f.; Burn 1987, pl. 35.
50. Akr. 433; Beazley 1942.216, no.19 (not in Beazley 1963); Kron 1976.74–75. Cf. the even better known red-figure cup Akropolis 396, showing Athena with the boy Erichthonios sipping from a phial: Beazley 1942.628, no.1 (not in Beazley 1963); Kron 1976.73–74.
51. Cf. S. Morris 1992.328, who would lower the dating of this cup to after 480.
52. On Ge Kourotrophos see Hadzisteliou-Price 1978.104–9. A sacrificial calendar of the fifth century associates Ge Kourotrophos with Zeus Polieus and Erechtheus: Kron 1976.47. A somewhat later inscription (*IG* II/III[2] 1039) records that the Athenian ephebes sacrificed to Athena, Pandrosos, and Ge Kourotrophos. Furthermore, Erechtheus himself was later said to have founded the cult of Ge Kourotrophos on the Akropolis: Suda, *s.v. kourotrophos.*
53. Loraux 1993.64. That the story of Erichthonios' conception, resulting from Hephaistos' amorous pursuit of Athena, was known in Athens by the mid-fifth century is suggested by a single representation of the pursuit, on a red-figure Nolan amphora, Bologna 158; Beazley 1963.636, no.19; fig. 7. Surprisingly, the subject is first attested on a non-Athenian monument, the Lakonian Throne of Amyklai (Paus. 3.18.13). According to Harpokration, *s.v. autochthones,* both Pindar and the author of a lost *Danais* told of Hephaistos being the father of Erechtheus.
54. Boedeker 1984.111.
55. I borrow the description from Harrison 1977a.411. Cf. Lévêque 1992; Neils 1983, who characterizes the birth of Erichthonios as a "Greek nativity." In scenes such as that on the Munich stamnos (fig. 3), Hephaistos seems to me deeply involved in the moment of birth and not, as Lévêque 1992.319, believes, "lointain et indifférent."
56. On this relationship, see most recently Shapiro 1995a.13–14.
57. Harrison 1977a.137–78.
58. S. Morris 1992.330; Hurwit 1995.181–84.
59. Kron 1976.56 and pl. 1.
60. See Kaempf-Dimitriadou 1979.34, 38.
61. Cf. Harrison 1979; Kron 1976.101–2, 261; and add two important new vases: the ram's head rhyton (Richmond, Virginia Museum of Fine Arts, 1979.100 [fig. 8]; Guy 1983) which shows a gathering of Athenian heroes as symposiasts, including Kekrops, Pandion, Theseus (all labelled), and two others; and the cup Malibu 84.AE.569 (*LIMC* VI, *s.v.* Kekrops, 1087, no.23) with Kekrops and Pandion (both labelled) and a third king witnessing the abduction of Kephalos by Eos.
62. On the different versions, see Schmidt 1968.202.
63. See below at n.95.
64. The earliest example of the combination is the pelike Leipzig T 654; Beazley 1963.585, no.35; figs. 9, 10. The earliest scene clearly showing the Daughters of Kekrops actually present at the birth of Erichthonios is on the Kodros Painter's cup (figs. 5, 6).

65. On the representations of the basket and its lid see Oakley 1982.
66. Kron 1976.59.
67. Burkert 1966, elaborated by Schmidt 1968.203; Boedeker 1984, chap. 5, and challenged by N. Robertson 1983.
68. London E 182; Beazley 1963.580, above, no.2. On the ritual nature of the embroidered cloth in which Athena receives the baby here, see Simon 1959.51.
69. See Simon 1978.1423.
70. For additional illustrations of the rhyton London E 788 (Beazley 1963.764, no.8) and the interpretation as a celebration of the birth of Erichthonios, see Shapiro 1995b.45.
71. Cf. Kron 1976.59–60.
72. On the "timeless" quality of early Attic heroes, which made it difficult to establish anything like an ordered genealogy, see Kearns 1989.110.
73. Schloss Fasanerie 77; Beazley 1963.1346, no.1.
74. Simon & Hirmer 1976.152–53. Cf. Jeppesen 1987.46–52; 1988. The kingly figure with scepter seated at the lower left is surely Zeus, as Simon argues (and as anticipated by the hydria in London, fig. 11), and not Erechtheus, as Jeppeson 1988 believes, following Brommer 1956.34. The only truly enigmatic figure is the woman seated behind Athena and holding the latter's helmet and shield. She cannot be a second Athena (e.g., Athena Nike), as argued by Jeppesen 1987.49–51, for the vase painters never show two versions of the same divinity in such proximity. Simon's suggestion of Zeuxippe (Simon & Hirmer 1976.153), ancestress of the Eteobutadai, who furnished the priest and priestess in the Erechtheion, is rather abstruse in this company of major gods and goddesses. Now that we have good evidence for Aphrodite at the birth of Erichthonios, on the contemporary krater by the Nikias Painter (fig. 14), we should consider this identification also for the figure on the Adolphseck krater. The crossed straps at her breasts, which Simon took as attributes of the charioteer, are a fashion worn by several goddesses in this period: see Harrison 1977b.155–56.
75. For the cult of Poseidon in the Erechtheion, see Travlos 1971.218 (B on the plan).
76. See Frazer 1969.264 for the suggestion that the divinity referred to at *Iliad* 2.550 is Poseidon-Erechtheus; but cf. also below at n.101 and Lacore 1983, who argues that the fusing of Poseidon and Erechtheus is an invention of Euripides (*Erechtheus* fr. 65.93–94). A possible argument for the early association of the two is the suggestion of Papachatzis 1989.175, that the etymology of Erechtheus' name (from *erechthōn*, "rending the earth") recalls Poseidon's epithet *enosichthōn* (earth-shaker).
77. Richmond, Virginia Museum of Fine Arts, 81.70; Oakley 1987.
78. On the cult, see Simon 1970; Pirenne-Delforge 1994.26–34. There may also be a reference to the sanctuary of Aphrodite on the north slope of the Akropolis, to which the Arrhephoroi carried the mystic chest: Paus. 1.27.3.
79. On the centrality of the theme of autochthony to this entire play, see Loraux 1993.184–236; Saxonhouse 1992.76–89. As the child of Erechtheus' daughter, Ion in

a sense inherits the autochthony of the Athenian royal house. Though Ion's birth was not autochthonous, it did take place in a cave of the Akropolis, and parallels between him and Erechtheus are drawn throughout the play.

80. See Kaspar-Butz 1990.185–87.
81. Moret 1982.
82. Burn 1987, chap. 2.
83. Cleveland 82.142; Neils 1983. The second uninscribed vase is the squat-lekythos Athens A21903; Beazley 1963.1314, no.15; Kokkorou-Alevra 1988. If this vase does depict Erichthonios, as I believe, then it is a slightly later moment in the story, since the baby is not being handed up by Ge to Athena, but is already held by one of her attendants (a Kekropid?).
84. So Neils 1983.282–83.
85. Athens, Archaeological Collection A8922; *Archaiologikon. Deltion* 31 (1976) B 1 pl. 35 and p. 30 for the inscriptions. Aside from a partial illustration, the vase remains unpublished.
86. On these personifications, see Shapiro 1993.37–38; Parker 1987.196. On the concept of *sōtēria,* see also Kearns 1989.324. On the question of whether Basile and Basileia represent the same or different figures, see Burn 1989.66–67.
87. For the latter see Boersma 1970.171.
88. An old theory proposed the birth of Erichthonios as the subject of the East Pediment of the Hephaisteion: Sauer 1899.51–72. But there is little evidence to support this: cf. Thompson 1949.243–46.
89. Harrison 1977a.265–87; Papaspyridi-Karusu 1954–55.
90. Boulter 1970.14, n.37. This theory was fully argued by Pallat 1937. But cf. Felten 1984.112–17, who rejects all mythological narrative interpretations and argues instead for a festival procession (as on the Parthenon Frieze), that of the Skirophoria.
91. Harrison 1977a.281, n.59. On Ion's tent see Zeitlin 1994.147–56.
92. For the sources on the war between Erechtheus and Eumolpos see Kearns 1989.113–15; S. Morris 1992.322. The central importance of the story for classical Athens is suggested by a statue group on the Akropolis showing Erechtheus and the defeated Eumolpos (Paus. 1.27.4). If the association of this monument with the sculptor Myron is correct (Paus. 9.30.1), then it should belong to the second quarter of the fifth century. Cf. Hölscher 1969.418, 425 and *Bulletin de correspondance hellénique* 118 (1994) 698 for the recent discovery of blocks belonging to this monument. For the suggested identification of Erechtheus and either Eumolpos or his son Immarados on Parthenon South Metope XVI, see Brommer 1967.101–2 and pls. 202, 203.
93. Cf. Simon, in *LIMC* V 702–4, with an attempt to identify Ion on the Parthenon West Pediment.
94. For the dating of the play to 422, see Calder 1969 and, for its topicality, Treu 1971. For the interpretation of the West Pediment as referring to the war between Erechtheus and Eumolpos, see Weidauer 1985.203–7; Spaeth 1991; for the Frieze, see Connelly 1996, suggesting that the East Frieze shows the sacrifice of the Daugh-

ters of Erechtheus. Earlier, Weidauer & Krauskopf 1992.14 had proposed that this sacrifice is alluded to on the West Pediment. A still earlier mythological reading of the East Frieze, by Kardara 1966, also connected it with the family of Erechtheus. But instead of the sacrifice of the Daughters, she saw the scene as the child Erichthonios giving the first peplos to Kekrops, in his guise as priest of Athena, at the founding of the Great Panathenaia. For the suggestion that the sacrifice of the Daughters of Erechtheus might be depicted on the frieze of the Erechtheion, see Boulter 1970.18, n.50.

95. See Wilamowitz 1926.2–9; Saxonhouse 1992.80; Dougherty 1996; but cf. Gantz 1993.244–45, who is more cautious. The unexpected presentation of Apollo as Ion's "real" father (rather than Xouthos) was probably not as jarring to the Athenian audience as we may think. As Erika Simon pointed out in discussion, several heroes, e.g., Herakles and Theseus, have two fathers, one mortal and one immortal.
96. Cf. the peculiar attempt of Dörig 1985.72–73 to recognize the war between Erechtheus and Eumolpos on the East Frieze of the Hephaisteion, with the further suggestion that this frieze inspired Euripides in shaping the material for his play. For the suggestion that this war is the subject of one or more of the friezes of the Nike Temple, see Hölscher 1973.92.
97. Above n.58. Cf. also Loraux 1993.10, 114–15.
98. For the sources see Palagia 1992.40.
99. Palagia 1992.42; Weidauer & Krauskopf 1992.
100. On Kekrops as *heros archēgetēs* and the traditions surrounding him, see Kearns 1989.113.
101. In an alternative version (Vergil, *Georgics* 1.12–14) Poseidon's gift was the horse. The place where Poseidon's trident struck the earth to produce the salt spring was visible in the Erechtheion: Travlos 1971.218 (H on the plan).
102. On this story, preserved in Augustine, *De civitate Dei* 18.9.1, see Tyrrell 1984.28–31; for the suggestion that the West Pediment explicitly alludes to this version, Castriota 1995. In other respects, too, women do not fare well within the ideology of autochthony. Their role in giving birth is entirely bypassed, and in the case of both Kekrops and Erechtheus, daughters serve a useful purpose only as sacrificial virgins. On the implications of autochthony for relations between the sexes see most fully Loraux 1993.17 and *passim*.
103. Palagia 1992.44–48.
104. Delivorrias 1987.204–5; cf. Weidauer & Krauskopf 1992.5, with n.17. As they show (p. 8), the connection between the contest of Athena and Poseidon and the war of Erechtheus against Eumolpos was made explicit on the Pella hydria and was probably implicit on the West Pediment. Cf. also Spaeth 1991.343.
105. Simon 1980.246–48.
106. E.g., at Euripides, *Suppliants* 403–8.
107. For Theseus and the Amazon invasion, see Tyrrell 1984.9–22. On Theseus as an emblem of Athenian imperialism, see Shapiro 1992c; Calame 1990 (1996); Mills 1997.

108. Cf. Loraux 1993.48, who sees the relationship rather in terms of a rivalry between Theseus and Erechtheus, the one responsible for the synoicism, the other the founding king. I would see it more as a complementary relationship.
109. See Mikalson 1976.
110. Calyx-krater, Bologna 303; Beazley 1963.1184–85, no.6. The date is ca. 410–400.
111. Brommer 1956.36–37 and pls. 49, 50.
112. Harrison 1966.129–32, arguing that these figures bring the Amazonomachy on the shield into line with the emphasis on the theme of autochthony in the West Pediment. For Kekrops' role on the shield, see Stephanidou-Tiveriou 1987.
113. Loraux 1993.38.
114. See Boedeker, this vol.

Chapter 7 Notes

I thank Deborah Boedeker and Kurt Raaflaub for useful comments and for helping to improve my English text.

1. All dates are B.C.E.
2. Ridgway 1970. Concepts of time and space: Krahmer 1931; Schweitzer 1969.188–99; Csapo & Miller, this vol.
3. The most explicit declaration of this view, laden with ideological overtones, was the Washington and New York exhibition "The Greek Miracle" of 1992, celebrating the 2,500th anniversary of Athenian democracy: see Buitron-Oliver 1992 and the editors' introduction to this volume.
4. Pollitt 1972; Hölscher 1989; Morris, this vol.
5. See generally Stähler 1992, 1993. I am preparing a monograph on Greek political monuments.
6. See especially the contributions by French and other scholars on monuments of Delphi, uncovered since 1891.
7. Gauer 1968b; Hölscher 1973.
8. Fehr 1979–81.
9. Hölscher 1974, followed by Stewart 1990.89–92.
10. Generally on the notion of "monument," see Mai 1989.
11. My view of the origin of the tropaion differs from most previous research: Charles-Picard 1957.17–64; Lammert 1939; Pritchett 1974.246–75. I will deal with this problem elsewhere.
12. Snodgrass 1980.105–7; Pritchett 1979.240–95.
13. See below at nn.34, 53ff.
14. Vanderpool 1966. A similar tropaion seems to have been erected after the battle of Salamis: Wallace 1969. See also West 1969.
15. On these monuments see Ioakimidou 1997.
16. Pausanias 10.1.10. Ioakimidou 1997. 135–43, no. 2.
17. Ioakimidou 1997. 157–66, no. 8; 200–13, no. 12; 173–79, no. 10; 243–55, nos. 16–17.
18. Gauer 1968b.

19. See Morris, this vol.
20. Brunnsåker 1971; Fehr 1984; Taylor 1991; Boedeker, this vol.
21. Timaios Sophistes, *Lexicon Platonicum*, *s.v.* orchestra. On the Pnyx, see Boedeker & Raaflaub, this vol., chap. 15, text at n.47.
22. Generally on Theseus in classical Athens: Schefold 1946; Connor 1970; Calame 1990; Castriota 1992.33–63.
23. Neils 1987.
24. Here I differ from Boardman's interpretation (e.g., Boardman 1984). See my forthcoming book on representations of Greek myths.
25. Thompson & Wycherley 1972.124–26.
26. Kron 1976.
27. Shear 1970; see Hölscher 1969; Thompson & Wycherley 1972.38–41; Kron 1976.282–332; Ioakimidou 1997.
28. See Eckstein 1958; Richter 1961.38–39, 53; Zinserling 1965; Stupperich 1977.71–86; Clairmont 1983; Garland 1989; I. Morris 1992.128–55.
29. Cicero, *De legibus* 2.64–65.
30. E.g., Kouros Kerameikos: Knigge 1983. Women's stele Athens: Richter 1961.55–56, fig. 174. Significantly, various scholars have interpreted these and other late specimens as votive offerings.
31. See I. Morris 1992, who draws a broad picture of self-restraint in burial customs all over Greece from around 500 and proposes an interesting model of interpretation.
32. See Hölscher 1991.370–72; 1996.
33. Herodotus 5.77; Pausanias 1.28.2; Raubitschek 1949.191–94, no.168; 201–5, no.173. See also Boedeker, this vol.
34. In the early fourth century, an inscription in Olympia stresses that a gilded statue of Gorgias was set up in Delphi not for the glory of the famous orator but to honor the god: Fränkel 1877.43–47. If the personal and nonreligious aspect of this votive offering needed to be rejected so forcefully, it must have been rather widespread.
35. Gauer 1968b.
36. Gauer 1968b.71–72, 75–98.
37. Herodotus 8.27; Pausanias 10.13.7; Ioakimidou 1997. 143–48, nos. 3–4.
38. Pausanias 2.20.5; 10.10.3–4. For the Delphic monument, see Bommelaer & Laroche 1991.113–14, no.112; Ioakimidou 1997. 226–42, nos. 14–15. For Argos: Pariente 1992.195–98.
39. I am planning a separate study on this system of public spaces.
40. ML no. 26 (pp. 54–57); Matthaiou 1988; Barron 1990.
41. Herodotus 6.14.
42. Wycherley 1957, nos.301, 304, 309; Thompson & Wycherley 1972.94–96; see La Genière 1960.
43. Harrison 1965.108–17.
44. Travlos 1960.40–42; Lauter-Bufé & Lauter 1975.
45. Hölscher 1973.50–84; see a forthcoming article by F. De Angelis.

46. See below at n.91.
47. See also Boedeker, this vol.
48. Niemeyer 1960.76–86; Gauer 1968b.102–5; Höcker & Schneider 1993.58–60. The name "Promachos" is uncertain for the fifth century; see Harrison 1996.
49. Thomas 1976; Knell 1990.95–108; Castriota 1992.134–83. See my forthcoming book on representations of myths.
50. See Cartledge 1993.
51. Boardman 1985; Knell 1990.108–26; cf. Maurizio, this vol.
52. Stupperich 1977.4–70; Clairmont 1983.
53. Amandry 1953.33–121.
54. Amandry 1954; Gauer 1968b.105–7; Stähler 1989. See the rf. skyphos, Lambrinudakis 1984, no.352: Apollo seated on palm tree.
55. Gauer 1968b.56–70; Kron 1976.215–27.
56. See, in general, Gauer 1968a.
57. Aischines, *Ktesiphon* 186; Hölscher 1973.55–56.
58. Plutarch, *Kimon* 8; cf. Herodotus 8.125.
59. Demosthenes, *Leptines* 112; Aischines, *Ktesiphon* 183–85.
60. Demosthenes, *Leptines* 70; schol. on Demosthenes, *Meidias* 62.
61. *IG* II^2 450.b7–12; 646.37–40; 1039.39; Plutarch, *Lives of the Ten Orators* 852e.
62. Wycherley 1957.207–17.
63. Pausanias 10.14.5–6.
64. Furtwängler 1893.4–43. Hartswick 1983 doubts the identification; Protzmann 1984 contests it. Location: Hölscher 1975.192–93; Höcker & Schneider 1993.99–104.
65. If Plutarch, *Perikles* 17 is authentic: see Stadter 1989.201–4.
66. Identification and date in the 440s: Willers 1967.
67. Buschor 1953; Berger 1969.
68. Despite endless discussions on the Ephesian Amazons, little useful research exists on their historical significance. Exceptions: Gauer 1980, 1992; Höcker & Schneider 1993.104–10; Schmaltz 1995. See work in preparation by R. Bol; Hölscher forthcoming.
69. Gauer 1980, 1992 sees the Amazon group as a monument of Athens or the Delian League, based on the Athenian view of the Amazons as paradigmatic enemies. According to the Ephesian version, however, the Amazons played a positive role in the Artemision.
70. Devambez 1976.272.
71. See Kallet, this vol.
72. Sanctuary: Mark 1993. Sculptural decoration: Simon 1985, 1985/86; Stewart 1985; and an article of mine currently in preparation.
73. This has been demonstrated, I hope definitively, by Mark 1993.115–22, 140.
74. Despinis 1974.
75. Boulter 1969.
76. Hölscher 1973.91–98; Simon 1985.274–80; 1985/86.15–21; Stewart 1985.58–66.

77. Simon 1985.280–86; 1985/86.21–27; Stewart 1985.
78. Goulaki-Voutira 1992, no.352.
79. Especially on documentary reliefs: Kasper-Butz 1990.59–65, 115–29.
80. Raaflaub 1984.68–72; 1985.244–48.
81. Hölscher 1974.
82. Pausanias 3.17.4.
83. Pausanias 3.18.8.
84. Pausanias 10.9.7–11; Bommelaer 1971; Bommelaer & Laroche 1991.108–10, no.109; Ioakimidou 1997.
85. Willemsen 1977; Lysias, *Epitaphios* 63.
86. See also Shapiro, this vol.
87. Hölscher 1973.38–49; Raeck 1981.101–61.
88. Schauenburg 1975.
89. Simon & Hirmer 1976 (1981).105–6, pls. 128–29. Such compassion was also expressed in tragedy.
90. Hölscher 1989.18–20; see Miller 1997.
91. Plutarch, *Themistokles* 18. On the origins of Greek portraits, see Metzler 1971; Hölscher 1973.207–11; Himmelmann 1994.49–88.
92. Xenophanes, fr. B18 DK. See Meier 1980.435–99 (1990b.186–221); Hölscher 1974.88–111.
93. Pausanias 3.11–18.
94. Thucydides 1.10.2.
95. See Meier 1996.

Chapter 8 Notes

1. For the scope of these innovations see Raaflaub, this vol.; for innovationism, Csapo & Miller, this vol. It is a pleasure to thank these three collaborators, as well as the other participants in the colloquium, for fruitful criticism and suggestions. I am grateful also to Paul Cartledge, Carolyn Dewald, John Marincola, and Lukas Thommen, who offered generous advice at various stages of this project.
2. On the monuments see Hölscher, this vol.
3. All unspecified dates are B.C.E. The dating of the Athenian treasury is controversial; most recently, Büsing 1994 argues that it was not built until well into the fifth century.
4. Cf. Tyrrell 1984.1–22 for a brief summary of the Amazons in sixth- and fifth-century Athenian art, including funeral orations.
5. Cf. Burn 1989.
6. Francis 1990.8–15, 25–26. The method is used to interpret vase paintings as well, e.g. ibid. 40–41.
7. E.g., Hölscher 1973.69. Burn 1989.63 quotes Ridgway 1981.85 on the frustrating, perhaps intentional ambiguity of classical Athenian sculptural decoration; vase paintings on the other hand are often quite specific, with characters frequently named; on the "recurrent uncertainty" of figures in fifth-century Athenian architectural sculpture see also Robertson 1975.349.

8. Hölscher, this vol, text at n.50.
9. Cf. Castriota 1992.96–118; M. Miller 1995.452–54.
10. Castriota 1992.58–63; Barron 1980. Bacchylides fr. 17 was performed not in Athens but by a chorus on Keos, but as Castriota argues, the ode must have been influenced by Athens' claim to dominion of the Aegean. Francis 1990.62 calls this version of the story "a manifesto for the Delian League."
11. On the Amazonomachy cf. Tyrrell 1984.3–22; Castriota 1992.43–58, 80; Harrison 1966.
12. Castriota 1992.179–80 summarizes interpretations of the Nike friezes, citing Felten 1984 for the Trojan War thesis; cf. also Gauer 1968b.17–18, who accepts Furtwängler's argument that the battle of Plataea is shown in the South, North and West friezes. Burn 1989.68–70 argues plausibly that the very ambiguity of such images encouraged viewers to draw analogies between recent events and the heroic battles typical of architectural sculpture; she notes (70) that by the late 420s, Marathon and Plataea were already "assimilated into the heroic past of Athens and so might have been legitimate subjects for the frieze."
13. As C. Keesling argues in a forthcoming study of dedicatory sculpture on the Akropolis.
14. On Archaic Athenian dedicatory inscriptions cf. Raubitschek 1949, esp. 455–78.
15. On the Tyrannicides from a different perspective, see Hölscher, this vol., text at nn.20ff., and Csapo & Miller, this vol., text at n.40. For a summary of recent discussions, see Versnel 1995.380–82 with bibliog.
16. See below, at nn.69, 94.
17. Keesling forthcoming says these seem to originate in Athens, especially in the late fifth century.
18. This would be all the more true if indeed the Archaic kouroi and korai statues represented gods and goddesses rather than individuals.
19. Robertson 1975.55–56; Pemberton 1988. Pemberton suggests that large-scale paintings were introduced while Athens was still observing the oath of Plataea, which prohibited reconstruction of temples damaged by the Persians.
20. Cf. Barron 1972 for detailed study of the Theseion murals.
21. Barron 1972 discusses differences between the portrayal of Amazons in the Theseion and the Stoa Poikile: in the earlier building, at least one Amazon (presumably the wife of Theseus) was portrayed fighting on the Athenian side; in the later, all the Amazons were battling against Athenians. The change may indicate a hardening of the category "Athenian-barbarian." Cf. also Tyrrell 1984.3–21; Castriota 1992.43–58, 80.
22. The Stoa was originally named after Kimon's brother-in-law Peisianax, as the individual responsible for its construction (Plutarch, *Kimon* 4.5). Pemberton 1988.185–86 is confident that the Anakeion was a Kimonian building as well, since it was dedicated to the very Spartan Dioskouroi, and Kimon (whose son was named Lakedaimonios) was famous for his pro-Lakonian disposition.

23. Quoted by Francis & Vickers 1985.111. Even more remarkably, Paus. 10.10.1–2 mentions a statue of Miltiades with Apollo and Artemis, erected at Delphi as part of the Athenian dedication there from the spoils of Marathon; cf. Gauer 1968b.66–70.
24. Cf. Hölscher 1973.68–70; this vol., text at n.45.
25. Jeffery 1965.50–51. Thomas 1976.75, following Hölscher 1973.68–70, accepts Pausanias' testimony for the representation of the battle on the Stoa Poikile. Francis & Vickers 1985 argue for the historicity of the battle but against its representation in the Stoa Poikile. Andrewes 1975 raises practical questions about where the battle described by Pausanias could possibly have been fought in the terrain around Oinoe, and concludes that Pausanias must have made an error in naming Oinoe in the Stoa Poikile.
26. Francis & Vickers 1985.99–113, with literature. Hölscher, this vol. with others still thinks it is the battle in the Argolid.
27. Cf. Francis & Vickers 1985.108, but I find their structural parallels unnecessarily rigid: a visitor to the Stoa could view the "recent-past-past-recent" (Oinoe-Amazons, Troy, Marathon) paintings in any order, but the audience of an ode would be constrained to hear the "recent-past-recent" order of the song.
28. Cf. Jacoby 1945.185–211; Hölscher, this vol.
29. *Iliad* 2.553–54.
30. Simonides, elegy fr. 11.13–28. On the "new Simonides" fragments, see Boedeker & Sider 1996, with bibliog.
31. Cf. Aloni 1994; Boedeker 1995.
32. See Hölscher, this vol.
33. Loraux 1986; cf., e.g., Kierdorf 1966.
34. Thomas 1989.110–18, citation 117.
35. Knox 1979.1–24 on tragedy and the past. For recent studies of tragedy and contemporary Athens see also Meier 1993b; Griffith 1995; Easterling 1997; Pelling 1997; Saïd, this vol.
36. Aeschylus' lost *Eleusinians,* also set in Attika, treated the same myth; but in this earlier version the Athenians did not fight the Thebans but were able to persuade them. On the *Suppliants* see Michelini 1994. Cf. Saïd, this vol. for the polis-*oikos* conflict in the *Suppliants.*
37. As Margaret Miller and Eric Csapo remind me, the much-debated "Gyges tragedy," which has been dated to the Hellenistic period as well as to the fifth century, also deals with an Asian monarch who attacked Greek cities (cf. Her. 1.15). The same would be true of the "Kroisos tragedy" that may underlie the narrative about Kroisos (the first foreign king to subject Greek cities, cf. Her. 1.5) and his son Atys in Herodotus 1.34–45.
38. In the opinion of Csapo & Slater 1995.167, this famous story should be seen as part of "a bitter factional struggle" about the still lively connection between Persians and Peisistratids in contemporary Athens. But see Rosenbloom 1993.
39. Especially Dorians, who could be seen (Parker 1987.194–95) as "mere immigrants,

a motley rabble tainted with foreign blood." Cf. now Dougherty 1996 on democratic concerns in the *Ion*.

40. Cf. Jeffery 1965.50 and Hölscher 1973.34–35 on a painting by a certain Boularchos, showing the defeat of the Magnesians, reported by Pliny to have been owned by the early-seventh-century Lydian king Kandaules.
41. Hölscher 1973.35–37. Heleen Sancisi-Weerdenburg points out to me (personal communication) that Achaemenid art does not represent historical events as such, but rather attempts to give a permanent image of kingly power.
42. On this subject the fullest treatment is still Gauer 1968b; for representations of the Persian Wars see Kierdorf 1966. Hölscher, this vol., text at n.93, postulates that Sparta may even have rivalled Athens in monuments to the Persian Wars, although it may be that some of the Spartan monuments were erected much later.
43. E.g., the Corinthian epitaph for those who died at Salamis; cf. Gauer 1968b.13.
44. Cf. Gauer 1968b.22–41 for an overview.
45. Gauer 1968b.16–20 collects the evidence. One wonders whether, paradoxically, this development in the direction of historical representation was due in part to Persian influence, as was surely the case for the painting dedicated by Mandrokles of Samos, as discussed above: Greeks adopted the practice of making public displays of their great deeds, as did their enemies Darius and Xerxes.
46. See above at n.25.
47. See above at n.12.
48. Cf. Strasburger 1958.21–24.
49. Cf. Castriota 1992; Hölscher, this vol.
50. The question of how the ideological message is communicated and received is of special interest to Castriota 1997. Cf. also Burn 1989.
51. Cf. Boedeker 1998 for a discussion of the fragment from this point of view.
52. This volume, text at n.47. Cf. also Csapo & Miller, this vol., text at nn.21–22
53. Castriota 1992.96.
54. Francis 1990.46 and *passim;* Parker 1987.187, referring to the book of that name edited by Hobsbawm & Ranger 1983. For a more nuanced view of this process cf. Dougherty 1996.
55. Morris 1993.
56. Cf. Lincoln 1989.
57. Goody & Watt 1968.
58. Cf. Raaflaub, this vol.
59. Cf. Connor 1994.
60. The title of van Groningen 1953.
61. It is hardly necessary to point out that many contemporaries, Athenians included—from philosophers like Plato to political pamphleteers like the "Old Oligarch"—heartily criticized this political system. On violent clashes that erupted when full-fledged democracy was introduced cf. Meier 1987a. See especially Csapo & Miller, this vol. on Athenian orientations to time.

62. Connor 1994.37–38 on some democratic aspects of autochthony, particularly the way it "*masks* divergences in status and situation."
63. This volume, text at n.92.
64. Athenians could easily justify their empire: they had won it by their role in the Persian Wars, and used their power justly for good ends (cf. Thucydides 1.73–75); cf. Raaflaub 1985.218–23. But fifth-century literature from Athens and elsewhere indicates that there were many "constitutional debates" (as in Herodotus 3.80–82; Euripides, *Suppliants* 403–41) and arguments for and against democracy (Pseudo-Xenophon, *Constitution of the Athenians* 1.1–9). Cf. Raaflaub 1989.
65. Cf. Shapiro, this vol.
66. Cf. Loraux 1973; Kierdorf 1966, chap. 3.
67. Cf. also Herodotus' report (7.161) of the Athenian refusal to yield command of the naval alliance to Gelon of Syracuse, on grounds of their autochthony and (as in the Eion poem) Homer's praise of Menestheus at Troy (Marathon is not mentioned in this context). Such reasoning is not restricted to Athenians in Herodotus: the Spartans refuse to yield command to Gelon by imagining Agamemnon's response to such a travesty (Herodotus 7.159).
68. Here, the Persian Wars have almost entirely replaced legendary events as the basis of the Athenian claim to leadership (i.e., empire), a process that had begun in the speech of Herodotus' Athenians at Plataea (9.27). In Thucydides' report of the Athenian Euphemos' speech at Kamarina, dated to 415/14, the speaker does not even allude to legendary deeds, and attributes Athens' role in the Persian Wars primarily to the city's self-interested desire to avoid being enslaved to Persia (6.82–83).
69. Cf. Boardman 1993.92.
70. So Kierdorf 1966, chap. 3.
71. Cf. Burn 1989.65–68 and *passim* for concise discussion of the use of (especially) Athenocentric myths as allusions to contemporary events on fifth-century vase paintings.
72. Lissarrague 1989.44.
73. E.g., in Lissarrague 1989.49–51.
74. For a review of the subject that challenges some of Felix Jacoby's views on the development of Greek historiography in the late Archaic and early classical period, cf. Fowler 1996.
75. Meier 1987b; cf. id. 1973. Farrar 1988 proposes the same for Thucydides.
76. Pearson 1942.7. The date of Hellanikos is much discussed. Fornara 1983b.17, following Jacoby, argues that Hellanikos wrote the first local history of Attika only at the end of the fifth century. See most recently Fowler 1996.64, who concludes that Hellanikos and Herodotus were near-contemporaries.
77. Maddoli 1985, discussing Herodotus 1.63 and Aristotle, *Constitution of the Athenians* 15.3–4.
78. Castriota 1997 comments on the apparent widespread "need" for genealogies.
79. An aspect emphasized by van Groningen 1953.

80. M. West 1985.103–9. Cf. also Fornara 1983b.1.
81. Similar tendencies may be reflected in the lists of kings in Sparta (on which see Cartledge 1979.341–46), priestesses of Hera in Argos, and athletic victors at Olympus, all of which seem to be first attested in the fifth century.
82. Vansina 1985.23–24 and *passim*. On the situation in Athens cf. Raaflaub 1988. The tradition on early Rome offers an impressive analogy: cf. Ungern-Sternberg 1988.
83. For a different view of Thucydides' relationship to Athens cf. Badian 1993.
84. Ober 1994a.105. On the political background see Munn forthcoming.
85. Connor 1994 and other chapters in Boegehold & Scafuro 1994.
86. For recent discussions cf. Hansen 1996b; Parker 1996, chap. 10.
87. Cf. Mink 1978.
88. Cf. Miller & Csapo, this vol. for a perceptive study of classical Athens' new view of time.
89. As Loraux 1986.134 says of the funeral oration, "In [its] historical excursus . . . we do not find the unfolding of a continuity, but the repetitive and exemplary enactment of a single arete."
90. The dedication was destroyed during the Persian sack of Athens and apparently reerected in the mid-fifth century. Cf. ML 15; Fornara 1983a, no.42; Raubitschek 1949, no.173. Cf. West 1985.283–85 for a brief discussion of this epigram, including references (n.20) to the archaeological evidence for the dedication. See also Raubitschek 1949.458; Hölscher, this vol., text at n.33.
91. Cf. Loraux 1986.132 and *passim* on how the version of "history" presented in Athenian funeral orations "effac[ed] the problems that a critical [historical] study reveals."
92. Cf. n.7 above.
93. The fourth-century Athenian orator Hypereides (*Against Philokrates* 3) mentions a law forbidding ridicule of Harmodios and Aristogeiton. On freedom of speech and its limits in Athens, see Henderson, this vol.
94. Cf. Kinzl 1978. The krater, attributed to the Copenhagen Painter, is now in Boston.
95. See, for Herodotus, Raaflaub 1987; for Thucydides, id. 1979.

Chapter 9 Notes

Versions of this text have been delivered at the University of Chicago and the Università degli studi di Urbino, as well as the Center for Hellenic Studies; an earlier draft was read by Richard Bett. I am grateful for all comments received, and in particular I must commend both editors for the unrivalled care they have taken with my manuscript. Translations are my own, typically adapted from standard versions. References to the sophists and other pre-Socratic philosophers are by numbers in Diels-Kranz 1952 (DK).

1. De Romilly 1992.4. Protagoras: e.g., Sprague 1972.3; de Romilly 1992.viii.
2. Ostwald 1986.242.

3. Kerferd 1981a.15.
4. E.g., Kerferd 1981a.15–17; de Romilly 1992.19–26.
5. Müller 1986.192.
6. Kerferd 1981b.3.
7. Ostwald 1992.341, 343.
8. Kerferd 1950; see also Rankin 1983.13; de Romilly 1992.1.
9. Braudel 1972.103–67.
10. Lloyd points out that "acceptance of money for instruction in such *technai* as medicine or sculpture was a well-established and uncontroversial practice" (1987.92–94, nn.152, 153). However, these tasks may have been considered more banausic than the teaching of wisdom.
11. See esp. Kerferd 1981a.55–57; 1981b.4–5. Cf. in particular Sokrates' love of argument amid a crowd of rich young Athenians, his characteristic use of the antilogic method in the exploration of ethical and other human questions which often led to *aporia,* and his constant challenges to received opinion.
12. See also Plato, *Meno* 90d, 91b. Kerferd 1981a.26.
13. See Lloyd, as in n.10.
14. Bett 1989.
15. See esp. Gorgias, *Helen* 13.
16. Adkins 1972.103.
17. On the earlier development of empirical research, see Comotti 1991.
18. de Romilly 1992.9.
19. For a general account of the methodologies associated with the Hippocratic authors, see Lloyd 1979.126–225 ("The development of empirical research").
20. For a recent assessment of these figures and further references, see Cole 1991a.22–25 and 1991b; but see Yunis, this vol.
21. Kerferd 1950.8.
22. For the educational role of Greek poets, see, e.g., Aristophanes, *Acharnians* 656–58; *Frogs* 1009–10, 1054–58; and Plato, *Protagoras* 325c–326c; see also Taplin 1983.332–33; Gentili 1988.155–61; Henderson 1990.271–72, 297–307, 312–13.
23. For the spread of education to lower social levels after the later sixth century, see Marrou 1956.36–43. See Pseudo-Xenophon, *Constitution of the Athenians* 2.10, that at least by the later fifth century the demos enjoyed aristocrat-style baths and the palaestra. See also the steady augmentation of slave labor as more and more citizens of what John Davies has called Athens' "rentier" or "leisure class" of several thousand heads-of-household (1981.10–14, 28–37; for the numbers, Rhodes 1982.1–9) spent significant amounts of time in traditionally aristocratic occupations such as governing; the early-fifth-century institution of the public funeral oration as a eulogy for all citizens (Loraux 1986); the public erection of great monuments and buildings (Hölscher, this vol.); and also the demos' assumption of myth as their own history in Attic tragedy (Boedeker, this vol.).
24. Detienne 1967.117. Antilogies: Yunis, this vol.

25. Vernant 1982. See the debate on the origins of democracy between Josiah Ober, Kurt Raaflaub, and myself in Morris & Raaflaub 1997.
26. Wallace 1995.
27. Gold 1987.21–30, with references.
28. Wallace 1995.
29. Simonides, fr. 11 West^2; cf. Boedeker & Sider 1996.
30. Lesky 1966.189; Detienne 1967.119.
31. Lesky 1966.190; see also Kerferd 1981a.46–47.
32. Gentili 1988.161–62.
33. See Morris, this vol.
34. For the widespread success of philosophers throughout the Greek world in the fourth century and later, see McKechnie 1989.150–52.
35. Knox 1979.87–95.
36. Luce 1992.82.
37. Kerferd 1981a.50; cf., e.g., Guthrie 1969.293–94; Romeyer-Dherbey 1985.95.
38. On the *patrios politeia,* see Finley 1971; Fuks 1953.
39. Rankin 1983.65.
40. For ancient opinions on the question of one or two Antiphons, see Gagarin 1990 and Pendrick 1993, with references. Wiesner 1994 again identifies the two. I am grateful to Michael Gagarin for helpful comments on Antiphon.
41. E.g., Guthrie 1969.168, 290–91.
42. Kerferd 1981a.18.
43. Stadter 1991. It is unsafe to regard Perikles' companion Aspasia as a legitimate philosophical figure: see my review of Henry 1995 in *Bryn Mawr Classical Review* 7 (1996) 210–17.
44. Anaxagoras: Isokr. *Antid.* 235; Plato, *Phaedr.* 269e–270a, and Plato? *I Alcibiad.* 118c. Damon: Isokr. *Antid.* 235; Plato? *I Alcibiad.* 118c; cf. Arist. *Const. of the Athenians* 27.4. Pythokleides: Plato? *I Alcibiad.* 118c and Arist. ap. Plut. *Per.* 4 (perhaps in error for Plato).
45. Contrast esp. Mansfeld 1979–80.
46. See generally Isokr. 8.121–31, and also, e.g., Arist., *Pol.* 1320a4–6; among modern works, above all Connor 1971.
47. Connor 1971.166, n.54.
48. See above all Carter 1986.52–75 (chap. 3: "Noble Youths").
49. I. Morris 1992, chap. 5; cf. id., this vol.
50. Forrest notes that this was "the course adopted in real life by Alkibiades. He must learn the tricks and join in the demagogic rat-race. He must beat the demagogues at their own game. He must be more extreme, more flattering" (1975.47). Cf. Adkins 1972.145: "Those—of wealthy families . . . —who wished, and were able, to benefit fully from sophistic instruction in the 'political art', but did not wish to be 'champions of the people', must have been unable to exercise effectively that superior skill that they believed themselves to possess, or to rule over others as an agathos should."

51. Tr. Forrest 1975.41–42.
52. See Natali 1987, which however does not attempt to situate these comments in their evolving historical contexts.
53. See Dover 1968b.31–32, 39, 42–43, arguing for 420–15, and Waterfield 1993.380, arguing for ca. 420 (while the Megarian battle mentioned in 368a is probably that of 409).
54. Forrest 1975.49.

Chapter 10 Notes

I am grateful to the members of the CHS colloquium, especially the editors of this volume, for much constructive criticism; to Hilary Mackie, David Nirenberg, Carol Quillen, John Gibert, Brian Vickers, and George Kennedy for reading and criticizing an earlier version; and to the Center for the Study of Cultures of Rice University for support during the writing of this chapter.

1. Attribution to Anaximenes on the basis of Quintilian, *Institutio* 3.4.9; see Mirhady 1994.55–61.
2. For an overview of the history of rhetoric, see Kennedy 1980; Conley 1994. Kennedy's studies of particular periods of the ancient world are highly useful: 1963 on classical Greece, 1972 on Rome and the Hellenistic world, 1983 on Byzantium; these volumes have now been revised and abridged in a single volume, Kennedy 1994. On the Aristotelian tradition in rhetoric, see Solmsen 1941; Fortenbaugh & Mirhady 1994. Vickers 1988 treats rhetoric historically and thematically. On the systematic content of ancient rhetoric, see Volkmann 1885; Josef Martin 1974. Pernot 1993, primarily concerned with encomium, is a superb resource for ancient rhetoric generally.
3. On rhetoric and religion, see Murphy 1974.269–355; Kennedy 1980.120–60; Shuger 1988. The close connection of rhetoric and literature begins with Aristotle and has grown ever since; see Kennedy 1980.108–19 for an introduction. On rhetoric and the arts, see Vickers 1988.340–74.
4. See Hesiod, *Theogony* 81–93 for the archaic attitude of eloquence bestowed by the Muses; Homer, *Iliad* 3.204–24 for the eloquence traditionally ascribed to Odysseus; and Martin 1989 on speech and performance in the *Iliad*. On Homer and other preclassical, poetic influences on rhetoric, see Kennedy 1963.35–48; Kennedy 1980.9–15; Race 1990; Cole 1991a. On persuasion in Athenian tragedy see Buxton 1982. Cicero, *De oratore* 1.146; Quintilian, *Institutio* 3.2.3 contrast art and eloquence.
5. On the early usage of *rhētorikē*, see Schiappa 1990b; O'Sullivan 1993. *Rhētorikē* does not occur in Isokrates or the other fourth-century Athenian orators. See Classen 1976b on the study of language by Socrates and his contemporaries.
6. Hamberger 1914; Baumhauer 1986 treat the passage at length.
7. See Cicero, *De inventione* 2.6–7; *Brutus* 46–48; and Schöpsdau 1994 on Aristotle's "Collection of Arts." Since *technē* could refer to a treatise on any subject, we ought not to assume that Aristotle's "Collection" was restricted to *technai* on rhetoric.

Radermacher 1951 is the standard collection of ancient evidence on non-Platonic, pre-Aristotelian rhetorical theory. Isokrates occasionally mentions predecessors but only in general terms, for example, 13.19, 15.197, 295.

8. Blass 1887–98.1:1–46; Navarre 1900.3–77; Süss 1910.2–3, 15–17; Kroll 1940.1041–44; Kennedy 1963.52–61; Eisenhut 1982.8–21; Baumhauer 1986. Recently Jarratt 1991; Enos 1993; and Thomas & Webb 1994 maintain the fourth-century story of fifth-century rhetoric.
9. Schiappa 1990a; Cole 1991b reject the traditional accounts of Korax and Teisias. On *prōtos heuretēs,* see Kleingünther 1933; Thraede 1962. The entire tradition of Sicily as the place where rhetoric originated is fundamentally weak (*pace* Martin 1976.157–58): it rests merely on the prominence of Gorgias of Leontini and his famous visit to Athens in 427 (Plato, *Hippias maior* 282B; Diodorus 12.53; Dionysios of Halikarnassus, *Lysias* 3) and on an isolated report that Aristotle regarded Empedokles of Akragas as the "first to discover (*prōton heurein*) rhetoric" (Diogenes Laertius 8.57).
10. Cole 1991a.ix.
11. Halliwell 1994.231 claims that Plato exploited but did not invent the form/content dichotomy; to Halliwell's citations (Thuc. 1.22.1; Lysias 10.7; Isokrates 9.10–11, 13.16–17) should be added Sophokles, *Oedipus at Colonus* 292–94; Alkidamas, *On the Sophists* 19. Yet Cole argues not that Plato first noticed the form/content dichotomy, but that he first systematically applied it to communication; see Cole 1991a.152–53. On Plato's innovation of conceiving rhetoric as a universal *technē* of discourse, see Yunis 1996.172–210. On pre-Platonic theorizing about persuasion, see now Gondos 1996; Wardy 1996.
12. By an utterly different method, Classen 1959 reaches a view of Plato much like Cole's. Usener 1994, a well-executed study of fourth-century prose reading and performance texts, corroborates Cole's account of that subject.
13. Cole 1991a.71–94, anticipated in certain respects by Gercke 1897.
14. On fourth-century innovations in *technē,* see Heinimann 1961; Pfeiffer 1968.57–58, 68. On fourth-century debates on *technē,* which included physicians, sophists, rhetoricians, and philosophers, see Kube 1969; Hutchinson 1988; Allen 1994. On Plato's theory of *technē,* see Irwin 1977; Cambiano 1991. See Plato, *Phaedr.* 269A–270E, Arist. *Topics* 1.3 for summaries of the theoretical basis of rhetorical *technē* and the analogy between rhetoric and medicine as similarly theoretical *technai.* For Aristotle's view of sophistic rhetorical *technē,* see *Rhetoric* 1.1.3, 1.2.4; *Sophistical Refutations* 183B25–184B8.
15. On Isokrates' ideas on rhetoric, see Eucken 1983; Too 1995.
16. On Demosthenes' art and its sources, see Pearson 1976; on the influence of Thucydides and Plato, see Yunis 1996.237–77. The ancient evidence for Demosthenes' rhetorical education is unreliable; see Blass 1887–98.3.1:11–25. See Kroll 1940.1065–71 on the independence of fifth- and fourth-century rhetorical practice from theory.
17. On Plato's treatment of Lysias in the *Phaedrus,* see Vickers forthcoming.
18. See *Gorgias* 449A, 466A–D, 502D–503A; Yunis 1996.117–53.

19. See Hansen 1983; Ober 1989.104–12 on the term *rhētōr*.
20. On the evolution of Athenian democracy, a contested subject, see Meier 1990b; Bleicken 1994, chap. 1; 1995; Raaflaub 1995; Morris & Raaflaub 1997. Although Athenian democracy continued to evolve, it is false to distinguish between a radical democracy of the fifth century and a moderate democracy of the fourth; see Bleicken 1987; Ober 1989.95–103. Democratic deliberation and decision-making were the backbone of the democracy and were consistently maintained throughout the classical period. Wülfing 1969, 1975 focuses on democracy as the origin of rhetoric.
21. The political consequences of this rhetorical situation are described by Ober 1989.104–55. Bleicken 1994 explains how a political system of this kind could function effectively. See Bitzer 1968 on the concept of the rhetorical situation.
22. See Meier 1993b.78–137 on the political import of Aeschylus' *Suppliants* and *Oresteia;* Buxton 1982.67–114 on persuasion in Aeschylus. Thucydides commends Themistokles' rhetorical skill in terms that recall Perikles (1.138.3).
23. See Connor 1971; Kallet-Marx 1994.
24. See Yunis 1996.36–58 on the sources mentioned in this paragraph as well as other contemporary sources not mentioned here.
25. See Adkins 1985.106–32 (but see Raaflaub 1996c.1035–42) on Solon; Kurke 1991 on Pindar.
26. See Arist. *Nic. Ethics* 1180B 29–1181A 17, and Martin 1976.145, esp. n.10 on political action as the goal of sophistic teaching. See Kerferd 1981a.139–62 on sophistic, especially Protagorean, politics.
27. Thuc. 8.68.1 on Antiphon; Plato, *Phaedrus* 261B–E; *Sophistes* 232D; Arist. *Nic. Ethics* 1180B 29–1181A 17; and see Wilcox 1942.
28. Matters requiring expertise: Xenophon, *Memorabilia* 3.6; Plato, *Alcibiades I.*106C–107D; Arist. *Rhetoric* 1359B 18–60B 1, 1396A 3–12. Arist. *Rhetoric* 1404A 13–15 mentions Thrasymachos on delivery; on Hippias' famed art of memory, see Plato, *Hippias minor* 368D; *Hippias maior* 285E. Collections of preambles are recorded for Antiphon (*Suda s.vv. aisthesthai, hama, mochthēros*); Thrasymachos (Athenaeus 416A), and Kritias (Hermogenes, *On Ideas* 402.6 Rabe). See Burckhardt 1924 on other early sources.
29. See Plato, *Phaedr.* 266D–267D; Arist. *Rhetoric* 1354B 16–19; Solmsen 1941.37–39.
30. See Ludwig 1957 on Euripides; Murphy 1938 on Aristophanes; Solmsen 1975 on Thucydides.
31. See Lavency 1964; Dover 1968b.148–74 on speechwriting for the courts. See Stadter 1991 on Perikles' relation to Protagoras and other sophists. On Perikles' rhetorical reputation and Thucydides' version of Perikles' rhetoric, see Yunis 1996.59–86. On Andokides, see Kennedy 1958; Missiou 1992.
32. On Antiphon, see Plato, *Menexenos* 236A; Thuc. 8.68.1; Gagarin 1994. On Thuc. 3.37–38 and Plato, *Phaedr.* 257E–258C, reproaching epideictic display in the assembly, see Yunis 1996.87–92, 181–88.
33. Popular distrust of sophistic expertise is a common theme of Attic oratory: see

[Demosth.] 35.40–43; Plato, *Apology* 19BC; Ober 1989.170–74. Denniston 1952.17–18 drew attention to a marked difference in style in the fourth century between epideictic on the one hand and deliberative and judicial on the other: poetic diction flourished in epideictic, but in deliberative and judicial it was found inappropriate and fell out of use. In Arist. *Rhetoric* 3.12, the style of "agonistic" (i.e., deliberative and judicial) is opposed to that of "written" (i.e., epideictic) rhetoric (1414A 17–18); see also Alkidamas, *On the Sophists* 12–13. On the distinction between real political rhetoric and artistic epideictic rhetoric, see Isokrates 4.11; Arist. *Rhetoric* 1358B 2–6, 1377B 21–22, 1391B 17–21; and Epicurus, fr. 20.4 Arrighetti[2].

34. See Martin 1976; Guthrie 1969; Wallace, this vol.
35. See *Phaedr.* 257E–258C, 261A–E, 272A; and Yunis 1996.172–210.
36. See Solmsen 1941.42–43; Hellwig 1973.65–68 on Aristotle's three genres; Vickers 1988.53–62 surveys the later development of these genres. See Lord 1981; Cooper 1994 on the *Rhetoric* and politics.
37. See Solmsen 1975.10–46 on the forms of antithetical argument. For Plato *antilogikē* and eristic are not identical; see Kerferd 1981a.59–67.
38. Thus the common literary model for debate in the assembly is the pro and contra of two opposed parties: cf. Aristophanes' *Knights,* Thucydides' depiction of post-Periklean debates in the assembly (n.46 below), and Demosthenes' presentation of his contest against Aischines (19.19–24). On voting in the assembly, see Hansen 1987.41–46.
39. Rhetorical thinkers before Aristotle recognized the antithetical nature of political debate in the notion of "agonistic" rhetoric (*agōnistikon*); see Buchheit 1960.124–25; Hellwig 1973.129–46; Yunis 1996.181–84.
40. Protagoras as originator: 80 A20–21, B6, 6a DK; see Schiappa 1991 on Protagoras. Prodikos: Xenophon, *Memorabilia* 2.1.21–34; see Binder & Liesenborghs 1976 on the Prodikean fragment on contradiction. *Double Arguments:* DK 90. Antisthenes: Radermacher 1951.B19.11–12. Carawan 1993 renews the debate on the provenience of Antiphon's tetralogies and suggests a date in the fourth century. See Lloyd 1966.103–27 on antithetical argument in earlier Greek thought; Kudlien 1974 on antithetical argument in Greek medicine; Moraux 1968 on antithetical dialectic in Arist. *Topics* Bk. 8. Navarre 1900.51–66 summarizes the sophistic arguments in Plato, *Euthydemus* and Arist. *Sophistical Refutations.*
41. Plato attributes these arguments to Teisias, Aristotle to Korax (*Rhetoric* 2.24.11); cf. n.9 above. With respect to arguments of this kind, legal advocacy has changed little since classical Athens.
42. See Gagarin 1994 on the limited scope of probability arguments. Prodikos' discourse is virtually a moral sermon (Xenophon, *Memorabilia* 2.1.21–34). See Kranz 1937 on the subject matter of the *Double Arguments.*
43. As pointed out by Dover 1968a.258–63 (on *Clouds* 1399–1451), Pheidippides recycles words and arguments used by the Weaker Argument in the earlier contest. See O'Regan 1992 on *Clouds,* rhetoric, and sophists.

44. Arist. *Rhetoric* 1.15.26 recommends precisely these arguments on torture; Carey 1989.135–36 collects further examples from Athenian oratory.
45. On the *agōnes* in tragedy, see Duchemin 1945; on Euripidean *agōnes,* see Lloyd 1992. On rhetoric and fifth-century tragedy, see Bers 1994. On rhetoric and fourth-century tragedy, see Arist. *Poetics* 1450B 4–8; Xanthakis-Karamanos 1979.
46. The following are the formal antilogies in Thucydides: Corinthians and Corcyreans in Athens (1.31–44); Corinthians and Athenians in Sparta (1.68–78); Kleon and Diodotos concerning Mytilene (3.36–49); Plataeans and Thebans (3.52–68); the Melian dialogue (5.84–114); Nikias and Alkibiades (6.8–26); Hermokrates and Athenagoras in Syracuse (6.32–41); Hermokrates and Euphemos in Kamarina (6.75–88).
47. See Yunis 1996.59–66 on Thucydides' speeches. On the literary artifice in two Thucydidean antilogies, see de Romilly 1956.186–94 on the debate at Kamarina; and Moraux 1954; Winnington-Ingram 1965; Macleod 1978 on the Mytilenaean debate.
48. Recall Aristotle's definition of rhetoric: "the ability to perceive the available means of persuasion in each particular case" (*Rhetoric* 1355B 25–26). On Thuc. 1.22.1, the much disputed passage in which Thucydides announces that his speeches contain the gist of the original while expressing what seems to him necessary for the case, see Badian 1992; Egermann 1972.575–86; Woodman 1988.11–14. On the didactic features of Thucydides' history, announced in 1.22.4, see Erbse 1969; de Ste. Croix 1972.5–33.
49. Contrast the debate on Pylos (4.27–28), where Thucydides omits speeches of his own, reports the gist of the original speeches, and records the outcome.
50. See de Romilly 1956.194–239; Woodruff 1994 on Thucydidean antilogy as a tool of analysis and a step in the development of dialectic.
51. Caplan 1944 discusses the ancient debate on rhetoric and free speech. Demosthenes (19.23–24) and Plato's Socrates (*Apology* 32A–C) complain that the assembly effectively silenced them. On the audience of the new political literature, see Jähne 1991; Usener 1994. On the development and publication of written political literature in the fourth century, see Canfora 1988; Johne 1991.
52. On the unconventional arguments in Thucydides' speeches, see de Ste. Croix 1972.11–16; Strasburger 1958; Meyer 1899.389–94. On Thucydides' unconventional style, see Dionysios of Halikarnassos, *Thucydides* 24; Norden 1915.1:95–101; the difficulty of this style was noted by Dion. Hal. *Thuc.* 55.4; Cicero, *Orator* 30–31; *Brutus* 287; *De opt. gen.* 15–16. On the differences in fourth-century Athens between reading texts, hearing texts, and delivery to live political audiences, see Usener 1994. See Jeffrey Henderson's contribution to this volume for Aristophanes' reluctance to criticize the democracy bluntly.
53. Cole 1991a.104–12, esp. 111.
54. Formerly a common view; for example, Moraux 1954; Kennedy 1963.47–51.
55. The difficulties of Thuc. 1.22.1 reflect, it seems to me, Thucydides' struggle to express the notion of the best possible case; cf. n.48 above. Gondos 1996 documents Thucydides' ability to discuss persuasive discourse critically.

56. Beyond the works of the Athenian orators, Plato created literary representations of political rhetoric in *Apology of Sokrates, Menexenos,* and the formal preambular speeches of the *Laws*. Isokrates "addresses" an assembly in *Areopagitikos, Peace,* and *Plataikos,* and a court in *Antidosis*. The influence of Antiphon, the earliest logographer, on Thucydides is virtually acknowledged by the latter (8.68.1).
57. Cf. the concept of *letteraturizzazione* employed by Kennedy 1980.110–12.

Chapter 11 Notes

1. Here I take a standard view of what constitutes "philosophy" in the context of ancient thought: one that allows in the "Presocratics" (to the degree that they were engaged systematically in the disinterested search for knowledge, i.e., *philosophia* in the, or a, Greek sense), and probably excludes the sophists (insofar as they were not). In these two categories, in the fifth century, the only two significant individuals are likely to be Demokritos and Protagoras; on these, see below. (Plato himself, of course, has his own definition of philosophy, which would exclude Presocratics and sophists alike.)
2. For a recent treatment of the general question of the influence of philosophy on practical politics, see the last three chapters of Brunt 1993, and Cartledge's review of Brunt (Cartledge 1992). In general, it seems reasonable to share the sceptical attitude suggested (I think) by the list of examples of *epagōgē* (induction) in Aristotle's *Rhetoric* which ends, "and at Thebes, the city began to flourish at just the time that those in charge became philosophers" (1398b 18–20). (The view of T. J. Saunders, cited by Cartledge against Brunt, hardly touches Brunt's case: if Plato's Academicians "were engaging in an educational enterprise of the first importance . . . attempting to convey to rulers and states . . . certain standards of moral and political conduct, . . . with the aim of seeing those standards applied in day-to-day life" [Saunders 1986.209], it will still be a legitimate question whether he, or they, actually succeeded to any extent.) The ancient evidence for the involvement of members or former members of the Academy—including Plato himself—in practical politics (see Morrow 1960.8–9) is by itself hardly decisive; would President Clinton's sojourn at the University of Oxford count as evidence for that institution's involvement in the day-to-day politics of the United States?

   The distance between philosophical reflection and political reality at Athens is beautifully illustrated by Cicero's report (*Orator* 151) that Plato's *Menexenos* was in his time being used for the annual celebration of the war dead: if Cicero's report is accurate (and only its paradoxical quality seems to be against it), then a parody of a funeral speech, and of Athenian self-perceptions, has become the real thing. But nevertheless the possibility exists that where individuals were able to shape legislation or initiate political change, specific philosophical influences might show themselves: thus, for instance, Morrow claims that Platonic influence, mediated through Aristotle and Theophrastus, is clearly visible in the legislation of Demetrios of Phaleron (Morrow 1960.9)—and much later the *Republic* could serve as an inspiration for radical thinkers at the time of the French Revolution. It may also be that democratic society itself sometimes perceived philosophers and intellectuals as a threat: the decree of Diopeithes and the prosecution of Anaxagoras, if not that of Sokrates, constitute decent evidence for this (see esp. Ostwald 1986). However, such popular reactions were evidently random and fitful, and not well justified. The intellectuals could by and large be safely ignored.

3. See now Nightingale 1995.
4. Farrar 1988.1, 14.
5. See n.1 above.
6. Finley 1974.9 (other references at Raaflaub 1989.33).
7. Momigliano 1960.534.
8. See, e.g., Ostwald 1986. The basic tests for the "survival of democracy" will presumably be that the citizen body continues to decide at least some important issues, and that the criteria for citizenship do not become too restrictive; the more restrictive they become, and the further the competence of the citizens is reduced, the lesser the degree of democracy (or, from the point of view of its critics, the greater its degree of moderation): see, e.g., Pennock 1979.15, and for the case of Athens, Hansen 1991.150ff. According to Raaflaub (1989.35), "there is a substantial difference between the fifth and fourth centuries not only in the constitutional structure and in the working and spirit, but also in the perception of democracy by the contemporaries and in their attitude towards it"; even if so, it is still—evidently—a perception of "democracy."
9. Raaflaub 1989; see also, e.g., Dover 1974.
10. See n.53 below.
11. "Self-rule" (which is shorthand for the phrase "to rule and be ruled," *archein kai archesthai*) is of course qualified by two higher principles: that the younger should be ruled by those who have already proved themselves "slaves of the laws" (*Laws* 762E), and that those with an unequal share of relevant qualities should have an unequal share of power (757E)—but all at least partly under the scrutiny of all the citizens (767C–768A; Brunt's view [1993.257] that this passage is "nullified" by others seems overstated).
12. When democracy began at Athens is of course a matter of dispute. But in the present context the question is mostly irrelevant: Plato usually discusses democracy only in the most general terms; even when, as in the *Laws*, he focuses directly on the history of democracy at Athens (apparently making it predate the Persian Wars), he gives only the sketchiest and most general of accounts, with no precise chronological coordinates, and in particular he ignores entirely the more restricted democracy of the fourth century (see n.8 above).
13. Conversely, according to one recent writer, *women* would gain extra rights (Cohen 1987, esp. 37); but see Saunders 1995.591–609.
14. Cf., e.g., Ostwald 1986.xxii.
15. More easily, in fact, than from an oligarchy, because in the latter case "the number

of persons of influence is greatest" (Taylor's translation). "Persons of influence" here translates *dunastai;* the point is presumably that power is concentrated in fewer hands, from which it would be more difficult to dislodge (cf. *Politicus* 303A).

16. In contrast to Aristotle: see below.
17. Contrast, e.g., E. Lévy: "même l'emploi, déjà courant, de *politeia* pour désigner le régime plus ou moins censitaire qui avait le faveur des milieux modérés est rattaché au sens habituel du mot: cette *politeia* n'est jamais que la *politeia* par excellence, non pas la *politeia* idéale à la manière platonicienne, mais celle qui est plus *politeia* que les autres" (Lévy 1993.90). However, it is difficult to see how the polity is "more of a constitution" than kingship and aristocracy, which are for Aristotle species of the best constitution, and appear in the same list of "correct" (*orthai*) constitutions.
18. The hoplite state is presumably what he thinks of as one (preferred, but usually less practicable) way of achieving such a compromise; the "middle" constitution, if distinguishable from it, would be another. Plato's own suggestions for "mixing" constitutions seem to me ultimately to tend in precisely this sort of direction; in other words, Aristotle's polity is a vision of what the "third city" of *Laws* 739 (or even the fourth?) might have looked like. For the relationship between polity and the ideal city of *Politics* VII–VIII, see my chapter on "Aristotelian Constitutions" in Rowe & Schofield 1999.
19. *Politics* VI.2, 1317b 2, 17ff.; cf. Hansen 1991.313–14; Finley 1983.74.
20. Most notably, insofar as both are implacably opposed to what they see as the inevitable polarization in a democracy; that is what they take "democracy" to *mean* (cf., e.g., *Laws* 757D 3: justice and equality in opposition to "a few tyrants or a single one, or even the power [*kratos*] of the people"). On democratic equality, see Raaflaub 1996b; Cartledge 1996.
21. I refer here above all, of course, to Popper 1952. For Popper, Plato is unqualifiedly a "totalitarian," where totalitarianism is defined by opposition to the freedom of thought and action that characterizes "democracy." But if government is, for Plato, to be philosophically based, and he always (as I propose) understands "philosophy" in a distinctly Sokratic sense, then Popper's analysis will be too simplistic to fit the case.
22. On the standard account, in fact, though not on Popper's, Plato's opposition to democratic government gives way to a reluctant, even despairing, acceptance that some version, or admixture, of democracy is necessary in the real world of politics. I believe that this interpretation rests on unprovable assumptions about Plato's psychology, and on equally unprovable (if equally plausible) assumptions about the development of his thinking; see further below.
23. I.e., as marking some kind of "transition" to the "middle," where "Sokrates" is surely not identical in some respects to the historical figure, whatever he might have been in the "early" dialogues.
24. See most recently de Strycker & Slings 1994; and the series of essays by Charles Kahn, beginning with Kahn 1981.

25. Klosko 1986.46.
26. For further evidence, including material from the *Apology* and the *Crito,* see Kraut 1984, chaps. 7, 8. Kraut's book is by far the most impressive contribution so far on what we might term "Sokrates' political theory" (but see Terry Penner's criticisms in Rowe & Schofield 1999). The larger part of the book is concerned with the arguments of the *Crito,* which provide the bulk of that theory but are not directly relevant to my present concerns (see, e.g., Kraut 1984.9, n.15).
27. Similarly Kraut ("I hope I have explained why it is inaccurate to portray Socrates as either a simple enemy or a simple friend of democracy," 1984.244).
28. On Kraut's view, this is one respect in which Sokrates prefers the laws of Athens to those of Sparta and Crete (e.g., 226).
29. So, e.g., by his greatest modern exponent, Gregory Vlastos (see esp. Vlastos 1991).
30. *Gorgias* 521D 6–8, in Vlastos' translation. Vlastos (1991.241) is right to say that "doing politics" is here understood in a "wilfully idiosyncratic sense"; but it is clear that Plato is entirely serious, insofar as Sokrates is the only one doing what politicians/statesmen *ought* to do.
31. Cf. *Memorabilia* IV.2.11 (with 6–7), where Sokrates is found advocating an "art of kingship" reminiscent of that of the *Euthydemus* (291B–292E; but Xenophon's report here may well draw on the *Euthydemus* itself).
32. Like Sokrates at *Gorgias* 520A, I propose to make no great distinction between orators and sophists; the category "orators" is meant to refer primarily to professional orators, i.e., *teachers* of the subject, like Gorgias himself. Plato regularly suggests that "politicians," *politikoi,* who in normal parlance are themselves *rhētores,* are at odds with sophists; but—as is suggested by the passage from the *Republic* quoted in my text below—this is explicable simply in terms of professional (or occupational?) rivalry. See, however, Yunis, this vol.
33. See also *Republic* VI, 493A–C.
34. The true statesman, by contrast, tells the plain truth—or at least according to the *Gorgias.*
35. Plato's opposition to imperialism, which he regards as the public counterpart of private injustice, is implicit but clear: so most obviously in the contrast between the virtuous Athens that opposed the latterly vicious and imperialistic Atlantis in the *Timaeus-Critias* (if Atlantis is not itself in part a picture of Periklean Athens [Vidal-Naquet 1986, chap. 13]), and in the siting of Magnesia in the *Laws* away from the sea.
36. The phrase is borrowed immediately from Ober 1993b.
37. So, e.g., Klosko (1986.199) talks of the "decidedly grim" mood of the *Laws,* as Plato gives way to pessimism.
38. See esp. Morrow 1960, e.g., 534; the same general view is endorsed, with modifications and qualifications, by Charles Kahn in his introduction to the second edition of Morrow's book (xxi): "Plato has gone as far as he could to make a place for the Athenian tradition in his city, and to unite 'freedom' with wisdom (represented by the higher magistrates) and friendship (i.e., class harmony)."

39. Stalley 1983.94. See also Brunt 1993.259: "It is . . . astounding that Morrow could think that [the] 'basic political structure' [of Magnesia] is 'thoroughly Athenian'." Brunt also criticizes Morrow, in the same context, for saying that Plato in the *Laws* is harking back to "the Athens of an older time" (Morrow 1960.592). Christopher Gill, for his part, takes a position that might be identified as somewhere between Stalley's and Klosko's, though in the end it probably has more in common with the latter; so for example he sees the philosopher-kings as amounting to a positive proposal, but one hedged about with as many qualifications as the idea of direct rule by an ideally wise king in the *Politicus* and the *Laws* (Gill 1995b; see also Gill 1995a.56, where he interestingly refers to the constitution of Magnesia as a kind of "hoplite democracy": cf. above, at n.21).
40. Cf. Laks 1990, 1991. On the second point, contrast Klosko (1986.173–74): Although "Plato is often thought of as an extremely unworldly, 'utopian' political thinker, it can be seen that he took the question of practical political reform seriously . . . It is a political program to the realization of which Plato did give serious thought."
41. Quoted in Laks' translation (1990.215).
42. Cf. Laks, ibid.: "insofar as it is a condition for approximating to the paradigmatic city, the coincidence in one individual of the philosopher and the ruler must be possible, in a sense that falls under the distinction *lexis/praxis* [i.e., as laid out at 473A]." Myles Burnyeat (1992.177) also argues for an interpretation of "possible" in the *Republic* in terms of "whether a reasonable approximation to it is a practicable possibility."
43. The position that I adopt on the *Republic* is in the end pretty close to one that Klosko rejects (1986.174), "[an employment] of the imaginary to project the ideal," i.e., as I take it, to provide a standard to aim at. In the whole construction of the *Republic,* what matters above all else is the principle that institutions and laws will be based on reason and knowledge; *that* is what we must attempt to approximate to.
44. I here perhaps go beyond what is explicit in Laks 1990; but the expansion seems consistent with Laks' account.
45. That is, to the city that I have identified with the "first-best" of the *Laws.*
46. This, however, might not be counted as particularly significant, insofar as the *Laws* is primarily concerned with human corruptibility rather than with the possible limits of human understanding. (Plato in the *Laws* seems to allow that even absolute knowledge would not be sufficient to keep corruption at bay: the implication of 711–12 and 875 is evidently that human beings, however knowledgeable, remain essentially corruptible. *Pace* Laks [1990.217], I believe the same to be true even of the ideal philosopher of the *Republic.*)
47. See, e.g., *Timaeus* 19A.
48. This is, I think, the implication of 473C–D itself; it is also strongly suggested by the terms of the discussion of the "possibility" of the proposal in VI.
49. What I have in mind here is of course not primarily the *Menexenos* itself (and the *Protagoras*) but its models in Lysias and Perikles and/or Thucydides. One difference

is that Plato does not regard the participation in government by all the citizens as itself a fundamental principle (see, e.g., *Laws* 757D); that requirement is rather, as I have suggested, a consequence of the unavailability of the ideal, expert ruler or rulers who would provide the only true justification for monarchy or oligarchy/aristocracy.

50. Or, more strictly, his second-best constitution, if we count in that of Kallipolis.
51. On Morrow's account (see n.38 above), this is what Plato thought Athens once was, but had ceased to be; thus the *Laws* as a whole is advocating a return to a kind of ancestral constitution. Pressing this point in discussion, Harvey Yunis pointed to *Laws* 698Aff., where the Athenian explicitly praises the Athens of the time of the Persian Wars, specifically because there was a *politeia . . . palaia* and the citizens were properly subservient to the laws. But see n.39 above; and further below.
52. See above, at n.15, and cf. *Laws* 832B–D, 962D–E. For the general interpretation I have adopted of 693D–E, cf. Stalley 1983.120–22.
53. Suzanne Saïd, in discussion, asked why we should see any connection with democracy here; why is Plato not just proposing a *politeia* in the orators' sense, i.e., a non-tyranny, and in that case is the point not rather that it is a *mixed* constitution that is being proposed? My response now, if not at the time, is that the mixture is there to ensure the presence of geometrical as well as arithmetical equality, i.e., to prevent the emergence of simple majority rule. Hence my claim, at n.10, that "the base of the mix is provided by democracy."
54. At n.38.
55. See *Laws* 951B–C.
56. It is in this sense that I should now reply to those participants in the colloquium—notably Suzanne Saïd and Lisa Kallet—who insisted that Magnesia looked as much like Sparta as Athens, and probably more like Sparta. Plato was not a Laconiser, or anything else, at least so far as concerns his writing. (I should like to thank all members of the colloquium—and also those who heard a heavily revised version of the original paper at a meeting of the North-East Classical Research Seminar in Durham, England, in January 1996—for helping me to see more precisely what my thesis is. Michael Stokes and John Moles were particularly helpful on the latter occasion.)
57. See Rowe 1995, esp. 14–18.
58. See n.39 above.

Chapter 12 Notes

1. On the factor of productivity see Kannicht 1983. The comic fragments are cited according to *PCG*.
2. Raaflaub 1990 includes tragedy in his survey of fifth-century perceptions of democracy but omits comedy and oratory.
3. Though tyranny was hardly an actual threat to the Athenians, they feared it much more than oligarchy, the real threat. But after all, oligarchy can be (and in 411 was)

"democratic"; from a modern vantage point the fifth-century democracy itself could be called oligarchic; see Brock 1989.161–62. For the centrality of freedom see Raaflaub 1985.

4. On this question see Lewis 1971.
5. Davies 1975.378.
6. Cf. Thuc. 2.37.1, 6.39.1; Hansen 1991.83–84.
7. Sinclair 1988.41.
8. *Parrhēsia* as plain speech: Aischines 1.51; 2.104; as truth telling, associated with pride and freedom: Aischines 2.70; Arist. *Nik. Ethics* 1124b; Demokritos 18, 43; Euripides, *Hippolytos* 421–23; Plato, *Gorgias* 492d, 521a; Menander, *Epitrepontes* 623. In general see Raaflaub 1980; Spina 1986.
9. Herodotus 3.80.6; Thucydides 2.37.1; Euripides, *Suppliants* 438–41; *Phoenician Women* 1015; cf. Monoson 1994b.182–83.
10. Euripides, *Suppliants* 433–41; Nikostratos com. 1.11–16 ("poverty's weapon").
11. Opposed to slavery: Eurip. *Ion* 672–75; *Phoenician Women* 391–92; opposed to tyranny, oligarchy, or Sparta: Aeschylus, *Persians* 691–94; Aischines 1.180–81, 3.6; Demosth. 20.105–8, 22.32; Plato, *Republic* 567b; Arist. *Politics* 1272a, 1313b; Nikostratos com. 1.11–16. In general see Ostwald 1995a, who underlines the close association between freedom and free speech in the fifth century.
12. E.g., Demosth. 1.1; *Exord.* 27.
13. Demosth. 3.3, 10.76; see Ober 1989.323.
14. Cf. Diodotos vs. Kleon in Thuc. 3.42–43 and Aristophanes' portrayal of Kleon as both a flatterer of Demos and an intimidator of opponents (*Knights* 45–70 and *passim*).
15. E.g., Demosth. 22.31, 60.25–26.
16. Her. 5.78; Thuc. 2.39.1, 40.1–2; *parrhēsia* was not an inappropriate name for a trireme (*IG* II^2 1624.81).
17. Cf. Perikles in his Funeral Oration (Thuc. 2.37.2–3).
18. See in general Halliwell 1991b; for festivals Henderson 1991a.13–18.
19. Cf. Isokrates 11.40; Plato, *Republic* 908c.
20. Cf. the portrayal of market-women in Aristophanes, *Wasps* 469–99, 1388–1414 (with Henderson 1987b.121), the chorus in *Lysistrata* 379, and the silenced wife, ibid. 507–28 (in pointed contrast with Andromache in *Iliad* 6).
21. Cf. Menander, *Monostichoi* 60 (Jaekel), "an undowered girl has no *parrhēsia*."
22. Pseudo-Xenophon, *Constitution of the Athenians* 1.2, 12; Demosth. 9.3.
23. Cf. Eurip. *Elektra* 1049–56 (of a parent); *Bakchai* 668–73; Menander, fr. 370 (of masters); Plato, *Symposium* 694b (of Kyros); Xenophon, *Agesilaos* 11.5 (of Agesilaos).
24. Cf. Aischines 1.14; Demosth. 22.30–32, 25.28, 59.28.
25. See generally Wallace 1994a.
26. For the rewards of leadership see Sinclair 1988.163–90.
27. Sinclair 1988.33–34.
28. See Hansen 1987.59–61, 63–66.

29. See Rhodes 1981.345; Henderson 1990.279–80.
30. See Sinclair 1988.68–73, 77–83, 152–61; for quietism see Carter 1986.
31. Cf. Pseudo-Xenophon, *Const. of the Athenians* 2.17; Thuc. 3.42–43; Xenophon, *History of Greece* 1.7.35.
32. For the claim of sincerity cf. Monoson 1994b.175.
33. Cf. Thuc. 6.13.1, 24.4; Pseudo-Xenophon, *Const. of the Athenians* 2.18; Aristoph. *Acharnians* 290, 493, 515–16; *Thesmophoriazousai* 540–47; *Wealth* 948; Isokrates 7.58, 8.14; Demosth. 21.14; Sokrates' rationale for avoiding politics, Plato, *Apology* 31c8–32a3; Hansen 1987.69–72.
34. E.g., Thuc. 2.65, 3.42–43; Aristoph. *Knights passim*; Arist. *Const. of the Athenians* 28.3.
35. For abusive speech as a feature of public life cf., e.g., Aristoph. *Acharnians* 38; *Knights passim*; *Clouds* 1140–41; *Wasps* 1183–84; *Peace* 635–47; *Birds* 1541; *Frogs* 857–58; *Ekklesiazousai* 142–43, 248–55, 399ff., 567; Pseudo-Xenophon, *Const. of the Athenians* 2.18; Plato, *Laws* 11.934d–36b.
36. For shame as a self-inhibiting factor in public speaking cf. Halliwell 1991b.289–90.
37. Kleon formally renounced his *philoi* so as to demonstrate his allegiance to the demos and not to a clubby circle (cf. Henderson 1990.280), and for Thucydides ruthless competition between politicians endangered the democratic process (2.65).
38. Before Ephialtes' reforms the Areopagos may have had, like similar bodies in Sparta and other states, *cura morum* and power to punish private behavior; cf. Cawkwell 1988.
39. For the historicity of the charges see Brickhouse & Smith 1989.30–34.
40. See Wallace 1994b for the prosecutions of these and other intellectuals.
41. See Henderson 1993b.597–99.
42. Murray 1990. Blaspheming the Mysteries was a stock charge even before 415: see Aristoph. *Wasps* 377–80, with Henderson 1993b.598. For the charge of *asebeia* generally see Ostwald 1986.528–36.
43. Plato's defense of *parrhēsia* in terms of philosophical as opposed to democratic (rhetorical) practice, especially in *Republic* Bk. 8, is especially trenchant: see Monoson 1994b.
44. For fuller accounts see Kraus 1985.25–30; Henderson 1990; Mastromarco 1994a.171–82.
45. So Halliwell 1991a.54–66, with earlier bibliog.
46. Gomme 1938 is the classic formulation of this view.
47. For a good recent discussion see Mastromarco 1994b.
48. Schol. Aristoph. *Acharnians* 67, naming the archons (not inferable from the commented text).
49. A similar rationale had motivated the fining of the tragic poet Phrynichos for his play of 493 on the recapture of Miletos by the Persians the previous year (Her. 6.21); for a recent discussion see Rosenbloom 1993.
50. Kallet, this vol.

51. If Phrynichos did not in fact write these words, as some suspect, then why would anyone have attributed such a decree to Syrakosios?
52. As Sommerstein 1986 has shown. Eric Csapo suggests that this avoidance may rather be due to self-restraint by the poets, but that begs the question: Syrakosios' decree forbade *something* that the poets could not be trusted to avoid voluntarily. Some clear examples of comic self-restraint are discussed below.
53. So Halliwell 1991a.61–63; D. M. MacDowell (as reported by Wallace 1994a.114).
54. So Atkinson 1992.
55. Aristoph. *Acharnians* 370–82, 496–519, 628–32; cf. Atkinson 1992.60–61.
56. See most recently Mastromarco 1994b.
57. See MacDowell 1995.352–53.
58. See Halliwell 1980.
59. For the novelty and daring of Aristophanes' "demagogue-comedies" see Lind 1990.217–57.
60. Wallace 1994a.110.
61. On the essential similarities see Dover 1974.23–33; Heath 1997.
62. Sommerstein 1986.104.
63. See Henderson 1990.295.
64. MacDowell 1993.
65. Cf. Pseudo-Arist. *Problemata* 29.14: "if a man reviles a magistrate the fines are heavy, but if he reviles a private individual there is no penalty."
66. See Sommerstein 1980; Henderson 1987b.
67. For this ancient satirical technique (*emphasis*) see Ahl 1984. Halliwell 1991a.58, n.41 questions whether this *emphasis* was defensive "since it was used *in the same period* as the growth of *onomasti komōidein* [ridicule by name]," but surely there were differences in the relative danger posed by given targets.
68. So Harding 1994.
69. For example, Halliwell 1991a.54.
70. See Rosen 1988 for comedy's iambic heritage.
71. For vulgarity as a traditional popular entertainment see Henderson 1991a.1–29; for shame and self-restraint see Halliwell 1991b.289–90.
72. For the connection in comedy between tone and earnestness see de Ste. Croix 1972, Appendix XXIX.
73. Cf. Aristoph. *Knights passim;* Thuc. 3.36.6; Arist. *Const. of the Athenians* 28.3. For democracy as a saturnalian polity see Edwards 1993, and for comic influence on oratory see Harding 1994.
74. But does not disappear entirely: cf. Nesselrath 1997.
75. For an overview see Halliwell 1991b.
76. See Halliwell 1991b.285–87.
77. See Goldhill 1990; Easterling 1997; Pelling 1997; Saïd, this vol.
78. See Lind 1990.217–57; Sommerstein 1992.
79. For a survey see Sommerstein 1992.

80. For the institutional structures and procedures see Goldhill 1990.97–106; Henderson 1990.285–93; Cartledge 1997b. Csapo & Slater 1995 provide the major testimonia.
81. See Csapo & Slater 1995.420–21; for its symbolic importance cf. Sinclair 1988.59.
82. See Sinclair 1988.67.
83. Connor 1990 argues that the Dionysia was *newly* created as an element of the Kleisthenic reforms as "a celebration of civic freedom" (23); for qualms see Sourvinou-Inwood 1994 and Quass 1995.28–29.
84. Cf. Arist. *Poetics* 1448a 28–40 on sixth-century Megara; Csapo & Slater 1995.174.
85. See Arist. *Const. of the Athenians* 22.5, with Rhodes 1981; on ostracism and comedy see Christ 1992; Rhodes 1994.
86. See Csapo & Slater 1995.166.
87. And vice versa in some respects: cf. Halliwell 1991b.293–94.
88. For the concept of notional versus actual audience see Henderson 1991b.
89. See Ober & Strauss 1990.
90. For the social background of the dramatic poets see Henderson 1990.291–92.
91. For elements of the traditional role of lone advisor, moralizer, and castigator of the group that were shared by poet and orator see Dover 1974.23–33.
92. For this dissonance in tragedy see Griffith 1995.
93. Foreigners did not attend the Lenaia (Aristoph. *Acharnians* 504–6) because it was held in winter, not because they were barred.
94. For women's attendance see Henderson 1991b. Goldhill 1994 is still skeptical, but his attempt to discredit the ancient evidence is strained, and his main argument, that the theater was civic space and therefore (as theory predicts) off-limits to women, fails to explain why other noncivic categories *could* attend.
95. For the audience generally see Csapo & Slater 1995.286–90.
96. Henderson 1993a.
97. The liability of comic speech to the rules governing *parrhēsia,* its civic integration, and its political *tendenz* (see below at n.102) all differentiate it from the "fool's privilege" of the medieval *Hofnarr* or the komastic flyting of such carnivalesque events as the Basel *Fastnacht* (described by Gelzer 1992; for festive Greek analogues see Dover 1993.247–48).
98. Plato, *Apology* 18b–d, 19b–c, 23c–d.
99. See Sommerstein 1993; Dover 1993.73–75; MacDowell 1995.299–300.
100. Plutarch, *Perikles* 32 connects Hermippos with the prosecution of Aspasia.
101. For statistics see Sommerstein 1996; for Nikias see Connor 1971.168–69; Ostwald 1986.214; for comic criticism of policies as well as style see Edwards 1993.115, n.49.
102. For the polarization of aristocracy and demos in the 430s and 420s see Ostwald 1986.175–205; Wallace, this vol.
103. Sommserstein 1997 suggests that, before the institution of the *theōrikon,* the (radical) poor were indeed underrepresented in the theater.
104. For example, Edwards 1993.101.

105. For this line see, e.g., Demosth. 3.30–31. In *Ekklesiazousai* the entire demos is ousted and replaced by their own wives, but by democratic means.
106. See Meiggs 1972.391–96.
107. Dover 1993.72.
108. So Carey 1994.75.
109. See Ober 1994b.170.

Chapter 13 Notes

1. Griffith 1995.63. On many issues discussed in this chapter, see now also Easterling 1997; Pelling 1997.
2. Connor 1990.
3. Pickard-Cambridge 1968; Kolb 1979.517–22.
4. Pickard-Cambridge 1968.71–99; Csapo & Slater 1995.139–57, 414.
5. The date is highly controversial; suggestions range from Perikles to the mid-fourth century: Csapo & Slater 1995.287–88, 420–21.
6. Poets: Csapo & Slater 1995.105, 108–9. Strategoi: Plutarch, *Kimon* 8.7–9.
7. The testimonia in *TGF* list only seven foreigners among forty-nine poets, and the first fourteen tragic poets are all Athenians. Chorus: Schol. Aristoph. *Plutos* 954 (quoted by Csapo & Slater 1995.135).
8. Plato, *Symp.* 175e: about 30,000; even if wrong, this figure is significant, for it is also the conventional number of Athenian citizens (Redfield 1990.318). Pickard-Cambridge 1968.236: 14,000 to 17,000.
9. Csapo & Slater 1995.289, 298–300.
10. Winkler 1990a.37–40; Csapo & Slater 1995.289–90.
11. Csapo & Slater 1995.157–65, 414–15.
12. Goldhill 1987.59–64; 1990.100–106; Meier 1988.62–74.
13. Demosthenes, *On the Crown* 120.
14. Isokrates, *Peace* 82; Aischines, *Against Ktesiphon* 154.
15. Kolb 1979.507–15; 1981.
16. Esp. Demosthenes, *On the Crown* 169–70.
17. McDonald 1943.
18. Gregory 1991.1–4; Croally 1994.20–22.
19. *Rep.* 595c, 598d, 607a; Salkever 1986.278–85; Croally 1994.23–26 (concise bibliog.: 23, n.19).
20. *Gorgias* 502c; *Laws* VII 817c; cf. Aristoph. *Clouds* 1088–94.
21. *Gorgias* 502b–c; *Rep.* X 602b; *Laws* VII 817b–d.
22. E.g., *Minos* 320d–321a. Praise: *Rep.*VIII 568c.
23. Macleod 1982.131, n.28; Rosenbloom 1993.161–68.
24. See Conradie 1981; Sartori 1988.
25. Lanza 1977a.3 aptly quotes Piscator's program for his proletarian theater.
26. Forrest 1986.229, citing Conacher.
27. Schwinge 1992 is an exception.

28. E.g., de Romilly 1965.46: "Les tragédies grecques sont bien souvent politiques par nature, de naissance, en vertu d'un état de fait"; Lanza 1977a.15: "Il teatro è in Atene costituzionalmente politico: fa parte della vita politica della città"; Taplin 1986.167: "Greek tragedy is through and through political"; Gregory 1991.6.
29. Rösler 1980b; Corsini 1986–88; Euben 1986; Meier 1988; cf. the titles of Euben 1990; Sommerstein et al. 1993; Seaford 1994.
30. Raaflaub 1989.49.
31. Bengl 1929; Zielinski 1931; Eberhardt 1944; Frei 1946; Webster 1948.
32. Webster 1948; Podlecki 1966; Diano 1969; Zuntz 1955.
33. Dover 1957; Dodds 1960.
34. Macleod 1982.132.
35. Delebecque 1951.26, 47; Ehrenberg 1954.11; Podlecki 1966.vii; Degani 1979.255; cf. Conradie 1981.24 (in a survey of various political interpretations of tragedy): "Critics show a preference for the term 'reflect' to describe the influence of the contemporary events on Greek tragedy."
36. Grégoire & Goossens 1940; Goossens 1962; Delebecque 1951 (cit. 28), 1962, 1969.
37. Zuntz 1955, 1958.
38. Zuntz 1955.63; similarly Garvie 1969.143.
39. Macleod 1982.124–33; Dodds 1960 (1973).45–53.
40. Post 1950; Stoessl 1952.
41. Kolb 1979.539.
42. E.g., Hall 1993b.267.
43. Knox 1957; Meier 1990b.133; cf. Rosenbloom 1995.106 (Aeschylus' *Agamemnon* and Athenian naval hegemony).
44. Conradie 1981.26.
45. Garvie 1969.148; cf. Burian 1974.
46. E.g., Meier 1988.110–11 (Aesch. *Suppliants* 370 refers to Ephialtes, because it does not fit the context).
47. Conradie 1981.24.
48. Vernant 1972.25; Lanza 1983.119; Vidal-Naquet 1992b.18 (cit.).
49. Taplin 1986.167.
50. Redfield 1990.325.
51. Jameson 1956; Hall 1993b.267.
52. Boegehold 1982.147.
53. Mastronarde 1994.14.
54. Cf. Thuc. 2.65.7, 3.82.8, 8.89.3; Aristoph. *Frogs* 359–61, 1427–30; de Romilly 1965. On *Orestes* and *Iphigenia at Aulis,* produced after the oligarchy of 411, as exposing the corruption of Athenian democracy, see, e.g., de Romilly 1972; Hall 1993b.267–71.
55. Stoessl 1952.115.
56. Delebecque 1951.18.
57. Webster 1948.33–34; Davison 1966.101–2; Podlecki 1966.125; Culasso-Gastaldi 1986.39.

58. Levi 1977/1978.
59. Salanitro 1965; Melchinger 1974.47; Hahn 1981; Rosenbloom 1995.93–94.
60. Müller 1833; Blass 1907; Salanitro 1966; Lloyd-Jones 1970.273–75; Cole 1977; Hahn 1981.184; Rhodes 1981.312; Farrar 1988.35.
61. Jacoby, *FGrH* IIIB Suppl. I.25; Dover 1957; Quincey 1964; Degani 1979.273; Kuch 1981.143; Forrest 1986; Wallace 1989.87–93.
62. Podlecki 1966.94.
63. Dodds 1960 (1973).48.
64. Cauer 1895; Livingstone 1925; Smertenko 1932; Headlam & Thomson 1966; Webster 1948.38; Stoessl 1952.138; Costa 1962.31; Sommerstein 1989.31–32.
65. Meier 1990b.114; cf. Gülke 1969; Schaps 1993.514.
66. Schröder 1914; Butts 1947; Grossmann 1970.111–61; Blundell 1993.
67. Lattimore 1943.
68. Loraux 1980.229–30; Macleod 1982; Saïd 1983, 1993.
69. Zeitlin 1986.117.
70. Easterling 1984.40. See also Davie 1982; Donini 1986; Blundell 1993; Seaford 1994.346.
71. Thebes: Grossmann 1970.154–61; Zeitlin 1986 (with Croally's criticism [1994.38–42]).
72. Raaflaub 1989.49.
73. Meier 1980.144–246; 1990b.82–139; Farrar 1988.28–38; cf. Euben 1986; 1990.45 (cit.).
74. Costa 1962.22; foreigners: Vidal-Naquet 1992a.
75. de Romilly 1969, 1977, 1983; Petre 1971; Lanza 1977a.95–159 (tyranny); Mette 1981; Lotze 1981; Turasiewicz 1981; Knox 1982; Saïd 1984; Hall 1989.
76. Easterling 1984.42.
77. Pelasgos: Stoessl 1952; Grossmann 1970.149–53; Podlecki 1986.82–86.
78. Callahan 1944; de Romilly 1969; Lanza 1977a; Easterling 1984; Podlecki 1986, 1993.
79. Arrowsmith 1963.33.
80. Croally 1994.37.
81. Euben 1986.23.
82. Ibid. 24.
83. Di Benedetto 1971, 1978; Cerri 1979 (cit. 269); Citti 1978 (with reviews by Portulas 1981; Scarcella 1982); Kuch 1979, 1980, 1981, 1983.
84. Maitland 1992.28; Rösler 1980b.18 (speaking of the "Konsolidierungsfunktion" of tragedy and its reinforcement of the citizen's "Identifikation mit dem demokratischen Status quo"); Lanza 1977a.12.
85. Segal 1986.47; Longo 1990.14, 19.
86. Meier 1990b.116.
87. Ober 1989; Kurke 1991; Griffith 1995 (cit. 65).
88. Longo 1990.18.
89. Ober & Strauss 1990.263; de Romilly 1965.

90. Griffith 1995.109; Lanza et al. 1977.25.
91. Lanza 1983.119.
92. Longo 1990.18–19.
93. Gregory 1991.8, 185.
94. Loraux 1986; Meier 1990b.89; Bowie 1993.11.
95. Meier 1990b.106–7.
96. Solmsen 1949; Saïd 1985.284–344.
97. Finley 1966; Meier 1990b.112.
98. Segal 1986.47 (cf. Zeitlin 1986.116); Goldhill 1987.73–74; Croally 1994.43–44.
99. Vernant 1972.
100. Goldhill 1987.73; 1990.
101. Osborne 1993a.34.
102. Seaford 1994.203.
103. Goldhill 1988.191.
104. Rosenbloom 1993.191.
105. Luschnig 1976; Buxton 1982.170–86; Gregory 1991.85–120; Croally 1994.
106. Hall 1989; cf. Saïd 1984.
107. Michelini 1994 (a brilliant interpretation).
108. Jones 1962.83–84: *oikos* "is at once house and household, building and family, land and chattels, slaves and domestic animals, hearth and ancestral graves: a psycho-physical community of the living and the dead and the unborn"; cf. MacDowell 1989.10–21; Strauss 1990.104.
109. Foxhall 1989.42; Aristotle, *Politics* 1276b 1.
110. Strauss 1990.105–6; Aristotle, *Politics* 1253b 3.
111. Wolff 1978.12.
112. Humphreys 1983.69–70.
113. Ibid. 73.
114. 73, 232, 278, 335, 454, 479, 482.
115. 71–73, 190, 418, 454, 479, 482. Cf. Maitland 1992.30–31.
116. Winnington-Ingram 1983.18–19, with short discussion and good bibliography.
117. 655, 695, 709, 720ff., 766, 784–85, 819, 831–32, 841, 887, 976–77. *Trophē:* 786; on the two possible interpretations ("the tendance of Oedipus by his sons" or "the rearing of the sons by Oedipus"), see Thalmann 1978.19–20; Winnington-Ingram 1983.46–48.
118. 636: Polyneikes; 676–81, 685–87, 691–93: Eteokles.
119. 750 (*philoi*). It is tempting to see here, with the scholiast and Winnington-Ingram 1983.45, a reference to bad advice given to Laios by his wife. By attributing responsibility to Jocasta, Aeschylus might therefore emphasize the role of women in powerful families and the pernicious influence of private interests on the public sphere.
120. On Laios' oracle, see Thalmann 1978.9–15.
121. Winnington-Ingram 1983.51–52.
122. City: 74, 120, 136, 302–3, 823, 1006. Kadmeians: 9, 39, 47, 531, 543, 679, 1015, 1025, 1026.

123. For various criticisms of this view, see Di Benedetto 1971.112; Cerri 1982a.154; Rösler 1980b.13–15; Sourvinou-Inwood 1989; Bennett & Tyrrell 1990.
124. Knox 1982.13; Sourvinou-Inwood 1989.
125. Ehrenberg 1954.67ff.
126. Sorum 1982.205.
127. 178–81, 208, 288, 320, 565, 571, 651, 652. Blundell 1989.117.
128. It is uncertain whether Athenian law prohibited burial of a traitor (Cerri 1982b.123–29); nor was prolonged public exposure of a corpse normal practice of Greek states (Rösler 1980b.13–14; Parker 1983.44, quoted approvingly by Foley 1995.136).
129. On the ambiguity of 44, *aporrhēton polei* (forbidden by or for the city?), see Blundell 1989.111, n.24.
130. Blundell 1989.126, quoting 173–74.
131. Easterling 1984.42 rightly on 269ff.
132. Strauss 1990.120; cf. Funke 1966; Lanza 1977a.50–58; Cerri 1982a.138–49; Nussbaum 1986.55–56; Blundell 1989.125–27; Bennett & Tyrrell 1990.442.
133. Knox 1982.17; Nussbaum 1986.63–66; Blundell 1989.106–15.
134. Bennett & Tyrrell 1990; see Foley 1995.140–42 for the difficulties and advantages of this argument.
135. Knox 1982.16; Blundell 1989.146.
136. Zuntz 1955.5; Michelini 1994.220.
137. Fitton 1961.439, 444–45.
138. Fitton 1961.435; Burian 1985.131–38.
139. For various interpretations of this problematic speech, see Fitton 1961.436–40; Collard 1972; Lanza 1977b.63, 74; Michelini 1994.241–44; Burian 1985.146–49.
140. Michelini 1994.245–47.
141. 3–5, 28, 293 (Aithra); 382, 562, 1168 (Theseus).
142. Musti 1963; Curty 1995.
143. 1152, 1215: *ekdikazein,* echoed by 154, *ekdikazon* (corr. Hermann), and 833, 1222 (*pikros*).
144. Riemschneider 1940; Ebener 1963; de Romilly 1965; Rawson 1970.112.
145. 217–18, 241–49, 291–92, 676–82, 828–29.
146. Rawson 1970.122.
147. Ibid. 120.
148. 1317, 1342, 1480–81, 1495–97, 1500, 1504, 1579–83.
149. 80, 482–83, 591, 601, 635, 1655. House: 260, 473–74, 482–83, 486, 547, 602.
150. 488, 605, 609, 1376, 1629 (*patris*); 573 (*patra*); 432–33, 570, 1628, 1652 (polis); 511 (*gē*).
151. Mastronarde 1994.391.
152. 1464, which I interpret, with Paley and Mastronarde, as "now that they are dead, victory is nowhere to be found."
153. Mastronarde 1994.597.
154. Despite Mastronarde 1994 ad loc., I think that Antigone's words in 1657 argue for

interpreting *tōn aporrhētōn polei* as "the things forbidden by [and not "for"] the city."

155. 45–54, 1047–50, 1352–53, 1502–7.
156. *Contra* Rawson 1970.112.
157. Mastronarde 1994.330.
158. Maitland 1992.30.
159. Foley 1995.145.

Chapter 14 Notes

I owe thanks to all participants in the CHS colloquium, especially Deborah Boedeker, Eric Csapo, Albert Henrichs, Margaret Miller, Martin Ostwald, and Kurt Raaflaub, as well as W. R. Connor, Michael Jameson, Steve Johnstone, and Victoria Wohl.

1. This study has been informed by the following work on the Panathenaia: Pfuhl 1900; Leacock 1900; Deubner 1932.22–35; Nilsson 1951; Bömer 1952; Davison 1958, 1959; Parke 1977.33–50; Simon 1983.55–72; N. Robertson 1985, 1992; Neils 1992, 1996; Loraux 1993; Goldhill 1994.
2. Bömer 1952.1894. Figueira (1984.469) succinctly captures the reasons why scholars have viewed the Panathenaia as democratic or "populist": "from its name, from its association with Peisistratos, and from its subsequent elaboration in Periklean Athens," and because it embraces a broad section of the population; but see Parker's reservations (1996.76).
3. Arist. *Const. of the Athenians* 18; Thuc. 6.54–58; Her. 5.55. See Wohl (1996.36–51), whose study, the only that treats the Panathenaia not merely as a celebratory expression of democratic principles, but as site of political contestation between elites and nonelites, has informed my appreciation of how this collection of tales informed and reflected ritual behavior at the Panathenaia.
4. Neils 1992.27, discussed by Wohl 1996.26, n.4. The view that the Panathenaia was inclusive is pervasive; see, e.g., Osborne 1994b.145.
5. For a critique of such a Durkheimian reading of ritual, wherein festivals are viewed as harmonious effervescences of community spirit, see Lindenbaum 1994.171–73.
6. Jameson 1997 argues that many features of Greek religion remained constant from before democracy developed in Athens, and did not change thereafter. Parker 1996 also challenges functionalist analyses that treat religious structures and changes within them as a direct reflection of political life. Theseus: Castriota 1992.33–63; 1997. See also Shapiro 1989.143–49.
7. On the participation of freed slaves, see Bekker, *Anecd.* I (1814).242,3.
8. *IG* II^2 334; Lewis 1959. Demesmen would have marched at the end of the procession proper, behind those with marked processional roles. Although they too were arranged in groups, marshalled by demarchs (*Suda, s.v. dēmarchoi;* scholia to Aristophanes, *Clouds* 37), they would have been barely distinguishable from onlookers (on Panathenaic *theōrika,* see Demosth. 44.37) and unable to see the procession.

For these reasons, perhaps, demesmen stopped marching; the inscription demands that they march in order to receive their meat portions.

9. "Carriers of secret things" (*arrhēphoroi*) were selected on account of their "good birth" (Harpocration, p. 57.1 Dindorf; Bekker, *Anecd.* I.446,18; 202,4) by the Basileus (*Etym. Magnum* p. 362,38; *Suda* E 2504, II p. 373,1 Adler). The same criterion applied to basket-carriers (Phot. *Lex. s.v. kanēphoros;* Bekker, *Anecd.* I.270, 31) and weavers (*ergastinai*); see n.48 below and Turner 1983.323–69 for a prosopographical study of these groups.
10. For a fuller description of the procession proper, see n.25 below; on thetes, Raaflaub, this vol., at n.110.
11. See Leacock 1900; Bömer 1952; Rotroff 1977.
12. Cited and discussed throughout the following presentation.
13. Summarized by Jenkins 1994. For a list of all the cruces, see Boardman 1984. The frieze's rejection, by Connelly 1996, among others, as a representation of the Panathenaic procession rests on the anomaly that a historical, rather than mythological, subject on a temple poses. Castriota 1992.184–229 provides parallels and precedents for the Parthenon frieze and demonstrates that it is less anomalous than formerly thought. Csapo & Miller, this vol., offer an overview of the effects of democracy on art that may account for the frieze's seemingly anomalous features.
14. A detailed discussion would go beyond the scope of this chapter. See Kroll 1979 (the frieze as a votive relief writ large with the Athenian populace elevated to almost heroic status in their intimate role as Athena's worshippers), describing a convincing sculptural and cultural context for this interpretation. For an overview of the frieze and the location of its marchers, see figure 1.
15. For one such attempt to reconcile the frieze with such sources, see Rotroff 1977. In contrast to Rotroff and others I do not attempt to establish a one-to-one correspondence between the figures on the frieze and hypothesized actual marchers.
16. The horsemen have been variously identified as ephebes (Reinmuth 1971.137; Simon 1983.59–61), Marathonian war dead (Boardman 1977.39–49), or newly formed cavalry (Bugh 1988.77; Spence 1993.267–71).
17. Osborne 1987b.104.
18. Bugh 1988.74–78; Castriota 1992.218–20.
19. Ridgway 1966.
20. Bonfante 1989.556.
21. The institution of Athens' state-sponsored cavalry has similarly been interpreted in opposed ways, as recognition of the elite's "status, or at least its wealth" (Gomme, Dover, & Andrewes 1945–81.1:328) or as an effort to make the cavalry more democratic by facilitating the inclusion of those who could not otherwise afford to maintain a horse (Bugh 1988.75). For other possible democratic appropriations of elite traits, see Ober 1989.262–63.
22. Reproduced in van Straten 1995, pl. 2, who discusses the association of this procession with the Panathenaia (1995.14–18, 203, with full bibliog.).

23. Miller 1992.104 dates the inclusion of metics as parasol- and tray-bearers to shortly after Pericles' citizenship law of 451/50. Aeschylus' *Oresteia*, however, indicates that the metics were included in the procession in some capacity even earlier: Thomson 1966.315–19. Institution of *metoikia:* Whitehead 1977.140–51. See Raaflaub, this vol., at n.103.
24. See *Iliad* 6.288–303, with Schefold 1964, pl. 30/31.
25. Modified from Pfuhl 1900.26–28. The distinction between procession proper and procession is mine.
26. See n.46 below.
27. Aelian, *Varia Historia* 6.1; Aristophanes, *Birds* 1550–52, with scholia; *Ecclesiazusae* 734.
28. Hesychius, *s.v. diphrophoroi;* Aristoph. *Birds* 1508, 1550–52, with scholia; *Ecclesiazusae* 734.
29. See nn.9, 48.
30. Ibid.
31. Photius *s.v. skaphai;* Harpocration, *s.v. skaphēphoroi;* Pollux 3.55; Zenobius 5.95; Hesychius, *s.v. systomoteron skaphas;* Aelian, *Varia Historia* 6.1.
32. Harpocration, *s.v. skaphēphoroi.*
33. For the order of the following marchers, see Pfuhl 1900; Leacock 1900; Rotroff 1977.
34. Bekker, *Anecd.* I (1814).242,3.
35. Here I follow Simon 1983.68. It seems more likely that these girls carry sacred furniture and are elite Athenian females rather than metic stool-bearers (*diphrophoroi*).
36. According to Rotroff 1977, the absence of parasol- and stool-bearers suggests that the frieze depicts the Panathenaic procession as it regrouped on the Acropolis before the sacrifice.
37. Simon 1983.64 identifies the frieze's water-bearers as the winners of the torch race, not the daughters of metics, and thus explains their gender. Interestingly, these hydriai strikingly resemble those used to collect tribute: Meritt, Wade-Gery, & McGregor 1939–53.1:123; Raubitschek 1941.359 on Aristoph. *Knights* 313, with scholia. See also Aristoph. *Birds* 602, with scholia.
38. Because these older men do not carry branches and there are no holes for metal attachments, they have been alternatively identified as Athenian magistrates: Simon 1983.62.
39. According to Dikaiarchos (schol. Aristoph. *Wasps* 544), women too processed as branch-bearers (*thallophoroi*).
40. Leacock 1900.33. There is evidence outside of Athens of contests and sortition to determine who should lead certain processions (Athenaeus 13.565f; Paus. 9.3.5–7).
41. See Bourdieu 1977.120: "Ritual practice . . . never defines beings or things otherwise than in and through the relationship it establishes practically between them."
42. Brulé 1987.287–323 links the function of *kanēphoroi* with the stage in a girl's life right before marriage. See also n.101 below.

43. See n.8 above.
44. Simon 1983.69–70; Shapiro, this vol., at n.52.
45. The offering bowls, pitchers, and incense burners carried by females on the east frieze may have been used in the sacrifice: Rotroff 1977.
46. *Kanēphoroi* are usual in public processions: van Straten 1995.10–12, 31–42; cf. Schelp 1975.
47. *IG* II^2 334. In the fourth century, Lycurgus supplied one hundred basket-bearers with silver and gold baskets as well as ornaments. See Paus. 1.29.16; Plut. *Vit. X Orat.* 852b; *IG* II^2 457.
48. The identity, age, and roles of those involved in weaving Athena's peplos are contested. Brulé 1987.99–105 distinguishes the *arrhēphoroi* from the *ergastinai* and reads the latter as recipients of honors in four inscriptions (*IG* II^2 1034, 1036+1060, 1942, 1943). Mansfield 1985.277–87 considers the two groups identical and thinks the inscriptions honor yet another group of females (about one hundred in number) who prepared the wool for the *arrhēphoroi-ergastinai*. On the *arrhēphoria*, see also Burkert 1966; Boedeker 1984, chap. 5; Shapiro, this vol.
49. See Miller 1992 *passim*; Kurke 1992.98. The stool carried for Athenian basket-bearers also had Eastern associations (Her. 3.146; Dinon in Athenaeus 514c). A similar folding stool was carried by slaves for Athenian men (Aelian, *Varia Historia* 4.22; Aristoph. *Knights* 1384–86, with scholia; Heraclides Ponticus in Athenaeus 514c). Rotroff 1977 attributes the absence of parasol- and stool-bearers on the frieze to their unimportance in the sacrifice that followed the procession (see n.36 above). Alternatively, their absence may indicate a deliberate erasure of metics from the frieze or some hesitation to include identifiable Eastern customs on the Parthenon.
50. Miller 1992.104.
51. Aelian, *Varia Historia* 6.1; Menander, fr. 191 K; *Com. adesp.* 1144, with Whitehead 1977.87.
52. Hesychius, *s.v. skaphēphoroi,* with Whitehead 1977.88.
53. Aeschylus, *Eumenides* 992, 1034.
54. Suda s.v. *askophorein.*
55. Aeschylus, *Eumenides* 1028–32, with Thomson 1966.315–16.
56. See Thomson 1966.315–19 for thorough discussion. On the color of the ephebes' cloaks, see also Maxwell-Stuart 1970.
57. Whitehead 1977.87.
58. Xenophon, *Symposium* 4.17; Aristoph. *Wasps* 542–44, with scholia.
59. Alexis in Athenaeus 3.64.10; on awards given to elites, see Demosth. 18.116.
60. De Polignac 1995.81–88; Osborne 1994a.143–60.
61. De Polignac 1995.84.
62. In his study of Montpellier, Robert Darnton writes (1985.124) that the city's main procession "ordered reality. It was not merely aimed at some utilitarian objective . . . It existed the way many statements and works of art exist—as sheer expression, a social order representing itself to itself." On processions, I have also found useful:

Muir 1981; Davis 1986; Smith 1987; Ryan 1989; Brooks 1988; Hanawalt & Reyerson 1994.

63. On the wealth of the *athlothetai,* the ten officials who organized the festival, see Nagy 1992.65. Wohl 1996 points out that the Panathenaia provided more opportunities for liturgies than any other state festival (Davies 1967.40); a large portion of the wealthiest class in Athens therefore invested large amounts of personal and monetary capital in this festival.
64. Connor, *Democracy and the Panathenaia* (emphasis in the original).
65. Raaflaub 1994.138–44.
66. Since the advent of cultural studies, classical scholars have become increasingly aware of how religious practices as well as political factors shaped Athens' civic life and what important role women played in religious rituals: e.g., Lonis 1994.52–53; Sourvinou-Inwood 1995a; see also Raaflaub, this vol., at n.137, with more bibliog.
67. Loraux 1993.47.
68. Raubitschek 1949, no.326.
69. Mette 1955, *s.v. agōn.*
70. Bourdieu 1991.115–16.
71. Cohen 1995.63.
72. For the size and composition of the liturgical class, see Davies 1981.1–37; for the function of liturgies, see Kallet, this vol.
73. On the relationship established between elites and nonelites through the exchange of "gifts" and rewards, embodied in the Greek word *charis,* see Davies 1981.91–96; Ober 1989.243–44.
74. Cohen 1995.62–64.
75. Pickard-Cambridge 1968.95–99.
76. Ober 1989.104–55.
77. Xenophon, *Hiero* 7.3–4, discussed by Cohen 1995.63 (tr. mine).
78. See, for example, the inscriptions discussed in n.48 above.
79. Aristotle equates office holding with honor (*Politics* 1278a 35f., 1281a 29f.). See also Thuc. 6.16.1–4.
80. Leitch 1992.22–23.
81. Demosth. *Against Meidias* 180.
82. Ibid. 171–74.
83. Johnstone 1994.219–40, whose approach to Xenophon's *Oeconomicus* and *On Hunting* is applicable here.
84. Aeschines, *On the Embassy* 151; Demosth. *On the Embassy* 287.
85. Demosth. *Ag. Meidias* 22, 25.
86. Isokrates, *Areopagiticus* 53–54.
87. Plato, *Republic* 327a4.
88. Lysias, *Against Agoratos* 80–81.
89. To generalize from this episode may be foolhardy. However, that Athenian marchers did value and monitor the privilege of marching is exemplified by Aeschines,

Against Timarchos 43, describing a row about who will march with whom in the procession (Goldhill 1994.361).

90. On the possible impact of ritual behavior outside of ritual contexts, see Jay 1992.6; Skorupski 1976.93; Bourdieu 1991.107–16.
91. Headlam 1906.
92. On the importance of a procession for declaring the identity of a newly formed city and thereby creating and assuring its existence, see Aristophanes, *Birds* 846–50.
93. Figueira 1984.466–69 suggests that there was greater political unrest during the years of the Greater Panathenaia, as though whatever picture the city created of itself at this time had a certain potency to imprint itself on the following four years. For a modification of this view, see Connor 1987.41, n.8.
94. Bourdieu 1991.121.
95. We can read their acts as so intentioned. For even if such actors do not create or understand the rules of ritual behavior, they certainly do think that their rituals have meaning. Skorupski 1976.50–52.
96. Goldhill 1994.357, 360, 369 only begins to explore the implications of imagining women as performers and spectators at ancient festivals. Stehle & Day 1996 study women as active spectators and interpreters of temple sculpture, Foxhall 1995 as active participants in religious festivals who "did not always allow themselves to be passively constituted" (108). Foxhall's thesis fits well with my present argument.
97. Geertz 1994.8.
98. On the colors (yellow, purple, and variegated) and function of these garments, see Leacock 1900.14–16. On the white garments of the *ergastinai* or *arrhēphoroi,* see the inscriptions listed in n.48.
99. An inscription from Andania in Messenia on the performance of mysteries details how different statuses of female initiates, their daughters, and slaves are to be demarcated by their clothing and jewelry, and regulates the clothing of female hierophants. The accoutrements, makeup, and entourage used by these females while processing receives particular attention. Interestingly, female hierophants are to use wicker, not purple, parasols: Sokolowski 1969, nos.65, 15–26, translated and discussed in Mills 1984.259.
100. On the social significance of women's clothing, competition, and sumptuary laws, see Mills 1984; Culham 1986. On women's competition more generally, Frasca 1991.
101. For stories of young girls seduced or pursued while marching, see Diodorus 9, fr. 37.1; cf. Polyainos, *Strategemata* 5.14, p. 251.1 Melber; Valerius Maximus 5.1, ext. 2; Plutarch, *Moralia* 189c (Peisistratos' daughter, when basket-bearer, is kissed by Thrasyboulos during a procession); Menander, fr. 558 K, with Plautus, *Cistellaria* 89–93 (a young woman is followed home after a procession and flattered). Aristophanes, *Acharnians* 241–83, a highly informative scene, suggests, as Brulé argues (1987.287–323), that *kanēphoroi* were on the brink of marriage and that the Panathenaia, like a "bal des débutantes," announced their eligibility.

102. See n.48 above.
103. *IG* II^2 1136, tr. in Lefkowitz & Fant 1982.118.
104. On metics' cloaks, see n.56 above.
105. Whitehead 1983.67–68; Pečirka 1966.
106. This claim of membership was also implicit in the metics' liturgical service which Davies 1981.92 calls "a deliberate investment in the goodwill of public opinion. The interest on this investment was to be drawn for the personal benefit of the investor; he was, or he fancied himself to be entitled to *charis*."
107. De Polignac 1995.78. This sentiment is remarkably reminiscent of Geertz's description of the formation of the Balinese festival state (1973.335). Reversing the priority usually given to political processes over religious ones, the Balinese rulers reenacted and staged an ideal religious order: "Power served pomp, not pomp power."
108. Aristotle explicitly states that residency does not provide qualification for citizenship (*Politics* 1275a 6–10). "Passive citizen": Mossé 1967, 1979.
109. Aristotle, *Politics* 1275a 23–25, 1275b 19–21, with Mossé 1967.19.

Chapter 15 Notes

For helpful comments we thank the contributors to this volume, especially Eric Csapo, Margaret Miller, Christopher Rowe, Alan Shapiro, and Harvey Yunis.

1. Morris, this vol. (introduction).
2. I. Morris 1992, chap. 5; Hölscher this vol., at nn.28–31; Shapiro, this vol., at n.7.
3. Morris, this vol., at n.69.
4. Renfrew 1986 (cf. Snodgrass 1986); Herman 1987.
5. See below, at n.78.
6. So, e.g., Ostwald 1992.
7. *Dēmiourgoi:* e.g., *Odyssey* 17.382–86; cf. Finley 1977.36–37, 56. Poets: Kurke 1991.
8. Harvey Yunis, commenting on an earlier version of this chapter, disagrees: "True, many fifth-century intellectuals and artists were not Athenian by birth, and they travelled around Greece, but that does not mean that they acquired their skills elsewhere . . . As the cultural center of Greece, Athens was precisely the place were many non-Athenians, as well as Athenians, improved, honed, and practiced, even acquired their art, even if they did not come to Athens devoid of all training."
9. References are cited by Wallace, this vol., at nn.3–4; see Webster's statement, this vol., introduction at n.33.
10. See Yunis, this vol., summarized below at n.76.
11. This seems to be indicated by the setting of several Platonic dialogues, especially the *Protagoras*.
12. Wills 1992.48 (author's emphasis).
13. Davies 1993.87, 94.
14. See Raaflaub, this vol., at n.30ff.
15. For patronage in the Greco-Roman world, see Gold 1987; Wallace-Hadrill 1989.
16. See also Davies 1993.96.

17. Kallet, this vol., at n.34; cf. Csapo & Slater 1995.140–41.
18. On details (for the following paragraph as well) and the liturgies, see Kallet, this vol., with bibliog.
19. Kallet, this vol., at n.73.
20. Hölscher 1996.180–87 (cit. 187, our tr.). On the disappearance of funeral sculpture, see above, n.2.
21. Kallet, this vol., at n.58.
22. As it is expressed in the ideology of the "freest and greatest city (*eleutherōtatē kai megistē polis*)," formulated around the outbreak of the Peloponnesian War and realized in the construction, at that time, of the Stoa of Zeus Eleutherios in the Agora: Raaflaub 1985.233–48.
23. Harrison 1989, esp. 55: "A contradiction between democracy and imperialism did not exist for the ancient Athenians."
24. See Goldhill 1990. The linkages explored in Kallet's chapter confirm "that it is necessary to examine the intersection of areas of Athenian life that were traditionally seen as having separate and separable histories. This applies to democracy, empire, the arts, and religion, but also the realms of finance and economy" (Kallet, this vol., conclusion).
25. E.g., Metzler 1988; Osborne 1994b; Shapiro 1996b; cf. Smarczyk 1990.31–57, 298–317.
26. Castriota 1997.197–201 (cit. 201).
27. On all this, see Hölscher, this vol. Outside enemies: Aeschylus, *Eumenides* 861–66, with Meier 1990b.116–17.
28. Shapiro, this vol., at n.15.
29. Ibid., at n.12.
30. See esp. Castriota 1992.33–133; 1997; Boedeker, this vol. To some extent this is visible already in Aeschylus' *Persians*, performed in 472.
31. Hölscher, this vol., after n.49.
32. Polar opposites: Lloyd 1966; cf. Cartledge 1993 (1997a). Odysseus: Vidal-Naquet 1986.15–38. On Greeks and others, e.g., Reverdin & Grange 1988; Georges 1994; Dihle 1994.
33. Hölscher, this vol., after n.50.
34. Hölscher, this vol., after n.32; so, too, J. J. Pollitt, in an unpublished manuscript on "Democracy and Ancient Greek Art": "democracy is not . . . a major theme in the art of the fifth century." But see in this volume Csapo & Miller, as well as Boedeker at n.59.
35. See recently Castriota 1997.200–201. On personification, see Shapiro 1993, whose main sources are vase and wall paintings. The latter would have been a suitable medium, but representation of personifications was inspired largely by literature and cult; see below. Vases show many hoplites and cavalry (for the larger context of such representations in Athenian imagery, see Lissarrague 1989, 1990; Boedeker, this vol.) but few allusions to naval warfare. In fact, warships and even naval battle

scenes are frequent on Archaic but very rare in classical art (Morrison & Williams 1968.73–117, 169–80, with pls.). Triremes appear in mythical scenes (e.g., representing the Argo on the "Talos Vase," ibid. 173–76, with pl. 26a) or on funeral stelai (representing death at sea, in whatever context, e.g., on the stele of Demokleides, cf. Ridgway 1983.202, with pl. 13.14). Depictions of triremes in full movement are known from the late fifth century (the "Lenormant relief," cf. Morrison & Williams 1968.170–73, with L. Beschi's reconstruction in Ridgway 1983.202, with pl. 13.13) and the late fourth century (the paintings of Protogenes on the Akropolis, Pliny, *Natural History* 35.101). What might have been done, but was apparently done only very late, is illustrated by the funeral pyre that Alexander erected for Hephaistion (Diodorus 17.115–16), the Nike of Samothrake, or the ship relief on the Akropolis of Lindos on Rhodos (Morrison & Williams 1968, pls. 27d, 28). As for "speaking names," an Archenautes is attested on an Attic red-figure stamnos of ca. 430 (BM E 456; Beazley 1963.1051.17; ill. in Shapiro 1996a.110) and an Aristonautes on a famous late-fourth-century funeral stele (Ridgway 1992), both without allusions to a naval context. Such names are not frequent and do not need to have military connotations (Ridgway 1992.271, with n.11). (For helpful suggestions on these issues we thank Ann Kuttner.) See also Csapo and Miller, this vol., at n.49.

36. Raubitschek 1962; Alexandri-Tzahou 1986. See also Lawton 1993; Palagia 1980.57–64; Pollitt, as in n.34. Kritias' tomb: schol. Aischines, *Ag. Timarchos*_39, doubted by many scholars, but defended by Pollitt (with reference to Hamdorf 1964.57) who adds, "I wonder, however, whether the scholiast has not garbled his information slightly. Could it be that the sculpture in question was a public monument set up by the victorious democracy after the fall of the Thirty which showed Demokratia giving the torch to Oligarchia? This seems to me more likely than that a monument was set up by the defeated oligarchs in order to taunt the followers of Thrasyboulos, although I admit that the latter is not impossible."

37. Despite the first oligarchic coup of 411/10 and the intermediate regime of the 5,000, after which democracy was restored without major violence, let alone war. After 404/3: Pollitt, as in n.35, with good comments.

38. Hansen 1991.83, with references. The reasons for the change in emphasis from *demos* to *demokratia* need to be explored further. Eric Csapo suggests that this shift could be indicative of "an emphasis on a general and abstract constitutional form of government" rather than the power relations by which one class dominates another. "This change seems more expressive of a propaganda of inclusion," characteristic of the conciliatory politics of the period after 403 (letter of Nov. 5, 1997).

39. *Demos* representing *demokratia:* Meier 1968, pt. 2 (= Kinzl 1995.144–53) and, more generally, 1970.36–52. Cult: Kron 1979.63–75. (The cult of Demos and the Charites [Graces] is much later: Kron 1979.66–67.) Parrhasios' painting of Demos: Pliny, *Natural History* 35.79: "His picture of the Demos of Athens also shows ingenuity . . . , since he displayed him in various moods (*varium*), as choleric, unjust and fickle, but also placable and merciful and compassionate, boastful, lofty and hum-

ble, fierce and timid—and all these at the same time"; see, e.g., Rumpf 1951. Such early personifications seem nevertheless rare; one decree relief possibly featuring a personification of Demos dates to 409/8 (Palagia 1980.62 D1; also identified as Kekrops or Erechtheus), compared to more than twenty in the fourth century.

40. Shapiro, this vol., at n.36.
41. Shapiro, this vol. (conclusion). See also Connor 1994.41, who emphasizes that such civic identity "had to be constructed and reconstructed in each generation by shared myths, by participation in cults, festivals, and ceremonies and by elaborate techniques of 'mixing.'"
42. Shapiro, this vol., at n.108.
43. Hölscher, this vol., at n.25. See also Walker 1995; Mills 1997.
44. Stupperich 1977; Clairmont 1983; Loraux 1986.
45. Hölscher, this vol. and 1996; see id. 1991.368–75. "Civic presence": Meier 1990b, chap. 4.
46. On the sixth-century Agora, see Shear 1978; Camp 1986.35–48; 1994. Changes after Kleisthenes: Camp 1986.48–77; von Steuben 1989; Shear 1994. Stoa Basileios: Camp 1986.53–57. Bouleuterion: Shear 1995. The dates of the Pnyx and the earliest theater of Dionysus are contested. For the Pnyx, with no external evidence, ca. 500 and ca. 460–440 have been proposed, simply tying it to the aftermath of Kleisthenes' or Ephialtes' reforms (Kourouniotes & Thompson 1932.107–13, esp. 109; Thompson 1982.136–37). Transfer of dramatic performances: Travlos 1971.537 proposes the Periklean period; the date of ca. 500, generally accepted before Travlos' revision, is defended by Newiger 1976, among others (see Csapo & Slater 1995.79–80, 410–11 for more bibliography).
47. See esp. Detienne 1965.
48. Hölscher 1996.171–78.
49. Harmodios Song: *Scol. anon.* 893, 896 Page (Athenaeus 15.50, 695ab); tr. in Fornara 1983a, no.39A. See also Csapo & Miller, this vol., at n.40 and after n.47. For bibliography and discussion of *isonomia* and its relation to Kleisthenes and democracy, see Raaflaub 1995.49–51.
50. Her. 5.55, 6.123; Thuc. 1.20, 6.54–59. For the political context of such debates, see Boedeker, this vol.; Munn 1999.
51. Hölscher, this vol., after n.21, with bibliog.; Castriota 1997; *contra,* Shapiro 1994b.124.
52. Hölscher, this vol., at n.27, with bibliog.; see also Mattusch 1994 and, on the problems of Athenian civic identity, Connor 1994.
53. See, however, Hölscher 1993.
54. Maurizio, this vol. (conclusion).
55. Ibid. On the relation between democracy and religion in fifth-century Athens, see Parker 1996, chaps. 7–9; Jameson 1997. For a brief summary, see Raaflaub, this vol., at n.148.
56. See also the beginning of Hölscher's chapter in this volume.

57. Adrados 1996.17 overemphasizes this phenomenon. See Csapo & Miller, this vol., after n.33.
58. Connor 1990; but see Sourvinou-Inwood 1994.
59. See Goldhill 1990; Saïd, this vol., at nn.3ff.; Henderson, this vol., at nn.79ff. On liturgies, Kallet, this vol.
60. Henderson, this vol., after n.85, after n.2, and after n.91; see also Connor 1996.
61. Henderson, this vol., after n.95.
62. Written before Easterling 1997 and Pelling 1997 were published.
63. Saïd, this vol., after n.113.
64. See also Adrados 1996.17. For recent discussion, see Kuch 1993; Easterling 1993. For democracy, see next note.
65. As argued, for example, by Ostwald 1986; Sealey 1987; Eder 1995a, 1997.
66. See Kallet, this vol., at n.91. Origins: Csapo & Slater 1995.40, 142.
67. See, e.g., Rosenbloom 1995; Mills 1997.
68. Csapo & Miller, this vol., at n.1.
69. Ibid., at n.28.
70. Widespread democracy: ibid., at n.1; empire, at n.3; conditions for change in mentality: at n.15.
71. Ibid., after n.9.
72. Ibid., at n.56.
73. The same could certainly be shown with political thought (see Farrar 1988; Meier 1993b), probably also with music (see Beschi 1996; Wallace, this vol.). We are much less certain about medicine and other sciences where Athens does not seem to play a major role at all.
74. Yunis, this vol., at n.14; Cole 1991a.
75. Yunis, this vol., at nn.21–25.
76. Ibid., after n.34.
77. Shapiro, this vol., at n.19. See Hölscher 1996.187.
78. See above at nn.1ff. "Artistic revolution": Hallett 1986; Hölscher, this vol., at nn.1–3.
79. Shapiro, this vol., at n.18; cf. Hölscher 1973.50–84; Pemberton 1988; Boedeker, this vol., at nn.19ff.
80. Hölscher, this vol., after n.19 and at n.38.
81. Ibid., at nn.46–49, and the summary in the conclusion of his chapter; also Boedeker, this vol.
82. Hölscher, this vol., at n.39 and before n.93.
83. Eric Csapo, while agreeing with our conclusion, places the emphasis differently. It "is not as if Athens remained part of the larger cultural matrix of Greece *despite* being democratic and imperialistic. Rather (1) the enabling conditions of democracy and imperialism were present throughout Greece, while (2) the fact of their actualization in Athens so completely transformed the broader cultural matrix that democracy and imperialism became essential constituents in the political consciousness of every state, even, and perhaps most especially, in those states which

most resisted it. The uniqueness of Athens lies largely in the fact that it eagerly embraced and developed common cultural trends which elsewhere met with a mixed or even predominantly hostile reception" (letter of Nov. 5, 1997).

84. Wallace, this vol., at n.52.
85. Rowe, this vol., n.1. Approaching the issues from a different angle, Wallace, this vol. (end of introductory section) considers sophists and Presocratics together.
86. Rowe, this vol., at n.2.
87. Ibid., at nn.10, 20 (our emphasis).
88. Ibid., at n.20.
89. Boedeker, this vol., after n.83, before n.95.
90. Ibid., after n.86.
91. Hölscher, this vol., after nn.94, 95.
92. Meier 1993b.
93. Meier 1996 (cit. 199, 209–10, 215; our tr.).
94. Raaflaub, this vol., at n.85.
95. Pollitt 1972.115; cf. Borbein 1995. See also Csapo & Miller, this vol., for a more ideological explanation of fifth-century art.
96. For a general survey, see Raaflaub, this vol., at n.148.
97. See esp. Auffarth 1995; Parker 1996, chaps. 9, 10; Jameson 1997.188–91.
98. See, e.g., Finley 1982, chap. 5; Wallace 1994b. On the most famous case, the trial of Sokrates, see recently Hansen 1996b, with bibliog.; Parker 1996, chap. 10.
99. Hölscher, this vol., at n.66.
100. See above, at n.85, and Csapo & Miller, this vol., at nn.23–25.

BIBLIOGRAPHY

CAH	*Cambridge Ancient History*. Cambridge: Cambridge University Press.
DK	Diels & Kranz 1952.
FGrH	*Die Fragmente der griechischen Historiker*. See Jacoby 1923–.
IG	*Inscriptiones Graecae*. Berlin: De Gruyter.
LIMC	*Lexicon Iconographicum Mythologiae Classicae*. Zurich: Artemis.
LSJ	Liddell, Scott, & Jones 1968.
ML	Meiggs & Lewis 1988.
PCG	*Poetae Comici Graeci*. See Kassel & Austin 1983–.
PMG	*Poetae Melici Graeci*. See Page 1962.
RE	*Paulys Realencyclopaedie der classischen Altertumswissenschaft*. Stuttgart: Druckenmüller.
SEG	*Supplementum Epigraphicum Graecum*. Leiden: Brill.
Supp. Hell.	*Supplementum Hellenisticum*. See Lloyd-Jones & Parsons 1983.
TGF	*Tragicorum Graecorum Fragmenta*. Several vols. by various authors. Göttingen: Vandenhoeck & Ruprecht, 1971–.

Accame, Silvio. 1961. "La concezione del tempo nell'età omerica e arcaica." *Rivista di filologia e di istruzione classica* n.s. 39, 359–94.

Adkins, Arthur W. H. 1960. *Merit and Responsibility: A Study in Greek Values*. Oxford: Clarendon Press.

——. 1972. *Moral Values and Political Behavior in Ancient Greece from Homer to the End of the Fifth Century*. New York: Norton.

——. 1985. *Poetic Craft in the Early Greek Elegists*. Chicago: University of Chicago Press.

Adrados, Francisco R. 1996. "La démocratie athénienne et les genres littéraires." In Sakellariou 1996.17–33.

Ahl, Fred. 1984. "The Art of Safe Criticism in Greece and Rome." *American Journal of Philology* 105, 174–208.

Aleshire, Sara B. 1994. "The Demos and the Priests: The Selection of Sacred Officials at Athens from Cleisthenes to Augustus." In Osborne & Hornblower 1994.325–37.

Alexandri-Tzahou, Olga. 1986. "Demokratia." *LIMC* 3.1, 372–74. (See also Tzachou-Alexandri.)

Allen, James. 1994. "Failure and Expertise in the Ancient Conception of an Art." In Thomas Horowitz & Alan I. Janis (eds.), *Scientific Failure*, 81–108. Lanham, Md.: Rowman and Littlefield.

Allen, James Turney. 1938. *On the Program of the City Dionysia during the Peloponnesian War*. Berkeley: University of California Press.

Aloni, Antonio. 1994. "L'elegia di Simonide dedicata alla battaglia di Platea (Sim. frr. 10–18 W^2) e l'occasione della sua performance." *Zeitschrift für Papyrologie und Epigraphik* 102, 9–22.

Amandry, Pierre. 1953. *Fouilles de Delphes* II A V: *La colonne des Naxiens et le portique des Athéniens*. Paris: De Boccard.

——. 1954. "Notes de topographie et d'architecture delphiques IV. Le palmier de bronze de l'Eurymédon." *Bulletin de Correspondance Hellénique* 78, 295–315.

Ameling, Walter. 1985. "Plutarch, Perikles 12–14." *Historia* 34, 47–63.

Amit, Moshe. 1965. *Athens and the Sea: A Study in Athenian Sea Power*. Collection Latomus 74. Brussels: Latomus.

Andreades, Andreas M. 1933. *A History of Greek Public Finance*. Tr. C. N. Brown. Cambridge, Mass.: Harvard University Press.

Andrewes, Antony. 1975. "Could There Have Been a Battle at Oinoe?" In Barbara Levick (ed.), *The Ancient Historian and His Materials. Essays in Honour of C. E. Stevens on His Seventieth Birthday*, 9–16. Westmead, England: Gregg International.

——. 1978. "The Opposition to Perikles." *Journal of Hellenic Studies* 98, 1–8.

——. 1982. "The Growth of the Athenian State." *CAH* III.3^2, 360–91.

Andronikos, Manolis. 1969. *Vergina* I: *To Nekrotapheion ton Tymvon*. Athens: Vivliothiki tis en Athinais Arkhaiologikis Etaireias.

——. 1984. *Vergina: The Royal Tombs and the Ancient City*. Athens: Ekdotiki.

——. 1987. "Some Reflections on the Macedonian Tombs." *Annual of the British School at Athens* 82, 1–16.

——, Makaronas, Ch., Moutsopoulos, N. & Bakalakis, G. 1961. *To Anaktoro tis Verginas*. Athens: Vivliothiki tis en Athinais Arkhaiologikis Etaireias.

Arnheim, M. T. W. 1977. *Aristocracy in Greek Society*. London: Thames & Hudson.

Arnott, W. Geoffrey. 1973. "Euripides and the Unexpected." *Greece & Rome* 20, 49–64.

Arrowsmith, William. 1963. "A Greek Theater of Ideas." *Arion* 2, 32–56.

Asheri, David (ed. & comm.). 1988. *Erodoto, Le Storie, Libro I: La Lidia e la Persia*. Milan: Mondadori.

Atkinson, J. E. 1992. "Curbing the Comedians: Cleon versus Aristophanes and Syracosius' Decree." *Classical Quarterly* 42, 56–64.

Auberson, Paul & Schefold, Karl. 1973. *Eretria. Arkhaiologikos Odhigos*. Tr. Petros G. Themelis. Athens: Yeniki Diefthynsis Arkhaiotiton kai Anastyloseos.

Auerbach, Erich. 1968. *Mimesis: The Representation of Reality in Western Literature*. Tr. W. R. Trask. Princeton: Princeton University Press.

Auffarth, Christoph. 1995. "Aufnahme und Zurückweisung 'neuer Götter' im spätklassischen Athen: Religion gegen die Krise, Religion in der Krise?" In Eder 1995b.337–65.

Auslander, Leora. 1996. *Taste and Power: Furnishing Modern France*. Berkeley: University of California Press.

Austin, Michel M. & Vidal-Naquet, Pierre. 1977. *Economic & Social History of Ancient Greece: An Introduction*. Tr. M. M. Austin. Berkeley: University of California Press.

Aymard, André. 1967. *Etudes d'histoire ancienne*. Paris: Presses Universitaires de France.

Badian, Ernst (ed.). 1966. *Ancient Society and Institutions: Studies Presented to Victor Ehrenberg*. Oxford: Blackwell.

——. 1992. "Thucydides on Rendering Speeches." *Athenaeum* 80, 187–90.

——. 1993. "Thucydides and the Outbreak of the Peloponnesian War." In id., *From Plataea to Potidaea. Studies in the History and Historiography of the Pentecontaetia*, 125–62. Baltimore: Johns Hopkins University Press.

Bakewell, Geoffrey W. 1997. "*Metoikia* and the *Supplices* of Aeschylus." *Classical Antiquity* 16, 209–28.

Bakhtin, Mikhail M. 1981. *The Dialogic Imagination*. Ed. Michael Holquist. Tr. Caryl Emerson & Michael Holquist. Austin: University of Texas Press.

Bakir, Güven. 1981. *Sophilos*. Mainz: von Zabern.

Balcer, Jack M. 1976. "Imperial Magistrates in the Athenian Empire." *Historia* 25, 257–87.

——, Gehrke, Hans-Joachim, Raaflaub, Kurt A. & Schuller, Wolfgang. 1984. *Studien zum Attischen Seebund*. Xenia 8. Konstanz: Universitätsverlag.

Baldry, H. C. 1971. *The Greek Tragic Theatre*. New York: Norton.

Barron, J. P. 1964. "Religious Propaganda of the Delian League." *Journal of Hellenic Studies* 84, 35–48.

——. 1972. "New Light on Old Walls: The Murals of the Theseion." Ibid. 92, 20–45.

——. 1980. "Bakchylides, Theseus and a Woolly Cloak." *Bulletin of the Institute of Classical Studies* 27, 1–8.

——. 1983. "The Fifth-Century *horoi* of Aigina." *Journal of Hellenic Studies* 103, 1–12.

——. 1990. "All for Salamis." In Elizabeth M. Craik (ed.), *Owls to Athens. Essays on Classical Subjects Presented to Sir Kenneth Dover*, 133–41. Oxford: Clarendon Press.

Barr-Sharrar, Beryl & Borza, Eugene (eds.). 1982. *Macedonia and Greece in Late Classical and Early Hellenistic Times*. Washington, D.C.: Smithsonian Institution.

Barthes, Roland. 1984. *Le bruissement de la langue*. Paris: Ed. du Seuil.

Baslez, Marie-Françoise. 1984. *L'étranger dans la Grèce antique*. Paris: Les Belles Lettres.

Baudrillard, Jean. 1968. *Le système des objets*. Paris: Fontemoing.

Baudy, Gerhard J. 1992. "Der Heros in der Kiste. Der Erichthonios-Mythos als Aition athenischer Erntefeste." *Antike und Abendland* 38, 1–47.

Baumhauer, O. A. 1986. *Die sophistische Rhetorik. Eine Theorie sprachlicher Kommunikation*. Stuttgart: Metzler.

Beazley, J. D. 1942. *Attic Red-Figured Vase-Painters*. Oxford: Clarendon Press.

——. 1956. *Attic Black-Figured Vase-Painters*. Ibid.

——. 1963. *Attic Red-Figured Vase-Painters*. 2d ed. Ibid.

Beloch, Karl Julius. 1886. *Die Bevölkerung der griechisch-römischen Welt*. Leipzig: Duncker & Humblot. Repr. Rome: L'Erma, 1968.

Bengl, Hans. 1929. *Staatstheoretische Probleme im Rahmen der attischen, vornehmlich euripideischen Tragödie*. Diss. Munich.

Bennett, L. J. & Tyrrell, William B. 1990. "Sophocles' *Antigone* and Funeral Oratory." *American Journal of Philology* 111, 441–56.

Bérard, Claude. 1974. *Anodoi.* Rome: Swiss Archaeological Institute.

Berger, Ernst. 1969. "Zum samischen Zeus des Myron in Rom." *Mitteilungen des Deutschen Archäologischen Instituts Rom* 76, 66–92.

—— (ed.). 1984. *Parthenon-Kongress Basel.* Mainz: von Zabern.

Bers, Victor. 1994. "Tragedy and Rhetoric." In Worthington 1994.176–95.

Beschi, Luigi. 1996. "La democrazia e il mondo della musica." In Sakellariou 1996.35–50.

Bett, Richard. 1989. "The Sophists and Relativism." *Phronesis* 34, 139–69.

Binder, Gerhard & Liesenborghs, Leo. 1976. "Eine Zuweisung der Sentenz *ouk estin antilegein* an Prodikos von Keos." In Classen 1976a.452–62.

Bitzer, L. F. 1968. "The Rhetorical Situation." *Philosophy and Rhetoric* 1, 1–14.

Blackman, David J. 1968. "The Ship-sheds." In Morrison & Williams, 1968. 181–92.

Blass, Friedrich. 1887–98. *Die attische Beredsamkeit.* 3 vols. 2d ed. Leipzig: Teubner.

——. 1907. *Die Eumeniden des Aischylos.* Berlin: Weidmann.

Bleicken, Jochen. 1987. "Die Einheit der athenischen Demokratie in klassischer Zeit." *Hermes* 115, 257–83.

——. 1994. *Die athenische Demokratie.* 2d ed. Paderborn, Germany: Schöningh.

——. 1995. "Wann begann die athenische Demokratie?" *Historische Zeitschrift* 260, 337–64.

Bloch, Maurice. 1977. "The Past and the Present in the Present." *Man* n.s. 12, 278–92.

Blundell, Mary W. 1989. *Helping Friends and Harming Enemies: A Study in Sophocles and Greek Ethics.* Cambridge: Cambridge University Press.

——. 1993. "The Ideal of Athens in *Oedipus at Colonus.*" In Sommerstein et al. 1993.287–306.

Blundell, Sue. 1995. *Women in Ancient Greece.* Cambridge, Mass.: Harvard University Press.

Boardman, John. 1974. *Athenian Black Figure Vases.* London: Thames & Hudson.

——. 1975. *Athenian Red Figure Vases: The Archaic Period.* Ibid.

——. 1977. "The Parthenon Frieze—Another View." In Höckmann & Krug 1977.39–49.

——. 1978. *Greek Sculpture: The Archaic Period.* London: Thames & Hudson.

——. 1984. "The Parthenon Frieze." In Berger 1984.210–15.

——. 1985. *The Parthenon and Its Sculptures.* London: Thames & Hudson.

——. 1988. "Material Culture [between 525 and 479 B.C.]." *CAH* IV^2, 414–30.

——. 1990. "The Greek Art of Narrative." In Jean-Paul Descoeudres (ed.), *Eumousia. Ceramic and Iconographic Studies in Honour of Alexander Cambitoglou,* 57–62. *Mediterranean Archaeology* Suppl. 1. Sydney: Meditarch.

—— (ed.). 1993. *The Oxford History of Classical Art.* Oxford: Oxford University Press.

Böckh, August. 1840. *Urkunden über das Seewesen das attischen Staates. Beilage zur Staatshaushaltung der Athener.* Berlin: G. Reimer.

——. 1842. *The Public Economy of Athens.* Tr. G. C. Lewis. London: John W. Parker.

Boedeker, Deborah. 1984. *Descent from Heaven: Images of Dew in Greek Poetry and Religion.* Chico, Calif.: Scholars Press.

——. 1995. "Simonides on Plataea: Narrative Elegy and Mythodic History." *Zeitschrift für Papyrologie und Epigraphik* 107, 217–29.

——. 1996. "Heroic Historiography: Simonides and Herodotus on Plataea." In Boedeker & Sider 1996.223–42.

——. 1998. "The New Simonides and Heroization at Plataia." In Nick Fisher & Hans van Wees (eds.), *Archaic Greece: New Approaches and New Evidence.* Cardiff: Wales Classical Press & London: Duckworth.

—— & Peradotto, John (eds.). 1987. *Herodotus and the Invention of History. Arethusa* 20.

—— & Sider, David (eds.). 1996. *The New Simonides. Arethusa* 29.2.

Boegehold, Alan L. 1982. "A Dissent at Athens ca 424–421." *Greek, Roman and Byzantine Studies* 23, 147–56.

——. 1991. "Three Court Days." In Michael Gagarin (ed.), *Symposion 1990: Vorträge zur griechischen und hellenistischen Rechtsgeschichte.* Cologne: Böhlau. Repr. (with footnotes) in Boegehold 1995.21–42.

——. 1994. "Perikles' Citizenship Law of 451/0 B.C." In Boegehold & Scafuro 1994.57–66.

——. 1995. *The Lawcourts at Athens: Sites, Buildings, Equipment, Procedure, and Testimonia.* The Athenian Agora 28. Princeton: American School of Classical Studies at Athens.

——. 1996. "Group and Single Competitions at the Panathenaia." In Neils 1996.95–105.

—— & Scafuro, Adele C. (eds.). 1994. *Athenian Identity and Civic Ideology.* Baltimore: Johns Hopkins University Press.

Bömer, Franz. 1952. "Pompa." *RE* 21.2, 1878–1994.

Boer, Willem den. 1967. "Herodot und die Systeme der Chronologie." *Mnemosyne* 4th ser. 20, 30–60.

——. 1979. *Private Morality in Greece and Rome: Some Historical Aspects. Mnemosyne* Suppl. 57. Leiden: Brill.

Boersma, Johannes S. 1970. *Athenian Building Policy from 561/0 to 405/4 B.C.* Groningen: Wolters-Noordhoff.

Bolkestein, Hendrik. 1958. *Economic Life in Greece's Golden Age.* New ed., rev. & annotated by E. J. Jonkers. Leiden: Brill.

Bommelaer, Jean-François. 1971. "Note sur les navarques et les successeurs de Polyclète à Delphes." *Bulletin de Correspondance Hellénique* 95, 42–64.

—— & Des Courtils, Jacques. 1994. *La salle hypostyle d'Argos.* Études péloponnésiens 10. Athens: Ecole française d'Athènes.

—— & Laroche, Didier. 1991. *Guide de Delphes. Le site.* Paris: De Boccard.

Bonfante, Larissa. 1989. "Nudity as a Costume in Classical Art." *American Journal of Archaeology* 93, 543–73.

Borbein, Adolf H. 1989. "Tendenzen der Stilgeschichte der bildenden Kunst und politisch-soziale Entwicklungen zwischen Kleisthenes und Perikles." In Schuller, Hoepfner, & Schwandner 1989.91–108 (with discussion).

——. 1995. "Die bildende Kunst Athens im 5. und 4. Jahrhundert v. Chr." In Eder 1995b.429–73 (with discussion).

Borza, Eugene. 1990. *The Shadow of Olympus: The Emergence of Macedon*. Princeton: Princeton University Press.

Boulter, Patricia Neils. 1969. "The Acroteria of the Nike Temple." *Hesperia* 38, 133–40.

——. 1970. "The Frieze of the Erechtheion." *Antike Plastik* 10, 7–28.

Bourdieu, Pierre. 1977. *Outline of a Theory of Practice*. Tr. Richard Nice. Cambridge: Cambridge University Press.

——. 1991. *Language and Symbolic Power*. Ed. John B. Thompson. Tr. Gino Raymond & Matthew Adamson. Cambridge, Mass.: Harvard University Press.

Bouzek, Jan & Ondrejová, Iva. 1988. "Sindos-Trebenishte-Duvanli." *Mediterranean Archaeology* 1, 84–94.

Bowie, Angus M. 1993. "Religion and Politics in Aeschylus' *Oresteia*." *Classical Quarterly* 43, 10–31.

Bradeen, Donald. 1964. "Athenian Casualty Lists." *Hesperia* 33, 16–62.

Braudel, Fernand. 1972. *The Mediterranean and the Mediterranean World in the Age of Philip II*. Tr. Siân Reynolds. New York: Harper and Row.

Braund, David. 1994. "The Luxuries of Athenian Democracy." *Greece & Rome* 41, 41–48.

Brecht, Bertolt. 1964. "A Short Organum for the Theatre." In John Willet (ed. & tr.), *Brecht on Theatre*, 179–205. London: Methuen.

Breckenridge, James D. 1968. *Likeness. A Conceptual History of Ancient Portraiture*. Evanston, Ill.: Northwestern University Press.

Bremer, Jan M. 1993. "Aristophanes on His Own Poetry." In Bremer & Handley 1993.125–72.

—— & Handley, Eric W. (eds.). 1993. *Aristophane*. Entretiens sur l'antiquité classique 38. Vandoeuvres-Geneva, Switzerland: Fondation Hardt.

Bremmer, Jan N. 1984. "Greek Maenadism Reconsidered." *Zeitschrift für Papyrologie und Epigraphik* 55, 267–86.

Bresson, Alain. 1993. "Les cités grecques et leurs *emporia*." In Bresson & Rouillard 1993.163–226.

—— & Rouillard, Pierre (eds.). 1993. *L'Emporion*. Paris: De Boccard.

Brickhouse, Thomas C. & Smith, Nicholas D. 1989. *Socrates On Trial*. Princeton: Princeton University Press.

Brilliant, Richard. 1984. *Visual Narratives: Storytelling in Etruscan and Roman Art*. Ithaca, N.Y.: Cornell University Press.

Brock, Roger. 1989. "Athenian Oligarchs: The Numbers Game." *Journal of Hellenic Studies* 109, 160–64.

Brommer, Frank. 1956. *Corpus Vasorum Antiquorum. Deutschland* 11: *Schloss Fasanerie (Adolphseck)* I. Munich: Beck.

——. 1957. "Attische Könige." In Konrad Schauenburg (ed.), *Charites. Studien zur Altertumswissenschaft*, 152–64. Bonn: Athenäum-Verlag.

——. 1967. *Die Metopen des Parthenon*. Mainz: von Zabern.

——. 1969. *Die Wahl des Augenblicks in der griechischen Kunst*. Munich: Heimeran.

Brooks, Lynn M. 1988. *The Dances of the Processions of Seville in Spain's Golden Age*. Kassel: Edition Reichenberger.

Brouskari, Maria. 1974. *The Akropolis Museum*. Athens: Commercial Bank of Greece.

Bruit Zaidman, Louise. 1992. "Pandora's Daughters and Rituals in Grecian Cities." In Schmitt Pantel 1992.338–76.

—— & Schmitt Pantel, Pauline. 1992. *Religion in the Ancient Greek City*. Tr. Paul Cartledge. Cambridge: Cambridge University Press.

Brulé, Pierre. 1987. *La Fille d'Athènes*. Annales littéraires de l'université de Besançon 363. Paris: Belles Lettres.

Brunnsåker, Sture. 1971. *The Tyrant-Slayers of Kritios and Nesiotes*. Stockholm: Svenska Institutet i Athen.

Brunt, Peter A. 1966. "Athenian Settlements abroad in the Fifth Century B.C." In Badian 1966.71–92. Repr. (with a postscript) in Brunt 1993.112–36.

——. 1993. *Studies in Greek History and Thought*. Oxford: Oxford University Press.

Buchanan, James J. 1962. *Theorika: A Study of Monetary Distributions to the Athenian Citizenry during the Fifth and Fourth Centuries B.C.* Locust Valley, N.Y.: J. J. Augustin.

Buchheim, Thomas. 1986. *Die Sophistik als Avantgarde normalen Lebens*. Hamburg: Felix Meiner.

Buchheit, Vinzenz. 1960. *Untersuchungen zur Theorie des genos epideiktikon von Gorgias bis Aristoteles*. Munich: Huber.

Buchner, Edmund. 1958. *Der Panegyrikos des Isokrates. Eine historisch-philologische Untersuchung*. *Historia* Einzelschrift 2. Wiesbaden: Steiner.

Bugh, Glenn R. 1988. *The Horsemen of Attica*. Princeton: Princeton University Press.

Buitron-Oliver, Diana (ed.). 1992. *The Greek Miracle: Classical Sculpture from the Dawn of Democracy. The Fifth Century B.C.* Washington, D.C.: National Gallery of Art.

Burckhardt, August. 1924. *Spuren der athenischen Volksrede in der alten Komödie*. Basel: Birkhäuser.

Burckhardt, Jacob. 1963. *History of Greek Culture*. Tr. Palmer Hilty. New York: Ungar.

Burford, Alison. 1965. "The Economics of Greek Temple Building." *Proceedings of the Cambridge Philological Society* n.s. 11, 21–34.

——. 1972. *Craftsmen in Greek and Roman Society*. Ithaca, N.Y.: Cornell University Press.

Burian, Peter. 1974. "Pelasgos and Politics in Aeschylus' Danaid Trilogy." *Wiener Studien* 8, 5–14.

——. 1985. "*Logos* and *Pathos*: The Politics of the *Suppliant Women*." In id. (ed.), *Directions in Euripidean Criticism: A Collection of Essays*, 129–55. Durham, N.C.: Duke University Press.

Burke, Edmund M. 1992. "The Economy of Athens in the Classical Era: Some Adjustments to the Primitivist Model." *Transactions of the American Philological Association* 122, 199–226.

Burkert, Walter. 1966. "Kekropidensage und Arrhephoria." *Hermes* 94, 1–25.

——. 1992a. "Athenian Cults and Festivals." *CAH* V^2, 245–67.

——. 1992b. *The Orientalizing Revolution*. Cambridge, Mass.: Harvard University Press.

——. 1996. "Isonomia und Polisreligion im kleisthenischen Athen." In Sakellariou 1996.51–65.

Burman, Rickie. 1981. "Time and Socioeconomic Change in Simbu." *Man* 16, 251–67.

Burn, Lucilla. 1987. *The Meidias Painter*. Oxford: Oxford University Press.

——. 1989. "The Art of the State in Late Fifth Century Athens." In Mary M. Mackenzie & Charlotte Roueché (eds.), *Images of Authority: Papers Presented to Joyce Reynolds. Proceedings of the Cambridge Philological Society* Suppl. 16, 62–81. Cambridge: Philological Society.

Burnyeat, Myles. 1992. "Utopia and Fantasy." In James Hopkins & Anthony Savile (eds.), *Psychoanalysis, Mind and Art: Perspectives on Richard Wollheim*. Oxford: Blackwell.

Buschor, Ernst. 1953. "Gruppe des Myron." *Mitteilungen des Deutschen Archäologischen Instituts Athen* 68, 51–62.

Büsing, Hermann H. 1994. *Das Athener Schatzhaus in Delphi*. Marburger Winckelmann–Programm, 1992. Marburg: Philipps-Universität.

Busolt, Georg. 1893. *Griechische Geschichte bis zur Schlacht bei Chaeroneia* I. 2d ed. Gotha: Friedrich Andreas Perthes.

Butts, H. R. 1947. *The Glorification of Athens in Greek Drama*. Diss. University of Iowa.

Buxton, R. G. A. 1982. *Persuasion in Greek Tragedy: A Study of Peitho*. Cambridge: Cambridge University Press.

Cahn, Herbert A. & Simon, Erika (eds.). 1980. *Tainia. Festschrift für Roland Hampe*. Mainz: von Zabern.

Calame, Claude. 1990. *Thésée et l'imaginaire Athénien*. Lausanne: Payot. 2d ed. 1996.

Calder, William M. III. 1969. "The Date of Euripides' *Erectheus*." *Greek, Roman and Byzantine Studies* 10, 147–56.

Callahan, Virginia W. 1944. *Types of Rulers in the Plays of Aeschylus*. Diss. University of Chicago.

Cambiano, Giuseppe. 1991. "Remarques sur Platon et la 'techne'." *Revue philosophique* 181, 407–16.

Camp, John McK. II. 1986. *The Athenian Agora: Excavations in the Heart of Classical Athens*. London: Thames & Hudson.

——. 1994. "Before Democracy: The Alkmaionidai and Peisistratidai." In Coulson et al. 1994.7–12.

Canfora, Luciano. 1988. "Discours écrit/discours réel chez Démosthène." In Marcel Detienne (ed.), *Les savoirs de l'écriture en Grèce ancienne*. Cahiers de Philologie 14, 211–20. Lille: Presses Universitaires de Lille.

Cannadine, David. 1994. "Gilbert and Sullivan: The Making and Unmaking of a British 'Tradition'." In Roy Porter (ed.), *Myths of the English*, 12–32. Cambridge: Polity Press.

Caplan, Harry. 1944. "The Decay of Eloquence at Rome in the First Century." In H. A. Wichelns (ed.), *Studies in Speech and Drama in Honor of Alexander M. Drummond*, 295–325. Ithaca, N.Y.: Cornell University Press. Repr. in id., *Of Eloquence: Studies in Ancient and Medieval Rhetoric*, 160–95. Ibid. 1970.

Carawan, Edwin. 1993. "The *Tetralogies* and Athenian Homicide Trials." *American Journal of Philology* 114, 235–70.

Carey, Christopher (ed.). 1989. *Lysias: Selected Speeches*. Cambridge: Cambridge University Press.

——. 1994. "Comic Ridicule and Democracy." In Osborne & Hornblower 1994.69–83.

Carpenter, Rhys & Bon, Antoine. 1936. *Corinth* III.2: *The Defences of the Lower Town*. Cambridge, Mass.: Harvard University Press.

Carr, Stephen L. 1980. "Verbal-Visual Relationships: Zoffany's and Fuseli's Illustrations of *Macbeth*." *Art History* 3, 374–87.

Carter, L. B. 1986. *The Quiet Athenian*. Cambridge: Cambridge University Press.

Cartledge, Paul. 1979. *Sparta and Lakonia: A Regional History 1300–362 B.C.* London: Routledge & Kegan Paul.

——. 1981. "Spartan Wives: Liberation or Licence?" *Classical Quarterly* 31, 84–105.

——. 1992. Review of Brunt 1993. *Polis* 11, 184–90.

——. 1993. *The Greeks*. Oxford: Oxford University Press. Rev. ed. 1997a.

——. 1996. "Comparatively Equal." In Ober & Hedrick 1996.175–85.

——. 1997b. " 'Deep Plays': Theatre as Process in Greek Civic Life." In Easterling 1997.3–35.

—— (ed.). 1997c. *The Cambridge Illustrated History of Ancient Greece*. Cambridge: Cambridge University Press.

—— & Harvey, F. D. (eds.). 1985. *Crux: Essays in Greek History Presented to G. E. M. de Ste. Croix*. Exeter: Imprint Academic & London: Duckworth.

Casson, Lionel. 1984. "Traders and Trading in Classical Athens." In id., *Ancient Trade and Society*, 23–34. Detroit: Wayne State University Press.

Castriota, David. 1992. *Myth, Ethos, and Actuality: Official Art in Fifth-Century B.C. Athens*. Madison: University of Wisconsin Press.

——. 1995. "Barbarian and Female: The Other on the West Front of the Parthenon." *Source: Notes in the History of Art* 15.1, 32–38.

——. 1997. "Democracy and Art in Late Sixth– and Fifth–Century Athens." In Morris & Raaflaub 1997.197–216.

Cauer, Friedrich. 1895. "Aischylos und der Areopag." *Rheinisches Museum* 50, 348–56.

Cavaignac, Eugène. 1908. *Etudes sur l'histoire financière d'Athènes au Ve siècle: Le trésor d'Athènes de 480 à 404*. Paris: A. Fontemoing.

Cawkwell, George L. 1988. "*Nomophulakia* and the Areopagus." *Journal of Hellenic Studies* 108, 1–12.

Ceccarelli, Paola. 1993. "Sans thalassocratie, pas de démocratie? Le rapport entre thalassocratie et démocratie à Athènes dans la discussion du Ve et du IVe siècle av. J.-C." *Historia* 42, 444–70.

Cerri, Giovanni. 1979. *Legislazione orale e tragedia greca. Studi sull'Antigone di Sofocle e sulle Supplici di Euripide*. Naples: Liguori.

——. 1982a. "Antigone, Creonte e l'idea della tirannide nell'Atene del V secolo (alcune tesi di V. di Benedetto)." *Quaderni Urbinati di cultura classica* 39, 137–55.

——. 1982b. "Ideologia funeraria nell'Antigone di Sofocle." In Gherardo Gnoli & Jean-Pierre Vernant (eds.), *La mort, les morts dans les sociétés anciennes,* 121–31. Paris: Maison des sciences de l'homme & Cambridge: Cambridge University Press.

Chambers, Mortimer. 1990. *Aristoteles, Staat der Athener, übersetzt und erläutert.* Berlin: Akademie-Verlag.

Charles-Picard, Gilbert. 1957. *Les Trophées Romains. Contribution à l'histoire de la religion et de l'art triomphal de Rome.* Paris: De Boccard.

Chartier, Roger. 1988. *Cultural History: Between Practices and Representations.* Tr. Lydia Cochrane. Ithaca, N.Y.: Cornell University Press.

Childs, William A. P. 1994. "The Date of the Old Temple of Athena on the Athenian Acropolis." In Coulson et al. 1994.1–6.

Christ, Matthew R. 1990. "Liturgy Avoidance and *Antidosis* in Classical Athens." *Transactions of the American Philological Association* 120, 147–69.

——. 1992. "Ostracism, Sycophancy and the Deception of the Demos: [Arist] *Ath. Pol.* 43.5." *Classical Quarterly* 42, 336–46.

Christiansen, Jette & Melander, Torben (eds.). 1988. *Ancient Greek and Related Pottery.* Copenhagen: Nationalmuseet, Ny Carlsberg Glyptothek & Thorvaldsens Museum.

Citti, Vittorio. 1978. *Tragedia e lotta di classe in Grecia.* Naples: Liguori.

Clairmont, Christoph. 1970. *Gravestone and Epigram.* Mainz: von Zabern.

——. 1983. *Patrios Nomos: Public Burial in Athens during the Fifth and Fourth Centuries B.C.* Brit. Arch. Rep. Intern. Ser. 161. 2 vols. Oxford: British Archaeological Reports.

——. 1986. "Some Reflections on the Earliest Classical Attic Gravestones." *Boreas* 9, 27–50.

Classen, Carl Joachim. 1959. *Sprachliche Deutung als Triebkraft platonischen und sokratischen Philosophierens.* Zetemata 22. Munich: Beck.

—— (ed.). 1976a. *Sophistik.* Wege der Forschung 187. Darmstadt: Wissenschaftliche Buchgesellschaft.

——. 1976b. "The Study of Language amongst Socrates' Contemporaries." In id. 1976a.215–47.

Cohen, David. 1987. "The Legal Status and Political Role of Women in Plato's *Laws.*" *Revue internationale des droits de l'antiquité* 31, 27–40.

——. 1989. "Seclusion, Separation, and the Status of Women in Classical Athens." *Greece & Rome* 36, 3–15.

——. 1991. *Law, Sexuality, and Society: The Enforcement of Morals in Classical Athens.* Cambridge: Cambridge University Press.

——. 1995. *Law, Violence and Community in Classical Athens.* Ibid.

Cohen, Edward E. 1992. *Athenian Economy & Society: A Banking Perspective.* Princeton: Princeton University Press.

Cole, John R. 1977. "The *Oresteia* and Cimon." *Harvard Studies in Classical Philology* 81, 99–111.

Cole, Thomas. 1991a. *The Origins of Rhetoric in Ancient Greece.* Baltimore: Johns Hopkins University Press.

——. 1991b. "Who was Corax?" *Illinois Classical Studies* 16, 65–84.

Collard, Christopher. 1972. "The Funeral Oration in Euripides' Supplices." *Bulletin of the Institute of Classical Studies* 19, 39–53.

Comotti, Giovanni. 1991. "Laso, Ippaso e il metodo scientifico sperimentale." In Robert W. Wallace & Bonnie MacLachlan (eds.), *Harmonia Mundi: Musica e filosofia nell'antichità*. Rome: Ateneo.

Conley, T. M. 1994. *Rhetoric in the European Tradition*. Chicago: University of Chicago Press.

Connelly, Joan B. 1996. "Parthenon and Parthenoi: A Mythological Interpretation of the Parthenon Frieze." *American Journal of Archaeology* 100, 53–80.

Connor, W. Robert. 1968. *Theopompus and Fifth-Century Athens*. Cambridge, Mass.: Harvard University Press.

——. 1970. "Theseus in Classical Athens." In Anne G. Ward (ed.), *The Quest for Theseus*, 143–74. London: Pall Mall Press.

——. 1971. *The New Politicians of Fifth-Century Athens*. Princeton: Princeton University Press. Repr. (with new introduction) Indianapolis, Ind.: Hakkett, 1992.

——. 1977. "Tyrannis polis." In John H. D'Arms & John W. Eadie (eds.), *Ancient and Modern: Essays in Honor of Gerald F. Else*, 95–109. Ann Arbor: University of Michigan Press.

——. 1987. "Tribes, Festivals and Processions." *Journal of Hellenic Studies* 107, 40–50.

——. 1988. "'Sacred' and 'Secular.' *Hiera kai hosia* and the Classical Athenian Concept of the State." *Ancient Society* 19, 161–88.

——. 1990. "City Dionysia and Athenian Democracy." In Connor et al. 1990.7–32.

——. 1991. "The Other 399: Religion and the Trial of Socrates." In Michael A. Flower & Mark Toher (eds.), *Georgica: Greek Studies in Honour of George Cawkwell*. Bulletin Suppl. 58, 49–56. London: Institute for Classical Studies.

——. 1994. "The Politics of Athenian Civic Identity." In Boegehold & Scafuro 1994.34–44.

——. 1996. "Festival and Democracy." In Sakellariou 1996.79–89.

——, Hansen, Mogens H., Raaflaub, Kurt A. & Strauss, Barry S. 1990. *Aspects of Athenian Democracy*. Copenhagen: Museum Tusculanum Press.

Conradie, P. J. 1981. "Contemporary Politics in Greek Tragedy. A Critical Discussion of Different Approaches." *Acta Classica* 24, 23–35.

Cook, A. B. 1940. *Zeus* III. Cambridge: Cambridge University Press.

Cook, R. M. 1959. "Die Bedeutung der bemalten Keramik für den griechischen Handel." *Jahrbuch des Deutschen Archäologischen Instituts* 74, 114–23.

Cooper, Frederick. 1992. "Colonising Time: Work Rhythms and Labour Conflict in Colonial Mombasa." In N. B. Dirks (ed.), *Colonization and Culture*. Ann Arbor: University of Michigan Press.

Cooper, John M. 1994. "Ethical-Political Theory in Aristotle's *Rhetoric*." In David J. Furley & Alexander Nehamas (eds.), *Aristotle's* Rhetoric: *Philosophical Essays*, 193–210. Princeton: Princeton University Press.

Corsini, Eugenio (ed.). 1986–88. *La polis e il suo teatro*. 2 vols. Turin: Editoriale Programma.

Costa, C. D. N. 1962. "Plots and Politics in Aeschylus." *Greece & Rome* 9, 22–34.

Coulson, W. D. E., Palagia, Olga, Shear, T. Leslie, Shapiro, H. Alan & Frost, Frank J. (eds.). 1994. *The Archaeology of Athens and Attica under the Democracy.* Oxbow Monogr. 37. Oxford: Oxbow Books.

Croally, N. T. 1994. *Euripidean Polemic: The Trojan Women and the Function of Tragedy.* Cambridge: Cambridge University Press.

Croissant, Francis. 1993. "Observations sur la date et le style du fronton de la gigantomachie, Acr. 631." *Revue des études anciennes* 95, 61–77.

Cropp, Martin, Fantham, Elaine & Scully, Stephen (eds.). 1986. *Greek Tragedy and Its Legacy: Essays Presented to D. J. Conacher.* Calgary: University of Calgary Press.

Csapo, Eric. Forthcoming. *Mimesis, Ambiguity, Enigma and the Spirit of the New Music: A Performance Commentary on the Dithyrambic Stasima of Euripides' Electra.*

—— & Slater, William J. 1995. *The Context of Ancient Drama.* Ann Arbor: University of Michigan Press.

Culasso-Gastaldi, E. 1986. "Temistocle, Eschilo, Simonide e il culto della vittoria." In Corsini 1986–88.1:31–45.

Culham, Phyllis. 1986. "Again, What Meaning Lies in Colour!" *Zeitschrift für Papyrologie und Epigraphik* 64, 235–45.

Curty, Olivier. 1995. *Les parentés légendaires entre cités grecques. Catalogue raisonné des inscriptions contenant le terme* suggeneia *et analyse critique.* Geneva: Droz.

Darnton, Robert. 1985. *The Great Cat Massacres and Other Episodes in French Cultural History.* New York: Vintage Books.

Dasen, Véronique. 1983. "Autour du dinos de Néarchos: Essai sur la bande dessinée chez les Anciens." *Études de Lettres* pt. 4, 55–73.

Davie, John. 1982. "Theseus the King in Fifth Century Athens." *Greece & Rome* 29, 25–34.

Davies, John K. 1967. "Demosthenes on Liturgies: A Note." *Journal of Hellenic Studies* 87, 33–40.

——. 1971. *Athenian Propertied Families, 600–300 B.C.* Oxford: Oxford University Press.

——. 1975. Review of Connor 1971. *Gnomon* 47, 374–78.

——. 1981. *Wealth and the Power of Wealth in Classical Athens.* Salem, N.H.: Ayer.

——. 1988. "Religion and the State." *CAH* IV², 368–88.

——. 1992a. "Greece after the Persian Wars." *CAH* V², 15–33.

——. 1992b. "Society and Economy." Ibid. 287–305.

——. 1993. *Democracy and Classical Greece.* 2d ed. Cambridge, Mass.: Harvard University Press.

——. 1995. "The Fourth Century Crisis: What Crisis?" In Eder 1995b.29–36.

Davis, Susan G. 1986. *Parades and Power: Street Theatre in Nineteenth–Century Philadelphia.* Philadelphia: Temple University Press.

Davison, J. A. 1958. "Notes on the Panathenaea." *Journal of Hellenic Studies* 78, 23–42.

——. 1959. "Addenda to 'Notes on the Panathenaea'." Ibid. 79, 141–42.

——. 1966. "Aeschylus and Athenian Politics 472–456 B.C." In Badian 1966.93–107.

Degani, Enzo. 1961. *Aion, da Omero ad Aristotele.* Università di Padova, Pubbl. Fac. di Lett. e Filos. 37. Padova: Cedam.

——. 1979. "Democrazia ateniese e sviluppo del dramma attico: la tragedia." In Ranuccio Bianchi Bandinelli (ed.), *Storia e civiltà dei Greci* III, 255–310. Milan: Bompiani.

——. 1993. "Aristofane e la tradizione dell'invettiva." In Bremer & Handley 1993.1–36.

Delebecque, Edouard. 1951. *Euripide et la guerre du Péloponnèse.* Paris: C. Klincksieck.

——. 1962. "Euripide et l'actualité de son temps." In J. Jacquot (ed.), *Le théâtre tragique,* 49–54. Paris: Editions du CNRS.

——. 1969. "Euripide et la Sicile." *Dioniso* 43, 227–45.

Del Grande, Carlo. 1936. *Intorno alle origini della tragedia e* altri *saggi.* Naples: Ricciardi.

Delivorrias, Angelos (ed.). 1987. *Greece and the Sea.* Exhibition Catalogue. Amsterdam: De Nieuwe Kerk.

Denniston, John D. 1952. *Greek Prose Style.* Oxford: Oxford University Press.

Descat, Raymond. 1986. *L'acte et l'effort: Une idéologie du travail en Grèce ancienne.* Paris: Belles Lettres.

Des Courtils, Jacques. 1992. "L'architecture et l'histoire d'Argos dans la première moitié du Ve siècle avant J.-C." In Piérart 1992.241–51.

Despinis, Giorgos. 1974. "Ta glypta ton aetomaton tou naou tes Athenas Nikes." *Deltion* 29, Meletai 1–24.

Detienne, Marcel. 1965. "En Grèce archaïque: Géométrie, politique et société." *Annales ESC* 20, 425–41.

——. 1967. *Les maîtres de vérité dans la Grèce archaïque.* Paris: F. Maspero. Engl. tr., Detienne 1996.

——. 1989. "The Violence of Wellborn Ladies: Women in the Thesmophoria." In id. & Jean-Pierre Vernant, *The Cuisine of Sacrifice among the Greeks,* 129–47. Tr. Paula Wissing. Chicago: University of Chicago Press.

——. 1996. *The Masters of Truth in Archaic Greece.* Tr. Janet Lloyd. New York: Zone Books.

—— & Vernant, Jean-Pierre. 1974. *Les ruses de l'intelligence. La mètis des Grecs.* Paris: Flammarion.

Dettenhofer, Maria H. 1993. "Die Frauen von Sparta: Gesellschaftliche Position und politische Relevanz." *Klio* 75, 61–75.

——. 1995. "Die Frauen von Sparta: Ökonomische Kompetenz und politische Relevanz." In id. (ed.), *Reine Männersache? Frauen in Männerdomänen der antiken Welt,* 15–40. Cologne: Böhlau.

Deubner, Ludwig. 1932. *Attische Feste.* Berlin: Akademie–Verlag.

Devambez, Pierre. 1976. "Les Amazones et l'Orient." *Revue archéologique,* 265–80.

Diano, Carlo. 1969. "Sfondo sociale e politico della tragedia greca antica." *Dioniso* 43, 119–30.

Di Benedetto, Vincenzo. 1971. *Euripide. Teatro e società.* Turin: Einaudi.

——. 1978. *L'ideologia del potere e la tragedia greca. Ricerche su Eschilo.* Turin: Einaudi.

Diels, Hermann & Kranz, Walther. 1952. *Die Fragmente der Vorsokratiker.* 3 vols. 6th ed. Berlin: Weidmann (many further repr. eds.).

Dihle, Albrecht. 1994. *Die Griechen und die Fremden.* Munich: Beck.

Dillon, Matthew. 1995. "Payments to the Disabled at Athens: Social Justice or Fear of Aristocratic Patronage?" *Ancient Society* 26, 27–57.

——. 1997. *Pilgrims and Pilgrimage in Ancient Greece.* London: Routledge.

Dilts, Mervin (ed.). 1971. *Heraclidis Lembi excerpta politiarum. Greek, Roman and Byzantine Studies* Monogr. 5. Durham, N.C.: Duke University Press.

Dinsmoor, William Bell. 1910. "The Choregic Monument of Nicias." *American Journal of Archaeology* 14, 459–84.

——. 1913. "Attic Building Accounts I." Ibid. 17, 53–80.

——. 1921. "Attic Building Accounts V." Ibid. 25, 233–45.

——. 1947. "The Hekatompedon on the Athenian Acropolis." Ibid. 51, 109–51.

Dobrov, Gregory W. (ed.). 1997. *The City as Comedy: Society and Representation in Athenian Drama.* Chapel Hill: University of North Carolina Press.

Dodds, E. R. 1960. "Morals and Politics in the *Oresteia.*" *Proceedings of the Cambridge Philological Society* 186, 19–31. Repr. in id., *The Ancient Concept of Progress,* 45–63. Oxford: Clarendon Press, 1973.

Dörig, Jose. 1969. "La Tte Webb, l'Harmodios d'Antenor, et le problème des copies romaines d'après des chefs-d'oeuvres archaïques." *Antike Kunst* 12, 41–50.

——. 1985. *La frise est de l'Héphaisteion.* Mainz: von Zabern.

Donini, Guido. 1986. "Sofocle e la città ideale." *Annali della scuola normale superiore di Pisa* 16, 449–60.

Donlan, Walter. 1980. *The Aristocratic Ideal in Ancient Greece.* Lawrence, Kans.: Coronado Press.

Dontas, George. 1983. "The True Aglaureion." *Hesperia* 52, 48–63.

Dougherty, Carol. 1996. "Democratic Contradiction and the Synoptic Illusion of Euripides' *Ion.*" In Ober & Hedrick 1996.249–70.

—— & Kurke, Leslie (eds.). 1993. *Cultural Poetics in Archaic Greece.* Cambridge: Cambridge University Press.

Dover, Kenneth J. 1957. "The Political Aspect of Aeschylus's *Eumenides.*" *Journal of Hellenic Studies* 77, 230–37.

——. 1968a. *Aristophanes,* Clouds. Ed. with Introduction and Commentary. Oxford: Oxford University Press.

——. 1968b. *Lysias and the Corpus Lysiacum.* Berkeley: University of California Press.

——. 1974. *Greek Popular Morality.* Oxford: Blackwell.

——. 1976. "Linguaggio e caratteri aristofanei." *Rivista di cultura classica e medievale* 18, 359–71.

——. 1993. *Aristophanes,* Frogs. Ed. with Introduction and Commentary. Oxford: Oxford University Press.

Drews, Robert. 1973. *The Greek Accounts of Eastern History.* Washington, D.C.: Center for Hellenic Studies.

Ducat, Jean. 1976. "Fonctions de la statue dans la Grèce archaïque: Kouros et kolossos." *Bulletin de Correspondance Hellénique* 100, 239–51.

Duchemin, Jacqueline. 1945. *L'agôn dans la tragédie grecque.* Paris: Belles Lettres.

Ducrey, Pierre. 1968. *Le traitement des prisonniers de guerre en Grèce ancienne.* Paris: De Boccard.

——, Metzger, Ingrid & Reber, Karl. 1993. *Eretria* VIII: *Le quartier de la maison aux mosaïques.* Lausanne: Payot.

Duncan-Jones, R. P. 1980. "Metic Numbers in Periclean Athens." *Chiron* 10, 101–9.

Dunn, John (ed.). 1992. *Democracy: The Unfinished Journey, 508 BC to AD 1993.* Oxford: Oxford University Press.

——. 1996. "The Transcultural Significance of Athenian Democracy." In Sakellariou 1996.97–108.

Eagleton, Terry. 1991. *Ideology.* London: Verso.

Easterling, Patricia. 1984. "Kings in Greek Tragedy." In J. Coz & J. de Hoz (eds.), *Estudios sobre los generos literarios,* 33–45. Salamanca: Universidad de Salamanca.

——. 1985. "Anachronism in Greek Tragedy." *Journal of Hellenic Studies* 105, 1–10.

——. 1993. "The End of an Era? Tragedy in the Early Fourth Century." In Sommerstein et al. 1993.559–69.

——. 1994. "Euripides outside Athens: A Speculative Note." *Illinois Classical Studies* 19, 73–80.

—— (ed.). 1997. *The Cambridge Companion to Greek Tragedy.* Cambridge: Cambridge University Press.

Ebener, Dieter. 1963. "Die Phönizierinnen des Euripides als Spiegelbild geschichtlicher Wirklichkeit." *Eirene* 2, 71–79.

Eberhardt, W. 1944. "Die griechische Tragödie und der Staat." *Die Antike* 20, 87–114.

Eckstein, Felix. 1958. "Die attischen Grabmälergesetze." *Jahrbuch des Deutschen Archäologischen Instituts* 73, 18–29.

Eddy, Samuel. 1977. "The Gold in the Athena Parthenos." *American Journal of Archaeology* 81, 107–11.

Eder, Walter. 1988. "Political Self-Confidence and Resistance: The Role of *Demos* and *Plebs* after the Expulsion of the Tyrant in Athens and the King in Rome." In Yuge & Doi 1988.465–75.

—— (ed.). 1990. *Staat und Staatlichkeit in der frühen römischen Republik.* Stuttgart: Steiner.

——. 1992. "Polis und Politai. Die Auflösung des Adelsstaates und die Entwicklung des Polisbürgers." In Irma Wehgartner (ed.), *Euphronios und seine Zeit,* 24–38. Berlin: Staatliche Museen zu Berlin.

——. 1995a. "Die athenische Demokratie im 4. Jahrhundert v. Chr.: Krise oder Vollendung?" In Eder 1995b.11–28.

—— (ed.). 1995b. *Die athenische Demokratie im 4. Jahrhundert v. Chr. Vollendung oder Verfall einer Verfassungsform?* Stuttgart: Steiner.

——. 1997. "Aristocrats and the Coming of the Athenian Democracy." In Morris & Raaflaub 1997.105–40.

—— & Hölkeskamp, Karl-Joachim (eds.). 1997. *Volk und Verfassung im vorhellenistischen Griechenland: Beiträge... zu Ehren von Karl-Wilhelm Welwei.* Stuttgart: Steiner.

Edmonds, John M. (ed.). 1957–59. *The Fragments of Attic Comedy*. 2 vols. Leiden: Brill.

Edwards, A. T. 1993. "Historicizing the Popular Grotesque: Bakhtin's *Rabelais* and Attic Old Comedy." In Scodel 1993.89–117.

Egermann, Franz. 1972. "Thukydides über die Art seiner Reden und über seine Darstellung der Kriegsgeschehnisse." *Historia* 21, 575–602.

Ehrenberg, Victor. 1951. *The People of Aristophanes: A Sociology of Old Attic Comedy*. 2d ed. Oxford: Blackwell.

——. 1954. *Sophocles and Pericles*. Oxford: Blackwell.

Eisenhut, Werner. 1982. *Einführung in die antike Rhetorik und ihre Geschichte*. 3d ed. Darmstadt: Wissenschaftliche Buchgesellschaft.

Enos, R. L. 1993. *Greek Rhetoric before Aristotle*. Prospect Heights, Ill.: Waveland Press.

Ensoli, S. 1987. *L'heróon di Dexileos nel Ceramico di Atene*. Rome: Accademia dei Lincei.

Erbse, Hartmut. 1969. "Die politische Lehre des Thukydides." *Gymnasium* 76, 393–416.

Euben, J. Peter (ed.). 1986. *Greek Tragedy and Political Theory*. Berkeley: University of California Press.

——. 1990. *The Tragedy of Political Theory: The Road not Taken*. Princeton: Princeton University Press.

——, Wallach, John R. & Ober, Josiah (eds.). 1994. *Athenian Political Thought and the Reconstruction of American Democracy*. Ithaca, N.Y.: Cornell University Press.

Eucken, Christoph. 1983. *Isokrates. Seine Positionen in der Auseinandersetzung mit den zeitgenössischen Philosophen*. Berlin: de Gruyter.

Fabian, Johannes. 1983. *Time and the Other: How Anthropology Makes Its Object*. New York: Columbia University Press.

Fantham, Elaine, Foley, Helene P., Kampen, Natalie B., Pomeroy, Sarah B. & Shapiro, H. Alan. 1994. *Women in the Classical World*. New York: Oxford University Press.

Farrar, Cynthia. 1988. *The Origins of Democratic Thinking: The Invention of Politics in Classical Athens*. Cambridge: Cambridge University Press.

Fehr, Burkhard. 1979–81. "Zur religionspolitischen Funktion der Athena Parthenos im Rahmen des Delisch-Attischen Seebundes." 3 parts. *Hephaistos* 1, 71–92; 2, 113–25; 3, 55–93.

——. 1984. *Die Tyrannentöter. Oder: Kann man der Demokratie ein Denkmal setzen?* Frankfurt/Main: Fischer.

Felten, Florens. 1984. *Griechische Tektonische Friese*. Waldsassen, West Germany: Stiftland Verlag.

Ferguson, William Scott. 1932. *The Treasurers of Athena*. Cambridge, Mass.: Harvard University Press.

Figueira, Thomas. 1984. "The Ten Archontes of 579/8 at Athens." *Hesperia* 53, 447–73.

——. 1991. *Athens and Aigina in the Age of Imperial Colonization*. Baltimore: Johns Hopkins University Press.

——. 1993. *Excursions in Epichoric History: Aiginetan Essays*. Lanham, Md.: Rowman and Littlefield.

Filow, Bogdan. 1927. *Die archaische Nekropole von Trebenischte*. Berlin: de Gruyter.

——. 1934. *Die Grabhügelnekropole bei Duvanlij in Südbulgarien.* Berlin: de Gruyter.

Finley, John H. 1966. "Politics and Early Greek Tragedy." *Harvard Studies in Classical Philology* 71, 1–15.

Finley, Moses I. 1971. *The Ancestral Constitution.* Inaugural Lecture. Cambridge: Cambridge University Press. Repr. in id. 1975.34–59.

——. 1973. *The Ancient Economy.* Berkeley: University of California Press. 2d ed. 1985.

—— (ed.). 1974. *Studies in Ancient Society.* London: Routledge & Kegan Paul.

——. 1975. *The Use and Abuse of History.* London: Chatto & Windus. 2d ed. 1986.

——. 1977. *The World of Odysseus.* 2d ed. London: Chatto & Windus.

——. 1978. "Empire in the Greco-Roman World." *Greece & Rome* n.s. 25, 1–15.

—— (ed.). 1979. *The Bücher-Meyer-Controversy.* New York: Arno Press.

——. 1980. *Ancient Slavery and Modern Ideology.* New York: Viking.

——. 1982. *Economy and Society in Ancient Greece.* New York: Viking.

——. 1983. *Politics in the Ancient World.* Cambridge: Cambridge University Press.

Fitton, J. W. 1961. "The *Suppliant Women* and the *Herakleidai* of Euripides." *Hermes* 89, 430–61.

Flickinger, Roy C. 1936. *The Greek Theater and Its Drama.* Chicago: University of Chicago Press.

Fogel, Robert W. 1983. " 'Scientific' History and Traditional History." In G. R. Elton & Robert W. Fogel (eds.), *Which Road to the Past?* 5–70. New Haven: Yale University Press.

Foley, Helene. 1995. "Tragedy and Democratic Ideology: The Case of Sophocles' *Antigone*." In Goff 1995.131–50.

Fornara, Charles W. (ed. & tr.). 1983a. *Archaic Times to the End of the Peloponnesian War.* 2d ed. Cambridge: Cambridge University Press.

—— 1983b. *The Nature of History in Ancient Greece and Rome.* Berkeley: University of California Press.

—— & Samons, Loren J. II. 1991. *Athens from Cleisthenes to Pericles.* Berkeley: University of California Press.

Forrest, W. George. 1975. "An Athenian Generation Gap." *Yale Classical Studies* 24, 37–52.

——. 1986. "The Stage and Politics." In Cropp, Fantham, & Scully 1986.229–39.

Forster, E. Morgan. 1927. *Aspects of the Novel.* New York: Harcourt Brace Jovanovich.

Fortenbaugh, William W. & Mirhady, David C. (eds.). 1994. *Peripatetic Rhetoric after Aristotle.* Rutgers University Studies in Classical Humanities 6. New Brunswick, N.J.: Transaction Publishers.

Fowler, Robert L. 1996. "Herodotos and His Contemporaries." *Journal of Hellenic Studies* 116, 62–87.

Foxhall, Lin. 1989. "Household, Gender and Property in Classical Athens." *Classical Quarterly* 39, 22–44.

——. 1993. "Farming and Fighting in Ancient Greece." In Rich & Shipley 1993.134–45.

——. 1995. "Women's Ritual and Men's Work in Ancient Athens." In Hawley & Levick 1995.97–110.

Fränkel, Hermann. 1960. *Wege und Formen frühgriechischen Denkens*. 2d ed. Munich: Beck.

——. 1973. *Early Greek Poetry and Philosophy*. 2d ed. Tr. Moses Hadas & James Willis. Oxford: Blackwell.

Fränkel, Max. 1877. "Inschriften aus Olympia." *Archäologische Zeitung* 35, 43–49.

Francis, E. D. 1990. *Image and Idea in Fifth-Century Greece: Art and Literature after the Persian Wars*. London: Routledge.

—— & Vickers, Michael. 1985. "The Oenoe Painting in the Stoa Poikile and Herodotus' Account of Marathon." *Annual of the British School at Athens* 80, 99–113.

Frasca, Rosella. 1991. *L'agonale nell'educazione della donna greca: Iaia e le altre*. Bologna: Patron Editore.

Frazer, R. M. 1969. "Some Notes on the Athenian Entry, *Iliad* B 546–56." *Hermes* 97, 262–66.

Frei, V. 1946. *Die Stellung der attischen Tragödie und Komödie zur Demokratie*. Diss. Zurich.

French, Alfred. 1964. *The Growth of the Athenian Economy*. London: Routledge & Kegan Paul.

——. 1993. "The Population of Fifth-Century Athens." *Ancient History: Resources for Teachers* 23, 74–94.

Freyer-Schauenburg, Brigitte. 1974. *Samos* XI: *Bildwerke der archaischen Zeit und des Strengen Stils*. Bonn: Habelt.

Friedrich, Johann. 1918. "Das Attische im Munde von Ausländern bei Aristophanes." *Philologus* 75, 301–3.

Frisch, Hartvig. 1942. *The Constitution of the Athenians: A Philological-Historical Analysis of Pseudo-Xenophon's Treatise De re publica Atheniensium*. Copenhagen: Gyldendal.

Froleyks, W. J. 1973. *Der Agon Logon in der antiken Literatur*. Diss. Bonn.

Froning, Heide. 1988. "Anfänge der kontinuierenden Bilderzählung in der griechischen Kunst." *Jahrbuch des Deutschen Archäologischen Instituts* 103, 169–99.

Frost, J. Frank. 1976. "Tribal Politics and the Civic State." *American Journal of Ancient History* 1, 66–75.

——. 1980. *Plutarch's* Themistocles. *A Historical Commentary*. Princeton: Princeton University Press.

——. 1984. "The Athenian Military before Cleisthenes." *Historia* 33, 283–94.

Fuks, Alexander. 1953. *The Ancestral Constitution*. London: Routledge.

Funke, Hermann. 1966. "*Kreon apolis*." *Antike und Abendland* 12, 29–50.

Furley, William D. 1996. *Andokides and the Herms: A Study of Crisis in Fifth-Century Athenian Religion*. Bulletin Suppl. 65. London: Institute of Classical Studies.

Furtwängler, Adolf. 1893. *Meisterwerke der griechischen Plastik*. Berlin: von Giesecke & Devrient.

—— & Reichhold, Karl. 1904–32. *Griechische Vasenmalerei. Auswahl hervorragender Vasenbilder*. 3 vols. Munich: F. Bruckmann.

Gabrielsen, Vincent. 1985. "The Naukrariai and the Athenian Navy." *Classica & Mediaevalia* 36, 21–51.

——. 1986. "*Phanera* and *aphanēs ousia* in Classical Athens." *Classica et Mediaevalia* 37, 99–114.

——. 1987. "The *Antidosis* Procedure in Classical Athens." Ibid. 38, 7–38.

——. 1994. *Financing the Athenian Fleet: Public Taxation and Social Relations*. Baltimore: Johns Hopkins University Press.

Gagarin, Michael. 1990. "The Ancient Tradition on the Identity of Antiphon." *Greek, Roman and Byzantine Studies* 31, 27–44.

——. 1994. "Probability and Persuasion: Plato and Early Greek Rhetoric." In Worthington 1994.46–68.

Gantz, Timothy. 1993. *Early Greek Myth: A Guide to Literary and Artistic Sources*. Baltimore: Johns Hopkins University Press.

Garlan, Yvon. 1975. *War in the Ancient World: A Social History*. Tr. Janet Lloyd. London: Chatto & Windus.

——. 1980. "Le travail libre en Grèce ancienne." In Garnsey 1980.6–22.

——. 1988. *Slavery in Ancient Greece*. Tr. Janet Lloyd. Rev. & exp. ed. Ithaca, N.Y.: Cornell University Press.

Garland, Robert S. J. 1982. "A First Catalogue of Attic Peribolos Tombs." *Annual of the British School at Athens* 77, 125–76.

——. 1985. *The Greek Way of Death*. Ithaca, N.Y.: Cornell University Press.

——. 1987. *The Piraeus from the Fifth to the First Century B.C.* Ibid.

——. 1989. "The Well-Ordered Corpse: An Investigation into the Motives behind Greek Funerary Legislation." *Bulletin of the Institute of Classical Studies* 36, 1–15.

——. 1992. *Introducing New Gods. The Politics of Athenian Religion*. Ithaca, N.Y.: Cornell University Press.

——. 1997. "Whose *Life* Is It Anyway?" (Review of Calame 1996). *Arion* 3d ser. 5.2, 207–21.

Garnsey, Peter (ed.). 1980. *Non-Slave Labour in the Greco-Roman World. Proceedings of the Cambridge Philological Society* Suppl. 6. Cambridge: Philological Society.

——. 1985. "Grain for Athens." In Cartledge & Harvey 1985.62–75.

——. 1988. *Famine and Food Supply in the Graeco-Roman World: Responses to Risk and Crisis*. Cambridge: Cambridge University Press.

Garton, Charles. 1957. "Characterisation in Greek Tragedy." *Journal of Hellenic Studies* 77, 247–54.

Garvie, A. F. 1969. *Aeschylus' Supplices: Play and Trilogy*. Cambridge: Cambridge University Press.

Gauer, Werner. 1968a. "Die griechischen Bildnisse der klassischen Zeit als politische und persönliche Denkmäler." *Jahrbuch des Deutschen Archäologischen Instituts* 83, 118–79.

——. 1968b. *Weihgeschenke aus den Perserkriegen. Istanbuler Mitteilungen*, Beiheft 2. Tübingen: Wasmuth.

——. 1980. "Die Gruppe der ephesischen Amazonen: ein Denkmal des Perserfriedens." In Cahn & Simon 1980.201–26.

——. 1992. "Die ephesischen Amazonen, das Bildnis des Artemon und der samische Krieg des Perikles." In Heide Froning, Tonio Hölscher & Harald Mielsch (eds.), *Kotinos. Festschrift Erika Simon,* 188–98. Mainz: von Zabern.

Gauthier, Philippe. 1973. "A propos des clérouquies athéniennes du Ve siècle." In Moses I. Finley (ed.), *Problèmes de la terre en Grèce ancienne,* 163–78. Paris: Mouton.

Geagan, Helen A. 1970. "Mythological Themes on the Plaques from Penteskouphia." *Archäologischer Anzeiger,* 31–48.

Geddes, A. G. 1987. "Rags and Riches: The Costume of Athenian Men in the Fifth Century." *Classical Quarterly* 37, 307–31.

Geertz, A. W. 1994. *The Invention of Prophecy: Continuity and Meaning in Hopi Indian Religion.* Berkeley: University of California Press.

Geertz, Clifford. 1973. *The Interpretation of Cultures.* New York: Basic Books.

Gehrke, Hans-Joachim. 1986. *Jenseits von Athen und Sparta. Das Dritte Griechenland und seine Staatenwelt.* Munich: Beck.

Gellie, George H. 1963. "Character in Greek Tragedy." *Journal of the Australasian Universities Language and Literature Association* 20, 241–54.

Gellner, Ernest. 1964. *Thought and Change.* Chicago: University of Chicago Press.

Gelzer, Thomas. 1992. "Die alte Komödie in Athen und die Basler Fastnacht." In Graf 1992.29–61.

Genette, Gérard. 1972. *Figures III.* Paris: Éditions du Seuil.

Gentili, Bruno. 1988. *Poetry and Its Public in Ancient Greece: From Homer to the Fifth Century.* Baltimore: Johns Hopkins University Press.

—— & Pretagostini, Roberto (eds.). 1988. *La musica in Grecia.* Bari: Laterza.

Georges, Pericles. 1994. *Barbarian Asia and the Greek Experience from the Archaic Period to the Age of Xenophon.* Baltimore: Johns Hopkins University Press.

Gercke, Alfred. 1897. "Die alte *technē rhētorikē* und ihre Gegner." *Hermes* 33, 341–81.

Gergova, D. 1993. "Common Elements in the Ritual Behaviour of Thracians and Macedonians." In *Ancient Macedonia/Archaia Makedonia* V: *Anakoinoseis kata to Pempto Diethnes Symposio Thessalonike 1989,* 471–78. Thessaloniki: Institute for Balkan Studies.

Gernet, Louis. 1968. *Anthropologie de la Grèce antique.* Paris: Maspero. Repr. Paris: Flammarion, 1982a. Engl. tr., id. 1981.

——. 1981. *The Anthropology of Ancient Greece.* Tr. John Hamilton & Blaise Nagy. Baltimore: Johns Hopkins University Press.

——. 1982b. *Droit et institutions en Grèce antique.* Paris: Flammarion.

Gill, Christopher. 1995a. *Greek Thought. Greece & Rome*: New Surveys in the Classics 25. Oxford: Oxford University Press.

——. 1995b. "Rethinking Constitutionalism in *Statesman* 291–303." In Christopher J. Rowe (ed.), *Reading the Statesman. Proceedings of the Third Symposium Platonicum,* 292–305. Sankt Augustin, Germany: Academia Verlag.

Giorgini, Giovanni. 1993. *La città e il tiranno. Il concetto di tirannide nella Grecia del VII–IV secolo a.C.* Milan: Giuffrè Editore.

Giovannini, Adalberto. 1990. "Le Parthénon, le trésor d'Athéna et le tribut des alliés." *Historia* 39, 129–48.

——. 1991. "Symbols and Rituals in Classical Athens." In Molho, Raaflaub, & Emlen 1991.459–78.

——. 1997. "La participation des alliés au financement du Parthénon: *aparchè* ou tribut?" *Historia, 46*, 145–57.

Goethe, Johann Wolfgang & Schiller, Friedrich. 1953. "Über epische und dramatische Dichtung." In W. Weber & H. J. Schrimpf (eds.), *Goethes Werke,* vol. 12, 249–51. Hamburg: Christian Wegner Verlag.

Goff, Barbara (ed.). 1995. *History, Tragedy, Theory: Dialogues on Athenian Drama.* Austin: University of Texas Press.

Gold, Barbara. 1987. *Literary Patronage in Greece and Rome.* Chapel Hill: University of North Carolina Press.

Golden, Mark & Toohey, Peter (eds.). 1997. *Inventing Ancient Culture: Historicism, Periodization, and the Ancient World.* London: Routledge.

Goldhill, Simon. 1987. "The Great Dionysia and Civic Ideology." *Journal of Hellenic Studies* 107, 58–76.

——. 1988. "Battle Narrative and Politics in Aeschylus' *Persians.*" Ibid. 108, 189–93.

——. 1990. "The Great Dionysia and Civic Ideology." In Winkler & Zeitlin 1990.97–129. Rev. from Goldhill 1987.

——. 1994. "Representing Democracy: Women at the Great Dionysia." In Osborne & Hornblower 1994.347–69.

Goldschmidt, Victor. 1970. *Questions platoniciennes.* Paris: Librairie Philosophique J. Vrin.

Gomme, Arnold W. 1933. *The Population of Athens in the Fifth and Fourth Centuries B.C.* Oxford: Blackwell. Repr. Chicago: University of Chicago Press, 1967.

——. 1938. "Aristophanes and Politics." *Classical Review* 52, 97–109.

——. 1951. "The Working of Athenian Democracy." *History* 36, 12–28.

——. 1945–81. *A Historical Commentary on Thucydides.* 5 vols. Oxford: Oxford University Press. [Vols. 4 and 5 completed by Kenneth J. Dover and Antony Andrewes.]

—— & Hopper, Robert J. 1970. "Population (Greek)." *Oxford Classical Dictionary,* 861–63. 2d ed. Ibid.

Gondos, Elizabeth Ann. 1996. *Auf dem Weg zur rhetorischen Theorie. Rhetorische Reflexion im ausgehenden fünften Jahrhundert v. Chr.* Tübingen: Niemeyer.

Goody, Jack & Watt, Ian. 1968. "The Consequences of Literacy." In Jack Goody (ed.), *Literacy in Traditional Societies,* 27–68. Cambridge: Cambridge University Press.

Goossens, Roger. 1962. *Euripide et Athènes.* Brussels: Palais des Académies.

Gostoli, Antonia. 1988. "Terpandro e la funzione etico-politica della musica nella cultura spartana del VII sec. a. C." In Gentili & Pretagostini 1988.231–37.

Goulaki-Voutira, Alexandra et al. 1992. "Nike." *LIMC* VI, 850–904.

Gould, John P. 1980. "Law, Custom and Myth: Aspects of the Social Position of Women in Classical Athens." *Journal of Hellenic Studies* 100, 38–59.

Graef, Botho & Langlotz, Ernst. 1925–33. *Die antiken Vasen von der Akropolis zu Athen*. 2 vols. Berlin: de Gruyter.

Graf, Fritz (ed.). 1992. *Klassische Antike und neue Wege der Kulturwissenschaften: Symposium Karl Meuli*. Basel: Verlag der schweizerischen Gesellschaft für Volkskunde.

Gray, Vivienne J. 1992. "Xenophon's *Symposion*: The Display of Wisdom." *Hermes* 120, 58–75.

Grégoire, Henri & Goossens, Roger. 1940. "Les allusions politiques dans l'*Hélène* d'Euripide." *Comptes-rendus de l'Académie des inscriptions et belles-lettres*, 206–27.

Gregory, Justina. 1991. *Euripides and the Instruction of the Athenians*. Ann Arbor: University of Michigan Press.

Griffith, Mark. 1995. "Brilliant Dynasts." *Classical Antiquity* 14, 62–129.

Groningen, B. A. van. 1953. *In the Grip of the Past. Essay on an Aspect of Greek Thought*. Leiden: Brill.

Grossmann, Gustav. 1970. *Promethie und Orestie. Attischer Geist in der attischen Tragödie*. Heidelberg: Winter.

Grütter, Heinrich-Theodor. 1997. "Die athenische Demokratie als Denkmal und Monument: Überlegungen zur politischen Ikonographie im 5. Jh. v. Chr." In Eder & Hölkeskamp 1997.113–32.

Gschnitzer, Fritz. 1981. *Griechische Sozialgeschichte von der mykenischen zum Ausgang der klassischen Zeit*. Stuttgart: Steiner.

Gülke, Christina. 1969. *Mythos und Zeitgeschichte bei Aischylos. Das Verhältnis von Mythos und Historie in Eumeniden und Hiketiden*. Meisenheim am Glan, Germany: A. Hain.

Günther, Linda-Marie. 1993. "Witwen in der griechischen Antike—Zwischen Oikos und Polis." *Historia* 42, 308–25.

Gurvitch, Georges. 1963. *La vocation actuelle de la sociologie*. Paris: Presses Universitaires de France.

——. 1964. *The Spectrum of Social Time*. Dordrecht: D. Reidel.

Guthrie, W. K. C. 1969. *A History of Greek Philosophy* III: *The Fifth-Century Enlightenment*. Cambridge: Cambridge University Press.

Guy, J. R. 1983. "A Ram's Head Rhyton Signed by Charinos." *Arts in Virginia* 21, 2–14.

Haas, C. J. 1985. "Athenian Naval Power before Themistocles." *Historia* 34, 29–46.

Hadzisteliou-Price, Theodora. 1978. *Kourotrophos*. Leiden: Brill.

Hafner, German. 1956. "Anakreon und Xanthippos." *Jahrbuch des Deutschen Archäologischen Instituts* 71, 1–28.

Hahn, Istvan. 1981. "Aischylos und Themistokles. Bemerkungen zu den *Persern*." In Schmidt 1981.173–86.

Hall, Edith. 1989. *Inventing the Barbarian: Greek Self-Definition through Tragedy*. Oxford: Oxford University Press.

——. 1993a. "Asia Unmanned: Images of Victory in Classical Athens." In Rich & Shipley 1993.108–33.

——. 1993b. "Political and Cosmic Turbulence in Euripides' *Orestes*." In Sommerstein et al. 1993.263–85.

Hall, Jonathan. 1995. "Approaches to Ethnicity in the Early Iron Age of Greece." In Nigel Spencer (ed.), *Time, Tradition and Society in Greek Archaeology: Bridging the Great Divide,* 18–27. London: Routledge.

——. 1997. *Ethnic Identity in Greek Antiquity*. Cambridge: Cambridge University Press.

Hallett, C. H. 1986. "The Origins of the Classical Style in Sculpture." *Journal of Hellenic Studies* 106, 71–84.

Halliwell, Stephen. 1980. "Aristophanes' Apprenticeship." *Classical Quarterly* 30, 33–45.

——. 1991a. "Comic Satire and Freedom of Speech in Classical Athens." *Journal of Hellenic Studies* 111, 48–70.

——. 1991b. "The Uses of Laughter in Greek Culture." *Classical Quarterly* 41, 279–96.

——. 1994. "Philosophy and Rhetoric." In Worthington 1994.222–43.

Halperin, David M. 1990. "The Democratic Body: Prostitution and Citizenship in Classical Athens." In Konstan & Nussbaum 1990.1–28.

Hamberger, Peter. 1914. *Die rednerische Disposition in der alten technē rhētorikē (Korax—Gorgias—Antiphon)*. Paderborn, Germany: Schöningh.

Hamdorf, Friedrich W. 1964. *Griechische Kultpersonifikationen der vorhellenistischen Zeit.* Mainz: von Zabern.

Hamilton, Richard. 1978. "Prologue, Prophecy and Plot in Four Plays of Euripides." *American Journal of Philology* 99, 277–302.

Hanawalt, Barbara A. & Reyerson, Kathryn L. (eds.). 1994. *City and Spectacle in Medieval Europe*. Minneapolis: University of Minnesota Press.

Hands, Arthur R. 1968. *Charities and Social Aid in Greece and Rome*. London: Thames & Hudson.

Hanfmann, George M. A. 1957. "Narration in Greek Art." *American Journal of Archaeology* 61, 71–78.

Hansen, Mogens Herman. 1980. "Seven Hundred *archai* in Classical Athens." *Greek, Roman and Byzantine Studies* 21, 151–73.

——. 1983. "The Athenian 'Politicians', 403–322 B.C." Ibid. 24, 33–55.

——. 1985. *Demography and Democracy. The Number of Athenian Citizens in the Fourth Century B.C.* Herning: Systime.

——. 1987. *The Athenian Assembly in the Age of Demosthenes*. Oxford: Blackwell.

——. 1988. *Three Studies in Athenian Demography*. Copenhagen: Munksgaard.

——. 1989. *Was Athens a Democracy? Popular Rule, Liberty and Equality in Ancient and Modern Political Thought*. Ibid.

——. 1991. *The Athenian Democracy in the Age of Demosthenes*. Oxford: Blackwell.

——. 1996a. "The Ancient Athenian and the Modern Liberal View of Liberty as a Democratic Ideal." In Ober & Hedrick 1996.91–104.

——. 1996b. "The Trial of Sokrates from the Athenian Point of View." In Sakellariou 1996.137–70.

—— & Raaflaub, Kurt (eds.). 1995. *Studies in the Ancient Greek Polis. Historia* Einzelschrift 95. Stuttgart: Steiner.

Hanson, Victor D. 1995. *The Other Greeks: The Family Farm and the Agrarian Roots of Western Civilization.* New York: Free Press.

——. 1996. "Hoplites Into Democrats: The Changing Ideology of Athenian Infantry." In Ober & Hedrick 1996.289–312.

——. Forthcoming. "Democratic Warfare." In McCann & Strauss forthcoming.

Harding, Philip. 1986. "An Education to All." *Liverpool Classical Monthly* 11, 134–36.

——. 1994. "Comedy and Rhetoric." In Worthington 1994.196–221.

Harrison, A. Robin W. 1968–71. *The Law of Athens.* 2 vols. Oxford: Oxford University Press.

Harrison, Evelyn B. 1965. *The Athenian Agora* XI: *Archaic and Archaistic Sculpture.* Princeton: American School of Classical Studies at Athens.

——. 1966. "The Composition of the Amazonomachy on the Shield of Athena Parthenos." *Hesperia* 35, 107–33.

——. 1972. "The South Frieze of the Nike Temple and the Marathon Painting in the Painted Stoa." *American Journal of Archaeology* 76, 353–78.

——. 1977a. "Alkamenes' Sculptures for the Hephaisteion." *American Journal of Archaeology* 81, 137–78, 265–87, 411–26.

——. 1977b. "The Shoulder-Cord of Themis." In Höckmann & Krug 1977.155–61.

——. 1979. "The Eponymous Heroes on the Parthenon and in the Agora." In Otto Mørkholm & N. M. Waggoner (eds.), *Greek Numismatics and Archaeology. Essays in Honor of Margaret Thompson,* 71–85. Wetteren: Cultura Press.

——. 1989. "Hellenic Identity and Athenian Identity in the Fifth Century B.C." In Susan J. Barnes & Walter S. Melion (eds.), *Cultural Differentiation and Cultural Identity in the Visual Arts,* 41–61. Washington, D.C.: National Gallery of Art.

——. 1996. "Pheidias." In Olga Palagia & J. J. Pollitt (eds.), *Personal Styles in Greek Sculpture,* 16–65. *Yale Classical Studies* 30. Cambridge: Cambridge University Press.

——. 1997. "The Glories of the Athenians: Observations on the Program of the Frieze of the Temple of Athena Nike." In Diana Buitron-Oliver (ed.), *The Interpretation of Architectural Sculpture in Greece and Rome,* 109–25. Ibid.

Hartswick, Kim J. 1983. "The Athena Lemnia Reconsidered." *American Journal of Archaeology* 87, 335–46.

Harvey, F. D. 1985. "*Dona ferentes*: Some Aspects of Bribery in Greek Politics." In Cartledge & Harvey 1985.76–117.

Hasebroek, Johannes. 1928. *Staat und Handel im alten Griechenland.* Tübingen: Mohr. Repr. Hildesheim: Olms, 1966. English tr., see id. 1933.

——. 1933. *Trade and Politics in Ancient Greece.* Tr. L. M. Fraser & D. C. MacGregor. London: Bell.

Havelock, Eric A. 1957. *The Liberal Temper in Greek Politics.* New Haven: Yale University Press.

Hawley, Richard & Levick, Barbara (eds.). 1995. *Women in Antiquity: New Assessments.* London: Routledge.

Headlam, Walter. 1906. "The Last Scene in the Eumenides." *Journal of Hellenic Studies* 26, 268–77.

—— & Thomson, George. 1966. *The Oresteia of Aeschylus*. 2d ed. Amsterdam: A. M. Hakkert.

Heath, Malcolm. 1997. "Aristophanes and the Discourse of Politics." In Dobrov 1997. 230–49.

Hedrick, Charles W., Jr. 1990. *The Decrees of the Demotionidai*. American Classical Studies 22. Atlanta: Scholars Press.

Heinimann, Felix. 1961. "Eine vorplatonische Theorie der *technē*." *Museum Helveticum* 18, 105–30.

Hellström, Pontus & Alroth, Brita (eds.). 1996. *Religion and Power in the Ancient Greek World*. Boreas 24. Uppsala: University of Uppsala.

Hellwig, Antje. 1973. *Untersuchungen zur Theorie der Rhetorik bei Platon und Aristoteles*. Hypomnemata 38. Göttingen: Vandenhoeck & Ruprecht.

Hemelrijk, Jaap M. 1970. Review of Himmelmann 1967. *Gnomon* 42, 166–71.

Henderson, Jeffrey. 1980. "*Lysistrata*: The Play and Its Themes." In id. (ed.), *Aristophanes: Essays in Interpretation*, 153–218. *Yale Classical Studies* 21.

——. 1987a. *Aristophanes, Lysistrata*. Ed. with Introduction and Commentary. Oxford: Clarendon Press.

——. 1987b. "Older Women in Attic Old Comedy." *Transactions of the American Philological Association* 117, 105–29.

——. 1990. "The Demos and the Comic Competition." In Winkler & Zeitlin 1990.271–313.

——. 1991a. *The Maculate Muse: Obscene Language in Attic Comedy*. 2d ed. Oxford: Oxford University Press.

——. 1991b. "Women and the Athenian Dramatic Festivals." *Transactions of the American Philological Association* 121, 133–47.

——. 1993a. "Comic Hero versus Political Elite." In Sommerstein et al. 1990.307–19.

——. 1993b. "Problems in Greek Literary History: The Case of Aristophanes' *Clouds*." In Rosen & Farrell 1993.591–601.

Henrichs, Albert. 1978. "Greek Maenadism from Olympias to Messalina." *Harvard Studies in Classical Philology* 82, 121–60.

——. 1994–95. " 'Why Should I Dance?' Choral Self-Referentiality in Greek Tragedy." *Arion* 3d ser. 3.1, 56–111.

Henry, Madeleine M. 1995. *Prisoner of History: Aspasia of Miletus and Her Biographical Tradition*. New York: Oxford University Press.

Herman, Gabriel. 1987. *Ritualised Friendship and the Greek City*. Cambridge: Cambridge University Press.

Higgins, Reynold N. 1986. *Tanagra and the Figurines*. London: Trefoil Books.

Hill, George F. 1951. *Sources for Greek History B.C. 478–431*. Rev. Russell Meiggs & Antony Andrewes. Oxford: Oxford University Press.

Himmelmann, Nikolaus. 1967. *Erzählung und Figur in der archaischen Kunst*. Abh. Akad. Mainz, geistes- und sozialwiss. Kl. 1967, 2. Wiesbaden: Steiner.

——. 1971. *Archäologisches zum Problem der griechischen Sklaverei*. Ibid. 1971, 13.

——. 1990. *Ideale Nacktheit in der griechischen Kunst*. Berlin: de Gruyter.

——. 1994. *Realistische Themen in der griechischen Kunst der archaischen und klassischen Zeit. Jahrbuch des Deutschen Archäologischen Instituts* 28, Ergänzungsheft. Ibid.

Hobsbawm, Eric & Ranger, Terence (eds). 1983. *The Invention of Tradition*. Cambridge: Cambridge University Press.

Hodkinson, Stephen. 1993. "Warfare, Wealth, and the Crisis of Spartiate Society." In Rich & Shipley 1993.146–76.

Höcker, Christopher & Schneider, Lambert. 1993. *Phidias*. Reinbek bei Hamburg, Germany: Rowohlt.

Höckmann, Ursula & Krug, Antje (eds.). 1977. *Festschrift für Frank Brommer*. Mainz: von Zabern.

Hölscher, Tonio. 1969. "Ein attischer Heros." *Archäologischer Anzeiger*, 410–27.

——. 1973. *Griechische Historienbilder des 5. und 4. Jahrhunderts v. Chr.* Würzburg: Triltsch.

——. 1974. "Die Nike der Messenier und Naupaktier in Olympia." *Jahrbuch des Deutschen Archäologischen Instituts* 89, 70–111.

——. 1975. "Die Aufstellung des Perikles-Bildnisses und ihre Bedeutung." *Würzburger Jahrbücher für die Altertumswissenschaft* 1, 187–208.

——. 1988. Repr. of Hölscher 1975. In Klaus Fittschen (ed.), *Griechische Porträts*, 377–91. Darmstadt: Wissenschaftliche Buchgesellschaft.

——. 1989. *Die unheimliche Klassik der Griechen*. Bamberg: Buchner.

——. 1991. "The City of Athens: Space, Symbol, and Structure." In Molho, Raaflaub, & Emlen 1991.355–80.

——. 1993. Review of Himmelmann 1990. *Gnomon* 65, 519–28.

——. 1996. "Politik und Öffentlichkeit im demokratischen Athen: Räume, Denkmäler, Mythen." In Sakellariou 1996.171–87.

——. Forthcoming. "Die Amazonen von Ephesos. Ein Monument der Selbstbehauptung." In *Festschrift für Lily Kahil*.

Hoepfner, Wolfram. 1994. "Überlegungen zum Städtebau klassischer Zeit." In Egert Pöhlman & Werner Gauer (eds.), *Griechische Klassik*, 199–212. Nürnberg: Verlag Hans Carl.

—— & Schwandner, Ernst-Ludwig. 1994. *Haus und Stadt im klassischen Griechenland*. 2d ed. Munich: Deutscher Kunstverlag.

Hopper, Robert J. 1979. *Trade and Industry in Classical Greece*. London: Thames & Hudson.

Hornblower, Simon. 1987. *Thucydides*. Baltimore: Johns Hopkins University Press.

——. 1991. *A Commentary on Thucydides* I. Oxford: Clarendon Press.

——. 1992. "The Religious Dimension to the Peloponnesian War, or, What Thucydides Does not Tell Us." *Harvard Studies in Classical Philology* 94, 169–97.

Houby-Nielsen, Sanne. 1992. "Interactions between Chieftains and Citizens? 7th Cent. B.C. Burial Customs in Athens." *Acta Hyperborea* 4, 343–74.

——. 1995. " 'Burial Language' in Archaic and Classical Kerameikos." *Proceedings of the Danish Institute at Athens* 1, 129–91.

How, Walter W. & Wells, Joseph. 1912. *A Commentary on Herodotus*. 2 vols. Oxford: Oxford University Press.

Humphreys, Sally C. 1974. "The Nothoi of Kynosarges." *Journal of Hellenic Studies* 94, 88–95.

——. 1978. *Anthropology and the Greeks*. London: Routledge & Kegan Paul.

——. 1980. "Family Tombs and Tomb-Cult in Classical Athens: Tradition or Traditionalism?" *Journal of Hellenic Studies* 100, 96–126. Repr. in Humphreys 1983 (1993).79–130.

——. 1983. *The Family, Women and Death: Comparative Studies*. London: Routledge. 2d ed. Ann Arbor: University of Michigan Press, 1993.

Hunt, Lynn (ed.). 1989. *The New Cultural History*. Berkeley: University of California Press.

Hurst, André. 1983. "Temps du récit chez Pindare (Pyth. 4) et Bacchylide (11)." *Museum Helveticum* 40, 154–68.

——. 1985. "Aspects du temps chez Pindare." In id. (ed.), *Pindare*. Entretiens sur l'antiquité classique 31, 155–97. Vandoeuvres-Geneva, Switzerland: Fondation Hardt.

Hurwit, Jeffrey M. 1985. *The Art and Culture of Early Greece, 1100–480 B.C.* Ithaca, N.Y.: Cornell University Press.

——-. 1995. "Beautiful Evil: Pandora and the Athena Parthenos." *American Journal of Archaeology* 99, 171–86.

Hutchinson, D. S. 1988. "Doctrines of the Mean and the Debate Concerning Skills in Fourth-Century Medicine, Rhetoric and Ethics." In R. J. Hankinson (ed.), *Method, Medicine and Metaphysics*, 17–52. Edmonton: Academic Printing and Publishers.

Immerwahr, Henry R. 1960. "*Ergon:* History as a Monument in Herodotus and Thucydides." *American Journal of Philology* 81, 261–90.

Ioakimidou, Chrissula. 1997. *Die Statuenreihen griechischer Poleis und Bünde aus spätarchaischer und klassischer Zeit*. München: tuduv-Verlag.

Irwin, Terence. 1977. *Plato's Moral Theory*. Oxford: Clarendon Press.

Isager, Signe & Hansen, Mogens. 1975. *Aspects of Athenian Society in the Fourth Century B.C: A Historical Introduction to and Commentary on the Paragraphe Speeches and the Speech against Dionysiodorus in the Corpus Demosthenicum*. Odense: Odense University Press.

Jackson, Alastar H. 1969. "The Original Purpose of the Delian League." *Historia* 18, 12–15.

Jacoby, Felix. 1923–. *Die Fragmente der griechischen Historiker*. Many vols. Berlin: Weidmann, then Leiden: Brill.

——. 1945. "Some Athenian Epigrams from the Persian Wars." *Hesperia* 14, 157–211.

Jähne, Armin. 1991. "Kommunikative Umsetzung gesellschaftlicher Problematik bei Isokrates." *Philologus* 135, 131–39.

Jameson, Michael. 1956. "Politics in the *Philoctetes*." *Classical Philology* 51, 217–27.

——. 1977. "Agriculture and Slavery in Classical Athens." *Classical Journal* 73, 122–41.

——. 1988. "Sacrifice and Animal Husbandry in Classical Greece." In C. R. Whittaker (ed.), *Pastoral Economies in Classical Antiquity. Proceedings of the Cambridge Philological Society,* Suppl. 14, 87–119. Cambridge: Philological Society.

——. 1997. "Religion in the Athenian Democracy." In Morris & Raaflaub 1997.171–95.

Jarratt, S. C. 1991. *Rereading the Sophists: Classical Rhetoric Refigured.* Carbondale, Ill.: Southern Illinois University Press.

Jay, Nancy. 1992. *Throughout Your Generations Forever: Sacrifice, Religion, and Paternity.* Chicago: University of Chicago Press.

Jeffery, Lillian H. 1965. "The *Battle of Oinoe* in the Stoa Poikile." *Annual of the British School at Athens* 60, 41–57.

Jenkins, Ian. 1994. *The Parthenon Frieze.* Austin: University of Texas Press.

Jeppesen, Kristian. 1987. *The Theory of the Alternative Erechtheion.* Aarhus: Aarhus University Press.

——. 1988. "On the Interpretation of the Principal Scenery on the Krater Schloss Fasanerie 77 by the Kekrops Painter." In Christiansen & Melander 1988.285.

Johne, Renate. 1991. "Zur Entstehung einer 'Buchkultur' in der zweiten Hälfte des 5. Jahrhunderts v. u. Z." *Philologus* 135, 45–54.

Johnstone, Steven. 1994. "Virtuous Toil, Vicious Work: Xenophon on Aristocratic Style." *Classical Philology* 89, 219–40.

Jones, A. H. M. 1957. *Athenian Democracy.* Oxford: Blackwell. Repr. Baltimore: Johns Hopkins University Press, 1986.

Jones, J. Ellis. 1975. "Town and Country Houses of Attica in Classical Times." In Herman F. Mussche, Paule Spitaels & F. Goemaere-de Poerck (eds.), *Thorikos and the Laurion in Archaic and Classical Times.* Miscellanea Graeca 1, 63–140. Ghent: Belgian Archaeological Mission in Greece.

Jones, John. 1962. *On Aristotle and Greek Tragedy.* London: Chatto & Windus.

Jones, L. A. 1987. "The Role of Ephialtes in the Rise of Athenian Democracy." *Classical Antiquity* 6, 53–76.

Jones, Nicholas. Forthcoming. *The Associations of Classical Athens: The Response to Democracy.* New York: Oxford University Press.

Jordan, Borimir. 1975. *The Athenian Navy in the Classical Period: A Study of Athenian Naval Administration and Military Organization in the Fifth and Fourth Centuries B.C.* Berkeley: University of California Press.

——. 1986. "Religion in Thucydides." *Transactions of the American Philological Association* 116, 119–47.

Judeich, Walther. 1931. *Topographie von Athen.* 2d ed. Munich: Beck.

Jung, Karl G. & Kerényi, Karl. 1969. *Essays on a Science of Mythology.* Bollingen Series 22. Princeton: Princeton University Press.

Just, Roger. 1989. *Women in Athenian Law and Life.* London: Routledge.

Kaempf-Dimitriadou, Sophia. 1979. *Die Liebe der Götter in der attischen Kunst des 5. Jahrhunderts v. Chr. Antike Kunst,* Beiheft 11. Bern: Francke.

Kahn, Charles. 1981. "Did Plato Write Socratic Dialogues?" *Classical Quarterly* 31, 292–305.

Kakridis, Johannes T. 1961. *Der thukydideische Epitaphios. Ein stilistischer Kommentar.* Munich: Beck.

Kallet-Marx, Lisa. 1989. "Did Tribute Fund the Parthenon?" *Classical Antiquity* 8, 252–66.

——. 1993a. *Money, Expense, and Naval Power in Thucydides'* History *1–5.24.* Berkeley: University of California Press.

——. 1993b. "Thucydides 2.45.2 and the Status of War Widows in Periclean Athens." In Rosen & Farrell 1993.133–43.

——. 1994. "Money Talks: Rhetor, Demos, and the Resources of the Athenian Empire." In Osborne & Hornblower 1994.227–51.

Kannicht, Richard. 1983. "Dikaiopolis. Von der Schwierigkeit, ein rechter Bürger zu sein." In Wilfried Barner (ed.), *Literatur in der Demokratie. Für Walter Jens zum 60. Geburtstag,* 246–57. Munich: Kindler.

Karavites, Panayotis. 1982. *Capitulations and Greek Interstate Relations.* Hypomnemata 71. Göttingen: Vandenhoeck & Ruprecht.

Kardara, Chrysoula. 1966. "Erichthonios Spendon." In *Charisterion eis Anastasion K. Orlandon* II, 22–24. Athens: Athenian Archaeological Society.

Kasper-Butz, Irmgard. 1990. *Die Göttin Athena im klassischen Athen.* Frankfurt/Main: Peter Lang.

Kassel, Rudolf & Austin, Colin (eds.). 1983–. *Poetae Comici Graeci.* Several vols. Berlin: De Gruyter.

Katayama, Y. 1970. "The Social Significance of Liturgies from the Viewpoint of the Participation of Metics." *Journal of Classical Studies (Japan)* 18, 40–51.

Katz, Marilyn. 1992. "Ideology and 'the Status of Women' in Ancient Greece." In *History and Feminist Theory. History and Theory,* Beiheft 31, 70–97. Repr. in Hawley & Levick 1995.21–43.

——. 1997. "Women, Children and Men." In Cartledge 1997c.100–138.

Kearns, Emily. 1985. "Change and Continuity in Religious Structures after Cleisthenes." In Cartledge & Harvey 1985.189–207.

——. 1989. *The Heroes of Attica. Bulletin of the Institute of Classical Studies,* Suppl. 57. London: Institute of Classical Studies.

——. 1995. "Order, Interaction, Authority: Ways of Looking at Greek Religion." In Powell 1995.511–29.

Keesling, Katherine. Forthcoming. *The City of Gods: Votive Statues in Archaic and Classical Athens.*

Kennedy, George A. 1958. "The Oratory of Andocides." *American Journal of Philology* 79, 32–43.

——. 1963. *The Art of Persuasion in Greece.* Princeton: Princeton University Press.

——. 1972. *The Art of Rhetoric in the Roman World: 300 B.C.–A.D. 300.* Ibid.

——. 1980. *Classical Rhetoric and Its Christian and Secular Tradition from Ancient to Modern Times.* Chapel Hill: University of North Carolina Press.

——. 1983. *Greek Rhetoric under Christian Emperors.* Princeton: Princeton University Press.

——. 1994. *A New History of Classical Rhetoric.* Ibid.

Kennell, Nigel M. 1995. *The Gymnasium of Virtue. Education and Culture in Ancient Sparta.* Chapel Hill: University of North Carolina Press.

Kerényi, Karl. 1940. *Die antike Religion.* Amsterdam: Pantheon.

Kerferd, George B. 1950. "The First Greek Sophists." *Classical Review* 1, 8–10.

——. 1981a. *The Sophistic Movement.* Cambridge: Cambridge University Press.

—— (ed.). 1981b. *The Sophists and Their Legacy.* Wiesbaden: Steiner.

Keuls, Eva C. 1985. *The Reign of the Phallus: Sexual Politics in Ancient Athens.* New York: Harper & Row. Repr. Berkeley: University of California Press, 1993.

Kierdorf, Wilhelm. 1966. *Erlebnis und Darstellung der Perserkriege. Studien zu Simonides, Pindar, Aischylos und den attischen Rednern.* Hypomnemata 16. Göttingen: Vandenhoeck & Ruprecht.

Kiilerich, Bente. 1989. "The Olive Tree Pediment and the Daughters of Kekrops." *Acta ad archaeologiam et artium historiam pertinentia* 7, 1–21.

Kinzl, Konrad. 1978. "DEMOKRATIA. Studie zur Frühgeschichte des Begriffes." *Gymnasium* 85, 117–27, 312–26 with Tafel I-II.

—— (ed.). 1995. *Demokratia: Der Weg zur Demokratie bei den Griechen.* Wege der Forschung 657. Darmstadt: Wissenschaftliche Buchgesellschaft.

Kleingünther, Adolf. 1933. *Prōtos heuretēs: Untersuchungen zur Geschichte einer Fragestellung. Philologus* Suppl. 26. Leipzig: Dieterich.

Kloft, Hans (ed.). 1988. *Sozialmassnahmen und Fürsorge. Zur Eigenart antiker Sozialpolitik. Grazer Beiträge* Suppl. 3. Horn, Austria: F. Berger.

Klosko, George. 1986. *The Development of Plato's Political Theory.* London: Methuen.

Kluwe, Ernst. 1976–77. "Die soziale Zusammensetzung der athenischen Ekklesia und ihr Einfluss auf politische Entscheidungen." 2 parts. *Klio* 58, 295–333; 59, 45–81.

——. 1984. "Die athenische Geldwirtschaft im 5. Jahrhundert und die Finanzierungsweise des Parthenon." In Berger 1984.11–14.

Knell, Heiner. 1990. *Mythos und Polis.* Darmstadt: Wissenschaftliche Buchgesellschaft.

Knigge, Ursula. 1976. *Kerameikos* IX: *Die Südhügel.* Berlin: De Gruyter.

——. 1983. "Ein Jünglingskopf vom Heiligen Tor in Athen." *Mitteilungen des Deutschen Archäologischen Instituts Athen* 98, 45–56.

——. 1988. *Der Kerameikos von Athen.* Athens: Krene.

Knox, Bernard. M. W. 1957. *Oedipus at Thebes.* New Haven: Yale University Press.

——. 1979. *Word and Action: Essays on the Ancient Theater.* Baltimore: Johns Hopkins University Press.

——. 1982. "Sophocles and the Polis." In Olivier Reverdin & Bernard Grange (eds.), *Sophocle.* Entretiens sur l'antiquité classique 29, 1–37. Vandoeuvres-Geneva, Switzerland: Fondation Hardt.

Knox, R. A. 1985. " 'So mischievous a Beaste?' The Athenian *Demos* and Its Treatment of Its Politicians." *Greece & Rome* 32, 132–61.

Kock, Theodor. 1888. *Comicorum Atticorum Fragmenta* III. Leipzig: Teubner.

Kohns, Hans P. 1964. "Die staatliche Lenkung des Getreidehandels in Athen (zu Lysias, or. 22)." In Horst Braunert (ed.), *Studien zur Papyrologie und antiken Wirtschaftsgeschichte, Friedrich Oertel zum achtzigsten Geburtstag gewidmet,* 146–66. Bonn: Habelt.

Kokkorou-Alevra, Georgia. 1988. "Ena gnosto-agnosto aggeio tou Zographou tou Meidia." In Eos Zervoudaki (ed.), *Proceedings of the XII International Congress of Classical Archaeology, Athens 1983,* II, 103–14. Athens: Ministry of Greek Culture.

Kolb, Frank. 1979. "Polis und Theater." In Gustav A. Seeck (ed.), *Das griechische Drama,* 504–45. Darmstadt: Wissenschaftliche Buchgesellschaft.

——. 1981. *Agora und Theater, Volks- und Festversammlung.* Berlin: Gebr. Mann.

Konstan, David. 1993. "Aristophanes' *Lysistrata*: Women and the Body Politic." In Sommerstein et al. 1993.431–44.

—— & Nussbaum, Martha (eds.). 1990. *Sexuality in Greek & Roman Society. Differences: A Journal of Feminist Cultural Studies* 2.1.

Kort, Wesley A. 1985. *Modern Fiction and Human Time: A Study in Narrative and Belief.* Tampa: University of South Florida Press.

Koselleck, Reinhart. 1979. *Vergangene Zukunft: Zur Semantik geschichtlicher Zeiten.* Frankfurt am Main: Suhrkamp.

Kourouniotes, K. & Thompson, Homer A. 1932. "The Pnyx in Athens." *Hesperia* 1, 90–217.

Kovacscovics, Wilfried K. 1990. *Kerameikos* XIV: *Die Eckterrasse.* Berlin: De Gruyter.

Krahmer, Gerhard. 1931. *Figur und Raum in der ägyptischen und griechisch-archaischen Kunst.* Hallesches Winckelmann-Programm 28. Halle: Niemeyer.

Kranz, Walther. 1937. "Vorsokratisches IV. Die sogenannten *Dissoi logoi.*" *Hermes* 72, 225–32.

Kraus, W. 1985. *Aristophanes' politische Komödien.* Sitzungsberichte Akad. Wien 453. Vienna: Verlag der Österreichischen Akademie der Wissenschaften.

Kraut, Richard. 1984. *Socrates and the State.* Princeton: Princeton University Press.

Kroll, John. 1979. "The Parthenon Frieze as Votive Relief." *American Journal of Archaeology* 83, 349–52.

Kroll, Wilhelm. 1940. "Rhetorik." *RE* Suppl. 7, 1039–1138.

Kron, Uta. 1976. *Die zehn attischen Phylenheroen. Athenische Mitteilungen,* Beiheft 5. Berlin: Gebr. Mann.

——. 1979. "Demos, Pnyx und Nymphenhügel. Zu Demos-Darstellungen und zum ältesten Kultort des Demos in Athen." *Athenische Mitteilungen* 94, 49–75.

——. 1992. "Frauenfeste in Demeterheiligtümern: Das Thesmophorion von Bitalemi. Eine archäologische Fallstudie." *Archäologischer Anzeiger,* 611–50.

——. 1996. "Priesthoods, Dedications and Euergetism. What Part Did Religion Play in the Political and Social Status of Greek Women?" In Hellström & Alroth 1996.139–82.

Kube, Jörg. 1969. *Techne und arete: sophistisches und platonisches Tugendwissen.* Berlin: De Gruyter.

Kuch, Heinrich. 1979. "Zur Interpretation der griechischen Tragödie." *Philologus* 123, 202–15.

——. 1980. "Von den historischen Voraussetzungen des griechischen Dramas." *Das Altertum* 26, 133–42.

——. 1981. "Der Dichter und die Demokratie." In Schmidt 1981.135–44.

——. 1983. "Individuum und Gesellschaft in der tragischen Dichtung der Griechen." In id. (ed.), *Die griechische Tragödie in ihrer gesellschaftlichen Funktion,* 61–84. Berlin: Akademie-Verlag.

——. 1993. "Continuity and Change in Greek Tragedy under Postclassical Conditions." In Sommerstein et al. 1993.545–57.

Kudlien, Fridolf. 1974. "Dialektik und Medizin in der Antike." *Medizinhistorisches Journal* 11, 187–200.

Kübler, Karl. 1976. *Kerameikos* VII.1: *Die Nekropole der Mitte des 6. bis Ende des 5. Jahrhunderts.* Berlin: De Gruyter.

Kuenzi, Adolphe. 1923. *Epidosis. Sammlung freiwilliger Beiträge zur Zeit der Not in Athen.* Bern: P. Haupt.

Kunstler, Barton. 1986. "Family Dynamics and Female Power in Ancient Sparta." *Helios* 13, 35–48.

Kurke, Leslie. 1991. *The Traffic in Praise: Pindar and the Poetics of Social Economy.* Ithaca, N.Y.: Cornell University Press.

——. 1992. "The Politics of *habrosynē*." *Classical Antiquity* 11, 91–120.

——. 1997. "Decentering Tragedy: The Impact of (on) Democracy." In Morris & Raaflaub 1997.155–69.

Kyrieleis, Helmut. 1986. "Neue archaische Skulpturen aus dem Heraion von Samos." In id. (ed.), *Archaische und klassische griechische Plastik,* 35–41. Mainz: von Zabern.

Lacey, W. K. 1968. *The Family in Classical Greece.* London: Thames & Hudson.

Lacore, Michelle. 1983. "Euripide et le culte de Poseidon-Erechthée." *Revue des études anciennes* 85, 215–34.

La Genière, Juliette de. 1960. "Une pélike inédite du Peintre de Pan au Musée du Louvre." *Revue des études anciennes* 62, 249–53.

Laks, André. 1990. "Legislation and Demiurgy: On the Relationship between Plato's *Republic* and *Laws*." *Classical Antiquity* 9, 209–29.

——. 1991. "L'utopie législative de Platon." *Revue philosophique* 4, 417–28.

Lambert, Stephen D. 1993. *The Phratries of Attica.* Ann Arbor: University of Michigan Press.

Lambrinudakis, Wassilis et al. 1992. "Apollon." *LIMC* II, 183–327.

Lammert, Friedrich. 1939. "Tropaion." *RE* VIIA 1, 663–73.

Lanza, Diego. 1977a. *Il tiranno e il suo pubblico.* Turin: Einaudi.

——. 1977b. "Lo spettatore sulla scena." In Lanza 1977a.57–78.

——. 1983. "Lo spettacolo." In Mario Vegetti (ed.), *Oralità, scrittura, spettacolo,* 107–39. Turin: Borighieri.

——. 1988. "Les temps de l'émotion tragique: Malaise et soulagement." *Mètis* 3, 15–39.

——, Vegetti, Mario, Caiani, Guglielmino & Sircana, Francesco. 1977. *L'ideologia della città*. Naples: Liguori.

Lattimore, Richmond. 1943. "Aeschylus on the Defeat of Xerxes." In *Classical Studies in Honor of William Abbott Oldfather, Presented by a Committee of his Former Students and Colleagues,* 83–93. Urbana: University of Illinois Press.

Lauffer, Siegfried. 1974. "Die Liturgien in der Krisenperiode Athens." In Elisabeth C. Welskopf (ed.), *Hellenische Poleis: Krise, Wandlung, Wirkung* I, 147–59. Berlin: Akademie-Verlag.

Lauter-Bufé, Heide & Lauter, Hans. 1975. "Die vorthemistokleische Stadtmauer Athens nach philologischen und archäologischen Quellen." *Archäologischer Anzeiger,* 1–9.

Lavency, M. 1964. *Aspects de la logographie judiciaire attique*. Louvain: Bibliothèque de l'université.

Lawall, Mark. 1995. "Premonetary and Monetary? A Note on Trade in the Fifth Century B.C." In Carole Gillis, Christina Risberg & Birgitta Sjöberg (eds.), *Trade and Production in Premonetary Greece: Aspects of Trade,* 139–57. Jonsered, Sweden: Paul Åström Förlag.

Lawton, Carol. 1993. "Representations of Athenian Democracy in Attic Document Reliefs." In Ober & Hedrick 1993.12–16.

Lazaridis, Dimitri, Romiopoulou, Katerina, & Tsouratsoglou, Yianni. 1992. *O Tymvos tis Nikisianis*. Vivliothiki tis en Athinais Archaiologikis Etaireias 121. Athens: Archaiologiki Etaireia.

Leach, Edmund R. 1961. *Rethinking Anthropology*. London: Athlone Press.

Leacock, Arthur G. 1900. "De rebus ad pompas sacras apud Graecos pertinentibus quaestiones selectae." *Harvard Studies in Classical Philology* 11, 1–47.

Lefkowitz, Mary R. 1981. *The Lives of the Greek Poets*. Baltimore: Johns Hopkins University Press.

—— & Fant, Maureen B. 1982. *Women's Lives in Greece and Rome*. Ibid.

Le Goff, Jacques. 1989. *Time, Work, and Culture in the Middle Ages*. Tr. Arthur Goldhammer. Chicago, University of Chicago Press.

Leitch, Vincent. 1992. *Cultural Criticism, Literary Theory and Post–Structuralism*. New York: Columbia University Press.

Lesky, Albin. 1966. *A History of Greek Literature*. Tr. James Willis & Cornelis de Heer. New York: Crowell.

Lessing, Gotthold E. 1769. *Hamburgische Dramaturgie*. Leipzig: Schwickert.

Lévêque, Pierre. 1992. "La naissance de la sainte famille." *Revue des études anciennes* 94, 315–24.

Levi, Mario A. 1977/1978. "Una lettura storiografica: I *Persiani* di Eschilo." *Atti Centro ricerche e documentazione sull'antichità classica* 9, 67–73.

Levine, Lawrence. 1991. "William Shakespeare and the American People." In Chandra Mukerji & Michael Schudson (eds.), *Rethinking Popular Culture,* 157–97. Berkeley: University of California Press.

Lévy, Edmond. 1993. "*Politeuma* et *politeia* chez Aristote." In Piérart 1993.65–90.

Lewis, David M. 1959. "Law on the Lesser Panathenaia." *Hesperia* 28, 239–47.

Lewis, J. D. 1971. "Isegoria at Athens: When Did It Begin?" *Historia* 20, 129–40.

Lezzi-Hafter, Adrienne. 1988. *Der Eretria-Maler*. Mainz: von Zabern.

Liddell, Henry G., Scott, Robert & Jones, Sir Henry S. 1968. *A Greek-English Lexicon*. New edition, with a supplement. Oxford: Clarendon Press.

Lincoln, Bruce. 1989. *Discourse and the Construction of Society. Comparative Studies of Myth, Ritual, and Classification*. New York: Oxford University Press.

Lind, Hermann. 1990. *Der Gerber Kleon in den "Rittern" des Aristophanes. Studien zur Demagogenkomödie*. Frankfurt am Main: Lang.

Lindenbaum, S. 1994. "Ceremony and Oligarchy: The London Midsummer Watch." In Hanawalt & Reyerson 1994.171–88.

Lissarrague, François. 1989. "The World of the Warrior." In Claude Bérard et al., *A City of Images: Iconography and Society in Ancient Greece*, 39–52. Tr. Deborah Lyons. Princeton: Princeton University Press.

——. 1990. *L'autre guerrier. Archers, peltastes, cavaliers dans l'imagerie attique*. Paris: La Découverte & Rome: Ecole française de Rome.

Livingstone, R. W. 1925. "The Problem of the *Eumenides* of Aeschylus." *Journal of Hellenic Studies* 45, 120–31.

Lloyd, G. E. R. 1966. *Polarity and Analogy: Two Types of Argumentation in Early Greek Thought*. Cambridge: Cambridge University Press.

——. 1979. *Magic, Reason and Experience*. Ibid.

——. 1987. *The Revolutions of Wisdom: Studies in the Claims and Practice of Ancient Greek Science*. Berkeley: University of California Press.

Lloyd, Michael. 1992. *The Agon in Euripides*. Oxford: Oxford University Press.

Lloyd-Jones, Hugh. 1970. *Aeschylus' Oresteia*. Tr. with Commentary. Englewood Cliffs, N.J.: Prentice Hall. Repr. Berkeley: University of California Press, 1993.

—— & Parsons, Peter (eds.). 1983. *Supplementum Hellenisticum*. Berlin: De Gruyter.

Loeb, Ehud H. 1979. *Die Geburt der Götter in der griechischen Kunst der klassischen Zeit*. Jerusalem: Shikoma.

Lohmann, Hans. 1993. *Atene: Forschungen zu Siedlungs- und Wirtschaftsstruktur des klassischen Attika*. 2 vols. Köln: Böhlau.

Long, Timothy. 1986. *Barbarians in Greek Comedy*. Carbondale, Ill.: Southern Illinois University Press.

Longo, Oddone. 1990. "The Theater of the Polis." In Winkler & Zeitlin 1990.12–19.

Lonis, Raoul (ed.). 1988–92. *L'étranger dans le monde grec*. 2 vols. Nancy: Presses Universitaires de Nancy.

——. 1994. *La cité dans le monde grec*. Paris: Nathan.

Loraux, Nicole. 1973. " 'Marathon' ou l'histoire idéologique." *Revue des études anciennes* 75, 13–42.

——. 1979. "L'autochthonie: Une topique athénienne. Le mythe dans l'espace civique." *Annales ESC* 1, 2–26. English tr. of rev. version in Loraux 1993.37–71.

——. 1980. "L'oubli dans la cité." *Le Temps de la réflexion* 1, 213–42. Repr. in Loraux 1997, chap. 1.

——. 1986. *The Invention of Athens: The Funeral Oration in the Classical City*. Tr. Alan Sheridan. Cambridge, Mass.: Harvard University Press.

——. 1993. *The Children of Athena: Athenian Ideas about Citizenship & the Division between the Sexes*. Tr. Caroline Levine. Princeton: Princeton University Press.

——. 1996. "Clistene e i nuovi caratteri della lotta politica." In Settis 1996.1083–1110.

——. 1997. *La cité divisée*. Paris: Payot.

Lord, Carnes. 1981. "The Intention of Aristotle's *Rhetoric*." *Hermes* 109, 326–39.

Lotze, Detlef. 1981. "Zum Begriff der Demokratie in Aischylos' *Hiketiden*." In Schmidt 1981.207–16.

——. 1983. "Entwicklungslinien der Demokratie im 5. Jh. v. Chr." *Oikumene* 4, 9–24.

——. 1997. "Zwischen Kleisthenes und Ephialtes." In Eder & Hölkeskamp 1997.89–98.

Luce, J. V. 1992. *An Introduction to Greek Philosophy*. London: Thames & Hudson.

Ludwig, Walter. 1957. *Sapheneia. Ein Beitrag zur Formkunst im Spätwerk des Euripides*. Bonn: Habelt.

Luginbühl, Marianne. 1992. *Menschenschöpfungsmythen. Ein Vergleich zwischen Griechenland und dem Alten Orient*. Frankfurt/Main: Lang.

Lullies, Reinhard & Hirmer, Max. 1979. *Griechische Plastik von den Anfängen bis zum Beginn der römischen Kaiserzeit*. Munich: Hirmer.

Luschnig, C. A. E. 1976. "Euripides' *Hecabe*: The Time is Out of Joint." *Classical Journal* 71, 227–34.

McCann, David & Strauss, Barry S. Forthcoming. *Democracy at War: The Korean War and the Peloponnesian War*. Washington, D.C.: Wilson Center Press.

McDermott, Emily A. 1989. *Euripides'* Medea*: The Incarnation of Disorder*. University Park: Pennsylvania State University Press.

McDonald, William A. 1943. *The Meeting Places of the Greeks*. Baltimore: Johns Hopkins University Press.

MacDowell, Douglas. 1971. *Aristophanes,* Wasps. Oxford: Oxford University Press.

——. 1978. *The Law in Classical Athens*. London: Thames & Hudson.

——. 1989. "The *oikos* in Athenian Law." *Classical Quarterly* 39, 10–21.

——. 1993. "Foreign Birth and Athenian Citizenship in Aristophanes." In Sommerstein et al. 1993.359–71.

——. 1995. *Aristophanes and Athens. An Introduction to the Plays*. Oxford: Oxford University Press.

McInerney, Jeremy. Forthcoming. *The Folds of Parnassos. Land and Ethnicity in Ancient Phokis*.

McKechnie, Paul. 1989. *Outsiders in the Greek Cities in the Fourth Century B.C.* London: Routledge.

Macleod, Colin. 1978. "Reason and Necessity: Thucydides III 9–14, 37–48." *Journal of Hellenic Studies* 98, 64–78. Repr. in id. 1983.88–102.

——. 1982. "Politics and the *Oresteia*." *Journal of Hellenic Studies* 102, 124–44. Repr. in id. 1983.20–40.

——. 1983. *Collected Essays*. Oxford: Clarendon Press.

McNiven, Timothy J. 1995. "The Unheroic Penis: Otherness Exposed." *Source: Notes in the History of Art* 15, 10–16.

Macve, Richard H. 1985. "Some Glosses on Ste. Croix's 'Greek and Roman Accounting.'" In Cartledge & Harvey 1985.233–64.

Maddoli, Gianfranco. 1985. "Attikà prima di Erodoto?" *Storia della storiografia* 7, 101–13.

Mai, Ekkehard (ed.). 1989. *Denkmal - Zeichen - Monument. Skulptur und öffentlicher Raum heute*. Munich: Prestel.

Maitland, Judith. 1992. "Dynasty and Family in the Athenian City State: A View from Attic Tragedy." *Classical Quarterly* 42, 26–40.

Makaronas, Chr. & Yiouri, E. 1989. *Oi oikies apragis tis Elenis kai Dionysou*. Athens: Vivliothiki tis en Athinais Arkhaiologikis Etaireias.

Manfredini, Mario & Piccirilli, Luigi. 1977. *Plutarco, La vita di Solone*. Milan: Mondadori.

Mann, Thomas. 1937. *Freud, Goethe, Wagner*. New York: Knopf.

Mannheim, Karl. 1927. "Das konservative Denken. Soziologische Beiträge zum Werden des politisch-historischen Denkens in Deutschland." *Archiv für Sozialwissenschaft und Sozialpolitik* 57, 68–142, 470–95.

——. 1936. *Ideology and Utopia*. London: Routledge & Kegan Paul.

Mansfeld, Jaap. 1979–80. "The Chronology of Anaxagoras' Athenian Period and the Date of His Trial." *Mnemosyne* ser. 4, 32, 39–69; 33, 17–95.

Mansfield, John. 1985. *The Robe of Athena and the Panathenaic "Peplos."* Diss. University of California at Berkeley.

Manville, P. Brook. 1990. *The Origins of Citizenship in Ancient Athens*. Princeton: Princeton University Press.

Mark, Ira S. 1993. *The Sanctuary of Athena Nike in Athens: Architectural Stages and Chronology*. *Hesperia* Suppl. 26. Princeton: American School of Classical Studies at Athens.

Markle, Minor M. III. 1985. "Jury Pay and Assembly Pay in Athens." In Cartledge & Harvey 1985.265–97.

Marrou, Henri I. 1956. *A History of Education in Antiquity*. Tr. George Lamb. London: Seed & Ward.

Martin, Jochen. 1974. "Von Kleisthenes zu Ephialtes. Zur Entstehung der athenischen Demokratie." *Chiron* 4, 5–42. Repr. in Kinzl 1995.160–212.

——. 1976. "Zur Entstehung der Sophistik." *Saeculum* 27, 143–64.

——. 1990. "Aspekte antiker Staatlichkeit." In Eder 1990.220–32.

Martin, Josef. 1974. *Antike Rhetorik. Technik und Methode*. Handbuch der Altertumswissenschaft II.3. Munich: Beck.

Martin, Richard. 1989. *The Language of Heroes: Speech and Performance in the* Iliad. Ithaca, N.Y.: Cornell University Press.

Marzi, Giovanni. 1988. "Il 'decreto' degli Spartani contro Timoteo (Boeth. *De inst. mus.* 1,1)." In Gentili & Pretagostini 1988.264–72.

Mastromarco, Giuseppe. 1994a. *Introduzione a Aristofane*. Rome: Laterza.

——. 1994b. "Teatro comico e potere politico nell'Atene del V secolo (Pseudo-Senofonte, 'Costituzione degli Ateniesi', II 18)." In *Storia poesia e pensiero nel mondo antico. Studi in onore di Marcello Gigante,* 451–58. Naples: Bibliopolis.

Mastronarde, Donald J. 1994. *Euripides: Phoenissae.* Ed. with Introduction and Commentary. Cambridge: Cambridge University Press.

Matthaiou, Angelos P. 1988. "Neos lithos tou mnemeiou me ta epigrammata gia tous Persikous polemous." *Horos* 6, 118–22.

——. 1994. "Two New Attic Inscriptions." In Osborne & Hornblower 1994.175–88.

Mattingly, Harold. 1961. "The Athenian Coinage Decree." *Historia* 10, 148–88. Repr. in id., *The Athenian Empire Restored: Epigraphic and Historical Studies,* 5–52. Ann Arbor: University of Michigan Press, 1996.

Mattusch, Carol C. 1994. "The Eponymous Heroes: The Idea of Sculptural Groups." In Coulson et al. 1994.73–81.

Maxwell–Stuart, P. G. 1970. "Remarks on the Black Cloaks of the Ephebes." *Proceedings of the Cambridge Philological Society* 16, 113–16.

Meier, Christian. 1968. "Drei Bemerkungen zur Vor- und Frühgeschichte des Begriffs Demokratie." In Marc Sieber (ed.), *Discordia concors. Festgabe für Edgar Bonjour* I, 3–29. Basel: Helbig & Lichtenhahn. Rev. repr. in Kinzl 1995.125–59.

——. 1970. *Entstehung des Begriffs "Demokratie": Vier Prolegomena zu einer historischen Theorie.* Frankfurt am Main: Suhrkamp.

——. 1973. "Die Entstehung der Historie." In Reinhard Koselleck & Wolf-Dieter Stempel (eds.), *Geschichte—Ereignis und Erzählung,* 251–305. Munich: Wilhelm Fink.

——. 1975. "'Fortschritt' in der Antike." In Otto Brunner et al. (eds.), *Geschichtliche Grundbegriffe* II, 353–63. Stuttgart: Klett.

——. 1978. "Entstehung und Besonderheit der griechischen Demokratie." *Zeitschrift für Politik* N.F. 25, 1–31. Rev. repr. in Kinzl 1995.248–301.

——. 1980. *Die Enstehung des Politischen bei den Griechen.* Frankfurt am Main: Suhrkamp. Engl. tr., id. 1990b.

——. 1983/84. "Arbeit, Politik, Identität: Neue Fragen im alten Athen?" *Chronik der Ludwig-Maximilians-Universität München,* 69–95.

——. 1985. *Politik und Anmut.* Berlin: Siedler.

——. 1987a. "Der Umbruch zur Demokratie in Athen (462/1 v.Chr.)." In Reinhart Herzog and Reinhart Koselleck (eds.), *Epochenschwelle und Epochenbewusstsein.* Poetik und Hermeneutik 12, 353–80. Munich: Fink.

——. 1987b. "Historical Answers to Historical Questions: The Origins of History in Ancient Greece." In Boedeker & Peradotto 1987.41–57.

——. 1988. *Die politische Kunst der griechischen Tragödie.* Munich: Beck. Engl. tr., id. 1993b.

——. 1990a. "Die Rolle des Krieges im klassischen Athen." *Historische Zeitschrift* 251, 555–605.

——. 1990b. *The Greek Discovery of Politics.* Tr. David McLintock. Cambridge, Mass.: Harvard University Press.

——. 1993a. *Athen*. Berlin: Siedler.

——. 1993b. *The Political Art of Greek Tragedy*. Tr. Andrew Webber. Baltimore: Johns Hopkins University Press.

——. 1996. "Kultur als Absicherung der attischen Demokratie: wieso brauchten die Athener ihre Kultur?" In Sakellariou 1996.199–222.

Meiggs, Russell. 1972. *The Athenian Empire*. Oxford: Oxford University Press.

——. 1982. *Trees and Timber in the Ancient Mediterranean World*. Ibid.

—— & Lewis, David (eds.). 1988. *A Selection of Greek Historical Inscriptions to the End of the Fifth Century B.C.* Ibid.

Meikle, Scott. 1995. "Modernism, Economics, and the Ancient Economy." *Proceedings of the Cambridge Philological Society* 41, 174–91.

Melchinger, Siegfried. 1974. *Das Theater der Tragödie. Aischylos, Sophokles, Euripides auf der Bühne ihrer Zeit*. Munich: Beck.

Mendilow, Adam A. 1972. *Time and the Novel*. New York: Humanities Press.

Meritt, Benjamin D. 1928. *The Athenian Calendar in the Fifth Century*. Cambridge, Mass.: Harvard University Press.

—— & Wade-Gery, H. T. 1963. "The Dating of Documents to the Mid-Fifth Century." *Journal of Hellenic Studies* 83, 100–117.

——, Wade-Gery, H. T. & McGregor, Malcolm F. (eds.). 1939–53. *The Athenian Tribute Lists*. 4 vols. Princeton: American School of Classical Studies at Athens.

Mette, Joachim (ed.). 1955. *Lexikon des frühgriechischen Epos*, I. Göttingen: Vanderhoeck & Ruprecht.

——. 1981. "Aischylos und das Problem des Krieges." In Schmidt 1981.154–60.

Metzger, Henri. 1976. "Athéna soulevant de terre le nouveau-né. Du geste au mythe." In Pierre Ducrey et al. (eds.), *Mélanges d'histoire ancienne et d'archéologie offerts à Paul Collart*, 295–303. Lausanne: Bibliothèque historique vaudoise.

Metzler, Dieter. 1971. *Porträt und Gesellschaft*. Berlin: Wasmuth.

——. 1980. "Eunomia und Aphrodite. Zur Ikonologie einer attischen Vasengruppe." *Hephaistos* 2, 181–97.

——. 1988. "Demokratie als Bauherr. Ideologische Aspekte der Architektur der Klassik." In id., *Praktika tou XII Diethnous Synedriou Klasikis Archaiologias, Athena 1983* IV, 129–33. Athens: Ypourgeio politismou kai epistemon.

——. 1992. "Archaische Kunst im Spiegel archaischen Denkens. Zur historischen Bedeutung der griechischen Kouros-Statuen." In Oliver Brehm & Sascha Klie (eds.), *Mousikos aner. Festschrift für Max Wegner zum 90. Geburtstag*. Antiquitas ser. 3, 32, 289–303. Bonn: Habelt.

Meyboom, P. G. P. 1978. "Some Observations on Narration in Greek Art." *Mededelingen van het Nederlands Instituut te Rome* 40, 55–82 & pls. 27–33.

Meyer, Eduard. 1899. *Forschungen zur Alten Geschichte* II. Halle an der Saale, Germany: Niemeyer.

Meyer, Elizabeth. 1993. "Epitaphs and Citizenship in Classical Athens." *Journal of Hellenic Studies* 113, 99–121.

Meyer, Marion. 1988. *Die griechischen Urkundenreliefs. Athenische Mitteilungen*, Beiheft 13. Berlin: Gebr. Mann.

Meyerson, Ignace. 1956. "Le temps, la mémoire, l'histoire." *Journal de Psychologie* 53, 333–54.

Michelini, Ann. 1994. "Political Themes in Euripides' *Suppliants*." *American Journal of Philology* 115, 219–52.

Michell, Humphrey. 1957. *The Economics of Ancient Greece*. Cambridge: W. Heffer & Sons.

Migeotte, Leopold. 1984. *L'Emprunt public dans les cités grecques*. Québec: Editions du Sphinx.

——. 1992. *Les souscriptions publiques dans les cités greques*. Geneva: Librairie Droz & Québec: Editions du Sphinx.

Mikalson, Jon D. 1975. *The Sacred and Civil Calendar of the Athenian Year*. Princeton: Princeton University Press.

——. 1976. "Erechtheus and the Panathenaia." *American Journal of Philology* 97, 141–53.

——. 1983. *Athenian Popular Religion*. Chapel Hill: University of North Carolina Press.

——. 1984. "Religion and the Plague in Athens, 431–423 B.C." In Alan L. Boegehold et al. (eds.), *Studies Presented to Sterling Dow on his Eightieth Birthday*. Greek, Roman, and Byzantine Monograph 10, 217–25. Durham, N.C.: Duke University Press.

Miller, Margaret C. 1992. "The Parasol: An Oriental Status–Symbol." *Journal of Hellenic Studies* 112, 91–105.

——. 1995. "Priam, King of Troy." In Jane B. Carter and Sarah P. Morris (eds.), *The Ages of Homer: A Tribute to Emily Townsend Vermeule*, 449–65. Austin: University of Texas Press.

——. 1997. *Athens and Persia in the Fifth Century B.C.: A Study in Cultural Receptivity*. Cambridge: Cambridge University Press.

——. Forthcoming. *The Orientalization of Greek Myth in Attic Art*.

Miller, Stella G. 1979. *Two Groups of Thessalian Gold*. Berkeley: University of California Press.

——. 1982. "Macedonian Tombs: Their Architecture and Architectural Decoration." In Beryl Barr-Sharrar & Eugene N. Borza (eds.), *Macedonia and Greece in Late Classical and Early Hellenistic Times*, 152–69. Washington, D.C.: National Gallery of Art.

Miller, Stephen G. 1995. "Old Metroon and Old Bouleuterion in the Classical Agora of Athens." In Hansen & Raaflaub 1995.133–56.

Miller, Walter. 1929–32. *Daedalus and Thespis: The Contributions of the Ancient Dramatic Poets to Our Knowledge of the Arts and Crafts of Greece*. 3 vols. New York: MacMillan.

Millett, Paul. 1983. "Maritime Loans and the Structure of Credit in Fourth-Century Athens." In Peter Garnsey, Keith Hopkins & C. R. Whittaker (eds.), *Trade in the Ancient Economy*, 36–52. Berkeley: University of California Press.

——. 1991. *Lending and Borrowing in Ancient Athens*. Cambridge: Cambridge University Press.

——. 1993. "Warfare, Economy, and Democracy in Classical Athens." In Rich & Shipley 1993.177–96.

Mills, Harrianne. 1984. "Greek Clothing Regulations: Sacred and Profane." *Zeitschrift für Papyrologie und Epigraphik* 55, 255–65.

Mills, Sophie. 1997. *Theseus, Tragedy, and the Athenian Empire.* Oxford: Oxford University Press.

Mink, Louis. 1978. "Narrative Form as a Cognitive Instrument." In R. H. Canary and H. Kozicki (eds.), *The Writing of History: Literary Form and Historical Understanding,* 129–49. Madison: University of Wisconsin Press.

Mirhady, David C. 1994. "Aristotle, the *Rhetorica ad Alexandrum* and the *tria genera causarum.*" In Fortenbaugh & Mirhady 1994.54–65.

Missiou, Anna. 1992. *The Subversive Oratory of Andokides: Politics, Ideology and Decision-Making in Democratic Athens.* Cambridge: Cambridge University Press.

Mitchell, W. J. Thomas. 1986. *Iconology: Image, Text, Ideology.* Chicago: University of Chicago Press.

Moggi, Mauro. 1972. "Autori greci di Persika, I: Dionisio di Mileto." *Annali della Scuola normale superiore di Pisa* ser. 3, 2, 439–42.

——. 1977. "Autori greci di Persika, II: Carone di Lampsaco." Ibid. ser. 3, 7, 1–26.

Molho, Anthony, Raaflaub, Kurt & Emlen, Julia (eds.). 1991. *Athens and Rome, Florence and Venice: City States in Classical Antiquity and Medieval Italy.* Stuttgart: Steiner & Ann Arbor: University of Michigan Press.

Momigliano, Arnaldo. 1960. Review of Havelock 1957. *Rivista storica* 72, 534–41.

——. 1966. "Time in Ancient Historiography." In id., *History and the Concept of Time. History and Theory,* Beiheft 6, 1–23. Middletown, Conn.: Wesleyan University Press.

Monoson, S. Sara. 1994a. "Citizen as *Erastes*: Erotic Imagery and the Idea of Reciprocity in the Periclean Funeral Oration." *Political Theory* 22, 253–76.

——. 1994b. "Frank Speech, Democracy, and Philosophy: Plato's Debt to a Democratic Strategy of Civic Discourse." In Euben, Wallach, & Ober 1994.172–97.

Montanari, Enrico. 1981. *Il mito dell'autoctonia. Linee di una dinamica mitica-politica ateniese.* 2d ed. Rome: Bulzoni.

Moon, Warren G. (ed.). 1983. *Ancient Greek Art and Iconography.* Madison: University of Wisconsin Press.

Moore, John M. 1975. *Aristotle and Xenophon on Democracy and Oligarchy.* Berkeley: University of California Press. 2d ed. 1983.

Moraux, Paul. 1954. "Thucydide et la rhétorique. Etude sur la structure de deux discours (III, 37–48)." *Les études classiques* 22, 3–23.

——. 1968. "La juste dialectique d'après le huitième livre des Topiques." In G. E. L. Owen (ed.), *Aristotle on Dialectic,* 277–311. Oxford: Clarendon Press.

Moret, Jean-Marc. 1982. "L'apollinisation de l'imagerie légendaire à Athènes dans la seconde moitié du Ve siècle." *Revue archéologique,* 109–36.

——. 1984. *Oedipe, la Sphinx et les Thébains. Essai de mythologie iconographique.* Bibliotheca Helvetica Romana 23. Geneva: Institut Suisse de Rome.

Moretti, Jean-Charles. 1993. *Théâtres d'Argos*. Sites et monuments 10. Athens: Ecole française d'Athènes.

Morgan, Catherine. 1991. "Ethnicity and Early Greek States." *Proceedings of the Cambridge Philological Society* 37, 131–63.

Morris, Ian. 1987. *Burial and Ancient Society: The Rise of the Greek City-State*. Cambridge: Cambridge University Press.

——. 1992. *Death-Ritual and Social Structure in Classical Antiquity*. Ibid.

——. 1992/93. "Law, Culture and Funerary Art in Athens, 600–300 BC." *Hephaistos* 11/12, 32–50.

——. 1993. "Poetics of Power: The Interpretation of Ritual Action in Archaic Greece." In Dougherty & Kurke 1993.15–45.

——. 1994a. "The Athenian Economy Twenty Years after *The Ancient Economy*." *Classical Philology* 89, 351–66.

——. 1994b. "Everyman's Grave." In Boegehold & Scafuro 1994.67–101.

——. 1996. "The Strong Principle of Equality and the Archaic Origins of Greek Democracy." In Ober & Hedrick 1996.19–48.

——. 1997a. "Archaeology as a Kind of Anthropology." In Morris & Raaflaub 1997.229–39.

——. 1997b. "An Archaeology of Equalities? The Greek City-States." In Thomas Charlton & Deborah Nichols (eds.), *The Archaeology of City-States*. Washington, D.C.: Smithsonian Institution.

——. 1997c. "The Art of Citizenship." In Susan Langdon (ed.), *New Light on a Dark Age: Exploring the Culture of Geometric Greece*, 9–43. Columbia: University of Missouri Press.

——. Forthcoming. *Darkness and Heroes: Manhood, Equality, and Democracy in Iron Age Greece*. Oxford: Blackwell.

—— & Raaflaub, Kurt A. (eds.). 1997. *Democracy 2500? Questions and Challenges*. AIA Colloquia Conference Papers 2. Dubuque, IA: Kendall/Hunt.

Morris, Sarah P. 1992. *Daidalos and the Origins of Greek Art*. Princeton: Princeton University Press.

Morrison, J. S. & Coates, J. F. 1986. *The Athenian Trireme: The History and Reconstruction of an Ancient Greek Warship*. Cambridge: Cambridge University Press.

—— & Williams, R. T. 1968. *Greek Oared Ships, 900–322 B.C.* Cambridge: Cambridge University Press.

Morrow, Glenn. 1960. *Plato's Cretan City. A Historical Interpretation of the Laws*. Princeton: Princeton University Press. 2d ed. 1993.

Mossé, Claude. 1967. "La conception du citoyen dans la Politique d'Aristote." *Eirene* 6, 17–22.

——. 1979. "Citoyens 'actifs' et citoyens 'passifs' dans la cité grecque." *Revue des études anciennes* 81, 241–49.

Mrozek, Stanislaw. 1989. *Lohnarbeit im klassischen Altertum*. Bonn: Habelt.

Müller, Karl O. 1833. *Aischylos' Eumeniden*. Göttingen: Dieterich.

Müller, Reimar. 1986. "Sophistique et démocratie." In Barbara Cassin (ed.), *Positions de la Sophistique, Colloque de Deris,* 179–93. Paris: J. Vrin.

Müller-Strübing, Hermann. 1873. *Aristophanes und die historische Kritik.* Leipzig: Teubner.

Muhly, James D. 1992. "The Crisis Years in the Mediterranean World: Transition or Cultural Disintegration?" In William A. Ward & Martha S. Joukowsky (eds.), *The Crisis Years: The 12th Century B.C. from beyond the Danube to the Tigris,* 10–26. Dubuque, Ia.: Kendall/Hunt.

Muir, Edward. 1981. *Civic Ritual and Renaissance Venice.* Princeton: Princeton University Press.

Muir, Edwin. 1957. *The Structure of the Novel.* London: Hogarth Press.

Munn, Mark. 1999. *Democracy and History at Athens in the Age of Socrates.* Berkeley: University of California Press.

Murphy, C. T. 1938. "Aristophanes and the Art of Rhetoric." *Harvard Studies in Classical Philology* 49, 69–113.

Murphy, J. J. 1974. *Rhetoric in the Middle Ages: A History of Rhetorical Theory from Saint Augustine to the Renaissance.* Berkeley: University of California Press.

Murray, Oswyn. 1990. "The Affair of the Mysteries: Democracy and the Drinking Group." In id. (ed.), *Sympotica: A Symposium on the Symposion,* 149–61. Oxford: Clarendon Press.

—— & Price, Simon (eds.). 1990. *The Greek City from Homer to Alexander.* Oxford: Clarendon Press.

Musti, Domenico. 1963. "Sull'idea di *suggeneia* in iscrizioni greche." *Annali della scuola normale superiore di Pisa* 32, 225–39.

Nagy, Blaise. 1992. "Athenian Officials in the Parthenon Frieze." *American Journal of Archaeology* 96, 55–69.

Nagy, Gregory. 1990. *Pindar's Homer.* Baltimore: Johns Hopkins University Press.

——. 1996. *Poetry as Performance: Homer and beyond.* Cambridge: Cambridge University Press.

Natali, Carlo. 1987. "*Adolescheia, Leptologia,* and the Philosophers in Athens." *Phronesis* 32, 232–41.

Navarre, Octave. 1900. *Essai sur la rhétorique grecque avant Aristote.* Paris: Hachette.

Neils, Jenifer. 1983. "A Greek Nativity by the Meidias Painter." *Bulletin of the Cleveland Museum of Art* 70, 274–89.

——. 1987. *The Youthful Deeds of Theseus.* Rome: Bretschneider.

—— (ed.). 1992. *Goddess and Polis: The Panathenaic Festival in Classical Athens.* Princeton: Princeton University Press.

——. 1994. "The Panathenaia and Kleisthenic Ideology." In Coulson et al. 1994.151–60.

——. 1995. "The Euthymides Krater from Morgantina." *American Journal of Archaeology* 99, 427–44.

—— (ed.). 1996. *Worshipping Athena: Panathenaia & Parthenon.* Madison: University of Wisconsin Press.

Nesselrath, Heinz-Günther. 1997. "The Polis of Athens in Middle Comedy." In Dobrov 1997. 271–88.

Neumann, Uwe. 1995. *Gegenwart und mythische Vergangenheit bei Euripides. Hermes* Einzelschrift 69. Stuttgart: Steiner.

Nevett, Lisa. Forthcoming. *House and Society: Domestic Space in the Classical and Hellenistic Greek World.* Cambridge: Cambridge University Press.

Newiger, Hans-Joachim. 1976. "Zwei Bemerkungen zur Spielstätte des attischen Dramas im 5. Jahrhundert v. Chr." *Wiener Studien* 89 (n.s. 10), 80–92.

Nielsen, Thomas Heine, Bjerstrup, Lars, Hansen, Mogens Herman, Rubinstein, Lene & Vestergard, Torben. 1989. "Athenian Grave Monuments and Social Class." *Greek, Roman and Byzantine Studies* 30, 411–20.

Niemeyer, Hans Georg. 1960. *Promachos.* Waldsassen, Germany: Stiftland-Verlag.

Nightingale, Andrea. 1995. *Genres in Dialogue: Plato and the Construct of Philosophy.* Cambridge: Cambridge University Press.

Nilsson, Martin P. 1940. *Greek Popular Religion.* New York: Columbia University Press. Repr. *Greek Folk Religion.* New York: Harper Torchbooks, 1961.

——. 1951. "Die Prozessionstypen im griechischen Kult." In id., *Opuscula Selecta* I, 166–214. Lund: Gleerup.

Nippel, Wilfried. 1982. "Die Heimkehr der Argonauten aus der Südsee. Ökonomische Anthropologie und die Theorie der griechischen Gesellschaft in klassischer Zeit." *Chiron* 12, 1–39.

Nixon, Lucia & Price, Simon. 1990. "The Size and Resources of Greek Cities." In Murray & Price 1990.137–70.

Norden, Eduard. 1915. *Die antike Kunstprosa.* 2 vols. 3d ed. Leipzig: Teubner.

Nussbaum, Martha. 1986. *The Fragility of Goodness: Luck and Ethics in Greek Tragedy and Philosophy.* Cambridge: Cambridge University Press.

Nylander, Carl. 1962. "Die sog. mykenischen Säulenbasen auf der Akropolis in Athen." *Opuscula Atheniensia: Acta Inst. Athen. Regni Sueciae* 4, 31–77.

Oakley, John H. 1982. "A Louvre Fragment Reconsidered: Perseus Becomes Erichthonios." *Journal of Hellenic Studies* 102, 220–22.

——. 1987. "A Calyx-Krater in Virginia by the Nikias Painter with the Birth of Erichthonios." *Antike Kunst* 30, 123–30.

—— & Rotroff, Susan. 1992. *Debris From a Public Dining Place in the Athenian Agora. Hesperia* Suppl. 25. Princeton: American School of Classical Studies at Athens.

Ober, Josiah. 1985a. *Fortress Attica: Defense of the Athenian Land Frontier, 404–322 B.C. Mnemosyne* Suppl. 84. Leiden: Brill.

——. 1985b. "Thucydides, Pericles, and the Strategy of Defense." In John W. Eadie & Josiah Ober (eds.), *The Craft of the Ancient Historian: Essays in Honor of Chester G. Starr,* 171–88. Lanham, Md.: University Press of America. Repr. in Ober 1996.72–85.

——. 1989. *Mass and Elite in Democratic Athens: Rhetoric, Ideology and the Power of the People.* Princeton: Princeton University Press.

——. 1993a. "The Athenian Revolution of 508/7 B.C.E.: Violence, Authority, and the Origins of Democracy." In Dougherty & Kurke 1993.215–32. Repr. in Ober 1996.32–52.

——. 1993b. "Thucydides' Criticism of Democratic Knowledge." In Rosen & Farrell 1993.81–98.

——. 1994a. "Civic Ideology and Counterhegemonic Discourse: Thucydides on the Sicilian Debate." In Boegehold & Scafuro 1994.102–26.

——. 1994b. "How to Criticize Democracy in Late Fifth- and Fourth-Century Athens." In Euben, Wallach, & Ober 1994.149–71. Repr. in Ober 1996.140–60.

——. 1996. *The Athenian Revolution: Essays on Ancient Greek Democracy and Political Theory*. Princeton: Princeton University Press.

——. 1997. "Revolution Matters: Democracy as Demotic Action." In Morris & Raaflaub 1997.67–85.

——. Forthcoming. "Thucydides on State Power and Domestic Politics: Realist Theory and Critical History." In McCann & Strauss forthcoming.

—— & Hedrick, Charles (eds.). 1993. *The Birth of Democracy*. Exhibition Catalogue. Princeton: American School of Classical Studies in Athens.

—— & Hedrick, Charles (eds.). 1996. *Demokratia: A Conversation on Democracies, Ancient and Modern*. Princeton: Princeton University Press.

—— & Strauss, Barry S. 1990. "Drama, Political Rhetoric and the Discourse of Athenian Democracy." In Winkler & Zeitlin 1990.237–70.

O'Neil, James L. 1973. *Greek Democratic Constitutions outside Athens*. Diss. Cambridge (unpublished).

——. 1995. *The Origins and Development of Ancient Greek Democracy*. Lanham, Md.: University Press of America.

Onians, Richard B. 1954. *The Origins of European Thought about the Body, the Mind, the Soul, World, Time and Fate*. 2d ed. Cambridge: Cambridge University Press.

O'Regan, D. E. 1992. *Rhetoric, Comedy, and the Violence of Language in Aristophanes'* Clouds. New York: Oxford University Press.

Osborne, Peter. 1995. *The Politics of Time: Modernity and Avant-Garde*. London: Verso.

Osborne, Robin. 1985. *Demos: The Discovery of Classical Attika*. Cambridge: Cambridge University Press.

——. 1987a. *Classical Landscape with Figures: The Ancient Greek City and Its Countryside*. Dobbs Ferry, N.Y.: Sheridan House.

——. 1987b. "Viewing and Obscuring the Parthenon Frieze." *Journal of Hellenic Studies* 107, 98–105.

——. 1993a. "Competitive Festivals and the Polis." In Sommerstein et al. 1993.21–37.

——. 1993b. "Women and Sacrifice in Classical Greece." *Classical Quarterly* 43, 392–405.

——. 1994a. "Archaeology, the Salaminioi, and the Politics of Sacred Space in Archaic Attica." In Susan E. Alcock and Robin Osborne (eds.), *Placing the Gods: Sanctuaries and Sacred Space in Ancient Greece*, 143–60. Oxford: Clarendon Press.

——. 1994b. "Democracy and Imperialism in the Panathenaic Procession: The Parthenon Frieze in Its Context." In Coulson et al. 1994.143–50.

——. 1995. "The Economics and Politics of Slavery at Athens." In Powell 1995.27–43.

—— & Hornblower, Simon (eds.). 1994. *Ritual, Finance, Politics: Athenian Democratic Accounts Presented to David Lewis*. Oxford: Oxford University Press.

Ostwald, Martin. 1986. *From Popular Sovereignty to the Sovereignty of Law*. Berkeley: University of California Press.

——. 1992. "Athens as a Cultural Centre." *CAH* V², 306–69.

——. 1995a. "Freedom and the Greeks." In R. W. Davis (ed.), *The Origins of Modern Freedom in the West*, 37–63. Stanford: Stanford University Press.

——. 1995b. "Public Expense: Whose Obligation? Athens 600–454 B.C.E." *Proceedings of the American Philosophical Society* 139, 368–79.

O'Sullivan, Neil. 1993. "Plato and *hē kaloumenē rhētorikē*." *Mnemosyne* 46, 87–89.

Overbeck, Johannes A. 1868. *Die antiken Schriftquellen zur Geschichte der bildenden Künste bei den Griechen*. Leipzig: W. Engelmann.

Page, Denys (ed.). 1962. *Poetae Melici Graeci*. Oxford: Clarendon Press.

Palagia, Olga. 1980. *Euphranor*. Leiden: Brill.

——. 1992. *The Pediments of the Parthenon*. Leiden: Brill.

Palavestra, Aleksandar. 1994. "Prehistoric Trade and a Cultural Model for Princely Tombs in the Central Balkans." In Kristian Kristiansen & Jørgen Jensen (eds.), *Europe in the First Millennium B.C.*, 7–30. Sheffield Archaeological Monographs 6. Sheffield: J. R. Collis Publications.

Pallat, Ludwig. 1937. "Zum Friese der Nordhalle des Erechtheion." *Jahrbuch des Deutschen Archäologischen Instituts* 52, 17–29.

Palmer, Hazel. 1964. "The Classical and Roman Periods." In Carl Blegen, Hazel Palmer, & Rodney Young, *Corinth* XIII: *The North Cemetery*, 65–327. Princeton: American School of Classical Studies at Athens.

Papachatzis, Nikolaos. 1989. "The Cult of Erechtheus and Athena on the Acropolis of Athens." *Kernos* 2, 175–82.

Papakonstandinou-Diamandourou, Despina. 1971. *Pella* I. Athens: Vivliothiki tis en Athinais Arkhaiologikis Etaireias.

Papaspyridi-Karusu, Semni. 1954–55. "Alkamenes und das Hephaisteion." *Athenische Mitteilungen* 69–70, 67–94.

Pariente, Anne. 1992. "Le monument argien des 'Sept contre Thèbes'." In Piérart 1992.195–225.

Parke, H. W. 1977. *Festivals of the Athenians*. Ithaca, N.Y.: Cornell University Press.

Parker, Robert. 1983. *Miasma: Pollution and Purification in Early Greek Religion*. Oxford: Oxford University Press.

——. 1987. "Myths of Early Athens." In Jan Bremmer (ed.), *Interpretations of Greek Mythology*, 187–214. London: Croom Helm.

——. 1994. "Athenian Religion Abroad." In Osborne & Hornblower 1994.339–46.

——. 1996. *Athenian Religion: A History*. Oxford: Oxford University Press.

Patterson, Cynthia. 1981. *Pericles' Citizenship Law of 451–450 BC*. New York: Arno Press.

——. 1986. "*Hai Attikai*: The Other Athenians." *Helios* 13, 49–67.

Patterson, Orlando. 1991. *Freedom I: Freedom in the Making of Western Culture.* New York: Basic Books.

Payne, Humfry & Young, Gerald M. 1936. *Archaic Marble Sculpture from the Acropolis.* London: Cresset Press.

Pearson, Lionel. 1942. *The Local Historians of Attica.* Philadelphia: American Philological Association.

——. 1976. *The Art of Demosthenes.* Beiträge zur Klassischen Philologie 68. Meisenheim am Glan, Germany: A. Hain.

Pečirka, J. 1966. *The Formula for the Grant of Enktesis in Attic Inscriptions.* Prague: Universita Karlova.

Pelling, Christopher (ed.). 1997. *Greek Tragedy and the Historian.* Oxford: Clarendon Press.

Pemberton, Elizabeth G. 1988. "The Beginning of Monumental Painting in Mainland Greece." In Robert I. Curtis (ed.), *Studia Pompeiana & Classica in Honor of Wilhelmina Jashemski,* 181–97. New Rochelle: Caratzas.

Pendrick, Gerard J. 1993. "The Ancient Tradition on Antiphon Reconsidered." *Greek, Roman and Byzantine Studies* 34, 215–28.

Pennock, J. Roland. 1979. *Democratic Political Theory.* Princeton: Princeton University Press.

Peradotto, John & Sullivan, J. P. (eds.). 1984. *Women in the Ancient World: The Arethusa Papers.* Albany: State University of New York Press.

Pernot, Laurent. 1993. *La rhétorique de l'éloge dans le monde gréco-romain.* 2 vols. Paris: Institut d'études augustiniennes.

Petersen, Eugen. 1915. *Die attische Tragödie als Bild- und Bühnenkunst.* Bonn: Friedrich Cohen.

Petre, Zoê. 1971. "Thèmes dominants et attitudes politiques dans les *Sept contre Thèbes.*" *Studii Clasice* 13, 15–28.

Petsas, Photios M. 1978. *Pella, Alexander the Great's Capital.* Thessaloniki: Arkhaiologiko Mouseio Thessalonikis.

Pfeiffer, Rudolf. 1968. *History of Classical Scholarship: From the Beginnings to the End of the Hellenistic Age.* Oxford: Oxford University Press.

Pfuhl, Ernestus. 1900. *De Atheniensium Pompis Sacris.* Berlin: Weidmann.

Philippson, Paula. 1944. *Untersuchungen über den griechischen Mythos.* Zurich: Rhein-Verlag.

Pickard-Cambridge, Arthur W. 1968. *The Dramatic Festivals of Athens.* 2d ed. rev. by John Gould & D. M. Lewis. Oxford: Oxford University Press. Repr. with additions, ibid. 1988.

Piérart, Marcel (ed.). 1992. *Polydipsion Argos. Bulletin de correspondance hellénique* Suppl. 22. Athens: Ecole française d'Athènes.

—— (ed.). 1993. *Aristote et Athènes. Actes de la table ronde du centenaire de la* Constitution d'Athènes, *23–25 Mai 1991.* Paris: De Boccard.

Pinney, Gloria F. 1983. "Achilles Lord of Scythia." In Moon 1983.127–46.

——. 1988. "Pallas and Panathenaia." In Christiansen & Melander 1988.465–77.

Pirenne-Delforge, Vinciane. 1994. *L'Aphrodite grecque. Kernos* Suppl. 4. Liège: Centre international d'étude de la religion grecque antique.

Podes, Stephan. 1992. "Zur Problematik der Diobelie und Obolos-Zahlungen." *Grazer Beiträge* 18, 35–45.

——. 1994. "The Introduction of Jury Pay by Pericles: Some Mainly Chronological Considerations." *Athenaeum* 82, 95–110.

Podlecki, Anthony J. 1966. *The Political Background of Aeschylean Tragedy*. Ann Arbor: University of Michigan Press.

——. 1986. "Polis and Monarch in Early Attic Tragedy." In Euben 1986.76–100.

——. 1993. "*Kat'archēs gar philaitios leōs*: The Concept of Leadership in Aeschylus." In Sommerstein et al. 1993.55–79.

Poliakoff, Michael B. 1987. *Combat Sports in the Ancient World*. New Haven: Yale University Press.

Polignac, François de. 1995. *Cults, Territory, and the Origins of the Greek City-State*. Tr. Janet Lloyd. Chicago: University of Chicago Press.

Pollitt, Jerome J. 1965. *The Art of Greece, 1400–31 B.C.* New York: Prentice Hall.

——. 1972. *Art and Experience in Classical Greece*. Cambridge: Cambridge University Press.

Pomeroy, Sarah B. 1975. *Goddesses, Whores, Wives, and Slaves: Women in Classical Antiquity*. New York: Schocken Books.

——. 1982. "Charities for Greek Women." *Mnemosyne* 35, 115–35.

——. 1984. "Selected Bibliography on Women in Classical Antiquity." In Peradotto & Sullivan 1984.315–72.

——. 1995. "Women's Identity and the Family in the Classical *Polis*." In Hawley & Levick 1995.111–21.

——. 1997. *Families in Classical and Hellenistic Greece: Representations and Realities*. Oxford: Clarendon Press.

Popper, Karl R. 1952. *The Open Society and Its Enemies*, I: *The Spell of Plato*. 2d ed. London: Routledge.

Porter, John R. 1994. *Studies in Euripides' Orestes*. Leiden: Brill.

Portulas, Jaume. 1981. "Tragédie et lutte des classes dans l'Athènes classique. A propos d'un ouvrage récent de V. Citti." *Faventia* 3, 31–46.

Post, L. A. 1950. "The *Seven against Thebes* as Political Propaganda for Pericles." *Classical Weekly* 44, 49–52.

Potts, Alex. 1994. *Flesh and the Ideal: Winckelmann and the Origins of Art History*. New Haven: Yale University Press.

Powell, Anton. 1988. *Athens and Sparta: Constructing Greek Political and Social History from 478 B.C.* London: Routledge.

—— (ed.). 1995. *The Greek World*. London: Routledge.

Powell, Benjamin. 1906. *Erichthonios and the Three Daughters of Cecrops*. Ithaca, N.Y.: Cornell University Press.

Price, Jonathan. 1999. *Internal Conflict in Thucydides*. Cambridge: Cambridge University Press.

Prinz, Friedrich. 1979. *Gründungsmythen und Sagenchronologie.* Zetemata 72. Munich: Beck.

Pritchard, David. 1994. "From Hoplite Republic to Thetic Democracy: The Social Context of the Reforms of Ephialtes." *Ancient History: Resources for Teachers* 24, 111–39.

Pritchett, W. Kendrick. 1953/1956. "The Attic Stelai." 2 parts. *Hesperia* 22, 225–99; 25, 178–317.

——. 1961. "Five New Fragments of The Attic Stelai." *Hesperia* 30, 23–29.

——. 1974. *The Greek State at War* II. Berkeley: University of California Press.

——. 1979. *The Greek State at War* III. Ibid.

Protzmann, Heiner. 1984. "Antiquarische Nachlese zu den Statuen der sogenannten Lemnia Furtwänglers in Dresden." *Jahrbuch der Staatlichen Kunstsammlungen Dresden* 16, 7–22.

Quass, Friedemann. 1995. Review of Connor et al. 1990. *Gnomon* 67, 27–33.

Quincey, J. H. 1964. "Orestes and the Argive Alliance." *Classical Quarterly* 14, 190–206.

Raaflaub, Kurt A. 1979. "Polis Tyrannos. Zur Entstehung einer politischen Metapher." In Glen W. Bowersock, Walter Burkert & Michael C. J. Putnam (eds.), *Arktouros: Hellenic Studies Presented to Bernard M. W. Knox*, 237–52. Berlin: De Gruyter.

——. 1980. "Des freien Bürgers Recht der freien Rede." In Werner Eck, Hartmut Galsterer & Hartmut Wolff (eds.), *Studien zur antiken Sozialgeschichte: Festschrift F. Vittinghoff*, 7–57. Cologne: Böhlau.

——. 1983. "Democracy, Oligarchy, and the Concept of the 'Free Citizen' in Late Fifth-Century Athens." *Political Theory* 11, 517–44.

——. 1984. "Athens 'Ideologie der Macht' und die Freiheit des Tyrannen." In Balcer et al. 1984.45–86.

——. 1985. *Die Entdeckung der Freiheit.* Vestigia 37. Munich: Beck.

——. 1987. "Herodotus, Political Thought, and the Meaning of History." In Boedeker & Peradotto 1987.221–48.

——. 1988. "Athenische Geschichte und mündliche Überlieferung." In Ungern-Sternberg & Reinau 1988.197–225.

——. 1989. "Contemporary Perceptions of Democracy in Fifth-Century Athens." *Classica & Mediaevalia* 40, 33–70. Repr. in Connor et al. 1990.33–70.

——. 1990. "Expansion und Machtbildung in frühen Polis-Systemen." In Eder 1990.511–45.

——. 1994. "Democracy, Power, and Imperialism in Fifth-Century Athens." In Euben, Wallach, & Ober 1994.103–46.

——. 1995. "Einleitung und Bilanz: Kleisthenes, Ephialtes und die Begründung der Demokratie." In Kinzl 1995.1–54.

——. 1996a. "Born to Be Wolves? Origins of Roman Imperialism." In Robert W. Wallace & Edward M. Harris (eds.), *Transitions to Empire: Essays in Greco-Roman History, 360–146 B.C., in Honor of E. Badian*, 273–314. Norman: University of Oklahoma Press.

——. 1996b. "Equalities and Inequalities in Athenian Democracy." In Ober & Hedrick 1996.139–74.

——. 1996c. "Solone, la nuova Atene e l'emergere della politica." In Settis 1996.1035–81.
——. 1997a. "Power in the Hands of the People: Foundations of Athenian Democracy." In Morris & Raaflaub 1997.31–66.
——. 1997b. "The Thetes and Democracy." In Morris & Raaflaub 1997.87–103.
——. Forthcoming. "Father of All—Destroyer of All: War in Late Fifth-Century Athenian Discourse." In McCann & Strauss forthcoming.
Race, W. H. 1990. *Style and Rhetoric in Pindar's Odes*. Atlanta: Scholars Press.
Radermacher, Ludwig (ed.). 1951. *Artium scriptores (Reste der voraristotelischen Rhetorik)*. Vienna: Rohrer.
Raeck, Wulf. 1981. *Zum Barbarenbild in der Kunst Athens im 6. und 5. Jh. v. Chr.* Bonn: Habelt.
Rankin, H. D. 1983. *Sophists, Socratics and Cynics*. London: Croom Helm.
Raubitschek, Antony. 1941. "Two Notes on Isocrates." *Transactions of the American Philological Association* 72, 356–64.
——. 1949. *Dedications from the Athenian Akropolis*. Cambridge, Mass.: Harvard University Press.
——. 1962. "Demokratia." *Hesperia* 31, 238–43.
——. 1984. "Die Bedeutung des Parthenon und seines Skulpturenschmuckes." In Berger 1984.19.
Rawson, Elisabeth. 1970. "Family and Fatherland in Euripides' *Phoenissae*." *Greek, Roman and Byzantine Studies* 11, 109–27.
Reden, Sitta von. 1995. *Exchange in Ancient Greece*. London: Duckworth.
Redfield, James. 1990. "Drama and Community: Aristophanes and Some of His Rivals." In Winkler & Zeitlin 1990.314–35.
Reeder, Ellen D. (ed.). 1995. *Pandora*. Exhibition Catalogue. Baltimore: Walters Art Gallery & Princeton: Princeton University Press.
Reinmuth, Oscar. 1971. *The Ephebic Inscriptions of the Fourth Century B.C.* Leiden: Brill.
Renfrew, Colin. 1986. "Introduction: Peer Polity Interaction and Socio-Political Change." In Renfrew & Cherry 1986.1–18.
—— & Cherry, John F. (eds.). 1986. *Peer Polity Interaction and Socio-Political Change*. Cambridge: Cambridge University Press.
Reverdin, Olivier & Grange, Bernard (eds.). 1988. *Hérodote et les peuples non Grecs*. Entretiens sur l'antiquité classique 35. Vandoeuvres-Geneva: Fondation Hardt.
Rhodes, Peter J. 1972. *The Athenian Boule*. Oxford: Oxford University Press.
——. 1980. "Athenian Democracy after 403 B.C." *Classical Journal* 75, 305–23.
——. 1981. *A Commentary on the Aristotelian* Athenaion Politeia. Oxford: Oxford University Press.
——. 1982. "Problems in Athenian *Eisphora* and Liturgies." *American Journal of Ancient History* 7, 1–19.
——. 1988. *Thucydides, History II*. Warminster, England: Aris & Phillips.
——. 1992a. "The Athenian Revolution." *CAH* V^2, 62–95.
——. 1992b. "The Delian League to 449 B.C." Ibid. 34–61.

——. 1994. "The Ostracism of Hyperbolus." In Osborne & Hornblower 1994.85–98.

Rhodes, Robin F. 1995. *Architecture and Meaning on the Athenian Acropolis.* Cambridge: Cambridge University Press.

Rich, John & Shipley, Graham (eds.). 1993. *War and Society in The Greek World.* London: Routledge.

Richter, Gisela. 1961. *The Archaic Gravestones of Attica.* London: Phaidon.

Ridgway, Brunilde S. 1966. "Some Notes on the Development of the Greek Frieze." *Hesperia* 35, 188–204.

——. 1970. *The Severe Style in Greek Sculpture.* Princeton: Princeton University Press.

——. 1977. *The Archaic Style in Greek Sculpture.* Ibid.

——. 1981. *Fifth Century Styles in Greek Sculpture.* Ibid.

——. 1983. "Painterly and Pictorial in Greek Relief Sculpture." In Moon 1983.193–208.

——. 1990. "Birds, 'Meniskoi,' and Head Attributes in Archaic Greece." *American Journal of Archaeology* 94, 583–612.

——. 1992. "Aristonautes' Stele, Athens Nat.Mus. 738." In Heide Froning, Tonio Hölscher & Harald Mielsch (eds.), *Kotinos: Festschrift für Erika Simon,* 270–75. Mainz: Philipp von Zabern.

Ridley, Ronald T. 1979. "The Hoplite as Citizen: Athenian Military Institutions in Their Social Context." *L'Antiquité classique* 48, 508–48.

Riemschneider, Wilhelm. 1940. *Held und Staat in Euripides' Phoenissen.* Würzburg: Konrad Triltsch.

Rimmon-Kenan, Shlomith. 1983. *Narrative Fiction: Contemporary Poetics.* London: Methuen.

Robert, Carl. 1881. *Bild und Lied. Archäologische Beiträge zur Geschichte der griechischen Heldensage.* Berlin: Weidmann.

——. 1919. *Archäologische Hermeneutik. Anleitung zur Deutung klassischer Bildwerke.* Ibid.

Roberts, Jennifer. 1986. "Aristocratic Democracy: The Perseverance of Timocratic Principles in Athenian Government." *Athenaeum* 64, 355–69.

——. 1996. "Athenian Equality: A Constant Surrounded by Flux." In Ober & Hedrick 1996.187–202.

Roberts, John W. 1984. *City of Sokrates: An Introduction to Classical Athens.* London: Routledge & Kegan Paul.

Robertson, Martin. 1965. "Greek Mosaics." *Journal of Hellenic Studies* 85, 72–89.

——. 1975. *A History of Greek Art.* 2 vols. Cambridge: Cambridge University Press.

——. 1982. "Early Greek Mosaic." In Barr-Sharrar & Borza 1982.240–49.

——. 1992. *The Art of Vase-Painting in Classical Athens.* Cambridge: Cambridge University Press.

Robertson, Noel. 1983. "The Riddle of the Arrhephoria." *Harvard Studies in Classical Philology* 87, 241–88.

——. 1985. "The Origin of the Panathenaea." *Reinisches Museum* n.s. 128, 231–95.

——. 1992. *Festivals and Legends: The Formation of Greek Cities in the Light of Public Rit-*

ual. Toronto: University of Toronto Press.

Robinson, David M. 1946. *Olynthus* XI: *Domestic and Public Architecture.* Baltimore: Johns Hopkins University Press.

—— & Graham, John W. 1938. *Olynthus* VIII: *The Hellenic House.* Ibid.

Robinson, Eric. 1997. *The First Democracies: Early Popular Government outside Athens. Historia* Einzelschrift 107. Stuttgart: Steiner.

Rösler, Wolfgang. 1980a. "Die Entdeckung der Fiktionalität in der Antike." *Poetica* 12, 283–319.

——. 1980b. *Polis und Tragödie. Funktionsgeschichtliche Betrachtungen zu einer antiken Literaturgattung.* Konstanz: Universitätsverlag.

Romeyer-Dherbey, Gilbert. 1985. *Les Sophistes.* Paris: Presses Universitaires de France.

Romilly, Jacqueline de. 1947. *Thucydide et l'impérialisme athénien.* Paris: Belles Lettres.

——. 1956. *Histoire et raison chez Thucydide.* Ibid.

——. 1965. "Les *Phéniciennes* d'Euripide ou l'actualité dans la tragédie grecque." *Revue philologique* 39, 28–47.

——. 1968. *Time in Greek Tragedy.* Ithaca, N.Y.: Cornell University Press.

——. 1969. "Il pensiero di Euripide sulla tirannia." *Dioniso* 43, 175–87.

——. 1972. "L'assemblée du peuple dans l'Oreste d'Euripide." In Salvatore Costanza, Rosario Anastasi, Giuseppina Basta Donizelli, Giovanni Salanitro & Giuseppe Spadaro (eds.), *Studi classici in onore di Q. Cataudella* I, 237–51. Catania: Università di Catania.

——. 1977. "La tragedia griega y la crisis de la ciudad." *Estudios Classicos* 21, 1–58.

——. 1983. "Le thème de la liberté et l'évolution de la tragédie grecque." In Zehnacker 1983.215–26.

——. 1992. *The Great Sophists in Periclean Athens.* Oxford: Oxford University Press.

Rosen, Ralph M. 1988. *Old Comedy and the Iambographic Tradition.* Atlanta: Scholars Press.

—— & Farrell, Joseph (eds.). 1993. *Nomodeiktes. Greek Studies in Honor of Martin Ostwald.* Ann Arbor: Michigan University Press.

Rosenbloom, Daniel. 1993. "Shouting Fire in a Crowded Theater: Phrynichos' *Capture of Miletus* and the Politics of Fear in Early Attic Tragedy." *Philologus* 137, 159–96.

——. 1995. "Myth, History and Hegemony in Aeschylus." In Goff 1995.91–130.

Rosivach, Vincent. 1985 [1993]. "Manning the Athenian Fleet." *American Journal of Ancient History* 10, 41–66.

——. 1987. "Autochthony and the Athenians." *Classical Quarterly* 37, 294–305.

——. 1998. "Enslaving *Barbaroi* and the Athenian Ideology of Slavery." Forthcoming in *Historia.*

Rotenberg, Robert. 1992. "The Power to Time and the Time to Power." In Rutz 1992.18–36.

Rotroff, Susan I. 1977. "The Parthenon Frieze and the Sacrifice to Athena." *American Journal of Archaeology* 81, 372–82.

Rowe, Christopher J. 1995. *Plato: Statesman* (with tr. and comm.). Warminster, England: Aris & Phillips.

—— & Schofield, Malcolm (eds.). 1999. *The Cambridge History of Greek and Roman Political Thought.* Cambridge: Cambridge University Press.

Rumpf, Andreas. 1951. "Parrhasios." *American Journal of Archaeology* 55, 1–12.

Ruschenbusch, Eberhard. 1966. *Solonos Nomoi. Die Fragmente des solonischen Gesetzeswerkes mit einer Text- und Überlieferungsgeschichte. Historia* Einzelschrift 9. Wiesbaden: Steiner.

——. 1978. *Untersuchungen zu Staat und Politik in Griechenland vom 7. - 4. Jh. v. Chr.* Bamberg: aku-Verlag.

——. 1979. *Athenische Innenpolitik im 5. Jh. v. Chr. Ideologie oder Pragmatismus?* Ibid.

Rusten, Jeffrey. 1989. *Thucydides, The Peloponnesian War, Book II.* Cambridge: Cambridge University Press.

Rutz, Henry J. (ed.). 1992. *The Politics of Time.* American Ethnological Society monogr. ser. 4. Washington, D.C.: American Anthropological Association.

Ryan, Mary. 1989. "The American Parade: Representations of the Nineteenth–Century Social Order." In Lynn Hunt (ed.), *The New Cultural History,* 131–53. Berkeley: University of California Press.

Saïd, Suzanne. 1983. "Concorde et civilisation: *Euménides* vv 858–866 et 976–987." In Zehnacker 1983.97–121.

——. 1984. "Grecs et barbares dans les tragédies d'Euripide: La fin des différences?" *Ktema* 9, 27–53.

——. 1985. *Sophiste et tyran ou le problème du Prométhée enchaîné.* Paris: Klincksieck.

——. 1993. "L'invention de la tradition: Le mythe de l'Aréopage avant Aristote." In Piérart 1993.155–81.

Ste. Croix, G. E. M. de. 1956. "Greek and Roman Accounting." In A. C. Littleton and B. S. Yamey (eds.), *Studies in the History of Accounting,* 14–74. Homewood, Ill.: Richard D. Irwin.

——. 1970. "Some Observations on the Property Rights of Athenian Women." *Classical Review* n.s. 20, 273–78.

——. 1972. *The Origins of the Peloponnesian War.* London: Duckworth.

——. 1981. *The Class Struggle in the Ancient Greek World.* Ibid. & Ithaca, N.Y.: Cornell University Press.

Sakellariou, Michel B. (ed.). 1996. *Colloque international: Démocratie athénienne et culture.* Athens: Ekdotike Athenon.

Salanitro, Giovanni. 1965. "Il pensiero politico di Eschilo nei Persiani." *Giornale italiano di filologia* 18, 193–235.

——. 1966. "L'Orestea e la politica estera di Atene." *Siculorum Gymnasium* 19, 153–73.

Salkever, S. G. 1986. "Tragedy and the Education of the *demos.*" In Euben 1986.274–303.

Sallares, Robert. 1991. *The Ecology of the Ancient Greek World.* Ithaca, N.Y.: Cornell University Press.

——. 1996. "Population, Greek." *Oxford Classical Dictionary,* 1221–23. 3d ed. Oxford: Oxford University Press.

Salmon, John B. 1984. *Wealthy Corinth: A History of the City to 338 B.C.* Oxford: Oxford University Press.

Salzmann, Dieter. 1982. *Untersuchungen zu den antiken Kieselmosaiken.* Berlin: Mann.

Samons, Loren J. 1993. "Athenian Finance and the Treasury of Athena." *Historia* 42, 129–38.

Sandbach, F. H. 1970. "Menander's Manipulation of Language for Dramatic Purposes." In E. G. Turner (ed.), *Ménandre.* Entretiens sur l'antiquité classique 16, 111–36. Vandoeuvres-Geneva, Switzerland: Fondation Hardt.

Sartori, Franco. 1988. "Teatro e storia nella Grecia antica: opinioni recenti su vecchi problemi." In Corsini 1986–88.2:11–48.

Sartre, Jean-Paul. 1948. *Qu'est-ce que la littérature?* Paris: Gallimard.

Sauer, Bruno. 1899. *Das sogenannte Theseion und sein plastischer Schmuck.* Leipzig: Geisecke & Devrient.

Saunders, T. J. 1986. "'The RAND Corporation of Antiquity'? Plato's Academy and Greek Politics." In J. H. Betts, J. T. Hooker & J. R. Green (eds.), *Studies in Honour of T. B. L. Webster* I, 200–210. Bristol, England: Bristol Classical Press.

——. 1995. "Plato on Women in the *Laws.*" In Powell 1995.591–609.

Saxonhouse, Arlene W. 1992. *Fear of Diversity: The Birth of Political Science in Ancient Greek Political Thought.* Chicago: University of Chicago Press.

Scafuro, Adele C. 1994. "Witnessing and False Witnessing: Proving Citizenship and Kin Identity in Fourth-Century Athens." In Boegehold & Scafuro 1994.156–98.

Scarcella, A. M. 1982. "Lotta di classe, potere e teatro nella società ateniese." *Klio* 64, 229–38.

Schaps, David. 1977. "The Woman Least Mentioned: Etiquette and Women's Names." *Classical Quarterly* n.s. 27, 323–30.

——. 1979. *Economic Rights of Women in Ancient Greece.* Edinburgh: Edinburgh University Press.

——. 1993. "Aeschylus' Politics and the Theme of the Oresteia." In Rosen & Farrell 1993.505–15.

Schauenburg, Konrad. 1975. "Eurymedon eimi." *Mitteilungen des Deutschen Archäologischen Instituts Athen* 90, 97–121.

Schefold, Karl. 1946. "Kleisthenes. Der Anteil der Kunst an der Gestaltung des jungen attischen Freistaates." *Museum Helveticum* 3, 59–93.

——. 1964. *Frühgriechische Sagenbilder.* Munich: Hirmer.

Scheidel, Walter. 1990. "Feldarbeit von Frauen in der antiken Landwirtschaft." *Gymnasium* 97, 405–31.

——. 1995–96. "The Most Silent Women of Greece and Rome: Rural Labour and Women's Life in the Ancient World." 2 parts. *Greece & Rome* 42, 202–17; 43, 1–10.

Schelp, Jochen. 1975. *Das Kanoun, der griechische Opferkorb.* Würzburg: K. Triltsch.

Schiappa, Edward. 1990a. "The Beginnings of Greek Rhetorical Theory." In David Zarefsky (ed.), *Rhetorical Movement: Essays in Honor of Leland M. Griffin,* 5–33. Evanston, Ill.: Northwestern University Press.

———. 1990b. "Did Plato Coin *Rhētorikē*?" *American Journal of Philology* 111, 457–70.

———. 1991. *Protagoras and Logos: A Study in Greek Philosophy and Rhetoric*. Columbia: University of South Carolina Press.

Schiffer, Michael B. 1987. *Formation Processes of the Archaeological Record*. Albuquerque: University of New Mexico Press.

Schmaltz, Bernhard. 1983. *Griechische Grabreliefs*. Darmstadt: Wissenschaftliche Buchgesellschaft.

———. 1995. "Zu den Ephesischen Amazonen." *Archäologischer Anzeiger* 335–43.

Schmidt, Ernst Günther (ed.). 1981. *Aischylos und Pindar*. Berlin: Akademie-Verlag.

Schmidt, Margot. 1968. "Die Entdeckung des Erichthonios." *Mitteilungen des Deutschen Archäologischen Instituts Athen* 83, 201–18.

Schmitt Pantel, Pauline (ed.). 1992a. *A History of Women in the West* I: *From Ancient Goddesses to Christian Saints*. Tr. Arthur Goldhammer. Cambridge, Mass.: Harvard University Press.

———. 1992b. *La Citê au banquet: Histoire des repas dans les citês grecques*. Rome: École française de Rome.

Schmitz, Winfried. 1988. *Wirtschaftliche Prosperität, soziale Integration und die Seebundpolitik Athens*. Munich: tuduv-Verlag.

Schneider, Lambert A. 1975. *Zur sozialen Bedeutung der archaischen Korenstatuen*. Hamburger Beiträge zur Archäologie 2. Hamburg: Helmut Buske.

Schöpsdau, Klaus. 1994. "Das Nachleben der *Technon synagoge* bei Cicero, Quintilian und in den griechischen Prolegomena zur Rhetorik." In Fortenbaugh & Mirhady 1994.192–216.

Schröder, Otto. 1914. *De laudibus Athenarum a poetis tragicis et ab oratoribus epidicticis excultis*. Diss. Göttingen.

Schuller, Wolfgang. 1974. *Die Herrschaft der Athener im Ersten Attischen Seebund*. Berlin: De Gruyter.

———. 1978. *Die Stadt als Tyrann: Athens Herrschaft über seine Bundesgenossen*. Konstanzer Universitätsreden 101. Konstanz: Universitäts-Verlag.

———. 1984. "Wirkungen des Ersten Attischen Seebunds auf die Herausbildung der athenischen Demokratie." In Balcer et al. 1984.87–101.

———, Hoepfner, Wolfram & Schwandner, Ernst Ludwig (eds.). 1989. *Demokratie und Architektur*. Munich: Deutscher Kunstverlag. Rev. ed. 1995.

Schwarze, Joachim. 1971. *Die Beurteilung des Perikles durch die attische Komödie und ihre historische und historiographische Bedeutung*. Munich: Beck.

Schweitzer, Bernhard. 1969. "Das Problem der Form in der Kunst des Altertums." In Ulrich Hausmann (ed.), *Handbuch der Archäologie: Allgemeine Grundlagen der Archäologie*, 163–203. Munich: Beck.

Schwenk, Cynthia. 1997. "Athens." In Tritle 1997.8–40.

Schwinge, Ernst-Richard. 1992. "Griechische Tragödie. Das Problem ihrer Zeitlichkeit." *Antike und Abendland* 38, 48–66.

Scodel, Ruth (ed.). 1993. *Theater and Society in the Classical World*. Ann Arbor: University of Michigan Press.

Seaford, Richard. 1994. *Reciprocity and Ritual: Homer and Tragedy in the Developing City-State*. Oxford: Oxford University Press.

Sealey, Raphael. 1966. "The Origins of the Delian League." In Badian 1966.233–55.

——. 1983. "How Citizenship and the City Began in Athens." *American Journal of Ancient History* 8, 97–129.

——. 1987. *The Athenian Republic: Democracy or the Rule of Law?* University Park: Pennsylvania State University Press.

Segal, Charles P. 1986. "Greek Tragedy and Society: A Structuralist Perspective." In Euben 1986.43–75.

——. 1992. "Tragic Beginnings: Narration, Voice and Authority in the Prologues of Greek Drama." *Yale Classical Studies* 29, 85–112.

Seidensticker, Bernd. 1995. "Dichtung und Gesellschaft im 4. Jahrhundert." In Eder 1995b.175–98.

Settis, Salvatore (ed.). 1996. *I Greci* II.1. Turin: Einaudi.

Sfyroeras, Pavlos. 1995. "The Ironies of Salvation: The Aegeus Scene in Euripides' *Medea*." *Classical Journal* 90, 125–42.

Shapiro, H. Alan. 1983. "Painting, Politics, and Genealogy: Peisistratos and the Neleids." In Moon 1983.87–96.

——. 1989. *Art and Cult under the Tyrants in Athens*. Mainz: von Zabern.

——. 1992a. "Mousikoi Agones: Music and Poetry at the Panathenaia." In Neils 1992.53–75.

——. 1992b. "Narrative Strategies in Euphronios." In id., *Euphronios. Atti del Seminario Internazionale di Studi,* 37–43. Florence: Il Ponte.

——. 1992c. "Theseus in Kimonian Athens: The Iconography of Empire." *Mediterranean Historical Review* 7, 29–49.

——. 1993. *Personifications in Greek Art*. Kilchberg, Switzerland: Akanthus.

——. 1994a. "Poet and Painter: Iliad 24 and the Greek Art of Narrative." *Quaderni ticinesi di numismatica e antichità classiche* 23, 23–48.

——. 1994b. "Religion and Politics in Democratic Athens." In Coulson et al. 1994.123–29.

——. 1995a. *Art and Cult under the Tyrants in Athens*. Suppl. Mainz: von Zabern.

——. 1995b. "The Cult of Heroines: The Daughters of Kekrops." In Reeder 1995.39–48.

——. 1996a. "Athena, Apollo, and the Religious Propaganda of the Athenian Empire." In Hellström & Alroth 1996.101–13.

——. 1996b. "Democracy and Imperialism: The Panathenaia in the Age of Perikles." In Neils 1996.215–25.

Shear, T. Leslie, Jr. 1970. "The Monument of the Eponymous Heroes in the Athenian Agora." *Hesperia* 39, 145–222.

——. 1978. "Tyrants and Buildings in Archaic Athens." In W. A. P. Childs (ed.), *Athens Comes of Age: From Solon to Salamis,* 1–19. Princeton: The Archaeological Institute of America.

——. 1994. "*Isonomous t'Athēnas epoiēsatēn*: The Agora and the Democracy." In Coulson et al. 1994.225–48.

——. 1995. "Bouleuterion, Metroon and the Archives at Athens." In Hansen & Raaflaub 1995.157–90.

Sherwin-White, Susan M. 1978. *Ancient Cos: An Historical Study from the Dorian Settlement to the Imperial Period.* Göttingen: Vandenhoeck & Ruprecht.

Shipley, Graham. 1987. *A History of Samos, 800–188 BC.* Oxford: Oxford University Press.

Shuger, D. K. 1988. *Sacred Rhetoric: The Christian Grand Style in the English Renaissance.* Princeton: Princeton University Press.

Siewert, Peter. 1982. *Die Trittyen Attikas und die Heeresreform des Kleisthenes.* Vestigia 33. Munich: Beck.

Simms, Ronda R. 1998. "Mourning and Community at the Athenian Adonia." *Classical Journal* 93.2, 121–41.

Simon, Erika. 1959. *Die Geburt der Aphrodite.* Berlin: De Gruyter.

——. 1970. "Aphrodite Pandemos auf attischen Münzen." *Schweizerische Numismatische Rundschau* 49, 5–24.

——. 1978. "Zeus, Teil III: Archäologische Zeugnisse." *RE* Suppl. 15, 1411–41.

——. 1980. "Die Mittelgruppe im Westgiebel des Parthenon." In Cahn & Simon 1980.239–55.

——. 1983. *Festivals of Attica: An Archaeological Commentary.* Madison: University of Wisconsin Press.

——. 1985. "La decorazione architettonica del tempietto di Atena Nike sull'Acropoli di Atene." *Museum Patavinum* 3.2, 271–88.

——. 1985/86. "Ta glypta tou naou kai tou thorakiou tes Athenas Nikes." *Archaiognosia* 4, 11–27.

—— & Hirmer, Max & Albert. 1976. *Die griechischen Vasen.* Munich: Hirmer. 2d ed. 1981.

Sinclair, R. K. 1988. *Democracy and Participation in Athens.* Cambridge: Cambridge University Press.

Sinn, Ulrich. 1989. "Die Votivgabe eines Athleten in Olympia." In Hans-Ulrich Cain, Hanns Gabelmann & Dieter Salzmann (eds.), *Beiträge zur Ikonographie und Hermeneutik. Festschrift für Nikolaus Himmelmann,* 65–70. Mainz: von Zabern.

Skorupski, John. 1976. *Symbol and Theory: A Philosophical Study of Theories of Religion in Social Anthropology.* Cambridge: Cambridge University Press.

Small, David B. 1997. "An Archaeology of Democracy." In Morris & Raaflaub 1997.217–27.

Smarczyk, Bernhard. 1990. *Untersuchungen zur Religionspolitik und politischen Propaganda Athens im Delisch-Attischen Seebund.* Munich: tuduv-Verlag.

Smertenko, Clara M. 1932. "The Political Sympathies of Aeschylus." *Journal of Hellenic Studies* 52, 233–35.

Smith, Michael French. 1982. "Bloody Time and Bloody Scarcity: Capitalism, Authority, and the Transformation of Temporal Experience in a Papua New Guinea Village." *American Ethnologist* 9, 503–18.

Snodgrass, Anthony M. 1980. *Archaic Greece: The Age of Experiment.* Berkeley: University of California Press.

——. 1982a. "Central Greece and Thessaly [in the Early Iron Age]." *CAH* III.1², 657–95.

——. 1982b. *Narration and Allusion in Archaic Greek Art*. London: Leopard's Head Press.

——. 1986. "Interaction by Design: The Greek City-State." In Renfrew & Cherry 1986.47–58.

——. 1987. *An Archaeology of Greece. The Present State and Future Scope of a Discipline*. Berkeley: University of California Press.

Sokolowski, Franciszek. 1969. *Lois sacrées des cités grecques*. Paris: De Boccard.

Solmsen, Friedrich. 1941. "The Aristotelian Tradition in Ancient Rhetoric." *American Journal of Philology* 62, 35–50, 169–90.

——. 1949. *Hesiod and Aeschylus*. Ithaca, N.Y.: Cornell University Press.

——. 1975. *Intellectual Experiments of the Greek Enlightenment*. Princeton: Princeton University Press.

Sommerstein, Alan S. 1980. "The Naming of Women in Greek and Roman Comedy." *Quaderni di storia* 11, 393–418.

—— (ed.). 1983. *Aristophanes*, Wasps. Warminster, England: Aris & Phillips.

——. 1986. "The Decree of Syrakosios." *Classical Quarterly* 36, 101–8.

——. 1989. *Aeschylus*, Eumenides. Cambridge: Cambridge University Press.

——. 1992. "Old Comedians on Old Comedy." In Bernhard Zimmermann (ed.), *Antike Dramentheorien und ihre Rezeption*. Drama: Beiträge zum antiken Drama und seiner Rezeption 1, 14–33. Stuttgart: M&P Verlag für Wissenschaft und Forschung.

——. 1993. "Kleophon and the Restaging of *Frogs*." In Sommerstein et al. 1993.461–76.

——. 1996. "How to Avoid Being a *komodoumenos*." *Classical Quarterly* 46, 327–56.

——. 1997. "The Theatre Audience, the Demos, and the *Suppliants* of Aeschylus." In Pelling 1997.63–97.

——, Halliwell, Stephen, Henderson, Jeffrey & Zimmermann, Bernhard (eds.). 1993. *Tragedy, Comedy and the Polis: Papers from the Greek Drama Conference, Nottingham, 18–20 July 1990*. Bari: Levante Editori.

Sorum, C. E. 1982. "The Family in Sophocles' *Antigone* and *Electra*." *Classical World* 75, 201–11.

——. 1989. "Assumptions and the Creation of Meaning: Reading Sophocles' *Antigone*." *Journal of Hellenic Studies* 109, 134–48.

——. 1990. "What is *Polis* Religion?" In Murray & Price 1990.295–322.

——. 1994. "Something to Do with Athens: Tragedy and Ritual." In Osborne & Hornblower 1994.269–90.

——. 1995a. "Male and Female, Public and Private, Ancient and Modern." In Reeder 1995.111–20.

——. 1995b. *'Reading' Greek Death: To the End of the Classical Period*. Oxford: Clarendon Press.

Spaeth, Barbette. 1991. "Athenians and Eleusinians in the West Pediment of the Parthenon." *Hesperia* 60, 331–62.

Spence, Iain. 1990. "Perikles and the Defence of Attika during the Peloponnesian War." *Journal of Hellenic Studies* 110, 91–109.

——. 1993. *The Cavalry of Classical Greece*. Oxford: Clarendon Press.

Spina, Luigi. 1986. *Il cittadino alla tribuna: Diritto e libertà di parola nell'Atene democratica*. Naples: Liguori.

Spivey, Nigel. 1994. "Psephological Heroes." In Osborne & Hornblower 1994.39–51.

——. 1996. *Understanding Greek Sculpture. Ancient Meanings, Modern Readings*. London: Thames & Hudson.

Sprague, Rosamond K. 1972. *The Older Sophists*. Columbia: University of South Carolina Press.

Stadter, Philip A. 1989. *A Commentary on Plutarch's* Pericles. Chapel Hill: University of North Carolina Press.

——. 1991. "Pericles among the Intellectuals." *Illinois Classical Studies* 16, 111–24.

Stähler, Klaus. 1989. "Die Palme der Herrschaft." In Nezih Basgelen & Mihin Lugal (eds.), *Festschrift Jale Inan*, 307–17. Istambul: Arkeoloji ve Sanat Yayinlari.

——. 1992. *Griechische Geschichtsbilder klassischer Zeit*. Münster: Ugarit Verlag.

——. 1993. *Form und Funktion. Kunstwerke als politisches Ausdrucksmittel*. Ibid.

Stahl, Michael. 1987. *Aristokraten und Tyrannen im archaischen Athen*. Stuttgart: Steiner.

Stalley, R. F. 1983. *An Introduction to Plato's* Laws. Oxford: Blackwell.

Stanier, R. S. 1953. "The Cost of the Parthenon." *Journal of Hellenic Studies* 73, 68–76.

Starr, Chester G. 1966. "Historical and Philosophical Time." In *History and the Concept of Time. History and Theory*, Beiheft 6, 24–35. Middletown, Conn.: Wesleyan University Press.

——. 1977. *The Economic and Social Growth of Early Greece, 800–500 B.C.* New York: Oxford University Press.

——. 1979a. "Religion and Patriotism in Fifth-Century Athens." In T. E. Gregory & A. J. Podlecki (eds.), *Panathenaia: Studies in Athenian Life and Thought in the Classical Age*, 11–25. Lawrence, Kans.: Coronado Press.

——. 1979b. "Thucydides on Sea Power." *Mnemosyne* 31, 343–50.

——. 1982. "Economic and Social Conditions in the Greek World [in the Archaic Age]." *CAH* III.3², 417–41.

——. 1986. *Individual and Community: The Rise of the Polis, 800–500 B.C.* New York: Oxford University Press.

Stedman Jones, Gareth. 1983. *Languages of Class*. Cambridge: Cambridge University Press.

Stehle, Eva & Day, Amy. 1996. "Women Looking at Women: Women's Ritual and Temple Sculpture." In Natalie B. Kampen (ed.), *Sexuality in Ancient Art*, 101–16. Cambridge: Cambridge University Press.

Stein-Hölkeskamp, Elke. 1989. *Adelskultur und Polisgesellschaft*. Stuttgart: Steiner.

Steinbrecher, Michael. 1985. *Der Delisch-Attische Seebund und die athenisch-spartanischen Beziehungen in der kimonischen Ära (ca. 478/7–462/1)*. Palingenesia 21. Stuttgart: Steiner.

Steiner, Ann. 1993. "The Meaning of Repetition. Visual Redundancy on Archaic Athenian Vases." *Jahrbuch des Deutschen Archäologischen Instituts* 108, 197–219.

Stephanidou-Tiveriou, Theodosia. 1987. "E sunthesi tes Pheidiakes Amazonomachias kai oi eroes Theseas kai Kekropas." In *AMETOS. Timetikos tomos yia to Kathegete Manoli Androniko* II, 839–57. Thessaloniki: Aristotelian University.

Steuben, Hans von. 1989. "Die Agora des Kleisthenes—Zeugnis eines radikalen Wandels?" In Schuller, Hoepfner, & Schwandner 1989.81–90 (including discussion).

Steuernagel, Dirk. 1991. "Der gute Staatsbürger. Zur Interpretation des Kuros." *Hephaistos* 10, 35–48.

Stevenson, G. H. 1924. "The Financial Administration of Pericles." *Journal of Hellenic Studies* 44, 1–9.

Stewart, Andrew F. 1978. "Lysippan Studies I. The Only Creator of Beauty." *American Journal of Archaeology* 82, 163–71.

——. 1985. "History, Myth, and Allegory in the Program of the Temple of Athena Nike, Athens." In Herbert Leon Kessler & Marianna Shreve Simpson (eds.), *Pictorial Narrative in Antiquity and the Middle Ages. Studies in the History of Art* 16, 53–73.

——. 1986. "When is a Kouros not an Apollo? The Tenea 'Apollo' Revisited." In Mario A. del Chiaro (ed.), *Corinthiaca. Studies in Honor of Darrell A. Amyx*, 54–70. Columbia: University of Missouri Press.

——. 1990. *Greek Sculpture. An Exploration.* New Haven: Yale University Press.

Stoessl, Franz. 1952. "Aeschylus as a Political Thinker." *American Journal of Philology* 73, 113–39.

Strasburger, Hermann. 1958. "Thukydides und die politische Selbstdarstellung der Athener." *Hermes* 86, 17–40.

Straten, F. T. van. 1995. *Hiera Kala: Images of Animal Sacrifice in Archaic and Classical Greece.* Leiden: Brill.

Strauss, Barry S. 1986. *Athens after the Peloponnesian War: Class, Faction and Policy 403–386 B.C.* Ithaca, N.Y.: Cornell University Press.

——. 1990. "*Oikos/Polis*: Towards a Theory of Athenian Paternal Ideology, 450–399 B.C." In Connor et al. 1990.101–27.

——. 1996. "The Athenian Trireme, School of Democracy." In Ober & Hedrick 1996.313–25.

——. 1997. "Genealogy, Ideology, and Society in Democratic Athens." In Morris & Raaflaub 1997.141–54.

Stroud, Ronald S. 1971. "Greek Inscriptions: Theozotides and the Athenian Orphans." *Hesperia* 40, 280–301.

Strycker, Emile de & Slings, Simon. 1994. *Plato's Apology of Socrates. A Literary and Philosophical Study with a Running Commentary. Mnemosyne* Suppl. 37. Leiden: Brill.

Stupperich, Reinhard. 1977. *Staatsbegräbnis und Privatgrabmal im klassischen Athen.* Diss. Münster.

——. 1994. "The Iconography of Athenian State Burials in the Classical Period." In Coulson et al. 1994.93–103.

Süss, Wilhelm. 1910. *Ethos. Studien zur älteren griechischen Rhetorik.* Leipzig: Teubner.

Takabatake, Sumio. 1988. "The Idea of *xenos* in Classical Athens: Its Structure and Peculiarities." In Yuge & Doi 1988.449–55.

Taplin, Oliver P. 1983. "Tragedy and Trugedy." *Classical Quarterly* 33, 331–33.

——. 1986. "Fifth-Century Tragedy and Comedy: A *synkrisis*." *Journal of Hellenic Studies* 106, 163–74.

Tausend, Klaus. 1989. "Theseus und der delisch-attische Seebund." *Rheinisches Museum* 132, 225–35.

——. 1992. *Amphiktyonie und Symmachie: Formen zwischenstaatlicher Beziehungen im archaischen Griechenland. Historia* Einzelschrift 73. Stuttgart: Steiner.

Taylor, Michael. 1991. *The Tyrant Slayers*. 2d ed. Salem, N.H.: Ayers.

Thalmann, W. G. 1978. *Dramatic Art in Aeschylus' Seven against Thebes*. New Haven: Yale University Press.

Thomas, Carol G. & Webb, E. K. 1994. "From Orality to Rhetoric: An Intellectual Transformation." In Worthington 1994.3–25.

Thomas, Eberhard. 1976. *Mythos und Geschichte*. Cologne: no publisher.

Thomas, Rosalind. 1989. *Oral Tradition and Written Record in Classical Athens*. Cambridge: Cambridge University Press.

Thommen, Lukas. 1996. *Lakedaimonion politeia: Untersuchungen zur Entstehung der spartanischen Verfassung. Historia* Einzelschrift 103. Stuttgart: Steiner.

Thompson, Edward P. 1967. "Time, Work-Discipline, and Industrial Capitalism." *Past & Present* 38, 56–97.

——. 1982. "The Pnyx in Models." In *Studies in Attic Epigraphy, History and Topography, Presented to Eugene Vanderpool. Hesperia* Suppl. 19, 133–47.

Thompson, Homer A. & Wycherley, R. E. 1972. *The Agora of Athens*. The Athenian Agora XIV. Princeton: American School of Classical Studies at Athens.

Thompson, Homer A. 1949. "The Pedimental Sculptures of the Hephaisteion." *Hesperia* 18, 230–68.

Thomsen, Rudi. 1964. *Eisphora: A Study of Direct Taxation in Ancient Athens*. Copenhagen: Gyldendal.

Thomson, George. 1966. *The Oresteia of Aeschylus*. Amsterdam: Hakkert.

Thornton, Harry & Agathe. 1962. *Time and Style: A Psycho-Linguistic Essay in Classical Literature*. Dunedin: University of Otago Press.

Thraede, Klaus. 1962. "Das Lob des Erfinders. Bemerkungen zur Analyse der Heuremata-Kataloge." *Rheinisches Museum* 105, 158–86.

Thür, Gerhard. 1989. "Wo wohnen die Metöken?" In Schuller, Hoepfner, & Schwandner 1989.117–21.

—— (ed.). 1994. *Symposion 1993. Vorträge zur griechischen und hellenistischen Rechtsgeschichte*. Cologne: Böhlau.

Tobin, Patricia D. 1978. *Time and the Novel: The Genealogical Imperative*. Princeton: Princeton University Press.

Tod, Marcus N. (ed.). 1946–48. *Greek Historical Inscriptions*. 2 vols. (vol. 1, 2d ed.) Oxford: Oxford University Press.

Todd, Stephen. 1990. "Lady Chatterley's Lover and the Attic Orators: The Social Composition of the Athenian Jury." *Journal of Hellenic Studies* 110, 146–73.

Too, Yun Lee. 1995. *The Rhetoric of Identity in Isocrates*. Cambridge: Cambridge University Press.

Toohey, Peter. 1997. "Trimalchio's Constipation: Periodizing Madness, Eros, and Time." In Golden & Toohey 1997.50–65.

Travlos, John. 1960. *Poleodomike exelixis ton Athenon*. Athenai: Konstantinide kai Mixala.

——. 1971. *Pictorial Dictionary of Ancient Athens*. London: Phaidon.

Trédé, Monique. 1992. *Kairos: L'à-propos et l'occasion (le mot et la notion d'Homère à la fin du IVe siècle avant J.-C.)*. Paris: Klincksieck.

Treu, Max. 1955. *Von Homer zur Lyrik*. Munich: Beck.

——. 1965. "Griechische Ewigkeitswörter." *Glotta* 43, 1–23.

——. 1971. "Der Erechtheus des Euripides als Zeugnis seiner Zeit." *Chiron* 1, 115–31.

Tritle, Lawrence A. (ed.). 1997. *The Greek World in the Fourth Century*. London: Routledge.

Tuplin, Christopher. 1985. "Imperial Tyranny: Some Reflections on a Classical Greek Political Metaphor." In Cartledge & Harvey 1985.348–75.

Turasiewicz, Romuald. 1981. "Remarks on Political Terms in Aeschylus." In Schmidt 1981.145–53.

Turner, J. A. 1983. *HIEREIAI: Acquisition of Feminine Priesthoods in Ancient Greece*. Diss. University of California, Santa Barbara.

Tyrrell, William. B. 1984. *Amazons: A Study in Athenian Mythmaking*. Baltimore: Johns Hopkins University Press.

Tzachou-Alexandri, Olga. 1993. "Personifications of Democracy." In Ober & Hedrick 1993.149–55. (See also Alexandri-Tzahou.)

Ungern-Sternberg, Jürgen von. 1988. "Überlegungen zur frühen römischen Überlieferung im Lichte der Oral-Tradition-Forschung." In Ungern-Sternberg & Reinau 1988.237–65.

—— & Reinau, Hansjörg (eds.). 1988. *Vergangenheit in mündlicher Überlieferung*. Stuttgart: Teubner.

Usener, Sylvia. 1994. *Isokrates, Platon und ihr Publikum. Hörer und Leser von Literatur im 4. Jh. v. Chr.* Tübingen: Narr.

Vanderpool, Eugene. 1966. "A Monument to the Battle of Marathon." *Hesperia* 35, 93–106.

Vansina, Jan. 1985. *Oral Tradition as History*. Madison: University of Wisconsin Press.

Vatin, Claude. 1984. *Citoyens et non-citoyens dans le monde grec*. Paris: SEDES.

Vattimo, Gianni. 1988. *The End of Modernity*. Oxford: Polity Press.

Vélissaropoulos, Julie. 1977. "Le monde de l'emporion." *Dialogues d'histoire ancienne* 3, 61–85.

Vernant, Jean-Pierre. 1965. "Travail et nature dans la Grèce ancienne." In id., *Mythe et pensée chez les Grecs* II, 16–36. Paris: Maspero.

——. 1972. "Tensions et ambiguïtés dans la tragédie grecque." In Vernant & Vidal-Naquet 1972.18–40. English in id. 1988a.29–48.

——. 1982. *The Origins of Greek Thought.* Ithaca, N.Y.: Cornell University Press.

——. 1988. *Mythe et pensée chez les Grecs.* 2d ed. Paris: Maspero.

——. 1989. *L'individu, la mort, l'amour.* Paris: Gallimard.

—— & Vidal-Naquet, Pierre. 1972 (1989). *Mythe et tragédie en Grèce ancienne.* Paris: La Découverte.

——. 1986. *Mythe et tragédie en Grèce ancienne* II. Ibid.

——. 1988. *Myth and Tragedy in Ancient Greece.* Tr. Janet Lloyd. New York: Zone Books.

Versnel, Henk S. 1990. *Inconsistencies in Greek and Roman Religion* I: *Ter Unus: Isis, Dionysos, Hermes. Three Studies in Henotheism.* Leiden: Brill.

——. 1995. "Religion and Democracy." In Eder 1995b.367–87.

Veyne, Paul. 1990. *Bread and Circuses: Historical Sociology and Political Pluralism.* Tr. Brian Pearce. London: Penguin.

Vian, Francis. 1963. *Les Origines de Thèbes: Cadmos et les Spartes.* Paris: Klincksieck.

Vickers, Brian. 1988. *In Defence of Rhetoric.* Oxford: Oxford University Press.

——. Forthcoming. "Plato's *Phaedrus* and the 'Reform' of Political Rhetoric." In id., *In Pursuit of Eloquence: Rhetoric and Its Goals, Good and Bad.* Oxford: Oxford University Press.

Vickers, Michael & Gill, David. 1994. *Artful Crafts: Ancient Greek Silverware and Pottery.* Oxford: Oxford University Press.

Vidal-Naquet, Pierre. 1983. *Le chasseur noir: Formes de pensée et formes de société dans le monde grec.* Paris: Maspero. Engl. tr., id. 1986.

——. 1986. *The Black Hunter: Forms of Thought and Forms of Society in the Greek World.* Tr. Andrew Szegedy-Maszak. Baltimore: Johns Hopkins University Press.

——. 1992a. "Notes sur la place et le statut des étrangers dans la tragédie grecque." In Lonis 1988–92.2:297–311.

——. 1992b. "Une invention: La démocratie." *Quaderni di storia* 35, 5–25.

——. 1996. "Democracy: A Greek Invention." Trans. David A. Curtis. In Pierre Lévèque and Pierre Vidal Naquet, *Cleisthenes the Athenian*, 102–18. Atlantic Highlands, NJ: Humanities Press.

Vlastos, Gregory. 1991. *Socrates: Ironist and Moral Philosopher.* Cambridge: Cambridge University Press.

Vokotopoulou, Ioulia et al. 1985. *Sindos. Katalogos tis Ekthisis.* Thessaloniki: Arkhaiologiko Mouseio Thessalonikis.

Volkmann, Richard. 1885. *Rhetorik der Griechen und Römer in systematischer Übersicht.* 2d ed. Leipzig: Teubner.

Wade-Gery, H. T. 1930. "The Year of the Armistice." *Classical Quarterly* 24, 33–39.

Walker, Henry J. 1995. *Theseus and Athens.* Oxford: Oxford University Press.

Wallace, Paul W. 1969. "Psyttaleia and the Trophies of the Battle of Salamis." *American Journal of Archaeology* 73, 293–303.

Wallace, Robert W. 1989. *The Areopagos Council to 307 B.C.* Baltimore: Johns Hopkins University Press.

——. 1994a. "The Athenian Laws Against Slander." In Thür 1994.109–24.

——. 1994b. "Private Lives and Public Enemies: Freedom of Thought in Classical Athens." In Boegehold & Scafuro 1994.127–55.

——. 1995. "Speech, Song and Text, Public and Private. Evolutions in Communications Media and Fora in Fourth Century Athens." In Eder 1995b.199–217.

——. 1996. "Law, Freedom, and the Concept of Citizens' Rights in Democratic Athens." In Ober & Hedrick 1996.105–19.

——. 1997. "Solonian Democracy." In Morris & Raaflaub 1997.11–29.

Wallace-Hadrill, Andrew (ed.). 1989. *Patronage in Ancient Society*. London: Routledge.

Wallinga, H. T. 1993. *Ships & Sea-Power before the Great Persian War: The Ancestry of the Ancient Trireme. Mnemosyne* Suppl. 121. Leiden: Brill.

Walter, Uwe. 1993. *An der Polis teilhaben. Bürgerstaat und Zugehörigkeit im Archaischen Griechenland. Historia* Einzelschrift 82. Stuttgart: Steiner.

Walter-Karydi, Elena. 1994. *Die Nobilitierung des Wohnhauses. Lebensform und Architektur im spätklassischen Griechenland*. Xenia 35. Konstanz: Universitätsverlag.

Wardy, Robert. 1996. *The Birth of Rhetoric: Gorgias, Plato and their Successors*. London: Routledge.

Waterfield, Robin. 1993. *Plato's Republic*. Oxford: Oxford University Press.

Watt, Ian. 1960. *The Rise of the Novel*. London: Chatto & Windus.

Weber, Max. 1958. *The City*. Tr. Don Martindale & Gertrud Neuwirth. Glencoe, Ill.: Free Press.

——. 1976. *The Agrarian Sociology of Ancient Civilizations*. Tr. R. I. Frank. Atlantic Highlands, N.J.: Humanities Press.

Webster, T. B. L. 1948. *Political Interpretations in Greek Literature*. Manchester, England: Manchester University Press.

——. 1972. *Potter and Patron in Classical Athens*. London: Methuen.

——. 1973. *Athenian Culture and Society*. London: Batsford.

Weidauer, Liselotte. 1985. "Eumolpos und Athen." *Archäologischer Anzeiger*, 195–210.

—— & Krauskopf, Ingrid. 1992. "Urkönige in Athen und Eleusis." *Jahrbuch des Deutschen Archäologischen Instituts* 107, 1–16.

Weiler, Ingomar. 1988. "Witwen und Waisen im griechischen Altertum. Bemerkungen zu antiken Randgruppen." In Kloft 1988.15–33.

Weitzmann, Kurt. 1947. *Illustrations in Roll and Codex. A Study of the Origin and Method of Text Illustration*. Princeton: Princeton University Press.

Welter, Gabriel. 1938. *Aigina*. Berlin: Gebr. Mann.

Welwei, Karl-Wilhelm. 1974. *Unfreie im antiken Kriegsdienst* I: *Athen und Sparta*. Forschungen zur antiken Sklaverei 5. Wiesbaden: Steiner.

——. 1992. *Athen. Vom neolithischen Siedlungsplatz zur archaischen Grosspolis*. Darmstadt: Wissenschaftliche Buchgesellschaft.

West, Martin L. 1985. *The Hesiodic Catalogue of Women: Its Nature, Structure, and Origins*. Oxford: Clarendon Press.

West, Stephanie. 1985. "Herodotus' Epigraphical Interests." *Classical Quarterly* 35, 278–305.

West, William C. III. 1969. "The Trophies of the Persian Wars." *Classical Philology* 64, 7–19.

Whitehead, David. 1977. *The Ideology of the Athenian Metic. Proceedings of the Cambridge Philological Society* Suppl. 4. Cambridge: Philological Society.

——. 1983. "Competitive Outlay and Community Profit: *philotimia* in Democratic Athens." *Classica et Mediaevalia* 34, 55–74.

——. 1984. "Immigrant Communities in the Classical Polis." *L'Antiquité classique* 53, 47–59.

——. 1986a. *The Demes of Attica 508–7 - ca. 250 B.C.: A Political Study.* Princeton: Princeton University Press.

——. 1986b. "The Ideology of the Athenian Metic: Some Pendants and a Reappraisal." *Proceedings of the Cambridge Philological Society* n.s. 32, 145–58.

Whitley, James. 1994. "The Monuments that Stood before Marathon." *American Journal of Archaeology* 98, 213–30.

Wickhoff, Franz. 1895. *Die Wiener Genesis. Beilage zum XV. und XVI. Band des Jahrbuches der Kunsthistorischen Sammlungen des allerhöchsten Kaiserhauses.* Vienna: F. Tempsky.

Wiesner, Jürgen. 1994. "Antiphon, der Sophist, und Antiphon, der Redner: ein oder zwei Autoren?" *Wiener Studien* 107, 225–43.

Wilamowitz-Moellendorff, Ulrich von. 1926. *Euripides, Ion.* Berlin: Weidmann.

Wilcox, Stanley. 1942. "The Scope of Early Rhetorical Instruction." *Harvard Studies in Classical Philology* 53, 121–55.

Will, Frederic. 1960. "Remarks on Counterpoint Characterization in Euripides." *Classical Journal* 55, 338–45.

Willemsen, Franz. 1977. "Zu den Lakedämoniergräbern im Kerameikos." *Mitteilungen des Deutschen Archäologischen Instituts Athen* 92, 117–57.

Willers, Dietrich. 1967. "Zum Hermes Propylaios des Alkamenes." *Jahrbuch des Deutschen Archäologischen Instituts* 82, 37–109.

Williams, Dyfri & Ogden, Jack. 1994. *Greek Gold. Jewelry of the Classical World.* New York: Metropolitan Museum of Art.

Williams, Raymond. 1977. *Marxism and Literature.* Oxford: Oxford University Press.

Wills, Garry. 1992. "Athena's Magic." *The New York Review of Books* Dec. 17, 47–50.

Winckelmann, Johann Joachim. [1764] 1880. *History of Ancient Art.* 2 vols. Tr. G. Henry Lodge. Boston: J. R. Osgood.

Winkler, John J. 1990a. "The Ephebes' Song: *Tragoidia* and *Polis.*" In Winkler & Zeitlin 1990.20–69.

——. 1990b. "The Laughter of the Oppressed: Demeter and the Gardens of Adonis." In id., *The Constraints of Desire: The Anthropology of Sex and Gender in Ancient Greece,* 188–209. New York: Routledge.

——. 1990c. "Phallos Politikos: Representing the Body Politic in Athens." In Konstan & Nussbaum 1990.29–45.

—— & Zeitlin, Froma I. (eds.). 1990. *Nothing to Do with Dionysos? Athenian Drama in Its Social Context.* Princeton: Princeton University Press.

Winnington-Ingram, R. P. 1965. "*Ta deonta eipein*: Cleon and Diodotus." *Bulletin of the Institute of Classical Studies* 12, 70–82.

——. 1983. *Studies in Aeschylus*. Cambridge: Cambridge University Press.

Wohl, Victoria. 1996. "*Eusebeias heneka kai philotimias*: Hegemony and Democracy at the Panathenaia." *Classica & Mediaevalia* 47, 25–88.

Wolff, Hans Julius. 1978. "Polis und Civitas." *Zeitschrift der Savigny-Stiftung für Rechtsgeschichte, Romanist. Abteilung* 95, 1–14.

Wolff, Hartmut. 1979. "Die Opposition gegen die radikale Demokratie in Athen bis zum Jahre 411 v. Chr." *Zeitschrift für Papyrologie und Epigraphik* 36, 279–302.

Wood, Ellen M. 1988. *Peasant-Citizen & Slave: The Foundations of Athenian Democracy*. London: Verso.

Woodman, Anthony J. 1988. *Rhetoric in Classical Historiography: Four Studies*. London: Croom Helm.

Woodruff, Paul. 1994. "Eikos and Bad Faith in the Paired Speeches of Thucydides." *Proceedings of the Boston Area Colloquium in Ancient Philosophy* 10, 115–45.

Worthington, Ian (ed.). 1994. *Persuasion: Greek Rhetoric in Action*. London: Routledge.

Wülfing, Peter. 1969. "Grundlagen und Anfänge der Rhetorik in der Antike." *Euphorion* 63, 207–15.

——. 1975. "Rhétorique et démocratie." *Les études classiques* 43, 107–18.

Wycherley, R. E. 1957. *The Athenian Agora* III: *Literary and Epigraphical Testimonia*. Princeton: American School of Classical Studies at Athens.

——. 1978. *The Stones of Athens*. Princeton: Princeton University Press.

——. 1992. "Rebuilding in Athens and Attica." *CAH* V^2, 206–22.

Xanthakis-Karamanos, Georgia. 1979. "The Influence of Rhetoric on Fourth-Century Tragedy." *Classical Quarterly* 29, 66–76.

Yuge, Toro & Doi, Masaoki (eds.). 1988. *Forms of Control and Subordination in Antiquity*. Leiden: Brill.

Yunis, Harvey. 1996. *Taming Democracy: Models of Political Rhetoric in Classical Athens*. Ithaca, N.Y.: Cornell University Press.

Zehnacker, Hubert (ed.). 1983. *Théâtre et spectacle dans l'antiquité*. Leiden: Brill.

Zeitlin, Froma. 1970. "The Argive Festival of Hera and Euripides' *Electra*." *Transactions of the American Philological Association* 101, 645–69.

——. 1986. "Thebes: Theater of Self and Society in Athenian Drama." In Euben 1986.101–41.

——. 1994. "The Artful Eye: Vision, Ecphrasis and Spectacle in Euripidean Theatre." In Simon Goldhill & Robin Osborne (eds.), *Art and Text in Ancient Greek Culture*, 139–96. Cambridge: Cambridge University Press.

Zerubavel, Eviatar. 1982. "The Standardisation of Time: A Sociohistorical Perspective." *American Journal of Sociology* 88.1, 1–23.

Zielinski, Tadeusz. 1931. "Les réflets de l'histoire politique dans la tragédie grecque." *Iresione* 1, 443–55.

Zimmermann, Bernhard. 1992. *Dithyrambos. Geschichte einer Gattung*. Göttingen: Vandenhoeck & Ruprecht.

——. 1993. "Aristophanes und die Intellektuellen." In Bremer & Handley 1993.255–80.

Zinserling, Verena. 1965. "Das attische Grabluxusgesetz des frühen 5. Jahrhunderts." *Wiss. Zeitschrift der Friedrich-Schiller-Universität Jena* 14.1, 29–34.

——. 1975. "Zum Beobachtungsgehalt des archaischen Kuros." *Eirene* 13, 19–33.

Zuntz, Günther. 1955. *The Political Plays of Euripides*. Manchester, England: Manchester University Press.

——. 1958. "Contemporary Politics in the Plays of Euripides." In *Acta Congressus Madvigiani: Proceedings of the Second International Congress of Classical Studies* I, 155–62. Copenhagen: Munksgaard. Repr. in id., *Opuscula selecta*, 54–61. Manchester, England: Manchester University Press, 1972.

THE CONTRIBUTORS

DEBORAH BOEDEKER is Professor of Classics at Brown University and Joint Director of the Center for Hellenic Studies in Washington, D.C. A specialist in Archaic and classical Greek poetry and religion, and the beginnings of historiography, she has published *Descent from Heaven: Images of Dew in Greek Poetry and Religion* (1984), *Herodotus and the Invention of History* (editor, 1987), and *The New Simonides* (coeditor, 1996).

ERIC CSAPO is Associate Professor of Classics at the University of Toronto, with main interests in Greek literature and social history, especially the history of the theater. He is coauthor of *The Context of Ancient Drama* (1995) and is currently writing a commentary on the choral odes of Euripides' *Electra* and a study of the representation of language and social class in Greek drama.

JEFFREY HENDERSON is Professor of Classics, Chair of the Department of Classical Studies, and Director of the College of Arts and Sciences Honors Program at Boston University. His main interests are Greek drama, Athenian social and political history, and textual criticism. His publications include *The Maculate Muse* (1975, 1990) and an edition and commentary of Aristophanes' *Lysistrata* (1987). He is currently working on a new edition and translation of Aristophanes in the Loeb Classical Library.

TONIO HÖLSCHER is Professor of Greek and Roman Archaeology and Director of the Archaeological Institute at the University of Heidelberg; he is a member of the Academy of Sciences of Heidelberg. His interests focus on the social, political, and aesthetic aspects of Greek and Roman art and archaeology. His books include *Griechische Historienbilder des 5. und 4. Jahrhunderts v. Chr.* (1973) and *Römische Bildsprache als semantisches System* (1988). He is currently working on a handbook of Roman state reliefs.

LISA KALLET is Associate Professor of Classics at the University of Texas, Austin. Her specialty is Greek history, with a strong interest in economic issues, and historiography. Her book *Money, Expense, and Naval Power in Thucydides'* History, *1–5.24* was published in 1993. She is currently working on *The Uses of Wealth: Money, Morality and Economic Thought in Thucydides.*

LISA MAURIZIO is Assistant Professor of Classics at the University of Massachusetts in Amherst. A specialist in Greek religion, she is working on a new book titled *Is Female to Male as Religion Is to Politics? Women and Religion in Ancient Greece.*

MARGARET MILLER is Associate Professor of Fine Arts at the University of Toronto. Her interests focus on Greek material culture, especially as studied through ceramic iconography, and Greek relations with the Near East. She is author of *Athens and Persia in the Fifth Century BC: A Study in Cultural Receptivity* (1997) and is currently engaged in a study of the iconographic orientalization of Greek myth in Attic art.

IAN MORRIS, a specialist in archaeology and social history, is Professor of Classics and Chair of the Department of Classics at Stanford University. His main publications are *Burial and Ancient Society: The Rise of the Greek City State* (1987) and *Death-Ritual and Social Structure in Classical Antiquity* (1992). He is currently working on the publication of Iron Age remains from Lerna and Koukounaries on Paros. His *Archaeology as Cultural History* is expected to be published soon.

KURT RAAFLAUB is Professor of Classics & History at Brown University and Joint Director of the Center for Hellenic Studies in Washington, D.C. His main interests are the social, political, and intellectual history of Archaic and classical Greece and the Roman republic. His books include *Die Entdeckung der Freiheit* (1985, 2d ed. in English forthcoming) and *Democracy 2500? Questions and Challenges* (coeditor, 1997). He is working on a new book titled *Early Greek Political Thought.*

CHRISTOPHER ROWE is Professor of Greek at the University of Durham. He is specialized in Greek philosophy, particularly Plato, and literature. He has published a series of commentaries on Platonic dialogues, including, most recently, the *Statesman* (1995) and *Symposium* (1998), and is joint editor of the *Cambridge History of Greek and Roman Political Thought* (planned for 1999).

SUZANNE SAÏD is Professor of Classics at Columbia University. Her interests focus on Greek literature from the classical to the Roman imperial period, especially tragedy, comedy, and the novel. Among her recent publications she lists *Sophiste et Tyran ou le problème du Prométhée enchaîné* (1985) and *Histoire de la littérature grecque* (coauthored, 1997). Her current projects include a book on *Dreams in Ancient Greece.*

ALAN SHAPIRO is Professor of Classics at Johns Hopkins University in Baltimore. A specialist in Greek iconography and religion, he is the author of *Art and Cult under the Tyrants in Athens* (1989, supplement 1995) and of *Personifications in Greek Art* (1993). He is currently completing an archaeological commentary on Athenian hero cults of the classical period.

ROBERT WALLACE is Associate Professor and Chair of Classics at Northwestern University, working primarily in the areas of Greek history, society, and culture, 800–300 BCE. His books include *The Areopagos Council, to 307 B.C.* (1989) and *Poet, Public and Performance in Ancient Greece* (coeditor, 1997). He is preparing two books on aspects of Athenian democracy, one on freedom and its limits, the other on Damon of Oa: philosophy and politics.

HARVEY YUNIS is Professor of Classics at Rice University in Houston. His interests include Athenian literature and thought and ancient rhetoric and rhetorical theory. He is the author of *A New Creed: Fundamental Religious Beliefs in the Athenian Polis and Euripidean Drama* (1988) and *Taming Democracy: Models of Political Rhetoric in Classical Athens* (1996). He is now working on a commentary on Demosthenes, *On the Crown.*

INDEX

(References to "Athens" are not indexed. Titles of ancient works are italicized, as are their book, line, and chapter numbers.)

Abdera: 65
Aegina: 16, 18, 357n7, 368n51
Aeschylus: 8–9, 59, 91, 92, 116, 117, 135, 191, 210, 230, 275–95, 332, 378n27; *Life of Aeschylus 11:* 9; *Agamemnon 536:* 378n27; *Eleusinians* 289; *Eumenides* 230, 280–81, 283, 305; *13:* 135; *Oresteia* 192, 195; *Persians* 280; *Prometheus Bound* 279; *Seven against Thebes* 279, 285–87; *Suppliants* 191, 195, 230, 279; *825–902:* 116
Agatharchos: 69
Agathon: 118, 120
Aglaureion: 132, 379n41
Aglauros, Herse, Pandrosos: 132–33, 136–38, 144
Agōn: see Competitions
Agora: 22, 24, 37, 69, 82, 129, 158–60, 162, 164–66, 169, 328, 336
Agriculture: 23, 25, 27, 30
Aischines: 54, 189, 264, 311; *1.11:* 54; *Against Ktesiphon* 264; *183:* 190; *186:* 189
Akropolis: 6, 18, 19, 22, 37, 40, 48, 50, 82, 127–151, 163, 167, 170, 171, 336, 346n13, 377n12
Alexis comicus: 306
Alkamenes: 171
Alkibiades: 52, 57, 69, 98, 259, 277, 303, 362n82, 363n102, 364n105, 364n114, 364n117, 367n32, 394n50
Alkidamas: 235
Alkmeonids: 201
Allies (Athenian): 6, 18, 23, 24, 25, 39, 44, 46, 47, 50, 52–54, 169, 171, 172
Amazonomachy: 119, 166, 167, 173, 186, 187, 189, 193, 194, 200, 325, 388n10, 388n21
Amazons: 161, 172, 173, 344
Amphipolis: 44, 357n6
Amyklai: 176
Anakeion: 129
Analogical history: 199
Anaxagoras: 217, 218, 259, 262, 401n2
Anaximenes of Lampsakos: 224
Andokides: 233, 367n32; *4.17:* 367n32
Antenor: 116
Antilogies: 234
Antiphon: 206, 207, 213, 216–17, 233, 235–36; *On Concord:* 216; *Truth:* 216
Antisthenes: 235
Anytos: 219
Aphrodision: 82
Aphrodite: 142, 381n74, 381n78
Apollo: 39, 50–51, 144, 145, 164, 168
Apollo Daphnephoros: 186
Archelaos: 81
Archetypes: 99, 100, 101, 114–21, 124
Architecture: 60, 128
Arginusae: 362n81
Argos: 63, 73–75, 82, 289–91, 293
Aristocracy (Elite): 10, 21–22, 27, 33–34, 52–54, 56–57, 59–86, 87–125, 128–29, 162, 210, 213–14, 219, 230, 258–59, 269, 299, 306–7, 310, 320, 330, 333–34, 338, 353n109, 362n87, 363n103, 364n114, 364n117
Aristophanes: 7, 21, 29, 47, 50, 53, 101, 116, 207, 216, 219, 231, 235, 263–65, 269, 270, 276–77; *Acharnians* 263; *Babylonians* 263; *Clouds* 231; *359–60:* 207; *Eccl. 219–*

220: 101, *456–57:* 101, *578–87:* 101; *Frogs* 276; *66ff.:* 8, *405:* 7, *686–705:* 270, *1417ff.:* 8; *Knights* 21, 231, 263; *188–92:* 219, *1111ff.:* 52, *1330ff.:* 52; *Lysistrata:* 35; *Peace:* 269; *Wasps* 50; *557 f.:* 47, *575:* 53, *587:* 53, *656 ff.:* 45
Aristotle: 16, 20, 35, 37, 52, 92, 98, 101, 117–18, 120, 204–5, 224, 227, 229, 234, 244, 266, 338–39, 345n5; *Constitution of the Athenians 21.6:* 37, *22.2:* 16, *22.3:* 345n5, *24:* 345n5, *24.3:* 20, *26.4:* 35, *27.1:* 345n5, *27.3:* 52, *27.4:* 30, 215; *Metaphysics 982a1:* 99; *Poetics 1449a6:* 110, *1451b14:* 120, *1453b22–23:* 118, *ch.9:* 117; *Politics 1268b26–69a28:* 101, *1341a28–32:* 205; *Rhetoric 1402a:* 204; *Sophistical Refutations 171b22–30:* 204
Arrhēphoroi: 138
Artemis: 172, 360n40
Artemision of Ephesos: 172–73
Arts: 1–12, 41, 59, 60, 83, 87–125, 153–83, 319–44
Asklepieion: 48
Assembly: 18–23, 95, 100, 102, 160, 163, 204, 209, 229–30, 235, 256, 267–68, 322, 328
Athena: 40, 48, 50, 58, 127–51, 168, 172, 174, 297, 304, 325, 361n60
Athena Lemnia: 169–71, 378n24
Athena Nike: 40, 117, 128, 139, 173–74, 176
Athena Parthenos: 136, 149, 151, 156, 173
Athena Promachos: 128, 167
Athena's treasury: 18, 48–51, 360n55
Athenian treasury at Delphi: 186, 327, 387n3
Athenocentrism: 11, 59–62, 81–83, 319–22
Attica: 64–70
Austerity: 59–86, 377n7
Autochthony: 127–51, 192, 195, 200, 286, 294, 327, 391n62, 391n67

Bacchylides: 187, 210; *fr. 17:* 187
Banking: 24
Barbarians: 116, 118, 187, 193, 195, 216, 284, 388n21
Bouleuterion: 129, 163
Building Program: 6, 20, 23, 44, 46, 48–52, 82, 128, 171, 173
Burials: see Graves, Grave Monuments

Casualties, Casualty Lists: 18, 31, 32, 84, 128
Chalkidike: 75, 81
Chalkis: 16, 71, 163, 182
Charis: 54, 364n112
Charondas of Katane: 354n117
Choirilos of Samos: 117, 373n25
Chorēgia: see Liturgy
Cicero: 9, 224, 366n13, 400n2; *Laws 2.64–65:* 366n13; *Orator 151:* 400n2
Citizens, civic life: 19–22, 26–34, 36, 38, 162, 181, 190, 242–45, 276, 283, 285, 297–317, 401
Citizenship Law: 29, 35, 131, 150
Civic identity: 153–83, 190, 195, 198, 200, 202, 309–13, 329, 424n41
Cleruchies: 18, 23, 29, 30, 169, 358n12, 378n24
Colonies: 18, 23, 29, 39, 51, 358n12
Comedy: 3, 8, 21, 54, 101, 116, 117, 255–73, 331–32, 344, 375n41; *Adesp. fr. 340 Kock:* 9
Competitions: 3, 5–6, 38, 98, 102–3, 237, 266, 284, 297, 309–13, 313–17, 331
Constitution: 248–53
Corinth: 63, 71–73, 82, 335, 352n85
Council: 18, 19–21, 235
Criticism of democracy: 229, 245–46, 258–59, 271, 283–84, 338, 391n64, 411n54
Croesus: 117
Cyprus: 18

Damon: 206–8, 212, 213, 215–17, 218, 221, 259, 262
Dedications: 127–28, 187–88, 199, 200–1, 388nn11, 12
Delia: 39
Delian League: 16, 17, 39, 50, 130, 144, 169–76, 327, 388n10
Delos: 39, 50, 145
Delphi: 5, 158, 165, 168–69, 176, 182, 314, 387n3
Demagogues: 8, 277
Demes: 36, 37, 39, 355n137, 363n92
Demeter: 34, 265
Demetrios of Phaleron: 58, 400n2
Democracy: 1–12, 19–22, 25–28, 32–39, 43–58, 59–60, 63, 82–83, 87–125, 128, 130, 131, 149, 151, 154–55, 158–63, 167–68, 169, 180–83, 203–22, 223–40,

241–53, 255–73, 277–84, 289, 297–317, 323–26, 339–44
Demokritos: 207–8, 241–42
Demos: 19–22, 28, 50–54, 56, 58, 83, 102, 118, 124, 129, 163, 204, 209, 214, 220, 230, 244, 253, 255–73, 284, 301, 327, 334, 362n81, 363n97, 378n22
Dēmosion sēma: see Kerameikos
Demosthenes: 6, 47, 66, 70, 113, 228, 239, 311, 312, 367n32; *3.25–26:* 70, *4.14:* 113, *4.35:* 47, *13.20:* 70, *21.147:* 367n32; *22.76–77:* 6, *23.207–8:* 70, *45.79:* 66
Diagoras of Melos: 259
Dinon: 117
Diodorus: 84, 89, 354n117; *12.30.1:* 89, *17.108.5:* 84
Dionysia: see Great Dionysia
Dionysos: 7, 265
Diopeithes, Decree of: 401n2
Dithyramb: 114

Economy: 22–26, 28, 29, 43–58, 59, 60, 99
Egalitarian, Egalitarianism: see Equality
Egypt: 2, 7, 18, 31, 355n145
Eion: 165
Eion elegies: 190–91, 193, 195, 391n67
Ekklesiastikon: 358n26
Eleusis: 39, 48
Elite: see Aristocracy
Empire: 1–12, 16–19, 21, 22–28, 30, 32–34, 39–40, 43–58, 59–60, 63, 82–83, 87–90, 101, 124, 129, 131, 149, 151, 166, 169–76, 180–83, 204, 214, 271, 284, 322–25, 333, 339–40, 340–44, 348n9, 355n146, 378n24, 403n35
Ephebes: 299, 305
Ephesos: 172, 173
Ephialtes: 20, 281, 327, 411n46
Epic: 92, 110–12, 118
Epicharmos: 267
Epidauros: 48
Eponymous Heroes: 37, 129, 136, 162, 329
Equality: 11, 19, 21, 34, 88, 89, 102, 124, 155, 158, 162–63, 169, 181, 197, 200, 205, 215–16, 229, 255–60, 268, 308, 325, 333, 363n97, 405n53
Erechtheion: 128, 145, 381n74
Erechtheus: 127–51, 327, 379n45
Eretria: 63–64, 70–71, 186
Erga: 2–5, 346n16
Erichthonios: 127–51, 198, 327, 379n45
Euboia: 357n7
Eupolis: 220; *Demes fr. 117:* 220
Euripides: 7–9, 27, 111, 117, 118, 120, 142–44, 145, 191, 192, 195, 199, 220, 231, 237, 275–95, 328, 373n25; *Bacchae 71:* 111; *Erechtheus fr.50.7–10:* 145; *Hippolytos 986–89:* 220; *Ion* 195; *595–601:* 220, *1163–65:* 145, *1595:* 118; *Medea 835:* 142–44; *Orestes 280; 1369–1526:* 116; *Phoenician Women* 280, 290–94; *Suppliants* 191, 195, 231, 280, 285, 289–94, 328; *403–8:* 199, *412–16:* 8, *417–422:* 27, *426–41:* 199
Eurymedon: 168
Expenditures: 20, 46–58, 66, 84–85

Family: 97–100, 285–95
Festivals: 3, 5, 7, 21, 34, 37, 39, 46–47, 54, 57, 185, 187, 200, 257, 265–69, 275–76, 284, 297–317, 324, 340, 342–44
Finances: 17, 19, 20, 22, 37, 43–58, 183, 322, 344
First Sacred War: 16, 348n4
Fleet: 16–18, 22–24
Freedom: 7, 9, 21, 26–27, 119, 124, 176, 205, 253, 256–57, 326, 403n38
Freedom of speech: 38, 255–73, 399n51; see also *Isēgoria*, *Parrhēsia*
French School: 93–94
Funeral Oration(s): 3–4, 30, 92, 120, 167, 174, 185, 190, 192–93, 196, 247, 281–84, 288, 290, 325, 346n13, 354n126, 392n91, 400n2

Gē: 133–36, 144, 304
Geistesgeschichte: 90, 92–94, 100, 116
Genre: 92, 96, 110, 114, 115
Gorgias: 8, 48, 54, 205, 208, 210–11, 213, 216, 229, 232–33, 247–48, 385n34; *Helen* 232, 235; *Palamedes* 232, 235
Gortyn: 32
Grain: 24, 25, 29, 351n74
Graves, Grave Monuments: 63–85, 128, 162, 168, 182, 301, 319–21
Great Dionysia: 31, 37, 39–40, 46, 54, 58, 262, 267, 275–76, 325, 331–32, 359n35
Gyges: 117

Hageladas: 155
Halieis: 18
Hallstatt culture: 78
Harmodios and Aristogeiton: 160, 329; see also Tyrannicides
Hekatompedon: 377n12
Heliodorus: 48
Hellenotamiai: 49–51, 57, 359n32, 360n38, 360n50
Hephaisteion: 48, 136, 145, 186, 196, 382n88, 383n96
Hephaistos: 48, 135–36, 139
Heraion: 82, 172
Herakleides Lembos: 117, 352n100
Herakles: 128, 160, 172
Hermes: 139
Hermes Propylaios: 171
Hermippos: 264, 270, 351n76
Herms: 165–66, 168–69
Hero cult, Heroes: 30, 65, 119
Herodotus: 2, 3, 7, 15, 16, 39, 92, 119, 134, 149, 192, 196–97, 199, 200–2, 210, 329, 345n7, 353n111, 365n10, 366n12, 379n33, 379n37; *1.4:* 199, *1.59.6:* 345n7, *2.35.1:* 2, *3.38:* 365n10, *3.60:* 2, *4.88:* 192, *5.62–63:* 201, *5.73:* 16, *5.74–75:* 16, *5.77–78:* 199, *5.78:* 16, 39, 197, 200, *5.96–97:* 16, *5.97:* 197, *5.97.2:* 353n111, *6.7–17:* 16, *6.90:* 379n33, *6.98:* 202, *6.102, 107:* 119, *6.103:* 366n12, *6.123.1–2:* 201, *7.139:* 197, *7.161.3:* 379n37, *8.41:* 134, *8.55:* 149, *8.57–58:* 210, *9.27:* 195
Hesiod: 194, 283; *Works and Days 109–201:* 194
Hippeis (Horsemen): 20, 120, 168, 299, 301, 304, 308, 329, 422n35
Hippias: 10, 207, 211, 373n25
Hippocrates: 208
Hippodamos of Miletus: 217, 351n79
History, Historiography: 10, 92, 94–95, 102, 112, 114, 117, 182, 185–202, 339, 343–44
Homer: 8, 88–89, 92, 98, 111, 114, 119, 132, 134, 193, 277, 346n15; *Il. 2.547:* 132, *2.548:* 134, *5.302–4:* 194; *Od. 4.613–19:* 98, *7.81:* 132
Hoplites: 16, 17–19, 20, 23, 28–31, 37, 101, 120, 253, 299, 301, 308, 329, 353n11, 422n35
Horsemen: see Hippeis
Houses: 63–86, 319–21, 365n10
Hypereides: 352n95

Identity: see Civic Identity
Ideology: 18, 21, 37, 39, 53, 63, 88–90, 93, 96, 98, 101, 114, 116, 122–25, 127–51, 153–83, 255–60, 276, 281–84, 294–95, 330, 333
Illyria: 78
Imperialism: see Empire
Innovationism: 101, 114–15, 271
Inscriptions: 18, 37, 44, 354n119; *IG* I[2] *334, 25–27:* 37; *IG* I[3] *259–90:* 44; *ML 33:* 18
Ion: 103, 133, 136, 145, 361n60, 381n79
Ion of Chios: 112
Ionia: 16, 39, 44, 99–100, 133, 195, 197, 361n60
Isēgoria: 200, 255–73, 326
Isokrates: 5, 24, 206, 223, 228, 239, 260–61, 312; *4.40–50:* 5, *4.42:* 24; *8.14:* 261, *15.155:* 206
Isonomia: 19, 155, 158–60, 163, 169, 181, 326, 329
Isthmos: 164

Kairos: 103–4
Kallias: 10, 217
Kallikles: 221, 247, 248
Kekropids: see Aglauros, Herse, Pandrosos
Kekrops: 130–31, 133
Kerameikos: 4, 30, 64–65, 128, 167–68, 176, 182, 328, 336
Kimon: 9, 10, 39, 48, 52, 54, 57, 158, 165–66, 188–89, 201, 279, 362n85, 363n103, 388n22
Kleisthenes, Kleisthenic reforms: 16, 19, 24–25, 37, 160, 162–63, 197, 287, 328, 378n29
Kleon: 23, 218–20, 237, 263, 265–66, 270, 272
Kleonymos: 264
Kleophon: 270, 279
Kodros: 130, 133
Konon: 169
Korax: 209, 226, 229
Kouroi: 83
Kratinos: 30, 264; *fr. 183 PCG:* 30
Kresilas: 172

Kritias: 206, 213, 326
Ktesias: 117
Ktesikles: 352n95

Lade: 16
Lamprokles: 212
Land distribution: 18, 23, 30, 45
Lasos of Hermione: 212
Laureion: 22, 48, 357n5
Law Courts: 19–21, 25, 30, 38, 47, 50, 95, 100, 102, 204, 229–30, 235, 256, 268, 322
Lenaia: 262
Lesbos: 357n7
Liturgies: 27, 45, 53–58, 323–24, 419n63
Lykourgos: 359n32, 364n112; *Leokrates 139–40:* 364n112
Lysander: 176
Lysias: 54, 56, 66, 228, 233, 239, 265, 312; *19.57:* 56, *21.5:* 54, *23:* 366n23, *32.21:* 66
Lysippos: 104

Macedonia: 64, 75–81
Maenadism: 355n137
Manufacture: 23, 25
Marathon: 9, 16, 39, 64, 105, 108, 119–20, 122, 128, 157–58, 161, 166, 168–69, 189, 353n111, 372n23
Marathonomachy: 105, 117, 119, 129
Megara: 16, 18
Metics: 17, 21–22, 26–29, 32, 34–35, 84, 124, 257, 260, 268, 299, 302–3, 305–6, 308–9, 311, 313–16, 330, 355n145
Mikon: 105, 119
Miletos: 262
Miltiades: 9, 119, 168–69, 176, 189, 389n23
Mimesis: 92, 111
Mimnermos: 194; *14.1–4W:* 194
Mixed Constitution: 243, 402n17, 405n53
Mnesiphilos: 210
Money: 25–26
Monuments: 2–4, 6–7, 18, 22, 39–40, 48–53, 56, 63–66, 82, 128, 153–83, 185–202, 328–30, 336, 343–44
Morychides, decree of: 262
Music: 207, 210, 212, 215, 218, 271
Mycenae: 3, 75
Myron: 116, 172, 382n92
Myth: 94, 98–99, 117, 119, 122, 129, 166–67, 178, 182, 185–202, 328
Mytilene: 16

Naval Power: 7, 16–18, 23, 39, 149
Naval Warfare: 22, 31–32, 101, 422n35
Neleus: 130
New Comedy: 267
"New politicians": 218, 256, 266, 270
Nike: see Athena Nike
Nike Temple: 119, 128–29, 173, 187, 189, 192–93, 383n96
Nikias: 219, 363n102, 363n103
Nikolaos of Damaskos: 352n100
Novel: 92, 121–23

Odeion: 218
Oikos: 257, 285–95, 413n108
Oinoe: 164, 166, 169, 189, 193, 389n25
"Old Oligarch": see Pseudo-Xenophon
Old Temple of Athena: 37, 128, 325
Oligarchs, Oligarchy: 7, 54, 101, 216, 244, 256, 267, 405n3
Olympia: 5
Olynthos: 81
Onatas: 155
Oral traditions: 190, 194, 198
Oratory: see Rhetoric
Orphans: 31–32, 276

Panathenaia: 37–39, 51, 54, 128, 145, 150, 171, 187, 218, 297–317, 325, 359n32, 359n35, 383n94
Panathenaic Procession: 106, 297–317, 329, 332, 378n25
Pandora: 136, 149
Panhellenic: 5, 11, 60–62, 82–83, 87, 160, 163, 164, 213, 271, 319–20, 331, 335–38
Panionia: 39
Parmenides: 208–9
Parrhasios: 327
Parrhēsia: 38, 255–73, 326
Parthenon: 6, 9–10, 17, 37, 40, 48–51, 58–59, 128–29, 136, 145, 149, 167–68, 173–74, 186, 325–26, 347n29
Parthenon Frieze: 37, 40, 106, 120, 145, 168, 299–303, 329–30, 378n25
Past, attitudes toward: 185–202
Patrios nomos: 30, 35, 354n118
Patrios politeia: 216, 405n51

Patronage: 10, 52–53, 57
Pausanias: 9, 105, 134, 142–44, 182, 377n5, 380n53, 381n78; *1.14.5:* 9, *1.15.3:* 105, *1.22.3:* 134, 142–44; *1.25.1:* 377n5, *1.27.3:* 381n78, *3.8.13:* 380n53, *3.11–18:* 182
Pay: 23–26, 30, 47, 204, 206–7, 210–11, 213, 215, 362n81, 363n97
Peace of Nikias: 269
"Peer polity interaction": 83
Peisistratids, Peisistratos: 16, 19, 37, 130, 188, 193, 196–97, 201, 353n117, 361n71, 379n41, 389n38
Peloponnesian War: 18, 26, 84, 191, 193, 342
Periander: 352n100
Peribolos Tombs: 65–67, 71, 83–84
Perikles: 3–7, 10, 18, 20, 24, 32, 36, 45–46, 48, 51–52, 57, 127–28, 131, 162, 169, 170–71, 173, 188, 197, 215–16, 217–18, 233, 270, 279–80, 327, 352n89, 354n117, 358n27, 361n57, 362n85, 377n5
Persian empire, Persians: 2, 16–17, 44, 117–19, 178, 188
Persian Wars: 19, 26, 117–20, 128, 158, 163–69, 173, 178, 181, 187–89, 190–93, 195, 197–200, 202, 325, 378n28, 390n42, 391n68
Personifications: 326–27, 422n35
Pheidias: 11, 59, 63, 128, 136, 154, 170, 172–73, 217, 344
Phenotype: 114–22
Pherekydes: 197, 378n27; *Autochthones*: 378n27
Philochorus: 353n108
Philosophers, Philosophy: 4, 5, 100, 203–22, 241–53, 271, 338, 343–44
Philotimia: 310–11, 314, 315
Phoenicia: 18
Phokis, Phokians: 158, 164
Photios: 354n117
Phratry: 36
Phrynichus: 117, 191, 262, 277
Phylai (tribes) 37
Pindar: 89, 91–92, 98, 210
Piraeus: 9, 17, 22–25, 28–29, 67, 347n29, 351n79, 359n32
Plague: 40, 84
Plataea: 164, 353n111
Plataea elegy: 190–91, 193
Plato: 8, 31, 101, 203–5, 207, 208–10, 217, 222, 224–29, 232–34, 236, 239, 241–53, 266, 277, 335, 338–39, 346n14, 346n18, 354n120, 400, 403n35; *Apology 21b–c:* 246, *29d:* 346n14, *31c:* 245; *Critias:* 251, 403n35; *Gorgias 452d:* 248, *452d–e:* 204, 232; *521d:* 246; *Hippias maior 281c–d:* 203; *Laws* 242–44, 249–53; *693d–e:* 252, *706–7:* 101, *739:* 250, *935d–e:* 266; *Menexenos* 400; *234–235:* 247, *238b:* 346n18, *248d–249c:* 31; *Phaedo 108d2–113c8:* 207; *Phaedrus 269e–270a:* 217, *266d–267d:* 226, *273b–c:* 236, *278d:* 251; *Politicus:* 242–44; *291e–292a:* 242, *299b–d:* 246; *Protagoras 316d–317c:* 209, *317b:* 203, *318d–e:* 208, *318e–319a:* 232, *319a:* 215; *323–25:* 215, *337d:* 204, *349a:* 204; *Republic* 249–53; *338e:* 247–48, *471–73:* 250, *592b:* 249; *Sophistes 231d:* 204; *Theaetetus 166d:* 215, *167a:* 217; *Timaeus* 250, 403n35
Plutarch: 6, 9, 47, 49–50, 54, 97, 134, 169, 207, 210–11, 346n13, 354n117, 355n146, 361n57, 364n114; *Alkibiades 10:* 364n114, *16:* 367n32; *Kimon 8:* 169; *Nikias 3:* 54; *Per.* 12: 49–50, 346n13; *12.1:* 6, *12.3:* 361n57, *14.1–2:* 52, *37.3–4:* 355n146; *Solon 31.3–4:* 354n117; *Themistokles 2.6:* 210, *10:* 134; *Moralia 345c–351b:* 9, *349a:* 47, *559c–d:* 97, *837b:* 207, *1141c:* 212, *1146b:* 210; *Glory of the Athenians 3:* 211
Pnyx: 163, 328
Polis: 36, 181, 209, 285–95
Polis tyrannos: 52–54, 58
Politeia: 244, 402n17, 405n53
Political Identity: 21, 28, 34, 153–83, 257
Political Theory: 10, 281
Politics, Politicians: 21–22, 27, 100–4
Politikē technē: 249
Polygnotos: 344
Polykleitos: 11, 155, 172–73
Polykrates of Samos: 7
Polypragmosynē: 21
Population Increase: 24–25, 29
Poseidippos: 104
Poseidon: 48, 142, 149, 164, 168, 359n32
Poteidaia: 44, 46
Power: 3, 95–96

Pratinas: 210
Praxiteles: 63
Prodikos: 204, 207, 235
Property: 33–34, 45, 285
Propylaia: 6, 48–51, 170–71, 173
Protagoras: 10, 203–4, 206–8, 211, 213, 215, 217, 229, 232, 234–35, 241–42, 245, 248
Prytaneis: 358n23
Pseudo-Xenophon: 7, 25, 29, 30, 47, 124, 262–63, 352n89; *Constit. of the Athenians 1.8:* 124, *1.10–12:* 29, 393n23; *1.13:* 54, *1.17:* 25, *2.9:* 7, *2.14–16:* 348n16, *2.18:* 262, *2.20:* 7, *3.2:* 47, *3.4:* 30
Pylos: 40
Pythagoras (sculptor): 155
Pythagoras of Selymbria: 65
Pythagoreans: 212
Pythokleides: 212, 217

Quintilian: 224

Religion: 32, 34, 36–40, 102–3, 127–51, 157, 165–66, 297–317, 324, 329–30, 340, 342–43, 355n137
Reserves (financial): 44, 51
Revenues: 18, 26, 28, 44–46
Rhamnous: 66
Rhetoric: 5, 8, 10, 101, 113–14, 120, 203–4, 207–9, 215, 218, 223–40, 247–48, 255, 260, 264, 266, 271, 322, 331, 334–35, 343–44
Rhodos: 31
Rituals: 18, 21, 32, 36, 38, 102, 117, 198, 316, 324
Rowers: 20, 24, 28

Sacrifices: 3, 5, 38, 47, 174, 299, 303, 359n32
Salamis: 119, 164, 168, 366n18
Sallust: 9
Samos: 2, 17, 46, 165, 172–73, 262, 335
Sculpture: 10, 60, 116, 127, 145, 153–83, 185, 187–88, 387n7
Second Athenian League: 45, 51
Serpent Column: 164
Shipsheds: 6–7, 9, 22, 346n21
Sicily: 18
Sikyon: 73, 82
Silver: 351n74
Simonides: 119, 190–91, 193, 211, 346n15
Slaves: 17, 22, 26–28, 33–34, 116, 120, 124, 257, 260, 268, 305
Sokrates: 2, 40, 198, 206–8, 213, 219, 221, 245–47, 259, 270, 272, 335, 338–39
Solon: 19, 26, 30, 31, 91, 210–11, 348n4, 354n117
Sophists: 4, 8, 10, 102, 123, 203–22, 223–40, 247–48, 257, 259, 321–22, 335, 338, 344, 403n32, 421n8
Sophocles: 9, 35, 100, 112, 114, 117, 130, 192, 214, 217, 275–95; *Ajax 131:* 112; *Antigone* 35, 287–89; *362:* 214; *OC 561–66:* 130; *OT* 279–80; *915–16:* 100; *Philoktetes* 280
Sparta: 4, 15–16, 18, 32, 165–67, 176, 187, 189–90, 201, 210, 271, 281, 350n40, 354n131, 379n35, 388n22, 390n42, 391n67, 391n81
Sphakteria: 176
Stoa Basileios: 129, 145
Stoa Poikile: 10, 119, 129, 166–67, 169, 174, 178, 189, 192–93, 195, 199, 389n25
Stoa of Zeus Eleutherios: 176, 422n22
Structuralism: 93
Synēgoroi: 358n23
Syracuse: 89
Syrakosios: 262–63

Taxes: 18, 20, 22, 24, 28, 54, 57, 362n81
Technai: 208, 226
Teisias: 209, 226, 229
Telesterion: 48
Temporality: 87–125, 320
Terpander: 210
Thasos: 31, 357n6
Theater: 3, 37, 355n137
Theater of Dionysos: 328
Thebes: 16, 131, 281, 285–95
Themistocles: 9, 169, 181
Theognis: 210
Theorikon: 358n26
Theseion: 10, 129, 161, 187, 188
Theseus: 39, 130, 131, 149, 150, 160, 161, 167, 168, 186–89, 191, 196, 198, 199, 201, 281, 289, 298, 290, 327, 328
Thessaly: 78
Thetes: 17–19, 23, 24, 29–30, 31, 299, 307, 308, 330
Thirty: 2, 6, 31, 222, 256

Tholos: 129
Thrasyboulos: 176
Thrasymachos: 221, 247, 248
Thucydides: 3–8, 18, 25, 32, 40, 44–46, 51–52, 98, 101, 112, 119, 124, 185, 196–99, 201–2, 214, 221, 233–34, 237–41, 259, 271, 329, 335, 339, 346n13; 349n19, 349n22, 356n172, 363n102, 364n105, 364n114, 370n58, 397n22, 399n48, 399n55; *1.1:* 112, *1.6:* 370n58, *1.10.1–2:* 3, *1.20–21:* 198, *1.21:* 112, *1.22:* 113, *1.22.1:* 399n48, 399n55; *1.70.2:* 101, *1.71.2:* 101, *1.71.3:* 214, *1.73–74:* 196, *1.96.1:* 51, *1.138.3:* 397, *1.142:* 101, *2.13:* 44, *2.13.3:* 45, 46, 51; *2.14.2:* 25, *2.36.1–2:* 119, *2.36.4:* 3, *2.37.2–3:* 259, *2.38.1:* 3, 5; *2.38.2:* 24, *2.40.1:* 3–4, 214, 346n13; *2.41.4:* 3–5; *2.42.1–2:* 346n16, *2.43.1:* 346n16, *2.43.3:* 4, *2.46.1:* 30, *2.52–53:* 40, *2.61.4:* 5, *2.63:* 202, *2.63.1:* 124, *2.63.2:* 51–52, *2.65:* 218, *2.95–101:* 370n58, *3.31.1:* 44, *3.37:* 202, 218, *3.37.2:* 52, *3.38.5:* 101, 214; *4.108.1:* 44, *5.26.5:* 198, *6.16.1:* 98; *6.16.2:* 364n114; *6.16.3:* 363n102, 364n105; *6.53–59:* 198, *6.54.5:* 345n7, *6.54.6:* 346n17; *Melian Dialogue:* 221, 238; *Mytilenian Debate:* 237–38
Thucydides, son of Melesias: 49–51
Timotheos: 116–17, 373n25
Tisias: 209
Town Planning: 11
Trade: 22–25, 99
Tragedy: 6, 8–9, 21, 41, 54, 91–92, 110–14, 116, 118, 185, 191–92, 195, 202, 237, 275–95, 332–33, 340–44, 389n35
Tribute: 18, 20, 23, 39, 44, 47, 50, 58, 276, 324, 358n10
Trierarchy: 18, 22, 54, 56–57, 364n112
Trireme: 16–17, 348n17, 423n35
Trojan War: 119, 166–67, 186–87, 189–90, 198, 200, 325
Tropaion: 157, 174
Tyrannicides: 37, 39–40, 116, 118–19, 130, 158–60, 162, 168–69, 182, 188, 192, 195–96, 198, 201–2, 298, 329, 361n73, 388n15
Tyranny, Tyrants: 16, 39, 52–54, 88, 119, 129, 157, 248, 253, 288–90, 292, 361n71, 364n114, 405n3

Urbanization: 24–25, 28–29
Utopias: 249, 307

Vases, Vase Painting: 59, 116, 129, 133–51, 176–80, 192, 196, 327, 387n7

Wall Paintings: 129, 185–86, 188, 192, 336, 388n19
War, Warfare: 16–18, 24, 30–32, 39–40, 88, 101, 325
War Victims: 30–32
Widows: 31–32, 354 n. 128
Women: 31–36, 260, 268, 290, 299, 302–3, 305, 307, 309, 311, 313–15, 330, 413n119, 420n96

Xenophanes: 181
Xenophon: 23, 45–46, 51, 112, 117, 119, 123, 204, 210, 246, 358n19, 362n81; *Anabasis* 112; *7.1.27:* 45–46; *Hellenika 2.3.48:* 123; *Kyropaideia* 119; *Memorabilia 1.1.10:* 246, *1.6.13:* 204, *3.7.6:* 23, *4.2.2:* 210; *Oeconomicus 11.9–10:* 51; *Poroi 1.1:* 51; *Symposion 4.31–32:* 362n81

Zeno: 206
Zeugites: 30–31
Zeus: 138–40, 142, 172, 344
Zeus of Olympia: 11, 164, 344
Zeuxis: 59, 81